The
Bomber Command
War Diaries

AN OPERATIONAL REFERENCE BOOK
1939-1945

The Bomber Command War Diaries

AN OPERATIONAL REFERENCE BOOK
1939-1945

Martin Middlebrook and Chris Everitt

MIDLAND

An imprint of
Ian Allan Publishing

The Royal Air Force Command Badge featured on the front cover
is acknowledged as a Crown Copyright / RAF photograph.

Front cover illustration: Armourers prepare a train of 250lb GP
bombs for an unidentified Vickers Wellington Ic. Although this
particular photograph was undoubtedly staged, it shows a scene
which was commonplace on many of the Bomber Command
airfields during the early years of the war once the 'operations on'
signal had been initiated. The Wellington along with the Handley
Page Hampden, provided the main strength of Bomber
Command's operations until the introduction of the four-engined
heavies in 1942. *Via Mike Hodgson*

Back cover: A Halifax of 6 Group attacking the Wanne-Eickel oil
refinery, which is covered by smoke, on 12 October 1944.
Imperial War Museum

First published in hardback by Viking 1985
Published in paperback by Penguin 1990

Revised paperback edition published 1996 by
Midland Publishing
This hardback edition published 2011 by Midland Publishing

ISBN 978 1 85780 335 8

Published by Midland Publishing

an imprint of Ian Allan Publishing Ltd, Hersham, Surrey
KT12 4RG.
Printed in England by Ian Allan Printing Ltd, Hersham, Surrey
KT12 4RG.

Visit the Ian Allan Publishing website at
www.ianallanpublishing.com

Distributed in the United States of America and Canada by
BookMasters Distribution Services

CONTENTS

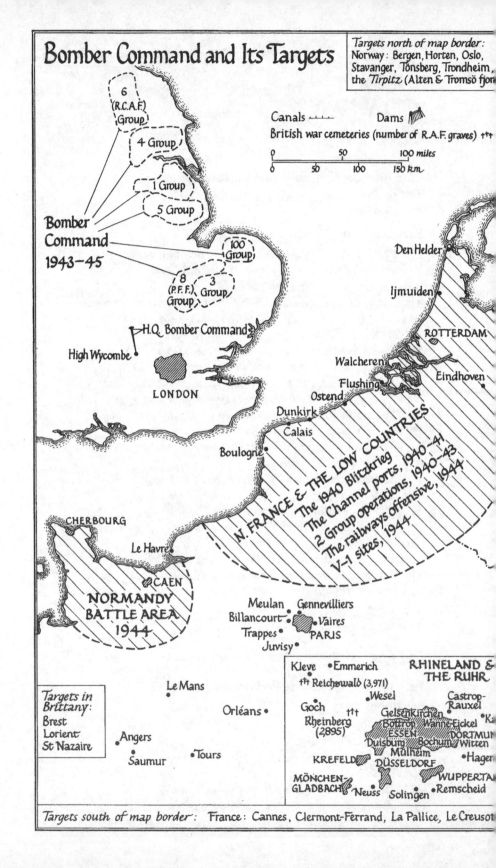

Bomber Command and Its Targets

Targets north of map border:
Norway: Bergen, Horten, Oslo,
Stavanger, Tönsberg, Trondheim,
the *Tirpitz* (Alten & Tromsö fjord)

6
(R.C.A.F.)
Group

4 Group

1 Group

5 Group

100
Group

8
(P.F.F.)
Group

3
Group

Bomber
Command
1943–45

H.Q. Bomber Command

High Wycombe

LONDON

Canals ---- Dams
British war cemeteries (number of R.A.F. graves) ╬

0   50   100 miles
0   50   100   150 km

Den Helder

Ijmuiden

ROTTERDAM

Walcheren

Flushing

Eindhoven

Ostend

Dunkirk

Calais

Boulogne

N. FRANCE & THE LOW COUNTRIES
The 1940 Blitzkrieg
The Channel ports, 1940–41
2 Group operations, 1940–43
The railways offensive, 1944
V-1 sites, 1944

CHERBOURG

Le Havre

CAEN

NORMANDY
BATTLE AREA
1944

Meulan   Gennevilliers
Billancourt   Vaires
Trappes   PARIS
Juvisy

Le Mans

Orléans

Kleve   •Emmerich   RHINELAND &
╬ Reichswald (3,971)   THE RUHR
            •Wesel
Goch   Castrop-
╬╬╬   Rauxel
Rheinberg   Gelsenkirchen   •Ka
(2,895)   Bottrop Wanne-Eickel
        ESSEN   DORTMUN
    Duisburg Bochum Witten
KREFELD   Mülheim   •Hager
MÖNCHEN- DÜSSELDORF
GLADBACH   WUPPERTA
    Neuss Solingen •Remscheid

Angers

Saumur

Tours

Targets east of map border:
Danzig, Gdynia, Königsberg

Hörnum
1st raid on German territory
Flensburg
Heligoland
Heidé
Daylight raids on shipping 1939–40
Wangerooge
Kiel Canal
KIEL Cemetery (865)
KIEL
Last raid of war
Warnemünde
Peenemünde
Wilhelmshaven
Emden
Lübeck
Wismar
Rostock
Pölitz
HAMBURG
†††Hamburg Cemetery (731)
STETTIN
Battle of Hamburg, 1943

BREMEN
†††Becklingen (895)
BERLIN
Early raids, 1940–41
Battle of Berlin, 1943–4
Mosquito raids, 1944–5

†††
Sage (713)
HANNOVER
Osnabrück
Rheine
Hannover Cemetery (1,841)
BRUNSWICK
Hildesheim
MAGDEBURG
Potsdam
†††Berlin Cemetery (2,937)
Dessau

Dortmund-Ems Canal
Münster
Paderborn

Hamm
Soest
LEIPZIG
Rhineland & The Ruhr see inset below
Möhne
THE DAMS
KASSEL
Merseburg (Leuna)
DRESDEN
Böhlen
Sorpe
Eder
Zeitz
Rositz
CHEMNITZ
Brüx
...sberg
Leverkusen
COLOGNE
Wesseling
Siegen
Fulda
Plauen
Komotau
...lich
HEN
Düren
Bonn
Urft Dam
Giessen
Bayreuth
Pilsen

Wiesbaden
FRANKFURT
Hanau
Bingen
Mainz
Hildesheim
Aschaffenburg
Darmstadt
Würzburg
NUREMBERG
The heaviest bomber loss, March, 1944
Trier
Worms
MANNHEIM
1st area raid, December, 1940
Ludwigshafen
Regensburg
Kaiserslautern
SAARBRÜCKEN
Zweibrücken
Heilbronn
KARLSRUHE
Pforzheim
STUTTGART
AUGSBURG
Ulm
MUNICH
Freiburg
Durnbach (2,652) †††
Berchtesgaden
Kembs Dam
Friedrichshafen
...ontbéliard

...ne, Montluçon, Poitiers, Royan, St Médard-en-Jalles. Italy: Genoa, La Spezia, Milan, Turin

LIST OF PLATES

INTRODUCTION

It is difficult to grasp the sheer scale of Bomber Command's unique and prolonged campaign against Germany in the Second World War. The bomber squadrons flew from the very first day of the war to within a few hours of the end, more than five and a half years later: more than a third of a million sorties; nearly 9,000 bomber aircraft destroyed by enemy defences or lost to the hazards of the skies; more than 50,000 airmen killed, men from the United Kingdom and from every Empire and Allied country in the world, enough fatal casualties to form seventy battalions of infantry or the crews of thirty modern battleships – and that was not counting the men taken prisoner of war, wounded or just worn out. It was a campaign which produced a scale of devastation in the cities and towns of Germany and of other European countries wildly beyond any pre-war conception of what a modern bomber force could achieve.

It is unlikely that the likes of that Second World War strategic bombing campaign will ever be seen again; the first atom bomb rendered such bomber fleets obsolete within months of the German surrender. It is not surprising that students of military history should have concentrated so intensely on this unique campaign. Book after book has appeared and still the interest does not seem to wane. And yet there has never been a published book which comprehensively covers the whole of Bomber Command's war in detailed reference form. THE BOMBER COMMAND WAR DIARIES attempts to fill this gap. Every single operation which Bomber Command mounted during the Second World War will somehow be listed, to produce an 'operational reference book' of use and interest we hope to all students of the air war and particularly to those men who flew with Bomber Command and survived; these last – and possibly the relatives of those who did not survive – may be helped to see how the efforts of an individual member of Bomber Command fitted into the greater pattern of the war which could not be seen at the time.

We do not intend this work to be in any way similar to the formal, academic study of the R.A.F. strategic bomber offensive which formed the British Official History, published in 1961. Neither will it contain any personal views on that sensitive subject, the so-called 'area bombing' campaign, to which such a large proportion of Bomber Command's efforts were devoted. References to bombing results will be confined to the inclusion of statistics for individual raids which have been obtained from Germany and the other countries where Bomber Command's targets were situated; these will be presented as fully as possible, whether they favour one side or other of the old argument about how worth while Bomber Command's operations were. We are determined to produce as accurate and reliable a reference work as possible and not to detract from any merit it might have by becoming involved in old arguments. The authors are mindful that a contribution to the bombing war was made by the R.A.F.'s Advanced Air Striking Force in France in 1939 and 1940 and greater contributions were provided by the Middle East, Mediterranean and 2nd Tactical Air Forces later in the war; we are also aware of the huge effort of the United States Army Air Forces in the second half of the war; but this study must confine itself strictly to the activities of the units flying under the operational control of R.A.F. Bomber Command.

The units of Bomber Command were in a uniquely favourable position to produce a reliable documentary record of their operations. A far-sighted Air Ministry had ordered that standard forms – the Air Force Forms 540 and 541 – were to be completed for every operational flight by every single aircraft. The aircraft's serial number, its crew, its bomb load and its take-off time were all recorded; if the aircraft returned safely, its landing time and a résumé of the crew's experiences during the flight were added. Squadrons made composite reports of the crews' flights; groups then consolidated the squadron reports; Bomber Command Headquarters finally produced an overall report of every raid. Because all links in the chain were home-based, none of these documents was lost to enemy action as were so many documents which failed to survive the war. There are minor gaps and errors due to clerical lapses but these are negligible. It is unlikely that any wartime operations were documented so comprehensively as those of Bomber Command. The records were transferred to the Public Record Office in 1971 and have been freely available to researchers since then. Chris Everitt, the researching half of this partnership, has spent much of the last four years studying them.

But these British records should be used with some care. Distinction must be made between what was definitely *known* to have happened and what the crews *believed* happened on their flights. If a report says that 500 bombers of various types took off to attack a German city and that 450 of the crews claimed on returning that they had released 1,500 tons of bombs on that city, only the first part of the statement – that 500 bombers had taken off – can be deemed to be completely reliable. All attempts by Bomber Command to provide raid reports based solely on the evidence of returning crews were soon found to be of little value and it was eventually found that there were many occasions when bombs were not released on the designated targets. Furthermore, a significant proportion of the bombs did not even explode; the city records of Cologne, for instance, state that *more than 10,000 unexploded wartime bombs* were found after the war – and these were only the high explosives; the unexploded incendiaries were never counted. Bomber Command established an Operational Research Section – staffed by mathematicians and scientists – to analyse the results of each raid and to try to establish what had actually happened to the bomb tonnages carried at such effort and cost to targets. But this process did not commence for night raids until February 1942 and did not properly cover day raids until the last weeks of the war. Even those raids which were analysed often produced little reliable result when the target concerned was covered by cloud at the time of the raid. Bomber Command had other methods of raid assessment, chiefly post-raid photographic reconnaissance, but there were frequent gaps in this cover. There was a half-hearted attempt to study the effects of raids when German civil and industrial documents were captured at the end of the war. A skeleton 'British Bombing Survey Unit' was established even before the war ended but the Government refused to allocate any large-scale manpower to it on the grounds that its report would not be completed until after the war with Japan was expected to finish. The needs of post-war historians were not considered. Some research was carried out by this small unit but, unlike the work of the American bombing survey, little was published.

So, in an attempt to rectify that great gap in the knowledge of what actually happened to the bombs dropped, we mounted a separate effort in German civilian archives, many of which contain reliable information that has never been published. German municipal authorities were particularly diligent compilers of wartime records and an approach was made to every German city and town which had been the target for any significant Bomber Command raid. This search was extended into places which are now in the German Democratic Republic or Poland or even, in the case of one German target, Königsberg (now Kaliningrad), in Russia. Inquiries were also made at places in Italy, Norway, France, Belgium and Holland which had been wartime targets. Some of the research was carried out by amateur local historians whose valuable help is acknowledged elsewhere. All other contacts were direct with the relevant municipal authorities.

There had to be some limits to this search; to cover every Bomber Command raid would be impossible. In particular, the early war years saw a mass of light attacks on many targets – sometimes six or more cities in one night were each attacked by a handful of aircraft – and the daylight raids by 2 Group during the 1941–42 period were often against semi-military objectives or consisted of very small bomber forces sent out under heavy fighter escort as little more than a bait to draw the Luftwaffe into combat. These small raids could not be covered by the search. The following general policy was thus adopted. Only details from raids of outstanding interest in 1940 were requested. During 1941 and the first two months of 1942, targets where fifty or more aircraft claimed to have bombed were covered. During the remaining months of 1942 the limit was raised to 100 aircraft claiming to have attacked and then, in 1943, to 250 aircraft for the remainder of the war. No serious attempt was made to cover the many so-called nuisance raids by small forces of Mosquitoes against German cities nor the raids on the V-weapons sites and the purely military targets attacked in support of the invasion in 1944.

Results from this arrived in a wide variety of forms and will be seen in many of the diary entries. Little useful information came in from the countries of East Europe or from Italy but nearly every West German, French, Belgian and Norwegian town which was approached sent useful material. Some places sent complete diaries for the whole war, which enables comment to be added to some of the smaller raids.

It remains only to describe how the diary is laid out. The basic method of presentation is to divide the war into a series of time periods. Years or calendar months meant nothing to Bomber Command; its life was ruled by the general progress of the war, by the orders it received, by the policies of its commanders, by the ever changing tactical circumstances under which its crews flew. Each of the diary periods has been chosen because of its particular strategic, tactical or technical background. They vary in length from seven months for the 1939–40 period of the Phoney War to just ten days for the Battle of Hamburg in 1943. Each section is introduced by notes which establish the importance of the period and describe the main purpose and activity of the coming phase; we must acknowledge that Webster and Frankland's Official History has been invaluable for this purpose. The reader is also told of the main changes in Bomber Command's organization and strength which took place during each phase.

Thereafter the operations are simply listed on a daily and nightly basis. To indicate their relative importance, the names of the individual targets are printed in a range of weighted headings from bold capitals down to normal type: these weightings correspond to the proportion of Bomber Command's available strength involved:

STUTTGART   This would be a major raid carried out by more than half of the regular strength of bombers available for operations in the relevant period.

BREMEN   An important raid, but carried out by less than half of the available bomber strength.

OBERHAUSEN   A small raid, for most of the war by fewer than 100 aircraft.

Aachen   A very small raid, for most of the war by fewer than 30 aircraft.

When more than one target was attacked in one day or night, the raids are listed in order of the numbers of bombers involved, not in time sequence. A busy day or night may conclude with a composite entry listing the supporting and other minor operations carried out during the day or night and, finally, with a short statistical résumé.

The headings shown above – STUTTGART, BREMEN, etc. – are suitable for most of the war but more general headings have to be used for most of 1940 because it was the practice during that period for Bomber Command to send small numbers of aircraft to many targets and it is impossible to list each target. The size of the heading still indicates the proportion of the force used, for example: GERMANY, THE CHANNEL PORTS; BERLIN, ITALY; HAMBURG, LORIENT; The Ruhr, Airfields. Repetitive minor operations over a period sometimes find themselves consolidated into one entry, but every sortie flown by a Bomber Command aircraft is included somewhere.

The numbers of aircraft recorded for each raid *are the numbers dispatched, not the numbers which bombed*; no one will ever know the latter figure. An aircraft is deemed to have been dispatched if it started its take-off down the runway of its airfield, even if it crashed soon afterwards. Useless otherwise stated, the majority of the crews of the aircraft dispatched claimed to have bombed in the correct target area, but the reader can assume that a small percentage of aircraft always turned back with mechanical trouble and that other aircraft bombed alternative targets after having failed to reach the designated one. If, however, a considerable number of crews reported that they had not been able to find the target or if part of a force was officially recalled, those facts are noted in the diary entry.

Another regular item to be included in the diaries is the number of Bomber Command aircraft noted as 'lost'. This term should be explained further. Bomber Command wartime records and the public releases to press and radio at that time referred to aircraft as being 'missing'. A missing aircraft was one which had set off to its target but was then lost either over enemy-occupied territory or in other circumstances which were not known at the time. If a bomber crashed in the sea without trace, it was thus 'missing'; if, however, it crashed in the sea near the English coast and members of its crew were rescued, to avoid giving comfort to the Germans its loss was not announced publicly. Similarly, later in the war, bombers which managed to reach France or other territory held by Allied armies before crashing were not regarded as casualties and these losses were not announced. In this reference book, however, it was considered more useful to classify any aircraft crashing beyond the shores of the British Isles as being a permanent aircraft casualty, hence our term 'lost' rather than 'missing'. Also regarded as 'lost' are the small number of planes which were shot down over England in error by 'friendly' fighters or anti-aircraft guns, those which crashed after striking barrage-balloon cables in England and those shot down over England by German 'Intruder' aircraft.

Many further aircraft and personnel casualties occurred when bombers crashed in Britain, either after take-off or, more usually, on returning in damaged condition or in bad weather from a raid. Bomber Command's records contain details of the steady drain of such further casualties. But crew members of these planes sometimes survived and the planes themselves were sometimes salvaged for further use and it is impossible for us to identify which were completely wrecked. For this reason, such crashes are not regarded here as 'lost' and they are not normally mentioned in the diary entries or in the periodic statistical résumés unless they were particularly numerous or if there were other notable circumstances.

Part One

The Diaries

1. THE PHONEY WAR

3 September 1939 to 8/9 April 1940

At dawn on 1 September 1939 German forces invaded Poland. The British and French Governments threatened that they would declare war unless Germany agreed to withdraw her forces from Poland by 11.0 a.m. on 3 September. When the time limit for this ultimatum ran out without German agreement to this demand, Britain and France went to war. Sixty-three minutes later, a Blenheim reconnaissance bomber took off from Wyton airfield to carry out Bomber Command's first operational sortie of the Second World War.

Britain had been rearming since the mid-1930s and Bomber Command was ready to operate from bases in England from the moment war began. Bomber Command also had a detailed set of plans – the sixteen so-called 'Western Air Plans' – which had originated in a combined-services planning section in 1936. The main assumptions of the planners were that the Germans would immediately commence operations in Western Europe, either with intense bombing raids on the United Kingdom or with a land offensive through France and Belgium. Bomber Command's main war plans were designed to counter whichever of these German moves was made. If the Germans started bombing, the R.A.F. would attack the Luftwaffe's airfields and supply depots; if the Wehrmacht attacked France, the raids would be on the lines of supply to the land battle. A third major plan had been prepared for strategic raids to be made on German war industry, particularly on oil refineries and storage depots. The plans for these three possible uses of Bomber Command – Western Air Plans 1, 4 and 5 – had been prepared in great detail. There were further plans for other eventualities and for a variety of minor operations but no plans for giving any help to Poland; indeed it was difficult to see how Bomber Command could help Poland, the nearest point of which was 700 miles away from the bomber airfields in England.

There was an immediate, though not unwelcome, delay. On the day that Poland was invaded, President Roosevelt appealed to the countries at war and to those about to go to war to refrain from carrying out any bombing operations on undefended towns or on any target where civilians might be hit by the bombing. Britain and France gave suitable assurances at once; Germany did so on 18 September when the campaign in Poland was drawing to a close. So, at a time when the R.A.F.'s main war plans were found to be unrealistic because of the German troops moving east instead of west, Bomber Command received orders that, because of the difficulty of defining purely military targets in Germany and ensuring that no civilians were hit, no targets of any kind on German soil were to be raided. Bomber Command squadrons could attack German naval vessels – though not those alongside a dockyard wharf, only those ships moored in harbours or steaming at sea – and the bombers could also carry out flights over Germany for the purpose of dropping propaganda leaflets. Although the bomber crews may have been surprised by all these restrictions, the R.A.F. commanders were relieved not to have their units thrown into an immediate all-out campaign but to be allowed time to continue the build-up of strength and to gain experience gradually.

Bomber Command had lost part of its strength two days before Britain's declaration of war when, as planned previously, No. 1 Group, with ten squadrons of Fairey Battle light bombers, moved to France together with two Blenheim squadrons from another group to become the Advanced Air Striking Force. Because these units did not operate under Bomber Command control while in France, their operations are not included in this book until the return of the remnants to England after the fall of France. Five more squadrons of Battles were left in England but were reduced to a training and reserve basis. The restricted nature of operations after the outbreak of war gave Bomber Command the opportunity to withdraw a further nine of its squadrons from the home-based groups and add these to the reserve, leaving only twenty-three front-line squadrons which contained approximately 280 aircraft with trained crews. That part of Bomber Command which now stood ready to proceed with war operations was organized in the following manner:

> Headquarters Bomber Command at Richings Park, Langley, Buckinghamshire (but due to move in March 1940 to a new location being prepared at High Wycombe). The Commander-in-Chief was Air Chief Marshal Sir Edgar Ludlow-Hewitt.
>
> 2 GROUP. HQ: Wyton: Commander: Air Vice-Marshal C. T. Maclean. Nos. 21, 82, 107, 110, 114 and 139 Squadrons, all equipped with Bristol Blenheims; 101 Squadron non-operational.
>
> 3 GROUP. HQ: Mildenhall. Commander: Air Vice-Marshal J. E. A. Baldwin. Nos. 9, 37, 38, 99, 115 and 149 Squadrons, all equipped with Vickers Wellingtons; 214 and 215 Squadrons non-operational.
>
> 4 GROUP. HQ: Linton-on-Ouse. Commander: Air Vice-Marshal A. Coningham. Nos. 10, 51, 58, 77 and 102 Squadrons, all equipped with Armstrong-Whitworth Whitleys; 78 Squadron non-operational.
>
> 5 GROUP. HQ: St Vincent's House, Grantham. Commander: Air Commodore W. B. Callaway (Air Vice-Marshal A. T. Harris from 11 September). Nos. 44, 49, 50, 61, 83 and 144 Squadrons, all equipped with Handley Page Hampdens; 106 and 185 Squadrons non-operational.

The four types of aircraft in use were all of sound design and without major mechanical drawbacks. Maximum bomb loads varied from 1,000 pounds for the Blenheim to 8,000 pounds for the Whitley. The Blenheim had only a restricted range but the other three types could reach any part of Germany except the extreme east. It had always been intended that the main bombing operations would be carried out by tight, self-defending daylight formations and only the Whitley squadrons of 4 Group were trained in night bombing.

Bomber Command commenced its leaflets flights and its operations against the German fleet at once. The Whitleys of 4 Group carried out the first leaflet raids; the other groups shared the daylight work. Subsequent diary entries show how these first efforts fared. An important tactical feature of this period was the neutrality of Holland and Belgium, which effectively blocked the direct approaches to Germany and left only long approach flights north over the small German coastline on the North Sea or south over France. Dutch and Belgian defences often fired on damaged or wayward Whitleys flying over their territory. Daylight operations were found to be costly in casualties whenever German fighters were encountered and the self-defending bomber theory was severely tested even before this opening period of restraint in the west was over. But the night leaflet raids which continued throughout the period were found to be almost free from casualties except for those losses resulting from the hazardous weather conditions of winter nights. One satisfying feature of all operations during this period was the very low proportion of aircraft which could not carry out their tasks because of mechanical failure. This was a result of the efforts of the pre-war-trained groundcrews combined with the fact that squadrons were never called upon to dispatch more than a proportion of their available strength. These conditions would soon disappear and Bomber Command would never again be able to carry out operations with such a low rate of 'early returns' as in these early months.

The range of the leaflet operations was increased when some of the Whitleys started refuelling at airfields in France in the early months of 1940 and leaflets were thus delivered to such distant cities as Prague, Vienna and Warsaw. It is unlikely that the propaganda leaflets had any real effect upon the morale of the German civilians who received them but Bomber Command was gaining invaluable night-operating experience at modest cost. Wellingtons and Hampdens started a tentative move to evening and then night operations in January 1940 but the shorter-range Blenheims were restricted to increasingly unproductive daylight maritime sweeps. The bombing truce initiated by President Roosevelt held throughout this period, with one exception, in March 1940, which is described in the appropriate diary entry. Bomber Command's strength was carefully preserved and there was only that one occasion in March 1940 when as many as fifty of its aircraft set out on operations; this was less than one quarter of the strength available. No bombing operations could be undertaken to help Britain's Polish allies, who succumbed to the joint German–Russian invasion within a month of the war opening.

---

3 September 1939

North Sea

1 Blenheim reconnaissance plane, 18 Hampdens and 9 Wellingtons searched for German warships. The Blenheim photographed many ships north of Wilhelmshaven but the 2 bomber forces made no contact. There were no losses. The Blenheim was the first aircraft of the war to cross the German coast. It was Blenheim N6215, crewed by Flying Officer A. McPherson, Commander Thompson, R.N., and Corporal V. Arrowsmith.

Night of 3/4 September 1939

Leaflet Raids

10 Whitleys – 3 from 51 Squadron and 7 from 58 Squadron – carried 5·4 million leaflets to Hamburg, Bremen, and 9 cities in the Ruhr. There were no losses but 3 aircraft were forced to land at airfields in France.

| | | Appendix _____ | R.A.F. Form 541. |

OPERATIONS RECORD BOOK.

DETAIL OF WORK CARRIED OUT.

From ___ hrs 3/9/39 to ___ hrs. 3/9/39   By ___   No. of pages used for day

Aircraft Type and No.	Crew.	Duty.	Time Up.	Time Down.	Remarks.	References.
Blenheim Mk. IV N6215	F/O McPherson. Cdr. Thompson. c/2 Arrowsmith.	Photo Recce.	1510.	1650	Duty successful. 15 photos taken of German fleet. The first British Air Force aircraft to cross the German frontier.	

1. The first Bomber Command sortie of the war. Corporal Vincent Arrowsmith was dead before the end of the month, lost on a reconnaissance flight on 24 September.

4 September 1939

WILHELMSHAVEN AND BRUNSBÜTTEL

After an early Blenheim reconnaissance, 15 Blenheims and 14 Wellingtons were dispatched to bomb German warships. 5 planes from each force failed to find targets in low-cloud conditions. Most of the remaining Blenheims carried out low-level attacks on the pocket battleship *Admiral Scheer* and on the cruiser *Emden* in Wilhelmshaven harbour. At least 3 bombs hit the *Admiral Scheer* but they failed to explode; the *Emden* was damaged and suffered some casualties when a Blenheim crashed on to it. 5 Blenheims were shot down, all or most by anti-aircraft (Flak) fire; 107 Squadron lost 4 of its 5 planes on the raid. The first Bomber Command casualties of the war are believed to have been Flight Lieutenant W. F. Barton and his crew – Flying Officer J. F. Ross, navigator, and Corporal J. L. Ricketts, wireless operator/gunner – of 107 Squadron, all killed when Blenheim N6184 was shot down by anti-aircraft gunfire of the *Admiral Hipper*.

Little is known of the Wellington attacks on ships at Brunsbüttel in the mouth of the Kiel Canal. 4 crews reported that they had found targets to bomb. Owing to navigation error, 2 bombs were dropped on the Danish town of Esbjerg, 110 miles north of Brunsbüttel, and 2 people were killed there. Some of the Wellingtons were attacked by German fighters and 2 Wellingtons were lost.

Total effort for the day: 30 sorties, 7 aircraft (23·3 per cent) lost.

LEAFLET RAIDS, 4/5 September to 23/24 December 1939

Whitleys again carried out leaflet raids on the second night of the war and were to continue such operations regularly by night in following months. (The inclusion of a separate diary entry for every one of these flights would be of little practical use, so they have been consolidated into batches.)

The Whitleys operated in this role on 22 nights between 4/5 September and

WAR'S FIRST CASUALTY LIST

THE first R.A.F. casualties of the war were announced by the Air Ministry last night:—

Missing (believed killed):
549741, Aircraftman Second Class, K. G. Day.

Missing (believed prisoners of war):
561012, Sergeant G. F. Booth.
36187, Pilot-Officer L. H. Edwards.
548555, Aircraftman, Second Class, L. J. Slattery.

Missing:
34213, Flight-Lieutenant W. F. Barton.
546065, Aircraftman, First Class, G. T. Brocking.
531493, Leading Aircraftman H. Dore.
36138, Flying-Officer H. L. Emden.
537187, Aircraftman, First Class, R. Evans.
565602, Sergeant D. E. Jarvis.
546679, Aircraftman, First Class, E. W. Lyon.
580695, Sergeant A. S. Prince.
524808, Leading Aircraftman J. Quilter.
519859, Corporal J. L. Ricketts.
39340, Flying-Officer J. F. Ross.
552231, Aircraftman, First Class, G. Sheffield.
550292, Acting-Sergeant B. G. Walton.

2 (a and b). The first casualties, after the raid on German warships on 4 September 1939. The 'Missing' were all dead.

Leading Aircraftman Harry Dore of 9 Squadron, who was killed when his Wellington was shot down while attempting to attack ships at Brunsbüttel. He is wearing the pre-war 'winged bullet' air gunner's badge. All aircrew were soon promoted to at least the rank of sergeant.

23/24 December and a total of 113 sorties were flown. On some moonlit nights the Whitleys were ordered to make visual reconnaissance of certain places in Germany, their main task of leaflet dropping becoming a secondary role on those nights. A high proportion of the flights were carried out successfully; it is believed that 105 of the 113 sorties achieved at least part of their allocated tasks.

The first British aircraft of the war to fly over Berlin – from 10 Squadron – did so on 1/2 October; this was a round trip of at least 1,000 miles. Airfields in France, particularly Villeneuve near Paris, were often used as advanced refuelling bases for distant targets or as relief landing grounds on return from long flights.

From all these operations, 4 Whitleys were lost over Germany or crashed into the sea. The first loss was the aircraft of Squadron Leader C. Murray, of 102 Squadron, which crashed in Germany on 8/9 September; the crew were all taken prisoner. On the same night, another Whitley force-landed in Belgium and its crew were interned. A Belgian aircraft was also shot down, with 2 of its crew believed wounded, but it is not known whether the Whitley fired on it or whether it was hit by its own anti-aircraft fire. German fighters – believed to be Me 109s attempting to act as night fighters -- were encountered as early as the fifth night of the war but it is not thought that any of the Whitley losses in the period were caused by fighter attack.

RECONNAISSANCE FLIGHTS, 20 September to 25 November 1939

After the costly raid on German warships on the second day of the war, there was no day activity of any kind for Bomber Command squadrons until 20 September, when a series of photographic reconnaissance flights over Germany commenced. The purpose of these was to discover whether the Germans were carrying out a military build-up in Western Germany after the end of the Polish campaign and whether a German attack on France was likely to occur. Road and rail communications were thus frequently photographed. A watch was also kept on German airfields and naval bases. 2 sorties were also made to the Ruhr to photograph power stations there which were being considered as future bombing targets. These daylight reconnaissance flights were all carried out by Blenheims of 2 Group. The first phase can usefully be consolidated into this composite entry.

The Blenheims flew 37 of these sorties on 11 days during this period, the most sorties in any one day being 6 on 30 October. These dangerous and lonely flights were carried out with much determination, but at heavy cost; the Blenheim was no match for the German fighters which were often encountered. 5 Blenheims were shot down, including the plane of the commander of 110 Squadron on 28 September. This was Wing Commander I. M. Cameron, an Australian, who crashed near Kiel on the day when Hitler was there to present the first Knight's Cross to a U-boat commander. 3 other Blenheims were lost over the North Sea, including 2 planes of 114 Squadron which collided on 11 November.* The 7 planes lost in this period represented 19·4 per cent of the sorties flown. The reconnaissance flights over Germany were stopped on 25 November.

29 September 1939

NORTH SEA-HELIGOLAND

After a 25-day interval since the last bombing raid on German warships, 11 Hampdens in 2 formations were dispatched to search the Heligoland area. 6 aircraft bombed 2 destroyers but without scoring any hits. The second formation, of 5 aircraft of 144 Squadron, did not return; a German radio broadcast stated that it had met 'a hornet's nest' of fighters and all the Hampdens had been shot down. Post-war records show that 18 of the 24 aircrew were killed, including the commander of 144 Squadron, Wing Commander J. C. Cunningham.

NORTH SEA SWEEPS, 8 October to December 1939

Flights by formations of bombers searching for German ships to attack were made on 9 days between 8 October and 2 December. The bombers did not approach the German mainland and the normal 'beat' was the 125-mile stretch of sea between Borkum and Sylt which marked the outer limits of Germany's small North Sea coast.

A total of 61 sorties were flown – 55 by Wellingtons and 6 by Hampdens. No German ships were seen; no bombs were dropped; no aircraft casualties were suffered.

---

* Some of the details of the 2 Group operations comes from the very useful reference book, *2 Group R.A.F.*, by Michael J. F. Bowyer, Faber & Faber, 1974.

3 December 1939

NORTH SEA–HELIGOLAND

24 Wellingtons attacked German warships, claiming 1 hit on a cruiser. Me 109s and 110s, believed to have been alerted by a patrol ship, appeared and attacked the Wellington formations. In the ensuing combats, no bombers were lost but one Me 109 was hit and possibly shot down.

1 Wellington, from 115 Squadron, suffered a bomb 'hang-up' on its bombing run and this bomb later dropped accidentally on the island of Heligoland. This was the first bomb to drop on German soil during the war.

3 further Wellingtons sent out later to attack these German ships failed to make contact. There were no R.A.F. losses during this day's operations.

4 December 1939

North Sea Shipping Search

3 Hampdens failed to locate any targets.

9 December 1939

North Sea Shipping Search

3 Wellingtons failed to locate any targets.

10 December 1939

North Sea Shipping Search

3 Whitleys failed to locate any targets. This was the first Whitley daylight operation of the war.

11 December 1939

North Sea Shipping Search

3 Whitleys failed to locate any targets.

SEAPLANE-BASE PATROLS, 12 December 1939 to 14/15 January 1940

On 12 December, 8 Whitleys commenced this new type of operation to harass the German seaplanes which were laying mines off the English coast. Flying in relays, Whitleys flew during the evenings over suspected seaplane bases on the islands of Sylt, Norderney and Borkum. If flare-paths on the water were seen to be lit, bombs were dropped but only in the water because of the instructions given to bomber units, after President Roosevelt's bombing-restraint appeal at the outbreak of war, that no bombs should be dropped on any land targets.

These operations were flown on 17 nights between the evening of 12 December 1939 and the night of 14/15 January 1940. A total of 71 Whitley sorties were flown.

Bombs were dropped on suspected seaplane take-off areas on at least 3 occasions. One of these was the cause of 2 bombs falling on the Danish island of Römö, which was very close to Sylt, on 10 January 1940 and bombs also fell on the town of Westerland, on the island of Sylt, on 12 January. A suspected German U-boat was bombed on 13 December and a Flak ship on 16 December, but no results were claimed. The Whitleys suffered no casualties during these operations; the only attack made on them was by R.A.F. Spitfires off the coast of Lincolnshire on 17 December.

---

14 December 1939

NORTH SEA SHIPPING SEARCHES

23 Hampdens, 12 Wellingtons and 7 Whitleys on shipping searches; 2 Blenheims made reconnaissance flights to Sylt. This was the biggest operation of the war so far.

The Wellingtons found a convoy in the Schillig Roads, north of Wilhelmshaven, but because of low cloud and bad visibility could not get into a favourable bombing position. The Wellingtons remained in the area for half an hour, flying at low level and being engaged by Flak and by fighters. 5 of the Wellingtons were shot down. The R.A.F. was reluctant to concede that German fighters had achieved the success of shooting down nearly half of a bomber formation and it was officially hoped that the losses were due to Flak but a German radio broadcast attributed the Wellington losses to fighter attack; 1 German fighter was admitted to have been lost. No German ships were hit.

The other forces operating on this day saw no action.

---

15 December 1939

North Sea Shipping Search

5 Blenheims failed to locate any targets.

---

17 December 1939

North Sea Shipping Search

6 Blenheims failed to locate any targets.

---

18 December 1939

SHIPPING SEARCH OFF WILHELMSHAVEN

24 Wellingtons were dispatched and ordered not to attack at less than 10,000 ft so that they could avoid the worst effects of Flak. 22 aircraft reached the target area. German ships were seen off Wilhelmshaven and bombed from 13,000 ft. Weather conditions were cloudless and visibility was perfect. For the first time in the war, German fighters were directed on to this bomber force by a ground controller who was being given information from an experimental *Freya* radar station located on the nearby island of Wangerooge. The radar station had detected the Wellingtons when they were 70 miles out on their approach flight. Flak caused the bomber formations

to open out somewhat and, when German fighters of IV/JG 2 appeared, 12 of the 22 Wellingtons were shot down. 2 German fighters were also shot down.

This famous action, together with that of 14 December when 5 out of a force of 12 Wellingtons were shot down, had a major effect upon the policy of the British bomber commanders. Exactly half of the 34 Wellingtons dispatched had been shot down in these 2 actions without any penetration of the German mainland having taken place. The validity of the self-defending bomber formation was now seriously in doubt.

3 further Wellingtons and 2 Whitleys on separate patrols saw no action.

---

20 December 1939

NORTH SEA SHIPPING SEARCH

12 Blenheims were dispatched and bombed 11 German minesweepers whose location had been detected by Coastal Command. Results of the bombing are not known. No Blenheims lost.

---

21 December 1939

NORTH SEA SHIPPING SEARCH

24 Hampdens and 18 Wellingtons failed to locate any targets. Part of the Hampden force was mistakenly attacked by R.A.F. Spitfires of 602 Squadron when returning to land in Scotland; 2 of the Hampdens were shot down in the sea; it is believed that 1 man died, the remaining crew members being rescued.

---

23 December 1939

North Sea Shipping Search

2 Whitleys failed to locate any targets.

---

24 December 1939

NORTH SEA SHIPPING SEARCH

17 Wellingtons attacked shipping but no results were seen. 2 Blenheims made photographic reconnaissance flights to Wilhelmshaven. No losses.

---

25 December 1939

North Sea Shipping Search

12 Hampdens located one or more submarines but were not able to attack.

NORTH SEA SHIPPING SEARCHES, 26 December 1939 to 1 February 1940

Despite the recent heavy losses, the attempts to find and bomb German warships continued regularly, but the bomber forces involved were ordered not to fly as close to the mainland as on previous raids unless there was good cloud cover. These operations were carried out on 13 days in this period and 186 sorties were flown: 87 by Blenheims, 73 by Wellingtons, 18 by Hampdens and 8 by Whitleys. German fighters were encountered on two occasions. 2 Wellingtons were lost and 1 Me 109 was claimed shot down on 2 January; 1 Blenheim was lost and 2 Me 110s were claimed on 10 January. No German ships were seen on any of these raids and no bombs were dropped.

RECONNAISSANCE FLIGHTS, 27 December 1939 to 12 January 1940

Blenheims flew photographic reconnaissance flights on 4 days in this period. 8 sorties were flown from England to the German coast; 1 Blenheim was lost on 27 December. 7 sorties were flown on 2 January from French airfields to locations 'behind the German lines'; there were no casualties on this day.

LEAFLET RAIDS, 4/5 January to 19/20 January 1940

After a gap of 10 nights without any operations, leaflet raids recommenced on 4/5 January and were carried out on 7 nights during this period. Only 25 sorties were flown: 10 by Whitleys, 9 by Wellingtons and 6 by Hampdens. The first leaflet flights by Wellingtons – to Hamburg on the 11/12th – and by Hampdens – to Kiel on the following night – were the first night sorties of the war for these 2 types of aircraft and represent a tentative but significant move to night operations by 2 of the 3 bomber groups previously intended only for day operations. Of the Whitley flights in this period, the new distant targets of Prague and Vienna were reached, from forward airfields in France, on 12/13 January.

There were no losses from any of the above operations.

Because of severe winter weather at the English airfields, with heavy snowfalls, there were no night operations between 20 January and the night of 17/18 February and no day operations from 2 February to 17 February.

NORTH SEA SHIPPING SEARCHES, 11 and 13 February 1940

18 Wellingtons on the 11th and 12 on the 13th failed to locate any targets.

NORTH SEA SHIPPING SEARCHES, 14 February to 1 April 1940

The main daylight operations over the North Sea were now allocated to the Blenheims of 2 Group and operations were flown on 34 out of 47 days between 14 February and 1 April. Most of these flights were uneventful, though German ships were bombed on at least 6 occasions and the Blenheims several times encountered German fighters. A total of 250 Blenheim sorties were flown of which 9 were purely photo-reconnaissance flights to the German coast. 4 Blenheims (1·6 per cent of those dispatched) were lost; all were believed to have been shot down by fighters. In addition to the Blenheim operations, 26 Wellington and 21 Hampden sorties were flown but these are all recorded as 'training sweeps' and no contact was made with any German forces and no casualties were suffered.

There was one confirmed bombing success for a Blenheim. On 11 March Squadron Leader M. V. Delap of 82 Squadron attacked a U-boat off Borkum bombing from such a low altitude that his aircraft was damaged by the explosions and nearly crashed. German records show that this was their Type VIIIA submarine U-31 and that Squadron Leader Delap's bombs sank it. This U-boat was later salvaged and repaired but was sunk by the British destroyer *Antelope* in the Atlantic on 2 November 1940.

LEAFLET RAIDS AND SEAPLANE-BASE PATROLS,
17/18 February to 8/9 April 1940

Both types of operations continued, with Wellingtons and Hampdens increasingly joining in the leaflet raids and with Hampdens taking over the seaplane-base patrols. At least 1 of these 2 types of operations was flown on 37 out of 52 nights in this period but the number of aircraft dispatched was usually small.

A total of 228 leaflet sorties – 102 by Wellingtons, 64 by Hampdens and 62 by Whitleys – were dispatched between 17/18 February and 6/7 April. The only new feature was the inclusion of Poland in locations where leaflets were dropped, Poznań on 7/8 March and Warsaw on the 15/16th. One of the Whitleys returning from Warsaw – Flight Lieutenant Tomlin's aircraft of 77 Squadron – was running short of fuel and landed in a field as soon as he thought he had reached French territory. Members of the crew left the aircraft and asked the first person they met where they were. They soon realized they were in Germany and German soldiers were observed appearing. The crew managed to take off and were not fired upon until they were clearing the hedge of the field. They hedge-hopped safely over the Siegfried Line and landed in France. Only 6 of the leaflet-dropping planes were lost – 3 Wellingtons, 2 Whitleys and 1 Hampden. One of the Whitleys – again from 77 Squadron – was shot down by Dutch anti-aircraft fire while flying over Holland on 27/28 March; 1 crew member was killed and 4 interned. 7 more leaflet-operations planes crashed in England.

Anti-minelayer patrols were flown over German seaplane bases from 23/24 February until 8/9 April. The total number of sorties flown was 61 – 54 by Hampdens and 7 by Whitleys. No aircraft were shot down by the Germans but 4 Hampdens crashed in England.

20/21 February 1940

GERMAN WARSHIPS, HELIGOLAND

20 Wellingtons were dispatched, 2 as reconnaissance planes and 18 as the bombing force but a recall signal was sent because of fog. 1 Wellington was lost over the sea and 1 crashed in England.

This may have been an experimental raid with the object of finding and bombing German warships by night, to avoid the heavy casualties of recent daylight raids, but the attempt was not repeated.

19/20 March 1940

HÖRNUM SEAPLANE BASE

This was an important operation. While attacking British ships in Scapa Flow in the Orkney Islands, 2 nights earlier, German planes had dropped bombs on land which killed 1 civilian (on an airfield) and wounded 7 more civilians in a village. The British Government ordered Bomber Command to carry out a reprisal raid on one of the German seaplane bases but only where there was no nearby civilian housing. The seaplane base at Hörnum, on the southernmost tip of the island of Sylt, was chosen.

30 Whitleys and 20 Hampdens were dispatched. The Whitleys bombed first, being allocated a 4-hour bombing period; 26 Whitleys claimed to have found the target in clear visibility and to have bombed accurately. The Hampdens followed with a 2-hour bombing period and 15 crews claimed to have bombed accurately. This was the first real bombing operation for both types of aircraft after more than 6 months of war. 20 tons of high explosives and 1,200 incendiary bombs were dropped. Only 1 Whitley was lost.

This was the biggest operation of the war so far and the first raid on a German land target. R.A.F. commanders were gratified that so many crews reported accurate bombing. Proper photographic reconnaissance was not carried out until 6 April when photographs of poor quality were brought back; no damage could be seen but some repairs could have been carried out by the Germans in the interval.

SEARCHES FOR SHIPPING, GERMAN BIGHT TO DENMARK, 4 to 8 April 1940

Warships and troop-ships were known to be collecting in German ports and then sailing north for a possible invasion of Norway. Bomber Command aircraft patrolled the area every day; 45 Blenheim and 3 Hampden sorties were flown. Coastal Command aircraft were also involved in the search. 21 Blenheims found ships on 3 different days and bombed them but without obtaining any hits; the German battleships *Scharnhorst* and *Gneisenau* were among the targets. No aircraft were lost during these operations.

Operational Statistics, 3 September 1939 to 8/9 April 1940
(219 days/nights)

Number of day raids when bombs dropped: 18
Number of days with other operations: 75
Number of night raids when bombs dropped: 3
Number of nights with other operations, mostly leaflets: 69
Number of daylight sorties: 996, from which 48 aircraft (4·8 per cent) were lost
Number of night sorties: 531, from which 14 aircraft (2·6 per cent) were lost
Total sorties: 1,527, from which 62 aircraft (4·1 per cent) were lost
Approximate bomb tonnage dropped in period: 71 tons
Averages per 24-hour period: 7·0 sorties, 0·3 aircraft lost, 0·3 tons of bombs dropped

2. NORWAY AND DENMARK

9 April to 9/10 May 1940

German forces invaded Denmark and Norway at dawn on 9 April 1940. The move into Denmark was by land and, being virtually uncontested, that small country was occupied within hours. The attack on Norway, however, had to be carried out by sea and air landings and was opposed by Norwegian forces. Britain and France immediately declared support for the two countries. Nothing could be done to help Denmark but Bomber Command was ordered to do what it could to slow down the German advance in Southern Norway while an Anglo-French expeditionary force was landed at Narvik in the north.

The bomber squadrons were ill-fitted for their new task. The distance to the scene of operations, with round trips of up to 1,000 miles entirely over sea, was a severe handicap. There was no fighter escort of any kind. Only targets in Southern Norway – where the Germans were soon in full command – could be reached. Nothing could be done to give direct support to the British and French troops who landed in the north at Narvik. The early restrictions against bombing land targets in Germany were not relaxed, so the ports and communications in Northern Germany which were well within range of Bomber Command and which could have been attacked in relative safety at night were left untouched throughout the Norwegian campaign.

Bomber Command entered into its Norway operations with enthusiasm but almost immediately suffered a setback when nine Hampdens and Wellingtons were shot down, most of them by German fighters, in a daylight raid on shipping in the Stavanger area. These losses finally convinced Bomber Command that the self-defending daylight bomber formation theory was not valid and this day, 12 April 1940, marked the end of the pre-war bombing policy; it was undoubtedly the most important turning-point in Bomber Command's war. The Hampdens and Wellingtons were now diverted to night bombing and, except for a very few occasions, they and the more modern types of bomber which would succeed them would fly only by night for the next four years. Only the Blenheims of 2 Group were retained as a permanent day-bomber force, a role which would sometimes bring them heavy casualties, even in the limited radius within which they operated. These tactical rules would continue through the remainder of the Norwegian campaign and for long afterwards.

That campaign would be over within a month. Daylight raids continued when possible but were only successful when weather conditions were favourable. The Blenheims were not allowed to proceed when there was no cloud cover in which they could seek shelter if German fighters appeared and, when they did proceed, they could not find their targets if the cloud was too low. Most of the effort in the later stages was by night. Night casualties were not heavy but bombing results were poor. This was the dilemma posed by the failure of the self-defending bomber policy.

The strength and organization of Bomber Command remained almost unchanged during this period. One new squadron starting its operational life, with a Wellington raid on Stavanger airfield on 17/19 April, was 75 (New Zealand) Squadron, the first Bomber Command squadron with a direct link with one of the Dominions. The groups never operated at full strength; the conservation policy was still in effect. Even on the major daylight operation of 12 April, less than one third of aircraft available were dispatched. Only two squadrons of 2 Group – 107 and 110 – took part in the Norwegian campaign; these squadrons moved north to fly from Lossiemouth in Scotland, leaving the remainder of the group in East Anglia to face a German invasion of France and the Low Countries expected to take place any day. The command of 2 Group changed during this period, Air Vice-Marshal J. M. Robb taking over from Air Vice-Marshal Maclean, and Bomber Command itself received a new commander-in-chief a few days before the Germans invaded Denmark and Norway when Air Marshal Sir Charles Portal took over from Air Chief Marshal Ludlow-Hewitt. Both of these replacements were routine ones and were not a reflection upon the qualities of the outgoing commanders.

---

9 April 1940

GERMAN SHIPPING OFF NORWAY

24 Hampdens searched for German warships off Bergen. 12 aircraft recalled; 2 of remaining 12 bombed a cruiser and claimed hits. 8 Blenheims carried out reconnaissance patrols. No losses.

---

10 April 1940

2 Blenheims on photographic reconnaissance to Wilhelmshaven abandoned task because of weather. 2 Blenheims on North Sea patrol. No losses.

10/11 April 1940

6 Hampdens to patrol seaplane bases at Borkum and Sylt. No incidents.

---

11 April 1940

SHIPPING, STAVANGER AIRFIELD

6 Hampdens dispatched to search for shipping off Kristiansund but abandoned task because weather was too clear. 6 Wellingtons dispatched to bomb Sola airfield near Stavanger (henceforth called 'Stavanger airfield'). 3 aircraft bombed the airfield; 1 of the remaining 3 was shot down by German fighters. 2 Blenheims on reconnaissance, no incidents.

The raid by the Wellingtons – from 115 Squadron – on Stavanger airfield was the first intentional raid by Bomber Command on a European mainland target in the Second World War.

11/12 April 1940

SHIPPING IN SKAGERRAK AND KATTEGAT

23 Whitleys and 20 Hampdens; 4 aircraft attacked ships at various locations between Kiel Bay and Oslo. 1 Whitley scored a direct hit on a ship which was believed to be an ammunition ship and which appeared to explode. 1 Whitley lost.

12 April 1940

SHIPPING AT STAVANGER

83 aircraft – 36 Wellingtons, 24 Hampdens, 23 Blenheims – to attack shipping. Intense Flak and fighter opposition was met. 6 Hampdens and 3 Wellingtons lost. German radio admitted the loss of 5 fighters. The Blenheim formations were not attacked by German fighters.

This was the largest bombing operation of the war so far. It was also the last major daylight raid for Hampdens and Wellingtons.

13 April 1940

9 Blenheims on North Sea patrol. Two patrol vessels bombed. No losses.

13/14 April 1940

Minelaying, Reconnaissance

15 Hampdens on the first R.A.F. minelaying operation of the war. 14 aircraft laid mines in sea lanes off Denmark between German ports and Norway. 1 Hampden lost. 8 Blenheims sent to patrol Wilhelmshaven area abandoned task.

14 April 1940

8 Blenheims to patrol Wilhelmshaven area abandoned task because of lack of cloud cover.

14/15 April 1940

28 Hampdens minelaying off Denmark, 2 lost.

15 April 1940

STAVANGER AIRFIELD, NORTH SEA

11 Blenheims; 6 bombed and 2 German aircraft on the ground were hit. No losses.
2 further Blenheims bombed patrol boats off Wilhelmshaven; 1 Blenheim shot down by 1 of the German boat's defensive fire.

15/16 April 1940
STAVANGER AIRFIELD

12 Whitleys. 8 aircraft bombed and hits were seen on the airfield. No losses.

16 April 1940

STAVANGER AIRFIELD, WILHELMSHAVEN

6 Blenheims. 5 returned because of icing conditions in cloud; 1 reached Stavanger and bombed. 2 Blenheims on reconnaissance to Wilhelmshaven; the battleship *Tirpitz* observed. No losses.

16/17 April 1940

NORWEGIAN AIRFIELDS

20 Whitleys to Stavanger, Vaernes (Trondheim) and Kjeller (Oslo) airfields. Because of bad weather, only 4 planes bombed at Trondheim and 2 at Stavanger. No losses.

17 April 1940

12 Blenheims bombed at Stavanger airfield, 2 lost.

17/18 April 1940

NORWEGIAN AIRFIELDS, MINELAYING

20 Wellingtons and Whitleys to Stavanger, Trondheim and Oslo airfields. 11 Wellingtons bombed at Stavanger but other targets not located. 1 Wellington lost.
    33 Hampdens laid mines off north-west Denmark. No losses.

18/19 April 1940

9 Whitleys to attack shipping in the Oslo and Trondheim areas but because of bad weather only 3 bombed. 1 aircraft lost.

19 April 1940

9 Blenheims to bomb Stavanger airfield. 7 abandoned task because of weather. 1 bombed an airfield. 1 Blenheim lost.

19/20 April 1940

4 Whitleys carried out reconnaissance flights over Northern Germany. No incidents.

20 April 1940

3 Blenheims to Stavanger airfield but task abandoned.

20/21 April 1940

AIRFIELDS, SHIPPING, MINELAYING

36 Whitleys to bomb various airfields and shipping. 22 bombed targets including airfields at Stavanger and Kristiansund, and at Aalborg in Denmark; shipping was not located.

23 Hampdens laid mines in the Elbe estuary and some then patrolled seaplane bases at Borkum and Sylt.

There were no losses from any of these operations.

---

21 April 1940

12 Blenheims to Stavanger airfield abandoned task because of weather conditions.

21/22 April 1940

AIRFIELDS, MINELAYING

36 Hampdens minelaying; 25 laid mines, 1 lost.

12 Wellingtons bombed Stavanger and Aalborg airfields, 1 lost.

22/23 April 1940

AIRFIELDS

10 Whitleys. 7 aircraft bombed Fornebu and Kjeller airfields near Oslo, Aalborg and a seaplane base at Lake Jansavannet. 1 aircraft lost.

23/24 April 1940

AIRFIELDS, MINELAYING, SEAPLANE BASES

34 aircraft – 16 Whitleys, 12 Wellingtons, 6 Blenheims – to airfields. 4 airfields in Norway, Aalborg in Denmark and Westerland in Germany were all bombed, and shipping near Oslo and Trondheim was also attacked. 1 Whitley and 1 Blenheim lost.

30 Hampdens – 26 minelaying and 4 on seaplane-base patrols. 2 ships were bombed. No losses.

---

24 April 1940

6 Blenheims to bomb Stavanger airfield and 1 on a reconnaissance to Aalborg. All abandoned tasks because of weather. No losses.

---

25 April 1940

6 Blenheims to bomb shipping in fjords near Bergen. 5 bombed, 1 lost. 1 Do 18 shot down. 1 reconnaissance Blenheim abandoned its flight to Aalborg.

25/26 April 1940

STAVANGER, OSLO, MINELAYING

18 aircraft – 12 Wellingtons, 6 Whitleys – to attack shipping, airfields and oil-storage tanks at Stavanger and Oslo. 8 aircraft bombed without losses.

2 Whitleys made reconnaissance flights to Aalborg airfield; 1 aircraft was lost. 28 Hampdens were dispatched on minelaying tasks but bad weather prevented any mines being laid; 3 Hampdens were lost. One of the missing Hampdens was shot down near Sylt by Oberfeldwebel Hermann Förster of IV/JG 2, flying an Me 109. The Hampden involved is believed to have been the 49 Squadron aircraft of Pilot Officer A. H. Benson and was probably the first Bomber Command aircraft to be shot down at night by a German fighter. Pilot Officer Benson and his crew – Pilot Officer A. P. B. Hordern, Sergeant R. I. L. McKenzie and Leading Aircraftman J. D. Openshaw – were all killed. Sergeant McKenzie's body came ashore and is now buried in the Kiel War Cemetery but the bodies of the other crew members were never found. Oberfeldwebel Förster's unit was scattered along the German coast in small detachments to act as night fighters and later became the regular night-fighting unit III/NJG 1. Förster gained a further 6 night victories before being sent back to a day-fighter unit; he died in North Africa in December 1941 on his 287th operational flight.

27 April 1940

12 Blenheims to Stavanger airfield abandoned task because of weather conditions.

29 April 1940

2 Blenheims to Aalborg and Rye airfields abandoned task because of weather conditions.

29/30 April 1940

6 Whitleys bombed Fornebu airfield near Oslo. 1 aircraft was lost.

30 April 1940

6 Blenheims bombed Stavanger airfield, where an estimated 150 German aircraft were seen on the ground. 2 Blenheims were lost. 3 Blenheims on reconnaissance to Aalborg and Rye airfields; photographs taken at Rye showed 60 German aircraft on the ground.

30 April/1 May 1940

AIRFIELDS

50 Aircraft – 24 Whitleys, 16 Wellingtons, 10 Hampdens – to Stavanger, Fornebu and Aalborg airfields. 35 aircraft bombed these targets. 2 Wellingtons and 1 Whitley were lost; 4 further aircraft crashed in England.

---

1 May 1940

STAVANGER AIRFIELD

12 Blenheims; 9 bombed with good results observed. No losses.

1/2 May 1940

AIRFIELDS, MINELAYING

12 Whitleys and 6 Hampdens bombed Stavanger, Fornebu and Aalborg airfields. No losses.

11 Hampdens minelaying in Elbe estuary and in Helsingör harbour, Denmark; only 5 aircraft laid mines but 1 German seaplane was claimed shot down. No losses.

---

2 May 1940

AIRFIELDS

12 Blenheims bombed Stavanger and Rye airfields. No losses. The Blenheims were now completely withdrawn from Norwegian operations because a German offensive in France and the Low Countries was feared imminent.

2/3 May 1940

AIRFIELDS, MINELAYING, SEAPLANE-BASE PATROLS

24 aircraft – 12 Whitleys, 12 Wellingtons – to airfields. 22 of them bombed Stavanger, Rye and Fornebu.

26 Hampdens minelaying in Oslo Fjord and Kiel Bay.

4 Wellingtons patrolled seaplane bases.

There were no losses from any of these operations.

3/4 May 1940

10 Hampdens minelaying off Norwegian and German coasts. 2 Wellingtons sent to patrol seaplane bases were recalled. No losses.

4/5 May 1940

Minelaying, Seaplane Base Patrols

5 Hampdens laid mines in Oslo Fjord. 4 Whitleys patrolled German seaplane bases and ports. No losses.

5/6 May 1940

4 Wellingtons patrolled seaplane bases.

6/7 May 1940

12 Hampdens minelaying in Elbe estuary. No losses.

7/8 May 1940

AIRFIELDS, SEAPLANE-BASE PATROLS

9 Wellingtons to bomb Stavanger airfield; only 1 located the target, because of low cloud. 5 Wellingtons to patrol seaplane bases and harbours but only 2 carried out patrols. No losses.

9/10 May 1940

MINELAYING, STAVANGER, SEAPLANE BASES

31 Hampdens to minelaying operations off Kiel, Lübeck, Warnemünde and in the Elbe; 23 aircraft laid mines.

9 Whitleys to bomb Stavanger airfield were recalled because of bad weather; 1 did not pick up signal and bombed the target.

6 Wellingtons patrolled seaplane bases.

There were no losses from any of these operations.

Operational Statistics, 9 April to 9/10 May 1940
(31 days/nights)

Number of day raids when bombs dropped: 12
Number of days with other operations: 7
Number of night raids when bombs dropped: 16
Number of nights with other operations: 8
Number of daylight sorties: 268, from which 17 aircraft (6·3 per cent) were lost
Number of night sorties: 663, from which 19 aircraft (2·9 per cent) were lost
Total sorties: 931, from which 36 aircraft (3·9 per cent) were lost
Approximate bomb tonnage dropped in period: 198 tons*
Average per 24-hour period: 30·0 sorties, 1·2 aircraft lost, 6·4 tons of bombs dropped

* It is not possible to provide tonnages or numbers for mines laid.

3. BLITZKRIEG

10 May to 25/26 June 1940

The long-anticipated German offensive in the West opened early on 10 May with German troops crossing the borders of Belgium and Holland and with airborne landings at several points. This move through the Low Countries outflanked the famous Maginot Line and violent mobile warfare – the Blitzkrieg – commenced immediately. The French and British had foreseen an initial German move through Belgium – as in 1914 – and had prepared plans to move most of the British Expeditionary Force into Belgium to face this, but no cooperation of any kind had been possible with Holland and this country fell within days. The British and French troops in Belgium were steadily pressed back and were eventually encircled with their backs to the sea after a brilliant German armoured breakthrough in the south reached the Channel coast. The evacuation from Dunkirk followed between 26 May and 4 June. Italy came into the war on Germany's side on 10 June. France, which had held the Germans so gallantly for four years in the First World War, finally collapsed on 25 June, only six weeks after the first German attack. It was a period of almost unbelievable historical event.

Despite all the intelligence warnings and the daily reconnaissance flights over Germany before the offensive, Bomber Command had carried out no bombing of any kind to hinder the German preparations; the policy of bombing restraint had been held to the end. The French Government had been promised that the entire British bomber force would be used to help in what came to be called the Battle of France, and Bomber Command was immediately committed. Even though the Norwegian campaign would not end for another four weeks, the whole of the British bomber effort was immediately concentrated into supporting this new, much nearer, land battle.

The Blenheims of 2 Group were placed under the tactical control of the R.A.F.'s Advanced Air Striking Force in France, although the Blenheims continued to fly from their own airfields in England; within days the head of the German advance would be within 200 miles of those airfields. The Blenheims would operate by day throughout the battle and would sometimes suffer heavy casualties in doing so. But the more distant-ranging Wellingtons, Hampdens and Whitleys operated only by night and they would emerge from the battle with the light casualties which had characterized all night operations so far in the war. In return for this comparative immunity, however, they would continue to face almost insuperable problems with navigation, target-finding and bomb-aiming.

The targets for the Blenheims were always on or near the battlefield, where German fighters and mobile Flak batteries were a constant scourge. Initially, the Blenheims flew in formations of six, nine or twelve aircraft; if larger numbers of aircraft are recorded in the diary entries as operating on one day, such numbers usually represent several separate raids. The Blenheims would later learn to operate in larger formations combining several squadrons. The night bombers always flew singly, usually spreading out their raids over several hours of darkness. Initially they attacked the German road and rail communications to the battle front. Despite the ferocity of the German attack and the seriousness of the situation, these raids were restricted by the political order to locations west of the Rhine until 15 May, the day the Germans bombed Rotterdam, when the War Cabinet finally allowed the bombers to cross the Rhine and reach into the German heartland. That date, 15 May 1940, was another of the great turning-points in Bomber Command's war. The R.A.F. commanders could finally start implementing their pre-war plans and the true strategic-bombing offensive against Germany commenced that night when most of the 108 aircraft allocated to operations were sent to industrial targets in Germany; it was the first occasion that more than 100 aircraft were dispatched. But the realities of the situation prevailed and, after only five nights of industrial bombing, the night bombers had to be brought back to attack bridges and communications nearer the battle front. The full-moon period in the second half of May was fully used for this purpose.

A review of both day and night operations took place at the end of May. Although the ground battle still raged, the Blenheims could not continue at their earlier pace because casualties had been so heavy. Their operations were restricted to allow the squadrons to rest, bring in and train new crews, and generally conserve their strength for the next phase. The Battle of France was clearly being lost; a battle for Britain was likely to follow. In the night-bombing war, the tactical bombing behind the battle front slackened with the ending of the moon period and the bombers increasingly turned their attentions to Germany again. Railways, roads and bridges between Germany and the battlefield continued to be attacked but the greater weight of the offensive was now concentrated on German oil refineries and storage depots. On 4 June the wildly optimistic assessment was made that German oil supplies might be reduced by up to half a million tons within the next two or three months, but post-war German records showed that their oil production suffered a loss through bombing of only 150,000 tons *in the next three and a half years*! Such unrealism pervaded the whole night offensive to which nearly 70 per cent of Bomber Command's effort was devoted during the Battle of France. In addition to the attack on communications, other industrial targets were raided, the minelaying campaign was continued and there was even an attempt to burn the German forests during the dry summer nights. The greatest number of bombers used in one night during this period was only 142; the bomb tonnage dropped on any one target was negligible; the achievement of bombing accuracy by night – as has been stated before and as will be mentioned again and again – was proving incredibly difficult, although few of the bomber commanders were yet prepared to face that unpleasant fact. Some German town reports become available during this period and they illustrate that Bomber Command's night raids were to be little more than pinpricks for months to come.

And so Bomber Command played its part in those momentous battles across the English Channel, although it cannot be claimed that the efforts of the bomber crews and their losses – 147 aircraft in the period – significantly altered the course of the campaign. No new types of aircraft were introduced. The strength available on the outbreak of war had not been significantly increased. A force which had been prepared primarily for day operations was being progressively committed to night bombing. On the credit balance, the strategic bombing of Germany had at last commenced and, tactically, the German invasion of Holland and Belgium had given the bombers the freedom to overfly those countries and this would be their route to Germany for the years ahead.

---

10 May 1940

DUTCH AIRFIELDS

33 Blenheims to attack German troop-carrying planes and other targets at Waalhaven and Ypenburg airfields and on a beach north of The Hague; many German planes were reported hit. 3 Blenheims lost.

3. Early Blenheim crews at an unnamed airfield.

10/11 May 1940

WAALHAVEN AIRFIELD, COMMUNICATIONS

36 Wellingtons to Waalhaven airfield and 9 Whitleys to bomb bridges across the Rhine at Rees and Wesel and columns of road transport near Goch and Geldern. No losses.

---

11 May 1940

MAASTRICHT BRIDGES

23 Blenheims to vital road bridges and German troop columns in the Maastricht area; 2 lost.

6 Blenheims abandoned reconnaissance flights because of unfavourable weather.

11/12 May 1940

MÖNCHENGLADBACH

37 aircraft – 19 Hampdens and 18 Whitleys – to attack road and rail communications. This was the first raid of the war on a German town. 4 people were killed including one Englishwoman living there. 2 Hampdens and 1 Whitley lost.

---

12 May 1940

BRIDGES

42 Blenheims to Maastricht, Hasselt and Tongres to bomb bridges and buildings near the bridges in order to block roads. 11 Blenheims lost.

12/13 May 1940

ROAD JUNCTIONS

12 aircraft – 6 Wellingtons and 6 Whitleys – to the area between the Rhine and the Dutch border. No losses.

13/14 May 1940

BRIDGES, ROADS

12 aircraft – 6 Hampdens and 6 Whitleys – to Aachen–Maastricht–Eindhoven area. No losses.

6 Hampdens went minelaying in the Kiel Canal but only 1 did so successfully. No losses.

---

14 May 1940

THE MEUSE, HOLLAND

28 Blenheims to bomb bridges and German troops who were making a new breakthrough on the River Meuse; 6 Blenheims lost. 6 further Blenheims to bomb road junction at Breda, no losses.

14/15 May 1940

COMMUNICATIONS IN GERMANY AND HOLLAND

18 Wellingtons to the Aachen area, 12 Whitleys to Mönchengladbach, 12 Hampdens to Breda and Roosendaal. 1 Hampden lost.

22 Hampdens minelaying near Kiel and Copenhagen.

---

15 May 1940

BELGIUM

24 Blenheims to attack communications and bridges; 3 aircraft lost.

15/16 May 1940

RUHR INDUSTRY AND RAILWAYS

99 aircraft – 39 Wellingtons, 36 Hampdens, 24 Whitleys – to 16 different targets in the Ruhr area. Factories at Dortmund, Sterkrade and Castrop-Rauxel were designated as targets for 9 aircraft each; all other targets had fewer aircraft. 81 aircraft reported bombing at their primary targets or at alternatives over a wide area. This was the first strategic bombing of German industry in the Second World War. No aircraft were shot down over Germany but 1 Wellington, of 115 Squadron, blown off course by an unexpected wind, crashed into high ground at Burney near Rouen in France. Flight Lieutenant A. E. Pringle and his 4 crewmen were all killed, the first R.A.F. casualties of the strategic bombing war.

A report from Cologne says that bombs aimed at the I G-Werk at Dormagen hit a large farm and killed a dairyman, Franz Romeike, who became Cologne's first air-raid casualty, the first of approximately 20,000 Cologne people killed in air raids and artillery assault during the war. Another report says that Herr Romeike had switched on an outside light by mistake while on the way to the toilet and that this light promptly attracted a stick of high-explosive bombs. 5 more people in Cologne were wounded.

Another report, from Münster, describes the dropping of 6 bombs in the town which caused light damage and wounded 2 people, although Münster was not on the list of towns to be attacked and no bomber reported attacking it as an alternative. The Münster report continues: 'This bombing created a sensation and, for days on end, thousands of inquisitive people were attracted to the scene.'

12 further aircraft – 6 Wellingtons, 6 Whitleys – attacked German communications in Belgium without loss. This brought the total number of aircraft operating on this night to 111, the first time that more than 100 bombers were dispatched on one occasion since the war began.

16/17 May 1940

GERMAN TARGETS

12 aircraft – 6 Hampdens and 6 Wellingtons – to oil targets in the Ruhr; 1 Wellington lost. 9 Whitleys to bomb communications between Germany and the battle front, no losses.

---

17 May 1940

GEMBLOUX

12 Blenheims, all from 82 Squadron, sent to bomb German troops who had created a gap in the Allied lines. Flak forced the squadron to loosen its formation and German fighters then attacked. 11 Blenheims were lost; the only surviving plane was badly damaged and crash-landed in England.

17/18 May 1940

HAMBURG, BREMEN, COLOGNE, BELGIUM

48 Hampdens to Hamburg and 24 Whitleys to Bremen, all attacking oil refineries; 6 Wellingtons to railway yards at Cologne. 46 Wellingtons and 6 Hampdens attacked German troop communications in Belgium. By contrast with the almost complete loss of the Blenheim bomber formation the previous day, there were no losses from the 130 aircraft dispatched on this night.

A report from Hamburg lists 36 separate fires, the largest causing the complete gutting of the Mercksche fertilizer factory, and 160 buildings damaged by high-explosive bombs. The most seriously damaged building after the fertilizer factory was in the Reeperbahn. 34 people – 28 civilians and 6 servicemen – were killed and 72 people injured.*

In Bremen, 6 fires were started, the largest being in 2 warehouses at the docks which were full of furniture confiscated from emigrating Jews. 13 people were killed and 55 injured.

18 May 1940

LE CATEAU

13 Blenheims attacked German columns, 3 lost.

18/19 May 1940

GERMANY, BELGIUM

60 aircraft – 24 Wellingtons, 24 Whitleys, 12 Hampdens – to various oil refineries and railway yards in Germany, and to German troop communications in Belgium. 1 Whitley lost.

19/20 May 1940

GERMANY, BELGIUM AND FRANCE

78 aircraft – 36 Hampdens, 30 Wellingtons, 12 Whitleys – carried out widespread attacks on German troop communications in France and Belgium and on railway and industrial targets in Germany. 2 Whitleys lost.

*Most of the Hamburg reports quoted are from *Feuersturm über Hamburg* by Hans Brunswig, Stuttgart, Motorbuch, 1978. Brunswig was a senior fire officer in Hamburg during the war and his book, which includes as an appendix casualty figures from Hamburg's civil records, is a very useful reference work.

20 May 1940

BAPAUME–ARRAS ROAD

47 Blenheims attacked the German armoured thrust which was threatening to encircle the B.E.F. from the south. An R.A.F. fighter escort was provided and German fighters did not intervene. No Blenheims lost.

20/21 May 1940

NORTHERN FRANCE

92 aircraft – 32 Wellingtons, 24 Whitleys, 18 Hampdens, 18 Blenheims – were dispatched in an attempt to delay the new German breakthrough. The Blenheim contribution was an experiment in night operations for this type of aircraft, an attempt to avoid the heavy day casualties. 77 aircraft bombed a variety of targets. 3 Whitleys and 1 Wellington lost.

21 May 1940

NORTHERN FRANCE

61 Blenheims (3 on reconnaissance flights) to attack the German columns advancing rapidly through to the coast north of the River Somme. 57 aircraft found targets to bomb but some were hampered by the presence of French refugees on the roads. 3 Blenheims lost.

21/22 May 1940

GERMAN RAILWAYS

124 aircraft – 52 Whitleys, 47 Wellingtons, 25 Hampdens – to attack German railways leading to the battle front at many places between Mönchengladbach and Euskirchen, particularly in the Aachen area. 5 aircraft – 3 Wellingtons, 1 Whitley, 1 Hampden – lost. The pilot of the lost Hampden, Flight Lieutenant Coton of 83 Squadron, ordered his 3 crewmen to bale out soon after the aircraft was hit by Flak over Germany. The pilot managed to bring his plane to England but it was hit again by British anti-aircraft guns on the Essex coast. The pilot baled out safely and the Hampden crashed near Hornchurch.

22 May 1940

NORTHERN FRANCE

59 Blenheims (1 reconnaissance) attacked the German columns advancing to the French coast. 3 Blenheims lost.

22/23 May 1940

MERSEBURG, FRANCE, BELGIUM, HOLLAND

47 aircraft – 24 Whitleys, 12 Hampdens, 11 Wellingtons – to bomb numerous railway, bridge and road targets in France, Belgium and Holland. 35 Hampdens to the oil refinery at Merseburg near Leipzig, a very distant target for this period of the war; because of deteriorating weather conditions over the English airfields this force was recalled. 1 Hampden did not receive the recall signal and went on to bomb Merseburg.

No aircraft was lost from any of the above operations but 3 crashed in England.

23 May 1940

NORTHERN FRANCE

27 Blenheims to bomb German troop columns south of Arras; weather conditions were bad and only 16 aircraft bombed various targets. 3 Blenheims lost, including the aircraft of the commander of 40 Squadron, Wing Commander J. G. Llewelyn; this was the second commanding officer lost by 40 Squadron in 8 days.

23/24 May 1940

COMMUNICATIONS TO BATTLE FRONT

122 aircraft – 50 Hampdens, 48 Wellingtons, 24 Whitleys – to bomb trains, road and rail bridges and junctions over a wide area. The Hampdens were allocated targets in Germany west of the Rhine and in Holland; other aircraft were sent to France and Belgium. 2 Hampdens and 1 Whitley lost.

24 May 1940

CALAIS

69 Blenheims attacked German troops surrounding the British garrison at Calais. No losses.

24/25 May 1940

COMMUNICATIONS

59 aircraft – 29 Whitleys, 18 Hampdens, 12 Wellingtons – to attack communications between Germany and the battle front over a wide area. No losses.

25 May 1940

BRIDGES AND TRANSPORT

42 Blenheims to bomb troops and vehicles and vital bridges just behind the German front line, now closing in on the main body of the B.E.F., which had its back to the coast. 4 Blenheims lost.

25/26 May 1940

COMMUNICATIONS, TROOP POSITIONS

103 aircraft – 38 Wellingtons, 36 Whitleys, 29 Hampdens – to targets over a wide area. The Wellingtons attempted to bomb troop locations close to the battlefield in France and Belgium; the Whitleys and Hampdens mostly attacked communications further in the rear. 2 Hampdens and 1 Wellington lost.

A report from Cologne describes how a Whitley, despite thick cloud, accurately bombed the Südbrücke and how the gas main under the bridge was set alight. The wooden planking of the railway bridge started burning and the bridge was closed to traffic for at least 1½ hours. This would be a typical incident during these attempts to cut communications between Germany and the battle front.

26 May 1940

DUNKIRK AREA

34 Blenheims attacked positions behind the German forces which now surrounded the Dunkirk perimeter. There were no losses. The evacuation from Dunkirk commenced on the evening of this day.

26/27 May 1940

COMMUNICATIONS, AIRFIELDS

43 aircraft – 22 Wellingtons, 21 Hampdens – attacked troop columns, railways and airfields in France, Belgium and Holland. No losses.

27 May 1940

DUNKIRK AREA

48 Blenheims attacked German positions around Dunkirk, 2 lost.

27/28 May 1940

OIL, COMMUNICATIONS

120 aircraft – 49 Hampdens, 36 Whitleys, 35 Wellingtons.

24 Hampdens attacked oil refineries at Hamburg and Bremen. Hamburg records show that the raid here was not a success. Only 7 high-explosive bombs and a few incendiaries fell in the city, causing 1 small fire. One bomb fell in the Blohm & Voss shipbuilding yard and damaged the lighting system. In nearby Harburg, 3 bombs fell very close to a group of whale-oil tanks and 3,000 tons of oil leaked through the splinter holes. All but 32 tons of this was later reclaimed and pumped back into the tanks. There were no casualties in the Hamburg area.

The Whitleys attacked 6 railway yards in the Ruhr. The remainder of the Hampdens and all the Wellingtons attacked communications behind the battle front in France and Belgium.

There were no R.A.F. losses from any of these operations. A Whitley of 10

Squadron, piloted by Squadron Leader Hanafin, shot down a German fighter near Utrecht. This is believed to be the first German night fighter shot down in the war. The tail gunner whose fire hit the fighter was Aircraftman Oldridge.

---

28 and 28/29 May 1940

DUNKIRK

48 Blenheims by day and 34 Wellingtons and 13 Whitleys by night attacked German positions near the perimeter. 1 Blenheim and 1 Whitley lost.

---

29 and 29/30 May 1940

DUNKIRK

51 Blenheims by day and 15 Wellingtons by night continued the attacks in poor weather conditions. No aircraft were lost but the pilots of 4 Wellingtons ordered their crews to bale out on returning to England in bad weather; all of the pilots managed to land safely. One of the men who baled out was never found.

---

30 May 1940

DUNKIRK

68 Blenheims flew in poor weather conditions; only 44 were able to bomb. No losses.

30/31 May 1940

DUNKIRK, HAMBURG, BREMEN

28 Wellingtons attempted to bomb German positions around Dunkirk; 1 was lost. 18 Hampdens to oil targets at Hamburg and Bremen. Hamburg reports 1 person injured, no fires, No losses.

---

31 May, 31 May/1 June 1940

DUNKIRK

126 aircraft – 93 Blenheims by day and 33 Wellingtons by night – attacked German positions. This was the largest daylight operation so far by 2 Group's Blenheims. 2 Wellingtons lost.

---

1 June 1940

DUNKIRK

56 Blenheims to German positions, none lost.

1/2 June 1940

GERMANY, DUNKIRK

37 Hampdens and 28 Whitleys attacked a wide range of oil and communications targets in Germany from Hamburg to Koblenz but only 25 aircraft found suitable targets. 16 Wellingtons bombed German positions around Dunkirk. No losses.

2 June 1940

DUNKIRK

24 Blenheims attacked German positions. No losses.

2/3 June 1940

GERMANY, DUNKIRK

24 Whitleys and 6 Hampdens attacked oil and communications targets at many places between Hamburg and Frankfurt. 16 Wellingtons attacked positions near Dunkirk. No losses.

3 June 1940

DUNKIRK

18 Blenheims bombed, no losses.

This day saw the end of the evacuation from Dunkirk. 2 Group's Blenheims had flown on all but 3 days – days when weather conditions had been bad – since the opening of the German offensive; they had also flown 1 night operation. A total of 956 sorties had been flown and 57 aircraft lost. This was a loss rate of 6·3 per cent, or the equivalent of 4 complete squadrons from the 9 squadrons in 2 Group which were operational during most of this period.

The Blenheims were given 1 day's rest before resuming operations, this time in support of the French Army and the few remaining British units further south in France.

3/4 June 1940

COMMUNICATIONS, INDUSTRY

The night squadrons continued operations with their largest effort to date. 142 aircraft – 48 Hampdens, 48 Whitleys, 46 Wellingtons – attacked many targets from Hamburg to Frankfurt; a few of the Wellingtons made a last attack on German positions near Dunkirk. 1 Hampden was lost and another crashed into a barrage-balloon cable at Felixstowe when returning to England.

4/5 June 1940

GERMANY

57 aircraft – 23 Hampdens, 17 Wellingtons, 17 Whitleys – were sent to many targets in Germany. 1 Whitley lost.

5 June 1940

FRANCE

23 Blenheims attacked German troops and communications in the Bapaume–Peronne–Albert area (exactly the area of the Battle of the Somme in 1916). No losses.

5/6 June 1940

GERMANY, FRANCE

92 aircraft – 36 Hampdens, 34 Wellingtons, 22 Whitleys – attacked railways in Germany and communications in the Somme area. 1 Hampden and 1 Wellington lost. Hamburg reports a sharp raid with 10 fires (5 large) and 16 people killed. 6 Hampdens resumed the minelaying campaign by mining the Langelands channel in Denmark, no losses.

6 June 1940

ST-VALÉRY

38 Blenheims operated in support of the 51st (Highland) Division, still fighting at St-Valéry. 5 Blenheims lost.

6/7 June 1940

HAMBURG, FRANCE

24 Wellingtons and 17 Whitleys attacked troops and communications in France. 24 Hampdens were sent to Hamburg for bombing and minelaying in the River Elbe. 15 of 18 aircraft reported bombing their targets. Hamburg reports 5 fires, 16 people killed and 7 injured. Only 2 of the 6 minelaying aircraft carried out their task.

There were no losses from any of these operations.

NORTHERN FRANCE, 7 to 13 June 1940

Blenheims of 2 Group attacked German troops, columns and communications in the same general area of Northern France every day, using the same tactics. 355 sorties were flown and 23 Blenheims lost.

FRANCE, GERMANY, 7/8 to 10/11 June 1940

The night bombers also continued their operations in a regular fashion. 336 bombing sorties were flown – 114 Wellingtons, 111 Hampdens and 111 Whitleys. Most of the effort was on the German communications and military positions in the continuing Battle of France but the largest single raid was by 24 Hampdens on an oil refinery at Hannover on 7/8 June. 283 of these night sorties claimed to have bombed their targets.

Minelaying operations continued every night with 23 Hampden sorties; 16 successfully laid mines.

Only 1 aircraft was lost by night in this period, a Hampden from a bombing raid to Germany on 9/10 June.

11/12 June 1940

ITALY, GERMANY, FRANCE

Following Italy's declaration of war on France and Britain on 10 June, 36 Whitleys were dispatched to Italy. They refuelled in the Channel Islands before their long flight over France and the Alps to bomb factories in Turin. 23 aircraft were not able to reach Italy because of difficult weather over the Alps. 9 aircraft bombed Turin but not the designated factories; most bombed railway yards. Turin reports 17 people killed and 40 injured. 2 other aircraft bombed targets at Genoa. Both cities were fully lit up, as in peacetime, when the bombers arrived; Turin's lights were turned off during the raid but Genoa's were not. Heavy anti-aircraft fire was encountered over Turin. A Whitley of 77 Squadron crashed in flames near Le Mans on its return flight and Sergeant N. M. Songest and his crew – Sergeants R. C. Astbury, P. H. J. Budden, A. Findlay and E. Ombler – were all killed, the first casualties of Bomber Command's operations to Italy, which would continue spasmodically over the next three years. A further Whitley crashed in France.

59 aircraft – 31 Hampdens, 18 Wellingtons, 10 Whitleys – bombed various targets in Germany and France; 1 Hampden and 1 Whitley were lost. The Wellingtons all carried out incendiary raids in the Black Forest in an attempt to cause widespread forest fires. This was one of the Air Ministry's pre-war 'Western Air Plans'; there is no evidence that the forest attacks or the fire-raising attacks on the German harvest, both of which would continue for several weeks, brought any success; they were a considerable waste of effort at a time when the war was going very badly for Britain.

5 Hampdens went minelaying without loss.

12/13 June 1940

FRANCE

29 Hampdens and 8 Whitleys were sent to military objectives in France but only 15 found suitable targets. 1 Hampden was lost and another hit a balloon cable at Harwich, crashing and setting fire to a flour mill on the docks.

6 Hampdens minelaying without loss.

13/14 June 1940

FRANCE, BELGIUM, HOLLAND

163 aircraft – 65 Wellingtons, 64 Hampdens, 34 Whitleys – attacked a wide range of communications targets. Some of the Hampdens bombed Boulogne and Dunkirk docks and airfields at Flushing (Vlissingen) and Ostend. 1 Wellington lost.

NORTHERN FRANCE, 14 and 15 June 1940

2 Group's Blenheims continued their raids in support of the Battle of France. 60 sorties were flown on the 14th (the day Paris fell), with 4 lost, and 12 sorties on the 15th with 2 lost. A new type of target on the 14th was Merville airfield.

14/15 June 1940

FRANCE, GERMANY

43 Whitleys bombed targets in France in support of the land battle; 1 was lost. 24 Wellingtons and 5 Hampdens bombed targets in the Ruhr and in Southern Germany. 16 Wellingtons were sent as far south as Basle and Konstanz, on the Bodensee (Lake Constance); this was presumably an attempt to carry the bomber offensive to the extreme corners of this part of Germany.

15/16 June 1940

GENOA

Bomber Command established a small detachment at the French airfield of Salon, near Toulon, so that raids could more easily be carried out against Italian targets. 8 Wellingtons from this force were dispatched to Genoa but only 1 bombed. 1 Hampden from England made a reconnaissance flight over the North Sea. There were no losses.

16/17 June 1940

GENOA, MILAN

22 Wellingtons, 14 bombed. There were no losses.

MINELAYING, 16/17 to 25/26 June 1940

A regular force of 6 Hampdens was sent minelaying on every night during this period except 22/23 June. 54 sorties were dispatched, 42 laid mines successfully, 1 Hampden was lost on the night of 23/24 June.

17/18 June 1940

GERMANY

After a 2-night rest, the home-based night squadrons resumed intensive operations. 139 aircraft – 51 Whitleys, 49 Wellingtons, 39 Hampdens – were sent to Northern Germany and numerous targets in the Ruhr. 2 Whitleys were lost. A report from Cologne says that 20 high-explosive bombs fell in the city centre; 3 industrial premises were severely damaged and a Rhine cargo ship was sunk. 6 civilians were killed, the heaviest casualty list so far in Cologne.

18 June 1940

CHERBOURG

6 Blenheims attacked armoured vehicles near Cherbourg without loss.

18/19 June 1940

GERMANY

69 aircraft – 38 Whitleys, 26 Wellingtons, 5 Hampdens – were sent to oil targets at Hamburg, Bremen and in the Ruhr and to railways at many other places. 2 Whitleys and 1 Wellington were lost. Hamburg reports 9 fires, 6 of them large ones, 1 civilian killed and 6 injured.

19 June 1940

AIRFIELDS

30 Blenheims attacked airfields at Rouen and Amiens with good results observed and no losses.

19/20 June 1940

GERMANY

112 aircraft – 53 Hampdens, 37 Wellingtons, 22 Whitleys – to 15 oil and railway targets between Hamburg and Mannheim. 1 Wellington and 1 Whitley lost. Münster reports many bombs with 6 people killed, the town's first dead of the war. Hamburg reports 1 person killed but no fires.

20 June 1940

AIRFIELDS

47 Blenheims attacked airfields at Rouen and Schiphol with good results and no losses. 2 Blenheims abandoned photographic reconnaissance flights to the Ruhr because weather was too clear.

20/21 June 1940

GERMANY

39 Whitleys and 17 Hampdens attacked a wide variety of targets in the Rhineland; some Hampdens bombed Schiphol airfield. 1 Hampden and 1 Whitley lost.

---

21 June 1940

GERMANY

10 Blenheims, on a new kind of operation. Making use of cloud cover, the Blenheims were to fly to targets in Germany which had recently been attacked by night bombers. The bombing by the Blenheims was intended to extend the disruption at such targets through daylight hours, to take photographs of the night-bombing results and to draw the German day-fighter strength away from the Channel coast near England.

The cloud cover was not good on this day and only 2 Blenheims bombed targets, at Bremen and at Hamstede airfield. There were no losses.

21/22 June 1940

GERMANY

105 aircraft – 42 Hampdens, 33 Wellingtons, 30 Whitleys – attacked a wide range of targets in Northern Germany, the Ruhr and Central Germany. Schiphol airfield and Antwerp were also bombed. 1 Hampden and 1 Wellington lost.

---

22 June 1940

AIRFIELDS

18 Blenheims bombed Merville airfield; 3 further Blenheims abandoned flights to Germany and bombed Schiphol airfield. No losses.

22/23 June 1940

This was the first night without any Bomber Command raids since the opening of the German offensive in the West. There had been 44 continuous nights of operations but only rarely a 'maximum effort'. The night squadrons had not been as fully extended as the day squadrons and their casualty rate had been much lower (see statistics at end of section).

---

23 June 1940

GERMANY, BELGIUM

26 Blenheims to Osnabrück, Hamm and Soest. Some proceeded to these targets, others bombed airfields in Holland. 3 Blenheims lost.

23/24 June 1940

GERMANY

53 Hampdens and 26 Whitleys attacked Bremen and 11 other targets in the Ruhr and the Rhineland. No losses.

24 June 1940

DUTCH AIRFIELDS

8 Blenheims bombed Schiphol and Eindhoven; no losses.

24/25 June 1940

GERMANY

103 aircraft – 68 Wellingtons, 19 Hampdens, 16 Whitleys – attacked 21 targets in Germany between Hamburg and Mannheim. No losses.

25 June 1940

GERMANY, HOLLAND

25 Blenheims to targets in Germany. Most turned back because of lack of cloud cover. Rotterdam airfield and an iron foundry at Alkmaar were bombed. No losses.

25/26 June 1940

GERMANY

48 aircraft – 24 Hampdens, 12 Wellingtons, 12 Whitleys – dispatched and 21 different targets in Germany and Holland bombed. No losses.

The armistice which the French Government had agreed with the Germans on 21 June came into effect on 25 June.

Operational Statistics, 10 May to 25/26 June 1940
(47 days/nights)

Number of days with operations: 41
Number of nights with operations: 46
Number of daylight sorties: 1,601, from which 92 aircraft (5·7 per cent) were lost
Number of night sorties: 3,484, from which 53 aircraft (1·5 per cent) were lost
Total sorties: 5,085, from which 145 aircraft (2·9 per cent) were lost
Approximate bomb tonnage in period: 3,492 tons
Averages per 24-hour period: 108·2 sorties, 3·1 aircraft lost, 74·3 tons of bombs dropped

4. THE BATTLE OF BRITAIN

26 June to 12/13 October 1940

The fall of France and Norway left German forces in control of the coast of Europe from Norway to the Spanish border. Hitler's plan now was either to persuade England to make peace or to launch an invasion across the narrow English Channel or the North Sea and defeat the weakened British Army before winter. Great Britain stood nearly alone against what was seen at that time as the almost unbeatable victor of Europe. Her only allies were the members of the Empire, although Britain's forces would also be reinforced by the men who had fled the countries defeated by Germany. Replacement of lost equipment and time to reorganize the Army which had returned from France were Britain's main problems. The Royal Navy, although having lost many small ships at Dunkirk, was still powerful. Much of the R.A.F.'s strength had been carefully conserved and it was at least as strong, and certainly more experienced, than at the outbreak of war.

Led and inspired by her new Prime Minister, Winston Churchill, Britain had no intention of settling for peace with Germany. The Battle of Britain would have to be fought to its conclusion. On 16 July, three weeks after the fall of France, Hitler ordered his commanders to prepare *Unternehmung Seelöwe* (Operation *Sea Lion*) – the invasion of Southern England – preceded by the destruction of R.A.F. Fighter Command on its airfields or in the air. The first, probing, German air attacks soon followed, and they increased in intensity through August and into September, when the climax came. The outcome is well known. The R.A.F. was not destroyed; the invasion did not come. The Germans then turned their bombing operations to night, thus submitting to the same tactical rules which had forced most of the R.A.F. bomber force to abandon daylight operations when faced by determined fighter opposition. London and many other British cities had to endure a sustained offensive by German bombers.

The victory of the Battle of Britain belonged mainly to Fighter Command; the bomber squadrons were able to play no more than a supporting role. Six major directives were issued in rapid succession to Bomber Command during the period under review here. The Air Ministry was torn between maintaining the long-term strategic offensive against selective parts of German industry and the need to devote effort to targets which could bring immediate relief in the front line. Such diversions from the main aim to more immediate problems would plague Bomber Command operations for years to come. So – although some of the available bombers were sent to Germany night after night to attack industrial targets (oil was still the first priority), to bomb the German communications system and to attempt the burning of forests and even autumn crops according to those old pre-war plans – an increasing amount of effort had to be devoted to attacking the airfields from which the Luftwaffe was operating, and German aircraft factories, even though these factories were often distant and hard to find. There was also a prolonged series of raids on any form of German shipping, especially the concentrations of barges which the Germans brought from Europe's inland-waterway system and gathered in the ports along the Channel and North Sea coasts. The destruction of many of these barges was probably Bomber Command's greatest contribution to the Battle of Britain. The result of all these calls upon the bomber strength meant that there was no concentration of effort on any one system. This is not intended as a criticism; the needs of that historic period demanded that Bomber Command play a supporting role whenever it was required.

Bomber Command had lost 145 aircraft during the Battle of France, plus the further number which had crashed in England or been seriously damaged in action. These casualties were equivalent to at least half the front-line strength which had been available at the opening of the German offensive less than two months earlier. But there had been some increase in the number of squadrons available. Three squadrons created by Czech and Polish airmen were formed in September: 311 (Czech) Squadron, with Wellingtons, was the first to fly on operations on 10/11 September and was closely followed by 300 and 301 (Polish) Squadrons flying old Fairey Battles three nights later. The bomber squadrons of the Advanced Air Striking Force returned from France and were nominally available for operations but they had taken a severe mauling and the first of them – 103 and 150 Squadrons – would not fly for nearly a month. Most of the Battle squadrons would help to re-form the original No. 1 Group and would soon be given a more effective aircraft, the Wellington; 1 Group would eventually become one of the most powerful in Bomber Command. The other groups had to replace their recent losses and many aircraft required extensive repair or were retired to training units. The Blenheim losses in the Battle of France were replaced with particular speed and more squadrons were added; there were eleven Blenheim squadrons with 180 aircraft available for operations by the end of July.

There was still no significant increase in bombing accuracy. Nearly all night raids were carried out by small numbers of aircraft sent to numerous targets. Each crew was required to find its own way and navigation was always a more severe problem than any defence the Germans could present. Visual sightings of the ground could be useful on moonlit nights but, when such sightings were not possible, navigation was almost all by 'dead reckoning' – the theoretical working out of an aircraft's position using forecast winds. Any improvement on this system by the use of radio bearings, astro navigation or the detection of wind changes was a chancy business. Major navigational errors were frequent. If a crew did find the city which housed its designated target – the city itself was not yet the target – the bomber had to fly around for some time, at various heights depending on the determination of the crew, trying to establish the exact location of the target by means of map-reading and by the light of the moon or the single flares which aircraft released; there was never an attempt to concentrate the flares into a short period of the night. The darkness and the effective German black-out often concealed the target, and increasingly dense and effective Flak and searchlights forced the bombers to higher altitudes and made any waiting in the target area more hazardous. A few aircraft were now fitted with 'bombing cameras' which would take a flashlit photograph of the ground at the approximate moment of bomb impact. These were usually given to the most experienced crews and, if the results had been interpreted properly, would have shown glaring discrepancies between the claims of crews and the actual results of the bombing. But optimism usually prevailed.

A study of civil records from three German cities – Hamburg, Wilhelmshaven and Münster – gives some indication both of the small scale of the raids and of their lack of effectiveness during this period. The targets in Wilhelmshaven were the docks – home of the pre-war German navy – in Hamburg oil-storage depots and the docks, and in Münster the railway and canal system. Münster was bombed on fourteen nights in the three-and-a-half-month period covered by this part of the diary but on only one night did more than ten bombs fall in the city and that night was the only one when there were fatal casualties, two people being killed. Hamburg had raids on thirty-six nights, with fatal casualties – nineteen people killed – on only ten of those nights, and with 'large fires' occurring on only five nights. (Two day raids on Hamburg are described under their individual diary entries.) Wilhelmshaven was bombed twenty-one times. Houses were destroyed on one night, seriously damaged on two nights and slightly damaged on four nights. The only other buildings mentioned are a crematorium destroyed and a school and a water-pumping station damaged. Bombs fell in the dock area frequently but only caused 'trifling damage' (*'geringer Schaden'*) on two occasions. Four people were killed in Wilhelmshaven, three of them in the dock area. Again, it is not claimed that such records are comprehensive and it is possible that some of the more serious damage which might have occurred in such places as the naval dockyard at Wilhelmshaven would not be included in the basically civil records available, but the overall picture is one of dozens of small raids having only a very slight effect upon the German war effort.

The German defences were hardly more effective. The Luftwaffe was as unprepared for a night-bombing war over their own country as the R.A.F. had been to wage such a war. The total German night-fighter force at this period numbered no more than forty aircraft, mostly Messerschmitt 110s. The night-fighter crews had no radar aids and had to find the British bombers by moonlight or in searchlight beams, although the searchlights were stationed near cities at this period of the war and the German fighters were thus likely to be shot at by their own Flak. The general story is of a very late and slow start by the German night-fighter force.

The Blenheims continued to operate mostly by day, either escorted to short-range targets by fighters or being sent to fly singly to Germany on 'cloud-cover' raids. A few of the Blenheims operated by night, their speciality becoming the bombing of Luftwaffe airfields in France, Belgium and Holland.

---

26 June 1940

GERMANY

13 Blenheims – 12 bombing, 1 reconnaissance – but only 3 bombed various targets. 1 aircraft lost.

26/27 June 1940

GERMANY, HOLLAND, BELGIUM

107 Hampdens, Wellingtons and Whitleys to multiple targets and minelaying.* 3 Hampdens lost from the operations of this night, 1 of them being from the minelaying force.

---

* Henceforth, when aircraft of all three night-bombing types were dispatched in a single night, the diary refers to these only as 'aircraft' except, as noted in future entries, when other aircraft come into action with the night-bombing force. When numbers of aircraft on minelaying operations are not specified, it can be assumed that a routine force of 6 Hampdens was dispatched.

4. Hampden and a Wellington of an early wartime period. These particular aircraft belonged to training units, not to front-line squadrons. Bomber Command Wellingtons flew 47,409 operational sorties during the war and Hampdens 16,541 sorties.

27 June 1940

GERMANY, CHANNEL COAST

24 Blenheims, 12 bombing targets, 12 on extensive reconnaissance of the Channel coast. Only 6 aircraft bombed, 5 at Hannover. 1 aircraft lost.

27/28 June 1940

GERMANY, HOLLAND

96 aircraft to industrial targets in Germany, airfields in Holland and minelaying. 1 minelaying Hampden lost.

28 June 1940

MERVILLE

20 Blenheims to bomb Merville airfield and on reconnaissance flights; all abandoned operations because of weather. No losses.

28/29 June 1940

GERMANY, HOLLAND

108 aircraft to industrial targets in Germany, airfields in Holland and minelaying. No losses.

29 June 1940

ABBEVILLE

12 Blenheims to Abbeville airfield and all bombed. 6 Blenheims on reconnaissance. No losses.

29/30 June 1940

GERMANY, HOLLAND

83 aircraft to various targets. 2 Hampdens and 1 Whitley lost.

30 June 1940

FRANCE

18 Blenheims, 12 to Merville airfield and 6 to Vignacourt aircraft depot. 3 aircraft lost.

30 June/1 July 1940

GERMANY

88 aircraft, 82 to bomb Darmstadt, Hamburg, Hamm and Hanau and 6 minelaying. No losses.

Bomber Command's Operations Record Book includes the expression 'fire-raising attacks' for this night. There is no explanation for this phrase but it is believed to refer to the carrying of quantities of small fire-raising devices, code-named *Deckers* and *Razzles*, which were dropped on German forests and on the ripening German harvest after aircraft had carried out their normal bombing attack. The smaller devices, believed to be the *Deckers*, which were used in an attempt to burn the crops, were impregnated pieces of cloth with a delayed ignition process. When they fell near houses, people who collected them as souvenirs and carried them round in their pockets received a nasty surprise when the device suddenly burst into flames. (This report comes from Hamburg.)

1 July 1940

GERMANY, FRANCE

38 aircraft – 24 Wellingtons, 13 Whitleys, 1 Blenheim – on 'cloud-cover raids' to Germany. Most of the targets were in the Ruhr but 5 Whitleys attempted to bomb the battleship *Scharnhorst* at Kiel; results are not known. 1 Whitley lost.

24 Blenheims carried out extensive photographic reconnaissance of the French coast without loss.

1/2 July 1940

GERMANY

73 aircraft to Osnabrück and Kiel and minelaying. 1 Hampden and 1 Whitley lost.

One of the Hampdens attacking the *Scharnhorst* at Kiel was flown by Flying Officer Guy Gibson of 83 Squadron, who dropped the first 2,000-lb bomb of the war. He released it on the sixth shallow dive-bombing attempt but the bomb overshot the *Scharnhorst* and exploded in the town of Kiel. 10 people were killed in Kiel on this night.

---

2 July 1940

GERMANY

11 Blenheims dispatched; 10 returned because of lack of cloud cover, the remaining aircraft was lost while attempting to bomb the Dortmund–Ems Canal.

2/3 July 1940

GERMANY, HOLLAND, BELGIUM

66 aircraft, including Blenheims on this night, to various targets. No losses.

---

3 July 1940

GERMANY, HOLLAND, BELGIUM

33 Blenheims on various tasks; 24 aircraft bombed targets that included for the first time barges being brought up the Rhine near Rotterdam for the intended invasion of Britain.

A report from Hamburg tells of 1 Blenheim which suddenly appeared out of the clouds and dropped 4 bombs in a residential area 3 miles from the nearest docks, though industrial premises may have been near by. There was no warning siren and one of the bombs fell near a group of children playing in a street. 11 children and 8 adults were killed; 31 houses were damaged. Because it was daylight, no first-aid or rescue teams were on duty and many of the wounded were taken to hospital on the fire-engines of Hamburg's regular fire brigade.

3/4 July 1940

GERMANY, HOLLAND

27 Hampdens and Whitleys to bomb communications, airfields and barges and to lay mines. 2 Hampdens lost.

---

4 July 1940

GERMANY, HOLLAND

20 Blenheims; 11 bombed targets in Germany or airfields in Holland. 2 further Blenheims photographed airfields in France. No losses.

4/5 July 1940

GERMAN PORTS

73 aircraft to ports in Northern Germany and minelaying. 1 Hampden lost.

5 July 1940

GERMANY, HOLLAND

60 Blenheims, Hampdens, Wellingtons and Whitleys to carry out cloud-cover attacks on targets – mainly ports – in Germany and airfields in Holland. 2 Blenheims and 1 Wellington lost. 12 Hampdens carried out a minelaying operation.

A report from Hamburg tells how one bomber carried out an attack on the liners *Europa* and *Bremen*, which were being prepared for Operation *Sea Lion*. 3 bombs fell very close to the ships but caused no damage.

5/6 July 1940

KIEL

51 aircraft were dispatched to Kiel but many bombed alternative targets; 1 Wellington lost. 12 Hampdens minelaying. (The normal minelaying force dispatched each night had now been increased to 12 Hampdens.)

6 July 1940

BELGIUM

19 Blenheims to bomb airfields and barges; only 6 aircraft bombed, 1 lost.

6/7 July 1940

GERMANY, HOLLAND

43 aircraft to German ports, airfields in Holland, and minelaying. 1 Wellington and 1 Whitley lost.

7 July 1940

HOLLAND

24 Blenheims to attack airfields and barges; only 3 aircraft bombed, 2 aircraft lost.

7/8 July 1940

GERMANY, HOLLAND

54 aircraft to various targets and minelaying. 1 Hampden lost.

8 July 1940

HOLLAND, BELGIUM, FRANCE

51 Blenheims on various tasks; only 24 bombed. No losses.

8/9 July 1940

GERMANY, HOLLAND

64 aircraft to ports in N Germany, airfields in Holland and minelaying. 1 Whitley lost.

9 July 1940

NORWAY, HOLLAND, BELGIUM

26 Blenheims on various tasks. 7 of the 12 aircraft bombing Stavanger airfield were lost.

9/10 July 1940

GERMANY, HOLLAND

55 Hampdens and Wellingtons to various targets and minelaying. 19 of the Wellingtons were recalled because of weather conditions. No losses.

10 July 1940

FRENCH AIRFIELDS

40 Blenheims to Amiens and St-Omer. 6 aircraft lost. 107 Squadron lost 5 out of the 6 planes it sent to Amiens.

11 July 1940

GERMANY, FRANCE, HOLLAND

40 Blenheims dispatched but none reached their targets in Germany and only 10 bombed airfields in France and Holland. 1 aircraft lost.

11/12 July 1940

GERMANY, HOLLAND

64 aircraft to various targets but only 45 bombed. 3 aircraft – 1 Hampden, 1 Welling-

ton and 1 Whitley – lost. 1 further Wellington was sent to photograph the distant target of Stettin; it carried out this task and returned safely.

12/13 July 1940

KIEL, EMDEN

23 Whitleys dispatched, only 14 bombed, 1 lost.

---

13 July 1940

GERMANY, FRANCE, BELGIUM

22 Blenheims, only 8 bombed, 2 lost.

13/14 July 1940

GERMANY, HOLLAND

97 aircraft to widespread targets and minelaying. No losses.

---

14 July 1940

6 Blenheims to Kiel turned back because of clear weather conditions.

14/15 July 1940

GERMANY

80 aircraft to widespread targets and minelaying. 1 Wellington lost.

---

15 July 1940

FRENCH AIRFIELDS

17 Blenheims to Lisieux and Évreux but only 4 bombed; no losses.

15/16 July 1940

GERMANY

33 Hampdens to Hamborn, Hannover, Osnabrück and Paderborn and minelaying. No losses.

---

16 July 1940

BELGIUM, HOLLAND

15 Blenheims to attack airfields and barges, 1 lost. 2 further Blenheims on photographic reconnaissance to Dortmund–Ems Canal turned back.

---

17 July 1940

BARGES

13 Blenheims attacked barges in Dutch and Belgian ports, no losses.

17/18 July 1940

GERMANY, FRANCE

7 Wellingtons to Gelsenkirchen and 3 Hampdens minelaying. 6 Blenheims attempted to bomb airfields in France; 1 aircraft bombed Morlaix airfield. An aircraft of 15 Squadron, piloted by Squadron Leader Webster (the records give no initials), carried out what is believed to be the first Intruder attack of the war when he attempted to patrol at low level over an airfield near Caen, waiting to attack any aircraft seen operating there. He was not successful in this attempt on this night.

18 July 1940

SHIPPING AND BARGES

41 Blenheims to Belgian and Dutch ports, 40 bombed, 1 lost.

18/19 July 1940

GERMANY

68 Hampdens and Wellingtons to 6 targets. 1 Wellington lost.

3 further Wellingtons from the newly formed Operational Training Units (O.T.U.s) carried out leaflet raids to towns in France and 1 of them bombed an airfield. This was the first example of the short operational flights made by crews at the end of their training period. These flights were usually to short-range targets in Northern France; most of them were leaflet raids but sometimes bombs were dropped.*

19 July 1940

GERMANY

16 Blenheims to attack railways in Northern Germany lacked enough cloud cover and turned back.

19/20 July 1940

GERMANY, HOLLAND

89 aircraft to 5 targets in Germany, to airfields in Holland and minelaying. 3 aircraft – 1 of each type – lost.

---

* In later diary entries these are recorded as 'O.T.U. sorties' and can be assumed to be without loss unless casualties are recorded:

20 July 1940

FLUSHING AIRFIELD

24 Blenheims, only 1 bombed, 1 lost.

20/21 July 1940

GERMANY, HOLLAND

95 aircraft to 6 German targets, airfields in Holland and minelaying. 4 Hampdens and 2 Wellingtons lost.

Bomber Command records state that attacks with 'special bombs', possibly a type of mine, were carried out from 30–100 ft against the battleship *Admiral Scheer* at Wilhelmshaven. This must have been a dangerous method of attack; Wilhelmshaven records say that 2 bombers crashed in the town and 3 near by, all shot down by local Flak.

---

21 July 1940

1 Blenheim on reconnaissance to Waalhaven airfield returned early.

21/22 July 1940

GERMANY, HOLLAND, FRANCE

81 aircraft to 7 targets in Germany. 12 Blenheims attacked airfields in France. 6 Battles bombed barges in Dutch ports; these Battles – from 103 and 150 Squadrons – were the first Battle operations under Bomber Command control. 8 Hampdens minelaying. 5 O.T.U. sorties.

This was the largest night effort since the fall of France. 1 Whitley lost.

---

22 July 1940

AIRFIELD

12 Blenheims to an unnamed airfield returned early.

22/23 July 1940

GERMANY, FRANCE, HOLLAND

68 aircraft of all Bomber Command types, including Battles, attacked 5 targets in Germany, airfields in France, barges in Holland, and carried out minelaying. 1 Blenheim and 1 Whitley lost. 1 O.T.U. sortie.

---

23 July 1940

FRANCE, HOLLAND

15 Blenheims to airfields and shipping, only 4 bombed, no losses.

23/24 July 1940

GERMANY, HOLLAND

85 aircraft of all types* to various targets; 1 Blenheim lost. 6 O.T.U. sorties.

---

24 July 1940

ST-AUBIN AIRFIELD

10 Blenheims, only 1 bombed, no losses.

24/25 July 1940

GERMANY, HOLLAND

27 Hampdens and Whitleys dispatched in poor weather conditions; only 7 aircraft bombed. No losses.

---

25 July 1940

5 Blenheims to attack French airfields, none bombed, 1 lost.

25/26 July 1940

THE RUHR, HOLLAND

166 aircraft of all types to 7 targets in the Ruhr and to airfields in Holland. 7 aircraft – 3 Hampdens, 2 Blenheims, 2 Wellingtons – lost. 6 O.T.U. sorties.

---

26 July 1940

GERMANY, HOLLAND

14 Blenheims on bombing and reconnaissance operations, only 3 aircraft bombed. No losses.

26/27 July 1940

GERMANY, FRANCE

18 Wellingtons and 9 Whitleys attacked Hamm and Ludwigshafen;† 1 Whitley lost. 12 Hampdens minelaying. 6 O.T.U. sorties.

---

* 'Aircraft' now means Battles, Blenheims, Hampdens, Wellingtons and Whitleys.
† The Ludwigshafen attacked was Ludwigshafen on Rhine, referred to later simply as 'Ludwigshafen'.

27 July 1940

NAVAL TARGETS

15 Blenheims to Germany and Holland; 14 bombed various targets. No losses.

27/28 July 1940

NORTH GERMANY

24 Wellingtons and 19 Hampdens to bomb Hamburg, Bremen, Wilhelmshaven and Borkum. No losses. 8 O.T.U. sorties, 1 Wellington lost.

---

28 July 1940

LEEUWARDEN AIRFIELD

9 Blenheims bombed without loss.

28/29 July 1940

GERMANY, HOLLAND, BELGIUM, FRANCE

89 aircraft to bomb a variety of targets and on minelaying operations. 2 Battles and 1 Hampden lost.

---

29 July 1940

GERMANY, HOLLAND

14 Blenheims to targets in Germany and to Leeuwarden airfield. Only 6 aircraft bombed; 1 lost.

29/30 July 1940

GERMANY, HOLLAND

76 Hampdens, Wellingtons and Whitleys to Homberg, Cologne, Hamm, barges in Dutch ports and minelaying. No losses.

---

30 July 1940

FRENCH AIRFIELDS

24 Blenheims, 1 lost.

30/31 July 1940

COLOGNE, THE RUHR

14 Wellingtons, no losses.

---

31 July 1940

GERMANY

28 Blenheims to attack shipping and an aircraft depot at Paderborn. Only 11 aircraft bombed; 1 lost.

---

31 July/1 August 1940

GERMANY, HOLLAND, FRANCE

42 Battles, Blenheims and Hampdens to bomb a variety of targets and minelaying but only 13 bombed and 9 laid mines. On its outward flight, 1 Battle was shot down into the sea off Skegness by R.A.F. fighters and 3 Hampdens ditched in the sea on their return flights.

---

1 August 1940

HOLLAND

12 Blenheims to attack airfields, only 5 bombed, 1 lost.

1/2 August 1940

THE RUHR

43 Wellingtons and Whitleys attacked 7 targets in the Ruhr. No losses.

A proportion of these aircraft released leaflets as a secondary task. This economical method of carrying leaflets to Germany and on flights across occupied countries became a regular practice and continued for the remainder of the war, although training aircraft continued to make leaflet-only flights to France and Belgium. Bomber Command delivered at least 1,500 million leaflets during the war.*

---

2 August 1940

AIRFIELDS

36 Blenheims to Holland, Belgium and France, 1 lost.

---

* Public Record Office AIR 20/4865 gives further details and shows that 1,361·9 million leaflets were delivered after June 1941.

2/3 August 1940

GERMANY

62 Hampdens, Wellingtons and Whitleys to 6 targets in Germany and minelaying. 1 Wellington lost.

3 August 1940

OCCUPIED COUNTRIES

16 Blenheims to various targets, only 6 bombed, 1 lost.

3/4 August 1940

GERMANY, HOLLAND

71 Hampdens, Wellingtons and Whitleys to oil targets in the Ruhr, to Kiel, to a seaplane base in Holland, and minelaying. 3 aircraft – 1 of each type – lost.

4/5 August 1940

THE RUHR

11 aircraft attacked Sterkrade/Holten and Krefeld, no losses.

5 August 1940

HOLLAND, FRANCE

9 Blenheims to Dutch airfields and on a sea sweep off Dieppe; no targets were bombed and no aircraft lost.

5/6 August 1940

GERMANY, HOLLAND
85 Hampdens, Wellingtons and Whitleys to Hamburg, Kiel, Wilhelmshaven and Wismar, to Dutch airfields and to minelaying. No losses.

6 August 1940

LE BOURGET

40 Blenheims to Le Bourget airfield but only 1 bombed. 6 Blenheims on sea sweep. No losses.

6/7 August 1940

GERMANY, HOLLAND

26 Wellingtons to Homberg and Reisholz and to airfields in Holland. 12 Hampdens minelaying, 1 lost.

7 August 1940

AIRFIELDS

29 Blenheims to attack airfields, only 2 bombed. 6 Blenheims on sea sweep. No losses.

7/8 August 1940

GERMANY

50 Hampdens and Wellingtons attacked Emmerich, Hamm, Soest and Kiel and laid mines. No losses.

8 August 1940

AIRFIELDS

15 Blenheims attacked Schiphol and Valkenburg, 1 lost. 6 Blenheims on sea sweep.

8/9 August 1940

GERMANY

46 Hampdens and Wellingtons attacked 7 targets. 1 Hampden lost.

9 August 1940

AIRFIELDS

15 Blenheims to Brittany and the Channel Islands; only 2 bombed – at Brest and at Le Bourg in Guernsey. This was the first bombing of the British Channel Islands, now occupied by the Germans. No aircraft lost.

9/10 August 1940

GERMANY, HOLLAND

38 Wellingtons and Whitleys attacked Cologne, Ludwigshafen and Dutch airfields. 3 O.T.U. sorties. No losses.

10 August 1940

AIRFIELDS

22 Blenheims dispatched but only 8 bombed, 2 lost. 6 Blenheims on sea sweep.

10/11 August 1940

GERMANY

57 Hampdens, Wellingtons and Whitleys to 9 targets; 1 Hampden lost. 3 O.T.U. sorties.

One of the targets raided on this night was Hamburg, whose local historian, Hans Brunswig, notes that the first R.A.F. 250-lb petrol bombs were recorded at approximately this time. They were described as being packed with petrol-soaked rags – 'Churchill's old socks' suggest the Hamburg humorists.*

---

11 August 1940

AIRFIELDS

23 Blenheims, only 9 bombed, 1 lost. 6 Blenheims on sea sweep attacked shipping near Brest.

11/12 August 1940

THE RUHR

59 Hampdens, Wellingtons and Whitleys to 6 targets in the Ruhr; 1 Whitley lost. 16 Hampdens minelaying and on sea reconnaissance, 1 lost. 5 O.T.U. sorties.

---

12 August 1940

6 Blenheims made a sea sweep. 1 aircraft bombed De Kooy airfield in Holland. No losses.

12/13 August 1940

GERMANY, HOLLAND

79 Blenheims, Hampdens, Wellingtons and Whitleys to 5 targets in Germany, to airfields in France, and minelaying. 4 Hampdens and 1 Blenheim lost. 4 O.T.U. sorties.

11 Hampdens of 49 and 83 Squadrons were ordered to make low-level bombing attacks on the Dortmund–Ems Canal at a point, near Münster, where the canal crosses the River Ems by means of twin aqueducts. These were an important bottleneck link in the German inland-waterway system. The aqueducts had been attacked by 5 Group Hampdens on previous occasions and damaged. The German defences

---

* From *Feuersturm über Hamburg*, op. cit., 58.

had now been increased and low-level attacks were subject to intense light Flak. 2 Hampdens were shot down but 8 aircraft managed to drop their bombs and caused damage which was still holding up barge traffic more than a month later.

For making a particularly determined attack, in which his Hampden was badly hit, Flight Lieutenant R. A. B. Learoyd of 49 Squadron was awarded Bomber Command's first Victoria Cross of the war. The Dortmund–Ems canal would need to be attacked on many future occasions and a second Victoria Cross would be earned here in 1945, again by a member of 5 Group.

---

13 August 1940

AIRFIELDS

29 Blenheims to France and Holland; 16 bombed but 12 were lost, including 11 out of the 12 aircraft from a formation provided by 82 Squadron which was caught by German fighters while attacking Hamstede airfield in Holland. This was the second time during the summer of 1940 that a formation from this squadron was almost completely destroyed. 6 Blenheims on a sea sweep and 2 Blenheims on photographic reconnaissance to the Dortmund–Ems Canal operated without loss.

13/14 August 1940

GERMANY, ITALY, FRANCE

62 Hampdens and Wellingtons to 5 widely spread targets in Germany, 35 Whitleys to Milan and Turin – the first raid on Italy since the end of the Battle of France – 6 Blenheims to airfields and a seaplane base at Brest and 2 Wellingtons to photograph Stettin and Swinemünde on the Baltic coast. 98 of the 105 aircraft on these mostly lengthy operations reported that they had carried out their tasks. 1 Hampden was lost from the force bombing Germany and 1 Whitley returning from Italy crashed in the sea.

---

14 August 1940

AIRFIELDS, SEA SWEEP

30 Blenheims; most turned back because of lack of cloud cover and only 6 bombed, at Morlaix, Dinard and St-Omer; there were no losses.

14/15 August 1940

FRANCE, GERMANY, HOLLAND

92 Blenheims, Hampdens, Wellingtons and Whitleys to various targets, including raids on 3 oil refineries in France. 2 Blenheims and 2 Whitleys lost.

---

15 August 1940

6 Blenheims on sea sweep; no action, no losses.

This was the day on which the main German air offensive on airfields in England commenced, the true start of the Battle of Britain.

15/16 August 1940

VARIOUS TARGETS

83 Blenheims, Hampdens and Wellingtons to multiple targets in Germany, France and Holland and 4 Whitleys to Italy. 6 O.T.U. sorties. 2 Blenheims and 1 Whitley lost.

16 August 1940

6 Blenheims on an uneventful sea sweep.

16/17 August 1940

GERMANY, HOLLAND

150 Blenheims, Hampdens, Wellingtons and Whitleys to the Ruhr and Frankfurt, to the distant targets of Jena, Leuna and Augsburg, and to airfields in Holland. 118 aircraft reported bombing successfully; 7 aircraft – 4 Whitleys, 2 Hampdens, 1 Wellington – lost.

17 August 1940

FRANCE

9 Blenheims on sea sweep and bombing; 2 aircraft bombed targets in the Fécamp–Dieppe area. No losses.

17/18 August 1940

AIRFIELDS, GERMANY

102 Blenheims, Hampdens and Wellingtons to 5 targets in Germany, to airfields in Holland, Belgium and France, and minelaying. No losses.

Although no aircraft was detailed to attack Brunswick, this city recorded its first raid of the war, with 4 Germans and 3 foreign workers killed. This is the first report of foreigners being killed in air raids. They were the forerunners of more than 5 million people – prisoners of war or civilians – who were brought to work in Germany under varying degrees of force during the war and subjected to all the hazards of Allied bombing of German cities. Their danger was more acute than that of German civilians because they were usually allocated poorer air-raid shelters. It is not known how many foreigners were killed in air raids but the number must be considerable; many individual reports from German cities give examples in raids later in these diaries. The Brunswick records, for example, show that, of 2,905 people killed in the city by R.A.F. and U.S.A.A.F. bombing in 40 wartime raids, 1,286 (44·3 per cent) were foreigners; but this was probably an extreme example.

---

18 August 1940

6 Blenheims on an uneventful sea sweep.

18/19 August 1940

GERMANY, ITALY

20 Whitleys to Rheinfelden, Waldshut and Freiburg, 4 Whitleys to Turin. No losses.

---

19 August 1940

HOLLAND

17 Blenheims to airfields and sea sweeps. Only 2 aircraft bombed – at Flushing airfield and a Flak position north of Amsterdam. 1 aircraft lost.

19/20 August 1940

VARIOUS TARGETS

120 Blenheims, Hampdens, Wellingtons and Whitleys to 5 targets in north Germany, to Ambes oil refinery in France, to airfields in Holland, Belgium and France, and minelaying. 2 Blenheims and 1 Whitley lost.

---

20 August 1940

9 Blenheims on coastal sweep. Only 2 aircraft bombed – at Ostend and Schiphol. No losses.

---

21 August 1940

26 Blenheims on coastal sweeps from Zuider Zee to Channel Islands; 6 aircraft bombed various targets. No losses.

21/22 August 1940

GERMANY, HOLLAND

42 Hampdens to widely spread targets; only 29 bombed and 1 was lost.

---

22 August 1940

13 Blenheims to Merville airfield but only 1 bombed. 6 Blenheims on sea sweep. No losses.

22/23 August 1940

GERMANY, FRANCE

52 Hampdens and Wellingtons attacked 6 targets in the Ruhr and the Rhineland and laid mines; 1 of the minelaying Hampdens also attacked a U-boat. 33 Blenheims attacked airfields in France. There were no losses but 4 aircraft crashed in England.

23 August 1940

HOLLAND, GERMANY

19 Blenheims; 7 aircraft bombed airfields in Holland, Flushing docks and a railway bridge over the Dortmund–Ems Canal. 1 aircraft lost. 6 Blenheims on sea sweep.

23/24 August 1940

MINELAYING, OIL, AIRFIELDS

40 Hampdens on the largest minelaying operation so far. 35 Blenheims sent to attack airfields in Belgium and Holland. 10 Wellingtons attacked the oil refinery at Sterkrade/Holten. There were no losses from any of these operations.

24 August 1940

15 Blenheims on coastal raids and sweeps; 4 aircraft bombed Dutch airfields and shipping at Zeebrugge. No losses.

24/25 August 1940

GERMANY, FRANCE, ITALY

68 Wellingtons and Whitleys to 5 targets in Germany. 2 Whitleys lost. One of the targets was Stuttgart, which recorded its first casualties on this night, 4 people being killed and 5 wounded when bombs dropped into suburbs of the city, hitting some houses and a garage.

28 Wellingtons went minelaying, 25 Blenheims attacked targets in France and 10 further Whitleys attacked Milan.

25 August 1940

AIRFIELDS

18 Blenheims, only 6 bombed 4 airfields in Holland and 1 in Germany. 6 Blenheims on sea sweep. No losses.

25/26 August 1940

BERLIN, GERMANY, FRANCE

Following raids by German bombers on London and other English cities the previous night, the War Cabinet sanctioned the first raid on Berlin. 103 aircraft were dispatched on operations and approximately half of these, mostly Hampdens and Wellingtons, were sent to Berlin. (Bomber Command records on this night are not clear on the numbers dispatched to different targets.) Berlin was found to be covered by thick cloud, which prevented accurate bombing, and a strong head wind was encountered on the return flight. The Hampdens were at the limit of their fuel capacity in such conditions and 3 of them were lost and 3 more ditched in the sea on their return flight.

The only bombs falling within the city limits of Berlin destroyed a wooden summer-house in a garden in the suburb of Rosenthal and 2 people were slightly injured. The Berlin records show that many bombs were dropped in the country areas south of the city and that some of these fell into large farms – *Stadtgüter* – owned by the city of Berlin. The joke went round Berlin: 'Now they are trying to starve us out.'

Approximately 24 Whitleys and Wellingtons bombed Bremen, Cologne and Hamm, and 12 Blenheims attacked airfields in France and Holland. 3 Blenheims were lost.

---

26 August 1940

DUTCH AIRFIELDS

16 Blenheims, only 2 bombed. 6 Blenheims on sea sweep, 1 of these lost.

26/27 August 1940

GERMANY, ITALY

99 Blenheims, Hampdens and Wellingtons to Hannover, Leipzig, Leuna and Nordhausen; 1 Hampden lost. 11 Whitleys to Turin and Milan, 2 lost.

---

27 August 1940

HOLLAND

19 Blenheims on airfield raids and sea sweep. Only 1 aircraft bombed, at Alkmaar airfield. No losses.

27/28 August 1940

VARIOUS TARGETS

50 Hampdens, Wellingtons and Whitleys to many targets in Germany, Italy and France and minelaying. 1 Wellington lost.

---

28 August 1940

2 Blenheims to airfields in France and sea sweep. No bombs dropped.

28/29 August 1940

GERMANY, FRANCE

79 Blenheims, Hampdens, Wellingtons and Whitleys to 6 targets in Germany and to French airfields. 1 Blenheim and 1 Hampden lost. Berlin was one of the German cities attacked and it would be regularly included in routine raids from now onwards; the number of aircraft sent was usually small and normal targets for this period of the war – power stations, railway stations, etc. – were chosen for attack.

29 August 1940

DUTCH–GERMAN COAST

26 Blenheims; 7 bombed airfields and shipping. No losses.

29/30 August 1940

GERMANY, AIRFIELDS

81 Blenheims, Hampdens, Wellingtons and Whitleys to Bottrop, Essen, Mannheim and Soest, and to airfields in Holland and France. 1 Blenheim and 1 Hampden lost.

30 August 1940

AIRFIELDS, NORTH SEA

18 Blenheims, but no bombs dropped.

30/31 August 1940

GERMANY, AIRFIELDS

87 Blenheims, Hampdens, Wellingtons and Whitleys to 5 targets in Germany and to airfields in France, Holland and Belgium. 4 aircraft – 2 Whitleys, 1 Hampden, 1 Wellington – lost.

31 August 1940

6 Blenheims on sea sweep and 1 to Paderborn abandoned their flights. No losses.

31 August/1 September 1940

BERLIN, COLOGNE, AIRFIELDS

77 Blenheims, Hampdens, Wellingtons and Whitleys attacked Berlin, Cologne and airfields in Holland and Belgium. 1 Hampden lost.

1 September 1940

AIRFIELDS

18 Blenheims to airfields and 6 on a sea sweep. Only 3 aircraft bombed airfields in Belgium. No losses.

1/2 September 1940

GERMANY, HOLLAND, ITALY

131 Blenheims, Hampdens, Wellingtons and Whitleys to 10 targets in Germany, to airfields in Holland, to Turin and San Giovanni in Italy. All main and many alternative targets bombed. 2 Wellingtons were lost and 8 aircraft crashed in England.

---

2 September 1940

4 Blenheims on a sea sweep forced back by bad weather.

2/3 September 1940

GERMANY, FRANCE, HOLLAND, ITALY

84 Blenheims, Hampdens, Wellingtons and Whitleys to a wide variety of targets. 2 Whitleys and 1 Blenheim lost. Of particular interest was the effort by 30 Wellingtons to start fires in the Black Forest and the forests of Thuringia and the raid by 39 Hampdens to the U-boat base being established by the Germans at the French port of Lorient. The attack on Lorient was the first Bomber Command raid on this type of target. A report from Lorient says that in a series of 25 raids between September 1940 and July 1941 9 civilians were killed and 27 wounded and 25 civilian buildings were destroyed. There is no information on the effect of the bombing on the German base.

---

3 September 1940

6 Blenheims on an uneventful sea sweep.

3/4 September 1940

GERMANY, FRANCE

90 Blenheims, Hampdens, Wellingtons and Whitleys to Berlin, Magdeburg, the Ruhr and the German forests, and to airfields in France. No losses.

4/5 September 1940

GERMANY, FRANCE

86 Blenheims, Hampdens, Wellingtons and Whitleys to Stettin, Magdeburg, Berlin and the Black Forest, and to French airfields. 1 Hampden and 1 Whitley lost.

5 September 1940

6 Blenheims on sea sweep, 1 lost.

5/6 September 1940

GERMANY, FRANCE, ITALY

82 Blenheims, Hampdens, Wellingtons and Whitleys to many targets from Turin to Stettin. 3 Hampdens and 1 Wellington lost.

---

6 September 1940

5 Blenheims on cloud-cover flights to Germany turned back because of lack of cover.

6/7 September 1940

GERMANY, BELGIUM, FRANCE

68 Blenheims, Hampdens, Wellingtons and Whitleys to many targets. 1 Hampden and 1 Whitley lost.

---

7 September 1940

6 Blenheims on an uneventful sea sweep.

7/8 September 1940

BARGES, FORESTS, THE RUHR

92 aircraft of all Bomber Command types (including Battles on regular operations now) dispatched, most of the effort devoted to invasion barges being assembled in Channel coast ports. 3 O.T.U. sorties. There were no losses in any of these operations.

---

8 September 1940

BLENHEIM OPERATIONS

30 aircraft in cloud-cover raids to Germany, attacks on Dutch and Belgian airfields, reconnaissance of Channel ports and sea sweeps. 6 aircraft bombed various targets; 3 Blenheims lost.

8/9 September 1940

PORTS, BARGES

133 Blenheims, Hampdens, Wellingtons and Whitleys to Hamburg, Bremen, Emden, Ostend and Boulogne. The heaviest raid was by 49 Hampdens on the Blohm & Voss shipyard in Hamburg. 8 aircraft were lost, 5 Blenheims and 2 Wellingtons in the Boulogne and Ostend raids and 1 Hampden in the Hamburg raid.

9 September 1940

7 Blenheims to Belgian and Dutch ports turned back because of lack of cloud cover. 1 aircraft lost.

9/10 September 1940

GERMANY, BELGIUM, FRANCE

76 Battles, Blenheims, Wellingtons and Whitleys to 5 targets in Germany and to Channel ports. 1 Battle and 1 Whitley lost.

10 September 1940

8 Blenheims on sea sweeps and reconnaissance of Channel ports.

10/11 September 1940

CHANNEL, PORTS, GERMANY

106 aircraft of all types. Most of the effort was to bomb barges in the Channel coast ports, but 17 Whitleys attacked the Potsdamer Station in Berlin and Bremen docks and 3 aircraft were minelaying. 2 Hampdens and 2 Whitleys lost.

11 September 1940

9 Blenheims on sea sweep and ports reconnaissance; 1 aircraft bombed a convoy off Dutch coast.

11/12 September 1940

GERMANY, CHANNEL PORTS

133 aircraft to 8 targets in Germany and to the Channel ports. 2 Hampdens and 1 Wellington lost. 8 further Hampdens laid mines in the Rivers Elbe and Gironde without loss.

12 September 1940

14 Blenheims on sweeps and reconnaissance; most abandoned flight because of lack of cloud cover.

12/13 September 1940

GERMANY, BELGIUM

40 Wellingtons to attack docks and railway yards at 7 targets in Germany and at Brussels. No losses.

13 September 1940

22 Blenheims on sea and coastal sweeps; 10 aircraft bombed shipping and barges in various ports. No losses.

13/14 September 1940

CHANNEL PORTS

92 Blenheims, Hampdens, Wellingtons and Whitleys attacked barges in 4 ports. 1 Blenheim and 1 Hampden lost.

14 September 1940

14 Blenheims on sea and coastal sweeps. 1 aircraft bombed Haamstede airfield and a U-boat at sea but no hits were scored on the U-boat. No losses.

14/15 September 1940

BELGIUM, GERMANY, FRANCE

157 aircraft of all types to an oil depot at Antwerp (the biggest raid, by 43 Wellingtons), railway yards at Brussels and in Germany, and barges in the Channel ports. 2 Whitleys lost.

15 September 1940

12 Blenheims on sea and coastal sweeps but all bombing sorties abandoned because of too-clear weather. No losses.

This day saw the climax of the daylight phase of the Battle of Britain. The Luftwaffe lost 56 aircraft in air battles over England and, although it was not immediately known by the British, the German high command started to abandon their plans to invade England in 1940. There was, however, no immediate slackening in Bomber Command operations.

5. Briefing, believed to be at a Whitley station, on 14/15 September 1940. These crews were dispatched to various railway targets in Germany and are being briefed by the Station Commander (with 1914–18 medal ribbons) and the Squadron Commander. Compare this relaxed, informal scene with the sombre briefing in photograph number 35 later in the war.

15/16 September 1940

CHANNEL PORTS, GERMANY

155 aircraft on widespread operations. The biggest effort was on the Channel ports; small raids made on many places in Germany. No losses.

Bomber Command's second Victoria Cross of the war was awarded for the actions of Sergeant John Hannah, the 18-year-old wireless operator in an 83 Squadron Hampden attacking invasion barges in docks at Antwerp. The Hampden was hit by Flak and set on fire. Sergeant Hannah could have baled out but stayed and was badly burned putting the fire out. The Hampden returned to its base.

16 September 1940

21 Blenheims on sea and coastal sweeps. 10 aircraft bombed shipping and barges in ports. No losses.

17 September 1940

15 Blenheims to the Channel ports. 9 aircraft bombed. No losses.

17/18 September 1940

CHANNEL PORTS, GERMANY

After a night's rest, Bomber Command dispatched 194 aircraft, its greatest number of the war to date. Approximately two thirds of the effort was devoted to bombing barges in the Channel ports; minor raids were made on many targets in Germany. 187 aircraft, 96 per cent of those dispatched, reported carrying out their tasks. 2 Hampdens were lost, 1 attacking the Channel ports and 1 on a minelaying sortie.

18 September 1940

6 Blenheims on an uneventful sea sweep.

18/19 September 1940

CHANNEL PORTS, GERMANY

174 aircraft dispatched. The majority of the effort was to the Channel ports; most of the remainder was to German railway targets. 8 aircraft – 3 Whitleys, 2 Blenheims, 2 Wellingtons, 1 Hampden – lost.

19 September 1940

18 Blenheims on operations but only 1 aircraft bombed, shipping in Dunkirk harbour.

19/20 September 1940

CHANNEL PORTS, GERMANY

53 Hampdens and Whitleys to ports and railway targets and laying mines (8 aircraft) in the River Gironde. No losses.

20 September 1940

6 Blenheims on an uneventful North Sea sweep.

20/21 September 1940

CHANNEL PORTS, GERMANY

172 aircraft of all types. Most of the effort was to Channel ports but small raids on German railways and canals, French airfields and minelaying at St-Nazaire. 1 Wellington lost.

21 September 1940

18 Blenheims on sea and coastal sweeps. 9 aircraft bombed Belgian ports. No losses.

21/22 September 1940

CHANNEL PORTS

92 aircraft. 91 reported bombing. No losses.

---

22 September 1940

6 Blenheims on an uneventful sea sweep.

22/23 September 1940

CHANNEL PORTS

95 Blenheims, Hampdens and Wellingtons to Channel ports; all bombed. 9 Whitleys to an aluminium factory at Lauta, near Dresden.

There were no losses on any of these operations.

---

23 September 1940

12 Blenheims on uneventful sea and coastal sweeps.

23/24 September 1940

BERLIN

In a unique raid for this period of the war, Bomber Command decided to concentrate its main strength of bombers for an attack on targets in just one German city. 129 Hampdens, Wellingtons and Whitleys were dispatched to 18 separate targets in Berlin. These targets were: 7 railway yards, 6 electrical power-stations, 3 gasworks and 2 factories making aero engines or aircraft components. 112 aircraft reported having bombed in a 3-hour period and from heights between 4,500 and 16,000 ft. Many searchlights and a ground mist made identification of targets very difficult. 3 aircraft, 1 of each type, were lost.

Unfortunately the relevant pages for this raid are missing from Berlin's air-raid records, possibly being removed immediately after the raid so that a record of it should not remain available to any civilian official. It is believed that most bombs fell in the Moabit area of the city where a power-station was one of the selected targets. The famous Schloss Charlottenburg was slightly damaged. No other details are available.

CHANNEL PORTS

71 aircraft – 46 Blenheims and 12 Battles, with 8 Wellingtons and 5 Whitleys probably manned by new, 'freshman' crews – attacked Boulogne, Calais and Flushing, and 9 O.T.U. crews operated over France and the Channel Islands, all without loss.

The total number of aircraft dispatched on this night – 209 – was another new record and it was the first time that the 200 figure was exceeded.

---

24 September 1940

18 Blenheims on sea sweeps. One formation of 12 aircraft attacked some German patrol boats in the Channel, scoring near misses. There were combats with German fighters in which 1 Me 109 was shot down and 1 Blenheim was lost.

24/25 September 1940

CHANNEL PORTS, BERLIN

122 aircraft of all types – 100 to the Channel ports, 20 to a power-station in Berlin and 2 to Hamm railway yards. 1 Blenheim and 1 Whitley lost.

---

25 September 1940

13 Blenheims on sea and coastal sweeps; 2 aircraft bombed ships off the Dutch coast without scoring hits. No losses.

25/26 September 1940

CHANNEL PORTS, GERMANY

117 aircraft to Channel ports, Kiel docks and to 6 other German targets. No losses.

---

26 September 1940

12 Blenheims. 3 aircraft bombed ports; 1 aircraft lost.

26/27 September 1940

CHANNEL PORTS, GERMANY

77 Blenheims, Hampdens, Wellingtons and Whitleys to Channel ports, Dortmund and Kiel. 1 Blenheim and 1 Hampden lost.

---

27 September 1940

15 Blenheims. 9 aircraft bombed shipping on Channel coast. No losses.

27/28 September 1940

CHANNEL PORTS, GERMANY

86 Hampdens, Wellingtons and Whitleys to Channel ports, Lorient U-boat base and railway targets in the Ruhr. 1 Wellington lost.

28 September 1940

13 Blenheims. 3 aircraft bombed barges at Ostend. No losses.

28/29 September 1940

GERMANY, CHANNEL COAST

109 Blenheims, Hampdens, Wellingtons and Whitleys to numerous targets in Germany and to the Channel ports. Whitley crews sent to attack the Fokker aircraft factory at Amsterdam could not identify their target and returned without bombing. 2 Wellingtons lost.

29 September 1940

9 Blenheims on uneventful sweeps.

29/30 September 1940

GERMANY, CHANNEL COAST

88 Blenheims, Hampdens, Wellingtons and Whitleys to many targets. The Fokker factory at Amsterdam was bombed. 1 Hampden and 1 Wellington lost.

30 September 1940

9 Blenheims on uneventful sweeps.

Bomber Command Headquarters was informed on this day that the imminent danger of German invasion had passed.

30 September/1 October 1940

GERMANY, CHANNEL PORTS

104 Blenheims, Hampdens, Wellingtons and Whitleys to many targets and minelaying in the River Elbe. A force of bombers attacking Berlin on this night was given the German Air Ministry building, the Reichsluftfahrt-Ministerium, in the Leipzigstrasse, as their target. 17 aircraft claimed to have found this single building and aimed bombs at it. 3 Wellingtons and 2 Whitleys lost.

6. The crew of a Whitley and their aircraft. The Whitleys of 4 Group were the main long-range night bombers of the early war years, flying 9,858 sorties, and their crews suffered severely from cold during winter months.

Only 6 bombs fell in the whole of Berlin on this night, mostly in the western suburbs. The Air Ministry was not hit until 1944 when it sustained light damage in American raids.

---

1 October 1940

7 Blenheims on uneventful sweeps.

1/2 October 1940

GERMANY, CHANNEL COAST

99 Blenheims, Hampdens, Wellingtons and Whitleys to numerous targets in Germany, to Channel ports and minelaying. 1 Hampden, 1 Wellington and 1 Whitley lost.

---

2 October 1940

6 Blenheims on uneventful sweeps.

2/3 October 1940

GERMANY, OCCUPIED COUNTRIES

81 Blenheims, Hampdens, Wellingtons and Whitleys to 9 targets in Germany, Eind-hoven airfield, the Channel ports and minelaying. 1 Blenheim and 1 Whitley lost.

3 October 1940

Germany, North Sea

7 Blenheims on cloud-cover raids to Germany and the Channel ports. 5 aircraft bombed various targets. 6 further Blenheims on sea sweep. No losses.

3/4 October 1940

There is some confusion over what operations were carried out on this night. Bomber Com-mand's Operations Record Book says that no operations were carried out because of unfavour-able weather conditions but other records indicated that 6 Blenheims and 3 Wellingtons attacked various targets on the French and Dutch coasts. There were no losses.

4 October 1940

GERMANY, NORTH SEA

30 Blenheims on cloud-cover raids; 15 bombed. 6 further Blenheims on sea sweep. No losses.

5 October 1940

Germany, North Sea

8 Blenheims to oil targets in Germany; all turned back because of lack of cloud cover. 6 Blenheims on sea sweep; 1 aircraft bombed ships without scoring hits. No losses.

5/6 October 1940

Germany, Rotterdam

20 Hampdens attacked oil and rail targets at Cologne, Gelsenkirchen, Hamm, Osna-brück and Soest. 10 Hampdens minelaying in the Elbe. 4 Wellingtons to Rotterdam docks. 3 Hampdens lost, 2 of them on the minelaying operation.

6 October 1940

21 Blenheims on cloud-cover raids; none of the designated targets in Germany was reached but 11 aircraft bombed alternative targets. No losses.

7 October 1940

18 Blenheims to Germany and on sea sweep. Only 1 aircraft bombed barges in Holland. No losses.

7/8 October 1940

GERMANY, OCCUPIED COUNTRIES

140 Blenheims, Hampdens, Wellingtons and Whitleys to many targets, with the main raid being by 42 Wellingtons and Whitleys on 12 individual targets in Berlin. There were also 10 O.T.U. and 6 minelaying sorties. 1 Wellington from the Berlin force was lost.

---

8 October 1940

8 Blenheims. 2 aircraft bombed Boulogne harbour. No losses.

8/9 October 1940

GERMANY, FRANCE, HOLLAND

108 Blenheims, Hampdens, Wellingtons and Whitleys to many targets. The largest raids were by 38 Blenheims on the Channel ports and by 17 Hampdens on the battleship *Tirpitz* in Wilhelmshaven dry dock. There were no losses from any operations.

---

9 October 1940

8 Blenheims to Germany. 2 aircraft bombed in Germany and 3 in Holland. No losses.

9/10 October 1940

GERMANY, FRANCE, HOLLAND

70 Battles, Hampdens and Wellingtons to many targets. 1 Wellington lost. The largest raid was by 20 Hampdens on the Krupps armament works in Essen but only 3 aircraft reached this target because of icing conditions. There were also 6 minelaying and 4 O.T.U. sorties.

10/11 October 1940

GERMANY, OCCUPIED COUNTRIES

157 aircraft of all types to 13 targets in Germany, to the Channel ports, to Eindhoven airfield and minelaying. No losses.

---

11 October 1940

6 Blenheims on an uneventful sea sweep.

11/12 October 1940

GERMANY, FRANCE, BELGIUM

86 aircraft of all types to oil and shipbuilding targets in Germany, in minor raids to the Channel ports and minelaying. No losses.

12 October 1940

6 Blenheims on sea sweep and 1 to Hamburg. No losses.

12/13 October 1940

GERMANY, CHANNEL COAST

93 Battles, Blenheims, Hampdens and Wellingtons to 5 targets in Germany, to the Channel ports, minelaying and O.T.U. leaflet flights. There were no losses.

The 24 Blenheims and 6 Battles of the above force sent to bomb shipping in the Channel ports represent the last major raid on these targets in the invasion-threat period.

Operational Statistics, 26 June to 12/13 October 1940
(109 days/nights)

Number of days with operations: 105
Number of nights with operations: 102
Number of daylight sorties: 1,885, from which 66 aircraft (3·5 per cent) were lost
Number of night sorties: 8,804, from which 180 aircraft (2·0 per cent) were lost
Total sorties: 10,689, from which 246 aircraft (2·3 per cent) were lost
Approximate bomb tonnage in period: 6,010 tons
Averages per 24-hour period: 98·1 sorties, 2·3 aircraft lost, 55·1 tons of bombs dropped

5. WINTER LULL

13 October 1940 to 10 February 1941

With the longer nights of autumn came the lifting of the immediate threat of invasion but a deterioration in flying conditions. Germany was drawing breath after defeating six countries in just over a year but she was having to face up to the fact that Britain, backed by the Empire, had failed to yield and a long war was now in prospect. In the West, Germany satisfied herself with the bombing of London and other British cities and with the continuing build-up of the U-boat campaign and raids on British shipping in the Atlantic by warships. Only Italy had the inclination for offensive military action; she invaded Greece on 28 October but failed to obtain the type of quick victory to which her partner had become accustomed. Italy was further disappointed in December when British units in the Middle East opened offensives against superior Italian forces on two fronts, in Libya and in East Africa. Both attacks exceeded all expectations and Britain gained her first land successes of the war. Germany would later have to send troops both to Greece and North Africa to rescue her Italian ally from complete humiliation.

The Middle East was too far away for Bomber Command to intervene directly but it started to lose some squadrons which were dispatched to that theatre. On the face of it, the lack of further military action in the West seemed to present Bomber Command with a unique opportunity. The bomber commanders could now pursue a pure strategic bombing policy free, for the first time in the war, of either political restraint or of the need to divert effort to tactical bombing in support of hard-pressed land forces. But, although the bomber leaders had every intention of pursuing that policy, this did not immediately happen. Their squadrons, too, needed to draw breath after the historic events of the past summer. It was a time for taking stock; the all-out strategic effort would have to wait a little. The pace of operations slowed appreciably.

The leadership of Bomber Command had changed again. Sir Charles Portal left on 5 October 1940 after only six months in command. Portal became Chief of the Air Staff, effectively the commander-in-chief of the whole R.A.F., a position he would hold until the end of the war and one from which he would always have much influence over the direction of Bomber Command's efforts. Portal's successor was Air Marshal Sir Richard Peirse. (The only other change in command occurred when Air Vice-Marshal Harris left 5 Group on 22 November 1940, after only a little over a year in command. He became Deputy Chief of the Air Staff, the second deputy to Portal. His place at 5 Group was taken by Air Vice-Marshal N. H. Bottomley.) Three weeks after Peirse's appointment, he received a long directive from the Air Ministry. Oil was to be his continuing priority target – to be attacked by his best crews in the best weather conditions which were presented. But there was also a long list of other important targets: the bombing of named industries and railways in German cities, targets in Berlin, in Italy, a continuation of minelaying, more attacks on Channel ports in case the Germans should think again of an invasion in 1941, attacks on airfields where German bombers were based. There was nothing fresh in the list but the new commander-in-chief protested that he could not attack all these targets and still carry out a sizeable offensive against oil. A clarification of the directive was thus issued which, in simple terms, said, 'concentrate on the oil and attack the other targets if the opportunities arise'.

There are two aspects of these orders on which particular comment can be made. The first is the utter unreality of some of the forecasts being made about the effectiveness of the attacks by the available strength of aircraft against the oil targets. A typical raid of this coming period was on a synthetic-oil plant near Cologne whose name would become familiar to bomber crews in another oil campaign four years later – Wesseling. On 26/27 October 1940, for example, three Whitleys were dispatched in a routine raid to Wesseling with total bomb loads of three and a half tons. Only two of the Whitleys reported being able to bomb the target. In 1944, Bomber Command would judge that nearly 200 four-engined bombers carrying 1,000 tons of bombs would be a reasonable force to attack Wesseling. The second point of interest was the arguments now being put forward in favour of a general attack on industrial German cities instead of the attacks on particular industrial premises within those cities. Those who supported the general-attack concept did so on two grounds: firstly, that it would make better use of a bomber force which was obviously having some difficulty in finding small targets, though the full degree of that difficulty was still not appreciated; and, secondly, that it would be justifiable retaliation for the heavy and seemingly indiscriminate bombing of British cities being carried out that autumn by the Luftwaffe. But, with the exception of one night, the 'general attack' policy was firmly rejected at this time. The exception came on the night of 16/17 December 1940 when 134 bombers carried out what would later be described as an 'area bombing' raid on Mannheim as retaliation for recent German bombing.

Air Marshal Peirse had just cause to resist some of the demands made upon his force; Bomber Command was losing rather than gaining strength. When Peirse took over in October, the theoretical strength of the operational squadrons had doubled since the outbreak of the war. The daily return to the Air Ministry's War Room* now showed a strength of 532 aircraft – 217 Blenheims, 100 Wellingtons, 71 Hampdens, 59 Whitleys and 85 Battles. There was much difficulty in finding a useful role for the large force of Blenheims now that the invasion threat had passed and the Battles, which had come back from France, were obsolete and would fly their last operation on the night of 15/16 October. In the five months to be covered by this coming period of the diary, the Blenheim strength would fall to 150 aircraft, which could only be used in limited roles, and the Battles would depart completely. The Whitleys and Hampdens, both due for replacement by more modern types of aircraft, did no more than hold their own in numbers but the sturdy and reliable Wellingtons would almost double their strength, mainly in the establishment of 1 Group as a regular night-bombing force with this type. Operations under the new commander-in-chief thus commenced with a force of only 230 aircraft of types suitable for night operations in winter, of which a proportion were always manned by inexperienced crews or were suffering from servicing problems. Peirse's realistic maximum strength for night operations was no more than 150 aircraft.

So the pattern of raids continued, with a greater emphasis on Germany but with

---

*Public Record Office AIR 22/31–49 for the whole wartime years.

a significant slackening of numbers dispatched. Most of the operations were by night, with small numbers of aircraft sent to many targets still being the normal routine. But the new commander does seem to have selected the best moonlit night in each month and gathered his strength of aircraft for a concentration of effort on one German city. In this way, Hamburg was attacked by 130 aircraft in the middle of November and Mannheim and Gelsenkirchen by similar numbers in December and January. The relaxation of pressure did allow for the less experienced crews to be introduced to operations more gradually; these 'freshman crews' were usually sent to a relatively safe target on the coast of one of the occupied countries until judged ready to tackle more distant targets.

The employment of the 2 Group Blenheims continued to pose major problems. At least four squadrons left for conversion to Wellingtons with other groups but those squadrons which remained saw little action. A small proportion of the strength available continued to be used on night raids but daylight operations brought little satisfaction. In January 1941, a new type of Blenheim operation was introduced, the *Circus*. In this, a handful of Blenheim bombers was dispatched with a large escort of the R.A.F. day fighters now available in Britain and, like the Blenheims, freed from the threat of invasion. The targets attacked by the Blenheims were rarely of importance but the true purpose of these operations was to draw the Luftwaffe fighters into action. The British fighters would then join combat and, in this way, it was hoped, a successful war of attrition against the Luftwaffe could be waged. The whole concept was hampered by the limited range of R.A.F. fighters and only a small area of northwest France around the Pas de Calais and parts of Belgium could be reached. The Luftwaffe could join battle or decline to do so as it wished. Some thought it a poor employment of resources but the alternative was to keep unemployed the large forces of day bombers and fighters which might one day be needed to defend Britain from invasion if the Germans did resurrect their plans and whose successors would certainly be needed on that dimly distant day when Allied forces could re-invade Europe.

Night-bombing operations proceeded steadily in October and November, though with many more aircraft than before turning back or failing to find their designated primary targets for weather reasons. With midwinter came a definite reduction in the scale of operations and this period really just fizzled out on the quietest of notes in January and early February. The general level of operations during the whole period was less than half that of any time since the German invasion of France and the Low Countries in May 1940.

---

13 October 1940

6 Blenheims on an uneventful sea sweep.

13/14 October 1940

GERMANY, FRANCE

125 Battles, Blenheims, Hampdens and Wellingtons to the Ruhr, Wilhelmshaven, Kiel and the Channel Ports. The weather was bad and only 41 aircraft reported bombing primary targets. At Wilhelmshaven, to which 35 Hampdens were sent, the only report describes how an 80-year-old woman was killed in bed by a fragment of Flak shell. 1 Wellington lost.

---

14 October 1940

18 Blenheims, 12 on cloud-cover raids, 6 on sea sweep. 1 aircraft lost.

14/15 October 1940

GERMANY, FRANCE

78 Hampdens, Wellingtons and Whitleys to Berlin, Stettin, Bohlen, Magdeburg and Le Havre. 2 Hampdens and 1 Wellington were lost and a Whitley bound for Le Havre crashed after hitting a barrage-balloon cable at Weybridge; the crew were all killed.

15 October 1940

1 Blenheim to the Dortmund–Ems Canal was recalled.

15/16 October 1940

GERMANY, FRANCE

134 aircraft to bomb many targets in Germany, with much of the effort on oil targets, and to the Channel ports. A report from Kiel, attacked by Wellingtons, tells of an oil-storage tank set on fire and bomb damage in the naval dockyards but no civilian casualties.

3 Hampdens were also minelaying off Kiel and there were 2 O.T.U. sorties.

There were no losses from any of these operations. The raid by 9 Fairey Battles on Calais and Boulogne was the last occasion on which this aircraft operated with Bomber Command.

16 October 1940

12 Blenheims on sea and coastal sweeps. 1 aircraft bombed a convoy without scoring hits. No losses.

16/17 October 1940

GERMANY, FRANCE

73 Hampdens and Wellingtons attacked Bremen, Kiel, Merseburg and Bordeaux. The Merseburg force also dropped incendiary devices into the Harz forests. Kiel again reports many bombs from the Wellingtons attacking here, with 20 people injured, a garage with 12 vehicles inside destroyed, and much minor damage. 2 Hampdens and 1 Wellington were lost and 10 Hampdens and 4 Wellingtons crashed in England when fog covered their bases on return.

6 Hampdens laid mines without loss.

17 October 1940

8 Blenheims on cloud-cover raids but only 1 aircraft bombed, De Kooy airfield. No losses.

18 October 1940

1 Blenheim to Hamburg docks returned early because of lack of cover.

18/19 October 1940

HAMBURG, LÜNEN

28 Blenheims, Hampdens and Whitleys to Hamburg docks and Lünen aluminium works. No losses. Hamburg reports no fires but 4 people were injured.

19 October 1940

16 Blenheims on cloud-cover raids on a sweep; no bombs dropped and no losses.

19/20 October 1940

2 Whitleys and 1 Hampden to Osnabrück and Berlin but Berlin was not reached. No losses but 1 Whitley crashed in England.

20 October 1940

7 Blenheims on uneventful sea sweeps.

20/21 October 1940

GERMANY, ITALY, OCCUPIED COUNTRIES

139 aircraft* to many targets, 30 Hampdens to Berlin being the largest raid. 1 Hampden lost and 3 Whitleys returning from the most distant target ditched in the sea.

A Whitley of 58 Squadron, based at Linton-on-Ouse, was shot down by a German Intruder on this night and crashed near Thornaby-on-Tees. The Whitley had taken off to bomb the Škoda Works at Pilsen, in Czechoslovakia. The pilot, Pilot Officer E. H. Brown, and 3 other members of the crew were killed and the only survivor was injured. This was the first known success against a Bomber Command aircraft by a German Intruder over the mainland of Britain, though several German pilots had already claimed bombers shot down on the routes over the North Sea. The successful German pilot was Hauptmann Karl Hulshoff of I/NJG 2, the specialist

---

* 'Aircraft' now means a mixed force of Blenheims, Hampdens, Wellingtons and Whitleys.

German Intruder unit at that time. Hulshoff claimed the Whitley as a 'Hereford'; he survived the war.*

---

21 October 1940

18 Blenheims on sea and coastal sweeps. 5 aircraft found targets to bomb. No losses.

21/22 October 1940

GERMANY

31 Wellingtons and 11 Whitleys to Cologne, Hamburg, Reisholz and Stuttgart. 1 Whitley lost. Wellingtons sent to Hamburg, attempting to bomb the battleship *Bismarck*, caused 12 fires of which 8 are classed as large in the Hamburg report. 17 people were injured in Hamburg.

---

22 October 1940

1 Blenheim claimed bomb hits on a cargo ship off the Hook of Holland.

---

23 October 1940

14 Blenheims on sea sweeps and to French airfields. 2 aircraft bombed ships and 1 a factory near Antwerp. No losses.

23/24 October 1940

GERMANY, OCCUPIED COUNTRIES

79 aircraft (including O.T.U. aircraft) attacked many targets, the largest effort being by 12 Wellingtons which bombed Emden and 11 Wellingtons which reached and bombed Berlin. 2 Wellingtons lost.

---

24 October 1940

15 Blenheims on sea and coastal sweeps. 5 aircraft bombed various targets. No losses.

---

*Aircraft shot down over Britain by German Intruders and those accidentally shot down by British defences are counted as 'lost' in all statistical résumés; the bomber involved was usually destroyed and there were rarely any survivors.

7. Berlin, 23/24 October 1940. Eleven Wellingtons reached the target and incendiary bombs set fire to the roof of this elegant block of flats in the Wilmersdorf district.

24/25 October 1940

GERMANY, HOLLAND

113 aircraft to many targets. 1 Wellington was lost and a Whitley of 102 Squadron was shot down by a German aircraft while taking off from Tholthorpe.

Hamburg reports describe a particularly sharp raid on this night. The Wellington force attacking this target found that cloud conditions prevented observation of bombing results but 13 fires were started, of which 5 were large ones – 3 people were killed, 20 injured and 217 bombed out of their homes. A wooden dockyard warehouse was completely destroyed by fire but 18 loaded railway wagons were removed safely. The compensation claimed for damage in Hamburg on this night was nearly 3 million Reichsmarks (£300,000).

5 further Hampdens laid mines off Brest and there were 7 O.T.U. sorties. No losses.

---

25 October 1940

12 Blenheims on sweeps at sea and on the German coast but no bombs were dropped. No losses.

25/26 October 1940

GERMANY, OCCUPIED COUNTRIES

94 aircraft to many targets, mostly German oil and harbour targets. 1 Hampden attacking Kiel was lost.

5 Hampdens laid mines in Kiel Bay and the Elbe.

26 October 1940

11 Blenheims on sea sweeps and cloud-cover raids to Hamburg and Bremen. No targets attacked. No losses.

26/27 October 1940

GERMANY, OCCUPIED COUNTRIES

84 aircraft to many targets, the largest raid being to a power-station in Berlin by 17 Hampdens. 5 further Hampdens were sent minelaying in the River Gironde. No losses from any operation.

27 October 1940

9 Blenheims on sea and coastal sweeps. Ships attacked off Dutch coast. No losses.

27/28 October 1940

GERMANY, OCCUPIED COUNTRIES

82 aircraft to many targets. 76 aircraft bombed their targets; none were lost.

5 Hampdens minelaying off Lorient; 1 lost. 2 O.T.U. sorties.

28 October 1940

13 Blenheims to France, Belgium and on a sea sweep. 3 aircraft bombed coastal targets. No losses.

28/29 October 1940

GERMANY, BELGIUM, FRANCE

97 aircraft to various targets. The biggest raid was by 20 Hampdens to Hamburg, where 1 person was killed, 3 injured and 44 bombed out, but no fires were started. 1 Blenheim and 1 Whitley lost.

29 October 1940

13 Blenheims on a sea sweep and to France and Belgium. The docks at Rotterdam were bombed. 1 aircraft lost.

29/30 October 1940

GERMANY, HOLLAND

98 aircraft to many targets. The largest raid, by 30 Hampdens and Wellingtons, was to Berlin but, because of bad weather, only 4 aircraft reached that target. No losses.
    5 Hampdens minelaying off Copenhagen; 1 lost. 1 O.T.U. sortie.

30 October 1940

6 Blenheims to France. 3 aircraft bombed Cherbourg harbour. No losses.*

30/31 October 1940

GERMANY, BELGIUM, HOLLAND

28 Blenheims and Wellingtons to Duisburg, Emden, Antwerp and Flushing. No losses.

31 October 1940

14 Blenheims. 5 aircraft attacked various targets, mostly in France. No losses.

1 November 1940

1 Blenheim to the Dortmund–Ems Canal returned early because of lack of cloud cover.

1/2 November 1940

GERMANY, OCCUPIED COUNTRIES

81 aircraft to Berlin, Gelsenkirchen, Magdeburg and to airfields in Belgium, Holland and France. 2 Hampdens lost.
    8 Hampdens minelaying off Brest.

---

*The sea sweeps, which had been such a regular feature of recent Blenheim operations, were now discontinued for the time being, All later Blenheim daylight operations are cloud-cover raids by single aircraft unless otherwise stated.

2 November 1940

4 Blenheims dispatched but lacked cover and returned early.

3 November 1940

11 Blenheims. Only 2 aircraft bombed. No losses.

3/4 November 1940

KIEL

11 Hampdens; 1 lost. Kiel reports only a few bombs in the suburb of Wellingdorf, with no casualties.

4 November 1940

7 Blenheims; all turned back.

4/5 November 1940

10 Wellingtons to docks at Le Havre and Boulogne. The weather was bad and only 3 reported bombing these targets; fires were seen at Le Havre. No losses.

5 November 1940

1 Blenheim to Haamstede airfield turned back.

5/6 November 1940

GERMANY, ITALY, OCCUPIED COUNTRIES

97 aircraft to many targets. 2 Whitleys and 1 Hampden were lost. Hamburg, target for approximately 10 Wellingtons, reports 15 fires and casualties of 7 killed, 32 injured and 236 bombed out, some only temporarily.

8 Hampdens minelaying off the island of Rügen in the Baltic; 1 aircraft lost.

6 November 1940

9 Blenheims to Holland and Northern Germany. 5 aircraft bombed targets. No losses.

6/7 November 1940

GERMANY

64 Hampdens, Wellingtons and Whitleys to 6 German cities. The largest raid was by
18 Wellingtons to Berlin but only 1 aircraft reached that target. 1 Wellington and 1
Whitley lost.

---

7 November 1940

12 Blenheims dispatched but only 1 aircraft bombed (Haamstede airfield). 1 aircraft lost.

7/8 November 1940

ESSEN, COLOGNE, OCCUPIED COUNTRIES

91 aircraft. The largest raid was by 63 aircraft to the Krupps factory at Essen. The
British Official History* makes comment on the reports submitted by the crews of
different groups (2, 3 and 5 Groups) taking part in this raid. Bomber Command
Headquarters found many inconsistencies and came to the conclusion that a lot of
crews who had reported successful attacks on Essen must have been some distance
from that target. The only bombing photographs developed showed some woods. It
was probably a typical experience of this period.

It is possible that the 'many fires' reported by some crews were at a decoy fire
site in open country, an early example of a device which the Germans would later use
whenever possible. The largest decoy site for the city targets in the western part of the
Ruhr was near the small town of Rheinberg, a few miles north-east of Duisburg. By
coincidence, it was near Rheinberg that a large post-war Commonwealth War Graves
Commission cemetery was established for British airmen who were killed in this part
of Germany. Of the 3,326 graves in the cemetery, 2,895 are of R.A.F. men.

3 Hampdens were minelaying off Brittany ports and there were 2 O.T.U. sorties.
There were no losses from any of the above operations.

8/9 November 1940

GERMANY, ITALY, OCCUPIED COUNTRIES

106 aircraft to many targets. 4 Whitleys were prevented from taking off from Honington because of a German air raid there. 1 Wellington lost. There were 2 O.T.U.
sorties.

---

9 November 1940

10 Blenheims. 1 aircraft bombed an airfield near Le Havre. No losses.

---

* Vol. I, pp. 224–5.

9/10 November 1940

14 Blenheims and Hampdens to airfields and to a seaplane base at Lorient. No losses.

---

10 November 1940

7 Blenheims. 3 aircraft bombed at Calais and Boulogne. 1 aircraft lost.

10/11 November 1940
GERMANY, FRANCE

111 aircraft to many targets; the largest raid was by 25 Wellingtons to Gelsenkirchen.
2 Blenheims lost. There were 3 O.T.U. sorties.

---

11 November 1940

6 Blenheims. 3 bombed at St-Brieuc airfield and Lorient. No losses.

12/13 November 1940
GERMANY, FRANCE

77 aircraft to many targets; the largest raid was by 24 Wellingtons to Gelsenkirchen
but only 6 aircraft reached that target. Because of bad weather, only 19 of all aircraft
dispatched bombed their primary targets. 1 Whitley lost.

---

13 November 1940

9 Blenheims. 2 aircraft bombed targets in France. No losses.

13/14 November 1940
GERMANY

72 Hampdens, Wellingtons and Whitleys to 5 targets. 1 Hampden was mistakenly
shot down by a Spitfire soon after its take-off. A further Hampden and a Whitley
were lost. Only 15 aircraft reached primary targets.

Evening of 14 November 1940
INTRUDER OPERATION

35 Blenheims to attack known Luftwaffe bomber airfields in France and Belgium
because intelligence information had been received that a large-scale German raid
was to take place this night on an unknown English city. 10 Blenheims carried out

bombing attacks on airfields with results which were recorded as 'generally unobserved'. The German raid duly took place on Coventry. The Blenheims all returned safely.

14/15 November 1940

BERLIN, HAMBURG, AIRFIELDS

82 Hampdens, Wellingtons and Whitleys; the largest raid to Berlin by 50 aircraft, but only 25 of these reported reaching the city. The raids on the airfields – Schiphol and Soesterberg – were also to frustrate the suspected German bombing raid on England. 3 Hampdens were sent minelaying off Brest and Lorient.

10 aircraft – 4 Hampdens, 4 Whitleys, 2 Wellingtons – were lost from the bombing raids, the heaviest night loss of the war so far.

---

15 November 1940

1 Blenheim to Lorient turned back.

15/16 November 1940

HAMBURG, AIRFIELDS

67 Hampdens, Wellingtons and Whitleys to Hamburg in 2 separate waves 8 hours apart. Returning crews reported good bombing conditions. Hamburg records show that 68 fires were started and that heavy damage – for this period of the war – was caused at the Blohm & Voss shipyard. 26 people were killed, 102 injured and 1,625 bombed out. This was almost certainly the most successful Bomber Command raid of the war so far.

56 Blenheims, Wellingtons and Whitleys – mostly Blenheims – continued the raids on Luftwaffe bomber airfields in the occupied countries.

All operations on this night were free from loss.

---

16 November 1940

6 Blenheims to Northern Germany. 4 aircraft bombed but none of the targets were in Germany. No losses.

16/17 November 1940

HAMBURG

130 aircraft to 4 targets in Hamburg. Weather conditions were unfavourable. Only 60 aircraft reported bombing Hamburg; 25 bombed alternative targets. Hamburg records show 6 fires, 2 people killed, 36 injured and 786 bombed out. Kiel, 50 miles north of Hamburg, had 5 people killed and 16 injured on this night. 2 Wellingtons and 1 Blenheim were lost and 5 more aircraft crashed in England.

12 further aircraft bombed airfields and 3 were minelaying, all without loss.

---

17 November 1940

5 Blenheims to Northern Germany turned back.

17/18 November 1940

THE RUHR

49 Wellingtons and Whitleys to Gelsenkirchen and Hamm; only 22 reported bombing primary target. 2 Whitleys bombed Lorient. No losses.

---

18 November 1940

5 Blenheims to Northern Germany. 1 aircraft bombed a tanker but scored no hits. No losses.

18/19 November 1940

MERSEBURG

11 Whitleys to the Leuna synthetic-oil plant at Merseburg. 1 Whitley to Le Havre recalled. No losses.

---

19 November 1940

5 Blenheims to Northern Germany but none reached a target. 2 aircraft had combats with Ju 88s but all returned safely.

19/20 November 1940

GERMANY, PILSEN

63 Hampdens, Wellingtons and Whitleys to 5 targets in Germany and to the Škoda Works at Pilsen in Czechoslovakia. Only 17 aircraft reported bombing their primary targets. 1 Wellington and 1 Whitley lost.

---

20 November 1940

3 Blenheims dispatched but turned back.

20/21 November 1940

DUISBURG, AIRFIELDS, LORIENT

68 aircraft – 43 to Duisburg, 17 to airfields and 8 to the submarine base at Lorient. Good bombing was reported at Duisburg and the airfields but Lorient was completely cloud-covered. 1 Whitley lost.

21 November 1940

6 Blenheims; 3 of them bombed various targets in Holland. No losses.

22 November 1940

24 Blenheims on widespread cloud-cover raids. 1 aircraft bombed a factory at Solingen in the Ruhr and 6 aircraft bombed targets in Holland and France. No losses.

22/23 November 1940

THE RUHR, BORDEAUX

95 aircraft to Dortmund, Duisburg and Wanne-Eickel and to an aircraft factory at Bordeaux. 2 O.T.U. aircraft and 1 Blenheim carried out leaflet raids over France and Holland and 3 Hampdens were minelaying off Lorient. 1 minelaying Hampden lost.

23/24 November 1940

GERMANY, ITALY, FRANCE

70 aircraft to widespread targets. 4 aircraft – 2 Whitleys, 1 Blenheim, 1 Wellington – lost. 3 Hampdens laid mines in the Elbe.

24/25 November 1940

HAMBURG, FRANCE

42 Blenheims, Hampdens and Wellingtons to Hamburg. 1 Blenheim and 1 Hampden lost. Hamburg was completely covered by cloud but Hamburg records show 4 fires, 2 people killed, 34 injured and 86 bombed out.

8 Blenheims and Wellingtons to Boulogne docks and 3 Hampdens minelaying off Brittany. No losses.

25/26 November 1940

KIEL, WILHELMSHAVEN

36 Hampdens, Whitleys and Wellingtons; targets were difficult to locate. Wilhelmshaven reports only 1 bomb on an air-raid shelter, which was empty, and 2 bombs in open ground. Kiel reports sirens but no bombing incidents. 1 Wellington lost.

26 November 1940

2 Blenheims to Belgian airfields turned back.

8. An old man killed in a raid at Stuttgart in 1940, possibly the first fatal casualty in that city.

26/27 November 1940

GERMANY, ITALY, FRANCE

69 aircraft to widespread targets but less than half found primary targets. 2 Hampdens minelaying in Kiel Bay. No losses from any operation.

---

27 November 1940

7 Blenheims, only 2 bombed; 1 of these hit a merchant ship outside Wilhelmshaven harbour. No losses.

27/28 November 1940

COLOGNE, FRANCE

62 aircraft to 5 targets in Cologne, less than half reported bombing there. 1 Whitley lost.

8 aircraft to Channel ports and 4 minelaying off Brittany; no losses.

---

28 November 1940

6 Blenheims to Coxyde-les-Bains on Belgian coast to bomb a hotel – the Terynick – believed to be in use as a German headquarters. 2 aircraft bombed this target and 1 direct hit was claimed. No losses to the Blenheims.

28/29 November 1940

GERMANY, CHANNEL PORTS

77 aircraft to many targets, the largest raid being by 24 Blenheims to Düsseldorf. 1 Blenheim lost.

29/30 November 1940

GERMANY, PORTS, AIRFIELDS

42 aircraft to Bremen, Cologne, the Channel ports and airfields; 1 Blenheim lost. 2 Hampdens minelaying off Brest and 1 O.T.U. sortie.

1/2 December 1940

Wilhelmshaven

10 Hampdens, only 3 reported bombing the target. The Wilhelmshaven civil diary has no entry for this night. No aircraft losses.

2 December 1940

6 Blenheims; 2 aircraft bombed targets. No losses.

2/3 December 1940

Lorient

9 Whitleys encountered thick cloud and only 4 bombed. No losses but 4 aircraft crashed in England.

3/4 December 1940

GERMANY

20 Blenheims and Whitleys to Duisburg, Essen and Mannheim; only 5 aircraft bombed these targets. 1 Blenheim lost and 4 more aircraft crashed in England.

4 December 1940

7 Blenheims; 3 aircraft bombed. No losses.

4/5 December 1940

DÜSSELDORF, TURIN

83 aircraft to Düsseldorf and Turin; only 30 reached these targets. 1 Blenheim and 1 Wellington lost. 3 Hampdens minelaying off Brest.

5 December 1940

5 Blenheims to Lorient and Caen airfield abandoned the flight.

5/6 December 1940

5 Whitleys to Gelsenkirchen; only 1 bombed; no losses.

6/7 December 1940

ANTI-LUFTWAFFE OPERATIONS

55 Blenheims, Hampdens and Whitleys to Luftwaffe bomber airfields in the Occupied Countries. 2 Hampdens lost. A further 20 Hampdens carried out 'interruption patrols', attempting to engage German bombers raiding Bristol, but with no success. 1 O.T.U. sortie to Paris.

7 December 1940

2 Blenheims; 1 bombed Brest and 1 Zeebrugge. No losses.

7/8 December 1940

DÜSSELDORF, OSTEND, AIRFIELDS

69 aircraft, mostly to Düsseldorf. 5 aircraft – 3 Wellingtons, 1 Hampden, 1 Whitley – lost. 4 Hampdens minelaying off Brest.

8/9 December 1940

DÜSSELDORF, BORDEAUX, LORIENT, AIRFIELDS

90 aircraft; many crews reported good bombing. 1 Hampden and 1 Wellington lost. 2 O.T.U. sorties. 19 Hampdens patrolled over Bristol but made no contact with German bombers.

9 December 1940

5 Blenheims; 4 aircraft bombed various targets. No losses.

9/10 December 1940

BREMEN, PORTS

39 Blenheims and Wellingtons to Bremen, Antwerp, Boulogne and Lorient. 1 Blenheim lost.

10/11 December 1940

GERMANY, PORTS

62 aircraft to many targets; only 6 reached their primaries. 1 Blenheim and 1 Hampden lost. 5 Hampdens minelaying in the River Gironde; 1 was lost.

11 December 1940

1 Blenheim to Schiphol airfield turned back.

11/12 December 1940

GERMANY, FRANCE

42 Blenheims, Wellingtons and Whitleys to Mannheim and many other cities but less than half reached their targets. 1 Blenheim and 1 Wellington lost. 20 Hampdens attempted interceptions of Germany bombers over Birmingham without success.

12 December 1940

1 Blenheim to Emden turned back.

12/13 December 1940

DUISBURG

15 Hampdens and Whitleys; the force was recalled. One aircraft did not receive signal and bombed Duisburg. No losses.

13 December 1940

6 Blenheims to Lorient and Brest turned back.

13/14 December 1940

BREMEN, KIEL

33 Wellingtons and Whitleys. Most bombed but no results seen because of complete cloud cover. The Kiel diary has no mention of bombs in the town. 1 Whitley lost.

15/16 December 1940

BERLIN, FRANKFURT, KIEL

71 Hampdens, Wellingtons and Whitleys; less than half bombed primary targets. Kiel reports bombs in the naval yard and in other parts of Kiel with 2 people killed (1 a soldier) and 5 injured and some houses destroyed. 3 Whitleys lost.

8 Hampdens minelaying off Brittany without loss.

16/17 December 1940

MANNHEIM

This raid to Mannheim was probably the most interesting operation of this period of the war. Bomber Command was authorized by the War Cabinet to carry out a general attack on the centre of a German city in retaliation for the recent heavy bombing of English cities, particularly Coventry and Southampton. Mannheim was chosen and a force of 200 bombers was prepared under the code-name Operation *Abigail Rachel*. Weather forecasts indicated that conditions over the bomber airfields would deteriorate and the force was cut to 134 aircraft – 61 Wellingtons, 35 Whitleys, 29 Hampdens and 9 Blenheims – but this was still the largest force sent to a single target so far.

The raid was opened by 8 Wellingtons, flown by the most experienced crews available, who attempted to start fires in the centre of Mannheim using all-incendiary bomb loads. Following crews were supposed to use these fires as a guide and attempt to cause as much destruction as possible. For the first time in more than fifteen months of war, Bomber Command was deliberately aiming at a target which was not primarily military or industrial in nature. The general area of the centre of Mannheim was the target. It was an early forerunner of what the R.A.F. would later call 'area bombing' and the Germans called 'terror bombing'.

The weather over the target was mainly clear of cloud and there was a full moon; the Mannheim defences were not heavy. Bomber Command's own records – the Operations Record Book and the Night Bombing Sheets* give figures varying between 82 and 102 aircraft claiming to have bombed Mannheim. But the raid was not a success. The early Wellington 'fire-raisers' were not accurate and the largest fires were not in the centre of the city. The resultant bombing by the main force of bombers was scattered.

The Mannheim report (55 pages long!) shows that the majority of the bombs fell in residential areas. 240 buildings were destroyed or damaged by incendiary bombs and 236 by high-explosive bombs; included in these figures are 13 commercial premises, 1 railway station, 1 railway office, 1 school and 2 hospitals. The hospitals did not sustain serious damage although at one of them, a military hospital, 28 people, including 13 soldiers and 9 nursing sisters, were injured by flying glass caused by the blast of a nearby high-explosive bomb. 4 barges or river steamers were damaged. The total casualty list was: 34 dead, 81 injured and 1,266 bombed out. Of the dead, 13 were male civilians, 1 was a soldier, 18 were women and 2 were children. Of the bombed out, 223 were in the town of Ludwigshafen on the other side of the Rhine.

2 Hampdens and 1 Blenheim were lost and 4 more aircraft crashed in England.

---

*Public Record Office AIR 24/200 and AIR 14/2670.

17/18 December 1940

MANNHEIM, AIRFIELDS

9 Whitleys to Mannheim, 8 Blenheims to airfields in France. No losses.

18/19 December 1940

MANNHEIM, MILAN

17 Wellingtons and 9 Whitleys to Mannheim, 5 Wellingtons to the Pirelli factory at Milan. Fires were claimed started near Mannheim main railway station and 3 aircraft which reached Milan claimed a 'terrific blaze' there. 1 Wellington was lost.

19 December 1940

5 Blenheims to France turned back.

19/20 December 1940

COLOGNE, THE RUHR, FRANCE

85 aircraft to Cologne, Duisburg, Gelsenkirchen and on small raids on Boulogne and airfields, but only 23 aircraft bombed primary targets. 1 Blenheim lost. 8 Hampdens minelaying off Brittany.

20 December 1940

5 Blenheims on cloud-cover raids but only 1 aircraft bombed, at Flushing docks. No losses.

20/21 December 1940

GERMANY, CHANNEL PORTS

125 aircraft to Berlin, Gelsenkirchen and the Channel Ports. 4 Hampdens minelaying in Kiel Bay. No losses.

The 6 Wellingtons dispatched by 103 and 150 Squadrons to Ostend were the first Wellingtons from 1 Group.*

21 December 1940

1 Blenheim to Le Havre turned back.

*This was the first occasion when one type of aircraft was operated by more than one group in a night. From this point diary references to Wellingtons dispatched can mean that Wellingtons from 1 and/or 3 Groups are operating, unless there is need to be more specific. The majority of the Wellington effort continued to be dispatched by 3 Group for many months to come.

21/22 December 1940

GERMANY, ITALY, HOLLAND, BELGIUM

71 Blenheims, Wellingtons and Whitleys to many targets. 5 Hampdens minelaying in Kiel Bay. 1 O.T.U. sortie. No losses.

22/23 December 1940

GERMANY, HOLLAND, FRANCE

59 Blenheims, Hampdens and Wellingtons to 5 targets but less than half bombed primaries. 1 Wellington lost. 3 Hampdens minelaying off Cuxhaven and 1 O.T.U. sortie.

23/24 December 1940

GERMANY, CHANNEL PORTS

43 Blenheims, Wellingtons and Whitleys to Ludwigshaven, Mannheim and to the ports. 1 Whitley lost. 2 O.T.U. sorties.

26/27 December 1940

6 Hampdens to aircraft factory at Bordeaux; 3 aircraft bombed and hits were seen on the airfield near by. No losses.

27/28 December 1940

FRANCE

75 aircraft to aircraft factory at Bordeaux and to ports and airfields. 1 Blenheim and 1 Wellington lost; 4 aircraft crashed in England.

28/29 December 1940

PORTS

59 Hampdens, Wellingtons and Whitleys to Rotterdam, Antwerp, Boulogne and Lorient. 1 Hampden and 1 Whitley lost. 7 Hampdens minelaying off Kiel and St-Nazaire.

29/30 December 1940

GERMANY, FRANCE

27 Blenheims, Wellingtons and Whitleys to Frankfurt, Hamm, Boulogne and airfields, but few aircraft reached these targets. 2 Wellingtons were lost.

30 December 1940

2 Blenheims to north Germany turned back.

---

31 December 1940

22 Blenheims on single flights to Germany and Holland. 6 aircraft bombed various targets. 2 aircraft lost.

---

1 January 1941

9 Blenheims to Germany turned back.

1/2 January 1941

BREMEN

141 aircraft to Bremen and in smaller raids to ports in Holland, Belgium and France. Many fires seen in target area.

Bremen reports accurate bombing, particularly by the first wave of aircraft, which hit the Focke-Wulf factory in the southern suburb of Hemelingen. 2 other industrial firms received serious damage and several others light damage. A large fire was started in stacks of straw and hay at an army depot. Fire units from outside Bremen were called in to help and the firemen had a difficult time in the prolonged bombing raid in a temperature of -12° Celsius. The bombing spread to the town centre where 14 housing units (blocks of flats) were destroyed and 313 damaged, though much of the damage consisted only of broken windows. 11 people were killed (including 3 firemen) and 30 people injured.

No aircraft were lost but 4 crashed in England.

---

2 January 1941

1 Blenheim to Dortmund–Ems Canal turned back.

2/3 January 1941

BREMEN

47 Hampdens, Wellingtons and Whitleys to Bremen and small raids to Emden and Amsterdam. 1 Whitley lost. 2 O.T.U. sorties.

This raid was not as effective as that of the previous night. About 15 bomb loads hit Bremen, mainly in the town centre and harbour area, where a store of 50,000 new jute sacks was burnt out. Reinforcement fire units were called in over icy roads and through snow showers from as far away as Hannover and Hamburg. 7 houses were destroyed and 576 damaged, mostly lightly. 8 people were killed and 44 injured.

3/4 January 1941

BREMEN

71 aircraft dispatched and reported good bombing results with numerous fires. Bremen again reports many fires and some casualties. Hamburg, to which no bombers were dispatched, also records 12 fires, 6 of which were classified as large, but no casualties. 1 Whitley lost.

---

4 January 1941

2 Blenheims turned back.

4/5 January 1941

BREST, HAMBURG

53 Hampdens, Wellingtons and Whitleys to attack major German naval units believed to be in Brest harbour. Cloud and heavy Flak produced indecisive bombing results. 24 Blenheims to Hamburg but weather conditions were poor and Hamburg records contain no mention of any attack.

Minor Operations: 9 Wellingtons to Duisburg, 4 Blenheims to Rotterdam, 5 Hampdens mine-laying off Lorient and 2 O.T.U. sorties.

There were no losses in any operation on this night.

---

5 January 1941

4 Blenheims; 1 aircraft bombed Flushing. No losses.

5/6 January 1941

12 Hampdens minelaying at Brest, Lorient and St-Nazaire. 1 aircraft lost.

---

6 January 1941

3 Blenheims; 1 aircraft bombed and hit a tanker off the Hook of Holland. No losses.

---

7 January 1941

1 Blenheim to Bremen turned back.

8 January 1941

5 Blenheims to Holland turned back.

8/9 January 1941

WILHELMSHAVEN, EMDEN

48 Hampdens, Wellingtons and Whitleys, 32 to Wilhelmshaven, 16 to Emden. The target at Wilhelmshaven was the battleship *Tirpitz*. Crews reported bombs straddling the *Tirpitz* and many fires. Wilhelmshaven reports heavy damage in various parts of the town with 12 people killed and adds the comment that this was the first large raid for the local air-raid services.

9 Hampdens minelaying in the Elbe. No losses from any operation.

---

9 January 1941

1 Blenheim to Antwerp turned back.

9/10 January 1941

GELSENKIRCHEN

135 aircraft – 60 Wellingtons, 36 Blenheims, 20 Hampdens and 19 Whitleys – to bomb synthetic-oil plants. Only 56 aircraft reported bombing the designated targets. Gelsenkirchen reports bombs in the city and in the surrounding towns of Buer, Horst and Hessler. One person was killed in Gelsenkirchen. 1 Whitley lost.

Minor Operations: 15 Wellingtons to Rotterdam, 1 Blenheim to Calais and 4 Hampdens minelaying in Kiel Bay. No losses.

---

10 January 1941

6 Blenheims of 114 Squadron were escorted by 72 fighters in this first *Circus* operation. The Blenheims bombed a German ammunition depot in the Forêt de Guines, south of Calais. None of the Blenheims were lost.

2 further Blenheims dispatched on cloud-cover raids to Emden and Nordholz turned back.

10/11 January 1941

12 Whitleys to attack warship in Brest harbour. No losses.

---

11 January 1941

19 Blenheims on widespread cloud-cover raids; 9 bombed targets. 1 aircraft lost.

11/12 January 1941

WILHELMSHAVEN

35 Hampdens and Wellingtons; 17 claimed to have bombed primary targets. No losses. Wilhelmshaven reports 1 house burnt down, a barn destroyed by an exploding Flak shell and a boy killed by a falling Flak-shell splinter.

Minor Operations: 11 Wellingtons to Turin and 5 Hampdens minelaying in the Baltic north of Lübeck. 1 Wellington, of 9 Squadron, returning from Turin force-landed in Vichy France and the crew destroyed the plane by fire before being interned.

12 January 1941

6 Blenheims; 1 bombed Flushing docks. No losses.

12/13 January 1941

BREST, MINOR OPERATIONS

26 Hampdens and Wellingtons to Brest, 21 Blenheims to airfields in France, 9 Wellingtons to Italy, 3 Wellingtons to Regensburg, 8 Hampdens minelaying off Brest and Lorient, 3 O.T.U. sorties. 1 Wellington lost from the Italian raid.

13 January 1941

1 Blenheim to Nordhorn airfield, just over the German border with Holland, did not return.

13/14 January 1941

WILHELMSHAVEN, FRENCH PORTS

24 Wellingtons and Whitleys to Wilhelmshaven, Dunkirk and Boulogne. Good bombing claimed at Wilhelmshaven but the town diary has no entry; cloud over the French ports. 12 Hampdens minelaying off Brittany ports. No losses from any operation.

14 January 1941

3 Blenheims turned back.

15 January 1941

2 Blenheims; 1 bombed a ship off Dutch coast but scored no hits. No losses.

15/16 January 1941

WILHELMSHAVEN

96 aircraft; most crews reported good bombing results. 1 Whitley lost. Wilhelmshaven reports much damage and many fires. Among buildings destroyed or damaged were: the head post office, the main police station, an army barracks, a naval technical school, the main dock offices, 7 large commercial premises and 2 hospitals. At least 22 fire-fighting teams were called in from towns in a radius of 120 km; the men of these teams had to travel in open vehicles over icy roads and then had to fight fires in freezing temperatures. 21 people were killed and 34 injured. The diarist says: 'The year of 1941 would bring many more heavy raids but none causing such heavy damage as this one.'

Minor Operations: 8 Wellingtons and 1 Whitley to Emden and Rotterdam. No losses.

16/17 January 1941

WILHELMSHAVEN

81 aircraft attempted to follow up the successful raid of the previous night but fewer crews found the target. Wilhelmshaven reports only light damage with 2 people killed. 5 aircraft – 2 Wellingtons, 2 Whitleys, 1 Hampden – lost.

Minor Operations: 3 Wellingtons to Emden and Rotterdam, 2 Blenheims to Boulogne, 4 Hampdens minelaying off Brest. No losses.

17/18 January 1941

1 O.T.U. leaflet sortie to Paris and Lille.

18 January 1941

1 Blenheim to Flushing turned back.

22 January 1941

12 Blenheims to Germany and Holland; 2 aircraft bombed at Flushing and Ghent. 1 aircraft mistakenly shot down over Lowestoft by anti-aircraft fire.

22/23 January 1941

DÜSSELDORF

28 Wellingtons and 12 Blenheims. No losses.

25 January 1941

8 Blenheims to oil targets in Holland turned back.

---

26 January 1941

1 Blenheim to Holland turned back.

26/27 January 1941

HANNOVER

10 Whitleys and 7 Wellingtons to attack the main post office and telephone exchange. No losses.

---

27 January 1941

1 Blenheim to Antwerp but turned back. It then had a combat with a Ju 88 off the Essex coast and claimed hits on it.

---

29 January 1941

1 Blenheim to Amsterdam turned back.

29/30 January 1941

WILHELMSHAVEN

25 Wellingtons and 9 Hampdens. The target was the *Tirpitz* but it could not be located and only 19 aircraft reported bombing in the target area. Wilhelmshaven reports many houses and an old water-tower destroyed and 18 people killed with many injured. No aircraft lost.

---

31 January 1941

7 Blenheims to Holland turned back.

---

1 February 1941

3 Blenheims; 1 aircraft bombed a ship off the Dutch coast but scored no hits. No losses.

1/2 February 1941

BOULOGNE

13 Wellingtons but cloud obscured bombing results. No losses.

2 February 1941

5 Blenheims with a large fighter escort in a *Circus* operation. 4 aircraft bombed Boulogne docks. No losses to Blenheims.

2/3 February 1941

BREST

12 Hampdens to attack warships but cloud prevented accurate bombing. 2 Hampdens minelaying off Lorient. No losses.

3 February 1941

1 Blenheim; turned back.

3/4 February 1941

BRITTANY PORTS

7 Wellingtons to Brest and 11 Hampdens minelaying off Brest and Lorient. No losses.

4 February 1941

7 Blenheims; 1 bombed a gun position on Borkum airfield. No losses.

4/5 February 1941

An increased effort was dispatched with the approach of the full moon period and, for the first time in night raids, the aircraft of each group were allocated their own separate target area.

DÜSSELDORF

30 Hampdens but heavy cloud over target. 1 aircraft lost.

BREST, LE HAVRE

38 Wellingtons; a direct hit was claimed on a cruiser at Brest. No losses.

BORDEAUX AIRFIELD, CALAIS

31 Whitleys; good bombing results claimed at Bordeaux but the freshmen crews found Calais covered by cloud. No losses.

DUNKIRK, OSTEND, QUIBERON, AIRFIELDS

37 Blenheims; no losses.

6 Hampdens minelaying off St-Nazaire. 1 aircraft lost.

---

5 February 1941

12 Blenheims on *Circus* operation to St-Omer airfield; 9 bombed. 1 further Blenheim to Le Havre turned back. No losses.

6/7 February 1941

BOULOGNE, DUNKIRK

25 Wellingtons to Boulogne, 24 Whitleys to Dunkirk. The force attacking Boulogne included a Photographic Reconnaissance Unit Wellington but its cameras failed. 1 Wellington lost.

7/8 February 1941

BOULOGNE, DUNKIRK

37 Wellingtons to Boulogne, 27 Hampdens to Dunkirk. Good bombing results claimed at both targets. 2 O.T.U. sorties. No losses.

---

8 February 1941

9 Blenheims to Holland and Germany; 2 aircraft bombed at Flushing and Rotterdam. No losses.

8/9 February 1941

MANNHEIM

15 Hampdens; the target was cloud-covered and no bombing results were seen. No losses.

---

9 February 1941

11 Blenheims; 4 aircraft bombed various targets. No losses.

9/10 February 1941

WILHELMSHAVEN

23 Hampdens; the target was cloud-covered and only 1 aircraft claimed to have bombed there; 13 other aircraft bombed estimated position of target. Wilhelmshaven diary has no entry. No losses.

10 February 1941

6 Blenheims on *Circus* raid to Dunkirk – all bombed – and 6 other Blenheims on cloud-cover raids; 4 of these bombed various targets. No losses.

Operational Statistics, 13 October 1940 to 10 February 1941
(120½ 24-hour periods)

Number of days with operations: 83
Number of nights with operations: 93
Number of daylight sorties: 567, from which 9 aircraft (1·6 per cent) were lost
Number of night sorties: 6,030, from which 117 aircraft (1·9 per cent) were lost
Total sorties: 6,597, from which 126 aircraft (1·9 per cent) were lost
Approximate bomb tonnage in period: 4,350 tons
Averages per 24-hour period: 54·7 sorties, 1·0 aircraft lost, 36·1 tons of bombs dropped

6. A NEW START

10/11 February to 12 March 1941

The prospect for Bomber Command's future operations now appeared to be more favourable than at any time since the beginning of the war. There was no military action in the West that could distract from the bomber effort. There could be no threat of a German invasion of England until the early summer, and even then only if the Luftwaffe could defeat Fighter Command first. The bombers available and suitable for operations were now more numerous than ever before. The increasing number of experienced crews had not been pressed too hard in recent weeks; many new crews had received a valuable introduction to operations in raids on the easy 'freshman' targets. The German night-fighter defences had still not been reinforced to any dangerous extent and it was hoped that the worst of the winter weather was now over.

On 15 January 1941, the Air Ministry had sent Sir Richard Peirse the most concise, clear and forceful directive yet produced.* It was assumed that 'oil position of the Axis Powers will be passing through their most critical period . . . during the next six months' and that, if the scale of attack on Germany's synthetic-oil industry could be increased, 'there will be widespread effects on German industry and communications, while it is even probable that within this time an appreciable effect may be felt in the scale of effort of her armed forces'. Sir Richard Peirse was therefore told that 'the sole primary aim of your bomber offensive, until further orders, should be the destruction of the German synthetic oil plants'. A list of seventeen places where oil was being produced from nearby deposits of cheaply mined brown coal (lignite) was added and it was judged that a reduction of 80 per cent in Germany's internal production of oil could be achieved if the first nine of these plants could be destroyed. The leading nine plants were: Leuna, Pölitz, Gelsenkirchen (the Nordstern plant), Zeitz, Scholven/Buer, Ruhland, Böhlen, Magdeburg and Lützkendorf.

The intentions of Sir Richard Peirse on receiving these orders were quite clear. He would wait for the February new moon, make the large once-a-month attack on a large industrial city to which he had become accustomed, and then set to work to concentrate on those oil plants. The serious attack on the oil targets would, of course, be carried out almost entirely by night. He would be able to dispatch 265 aircraft on his February 'big night'; this was fifty-six more than the previous highest total, achieved in September 1940. Hannover would be chosen for this attack. The number of aircraft Peirse would send to Hannover would be 222, which well exceeded the previous largest concentration on one target, 135 to Gelsenkirchen in the January 1941 moon period. There should be no reason why a substantially increased effort by the current types of bombers should not be available for operations for a prolonged

---

*Official History, Vol. IV, pp. 132–3.

period, and new, improved, types were also beginning to appear. The Manchester and the four-engined types, Stirling and Halifax, the new generation of aircraft with much increased bomb-carrying capacity and, it was hoped, better all-round performance, were all due to make their operational début within the next month. There was only one change in command at this time: Air Vice-Marshal D. F. Stevenson succeeded Air Vice-Marshal J. M. Robb in the command of the still operationally trouble-ridden 2 Group.

The new period was due to get off to a good start but would then run into further weather problems. The clearest of conditions were needed for the finding of the oil plants; when these conditions were not available, the bombers had to be sent to less important targets. It was in this way that Cologne, the comparatively short-range target and one that was outside the main Ruhr Flak and searchlight defences, came to be chosen for attack on numerous nights of marginal weather conditions. When the weather was really bad, the bomber force often had to be stood down completely. Sometimes risks were taken to keep the offensive going and the bombers suffered heavy casualties in crashes around their home airfields or in the more distant parts of the United Kingdom to which they were sometimes diverted. Nearly three quarters of the aircraft casualties incurred in the following weeks would be the result of crashes in the United Kingdom.

Unhappily for Bomber Command, the great oil offensive never really got under way. Frustrated immediately by the weather, it was soon to be cut off completely by yet another diversion of effort. The clear run for which Bomber Command Headquarters had hoped was destined to last for just one month.

10/11 February 1941

HANNOVER

222 aircraft – 112 Wellingtons, 46 Hampdens, 34 Blenheims, 30 Whitleys – to industrial targets in Hannover. 4 aircraft – 2 Wellingtons, 1 Blenheim, 1 Hampden – were lost and 3 more aircraft were shot down in England by German Intruders.

183 aircraft claimed to have bombed their primary targets; 32 aircraft bombed alternative targets. Crews reported good visibility, large explosions and many fires started. No report is available from Hannover.

ROTTERDAM

43 aircraft to oil-storage tanks at Rotterdam. Included in this force were 3 Stirlings, of 7 Squadron, making the first operational flights of this new type of aircraft. There were no losses.

The 119 Wellingtons provided by 3 Group on this night represented the first time a group had dispatched more than 100 aircraft.

---

11 February 1941

6 Blenheims to Channel ports turned back.

11/12 February 1941

BREMEN

79 Hampdens, Wellingtons and Whitleys but only 27 claimed to have bombed Bremen. No aircraft lost but 22 aircraft – 11 Wellingtons, 7 Whitleys and 4 Hampdens – crashed in England when unexpected fog descended on most of the bases. Most of their crews parachuted safely but 5 men were killed.

HANNOVER

18 Wellingtons and 11 Hampdens. No losses.

1 Wellington to Rotterdam bombed there.

---

12 February 1941

1 Blenheim to oil depot on Kiel Canal turned back.

---

14 February 1941

4 Blenheims; 1 bombed Calais docks. No losses.

14/15 February 1941

GELSENKIRCHEN

44 Wellingtons to the Nordstern oil plant but only 9 aircraft claimed to have hit the target. No losses. On the return of the bombers to England, what appeared to be a German aircraft landed among Hampdens of 57 Squadron at Feltwell. The flarepath was extinguished and the aircraft took off again.

HOMBERG

22 Blenheims and 22 Wellingtons to oil plant; 16 claimed to have bombed target. No losses.

11 Hampdens minelaying in Gironde; 1 lost.

---

15 February 1941

5 Blenheims; 1 bombed Calais docks. 1 aircraft lost.

15/16 February 1941

STERKRADE

73 aircraft – 46 Wellingtons and 27 Whitleys – to the Holten oil plant. 1 Wellington and 1 Whitley lost.

HOMBERG

37 Blenheims and 33 Hampdens; the local oil plant was difficult to identify because of searchlight glare but 40 aircraft bombed. No losses.

BOULOGNE

43 aircraft to docks; many fires seen. No losses.

---

16 February 1941

9 Blenheims to Holland and France. 5 aircraft bombed oil-storage tanks and shipping at various docks. No losses.

---

17 February 1941

5 Blenheims; 4 turned back; 1 lost.

---

20 February 1941

1 Blenheim to oil depot on Kiel Canal but bombed alternative target, docks at Ijmuiden.

---

21 February 1941

1 Blenheim to oil depot at Ghent turned back.

21/22 February 1941

WILHELMSHAVEN

34 Wellingtons; 19 bombed; 1 lost. Wilhelmshaven diary has no entry.

42 Hampdens minelaying off Brest. No losses.

Minor Operations: 7 Whitleys to Düsseldorf, 7 Blenheims to airfields in France and Holland, 3 Wellingtons to Boulogne. 1 Wellington lost.

---

22 February 1941

2 Blenheims; turned back.

22/23 February 1941

BREST

29 Wellingtons dispatched to attack warships in harbour but only 11 bombed. No losses but 4 aircraft crashed in England.

---

23 February 1941

3 Blenheims; 1 bombed Boulogne docks. No losses.

23/24 February 1941

BOULOGNE

35 Wellingtons and 17 Blenheims. The Blenheims were recalled but 26 Wellingtons bombed. 1 Wellington lost.

Minor Operations: 16 Whitleys and 1 Blenheim to Calais, 3 Blenheims to Den Helder and 6 O.T.U. sorties to Paris. No losses.

24/25 February 1941

BREST

57 aircraft – 30 Wellingtons, 18 Hampdens, 6 Manchesters, 3 Stirlings – to bomb warships. No losses. The Manchester sorties, from 207 Squadron, were the first operational flights by this type of aircraft; 1 Manchester crashed in England.

1 Wellington bombed Boulogne docks.

25 February 1941

4 Blenheims; 1 bombed Flushing docks. No losses.

25/26 February 1941

DÜSSELDORF

80 aircraft – 43 Wellingtons, 22 Hampdens, 15 Whitleys. 1 Wellington lost.
   64 aircraft bombed through complete cloud cover. A detailed report from Düsseldorf lists the results of approximately 7 loads of bombs which fell in the city. 4 small fires were soon put out; the only claim for compensation was by a farmer for 1,000 Reichsmarks (£100) damage to a barn. 1 civilian was slightly hurt fighting a fire and 2 Flak gunners slightly injured when a high-explosive bomb fell near their position.

Minor Operations: 17 Blenheims to airfields, 4 Blenheims and Wellingtons to Boulogne and 2 O.T.U. sorties. No losses.

26 February 1941

12 Blenheims on a *Circus* operation; 11 aircraft bombed Calais. 1 Blenheim on cloud-cover raid to Germany turned back. No losses.

26/27 February 1941

COLOGNE

126 aircraft of all types except Stirling to 2 targets in Cologne. 106 aircraft bombed and reported large fires. Cologne only reports 10 high-explosive and 90 incendiary bombs on the western edge of the city and more bombs in 3 village areas to the west. (This was out of 353 high-explosive and 15,060 incendiary bombs carried by the bomber force.)

Minor Operations: 9 Blenheims and Wellingtons to Boulogne and 5 Hampdens minelaying off Cuxhaven. 1 Blenheim lost.

28 February 1941

8 Blenheims on widespread cloud-cover raids; 7 aircraft bombed at Flushing, Den Helder and Lorient. No losses.

28 February/1 March 1941

WILHELMSHAVEN

116 Blenheims, Hampdens, Wellingtons and Whitleys in an attempt to bomb the battleship *Tirpitz* in Wilhelmshaven harbour. 75 crews reported bombing but Wilhelmshaven has no diary report. 1 Blenheim lost.

6 Blenheims to Boulogne but only 2 bombed. No losses.

1/2 March 1941

COLOGNE

131 Blenheims, Hampdens, Wellingtons and Whitleys to 2 targets in Cologne. 5 Whitleys and 1 Wellington lost; 14 further aircraft were abandoned and crashed in fog over England with 12 crew members killed, 2 missing and 5 injured.

Cologne reports a sharp raid, particularly in the dock areas on both banks of the Rhine near the city centre. A military stores and fodder depot and 13 warehouses and other commercial buildings were burnt out. 2 Rhine passenger steamers were sunk and 3 more damaged. 6 assorted commercial premises suffered serious damage. 80–90 houses were destroyed and 160 badly damaged. 21 people were killed and 35 injured.

3 Wellingtons to Boulogne. No losses.

2 March 1941

1 Blenheim bombed a seaplane base on the island of Sylt.

2/3 March 1941

BREST

54 aircraft, mostly Wellingtons, to bomb warships at Brest. 1 Wellington lost.

Minor Operations: 13 Blenheims to airfields and 2 Blenheims to Rotterdam oil tanks. 1 aircraft lost.

3/4 March 1941

COLOGNE

71 Hampdens, Wellingtons and Whitleys. 1 Hampden lost.
   Partial cloud hampered bombing but many fires were reported. Cologne records no bombs in the main city but a few on western outskirts. An opencast coal mine claimed 300–500 Reichsmarks (£30–£50) compensation for damaged equipment.

Minor Operations: 8 Wellingtons bombed Boulogne without loss. 7 aircraft to Brest with 1 Stirling lost. This was the first Stirling to be lost; Squadron Leader J. M. Griffiths-Jones, D.F.C., of 7 Squadron, and his crew all died; their names are on the Runnymede Memorial to the Missing.

The night squadrons of Bomber Command were stood down because of bad weather for the next week.

---

4 March 1941

1 Blenheim to Ghent turned back.

---

5 March 1941

6 Blenheims on a *Circus* operation; they bombed Boulogne docks without loss.

---

6 March 1941

5 Blenheims to oil depots in Belgium and Holland; 1 aircraft bombed Sluiskil. No losses.

---

8 March 1941

8 Blenheims to Holland and German islands; 2 aircraft bombed Den Helder. No losses.

---

10 March 1941

1 Blenheim on weather reconnaissance turned back.

10/11 March 1941

COLOGNE

19 Hampdens; 1 aircraft lost.

Some fires were claimed to have been started. Cologne reports 24 people killed and 60 injured but no serious industrial damage was caused.

LE HAVRE

8 Blenheims and 6 Halifaxes. This was the first Halifax operation of the war. No aircraft were lost but the Halifax of Squadron Leader Gilchrist, 35 Squadron, was mistakenly shot down over Surrey by an R.A.F. fighter while returning from the raid. Only the pilot and one other man survived.

ST-NAZAIRE

14 Whitleys; only 4 bombed the main target. No losses.

11 March 1941

4 Blenheims to Holland; 2 bombed. No losses.

11/12 March 1941

KIEL

27 Wellingtons; many hits claimed on shipyards. Kiel reports 6 people killed and 17 injured. No aircraft lost.

12 March 1941

6 Blenheims to Holland; 2 aircraft bombed a merchant ship near Ijmuiden but no hits reported. No losses.

Operational Statistics, 10/11 February to 12 March 1941 (30 days/nights)

Number of days with operations: 21
Number of nights with operations: 16
Number of daylight sorties: 94, from which 2 aircraft (2·1 per cent) were lost
Number of night sorties: 1,635, from which 26 aircraft (1·6 per cent) were lost
Total sorties: 1,729, from which 28 aircraft (1·6 per cent) were lost, but 70 further aircraft crashed in England
Approximate bomb tonnage in period: 1,517 tons
Averages per 24-hour period: 57·6 sorties, 0·9 aircraft lost, 50·6 tons of bombs dropped

7. MARITIME DIVERSION

12/13 March to 7 July 1941

Bomber Command now suffered a new diversion from its main campaign. German successes at sea, particularly by U-boats on the North Atlantic convoy run, had been running at a dangerously high figure in recent months. Nearly 900 British, Allied and neutral ships carrying stores for Britain had been sunk by German naval forces and aircraft since the fall of France the previous summer. The Royal Navy was short of escort vessels; there was not yet even continuous surface-escort cover for convoys over the whole Atlantic run. Long-range air escort was non-existent. The German battle-cruisers *Scharnhorst* and *Gneisenau* were out in the Atlantic, sinking or capturing twenty-two merchant ships. No British warship was fast enough to catch these modern ships and then have the ability to engage them successfully. Other, larger German ships, like the battleship *Bismarck*, were almost ready to sail and carry on this work. Long-range German bombers, Focke-Wulf Kondors, were also a scourge for British merchant shipping. What Hitler had failed to achieve by air attack and intimidation in 1940, his U-boats, surface warships and maritime bombers were close to achieving in 1941. Britain faced the possibility of its absolutely vital ocean links with the Americans being severed. The Prime Minister issued a simple instruction. For the next four months, Bomber Command's main operational effort was to be directed against those targets which housed the sources of the threats to British shipping.

The Air Ministry passed on these orders to Bomber Command in a directive dated 9 March 1941. The initial emphasis was on the U-boat and long-range aircraft threats. The directive repeated Churchill's own words: 'We must take the offensive against the U-boat and the Focke-Wulf wherever we can and whenever we can. The U-boat at sea must be hunted, the U-boat in the building yard or in dock must be bombed. The Focke-Wulf, and other bombers employed against our shipping, must be attacked in the air and in their nests.'* There was a list of targets: Kiel, with three U-boat shipbuilding yards. Hamburg, with two yards, Bremen and Vegesack, each with one yard; the cities of Mannheim and Augsburg with their marine diesel-engine factories (Augsburg was soon removed from the list because of its extreme range for the approaching shorter nights); Dessau and Bremen again with aircraft factories; Lorient, St-Nazaire and Bordeaux with their U-boat bases; the Focke-Wulf Kondor airfields at Stavanger in Norway and at Mérignac near Bordeaux. The Air Ministry did secure one concession; Sir Richard Peirse was allowed to devote a proportion of the operational effort on the old oil targets. The written directive was later amended by verbal order when the *Scharnhorst* and *Gneisenau* came into Brest from their

*Official History, Vol. IV, p. 133.

successful Atlantic sweep. A great tonnage of bombs was due to be thrown at those two ships.

Sir Richard Peirse was not happy to be taken off the strategic bombing of Germany just when he felt that his force was on the verge of potential success in the improving weather of spring. But Sir Charles Portal, Chief of the Air Staff, was probably less unhappy and did not oppose the order from Churchill. Portal, sometimes known as 'the big thinker', was coming to realize that Bomber Command's claims of accurate results in the bombing of the comparatively small oil targets were not justified. The Official History makes this comment:

> Whether Sir Charles Portal really believed that this directive would get the Admiralty out of its 'mess' or not, it was in effect the Admiralty which had got the Air Ministry out of a 'mess', for if Bomber Command had, at this stage, been left free to carry out the oil plan it would probably have done a great deal more damage to its prestige than to its targets.*

There were a few further words in the directive which were of the utmost significance to the unfolding story of the bombing war. In that 9 March directive, signed by Air Chief Marshal Sir Wilfred Freeman, Vice-Chief of the Air Staff, were these words referring to the list of German cities connected with the U-boat and long-range aircraft threat: 'Priority of selection should be given to those [targets] in Germany which lie in congested areas where the greatest moral [sic] effect is likely to result.' In a small amending directive, written on 18 March and signed by the Deputy Chief of the Air Staff Air Vice-Marshal Harris, Harris writes of Mannheim and the newly added target of Stuttgart, with its U-boat engine and accessory factories, 'Both are suitable as area objectives and their attack should have high morale value.'† In other words, the general bombing of city areas in an effort to break the morale of German civilians was progressively being introduced as a Bomber Command weapon. Freeman and Harris did not originate these ideas; they were merely putting the wishes of Portal and the Air Staff on paper. There were senior officers, however, besides Portal who were moving at various speeds to the conclusion that, until Bomber Command received some of the sophisticated aids to bombing accuracy being prepared, 'area bombing' against German cities with a view to breaking civilian morale was the most useful means of employing the bomber force. A pattern in the operations of Bomber Command thus developed during the coming period. One part of a force dispatched to a city might be given a specific industrial or port installation as its target while other parts of the force were directed to aim at the city centre in order to create general destruction, dislocation and disorder. It was now reckoned that really accurate bombing of small targets was possible on only the nine most moonlit nights in the month, even by experienced crews. During the remainder of the month, most bombing would become area bombing even though the aiming points were nominally industrial. These methods would inevitably produce heavier civilian death tolls. For example, during the coming four months during which the bombing was directed in support of the maritime campaign, Hamburg would suffer 331 deaths in eighteen raids compared with 125 deaths in its first seventy-two raids of the war, and Kiel would have 254 deaths in seventeen raids compared with only twenty-five deaths in its first sixteen raids.

*Official History, Vol. I, pp. 165–6.
†Official History, Vol. IV, p. 135.

So, the bomber squadrons were sent to attempt the destruction of the ports of Germany and France and the inland towns connected with the manufacture of U-boats and long-range bombers. 2 Group would join in the shipping offensive, being pressed more vigorously than in recent months in a variety of operations along the German-controlled coastline of Europe. There was still no basic increase in bomber strength; the transfers of squadrons to Middle East and to Coastal Command cancelled out the increase in new squadrons formed. The new types of aircraft being introduced made their first flights to Germany, but not in any strength during the coming period. It was the old Wellington which was emerging as the undisputed backbone of Bomber Command's strength. The original Wellington group, 3 Group, was now the most powerful in Bomber Command; the Wellington was also in service with 1 Group and some of the 4 Group squadrons would start operating this reliable aircraft in May. Wellingtons sometimes comprised more than half of a force of bombers dispatched. The first of many Canadian squadrons, 405 (Vancouver) Squadron, started to operate in June, flying Wellingtons in 4 Group, and the first 4,000-pound bombs would be dropped during the next few weeks. The only change of command in the coming period was the departure of Air-Vice-Marshal Bottomley from 5 Group on 12 May; Bottomley moved to the Air Ministry to replace as Deputy Chief of the Air Staff Air Vice-Marshal Harris, who was sent to lead an R.A.F. delegation to the United States. The new commander of 5 Group was Air Vice-Marshal J. C. Slessor.

The maritime campaign ran its full four-month course, uninterrupted by bad weather or diversion to any other priority. It is difficult to assess the overall benefits produced by the bombing. Much damage was caused in the German ports where U-boats were made and this must have affected new construction, although production figures do not reveal any dramatic setback. The bombing of the U-boat bases in France certainly moved the Germans to action and they commenced the construction of huge, bomb-proof shelters for the U-boats which operated from the French ports. A major effort was directed on to the warships sheltering in Brest, not in the expectation that accurate bombing would pound these ships to destruction but in the hope that an odd hit now and then would prevent their sailing out into the Atlantic again. This was achieved. Not much is known about the bombing of the long-range aircraft factories and bases. As for the secondary aim of lowering morale in the German cities selected for attack, the optimists who felt that the German spirit would crack were as much in error on this subject as they would continue to be throughout the rest of the war. It can be said, however, that this coming period of bombing had a greater effect upon the German war effort than the continuation of the oil campaign would have done; there had never been the slightest chance that the strength of bombers available and the methods being employed in 1941 could have stopped Germany's supply of synthetic oil.

Elsewhere, the war unfolded dramatically. On 30 March, a German offensive in North Africa drove back the British forces which had made such good earlier progress against the Italians. On 6 April, the Germans invaded Greece and Yugoslavia and, on 22 June, came that great watershed, the German invasion of Russia.

12/13 March 1941

HAMBURG

88 aircraft – 40 Hampdens, 25 Whitleys, 16 Wellingtons, 4 Manchesters, 3 Halifaxes – to attack the Blohm & Voss U-boat yards and other industry. This was the first time that Manchesters and Halifaxes had been sent to a target in Germany. No aircraft were lost from this raid.

Hamburg reports that 20 high-explosive and 300–400 incendiary bombs fell in the Blohm & Voss yard, causing damage to the main office block and other parts of the premises, including two slipways on which U-boats were being built. 4 other shipbuilding firms were hit and a large harbour warehouse and its contents were burnt out. A total of 205 fires (18 classed as large) were started; 8 people were killed, 96 injured and 414 bombed out.

BREMEN

86 aircraft – 54 Wellingtons, 32 Blenheims – dispatched, the Wellingtons to attack the Focke-Wulf aircraft factory and the Blenheims the town centre. 2 Wellingtons and 1 Blenheim lost. Photographic reconnaissance showed that 12 high-explosive bombs hit the aircraft factory.

BERLIN

72 aircraft – 30 Hampdens, 28 Wellingtons, 14 Whitleys – to two targets. 3 aircraft, one of each type, lost.

The bombing was very scattered with more bombs in the southern districts of the city than elsewhere. 60 buildings of many kinds were hit, though none was classed as destroyed and only 3 as being severely damaged. 11 people were killed, 24 injured and 80 bombed out.

Minor Operations: 8 aircraft to Calais and Boulogne. 2 O.T.U. sorties, 1 Hampden minelaying in the Elbe. 1 Wellington from the Boulogne raid was lost.

Total effort for the night: 257 sorties, 7 aircraft (2·7 per cent) lost.

---

13 March 1941

6 Blenheims on a *Circus* operation to Calais/Marck airfield; all bombed. No Blenheims lost.

13/14 March 1941

HAMBURG

139 aircraft – 53 Wellingtons, 34 Hampdens, 24 Whitleys, 21 Blenheims, 5 Manchesters, 2 Halifaxes. 6 aircraft – 2 Wellingtons, 2 Whitleys, 1 Blenheim, 1 Hampden –were lost and 1 Manchester was shot down soon after take-off by an Intruder, the first Manchester lost on operations. There was only one survivor from the Manchester crew, which was captained by Flying Officer Hugh Matthews of 207 Squadron.

In Hamburg, the Blohm & Voss shipyard was again hit and there was much other damage including a large fire in a timber-yard and a direct hit on the main fire station which damaged the reserve fire-hose store. A total of 119 fires – 31 large – were started; 51 people were killed, 139 injured and 95 bombed out. This was the heaviest death toll in Hamburg so far in the war.

Minor Operations: 14 aircraft to oil-storage tanks at Rotterdam, 3 O.T.U. sorties, 1 Hampden minelaying at Ameland. No losses.

---

14 March 1941

4 Blenheims on sea sweep; 2 bombed ships off Ostend but scored no hits. No losses.

14/15 March 1941

GELSENKIRCHEN

101 aircraft – 61 Wellingtons, 21 Hampdens, 19 Whitleys – to bomb oil plants. 1 Wellington lost.

Gelsenkirchen reports its worst raid of the war so far. The city itself was not badly hit; the worst damage was caused by Flak shells exploding on descent! But one of the oil plants, the Hydriewerk Scholven, was hit by an estimated 16 aircraft bomb loads. Much damage was caused, 5 fires started and 5 workmen killed. The company housing estate near by was also bombed. Total casualties were 9 killed. Production at the plant stopped completely but it is not stated for how long.

DÜSSELDORF

24 Blenheims. No losses.

ROTTERDAM

7 Whitleys and 5 Blenheims attacked the oil-storage tanks and fires were started. No losses.

---

15 March 1941

4 Blenheims on coastal sweep; shipping bombed off Dunkirk and Ostend. No losses.

15/16 March 1941

LORIENT, DÜSSELDORF

37 Wellingtons and Whitleys to Lorient submarine base but haze prevented accurate bombing. 21 Hampdens to Düsseldorf. 5 Blenheims on a 'special operation', probably airfield Intruder work. 4 of them bombed Vannes airfield.

There were no aircraft losses on this night.

16 March 1941

5 Blenheims to Brittany coast returned because of fog.

17 March 1941

9 Blenheims to bomb oil tanks and shipping at Flushing. All bombed but cloud prevented observations. No losses.

17/18 March 1941

BREMEN, WILHELMSHAVEN

57 Hampdens, Wellingtons, Whitleys and 1 Stirling (the first Stirling to attack a German target) to Bremen; 21 Blenheims to Wilhelmshaven. No aircraft lost over Germany but 1 Wellington shot down by an Intruder. Good bombing results reported at both targets.

2 Blenheims and 1 Stirling to Rotterdam. No losses.

18 March 1941

11 Blenheims on sweeps of enemy coasts; all aircraft bombed ships but scored no hits. No losses.

18/19 March 1941

KIEL

99 aircraft – 40 Hampdens, 34 Wellingtons, 23 Whitleys, 2 Manchesters; none lost. Kiel reports this as its heaviest raid so far, with special mention of increased incendiary attack. Damage was caused in the Deutsche Werke U-boat yard and in many city-centre-type buildings – large shops, banks, hospitals. 5 people were killed and 10 injured.

WILHELMSHAVEN

44 Blenheims; 1 was lost.

ROTTERDAM

19 aircraft; no losses.

19 March 1941

4 Blenheims on an uneventful sea sweep to Brest and the Channel Islands.

19/20 March 1941

COLOGNE

36 Wellingtons; none lost. Cologne records 2 industrial buildings damaged, 4 houses destroyed, 6 people injured.

1 Wellington and 1 Stirling to Rotterdam without loss.

20 March 1941

10 Blenheims to enemy coast; many trawlers and small vessels bombed. No losses.

20/21 March 1941

LORIENT

21 Whitleys and 3 Manchesters to attack the U-boat base. No aircraft lost.

42 Hampdens on minelaying operations off Brest, Lorient, and St-Nazaire. 1 aircraft lost.

1 Blenheim attacked Le Bourget airfield.

21 March 1941

9 Blenheims to Frisian Islands. Many attacks made on ships and 1 tanker was claimed hit. No aircraft losses.

21/22 March 1941

LORIENT

66 aircraft – 34 Wellingtons, 19 Blenheims, 12 Hampdens, 1 Stirling – to bomb the U-boat base but bad visibility caused poor bombing. 1 Blenheim and 1 Hampden lost.

Minor Operations: 6 aircraft to Ostend, 7 Hampdens minelaying off Bordeaux, 1 O.T.U. sortie. 1 Wellington lost on the Ostend raid.

22 March 1941

6 Blenheims on coastal sweep. 1 aircraft attacked a convoy off Holland. No aircraft lost.

23 March 1941

5 Blenheims on coastal sweep. 2 aircraft attacked 5 minesweepers and a destroyer off the Frisians but scored no hits. No aircraft lost.

23/24 March 1941

The operations of this night were typical of those dispatched on nights of no moon and marginal weather conditions. Small forces of bombers were sent, more with the intention of causing general damage in German cities than of obtaining any outstanding bombing success.

BERLIN

35 Wellingtons and 28 Whitleys; bombing results were not seen because of cloud and heavy Flak. No losses.

KIEL

31 Hampdens; none lost. Bombing was very scattered but one heavy bomb destroyed a house, killing 10 and injuring 6 people who were sheltering in the basement cellar.

HANNOVER

26 Blenheims; 1 lost. Bomb bursts and one big fire were seen in the target area.

Minor Operations: 7 aircraft to Calais and Rotterdam, 5 Hampdens minelaying off Kiel. No losses.

---

24 March 1941

9 Blenheims on coastal sweeps. 1 fishing vessel was sunk off the Dutch coast. 1 aircraft lost.

---

25 March 1941

5 Blenheims off Holland and the Frisian Islands. Convoy attacked and 1 ship claimed as hit. No aircraft lost.

---

26 March 1941

18 Blenheims on coastal sweeps. Several aircraft attacked small ships. No aircraft lost.

---

27 March 1941

10 Blenheims on coastal sweeps; warships and a submarine were attacked but no hits were scored. No aircraft lost.

27/28 March 1941

COLOGNE

38 Wellingtons and 1 Stirling. 1 Wellington lost.

DÜSSELDORF

39 aircraft – 22 Hampdens, 13 Whitleys, 4 Manchesters. 1 Manchester and 1 Whitley lost.

Minor Operations: 13 aircraft to Brest, Calais and Dunkirk. No losses.

---

28 March 1941

18 Blenheims on coastal sweeps but no shipping seen.

---

29 March 1941

4 Blenheims off Belgium and Holland. 1 aircraft attacked a tanker heavily defended by Flak ships. 6 further Blenheims to attack the *Scharnhorst* and *Gneisenau*, now reported off Brest after their raid on shipping in the Atlantic; the Blenheims returned because of lack of cloud cover. No losses on this day.

29/30 March 1941

25 Hampdens minelaying off Brest; only 14 succeeded in laying mines. 1 aircraft lost.

---

30 March 1941

12 Hampdens to Brest turned back, no cloud cover. 6 Blenheims off the Frisians attacked a cargo vessel. No losses.

30/31 March 1941

BREST

109 aircraft – 50 Wellingtons, 24 Whitleys, 16 Blenheims, 15 Hampdens, 4 Manchesters – attacked the *Scharnhorst* and *Gneisenau* in Brest harbour but no hits were achieved.

Minor Operations: 13 Wellingtons to Calais, 10 Hampdens minelaying off Brest, 2 O.T.U. sorties.

There were no losses on this night.

31 March 1941

20 Blenheims on coastal sweeps from France to Germany. Two destroyers were bombed from low level and one was hit; other ships were attacked and some hit. This was the first day of what was known as 'Fringe Operations', when the Blenheims were ordered to attack land targets along the coasts they were patrolling. Several German gun positions and a parade of troops were attacked in Holland. 2 Blenheims lost.

31 March/1 April 1941

BREMEN

28 Wellingtons; haze and cloud prevented accurate bombing. 1 aircraft lost.

Minor Operations: 6 Wellingtons to Emden and 5 to Rotterdam. 1 aircraft each from 9 and 149 Squadrons dropped the first 4,000-lb bombs of the war on Emden. These 'high-capacity' blast bombs, called 'blockbusters' or 'cookies' by the British and '*Luftminen*' by the Germans were due to become one of Bomber Command's main weapons. No aircraft lost.

1 April 1941

12 Blenheims to Belgian coast; several ships were attacked. No losses. 11 Hampdens to Brest turned back; 1 lost.

2 April 1941

19 Blenheims to Belgian, Dutch and Danish coasts; many targets attacked. 1 aircraft lost.

3 April 1941

12 Hampdens to Brest were recalled. 1 aircraft did not receive the signal and went on to bomb the German warships in Brest harbour. 11 Blenheims to the French coast but no targets were seen. No losses.

3/4 April 1941

BREST

90 aircraft – 51 Wellingtons, 27 Whitleys, 11 Blenheims, 1 Stirling – reported that the warships were difficult to locate. 1 Blenheim and 1 Whitley were lost and 1 Wellington was shot down over England by an Intruder.

Minor Operations: 15 Hampdens minelaying off Brest and La Pallice; 1 aircraft lost. 7 aircraft to Ostend and Rotterdam.

4 April 1941

14 Blenheims to French and Danish coasts; shipping attacked and 1 trawler hit. 1 aircraft lost.

4/5 April 1941

BREST

54 aircraft – 39 Wellingtons, 11 Hampdens, 4 Manchesters; 1 Hampden was lost.
 A direct hit was claimed on one of the German cruisers.
 German records show that one bomb fell in the dry dock in which the *Gneisenau* was lying. The bomb remained in the water left in the bottom of the dock alongside the cruiser. Further bombs hit the Continental Hotel in Brest just as the evening meal was being served. Several German naval officers, including some from the *Scharnhorst* and *Gneisenau*, were believed to have been killed.
 Next day the captain of the *Gneisenau* decided it would be safer to move his ship and he did so, mooring at a buoy out in Brest harbour. While there, *Gneisenau* was attacked by a Coastal Command Beaufort daylight torpedo bomber which scored a direct hit and inflicted serious damage that required six months to repair. The Beaufort was shot down and its crew all killed; its pilot, Flying Officer K. Campbell, was awarded a posthumous Victoria Cross.*

Minor Operations: 16 aircraft to Cologne, Rotterdam and Dunkirk but thick cloud prevented good bombing. 6 Hampdens minelaying off Brest. 2 O.T.U. sorties. No losses.

---

5 April 1941

10 Hampdens to Brest but only 1 aircraft bombed, because of cloud. 1 aircraft lost.

---

6 April 1941

14 Blenheims to Belgian and Dutch coasts. Shipping and harbours were attacked. No losses.

6/7 April 1941

BREST

71 aircraft – 65 Wellingtons, 4 Manchesters, 2 Whitleys; only 47 aircraft located the target in bad weather. No losses.

Minor Operations: 19 aircraft to Calais, Rotterdam and airfields, 24 Hampdens minelaying off Brittany and Frisians. 1 minelaying Hampden lost.

---

*Some of the details of this raid on Brest and later raids on the German warships come from *Scharnhorst and Gneisenau* by Richard Garrett, David & Charles, 1978.

7 April 1941

25 Blenheims to Dutch and Danish coasts. Several ships were attacked and 8 aircraft bombed industrial targets at Ijmuiden. 1 aircraft lost.

7/8 April 1941

KIEL

229 aircraft – 117 Wellingtons, 61 Hampdens, 49 Whitleys, 2 Stirlings – on the largest raid to one target so far in the war. 2 Wellingtons and 2 Whitleys lost.

Visibility was perfect and bright moonlight toned down the intensity of searchlights. The raid lasted nearly 5 hours and, at the end of it, the Kiel electric-light supply failed. Numerous fires were started requiring outside reinforcement of the fire services. Widespread damage of naval, industrial and civilian housing was caused. Particular damage is reported in the eastern dock areas and the night shifts at the Deutsche Werke and at the Germania Werft, both making U-boats, were sent home during the raid and both yards were out of action for several days. A fire in a naval armaments depot burnt for 2 days. 88 people were killed and 184 injured.

BREMERHAVEN

24 Blenheims. No losses.

Minor Operations: 9 aircraft to Emden, 2 O.T.U. sorties. No losses.

8 April 1941

17 Blenheims on coastal operations. Many targets were attacked. There were no losses.

8/9 April 1941

KIEL

160 aircraft – 74 Wellingtons, 44 Whitleys, 29 Hampdens, 12 Manchesters, 1 Stirling. 4 aircraft – 2 Wellingtons, 1 Hampden, 1 Manchester – lost and 9 further aircraft crashed in England.

The bomber crews claimed another successful raid. From the Kiel reports, it seems that this attack fell more in the town than in the dock areas. A long list of buildings damaged includes a bank, a museum, an engineering college and the gasworks. Gas and electricity were cut off and in some areas the water supply also failed, causing great difficulty. 125 people were killed and 300 injured. This casualty list is believed to be the heaviest of the war so far in a German town. 8,000 civilians and 300 naval personnel were bombed out and large numbers of civilians decided to leave the city by any means possible, including on foot. These two raids on Kiel in consecutive nights were probably the most successful of the war on any target till then.

BREMERHAVEN

22 Blenheims; claimed good bombing. No losses.

Minor Operations: 10 Hampdens minelaying off Brest and Calais, 5 Wellingtons to Rotterdam, 2 Blenheims to Emden. 1 minelaying Hampden lost.

---

9 April 1941

20 Blenheims to Belgian, Dutch and Danish coasts. Many attacks on ships and land targets. No losses.

9/10 April 1941

BERLIN

80 aircraft – 36 Wellingtons, 24 Hampdens, 17 Whitleys, 3 Stirlings. 5 aircraft – 3 Wellingtons, 1 Stirling, 1 Whitley – lost.

Minor Operations: 9 aircraft to Vegesack, 7 to Emden and 3 Hampdens minelaying in the East Frisians. 2 Wellingtons lost from the Vegesack raid and 1 Wellington from the Emden raid. The Wellington lost on the Emden raid was from 12 Squadron, which was flying its first operation with Wellingtons on this night; the pilot was the squadron commander, Wing Commander V. Q. Blackden, who was killed and is buried at Lemsterland in Holland.

---

10 April 1941

21 Blenheims on coastal raids in the Frisians and the German Bight. Several targets were attacked. 1 aircraft lost.

10/11 April 1941

BREST

53 aircraft – 36 Wellingtons, 12 Blenheims, 5 Manchesters – reported good bombing. It was later established that 4 bombs hit the *Gneisenau*, recently damaged by a Coastal Command torpedo bomber, during this raid and 50 Germans were killed and 90 injured. 1 Wellington lost.

DÜSSELDORF

29 Hampdens and 24 Whitleys. 5 Hampdens lost.

Minor Operations: 11 Wellingtons to Bordeaux/Mérignac airfield and claimed hits there, 3 Wellingtons to Rotterdam. 1 aircraft lost from the Mérignac raid.

---

11 April 1941

20 Blenheims to Emden, Heligoland, Rotterdam and shipping patrols. 1 aircraft lost.

12 April 1941

20 Blenheims to Düsseldorf, Gelsenkirchen and inland targets in Holland. 1 aircraft lost.

12/13 April 1941

BREST

66 aircraft – 35 Wellingtons, 13 Whitleys, 12 Hampdens, 6 Manchesters. Only 37 aircraft bombed at Brest, in poor cloud conditions; most other aircraft bombed Lorient as an alternative. No losses.

BORDEAUX

24 aircraft attacked Mérignac airfield; 1 Wellington lost.

6 Hampdens minelaying off Brest. No losses.

13 April 1941

16 Blenheims to industrial targets in Holland and to Borkum. These targets were not reached but shipping was attacked. 1 aircraft lost.

13/14 April 1941

17 Hampdens minelaying off La Pallice and 11 Whitleys bombing at Mérignac airfield. No losses.

14 April 1941

16 Blenheims attacked Leyden and Haarlem power stations. 14 Blenheims on shipping patrols; a convoy off Holland was bombed. 1 Blenheim lost.

14/15 April 1941

BREST

94 aircraft – 46 Wellingtons, 25 Hampdens, 20 Whitleys, 3 Stirlings – but bombing was poor because of cloud. No losses.

15 April 1941

29 Blenheims on coastal operations from France to Norway. 4 ships were attacked and 2 of these were claimed as sunk. Borkum was also bombed. 1 aircraft lost.

15/16 April 1941

KIEL

96 aircraft – 49 Wellingtons, 21 Whitleys, 19 Hampdens, 5 Halifaxes, 2 Stirlings. 1 Wellington lost.

Cloud hindered the bombing and Kiel reported only light damage compared to recent raids. 5 people were killed and 13 injured.

BOULOGNE

23 'freshmen' crews attacked the docks. 1 Whitley lost.

5 Hampdens minelaying off Brest. No losses.

16 April 1941

30 Blenheims on coastal raids. 11 aircraft bombed various targets. No losses.

16/17 April 1941

BREMEN

107 aircraft – 62 Wellingtons, 24 Whitleys, 21 Hampdens; mist and cloud prevented accurate bombing. Only 74 aircraft claimed to have bombed in the Bremen area. 1 Whitley and a Photographic Reconnaissance Unit Wellington accompanying the raid were lost.

Minor Operations: 9 Hampdens minelaying, of which 1 was shot down in England by an Intruder, 3 Wellingtons to Calais and Dunkirk, 1 O.T.U. sortie.

17 April 1941

35 Blenheims on coastal operations bombed ships – claiming 1 probably sunk – and Cherbourg docks. 1 aircraft lost.

17/18 April 1941

BERLIN

118 aircraft – 50 Wellingtons, 39 Hampdens, 28 Whitleys, 1 Stirling – to two aiming points but haze prevented concentrated bombing. 8 aircraft – 5 Whitleys, 2 Hampdens, 1 Wellington – lost.

Minor Operations: 13 Wellingtons and Whitleys to Rotterdam, 10 Wellingtons to Cologne, 3 Wellingtons to Mannheim, 6 Hampdens minelaying off Brest and the Frisians, 1 O.T.U. sortie. 3 Wellingtons were lost from the Cologne raid.

The 11 aircraft lost this night represent the largest total lost in night operations so far (not counting aircraft crashed in the United Kingdom).

---

18 April 1941

20 Blenheims and 6 Hampdens on operations to enemy coasts. A convoy off Holland was bombed and barges containing troops were also attacked. 1 Blenheim and 1 Hampden lost.

---

19 April 1941

34 Blenheims and 2 Hampdens on coastal operations. Many attacks on ships were made; 2 large merchant ships were hit and believed sunk; a tug was definitely sunk. No aircraft lost.

19/20 April 1941

5 Hampdens minelaying off Brest. No losses.

---

20 April 1941

22 Blenheims on coastal operations; 3 ships hit. No aircraft lost.

20/21 April 1941

COLOGNE

61 aircraft – 37 Wellingtons, 12 Whitleys, 11 Hampdens, 1 Stirling. Weather conditions were unfavourable and it was a poor raid. 2 Hampdens and 1 Wellington lost.

ROTTERDAM

17 Wellingtons and 7 Whitleys attacked the oil-storage depot without loss.

9 Hampdens minelaying off Brest without loss.

---

21 April 1941

36 Blenheims – 18 to Le Havre power station and 18 on shipping patrols. Le Havre was not reached and both forces made attacks on ships. No losses.

---

22 April 1941

14 Blenheims on coastal sweeps off Norway. 3 aircraft bombed a cargo ship, scoring one hit. No losses.

22/23 April 1941

BREST

24 Wellingtons and 2 Stirlings; the warships were not located because of intense Flak and searchlights. 1 Wellington lost. 6 Hampdens minelaying off Brest; no losses.

23 April 1941

31 Blenheims and 6 Hampdens on sweeps of Belgian, Dutch and German coasts. Ships and land targets bombed. 1 Blenheim lost.

23/24 April 1941

BREST

67 aircraft – 30 Wellingtons, 25 Whitleys, 10 Hampdens, 2 Stirlings. No losses. Hits were claimed on the *Scharnhorst* and *Gneisenau* but there is no confirmation of this.

14 Hampdens minelaying – 7 off Lorient, 7 off the East Frisians. No losses.

24 April 1941

24 Blenheims on coastal sweeps from Norway to the Channel Islands. A tanker was bombed and hit off Norway; a fishing vessel was sunk and a radio station ashore was bombed. No losses.

24/25 April 1941

KIEL

69 aircraft – 39 Wellingtons, 19 Whitleys, 10 Hampdens, 1 Stirling. 1 Whitley lost. Kiel reports a very scattered attack with no serious damage and 1 person killed and 3 injured.

Minor Operations: 12 aircraft to Le Havre, 10 to Ostend, 9 to Wilhelmshaven (where several houses were hit and a woman and 2 children killed), 8 Hampdens minelaying in Frisians and off Copenhagen, 4 O.T.U. sorties. No losses.

25 April 1941

27 Blenheims on sweeps of German and Danish coasts. Several attacks were made and at least 2 ships were hit. 1 aircraft lost.

25/26 April 1941

KIEL

62 aircraft – 38 Wellingtons, 14 Whitleys, 10 Hampdens. 1 Wellington lost. Kiel reports a scattered raid; places hit are listed: private housing, an old folks' home, a

coal-yard, a Catholic church, a mental home. 7 people were killed, all at one place, and 8 were injured.

Minor Operations: 5 aircraft to Bremerhaven, 4 each to Emden and Rotterdam, 3 to Berlin, 7 Hampdens minelaying off Aalborg, Denmark, and in the East Frisians. No losses.

---

26 April 1941

25 Blenheims on sea sweeps off Germany and Norway. 1 ship was damaged but 3 aircraft were lost while attacking convoys.

26/27 April 1941

HAMBURG

28 Hampdens and 22 Wellingtons. 1 Hampden lost. Cloud and heavy defences made bombing difficult. 44 aircraft claimed to have bombed but Hamburg records indicate approximately 16 bomb loads only in the city with no fires caused, 6 people killed, 12 injured and 121 bombed out.

4 Wellingtons attacked Emden without loss.

---

27 April 1941

18 Blenheims on coastal patrols attacked shipping but without scoring hits. 6 Blenheims, 2 Hampdens and 1 Stirling attempted cloud-cover raids to industrial targets in Germany; 2 Blenheims bombed Osnabrück and 2 Hampdens attacked targets in Holland. No losses.

---

28 April 1941

10 aircraft – 6 Hampdens, 3 Blenheims, 1 Stirling – on cloud-cover raids to Germany. Only the Stirling reached Germany and bombed Emden. 4 of the Hampdens bombed targets in Holland and ships. No losses.

6 Blenheims of 101 Squadron inaugurated *Channel Stop* in the Straits of Dover. In this operation, Blenheims with fighter escort attempted to prevent all German ships passing through this narrow part of the Channel by day. Motor torpedo boats attempted to keep up the blockade by night. It became a hard-fought battle between the Blenheims and German Flak ships and fighters. 1 fishing vessel was sunk on this day but 1 Blenheim was lost.

28/29 April 1941

BREST

22 Wellingtons and 3 Stirlings; only 9 aircraft bombed in poor weather conditions. No losses.

5 Hampdens minelaying off La Rochelle. 2 aircraft lost.

---

29 April 1941

COASTAL RAIDS

39 aircraft – 36 Blenheims, 2 Hampdens, 1 Stirling – operated over a wide area. Many attacks were made and 1 cargo ship was hit in a convoy off Norway, but 2 Blenheims attacking the convoy were shot down.

29/30 April 1941

MANNHEIM

71 aircraft – 42 Wellingtons, 15 Whitleys, 14 Hampdens. 1 Wellington was lost.

A report from Mannheim shows that approximately 15 aircraft bomb loads fell in Mannheim and Ludwigshafen. 4 houses were destroyed and 59 other buildings damaged but most of this was light damage. 2 small industrial premises were affected and suffered production loss of between 3 and 15 days. 4 people were killed and 4 injured.

ROTTERDAM

31 aircraft – 12 Hampdens, 11 Wellingtons, 8 Whitleys – to attack the oil depot. Fires were started but not in the oil depot. No losses.

30 April 1941

13 Blenheims on sweeps of Dutch and German coasts. 3 aircraft attacked a convoy off Holland. The defences of the convoy – 8 Flak-ship escorts for just 1 tanker, together with an Me 110 air cover – illustrate how the recent Blenheim operations forced the Germans to increase their protection of coastal shipping. 1 Blenheim was shot down attacking this convoy and another badly damaged; no hits were scored on the tanker.

30 April/1 May 1941

KIEL

81 aircraft – 43 Wellingtons, 25 Whitleys, 13 Hampdens. No losses.

The Kiel area was found to be completely cloud-covered and only 49 aircraft bombed the estimated position of the target. Kiel reports no bomb damage and no casualties. 28 aircraft bombed alternative targets.

Minor Operations: 10 Stirlings to Berlin but only 3 reached the city, 2 Wellingtons to Rotterdam. No losses.

1 May 1941

22 Blenheims on coastal operations to Holland. Bombs were dropped on the naval base at Den Helder and on ships at sea. 1 aircraft lost.

3 Hampdens on cloud-cover raid to Emmerich turned back.

2 May 1941

25 Blenheims on operations from France to Norway. 2 ships attacked off the Frisians were claimed probably sunk and a 2,000-ton ship off Ostend was also claimed sunk, the first success of the *Channel Stop* operation. No aircraft lost.

2/3 May 1941

HAMBURG

95 aircraft – 49 Wellingtons, 21 Whitleys, 19 Hampdens, 3 Manchesters, 3 Stirlings. 3 aircraft – 1 Hampden, 1 Manchester, 1 Whitley – were lost. Good bombing results were claimed. Hamburg reports no outstanding incidents but 26 fires were started – 13 large, 3 people were killed, 16 injured and 206 bombed out.

EMDEN

17 Wellingtons and 6 Whitleys. Ground haze spoiled bombing. 1 Wellington lost.

Minor Operations: 11 Hampdens minelaying in Frisians, 3 Wellingtons to Rotterdam, 8 O.T.U. sorties. No losses.

---

3 May 1941

21 Blenheims on coastal operations from France to Holland. Some ships attacked off Gravelines were hit but 2 Blenheims were shot down.

3/4 May 1941

COLOGNE

101 aircraft – 37 Wellingtons, 35 Whitleys, 27 Hampdens, 2 Manchesters; none lost. There was 9/10ths cloud and bombing was poor. Cologne reports approximately 8 to 10 bomb loads in the city, causing minor property damage, but 11 people were killed and 14 injured.

BREST

33 aircraft – 29 Wellingtons, 3 Stirlings, 1 Manchester; claimed accurate bombing of the docks. No losses.

Minor Operations: 9 Wellingtons and Whitleys to Rotterdam, 1 O.T.U. sortie; no losses.

---

4 May 1941

12 Blenheims on coastal operations from France to Denmark. 1 fishing vessel was hit. No aircraft lost.

4/5 May 1941

BREST

97 aircraft – 54 Wellingtons, 21 Hampdens, 21 Whitleys, 1 Stirling. No aircraft lost. Direct hits were reported on the *Scharnhorst* and the *Gneisenau* but these are not confirmed.

Minor Operations: 10 Wellingtons to Le Havre, 9 Blenheims to Antwerp and Rotterdam. No losses.

---

5 May 1941

11 Blenheims on operations off the French coast. Ships were bombed but there were no hits. 1 Stirling to Bremen turned back. No losses.

5/6 May 1941

MANNHEIM

141 aircraft – 70 Wellingtons, 33 Hampdens, 30 Whitleys, 4 Manchesters, 4 Stirlings. No losses. There was 10/10ths cloud all the way to the target and this hampered navigation but 121 aircraft claimed to have bombed in the target area.

A very detailed report from Mannheim lists the results of the raid. Approximately 25 bomb loads hit the city. 1 house and a barn were destroyed, 4 houses were badly damaged and 199 lightly damaged (mostly broken windows and roof tiles). There were 19 small fires. 1 electricity pylon collapsed; 1 water main was broken. Casualties: 4 people killed. Farm animals: 50 rabbits and chickens killed. Effect on industrial production: nil.

Minor Operations: 5 aircraft to Boulogne, 4 to Cherbourg, 4 Hampdens minelaying in Frisians. No losses.

---

6 May 1941

18 Blenheims on operations along coasts from France to Germany. Several ships were attacked. 2 aircraft lost. 1 Stirling to Emden turned back but attacked a ship at sea.

6/7 May 1941

HAMBURG

115 aircraft – 50 Wellingtons, 31 Whitleys, 27 Hampdens, 4 Manchesters, 3 Stirlings; few aircraft identified their targets, because of poor visibility. 81 aircraft claimed to have bombed Hamburg, 22 aircraft claimed to have attacked alternative targets. Hamburg records indicate some 12 bomb loads in the city. Crews reported large fires throughout the city but Hamburg only lists 4 fires – none large, with 2 people injured and 33 bombed out. No aircraft were lost from the raid.

LE HAVRE

16 Wellingtons; 1 lost.

AMELAND

10 Blenheims attacked a convoy by moonlight; no aircraft lost.

There were 7 minelaying sorties to Quiberon Bay and 4 O.T.U. sorties. No losses.

---

7 May 1941

16 Blenheims on coastal sweeps. 1 ship was attacked. 1 aircraft lost.

7/8 May 1941

BREST

89 aircraft – 43 Wellingtons, 28 Whitleys, 18 Hampdens; hits were claimed on both German cruisers in clear visibility but the hits are not confirmed. No aircraft losses.

ST-NAZAIRE

15 Wellingtons; 1 lost.

Minor Operations: 6 Blenheims on shipping strike off Ameland, 3 Stirlings to Bremen, 2 Hampdens minelaying in Frisians, 4 O.T.U. sorties. 1 Blenheim lost on the shipping operation.

---

8 May 1941

6 Blenheims on a sweep off Norway. 1 Flak ship was hit. 1 aircraft lost.

8/9 May 1941

HAMBURG

188 aircraft – 100 Wellingtons, 78 Hampdens, 9 Manchesters, 1 Stirling – 119 aircraft to shipyard targets and 69 to the city. 3 Wellingtons and 1 Hampden lost.

Returning crews claimed good bombing results and this is borne out by the Hamburg reports. 83 fires were started of which 38 were classed as large. The source from which most of the Hamburg information comes, Hans Brunswig,* selects 2 incidents for description, a large fire at an oil depot – the Deutschen Erdölwerken – from which many new lessons were learnt by the fire services (Brunswig was a fire officer), and the complete destruction by a 4,000-lb bomb of 10 substantial apartment buildings in the street named Tielch in a closely built-up area of the Barmbek district where 79 people were killed. These new bombs are described as causing many prob-

---

* *Feuersturm über Hamburg*, op. cit. pp. 89–92. As noted earlier, many Hamburg reports come from this source.

lems for the air-raid services. 185 people were killed in Hamburg on this night, 518 injured and 1,966 bombed out. It was the highest fatal casualty figure in Germany so far in the war.

BREMEN

133 aircraft – 78 Whitleys, 55 Wellingtons – to shipyards and city targets. 3 Wellingtons and 2 Whitleys lost.

Good bombing was claimed in clear weather conditions. Bremen reports widespread bombing in the town but no hits in the vital A.G. Weser submarine yards. The only casualties mentioned are 2 prisoners of war killed and 22 injured when a wooden camp in or near the harbour was hit by high-explosive bombs.

KIEL CANAL, BREMERHAVEN

23 Blenheims, most in an unsuccessful attempt to seal the Kiel Canal by sinking ships in it. 4 of the Blenheims were sent to Bremerhaven to attack the liner *Europa* but only the general dock area was bombed. No aircraft losses.

Minor Operations: 5 aircraft to Rotterdam, 5 to Berlin, 4 to Flushing, 3 to Emden and 3 minelaying in the Frisians. 1 Wellington lost on the Berlin raid.

Total effort for the night: 364 sorties, 10 aircraft (2·7 per cent) were lost. The effort on this night was a new record, the previous record being 265 sorties on 10/11 February 1941.

---

9 May 1941

13 Blenheims on sweeps of French and Norwegian coasts. 1 ship was hit and seen to be abandoned by its crew. 1 aircraft was lost.

9/10 May 1941

MANNHEIM/LUDWIGSHAFEN

146 aircraft – 69 Wellingtons, 42 Whitleys, 24 Hampdens, 11 Manchesters. 1 Wellington and 1 Whitley lost.

Mannheim's records show a successful raid on these two neighbouring cities. Totally destroyed buildings: military 1, war industry 4, other commerce 29, houses and shops 19. 11 railway wagons full of industrial fuel were burnt out. A large number of buildings of many kinds were damaged. 22 large and medium industrial plants suffered various production interruptions because of the damage. Casualties were: 64 killed, 122 injured and 3,533 bombed out (2,134 in Mannheim and 1,399 in Ludwigshafen). One third of the bombed out would return to their homes later.

Minor Operations: 5 aircraft to Berlin, 5 to Calais, 4 to Texel, 2 Hampdens minelaying in Frisians. No losses.

---

10 May 1941

5 Blenheims on shipping strike off La Pallice; ships were attacked but not hit. No aircraft lost.

10/11 May 1941

HAMBURG

119 aircraft – 60 Wellingtons, 35 Hampdens, 23 Whitleys, 1 Manchester – to shipyards, Altona power-station and the general city area. 3 Wellingtons and 1 Whitley lost.

The raid was carried out in perfect visibility. 128 fires – 47 large – were started in Hamburg with the worst of the fires in the city-centre area where a large department store (Kösters), a bank and part of the Hamburg Stock Exchange were among buildings destroyed by fire. 31 people were killed, 151 injured and 837 bombed out.

BERLIN

23 aircraft, of which only 12 reported bombing targets in the city. 3 aircraft – 2 Stirlings and 1 Manchester – lost.

Minor Operations: 18 Blenheims to the Dutch coast, 6 Wellingtons to Emden, 1 Hampden minelaying in the Frisians. There were no losses. A Wellington whose pilot, Pilot Officer Ball of 103 Squadron, and his crew were flying their first operation, claimed an Me 110 and a Ju 88 shot down on the Emden raid.

11/12 May 1941

HAMBURG

92 aircraft – 91 Wellingtons, 1 Stirling. 3 Wellingtons lost.

Good bombing was reported in clear conditions. Hamburg reports 88 fires – 26 large, 11 people killed, 44 injured and 1,096 bombed out. This series of 3 raids in 4 nights made a big impression on Hamburg. Brunswig reports that there were 3,000 separate bombing incidents causing damage resulting in claims for 100 million Reichsmarks (£10 million). It may be significant, however, that there was no mention of industrial damage in any of the reports; this shows the continuing tendency to attack general city areas rather than the industrial targets, which were often so difficult to find. The morale of Hamburg was further affected when the Battleship *Bismarck*, built in Hamburg, was sunk in the Atlantic on 27 May.

BREMEN

81 aircraft – 48 Whitleys, 31 Hampdens, 2 Manchesters. 1 Hampden lost.

62 aircraft claimed good bombing results. Bremen reports many bombs in the harbour area. A floating dock at A.G. Weser was sunk when hit by 2 bombs; several industrial premises in the dock area were damaged. The report goes on to stress, however, that most of the damage was in the general town area where 24 houses were destroyed, 49 seriously damaged and nearly 1,000 damaged. An office building at the Focke-Wulf factory was hit, by chance the Bremen report suggests. 8 people were killed and 31 injured.

Minor Operations: 4 Wellingtons to Dieppe, 2 Wellingtons to Rotterdam, 1 Stirling to Bordeaux. No losses.

Total effort for the night: 180 sorties, 4 aircraft (2·2 per cent) lost.

---

12 May 1941

8 Blenheims on coastal operations in Skagerrak. 1 ship was attacked but not hit. No losses.

12/13 May 1941

MANNHEIM/LUDWIGSHAFEN

105 aircraft – 42 Wellingtons, 41 Hampdens, 18 Whitleys, 4 Manchesters. 65 of these aircraft were detailed for Mannheim and 40 for Ludwigshafen.

Haze made identification of targets difficult. The local report suggests that no more than 10 aircraft succeeded in bombing the two targets. Damage was scattered and light. 5 people were killed and 3 injured.

26 aircraft reported that they had bombed alternative targets and there is an interesting report from Cologne where 16 aircraft reported bombing. Visibility must have been better at Cologne because direct hits were scored on several industrial premises and 1 bomb which hit the Hacketäuer Barracks killed 92 soldiers in an air-raid shelter. 8 other people were killed in Cologne.

Minor Operations: 4 Hampdens minelaying in the Frisians, 2 O.T.U. sorties.

111 sorties were dispatched on this night without any loss.

---

13 May 1941

44 Blenheims on coastal sweeps over a wide area. No ships were seen but docks at St-Nazaire and Heligoland were bombed. 2 aircraft were lost.

---

15 May 1941

20 Blenheims on coastal sweeps. Convoys were attacked off Rotterdam and near Heligoland and 3 ships were claimed as sunk. 1 aircraft was lost.

15/16 May 1941

HANNOVER

101 aircraft – 55 Wellingtons, 27 Hampdens, 18 Whitleys, 1 Stirling – with the main post office and telephone exchange as the aiming point, signifying that this was mainly an area attack. 2 Wellingtons and 1 Hampden lost.

Minor Operations: 14 Manchesters and Stirlings to Berlin, 11 Wellingtons to Dieppe, 9 Whitleys to Boulogne. 1 Manchester lost on the Berlin raid.

---

16 May 1941

8 Blenheims on coastal sweeps off Norway. 1 ship was claimed as sunk near Bergen. 1 aircraft lost.

16/17 May 1941

COLOGNE

93 aircraft – 48 Wellingtons, 24 Hampdens, 20 Whitleys, 1 Stirling. 1 Whitley lost.
    Bombing conditions were poor and Cologne reports only 7 high-explosive bombs in the city with 11 houses damaged and 1 person injured.

Minor Operations: 11 Wellingtons to Boulogne, 8 Blenheims on shipping searches – 1 ship claimed hit, 2 Hampdens minelaying in the Frisians, 4 O.T.U. sorties. No losses.

17 May 1941

5 Blenheims on an uneventful sweep off Cherbourg.

17/18 May 1941

COLOGNE

95 aircraft – 44 Wellingtons, 28 Whitleys, 23 Hampdens. 1 Hampden and 1 Whitley lost.
    Lack of moonlight and intense searchlights made identification of targets difficult but 82 aircraft claimed good bombing results. Cologne reports scattered bombing over a wide area but with some concentration in the southern districts of the city. 1 industrial building was destroyed and 22 damaged. 30 private houses were destroyed and 100 damaged. In the city centre, the Rathaus, a hospital, a department store and a well-known café, Café Bauer, were all damaged. 20 people were killed and 24 injured.

Minor Operations: 15 Wellingtons and Whitleys to Boulogne, 14 Blenheims to Rotterdam. No losses.

17/18 May 1941

KIEL

70 aircraft – 33 Wellingtons, 19 Whitleys, 18 Hampdens – to shipyards and the city. No losses. Kiel reports only a light raid with no serious damage but 5 people killed and 10 injured.

Minor Operations: 3 Whitleys to Emden, 4 Hampdens minelaying off Kiel. No losses.

21 May 1941

45 Blenheims on extensive coastal sweeps and on *Circus* operation to Béthune. No ships were seen but Heligoland town was attacked by machine-gun fire and an oil depot near Béthune was bombed. 2 Blenheims were lost.

22 May 1941

16 Blenheims on coastal sweeps from Holland to Denmark. 1 ship was attacked but not sunk. No losses.

23 May 1941

20 Blenheims on coastal sweeps. 1 ship was hit off Holland. No losses.

23/24 May 1941

COLOGNE

51 aircraft – 24 Hampdens, 22 Wellingtons, 5 Stirlings. None lost. The target was completely cloud-covered and bombing was poor. Cologne records only 13 high-explosive bombs and 200 incendiaries in the city, with 25 buildings damaged and 11 people injured.

2 Whitleys attacked Boulogne without loss.

24 May 1941

23 Blenheims on coastal sweeps. Shipping was attacked and 1 ship was hit. 1 aircraft lost.

25 May 1941

30 Blenheims on sweeps in the Frisians and off Denmark. Several ships were hit but German fighters were very active and 4 Blenheims were lost.

25/26 May 1941

48 Hampdens on minelaying operations off Brest and St-Nazaire; bad weather was encountered and only 27 aircraft laid mines. There were no losses.

26 May 1941

12 Blenheims on uneventful shipping sweeps off the Frisian Islands.

26/27 May 1941

38 Hampdens minelaying off Brest. No losses.

27 May 1941

PRINZ EUGEN

52 Wellingtons and 12 Stirlings searched over a wide area of sea for the cruiser *Prinz Eugen* after her partner ship, the *Bismarck*, had been sunk in the Atlantic. Nothing was seen.

14 Blenheims on shipping sweeps off Holland and Germany and 9 Blenheims attacked Lannion airfield, claiming German aircraft on the ground destroyed. No losses.

27/28 May 1941

COLOGNE

46 Whitleys and 18 Wellingtons to city centre but Cologne only records 31 high-explosive bombs and 300 incendiaries in the whole city although these damaged 167 buildings; 11 people were killed and 39 injured. No aircraft lost.

Minor Operations: 24 Wellingtons and Whitleys to Boulogne, 36 Hampdens minelaying off Brest and St-Nazaire. 1 Hampden lost.

28 May 1941

7 Blenheims to the mouth of the River Elbe. 1 ship was attacked but not hit. 1 aircraft lost.

28/29 May 1941

KIEL

14 Whitleys to bomb *Tirpitz* encountered thick cloud and storms. Only 3 aircraft claimed to have bombed Kiel, which reports, 'Considerable rain but luckily no bombs.' 1 Whitley lost.

30 May 1941

12 Blenheims on a coastal sweep but nothing seen. 1 Stirling on a photographic reconnaissance flight to Münster turned back.

2 June 1941

44 Blenheims on extensive shipping operations in cloudy weather. Some of the Blenheims tried again to block the Kiel Canal and several ships were bombed in that area. It is believed that 2 ships were sunk in the canal, blocking it for at least 10 days. 2 Blenheims lost.

2/3 June 1941

DÜSSELDORF

150 aircraft – 68 Wellingtons, 43 Hampdens, 39 Whitleys – to two aiming points but cloud conditions caused difficulties and only 107 aircraft claimed to have bombed Düsseldorf. 2 Hampdens and 1 Whitley lost.

Düsseldorf records only light and scattered damage with 5 people killed and 13 injured.

DUISBURG

25 Wellingtons; thick haze prevented accurate bombing. No aircraft lost.

BERLIN

8 Stirlings and 3 Wellingtons. 1 Stirling lost.

---

4 June 1941

54 Blenheims on coastal sweeps and airfield raids from Norway to Belgium. A 500-ton ship was claimed hit by 4 bombs. 2 aircraft lost.

---

5 June 1941

9 Blenheims on sweeps from Belgium to Norway. Ships were attacked off Zeebrugge. No aircraft lost.

---

6 June 1941

3 Blenheims to Cherbourg. Nothing was seen.

---

7 June 1941

22 Blenheims on shipping searches from the Frisians to Norway. A ship was set on fire off Terschelling. 3 aircraft lost.

7/8 June 1941

BREST

30 Wellingtons and 3 Stirlings to bomb the *Prinz Eugen*, which had now come into Brest from the Atlantic. No hits were scored and no aircraft were lost.

8/9 June 1941

DORTMUND

37 Whitleys; poor bombing owing to industrial haze. No losses.

---

9 June 1941

18 aircraft – 12 Blenheims, 4 Wellingtons, 2 Stirlings – operated on enemy coasts. Ships were attacked off Dunkirk, The Hague and Terschelling but without sure sinkings. 2 Blenheims and 2 Wellingtons lost.

10 June 1941

8 Blenheims bombed shipping off Stavanger. 2 Stirlings to Emden turned back but one claimed to have shot down an Me 109. No losses.

10/11 June 1941

BREST

104 aircraft – 39 Hampdens, 38 Wellingtons, 27 Whitleys – to bomb the 3 German warships now at Brest. Many bombs fell in the dock area but there were no hits on the ships. No aircraft lost.

9 Hampdens minelaying in Quiberon Bay. None lost.

11 June 1941

BREMERHAVEN

25 Blenheims to Bremerhaven and north-west Germany but 19 turned back. 1 aircraft sank a trawler and 1 aircraft bombed Ijmuiden docks. 1 aircraft lost.

11/12 June 1941

DÜSSELDORF

92 Wellingtons and 6 Stirlings; haze prevented accurate bombing. 6 Wellingtons lost.

DUISBURG

80 aircraft – 36 Whitleys, 35 Hampdens, 9 Halifaxes. 8/10ths cloud over target but good bombing reported. 1 Whitley lost.

There are no reports from the two main targets but Cologne reports bombs from aircraft which were either mistaking Cologne for the correct target or using it as an alternative. The main railway station was hit by 7 bombs and much damage was caused. Dock areas, a wagon works and 173 houses were also damaged. 14 people were killed and 36 injured. Because of its position just outside the main defences and industrial haze of the Ruhr, Cologne was always likely to be attacked in this way.

BOULOGNE

24 Wellingtons and 5 Whitleys; 1 of each type lost.

Minor Operations: 2 Wellingtons to Rotterdam, 20 Hampdens minelaying in Kiel Bay and the Frisians, 12 O.T.U. sorties. 1 minelaying Hampden lost.

Total effort for the night: 241 sorties, 10 aircraft (4·1 per cent) lost.

12 June 1941

12 Blenheims on coastal sweeps and to Brest. There was insufficient cloud for the Brest raid but other Blenheims attacked and hit a cargo ship off Gravelines. No aircraft lost.

12/13 June 1941

SOEST

91 Hampdens to the railway yards but visibility was poor and only 42 aircraft bombed the primary target. 2 aircraft lost.

SCHWERTE

80 Whitleys and 4 Wellingtons to railway yards but ground haze was encountered and only 41 aircraft bombed the primary target. 3 Whitleys lost.

HAMM

82 Wellingtons to attack the railway yards claimed good bombing results. No losses. Hamm reports that 7 bombs fell in the town. 6 exploded but did not cause any serious damage. The seventh bomb blew up later, killing 2 bomb-disposal men, the only fatal casualties of the raid.

OSNABRÜCK

61 Wellingtons to railway yards claimed good bombing. 1 aircraft lost. Local records describe this as a 'lively attack'.

HÜLS

11 Halifaxes and 7 Stirlings to the chemical works. Fires were started in the target area. No losses.

Minor Operations: 2 Wellingtons to Rotterdam, 1 Wellington to Emden. No losses.

Total effort for the night: 339 sorties, 6 aircraft (1·8 per cent) lost. 4 Wellingtons of 405 (Vancouver) Squadron sent to Schwerte on this night represent the first operational flight by the first of many Canadian squadrons to serve in Bomber Command.

13 June 1941

4 Blenheims to Norway recalled.

13/14 June 1941

BREST

110 aircraft – 69 Wellingtons, 37 Hampdens, 4 Stirlings – to attack the 3 warships

now at Brest but haze and smoke-screens concealed the targets and no hits were scored. No aircraft lost.

SCHWERTE

36 Whitleys and 6 Wellingtons to railway yards which were not located so the town was bombed instead. 1 Whitley lost.

Minor Operations: 5 Wellingtons to Boulogne, 4 Hampdens minelaying in the Frisians, 12 O.T.U. sorties. No losses.

---

14 June 1941

30 Blenheims on coastal sweeps, to Brest and on a *Circus* operation to St-Omer airfield. 1 aircraft lost.

14/15 June 1941

COLOGNE

29 Hampdens. The target was completely cloud-covered. 25 aircraft bombed estimated positions but Cologne reports only light damage with approximately 2 bomb loads in the city, 1 person killed and 1 injured. No aircraft lost.

---

15 June 1941

23 Blenheims on sweeps of Dutch and German coasts but most turned back because of lack of cloud cover. Ships off Terschelling and in the Ems estuary were attacked. 1 aircraft lost.

15/16 June 1941

COLOGNE

49 Wellingtons and 42 Hampdens to railway targets but Cologne reports only 3 or 4 bomb loads in the city with minor damage, 1 person killed and 2 injured. 1 Hampden lost.

DÜSSELDORF

31 Whitleys and 28 Wellingtons to railway targets but visibility was poor and bombing was scattered. No aircraft lost.

HANNOVER

16 aircraft; a large fire was started. No losses.

Minor Operations: 10 Wellingtons and 2 Whitleys to Dunkirk, 4 Hampdens minelaying in the Frisians, 1 O.T.U. sortie. The 2 Whitley freshmen crews sent to Dunkirk were both lost.

---

16 June 1941

25 Blenheims on coastal sweeps off Holland and Germany. Several ships were attacked including a trawler well out to sea and suspected of being a radio warning ship. One of the Blenheims attacking this ship was so low that it hit the trawler's mast and crashed into the sea. 3 Blenheims were lost on this day.

16/17 June 1941

COLOGNE

105 aircraft – 47 Hampdens, 39 Whitleys, 16 Wellingtons, 3 Halifaxes – but again bombing was poor with only 55 high-explosive bombs and 300 incendiaries recorded in Cologne, causing scattered damage, but 19 people were killed and 17 injured. 2 Whitleys and 1 Wellington lost.

DÜSSELDORF

65 Wellingtons and 7 Stirlings, haze prevented target identification. 58 aircraft claimed to have bombed Düsseldorf but the records show only 2 heavy bombs in the southern suburb of Wersten, which destroyed several houses, killing 4 people and

9. Thirty Wellingtons dispatched by 57 and 75 (New Zealand) Squadrons at Feltwell. This was a typical effort by 3 Group, which provided so much of the early strength of Bomber Command. The target for twenty-eight of these aircraft was Düsseldorf; the diary entry shows their bombing results. Two of the aircraft, flown by 'freshman' crews, bombed Boulogne. All the Wellingtons returned safely. The airfields shown on the bottom left of the board are the diversion airfields allocated to the Feltwell aircraft in the event of bad weather on their return.

injuring 23. A few bombs were reported in 4 other towns around Düsseldorf. No aircraft lost.

DUISBURG

39 Wellingtons; 1 lost.

BOULOGNE

7 Wellingtons; none lost.

Total effort for the night: 223 sorties, 4 aircraft (1·8 per cent) lost.

---

17 June 1941

23 Blenheims on a large *Circus* operation to a power-station near Béthune which was accurately bombed. No Blenheims were lost but 10 of the escorting fighters were shot down.

17/18 June 1941

COLOGNE

43 Hampdens and 33 Whitleys; thick haze obscured targets. 1 Whitley lost. Cologne reports only light bombing: 17 high-explosive bombs, 100 incendiaries, 11 people injured, 39 buildings damaged.

DÜSSELDORF

57 Wellingtons; none lost. Thick haze.

DUISBURG

26 Wellingtons; none lost. Thick haze.

Minor Operations: 11 aircraft to Hannover, 8 each to Boulogne and Rotterdam, 4 minelaying in Frisians, 8 O.T.U. sorties. No losses.

Total effort for the night: 198 sorties, 1 aircraft (0·5 per cent) lost.

---

18 June 1941

6 Blenheims on a *Circus* operation to a German camp at Bois de Licques. No Blenheims lost.

18/19 June 1941

BREMEN

100 aircraft – 39 Hampdens, 37 Wellingtons, 24 Whitleys. 3 Wellingtons and 3 Whitleys lost. Low cloud hindered the attack.

BREST

57 Wellingtons and 8 Stirlings; none lost. Haze and smoke-screens prevented identification of warship targets.

There were 2 O.T.U. sorties.

---

19 June 1941

36 Blenheims on a *Circus* operation to Le Havre docks. Only 9 aircraft bombed. No Blenheims lost.

19/20 June 1941

COLOGNE

28 Wellingtons; 1 lost. Good bombing was claimed but Cologne only reports 60 incendiary bombs in the city with no casualties.

DÜSSELDORF

20 Whitleys; 1 lost. Ground haze.

---

20 June 1941

11 Blenheims on coastal sweeps. 1 ship was claimed sunk off the Frisians. No aircraft lost.

20/21 June 1941

KIEL

115 aircraft – 47 Wellingtons, 24 Hampdens, 20 Whitleys, 13 Stirlings, 11 Halifaxes – in an attempt to identify and bomb the *Tirpitz*. No aircraft succeeded in doing so and the city was attacked instead. 2 Wellingtons lost. Kiel reports: much cloud, a few bombs dropped, 1 person injured, 'Flak fire in all directions', 1 barrage balloon shot down.

Minor Operations: 5 Wellingtons to Boulogne, 4 Hampdens on unspecified 'special tasks' to Essen and Cologne, 2 O.T.U. sorties. No losses.

---

21 June 1941

23 Blenheims on coastal sweeps and a *Circus* operation to St-Omer airfield. The airfield was bombed and a ship attacked off the Dutch coast. 1 Blenheim was lost.

21/22 June 1941

COLOGNE

68 Wellingtons; cloud and haze were encountered. Out of 500 high-explosive and nearly 5,000 incendiary bombs carried by the bombers, none are recorded as dropping inside Cologne's boundaries, only a few in villages to the west. No aircraft lost.

DÜSSELDORF

28 Hampdens and 28 Whitleys dispatched and claimed many fires started. No aircraft lost. Düsseldorf reports 2 loads of bombs in the city and 1 in nearby Neuss. There were no casualties and the only damage caused was broken windows.

Minor Operations: 18 Manchesters to Boulogne, 10 Wellingtons to Dunkirk, 2 O.T.U. sorties. 1 Manchester was shot down by an R.A.F. fighter over England and its crew were killed.

---

22 June 1941

17 Blenheims on coastal searches and a *Circus* operation. No ships were seen; Hazebrouck railway yards bombed. No Blenheims lost.

22/23 June 1941

BREMEN

45 Wellingtons and 25 Hampdens; the targets were haze-covered and bombing was scattered. 1 Hampden and 1 Wellington lost.

WILHELMSHAVEN

16 Wellingtons and 11 Whitleys. Wilhelmshaven reports bombing only in Cäciliengroden, a village on the coast 4 km to the south, where one house was hit and 'several' people were killed and wounded.

3 Wellingtons to Emden and 1 Hampden to Düsseldorf without loss.

---

23 June 1941

39 Blenheims on coastal sweeps and a *Circus* operation to Choques power-station. 2 Blenheims lost.

23/24 June 1941

COLOGNE

44 Wellingtons and 18 Whitleys. 1 Wellington lost. Cologne reports a few bombs but no casualties.

DÜSSELDORF

30 Hampdens and 11 Manchesters. No aircraft lost. Crews report: 'Fires started.'

KIEL

26 aircraft – 13 Stirlings, 10 Halifaxes, 3 Wellingtons. 1 Halifax lost. Little damage in Kiel but 1 person was killed and 8 injured when a large bomb appeared to explode in the air above the old town. The casualties are believed to have been in the open, watching a bomber trying to escape from a large searchlight cone. The bomber escaped from the mass of Flak being fired at it.

Minor Operations: 2 aircraft to Boulogne, 1 each to Bremen, Emden and Hannover, 1 minelaying in the Frisians, 7 O.T.U. sorties. No losses.

---

24 June 1941

18 Blenheims on a *Circus* operation to Comines power-station. No Blenheims lost.

24/25 June 1941

COLOGNE

32 Whitleys and 22 Wellingtons; the main city passenger station was the aiming point. No aircraft lost. Cologne reports only 11 bombs, 5 houses damaged, no casualties.

KIEL

25 Hampdens and 23 Wellingtons to dock areas. 1 Wellington lost. Kiel reports only a light raid with 11 people injured.

DÜSSELDORF

23 Wellingtons and 8 Manchesters, no losses.

Minor Operations: 3 Wellingtons to Emden, 1 to Boulogne and 2 O.T.U. sorties. 1 Wellington was lost from the Emden raid and the one sent to Boulogne was shot down into the sea off Harwich by 'friendly' anti-aircraft fire.

---

25 June 1941

24 Blenheims on *Circus* operations to Hazebrouck and St-Omer, 10 Blenheims on coastal sweep but no ships seen. 1 Blenheim lost.

25/26 June 1941

BREMEN

56 Wellingtons and 8 Whitleys; severe electrical storms prevented most aircraft reaching the target. 1 Wellington lost.

KIEL

30 Hampdens and 17 Wellingtons. 1 Hampden lost. Kiel reports light damage with 1 person killed.

Minor Operations: 6 aircraft to Rotterdam, 1 each to Cologne and Düsseldorf, 1 Hampden minelaying in Frisians, 7 O.T.U. sorties. No losses.

---

26 June 1941

23 Blenheims on a *Circus* operation to Comines power-station but the target was not reached. No Blenheims lost.

26/27 June 1941

COLOGNE

32 Wellingtons and 19 Whitleys; electrical storms allowed only 7 aircraft to claim attacks on the main target. 1 Wellington lost. Cologne reports no bombs.

DÜSSELDORF

30 Hampdens and 14 Wellingtons encountered thick cloud, snow and icing. Results of bombing not observed. 1 Wellington lost.

KIEL

41 aircraft – 18 Manchesters, 15 Stirlings, 8 Halifaxes – but ground haze spoiled bombing. 2 Manchesters lost. Light damage and no casualties in Kiel.

Minor Operations: 3 Wellingtons to Emden, 1 Hampden minelaying in Frisians, 3 O.T.U. sorties. No losses.

---

27 June 1941

23 Blenheims on a *Circus* operation to a steelworks at Lille which was bombed accurately. No Blenheim losses.

27/28 June 1941

BREMEN

73 Wellingtons and 35 Whitleys; they encountered storms, icing conditions and, reported for the first time in Bomber Command records, 'intense night-fighter attacks'. 11 Whitleys – 31 per cent of the Whitleys dispatched – and 3 Wellingtons were lost, the heaviest night loss of the war so far. No report is available from Bremen but many of the bombers must have found their way by mistake to Hamburg, 50 miles away. This city reports 76 bombing incidents, 14 fires, 7 people killed, 39 injured and 55 bombed out and 5 bombers shot down by night fighters over the city.

VEGESACK

28 Hampdens to attack U-boat construction yards. No losses.

Minor Operations: 4 aircraft to Dunkirk, 3 to Emden, 1 to Cologne, 1 to Düsseldorf, 3 Hampdens to the Frisians, 4 O.T.U. sorties. No losses.

---

28 June 1941

24 Blenheims on a *Circus* operation to Comines. 18 Blenheims to Bremen turned back. 6 Stirlings to Bremerhaven did not reach the target. 1 Stirling lost in the sea.

28/29 June 1941

34 Hampdens minelaying in Elbe and Heligoland areas, no losses.

29/30 June 1941

BREMEN

106 aircraft – 52 Wellingtons, 30 Hampdens, 24 Whitleys – of which 69 claimed good bombing results. 7 aircraft – 4 Wellingtons, 2 Hampdens, 1 Whitley – lost.

HAMBURG

28 aircraft – 13 Stirlings, 7 Wellingtons, 6 Manchesters, 2 Halifaxes. 4 Stirlings and 2 Wellingtons lost. Hamburg reports much damage with 8 people killed, 115 injured and 465 bombed out, also a large fire which completely destroyed a store containing 650 tons of rice and 200 tons of animal foods. 3 bombers were shot down over Hamburg by night fighters and the rice-store fire may have been started by a crashing bomber.

3 Hampdens laid mines in the Frisians without loss.

---

30 June 1941

28 Blenheims and 6 Halifaxes on cloud-cover raids to north-west Germany. 17 aircraft bombed at Bremen, Kiel, Norderney and Sylt. 1 Blenheim and 1 Halifax lost. 18 Blenheims on a *Circus* operation to Pont-à-Vendin power-station without loss.

---

30 June/1 July 1941

THE RUHR

64 aircraft – 32 Wellingtons, 18 Whitleys, 14 Hampdens – to Cologne, Duisburg and Düsseldorf. 2 Hampdens and 2 Whitleys lost. No reports of successful bombing.

---

1 July 1941

39 Blenheims and 6 Stirlings to various targets, mostly in north-west Germany. Only 6 aircraft bombed. 2 Blenheims and 1 Stirling lost.

1/2 July 1941

BREST

52 Wellingtons; good bombing claimed. 2 Wellingtons were lost on this raid and 1 of them is believed to have crashed alongside the *Prinz Eugen*. A bomb, possibly from the crashing Wellington, struck the *Prinz Eugen*, exploding inside the ship and causing serious damage. The executive officer and 60 other sailors were killed.

5 Wellingtons to Cherbourg; 1 was shot down by an R.A.F. fighter in Wiltshire.

2 July 1941

12 Blenheims on a *Circus* operation to Lille power-station. 2 Blenheims lost.

2/3 July 1941
BREMEN

67 aircraft – 57 Wellingtons, 6 Stirlings, 4 Halifaxes. Cloud and haze were encountered but good fires were claimed. 1 Wellington lost.

COLOGNE

33 Whitleys and 9 Wellingtons; haze covered the target. Cologne records only 20 incendiary bombs in the city and no casualties. 1 Wellington lost.

DUISBURG

39 Hampdens; only 18 claimed to have bombed Duisburg. 2 aircraft lost.

Minor Operations: 6 Wellingtons to Cherbourg, 7 O.T.U. sorties. No losses.

3 July 1941

12 Blenheims on a *Circus* operation to Hazebrouck. 1 Blenheim lost.

3/4 July 1941
ESSEN

61 Wellingtons and 29 Whitleys to Essen, attacking the Krupps armaments works and railway targets. 2 Wellingtons and 2 Whitleys lost.

Returning crews reported that bombing was difficult because of thick cloud. Essen reports only light housing damage with 2 people injured, but many bombs fell in the towns of Bochum, Dortmund, Duisburg, Hagen and Wuppertal as well as in other places.

BREMEN

39 Hampdens and 29 Wellingtons. Good bombing was claimed despite cloud and haze. 2 Wellingtons and 1 Hampden lost.

5 Wellingtons were sent to bomb Gilze-Rijen airfield. No losses.

---

4 July 1941

32 Blenheims on various operations.
    12 aircraft carried out a determined low-level raid on Bremen despite the lack of any cloud cover; 4 of them were shot down. For his leadership on this raid, Wing Commander Hughie Edwards, the Australian commander of 105 Squadron, was awarded the Victoria Cross.
    Other targets attacked by the Blenheims were Norderney and Choques power-station. Total Blenheim losses on this day were 6 aircraft.

4/5 July 1941
BREST

65 Wellingtons and 23 Whitleys; smoke-screens prevented accurate bombing of warship targets. 1 Whitley lost.

LORIENT

25 Hampdens and 22 Wellingtons; hits were claimed on the U-boat base in perfect visibility. No aircraft lost.

Minor Operations: 4 aircraft to Cherbourg, 2 each to Cologne and Dortmund, 1 each to Düsseldorf and Hamborn, 5 Hampdens minelaying in the Frisians, 2 O.T.U. sorties. The 2 Hampdens sent to Dortmund were lost.

---

5 July 1941

14 Blenheims on coastal sweeps off the Frisians and Holland, 3 Stirlings, escorted by fighters, to Lille and Abbeville. No losses.

5/6 July 1941
MÜNSTER

65 Wellingtons and 29 Whitleys; 1 Whitley lost. Crews reported a successful raid in good visibility and only light defences from this target, which had not been attacked for 5 months. Münster reports 21 people killed but no other details.

OSNABRÜCK

39 Hampdens; good bombing reported. 3 aircraft were lost.

BIELEFELD

33 Wellingtons; good bombing reported, including the gasworks, believed to have blown up. No aircraft losses.

Minor Operations: 13 Halifaxes and 3 Stirlings to Magdeburg, 14 Wellingtons to Rotterdam, 7 Hampdens minelaying in the Frisians, 5 O.T.U. sorties. No losses.

Total effort for the night: 208 sorties, 3 aircraft (1·4 per cent) lost.

---

6 July 1941

21 Blenheims on coastal sweeps; 2 lost. 9 Stirlings, escorted by fighters, to Le Trait shipyards and Lille without loss.

6/7 July 1941

BREST

88 Hampdens and 21 Wellingtons; smoke-screens concealed the warships. 1 Hampden and 1 Wellington lost.

MÜNSTER

47 Wellingtons; 2 lost. Crews claimed many fires in the target area but Münster reports only 30 incendiary bombs in the town and no casualties.

DORTMUND

31 Whitleys and 15 Wellingtons. 2 Whitleys lost. Haze was present over the target but fires were claimed.

Minor Operations: 5 Wellingtons to Rotterdam and 2 to Emden, 6 O.T.U. sorties. No losses.

Total effort for the night: 215 sorties, 6 aircraft (2·8 per cent) lost.

---

7 July 1941

20 Blenheims on coastal sweeps. Aircraft of 105 and 139 Squadrons made an attack on a convoy off Holland and hit 2 ships but lost 3 aircraft. 8 Stirlings made escorted raids to Northern France without loss.

Operational Statistics, 12/13 March to 7 July 1941
(117 days/nights)

Number of days with operations: 106
Number of nights with operations: 87
Number of daylight sorties: 2,189, from which 87 aircraft (4·0 per cent) were lost
Number of night sorties: 10,532, from which 234 aircraft (2·2 per cent) were lost
Total sorties: 12,721, from which 321 aircraft (2·5 per cent) were lost
Approximate bomb tonnage in period: 11,849 tons
Averages per 24-hour period: 108·8 sorties, 2·7 aircraft lost, 101·3 tons of bombs dropped

8. BACK TO GERMANY

7/8 July to 10 November 1941

Four months to the day after being forced to turn its attention from Germany to help with the war at sea, Bomber Command was released and was free to resume its main task. The danger at sea had receded, temporarily at least, and, because the main strength of both the Wehrmacht and the Luftwaffe was now deep into Russia, the prospects once again appeared to be favourable for an uninterrupted resumption of the bombing offensive against Germany.

A new directive arrived at Bomber Command Headquarters on 9 July 1941. It opened thus:

> Sir,
>
> I am directed to inform you that a comprehensive review of the enemy's present political, economic and military situation discloses that the weakest points in his armour lie in the morale of the civil population and in his inland transportation system. The wide extension of his military activities is placing an ever-increasing strain on the German transportation system and there are many signs that our recent attacks on industrial towns are having great effect on the morale of the civil population.
>
> 2 . . . I am to request that you will direct the main effort of the bomber force, until further instructions, towards dislocating the German transportation system and to destroying the morale of the civil population as a whole and of the industrial workers in particular.*

There was no mention of oil; it was finally realized that Bomber Command did not have the ability to make any impression on Germany's oil supplies at this stage of the war. The directive went on to list specific targets for attack. During the moon period of each month, the bombers were to be sent to a ring of targets around the Ruhr – Hamm, Osnabrück, Soest, Schwerte, Cologne, Duisburg and Düsseldorf – the destruction of whose railway installations should isolate the Ruhr and prevent war materials being moved from that large industrial area to Germany's fighting fronts. Inland waterway targets were also listed. On nights with no moon, the bombers were directed to attack the general city areas of Cologne, Düsseldorf and Duisburg which, all being situated on the distinctive Rhine, should be the easiest targets to find on dark nights. When the weather was unfavourable for raids on the Rhine city areas, more distant targets were listed for general attack: Hamburg, Bremen, Hannover, Frankfurt, Mannheim, Stuttgart. This directive would remain in force for the remainder of the summer and well into the autumn. The only minor diversion from raids on Germany was the requirement to

*Official History, Vol. IV, pp. 135–6.

pay occasional visits to U-boat bases in France and to the German warships in Brest harbour.

Although Sir Richard Peirse now had a reasonably clear run in what could be expected to be good flying weather, his force was still showing no increase in strength. The creation of new squadrons was still matched by the removal of squadrons for duty elsewhere. The new types of aircraft recently brought into service – Manchesters, Stirlings and Halifaxes – were meeting many technical problems when introduced to operational life and the combined numbers of these available during the coming period would never reach fifty aircraft. The main strength for night raids would continue to be provided by the Wellingtons, Whitleys and Hampdens, which had served so stoutly for what would soon be two years of war. The first Australian squadron to serve in Bomber Command commenced operations in August; this was 455 Squadron flying Hampdens from Swinderby. An interesting new aircraft about to appear as a high-altitude day bomber was the American-built B-17, the Flying Fortress. The only command change was the departure on 26 July of Air Vice-Marshal A. Coningham, who had commanded 4 Group since before the outbreak of war, for a position in the Middle East in which he would prove very successful. He was replaced by Air Vice-Marshal C. R. Carr, a New Zealander who would command 4 Group until almost the end of the war.

The new period got off to a good start with intensive operations to inland German targets and, although there was some slackening because of periods of unfavourable weather, particularly in August and October, the tonnage of bombs dropped was greater than in any previous period of the war. The pattern of recent months, with larger forces being dispatched in the moon period of each month and smaller raids to lower-priority targets on the darker nights, was continued. Most of the midsummer raids had to be confined to the Ruhr and Rhineland areas because of the shorter nights, but the bombers started to reach out to more distant targets as the nights lengthened. In this way, Italian cities appeared on the target lists again in the autumn. German reports will continue to illustrate the poor bombing results during this period. When a local expert in Cologne, Erich Quadflieg, was asked about a series of raids in 1941 which produced only a few bombs in Cologne, or sometimes even none, he was surprised to hear that 80 or 90 or even more than 100 bombers had been dispatched. The Cologne people had reckoned the true numbers to be three to five aircraft, with the larger numbers quoted in Britain's wartime newspapers being 'Churchill's propaganda'.

But, if the effort and the bomb tonnage increased, so did Bomber Command's casualties. The German night fighters were at last becoming established. Although much of the Luftwaffe departed to Russia, the growing night-fighter force remained; a German return shows 134 twin-engined night fighters with trained crews available in the West on 26 July 1941, most of them being based in Holland.* The early night-fighting technique had been for their pilots to attempt to find the R.A.F. bombers in the beams of searchlights over the target cities. This had rarely proved successful because of the German Flak barrages. The commander of the German night fighters, General Josef Kammhuber, then established a continuous belt of searchlights behind the coast, barring the way to the main bomber targets. The night fighters could thus hunt the bombers free from the danger of Flak. This move brought little improvement, however; the bombers were usually through the belt of searchlights before the German

---

* Luftwaffe Quartermaster-General return, quoted in the British Official History, Vol. I, pp. 187–8.

fighters could complete their interceptions. More technology was required. During 1941, Kammhuber was able to establish along the coast a chain of radar 'boxes', areas of sky in which fighters could be controlled from ground stations on to individual bombers passing through the boxes. If the fighter had not completed his interception before reaching the limits of the radar box, it could continue the chase into the searchlight belt which was situated as the next line of defence. The German fighters were next fitted with airborne radar sets and then their chances of successful interception really increased. These developments were now mostly complete. For most of the war to date, the rate of loss for night bombers had remained at a little below 2 per cent. The coming period would show a sharp rise and it was the German night-fighter force, particularly the units stationed in Holland, which was responsible for this.

Turning to daylight operations, the recently increased use of 2 Group's Blenheims in low-level attacks on shipping off the coasts of Europe, the costly *Channel Stop*, and the controversial fighter-escorted *Circuses* all continued. Attempts to raid inland targets in the expectation that the Germans had not left sufficient day fighters to defend the West produced heavy casualties. Similar attempts to breach the daylight defences by using small forces of the new four-engined bombers brought the same result. The tactical rules of daylight bombing remained unchanged. Unescorted bombers could not survive on any penetration in clear weather.

7/8 July 1941

COLOGNE

114 Wellingtons; 3 lost. Crews reported perfect weather and good bombing. Cologne reports its heaviest raid in 1941 with much damage in the centre and in the eastern areas of the city. There were 300 individual damage locations with 174 fires of which 62 were classed as large. The Maria Himmelfahrt church was burnt out. 3 railway lines were completely cut. 138 dwellings were destroyed and 7 industrial buildings badly damaged. Personnel casualties were: 45 killed, 114 injured and 5,450 bombed out.

OSNABRÜCK

54 Whitleys and 18 Wellingtons; 3 Whitleys lost. Good bombing of railway yards claimed. Osnabrück reports bombing in the south-western suburbs with no casualties and 3 buildings damaged but no mention of railway damage.

MÜNSTER

49 Wellingtons; 3 lost. The only report from Münster says many bombs in the town and 9 people killed.

MÖNCHENGLADBACH

40 Hampdens; 2 lost.

Minor Operations: 14 Halifaxes and 3 Stirlings to Frankfurt, 5 Wellingtons to Boulogne, 4 O.T.U. sorties. 1 Halifax lost.

Total effort for the night: 301 sorties, 12 aircraft (4·0 per cent) lost.

Sergeant J. A. Ward, a New Zealand second pilot in a 75 Squadron Wellington, was awarded the Victoria Cross for an action on this night. His aircraft was damaged by a night-fighter attack while returning from Münster and a fire broke out near the starboard engine. Sergeant Ward climbed out on to the wing, making holes in the canvas covering of the geodetic framework of the aircraft to obtain hand- and footholds. He was able to beat out sufficient of the fire to enable the Wellington to return to England.

---

8 July 1941

11 Blenheims on coastal sweep off Denmark and to targets in Northern France; 1 aircraft lost.

90 Squadron made the first raid of the war using Fortresses when 3 aircraft of this type were sent to bomb Wilhelmshaven. 2 aircraft were able to bomb; all returned safely. Wilhelmshaven reports accurate bombing of the dock area and of a post office which was completely destroyed. 14 people were killed and 25 injured.

8/9 July 1941

HAMM

45 Hampdens and 28 Whitleys; only 31 aircraft were able to bomb in the target area. 4 Whitleys and 3 Hampdens lost.

MÜNSTER

51 Wellingtons; 1 lost. Large fires were claimed in the railway-station area. Münster recorded 15 people killed.

BIELEFELD

33 Wellingtons to attack a power-station. No losses.

MERSEBURG

13 Halifaxes and 1 Stirling to the Leuna oil plant. 1 Halifax lost.

---

9 July 1941

15 Blenheims on uneventful sweep off the Frisians. 3 Stirlings to Mazingarbe; 1 lost.

9/10 July 1941

AACHEN

82 aircraft – 39 Hampdens, 27 Whitleys, 16 Wellingtons – on general area attack. 1 Hampden and 1 Whitley lost.

This was the first large raid on Aachen and the town was heavily bombed with many hits in the central areas. Property damage is listed as follows: 91 commercial premises hit of which 19 were destroyed; 1,698 houses (possibly housing 'units' in apartment blocks) destroyed or seriously damaged; the cathedral, the town hall and 2 hospitals were seriously damaged and 2 other churches were hit. Personnel casualties: 60 killed, 85 civilians and 21 air-raid workers injured, 3,450 people bombed out.

OSNABRÜCK

57 Wellingtons; 2 lost. Crews report 'Bursts in target area; several fires', but local reports show that no bombs fell in Osnabrück, only a few in two nearby villages – Holte and Georgsmarienhutte – with 1 person killed and 1 injured.

1 Wellington bombed Le Havre and returned safely.

---

10 July 1941

24 Blenheims on coastal sweeps from Le Havre to Cherbourg. Many aircraft attacked ships and land targets. 1 Blenheim was lost.

3 Stirlings to Chocques power-station in France. 1 aircraft lost, possibly shot down by an R.A.F. fighter (reports conflict).

10/11 July 1941

COLOGNE

98 Wellingtons and 32 Hampdens to two aiming points in the city centre and to the Humboldt works. Bad weather prevented an accurate attack and only 62 aircraft reported bombing in the Cologne area. Cologne reports only 3 high-explosive and 300 incendiary bombs, a few buildings lightly damaged and 1 person injured. 2 Wellingtons lost.

2 Wellingtons bombed Boulogne docks without loss.

---

11 July 1941

6 Stirlings to Le Trait shipyard and Hazebrouck. No losses.

10. The first of the four-engined bombers, Stirlings of 7 Squadron at Oakington. The aircraft in the foreground was lost on the Thousand-Bomber Raid to Bremen on 25/26 June 1942 while serving with a Conversion Unit; its mixed crew of instructors and pupils were all killed.

11/12 July 1941

WILHELMSHAVEN

36 Hampdens; good bombing results were claimed with no aircraft lost. Wilhelmshaven reports most of the bombs fell in open ground around the city and in the harbour. 1 fishing vessel was damaged and 1 barrack hut burnt down. 2 people were killed.

12 July 1941

38 Blenheims on sweeps off Dutch coast. Several attacks were made on ships. 1 aircraft lost.

3 Stirlings to Arques 'ship-lift' near St-Omer but most bombs missed the target and fell in the village. No aircraft lost.

11. The tail gunner in a Stirling with his four 0·303-inch machine guns, the standard defensive weapons of the wartime bombers. Just visible above the gunner's head are three spare bulbs for the reflector gun-sight. In a Stirling, the tail gunner was nearly eighty feet behind the pilot!

12/13 July 1941

BREMEN

33 Hampdens and 28 Wellingtons; 2 Hampdens lost.

13/14 July 1941

GERMAN PORTS

69 Wellingtons, 47 to Bremen, 20 to Vegesack and 2 to Emden. All forces encountered thick cloud and icing. 16 aircraft claimed to have bombed at Bremen, 1 at Vegesack but none at Emden. 2 aircraft were lost from the Bremen force.

14 July 1941

29 Blenheims on coastal sweeps from Cherbourg to Holland and to Hazebrouck railway yards. Many targets were attacked. 2 aircraft lost.

One of the Blenheims lost on this day was, according to our calculations, the 1,000th Bomber Command aircraft lost so far in the Second World War. Of these losses, 328 had occurred during day operations and 672 by night. The casualty rate by day so far in the war – 4·2 per cent – was exactly double the 2·1 per cent of the night casualty rate. A total of 40,346 sorties had been flown, 7,737 by day and 32,609 by night. Approximately 28,642 tons of bombs had been dropped since the beginning of the war.

14/15 July 1941

BREMEN

78 Wellingtons and 19 Whitleys to 3 aiming points, the shipyards, the goods station and the Altstadt. Crews reported 'the whole town was ablaze'. 4 Wellingtons lost.

HANNOVER

85 aircraft – 44 Hampdens, 21 Wellingtons, 14 Halifaxes, 6 Stirlings – to a rubber factory and the city centre. Many fires were observed. 2 Wellingtons lost.

Minor Operations: 6 Wellingtons to Rotterdam, 10 Hampdens minelaying in the Frisians and Elbe. No losses.

15/16 July 1941

DUISBURG

38 Wellingtons; bombing was difficult because of cloud and Flak. 4 aircraft lost.

16 July 1941

ROTTERDAM

36 Blenheims in low-level attacks on shipping in the docks. Dutch reports later told of 22 ships being damaged in this raid. 4 Blenheims were shot down by the intense Flak. 5 further Blenheims carried out sweeps off the Dutch coast without loss.

16/17 July 1941

HAMBURG

107 aircraft – 51 Wellingtons, 32 Hampdens, 24 Whitleys – encountered bad visibility. 52 aircraft reported bombing in the general area of Hamburg; 52 aircraft bombed alternative targets. 3 Wellingtons and 1 Hampden lost.

Hamburg reports 4 fires – none large, no major damage area, only 1 person injured but 154 bombed out.

Minor Operations: 9 aircraft to Boulogne but the target was cloud-covered and only 3 aircraft bombed, 5 Hampdens minelaying in the Frisians, 6 O.T.U. sorties. No losses.

17/18 July 1941

COLOGNE

50 Wellingtons and 25 Hampdens; claimed to have caused many fires. No aircraft lost. Cologne reports only 68 bombs of all types, no serious damage and no casualties.

5 Wellingtons sent to Rotterdam were unable to locate the target and 1 was shot down in England by an Intruder.

18 July 1941

5 Stirlings on cloud-cover raids to Holland and Germany turned back; 1 aircraft was lost in the sea. 3 Blenheims operating the *Channel Stop* attacked ships near Gravelines and scored hits but all 3 aircraft were shot down. Losses on this day were thus 50 per cent.

19 July 1941

21 Blenheims on coastal sweeps from Belgium to the Frisians. Ships were attacked and some set on fire. 2 aircraft lost. 3 Stirlings on an escorted raid to Lille power-station; 1 Stirling lost.

19/20 July 1941

HANNOVER

49 aircraft – 20 Whitleys, 17 Wellingtons, 12 Hampdens – with the main railway station as aiming point. 1 Wellington and 1 Whitley lost.

35 Hampdens on minelaying operation in mouths of the Elbe and Weser rivers. No losses.

20 July 1941

12 Blenheims on a coastal sweep off French coast. 1 ship was hit. 2 Blenheims lost. 3 Stirlings on a raid to Hazebrouck turned back.

20/21 July 1941

COLOGNE

113 aircraft – 46 Wellingtons, 39 Hampdens, 25 Whitleys, 3 Stirlings – to attack railway targets but thick cloud resulted in scattered bombing. Cologne reports only minor damage and 3 people killed.

Minor Operations: 15 Wellingtons and 9 Whitleys to Rotterdam caused fires in the dock area, 9 O.T.U. sorties.

There were no aircraft losses from any operation on this night.

21 July 1941

13 Blenheims on coastal sweeps and shallow raids into France. No losses.

21/22 July 1941

FRANKFURT

37 Wellingtons and 34 Hampdens on the first large raid against this target. No aircraft lost.

Frankfurt does not record this as a significant raid, merely mentioning 'bomb explosions' in its records, but Darmstadt, 15 miles away, suffered 15 buildings hit and 16 people killed.

MANNHEIM

36 Wellingtons and 8 Halifaxes; the centre of the town as the aiming point. 1 Wellington lost.

Mannheim reports only 4 high-explosive bombs – of which 1 was a dud – and 17 flares or incendiary bombs in the city and in nearby Ludwigshafen. 3 of the bombs fell in a Flak position but damage and casualties are not recorded.

Minor Operations: 6 Wellingtons to Cherbourg, 2 Hampdens minelaying in the Frisians, 1 O.T.U. sortie. No losses.

---

22 July 1941

6 Blenheims to Le Trait shipyards and 6 on a sweep off the French coast. No Blenheim losses.

22/23 July 1941

FRANKFURT

63 aircraft – 34 Hampdens, 16 Whitleys, 13 Wellingtons. No losses.

MANNHEIM

29 Wellingtons. No losses.

Minor Operations: 19 Wellingtons and Whitleys to Dunkirk, 5 Hampdens minelaying off Brest, 5 O.T.U. sorties. No losses.

---

23 July 1941

17 Blenheims on coastal operations; ships were attacked and set on fire but 6 Blenheims were lost. 12 further Blenheims on raids to Northern France; no losses.

There was an important development on this day in the continuing bombing campaign against the three German warships – *Scharnhorst*, *Gneisenau* and *Prinz Eugen* – sheltering in Brest. The *Scharnhorst* had not been hit in any recent bombing and the Germans had moved her stealthily to La Pallice, a small port more than 200 miles further south. A large tanker covered with camouflage netting was left in the *Scharnhorst*'s old berth at Brest. *Scharnhorst* was spotted by reconnaissance aircraft at La Pallice on 23 July. It was important to attack this powerful ship at once in case she was preparing for another Atlantic shipping foray. A formation of 6 Stirlings made the first attack on the evening of this day. 1 Stirling was shot down by German fighters.

23/24 July 1941

MANNHEIM

51 Wellingtons; haze obscured the target. No aircraft lost.

Mannheim reports only 17 high-explosive bombs and an unknown number of incendiary bombs, the only damage recorded being to a water main, broken glass and roof tiles in 12 houses, and crops damaged in some fields of cereals and tobacco. The only casualties recorded are 3 people killed in a village some distance from Mann-heim.

FRANKFURT

33 Hampdens; visibility was poor. 1 aircraft lost.

LA PALLICE

30 Whitleys. Bomb bursts were seen in the dock area. No losses.

Minor Operations: 8 Wellingtons to Le Havre and Ostend, 1 Hampden minelaying in the Frisians, 3 O.T.U. sorties. No losses.

---

24 July 1941

BREST

A major daylight operation against the German warships at Brest had been under preparation for some time. The original plan was to send approximately 150 aircraft but this had to be changed at the last minute because of the departure of the *Scharnhorst* for La Pallice. The force actually dispatched to Brest was 100 aircraft and the tactical plan was as follows:

1. 3 Fortresses bombing from 30,000 ft would, it was hoped, draw up German fighters prematurely.
2. 18 Hampdens, escorted by 3 squadrons of Spitfires with long-range fuel tanks, would complete the process of 'drawing-up' of the fighters.
3. The main bombing force of 79 Wellingtons, provided by 1 and 3 Groups, would then attack. No fighter escort was available for the Wellingtons.

The operation proceeded according to this plan in clear visibility. 6 hits were claimed on the *Gneisenau* but these cannot be confirmed. The German fighter op-position was stronger and more prolonged than expected and 10 Wellingtons and 2 Hampdens were lost to fighter attack or Flak.

CHERBOURG

As a diversion for the Brest raid, 36 Blenheims in several waves and all escorted by Spitfires, attacked Cherbourg docks with good bombing results but the diversionary aspect of the plan failed. No German fighters appeared. No Blenheims lost.

LA PALLICE

15 Halifaxes of 35 and 76 Squadrons carried out an entirely unescorted raid on the *Scharnhorst* at La Pallice. The Halifaxes met fierce fighter opposition and some Flak; 5 were lost and all the remainder damaged. 5 direct hits were scored on the *Scharnhorst* but 3 of these were armour-piercing bombs which passed straight through the ship, leaving small holes in the bottom only, and the 2 bombs which did explode caused only light damage. The Germans decided, however, that *Scharnhorst* should return at once for the better repair facilities and Flak cover at Brest and she sailed that night with much water inside the ship (reports vary between 3,000 and 7,000 tons of water). This operation was, therefore, a major success in that it ensured that this powerful warship was forced to stay in harbour for a further prolonged period, 4 months being required for repairs.

The total effort for the day: 151 sorties with 17 aircraft (11·3 per cent) lost.

24/25 July 1941

KIEL

34 Wellingtons and 30 Hampdens; 1 Hampden and 1 Wellington lost. Kiel reports only a few bombs with 2 people injured but 5 people were killed in the nearby village of Wellsee.

EMDEN

31 Whitleys and 16 Wellingtons; 2 Wellingtons lost.

Minor Operations: 4 Wellingtons to Rotterdam, 6 Hampdens minelaying in the Frisians. No losses.

25/26 July 1941

HANNOVER

30 Hampdens and 25 Whitleys; bombing results were not observed. 4 Whitleys and 1 Hampden lost.

HAMBURG

43 Wellingtons; 2 lost. Fires in the city and shipyards were claimed. Hamburg reports 4 large fires, 1 person killed and 6 injured with no particularly remarkable incidents.

Minor Operations: 7 Stirlings and 2 Halifaxes to Berlin of which 2 Stirlings and 1 Halifax were lost. 2 Wellingtons to Emden.

Total losses for this night: 10 aircraft out of 109 dispatched (9·2 per cent).

---

26 July 1941

2 Fortresses to Hamburg encountered thunderstorms and icing. 1 of the Fortresses bombed Emden. There were no losses.

---

27 July 1941

6 Blenheims to Yainville power-station turned back.

27/28 July 1941

Minor Operations

14 Wellingtons and Whitleys to Dunkirk, which was found to be cloud-covered, 36 Hampdens minelaying off Lorient and St-Nazaire, 3 O.T.U. sorties. 1 Hampden lost.

---

28 July 1941

6 Blenheims to Yainville were recalled.

28/29 July 1941

42 Hampdens minelaying in the Baltic; 1 lost.

---

30 July 1941

43 Blenheims to Kiel Canal and on sweeps off the Dutch and German coasts. Ships were attacked and hit but 7 Blenheims were lost.

30/31 July 1941

COLOGNE

116 aircraft – 62 Wellingtons, 42 Hampdens, 7 Halifaxes, 5 Stirlings – dispatched but the recent spell of bad weather continued; thunderstorms and icing were encountered and the crews could only report 'Cologne believed hit'. Cologne confirms only 3 high-explosive and 300 incendiary bombs, no casualties and 6 buildings damaged. 2 Hampdens and 1 Wellington were lost and 6 more aircraft crashed in England.

12 Whitleys to Boulogne turned back.

---

31 July 1941

4 Blenheims on an uneventful sweep off St-Valéry.

1 August 1941

3 Blenheims on the *Channel Stop* operation with fighter escort attacked ships off Nieuport but 2 Blenheims were lost.

2 August 1941

24 Blenheims on coastal sweeps between Cherbourg and Texel. Ships and land targets were attacked. 1 aircraft lost. 3 Fortresses to Kiel and Bremen but only Kiel was bombed. Kiel reports light damage, 1 person killed, 9 injured.

2/3 August 1941

HAMBURG

80 aircraft – 58 Wellingtons, 21 Whitleys, 1 Stirling – to bomb railway targets. 2 Wellingtons lost. Hamburg reports 5 people killed, 38 injured and 738 permanently or temporarily bombed out. There were 10 fires, 5 of them large ones. The most serious fire was caused by a concentration of incendiary bombs falling on a large dump of rolled cork stored in the open in the Billbrook area. This burned for 7 hours.

BERLIN

53 aircraft – 40 Wellingtons, 8 Halifaxes, 5 Stirlings; haze hampered bombing. 3 Wellingtons and 1 Stirling lost.

KIEL

50 Hampdens reported accurate bombing of the shipyards and the town. 5 aircraft lost. Kiel reports only 1 house hit with 1 person injured, though naval and shipyard damage may have been omitted from this report.

Minor Operations: 20 Wellingtons to Cherbourg, which was found to be cloud-covered, 5 Hampdens minelaying off Kiel. No losses.

Total effort for the night: 208 sorties, 11 aircraft (5·3 per cent) lost.

3/4 August 1941

FRANKFURT

39 Whitleys; weather conditions were poor. No aircraft lost.

HANNOVER

34 Wellingtons; the target was cloud-covered. 1 aircraft lost.

7 Whitleys to Calais docks. No losses.

---

4 August 1941

12 Blenheims on a sweep off the Frisians. 6 recalled; others attacked fishing vessels which was the only shipping seen. No aircraft lost.

---

5 August 1941

20 Blenheims on sweeps between the River Scheldt and the Frisians and on a *Circus* operation to St-Omer which was recalled. Several ships were attacked. No Blenheims lost.

5/6 August 1941

MANNHEIM

65 Wellingtons and 33 Hampdens; 2 Wellingtons and 1 Hampden lost. Good bombing results reported. The Mannheim–Ludwigshafen air-raid service recorded serious damage in several areas of Mannheim and in the northern part of Ludwigshafen. 5 commercial premises were totally destroyed – a cigar manufacturers, 2 paperworks, a shoe wholesalers and a railway office – and 3 more were damaged, including a rubber and celluloid factory badly damaged by fire when a bomber crashed on to it. The factory employed 2,200 people and production was reduced by 75 per cent for 8 days. 10 dwelling-houses were destroyed and 572 damaged. 27 people were killed and 55 injured, though it is not known whether the 12 people known to have been hurt by falling Flak splinters are included in this total.

KARLSRUHE

97 aircraft – 50 Hampdens, 28 Wellingtons, 11 Halifaxes, 8 Stirlings – to railway targets. 3 aircraft – 1 Halifax, 1 Hampden, 1 Wellington – lost. Karlsruhe reports bombing in the Rhine harbour and in the Weststadt and Mühlberg areas – all on the western side of the city; 34 people were killed.

FRANKFURT

46 Whitleys and 22 Wellingtons. 2 Whitleys and 1 Wellington lost. Good bombing claimed. Mainz, 20 miles away, reports that some bombs fell there.

Minor Operations: 13 Wellingtons to Aachen, 8 Wellingtons to Boulogne, 5 Hampdens mine-laying off the east coast of Denmark. 2 Wellingtons on the Aachen raid were lost.

Total effort for the night: 289 sorties, 11 aircraft (3·8 per cent) lost.

---

6 August 1941

25 Blenheims on coastal sweeps. 3 ships were attacked. 2 Fortresses to Brest jettisoned their bombs in the sea. No aircraft lost.

6/7 August 1941

FRANKFURT

34 Whitleys and 19 Wellingtons to railway yards. 2 Wellingtons and 2 Whitleys lost.

MANNHEIM

38 Wellingtons to railway workshops. No losses.

KARLSRUHE

38 Hampdens to railway workshops. 1 aircraft lost.

CALAIS

38 aircraft – 21 Hampdens, 11 Wellingtons, 6 Whitleys; only 14 could identify targets in the docks and were able to bomb. 1 Hampden lost.

2 O.T.U. sorties to France; 1 Wellington lost.

---

7 August 1941

12 Blenheims on *Circus* operations to St-Omer airfield and Lille power-station. Only St-Omer was bombed. There were no Blenheim losses.

7/8 August 1941

ESSEN

106 aircraft – 54 Hampdens, 32 Wellingtons, 9 Halifaxes, 8 Stirlings, 3 Manchesters – to attack the Krupps factory. 2 Hampdens and 1 Stirling lost.

Essen reports only 39 high-explosive and 200 incendiary bombs in the city, causing light damage. A bakery which was destroyed was the most serious incident. There were no casualties in Essen.

HAMM

45 Wellingtons and 1 Stirling to bomb the railway yards. No aircraft were lost. Large fires were started with smoke rising to 11,000 ft.

DORTMUND

20 Wellingtons and 20 Whitleys. No losses.

Minor Operations: 6 Wellingtons to Boulogne, 8 Hampdens minelaying in the Frisians and off Denmark, 2 O.T.U. sorties. No losses.

8/9 August 1941

KIEL

50 Hampdens and 4 Whitleys to attack the submarine yards. 2 Hampdens and 1 Whitley lost.

The Kiel diarist makes some interesting points on this raid.* The Flak barrage was so intense 'that it reminded old soldiers of 1914–1918 Western Front offensives'. 13 people were killed but 11 of these were Italian workers housed at an experimental farm outside Kiel. The survivors of 'our allies' then expressed a wish to return to Italy. There was little damage in Kiel; a gasometer is mentioned as having been damaged.

HAMBURG

44 Wellingtons to railway and shipyard aiming points. 1 aircraft lost. The target was cloud-covered and only scattered bombing resulted. 5 people were killed, 8 injured and 20 bombed out and the fire brigade had to deal with only one fire.

7 Hampdens minelaying in the Frisians, off Kiel and in the Norwegian fjords. No losses.

---

9 August 1941

5 Blenheims on a *Circus* operation to Gosnay power-station bombed an unidentified target at Gravelines instead, without loss.

---

10 August 1941

6 Blenheims on a sweep along the French coast. 3 aircraft claimed direct hits on ships off Gravelines. 2 aircraft lost.

11/12 August 1941

ROTTERDAM

31 Hampdens and 3 Wellingtons bombed dock targets. 1 further Wellington to Antwerp. No losses. Hampdens of 50 Squadron dropped 500 bags of tea from the Dutch East Indies for civilians during the Rotterdam raid.

KREFELD

20 Hampdens and 9 Whitleys to the railway yards; they encountered cloud over the target and only 1 aircraft claimed to have hit the yards. There were no losses.

---

* *Kiel im Luftkrieg 1939–1945, Tagebuch des Detlef Boelck*, Kiel, 1980, pp. 24–5.

MÖNCHENGLADBACH

29 Wellingtons to a railway target; the area was completely cloud-covered. No aircraft lost.

2 Wellingtons of 115 Squadron carried out the first trial of the new *Gee* navigation device on this raid. The trials were continued for a further 2 nights. They were successful but the flights then stopped to allow mass production of the equipment for later use to commence.

---

12 August 1941

COLOGNE POWER-STATIONS

This was another special daylight operation. In an attempt to help Russia by drawing German fighters back to the West, raids by 54 Blenheims were made on the important Knapsack and Quadrath power-stations near Cologne. 38 aircraft were dispatched to Knapsack and 18 to Quadrath. An extensive series of diversions and fighter-escort flights was also carried out, but the limit of the fighters' range was reached well short of Cologne.

The Blenheims, each carrying two 500-lb bombs, made fast, low-level approaches. Most crews reached the targets and reported accurate bombing but 10 aircraft were shot down by Flak or fighters – 18·5 per cent of the attacking force.

The diversions and supporting operations all proceeded according to plan. 2 forces each of 6 Hampdens carried out escorted raids to St-Omer and Gosnay and 6 Blenheims bombed Le Trait shipyard, all without loss. 4 Fortresses made high-level raids on Cologne, De Kooy airfield and Emden, also without loss. 175 Fighter Command sorties were flown, claiming 10 German fighters destroyed or 'probables' but losing 6 Spitfires. 2 Blenheims detailed to act as navigation leaders to R.A.F. fighter formations were both lost, bringing the Bomber Command losses to 12 aircraft, 15·4 per cent of the 78 bomber sorties dispatched.

12/13 August 1941

HANNOVER

65 Wellingtons and 13 Hampdens. 4 Wellingtons were lost including one of the *Gee* trial aircraft but the loss of this aircraft did not result in the Germans discovering any details of the still secret equipment.

BERLIN

70 aircraft – 40 Wellingtons, 12 Halifaxes, 9 Stirlings, 9 Manchesters; the Air Ministry building in the Alexander Platz was the aiming point but only 32 aircraft reached and bombed in the Berlin area and 9 aircraft – 3 Manchesters, 3 Wellingtons, 2 Halifaxes, 1 Stirling – were lost.

MAGDEBURG

36 Hampdens; none lost.

ESSEN

35 aircraft – 30 Wellingtons, 3 Stirlings, 2 Halifaxes; the target, the Krupps works, was not hit. 1 Wellington was shot down over England by an Intruder.

Minor Operations: 14 Wellingtons to Le Havre, 1 Stirling to Bielefeld. No losses.

Total effort for the night: 234 sorties, 14 aircraft (6·0 per cent) lost and 6 more crashed in England.

---

14 August 1941

26 Blenheims on coastal sweeps over a wide area. Ships off the Dutch coast and in Boulogne docks were bombed. 1 aircraft lost. 5 further Blenheims to Marquise shell factory turned back.

14/15 August 1941

HANNOVER

152 aircraft – 96 Wellingtons, 55 Whitleys, 1 Stirling – with railway stations as aiming points. 9 aircraft – 5 Wellingtons, 4 Whitleys – lost.

BRUNSWICK

81 Hampdens to railway targets. 1 aircraft lost.

MAGDEBURG

52 aircraft – 27 Wellingtons, 9 Halifaxes, 9 Stirlings, 7 Manchesters – to railway targets but visibility was poor and no bombing results were observed. 4 aircraft – 2 Wellingtons, 1 Halifax, 1 Stirling – lost.

Minor Operations: 13 Wellingtons to Boulogne, 9 Wellingtons and Whitleys to Rotterdam, 2 Wellingtons to Dunkirk, 5 Hampdens minelaying in the Frisians. No losses.

Total effort for the night: 314 sorties, 14 aircraft (4·5 per cent) lost.

---

16 August 1941

30 Blenheims on coastal sweeps and *Circus* operations to Marquise and St-Omer. No ships were seen but the Marquise shell factory was bombed. No aircraft were lost.

2 Fortresses to Brest and 2 to Düsseldorf. No aircraft were lost but 1 Fortress was attacked by 5 fighters over Brest; it crashed in England and was written off, to become the first R.A.F. Fortress casualty.

16/17 August 1941

COLOGNE

72 aircraft – 37 Wellingtons, 29 Whitleys, 6 Halifaxes – to railway targets. 7 Whitleys and 1 Wellington lost.

Haze and smoke obscured targets but a large fire was seen. Cologne reports only a few bombs with light damage and no casualties; the fire may have been a decoy.

DÜSSELDORF

52 Hampdens and 6 Manchesters to railways. 3 Hampdens and 2 Manchesters lost. Many fires were seen.

DUISBURG

54 Wellingtons to attack railway targets. 1 aircraft lost. 'Several fires' seen by crews.

Minor Operations: 10 Wellingtons to Rotterdam, 4 Hampdens and 2 Manchesters to Ostend, 1 O.T.U. sortie. No losses.

---

17 August 1941

20 Blenheims on coastal sweeps. Ships were attacked off Terschelling. No aircraft lost.

17/18 August 1941

BREMEN

39 Hampdens and 20 Whitleys, with the Focke-Wulf factory and the railway goods station as aiming points. 2 Hampdens lost. Hits were claimed on the Focke-Wulf factory.

DUISBURG

41 Wellingtons to railway targets. No losses. Weather was bad and bombing results were admitted to be poor.

Minor Operations: 1 Wellington to Dunkirk, 12 Hampdens minelaying off Denmark, 6 O.T.U. sorties. No losses.

---

18 August 1941

39 Blenheims on coastal sweeps off Holland and on *Circus* operations to Lille and Marquise. 2 trawlers were sunk and Lille was bombed. 1 Blenheim lost.

A Blenheim of 188 Squadron, flying on one of the *Circus* raids, dropped a spare artificial leg by parachute for Wing Commander Douglas Bader, who had recently been taken prisoner. It reached Bader safely.

18/19 August 1941

COLOGNE

62 aircraft – 42 Hampdens, 17 Whitleys, 3 Wellingtons – with the West Station as the aiming point. 5 Whitleys and 1 Wellington lost.

Crews reported many fires on the west side of the Rhine but Cologne reports few bombs, only 1 building damaged and no casualties, so this was probably another occasion when a decoy fire site attracted most of the bombs from a bomber force, which suffered nearly 10 per cent casualties.

DUISBURG

41 Wellingtons to attack railway yards. 2 aircraft lost. Good bombing results were claimed in clear weather.

Minor Operations: 11 Whitleys and 7 Wellingtons to Dunkirk, 1 O.T.U. sortie. No losses.

---

19 August 1941

18 Blenheims on *Circus* operations to Gosnay and Hazebrouck; only Hazebrouck was bombed. 3 Blenheims lost. 2 Fortresses to Düsseldorf turned back.

19/20 August 1941

KIEL

108 aircraft – 54 Wellingtons, 41 Hampdens, 7 Stirlings, 6 Halifaxes – to railway targets but icing conditions and thick cloud cover over Bremen resulted in only 67 aircraft claiming to bomb in the target area. 3 Wellingtons and 1 Hampden lost.

Kiel reports heavy rain during the raid, no casualties, 1 house hit by an unexploded Flak shell and swimming-bath buildings damaged by incendiary bombs. Bombs also fell on the airfield at Holtenau, just north of Kiel.

Minor Operations: 6 Wellingtons and 3 Whitleys to Le Havre, 3 Hampdens minelaying in the Frisians. No losses.

---

20 August 1941

18 Blenheims on coastal sweeps. Ships were attacked but not hit; Texel airfield was bombed. No losses.

---

21 August 1941

24 Blenheims in raids on Ijmuiden steelworks, which were bombed, and on Chocques chemical factory, but this target was not reached. No losses. 3 Fortresses to Düsseldorf turned back.

22 August 1941

18 Blenheims on uneventful coastal sweeps from France to the Frisians.

22/23 August 1941

MANNHEIM

56 Wellingtons and 41 Hampdens to 3 aiming points. 1 Hampden lost.

Crews reported many fires but Mannheim recorded only 6 high-explosive bombs in the city; 1 house was badly damaged and 5 houses lightly damaged. The only casualty was an air-raid worker who was injured when his lorry crashed on the way to a bombing incident.

Minor Operations: 23 aircraft – 11 Whitleys, 10 Wellingtons, 2 Stirlings – to Le Havre, 1 O.T.U. sortie. No losses.

---

24 August 1941

6 Blenheims on sweep in the Bremerhaven area. 1 ship was attacked but not hit. No aircraft lost.

24/25 August 1941

DÜSSELDORF

44 aircraft – 25 Whitleys, 12 Hampdens, 7 Halifaxes; only the estimated position of the target was bombed, through cloud. 2 Whitleys and 1 Halifax lost.

6 Hampdens were dispatched to the Wesel area for searchlight suppression operations in the German searchlight belt. These aircraft attacked any searchlight which was holding another bomber in its beam. The Hampdens dived to attack with small bombs and with machine guns; this usually caused the searchlight to lose the bomber which it had been holding. The Hampdens operating on this night found that, after 25 minutes of this type of attack, all the searchlights in the area became erratic and some were extinguished.

---

25 August 1941

6 Blenheims on uneventful sweep off the mouth of the River Scheldt.

25/26 August 1941

KARLSRUHE

37 Wellingtons and 12 Stirlings to the city centre; storms and thick cloud prevented accurate bombing. 2 Wellingtons and 1 Stirling lost.

MANNHEIM

38 Hampdens and 7 Manchesters to the city centre with moderate results claimed. 3 Hampdens lost.

---

26 August 1941

36 Blenheims on coastal sweeps. Many attacks were made and 2 ships claimed sunk but 7 Blenheims were lost. 6 further Blenheims on a *Circus* operation to St-Omer airfield bombed without loss to the Blenheims.

26/27 August 1941

COLOGNE

99 aircraft – 47 Wellingtons, 29 Hampdens, 22 Whitleys, 1 Manchester – to the city centre and to railway yards. 6 further Hampdens made searchlight suppression flights 10 miles west of Cologne without loss.

Good bombing was claimed in clear visibility. Cologne records indicate that most of the bombing was probably east of the city, with only about 15 per cent of the bombs dropped being inside the city limits. 8 people were killed in Cologne. 1 Wellington and 1 Whitley lost.

Minor Operations: 29 Wellingtons and Whitleys to Le Havre, 14 Wellingtons and 2 Stirlings to Boulogne, 17 Hampdens minelaying in the Frisians and off Kiel and the Danish coast. 1 minelaying Hampden lost.

---

27 August 1941

13 Blenheims on *Circus* operations to Lille and St-Omer were recalled.

27/28 August 1941

MANNHEIM

91 aircraft – 35 Hampdens, 41 Wellingtons, 15 Whitleys. No aircraft were lost but 7 Wellingtons and 1 Whitley crashed in England.

Good bombing and many fires were claimed though there was ground haze. Mannheim reports only 41 high-explosive and 25 incendiary bombs in the city, though the latter figure is probably too low. 13 premises were damaged – 2 store buildings on a military camp, 1 hotel, 2 shops, 5 houses, 1 factory air-raid post and 2 small warehouses. The only casualties were 13 people injured in the hotel incident.

Minor Operations: 2 Wellingtons to Boulogne, 2 to Dunkirk, 17 Hampdens minelaying in the Frisians. No losses.

28 August 1941

ROTTERDAM

18 Blenheims carried out a costly low-level raid on shipping in Rotterdam docks. 1 aircraft crashed on take-off and 7 other aircraft were lost during the raid. At least 2 large cargo ships were hit and possibly other damage was caused in the docks.

28/29 August 1941

DUISBURG

118 aircraft – 60 Wellingtons, 30 Hampdens, 13 Stirlings, 9 Halifaxes, 6 Manchesters – to railway targets. 6 aircraft – 3 Wellingtons, 1 Halifax, 1 Hampden, 1 Stirling – lost. 6 further Hampdens made searchlight-suppression flights near the target; 2 of these were lost.

Good bombing was claimed in clear visibility but Duisburg reports only 63 high-explosive and 500 incendiary bombs with no details of damage or casualties.

Minor Operations: 23 Wellingtons and Whitleys to Dunkirk and Ostend, 2 O.T.U. sorties. No losses.

---

29 August 1941

6 Blenheims on *Circus* operation to Hazebrouck but only 1 aircraft dropped bombs on this target. 1 Fortress to Düsseldorf turned back. No losses.

29/30 August 1941

FRANKFURT

143 aircraft – 73 Hampdens, 62 Whitleys, 5 Halifaxes, 3 Manchesters – on the first 100-plus aircraft raid on this city, with railways and harbours as aiming points. The first sortie by an Australian squadron was flown in this raid when Squadron Leader French (no initials recorded) and his crew took a 455 Squadron Hampden to Frankfurt and returned safely. 2 Hampdens and 1 Whitley lost.

Bad weather prevented accurate bombing and crews reported that the attack became general in the Frankfurt area. Frankfurt reports only light and scattered bombing, with damage to a gasworks, a cask merchant's depot and to several houses. 8 people were killed, 7 of them in one house which was struck by a bomb.

MANNHEIM

94 Wellingtons; 2 lost.

The weather was bad and Mannheim's report confirms that bombing results were poor with only scattered damage. 5 commercial firms, none employing more than 70 people, suffered production losses because of damage. 1 person was injured.

5 'freshmen' Wellingtons were sent to Le Havre. No losses.

Total effort for the night: 242 sorties, 5 aircraft (2·1 per cent) lost.

Resistance Operations

The first flights by Bomber Command in support of Resistance groups in the German-occupied countries were carried out on this night by an unknown number and type of aircraft from the newly formed 138 Squadron, based at Newmarket. This unit was joined in this work by 161 Squadron in February 1942. Both Squadrons belonged to 3 Group and a permanent base was later established for them at Tempsford. Supplies and agents were dropped regularly by parachute in many parts of Europe and sometimes agents or urgent packages were collected by small aircraft, usually Lysanders, which landed in fields. Many types of aircraft were used for the dropping of supplies or agents by parachute.

Bomber Command's Operations Record Books do not record details of these operations until the night of 7/8 January 1944 but, from the Record Books of 138 and 161 Squadrons, it appears that 2,654 sorties were flown and 73 aircraft were lost between the commencement of these operations and 7/8 January 1944. These sorties and losses, which cannot be included in the nightly diary entries or in the periodic operational statistics until January 1944, have been added into the final table at the end of the war.

---

30 August 1941

6 Blenheims on a Channel sweep recalled.

30/31 August 1941

5 Wellingtons and 1 Stirling attacked Cherbourg docks, starting fires. 2 Hampdens minelaying off Warnemünde. No losses.

---

31 August 1941

30 Blenheims on escorted raids to Lille power-station (12 aircraft), Lannion and St-Omer airfields and Le Trait shipyard (6 aircraft to each). Some alternative targets had to be bombed because of cloud. 3 Fortresses to Bremen, Hamburg and Kiel but only Bremen was bombed. No losses from any operation.

---

31 August/1 September 1941

COLOGNE

103 aircraft – 45 Wellingtons, 39 Hampdens, 7 Halifaxes, 6 Manchesters, 6 Stirlings – to railway targets and 5 further Manchesters on searchlight-suppression flights. 3 Hampdens, 1 Manchester and 1 Wellington were lost and a further Wellington was shot down by an Intruder over England.

The weather was bad and only the estimated position of Cologne could be bombed, through cloud, by 68 aircraft. Cologne reports a few bombs and 1 person killed.

ESSEN

43 Whitleys and 28 Wellingtons to the Krupps works. 1 Whitley lost.

Essen was also cloud-covered and bombing was poor. Only 1 house was damaged with 4 or 5 people killed (two reports differ) and 10 people were injured.

Minor Operations: 6 Wellingtons to Boulogne, 12 Hampdens minelaying in the Frisians and in Kiel Bay. 1 Wellington lost.

1/2 September 1941

COLOGNE

34 Wellingtons and 20 Hampdens bombed in good visibility. Many fires were claimed but some crews reported German decoy fires. Cologne reports only 35 bombs of all kinds, 1 house damaged, no casualties. 1 Hampden lost.

4 Hampdens minelaying off Denmark. No losses.

---

2 September 1941

6 Blenheims on a sweep from Dunkirk to Ostend set a merchant ship on fire but 1 Blenheim was lost. 3 Fortresses to Bremen, Duisburg and Hamburg but only Bremen was bombed. No losses.

2/3 September 1941

FRANKFURT

126 aircraft – 71 Wellingtons, 44 Whitleys, 11 Hampdens. 3 Wellingtons and 1 Hampden lost. The only report available from Frankfurt simply says 'bomb explosions' for this date; it is probable that not many bombs fell in the city.

BERLIN

49 aircraft – 32 Hampdens, 7 Halifaxes, 6 Stirlings, 4 Manchesters. 5 aircraft – 2 Halifaxes, 2 Hampdens, 1 Manchester – lost. The Manchester lost contained the commanding officer of 61 Squadron, Wing Commander G. E. Valentine, and Group Captain J. F. Barrett, the station commander of North Luffenham. Both officers were killed and are buried in the Berlin War Cemetery.

Minor Operations: 10 Wellingtons and Whitleys to Ostend, 16 Hampdens minelaying in the Frisians and off Denmark. 2 Hampdens and 1 Wellington lost.

Total effort for the night: 201 sorties, 12 aircraft (6·0 per cent) lost.

3/4 September 1941

BREST

140 aircraft – 85 Wellingtons, 30 Hampdens, 19 Whitleys, 4 Stirlings, 2 Manchesters. All aircraft of 1, 4 and 5 Groups were recalled, probably because of worsening

weather at bases, but 4 aircraft from these groups did not hear the signal and, with the 3 Group aircraft, proceeded to the target. 53 aircraft bombed the estimated positions of the German warships through a smoke-screen. No aircraft were lost but 2 Wellingtons and 1 Whitley crashed in England.

Minor Operations: 2 Wellingtons to Le Havre, 5 Hampdens minelaying off Denmark and Flensburg. No losses.

---

4 September 1941

18 Blenheims on escorted raids to Mazingarbe chemical works and Cherbourg docks. 3 Fortresses to Germany but none reached their targets; 1 aircraft bombed Rotterdam docks. 1 Blenheim was lost from the Mazingarbe raid.

6/7 September 1941

HÜLS

86 aircraft – 41 Whitleys, 27 Wellingtons, 18 Hampdens – to bomb a chemical factory. Good results were claimed in clear weather. 5 Whitleys and 2 Wellingtons lost.

24 Hampdens minelaying off Oslo. 1 aircraft lost.

---

7 September 1941

12 Blenheims on shipping attacks off the Dutch coast. 2 ships were hit and sunk or severely damaged. 2 Blenheims lost.

7/8 September 1941

BERLIN

197 aircraft – 103 Wellingtons, 43 Hampdens, 31 Whitleys, 10 Stirlings, 6 Halifaxes, 4 Manchesters – to 3 aiming points. 15 aircraft – 8 Wellingtons, 2 Hampdens, 2 Whitleys, 2 Stirlings, 1 Manchester – lost.

Good bombing was claimed by 137 crews in clear visibility. Berlin reports most bombs in the Lichtenberg and Pankow districts, which are east and north of the centre. Damage was reported to 4 war-industry factories, 10 transport and 13 public utilities, 2 public buildings, 1 zoo, 16 farms and 200 houses. 36 people were killed, 212 injured and 2,873 were bombed out, some only temporarily.

KIEL

51 aircraft – 30 Wellingtons, 18 Hampdens, 3 Stirlings – to bomb the Deutsche Werke submarine yard and the town area. 2 Hampdens and 1 Wellington lost.

Good bombing was claimed in clear weather. Kiel reports bombs in several areas with damage to 2 passenger ships, some warehouses and dwelling-houses. There were no casualties.

BOULOGNE

38 Wellingtons and 9 Whitleys; claimed excellent bombing results on dock areas in perfect visibility. No aircraft lost.

8 Hampdens minelaying in the Frisians. No losses.

Total effort of the night: 303 sorties, 18 aircraft (5·9 per cent) lost. This was the highest loss in one night so far in the war.

---

8 September 1941

4 Fortresses to attack the battleship *Admiral Scheer* at Oslo were intercepted by German fighters before reaching the target. 2 Fortresses were lost and 1 crashed in England.

8/9 September 1941

KASSEL

95 aircraft – 52 Wellingtons, 27 Hampdens, 16 Whitleys – to railway workshops and an armaments factory. No aircraft lost.

This was the first large attack on this target. The weather was clear and good results were claimed. Kassel reports that 2 industrial concerns – a railway-wagon works and an optical-instrument factory – were seriously damaged, 3 public buildings – the Landesbibliothek, the Rotes Palais and the main railway station – were hit and 11 houses were destroyed and 77 damaged. 15 people were killed and 39 injured.

Minor Operations: 7 Wellingtons to Cherbourg, 6 Hampdens minelaying in the Frisians and off Denmark. No losses.

---

10 September 1941

6 Blenheims on shipping sweep off the Dutch Frisians. Ships near Terschelling were attacked but not hit. No losses.

10/11 September 1941

TURIN

76 aircraft – 56 Wellingtons, 13 Stirlings, 7 Halifaxes. 4 Wellingtons and 1 Halifax lost. Bombing was affected by smoke and haze but good results were claimed in the centre of the city and on the Fiat steelworks.

There were 3 O.T.U. leaflet sorties to France without loss.

---

11 September 1941

23 Blenheims on shipping sweeps from Holland to Norway. A convoy off Holland was attacked without success. No aircraft lost.

11/12 September 1941

ROSTOCK

56 aircraft – 39 Hampdens, 12 Wellingtons, 5 Manchesters – to the Heinkel factory and to the harbour but there was much cloud and most crews attacked the town. 2 Hampdens lost.

KIEL

55 Wellingtons to shipyards. 2 aircraft lost.

Most crews bombed the town area. Kiel reports bombs in the Deutsche Werke U-boat yard, a margarine factory, a grain warehouse, a brickworks and on private housing. 4 people were killed and 2 injured.

WARNEMÜNDE

32 Whitleys to attack the docks but most crews bombed the general town area. 1 Whitley lost.

Minor Operations: 20 Wellingtons to Le Havre, 8 aircraft to Boulogne, 20 Hampdens minelaying in the Frisians and off Heligoland and Warnemünde. 1 Whitley from the Boulogne force was lost.

12 September 1941

11 Blenheims on sweeps off the Dutch coast. 1 ship was hit. No aircraft lost.

12/13 September 1941

FRANKFURT

130 aircraft – 71 Wellingtons, 31 Hampdens, 18 Whitleys, 9 Stirlings. 2 Wellingtons lost.

Thick cloud prevented accurate bombing but large fires were claimed. Frankfurt reports 75 high-explosive and 650 incendiary bombs in the city and in the nearby town of Offenbach. Nearly all the damage listed was in civilian housing although 2 bombs destroyed a workshop at the rubber factory in Offenbach. 38 fires were started. 8 people were killed, 17 injured and approximately 200 bombed out.

Mainz, nearly 20 miles from Frankfurt, reports many bombs with 19 people being killed.

Minor Operations: 21 Wellingtons and Whitleys to Cherbourg, 10 Hampdens minelaying in the Frisians and off Denmark. No losses.

13/14 September 1941

BREST

147 aircraft of 6 different types. The 3 warships in the harbour could not be spotted through smoke-screens. 120 aircraft bombed approximate positions. No aircraft lost.

Minor Operations: 8 Hampdens and Wellingtons to Le Havre, 1 O.T.U. sortie. No losses.

---

14 September 1941

12 Blenheims on sweep off the Dutch coast. Ships were attacked but not hit. No losses.

---

15 September 1941

8 Blenheims on sweeps off Holland and Norway. 3 ships were claimed sunk and a seaplane base at Haugesund was bombed. 1 Blenheim lost. 1 Fortress to Cologne turned back.

15/16 September 1941

HAMBURG

169 aircraft of 6 different types with railway stations and shipyards as aiming points. 8 aircraft – 3 Wellingtons, 2 Hampdens, 1 Halifax, 1 Stirling, 1 Whitley – lost.

Conditions were clear over Hamburg but crews found that searchlight glare prevented recognition of targets. Much damage was caused in various parts of Hamburg, with 26 fires – 7 of them large, 82 people killed, 229 injured and 1,441 bombed out. The worst incident was in the Wielandstrasse, a narrow street in the Wandsbek district, where a large block of densely populated flats was destroyed by a 4,000-lb 'blockbuster'. 66 people were killed and 171 injured here, most of the casualties being people who had not bothered to go to the basement shelter. Rescue work was made more difficult when a burning gas main set fire to the timber in the wreckage.

LE HAVRE

45 'freshmen' crews bombed the harbour in clear visibility but fires were started in the town as well as on the docks. 1 Wellington lost.

5 Hampdens minelaying off Warnemünde without loss.

Total effort for the night: 219 sorties, 9 aircraft (4·1 per cent) lost. Flying in one of the aircraft lost on this night, a 75 Squadron Wellington, was Sergeant James Ward, the young New Zealander who had won a Victoria Cross on 7/8 July 1941 by climbing out on to the wing of his aircraft to put out a fire. Sergeant Ward was killed when his Wellington was shot down on the Hamburg raid; his grave is in the Commonwealth War Graves Commission plot in Hamburg's main cemetery.

---

16 September 1941

18 Blenheims on sweep of Dutch and German coasts. 1 ship sunk near Den Helder. No aircraft lost.

16/17 September 1941

KARLSRUHE

55 Wellingtons; only 37 bombed the Karlsruhe area, in conditions of 'intense darkness'. No aircraft lost.

10 Wellingtons to Le Havre; no losses.

---

17 September 1941

24 Blenheims to Mazingarbe power-station and chemical works but only 10 bombed, 6 Hampdens to Marquise could not identify the target and did not bomb, 3 Blenheims on uneventful coastal sweeps. No losses of aircraft in any of the bomber forces.

17/18 September 1941

KARLSRUHE

38 Wellingtons; claimed large fires in the city centre. 1 aircraft lost.

Minor Operations: 1 Wellington to Le Havre, 14 Hampdens minelaying between Heligoland and the Elbe. No losses.

---

18 September 1941

11 Blenheims to a power-station, near Rouen, which was bombed and 5 Hampdens to Abbeville but their operation was unsuccessful and no bombs were dropped. There were no losses on these raids. 9 Further Blenheims carried out shipping patrols. 3 aircraft of 88 Squadron, taking their turn in the *Channel Stop* operation, made a successful attack on a large and strongly escorted tanker off Blankenberg. Their bombs blew off the stern of the ship, which is believed to have sunk, but 2 of the 3 Blenheims were shot down soon afterwards by German fighters.

18/19 September 1941

11 'freshmen' crews to Le Havre; no losses.

19/20 September 1941

STETTIN

72 aircraft, mostly Wellingtons; 60 reached and bombed this distant city but, most of

the individual targets allocated to crews were difficult to find. 1 Wellington and 1 Whitley lost.

---

20 September 1941

48 Blenheims and 6 Hampdens carried out an extensive series of sea sweeps and escorted raids to targets just beyond the French coast. Ships and land targets were bombed. 1 Fortress also bombed Emden. 3 Blenheims lost.

20/21 September 1941

BERLIN

74 aircraft; all were recalled because of worsening weather. 10 aircraft did not receive the signal and bombed alternative targets; none reached Berlin. 3 Wellingtons and 1 Whitley were lost and 12 more aircraft crashed in England.

FRANKFURT

34 aircraft dispatched but were recalled; some flew on and bombed Frankfurt. No aircraft lost but 3 crashed in England.

OSTEND

28 'freshmen' crews dispatched without loss.

---

21 September 1941

12 Blenheims and 6 Hampdens on *Circus* operations to Gosnay and Lille. No losses.

---

22 September 1941

24 Blenheims and 6 Hampdens; all were recalled.

22/23 September 1941

3 Wellingtons to Boulogne. No losses.

---

25 September 1941

1 Fortress to Emden was forced to turn back. This was the last attempt by the R.A.F. to operate Fortress bombers by day. The raids flown since 8 July by the handful of aircraft available to 90 Squadron had met with little success.

26/27 September 1941

COLOGNE, EMDEN, MANNHEIM, GENOA

104 aircraft to these targets were all recalled because of forecasts of fog at bases. 23 aircraft flew on and bombed various targets, including a solitary Wellington piloted by Sergeant Musalek of 311 (Polish) Squadron which reached and bombed Genoa. This aircraft returned safely but 1 Wellington was lost from the Emden raid and 4 more Wellingtons crashed in England.

27 September 1941

24 Blenheims on escorted raids to Amiens railway yards, which were bombed, and to Mazingarbe power-station which was not bombed. No Blenheims lost.

28 September 1941

3 Blenheims on an uneventful shipping sweep off Dunkirk.

28/29 September 1941

FRANKFURT

30 Hampdens and 14 Wellingtons. 1 Hampden and 1 Wellington lost; 5 aircraft crashed in England.

GENOA

39 Wellingtons and 2 Stirlings dispatched and claimed successful bombing. 3 Wellingtons lost.

EMDEN

6 Wellingtons and 1 Stirling. No losses.

29/30 September 1941

STETTIN

139 aircraft – 67 Wellingtons, 56 Whitleys, 10 Stirlings, 6 Halifaxes – to 4 aiming points in Stettin. 8 aircraft – 4 Whitleys, 2 Wellingtons, 2 Stirlings – were lost and 5 aircraft crashed in England. 95 aircraft claimed good bombing in conditions of slight haze.

HAMBURG

93 aircraft – mostly Hampdens and Wellingtons. 2 Wellingtons lost and 2 Hampdens crashed in England.

Searchlight glare prevented accurate bombing. Hamburg reports 9 fires, 48 people killed, 73 injured and 1,102 bombed out but no details of particular damage are available.

Minor Operations: 6 aircraft to Le Havre, 3 to Cherbourg, 5 Manchesters minelaying off Swinemünde. No losses, but 2 aircraft crashed in England. This was the first Manchester minelaying operation.

Total effort for the night: 246 sorties, 10 aircraft (4·1 per cent) lost, 9 further aircraft crashed in England.

---

30 September/1 October 1941

HAMBURG

82 aircraft – 48 Hampdens, 24 Wellingtons, 10 Whitleys. 1 Wellington lost.
    Cloud prevented accurate bombing. Hamburg recorded 14 fires, 8 people killed, 11 injured and 491 bombed out, some temporarily.

STETTIN

40 Wellingtons; 29 bombed. No losses.

Minor Operations: 41 'freshmen' crews to Cherbourg, 2 O.T.U. sorties. No losses.

1/2 October 1941

KARLSRUHE

44 Hampdens and 1 Wellington; all recalled because of fog forecasts at airfields. 3 aircraft flew on to Karlsruhe; 22 bombed alternative targets. 1 Wellington lost.

STUTTGART

27 Whitleys and 4 Wellingtons; only 10 aircraft claimed to have bombed in the Stuttgart area, through thick cloud. Stuttgart records only 1 load of bombs, in woods near the city. No aircraft lost.

Minor Operations: 7 aircraft to Boulogne, 2 Hampdens minelaying in the Frisians. No losses.

---

2 October 1941

6 Blenheims to Le Havre did not reach target.

2/3 October 1941

6 Halifaxes to Brest, bomb bursts claimed in area of warships. No losses.

---

3 October 1941

6 Blenheims bombed a power-station near Ostend without loss.

3/4 October 1941

103 aircraft carried out small raids on Rotterdam, Antwerp and Brest. The only casualty was a Stirling shot down over England by an Intruder.

There were no Bomber Command operations from 5 to 10 October, because of unfavourable weather conditions.

10/11 October 1941

ESSEN

78 aircraft to bomb the Krupps works; only 13 claimed to have bombed in the Essen area, because of bad weather. 2 Hampdens and 2 Whitleys were lost.

COLOGNE

69 aircraft; cloud and haze encountered. Cologne reports only minor damage, with 5 people killed and 6 injured. 5 Wellingtons lost.

Minor Operations: 5 Hampdens on searchlight-suppression flights in support of the Cologne and Essen raids, 23 Hampdens to Dunkirk, 22 Wellingtons and Whitleys to Ostend, 22 Wellingtons to Bordeaux, 13 Wellingtons to Rotterdam. 2 Wellingtons were lost from the Bordeaux raid and 1 Hampden from the Dunkirk raid.

11 October 1941

11 Blenheims were dispatched to the Dutch coast but their escort failed to rendezvous and the operation was abandoned without loss.

11/12 October 1941

EMDEN

27 Wellingtons; the target was cloud-covered and bombing was scattered. No aircraft were lost.

12 Hampdens minelaying in the mouths of the Elbe and Weser rivers. No losses.

12 October 1941

24 Blenheims bombed Boulogne docks without loss.

12/13 October 1941

NUREMBERG

152 aircraft – 82 Wellingtons, 54 Whitleys, 9 Halifaxes, 7 Stirlings – on the first large raid to this city. 8 aircraft – 5 Wellingtons, 1 each of the other types – lost and 5 more aircraft crashed in England.

Crews reported some fires started but some also said these were in villages 10 miles from Nuremberg. The city of Nuremberg reports only a few bombs in and around the city, with 1 person killed and 6 injured. Many more bombs fell on Schwabach, 10 miles south of Nuremberg, which suffered approximately 50 buildings destroyed and 8 or 10 (reports conflict) people killed.

By chance, a letter is available giving details of bombing on this night in the village of Lauingen, on the Danube *sixty-five miles* from Nuremberg. Bombs fell on this small community for 4 hours. Craters from 200 high-explosive bombs were later found and approximately 700 incendiaries fell in the village, with many more bombs falling in the surrounding countryside. 44 houses were destroyed. 4 people died, including the Bürgermeister, who had a heart attack when he saw his village on fire. The villagers could only think at the time that the raid was intended for the nearest industrial town, Ingoldstadt, which was 50 miles further east. Crowds of people came from surrounding areas to see this badly damaged village, so far from any major industrial target.

A further report, from Stuttgart, describes how 46 houses were hit in the small town of Lauffen, on the River Neckar, near one of Stuttgart's regular decoy fire sites. This location is *ninety-five miles* west of Nuremberg!

It is significant that both Lauingen and Lauffen were situated on wide rivers, as was Nuremberg, and it was probably this factor that persuaded a few hopelessly lost crews who were navigating on dead reckoning that they had found Nuremberg. Other crews were then attracted to the scenes of the bombing and joined in. These errors illustrate the navigation difficulties experienced by crews in changeable wind conditions when flying to inland targets, albeit they are extreme examples of such error.

BREMEN

99 aircraft – mostly Wellingtons and Hampdens. 65 aircraft bombed in cloudy conditions and fires were seen. 2 Wellingtons and 1 Hampden lost.

HÜLS

79 Hampdens and 11 Manchesters attempted to bomb the chemical factory at Hüls but this was completely cloud-covered and bombing was scattered. 1 Hampden and 1 Manchester lost.

Minor Operations: 8 Hampdens on searchlight-suppression and airfield attacks, 23 Wellingtons and 1 Whitley to Boulogne. No losses.

Total effort for the night: 373 sorties: this was, by a narrow margin, a new record; the previous highest number was 364 on the night of 8/9 May 1941. 13 aircraft (3·5 per cent) were lost in what was a most disappointing set of raids.

13 October 1941

18 Blenheims on *Circus* operations to Arques and Mazingarbe. 1 Blenheim lost.

13/14 October 1941

DÜSSELDORF

53 Wellingtons and 7 Stirlings; haze resulted in scattered bombing. 1 Wellington lost.

COLOGNE

30 Hampdens and 9 Manchesters; searchlight glare prevented target identification. Cologne reports only a few bombs, 6 people killed and 5 injured, and damage to 17 houses.

Minor Operations: 5 Wellingtons and 1 Stirling to Boulogne, 13 Hampdens minelaying in the Frisians and Kiel Bay. No losses.

14/15 October 1941

NUREMBERG

80 aircraft – 58 Wellingtons, 13 Whitleys, 5 Halifaxes, 4 Stirlings – were dispatched but conditions *en route* were very bad with icing and thick cloud. 51 aircraft bombed alternative targets; 14 aircraft claimed to have bombed the Nuremberg area but only one of these, a Whitley, claimed to have identified and bombed its allocated target in Nuremberg. 4 Wellingtons lost.

Nuremberg reports only 3 groups of bombs within the city area, although one of these hit the Siemens factory and destroyed a workshop there; these may have been the bombs of the individual Whitley quoted above. (This was the aircraft of Squadron Leader A. J. D. Snow, of 78 Squadron, which dropped 6 high-explosive bombs. Squadron Leader Snow was killed in a raid on Hamburg on 3/4 May 1942, just after 78 Squadron converted to Halifaxes. His body is buried at Sage War Cemetery, near Oldenburg.) Several houses were also hit in Nuremberg and 6 people were injured.

12 O.T.U. sorties were flown to France; 2 Wellingtons were lost.

---

15 October 1941

12 Blenheims on escorted raid to Le Havre docks. A tanker and a 10,000-ton merchant ship were claimed hit but the long, steady bombing run employed resulted in 2 Blenheims being shot down. 12 further Blenheims made sweeps off the Frisians and claimed 1 ship hit, but 5 of these aircraft were lost.

15/16 October 1941

COLOGNE

27 Wellingtons and 7 Stirlings. 3 Wellingtons lost.

Crews reported large fires in Cologne but the city recorded only a handful of bombs with no damage or casualties. Villages well east of the Rhine were hit, however, and in one of them, Lindenthal, a children's hospital was hit, though casualties are not mentioned. The synthetic-oil refinery at Wesseling, 7 miles south of Cologne, was hit by a high-explosive bomb which caused 8,000 tons of fuel production to be lost. Duisburg, 30 miles from Cologne, was also bombed, probably in error.

8 Wellingtons bombed Boulogne. No losses.

---

16 October 1941

12 Blenheims on an uneventful sweep off Cherbourg.

16/17 October 1941

DUISBURG

87 aircraft – 47 Wellingtons, 26 Hampdens, 14 Whitleys – with 8 further Hampdens carrying out searchlight-suppression flights. The target was cloud-covered and only estimated positions were bombed. 1 Wellington lost.

Minor Operations: 22 aircraft to Dunkirk, 15 aircraft to Ostend. 1 Wellington lost.

---

17 October 1941

12 Blenheims on an uneventful sweep off Cherbourg.

---

20 October 1941

8 Blenheims on sweep of Dutch coast. 1 Flak ship was attacked off Terschelling, with either a hit or a near miss. No Blenheims lost.

20/21 October 1941

BREMEN

153 aircraft – 82 Hampdens, 48 Wellingtons, 15 Stirlings, 8 Manchesters – to 2 aiming points. 5 aircraft – 2 Hampdens, 2 Wellingtons, 1 Manchester – lost.

Returning crews claimed to have started fires in the target area. The Bremen report records only that this was a 'small raid' and gives no details.

WILHELMSHAVEN

47 aircraft – 40 Whitleys, 4 Wellingtons, 3 Hampdens – none lost.

The weather was poor and crews reported scattered bombing. Wilhelmshaven reports 3 loads of bombs in areas of housing with 7 people killed and 7 injured.

EMDEN

35 Wellingtons and 1 Halifax. Fires were claimed on the docks and in the town. 1 Wellington lost.

ANTWERP

35 aircraft; complete cloud cover resulted in most crews retaining their bombs. 3 Wellingtons lost.

Minor Operations: 5 Hampdens and 5 Manchesters minelaying in the Frisians and the Baltic, 8 O.T.U. sorties. No losses.

Total effort for the night: 284 sorties, 9 aircraft (3·2 per cent) lost.

---

21 October 1941

17 Blenheims on coastal sweeps. Hits were claimed on 2 ships off Terschelling. 2 Blenheims lost.

21/22 October 1941

BREMEN

136 aircraft of 5 types to attack shipyards. 2 Wellingtons and 1 Hampden lost.

Crews reported industrial haze which caused difficulty in identifying targets. Bremen reports scattered bombing, mostly in housing areas, though damage was caused to 4 small industrial firms and 1 bomb fell in the Vulkan shipyard. 17 people were killed, 29 injured and 70 bombed out.

Minor Operations: 12 Hampdens and Wellingtons to Boulogne, 4 Manchesters minelaying in Kiel Bay. No losses.

---

22 October 1941

3 Blenheims on an uneventful sweep off the Dutch coast.

22/23 October 1941

MANNHEIM

123 aircraft – 50 Wellingtons, 45 Hampdens, 22 Whitleys, 6 Halifaxes. 3 Wellingtons and 1 Hampden lost.

Crews encountered thick cloud and icing conditions and only 58 crews claimed to have reached the Mannheim area. 42 aircraft bombed alternative targets. Mannheim reports a very light attack with 25 high-explosive and approximately 30 incendiary bombs. 1 house was destroyed and 35 damaged. 6 people were killed and 1 person injured.

Minor Operations: 22 aircraft to Le Havre, 6 Stirlings to Brest. 1 Wellington lost from the Le Havre raid.

---

23 October 1941

12 Blenheims to Lannion and Morlaix airfields. Only Lannion was found, and bombed in poor weather conditions. No Blenheims lost.

23/24 October 1941

KIEL

114 aircraft – 43 Wellingtons, 38 Hampdens, 27 Whitleys, 6 Manchesters – to attack shipyards. 1 Hampden lost.

Only 69 crews reached the target area. Kiel reports a raid in two widely separated waves. The second attack caused the most damage, with hits on the Deutsche Werke U-boat yard, the naval base, a bakery, a dance-hall and several houses. 4 people were killed – one on a ship in the harbour – and 5 people injured. The diarist, Detlef Boelck, records his great satisfaction and confidence in the local defences when 3 bombers were caught in searchlights at the same time and 1 was shot down while trying to dive out of the beams.

Minor Operations: 13 aircraft to Le Havre, 9 Stirlings to Brest, 4 aircraft to Cherbourg. 1 Hampden lost on the Le Havre raid.

---

24 October 1941

18 Blenheims on uneventful sweeps off the Dutch coast.

24/25 October 1941

FRANKFURT

70 aircraft; only 8 reported reaching the target area, in difficult weather conditions, 57 aircraft bombed elsewhere. 4 aircraft – 2 Wellingtons, 1 Hampden, 1 Whitley – lost.

Minor Operations: 12 Wellingtons to Emden, 6 Stirlings to Brest, 1 Wellington to Cherbourg. No losses.

---

25 October 1941

4 Blenheims on an uneventful sweep off Norway.

---

26 October 1941

8 Blenheims on a sweep off the Dutch coast. Ships were attacked but not hit. 1 Blenheim lost.

26/27 October 1941

HAMBURG

115 aircraft of 5 different types to shipyards and 2 city aiming points. 3 Wellingtons and 1 Hampden lost.

Crews reported good bombing in moonlight and Hamburg records confirm that more damage and casualties were caused than on average raids for this period. It is believed that 27 people were killed and 129 injured and that there were 10 to 12 fires but the table of figures consulted is not clear.

Minor Operations: 17 aircraft to Cherbourg, 5 Hampdens minelaying in Kiel Bay. No losses.

---

27 October 1941

6 Blenheims on sweeps off the Dutch coast. A convoy was attacked but no results were seen. 2 Blenheims lost.

28/29 October 1941

Minor Operations

17 Wellingtons and 7 Whitleys to Cherbourg but only 13 reached the target. 10 Stirlings to the Škoda works at Pilsen in Czechoslovakia but none reached the target; 8 bombed places in Germany. 2 O.T.U. sorties. No losses in any operation.

29/30 October 1941

SCHIPHOL AIRFIELD

40 Hampdens and 5 Manchesters; the airfield was not identified because of cloud. 1 Hampden lost.

BREST

16 Wellingtons attacked Brest but could not identify the locations of the warship targets. No losses.

30/31 October 1941

1 Stirling dropped leaflets over France and returned safely.

---

31 October 1941

9 Blenheims on sweeps off the Danish coast. 1 ship was claimed hit. No losses.

31 October/1 November 1941

HAMBURG

123 aircraft of 5 different types. 4 Whitleys lost.

Crews reported that visibility in the target area was bad and only 56 crews claimed to have bombed there. Hamburg reports no major incidents but 14 fires – 7 of them large ones, 1 person killed, 8 injured and 175 bombed out.

BREMEN

40 Wellingtons and 8 Stirlings; the weather was bad and only 13 crews claimed to have found the target. The Bremen diary has no entry for this night. 1 Wellington lost.

Minor Operations: 25 aircraft to Dunkirk, 7 to Boulogne, 17 Hampdens and 1 Manchester minelaying in the Frisians, the mouth of the Weser and in Kiel Bay, 2 O.T.U. sorties. 1 Halifax lost from the Dunkirk raid.

Total effort for the night: 223 sorties, 6 aircraft (2·7 per cent) lost.

1 November 1941

16 Blenheims on raids to airfields in Brittany and on uneventful sweeps off Norway. No losses.

1/2 November 1941

KIEL

134 aircraft – 72 Wellingtons, 32 Hampdens, 30 Whitleys – to attack harbour targets. 2 Whitleys and 1 Hampden lost.

Only 70 crews reported reaching the target area. Kiel's records state that searchlights could not penetrate thick, low cloud and that aircraft were heard to the east but no bombs fell in Kiel.

Minor Operations: 17 aircraft to Brest, 13 to Le Havre, 5 Hampdens and 2 Manchesters minelaying in Kiel Bay, 4 Hampdens made a night shipping patrol off the Frisians and bombed a convoy without scoring hits, 3 O.T.U. sorties. 1 Hampden from the shipping patrol was lost.

2 November 1941

4 Blenheims on an uneventful shipping sweep off Norway.

This day's sweep ended the long series of shipping searches and attacks carried out by the Blenheim squadrons of 2 Group. Since commencing these raids in March

1941, when Bomber Command was directed to turn its main attention on German U-boats and surface vessels, the Blenheims had pressed home their attacks on heavily defended ships in the most gallant manner. An Admiralty assessment committee estimated that 101 ships, totalling 328,000 tons, had been sunk or seriously damaged in this period. Post-war German records showed that 29 ships of 29,836 tons were actually sunk and 21 ships of 43,715 tons were seriously damaged.* The Blenheim squadrons lost 139 aircraft on low-level shipping and harbour raids during this period plus many more aircraft badly damaged. The Blenheim shipping campaign was now called off because these casualties could no longer be justified.

3/4 November 1941

Minor Operations

8 Wellingtons to Brest, 7 aircraft to Boulogne, 6 Hampdens on shipping patrol attacked a convoy in the Frisians, 10 Hampdens minelaying in the North Sea. No losses.

4/5 November 1941

ESSEN

28 Wellingtons; only 9 crews claimed to have found and attacked the Krupps works. No aircraft lost.

Minor Operations: 20 aircraft to Dunkirk and Ostend, 9 Hampdens on shipping patrols in the Frisians and in the Kiel area, 24 Hampdens and 4 Manchesters minelaying in Kiel Bay. No losses.

---

5 November 1941

3 Stirlings on cloud-cover raids to the Ruhr turned back.

5/6 November 1941

Minor Operations

22 Hampdens and 2 Manchesters to Cherbourg, 11 Hampdens on shipping patrols in the Frisians and in the Hamburg area, 24 Hampdens minelaying in Kiel Bay. 3 Hampdens from the shipping operations and 1 minelaying aircraft were lost.

6/7 November 1941

Minor Operations

9 Wellingtons to Le Havre, 6 Hampdens on patrols off the German coast and over the mainland, 15 Hampdens minelaying near Oslo, 3 O.T.U. sorties. 1 minelaying Hampden lost.

---

* Details from Bowyer, op. cit., p. 163.

7/8 November 1941

The operations of this night proved to be of great significance. No doubt frustrated by the recent long run of bad weather and poor bombing results, Sir Richard Peirse decided to mount a major effort on this night, with Berlin as the main target. He persisted in this decision despite a late weather forecast which showed that there would be a large area of bad weather with storms, thick cloud, icing and hail over the North Sea routes by which the bombers would need to fly to Berlin and back. Air Vice-Marshal Slessor of 5 Group objected to the plan and was allowed to withdraw his part of the Berlin force and send it to Cologne instead.

392 aircraft were sent out on the night's operations. This was a new record effort for Bomber Command and probably represents the maximum number of serviceable aircraft with crews available at that time.

BERLIN

169 aircraft – 101 Wellingtons, 42 Whitleys, 17 Stirlings, 9 Halifaxes – of 1, 3 and 4 Groups. 21 aircraft – 10 Wellingtons, 9 Whitleys, 2 Stirlings – were lost, 12·4 per cent of those dispatched.

12. A big fuss being made of an unexploded bomb which has been disarmed in a still intact street near the centre of Berlin. The men in striped clothes are political prisoners or criminals who could earn partial remission of their sentences if they volunteered to dig up unexploded bombs.

73 aircraft reached the general area of Berlin but could only claim fires on the outskirts of the city, with other results being 'unobserved'. Berlin reports scattered bombing in many areas. Premises hit by the bombing were: 1 industrial, 2 railway, 2 public utility (a gasometer at Staaken was burnt out), 2 official buildings, 30 houses, 16 wooden garden houses, and 1 farm building. The only buildings classed as 'de-

stroyed' were 14 of the houses. Casualties were: 11 people killed, 44 injured, 637 people bombed out and receiving official help, with a further number going to the homes of relatives and friends.

This was the last major raid on Berlin until January 1943.

COLOGNE

61 Hampdens and 14 Manchesters of 5 Group. No aircraft lost.

Crews reported many fires but Cologne recorded only 8 high-explosive and 60 incendiary bombs, with 5 people killed and 5 injured, 2 houses destroyed and 14 damaged; there was no industrial damage.

MANNHEIM

53 Wellingtons and 2 Stirlings of 1 and 3 Groups. 7 Wellingtons lost.

43 crews bombed in this area and reported a large fire. A specific request to Mannheim for a report for this particularly important night brought the reply that there was no record of any bombs falling in the city. It is not known where the bombs of this force fell.

Minor Operations: 30 Halifaxes, Hampdens, Wellingtons and Whitleys were sent on 'rover patrols' in the Essen and other areas; 6 aircraft – 2 Hampdens, 2 Wellingtons, 1 Halifax, 1 Whitley – were lost from these flights. 28 aircraft sent to Ostend and 22 to Boulogne operated without loss. 13 Halifaxes went minelaying near Oslo and 3 were lost.

Total effort for the night: 392 sorties, 37 aircraft (9·4 per cent) lost. This loss was more than double the previous highest for night operations. It is probable that many of the casualties crashed in the North Sea, suffering from icing or fuel exhaustion in the bad weather conditions there.

---

8 November 1841

11 Blenheims on escorted raids to Lille and Gosnay. Only the power-station at Gosnay was bombed. No Blenheims lost.

8/9 November 1941

ESSEN

54 aircraft; 35 bombed, claiming large fires. 6 aircraft – 3 Wellingtons, 2 Whitleys, 1 Hampden – lost. 8 further Hampdens made searchlight-suppression flights; 1 of these was lost.

Minor Operations: 18 aircraft to Dunkirk and 8 to Ostend. 1 Wellington was lost from the Dunkirk raid.

9/10 November 1941

HAMBURG

103 aircraft of 6 types. 1 Wellington lost.

71 aircraft claimed to have bombed Hamburg, starting fires in docks and city areas. Hamburg reports 3 large fires, 13 people killed, 56 injured and 393 bombed out. One bomb caused a major disappointment to the people of Hamburg when it set fire to the express-goods parcel store at the main railway station. It was 'film change-over day' in Hamburg and the entire stock of films for the area was destroyed. No other major incident was recorded.

Minor Operations: 9 aircraft to Ostend, 7 aircraft to Dunkirk, 5 Hampdens minelaying in the mouths of the Elbe and Weser rivers. 1 Hampden lost from the Ostend raid.

Operational Statistics, 7/8 July to 10 November 1941
(126 days/nights)

Number of days with operations: 83
Number of nights with operations: 92
Number of daylight sorties: 1,567, from which 112 aircraft (7·1 per cent) were lost
Number of night sorties: 11,991, from which 414 aircraft (3·5 per cent) were lost
Total sorties: 13,558, from which 526 (3·9 per cent) were lost
Approximate bomb tonnage in period: 14,851 tons
Averages per 24-hour period: 107·6 sorties, 4·2 aircraft lost, 117·9 tons of bombs dropped

9. WINTER QUARTERS

10/11 November 1941 to 22 February 1942

The two vital factors in any military campaign – the achievements compared to the casualties sustained – had now moved adversely against Bomber Command. It is an old maxim of warfare that heavy casualties can be sustained only as long as comparable results are being obtained. It was now quite obvious that Bomber Command was not gaining results to justify the recent run of heavy casualties either by night or by day.

Let us deal with the evidence available on bombing results first. Disturbing reports of the ineffectiveness of attacks on targets in Germany had been arriving at the Air Ministry through neutral countries for many months. During the first half of 1941, the R.A.F. had also been collecting its own evidence from three sources. Firstly, there was a multitude of verbal reports from returning bomber crews, processed and passed on with varying degrees of optimism by squadrons and groups to produce the final intelligence reports on which most public announcements were based. Then came the newly formed Photographic Reconnaissance Unit, although this had only been able to produce a very limited daylight cover of a very few targets. This evidence conflicted sharply with the crew reports but was too scanty to be accepted as conclusive. The only depth of sure evidence in the possession of the R.A.F. was the accumulated stock of individual aircraft bombing photographs taken by that proportion of the force whose planes were fitted with bombing cameras. In the middle of the year it was decided that a survey should be made of all such recent photographs. That decision was not made by Bomber Command or even by the Air Ministry; it was taken on the initiative of Lord Cherwell, scientific adviser to the Prime Minister and the War Cabinet. The actual work was carried out by Mr D. M. Butt, a civil servant in the War Cabinet secretariat.

The famous Butt Report was completed by 18 August. Its conclusions were a sensation. Mr Butt analysed 4,065 individual aircraft photographs taken in 100 night raids in June and July 1941. Despite the fact that it was usually the best crews in squadrons who were given these cameras, only one in four of the crews which claimed to have bombed a target in Germany were found to have been within five miles of that target. In the full-moon period, the proportion of crews whose bombs fell in the five-mile zone increased to two in five on all targets (about one in three over German targets) while, in the non-moon periods of each month, the five-mile zone was hit by one in fifteen crews on all targets (about one in twenty on German targets). In the Ruhr, which was usually affected by industrial haze, the proportion of successful crews was considerably less. These disappointing figures were further worsened by the fact that only the photographs of crews reporting successful bombing in the first place had contributed to the figures; one third of all crews dispatched did not even claim to have reached the target area!

Early in the war, Bomber Command had been forced to turn the majority of its effort to night bombing by the harsh fact that bombers could not defend themselves in daylight operations. Recent casualties in 2 Group confirmed that these rules had not changed, even though most of the Luftwaffe day-fighter force was in Russia. The Butt Report, taken with other evidence available, seemed to prove with equal harshness that Bomber Command, with its present navigation equipment, standard of crew training and methods of tactical employment, could not hit its targets with any accuracy, even on the best moonlit nights in summer weather. The Butt Report finally showed the R.A.F. what officials in German cities had been recording all the time and what this diary is revealing in its entries for night after night.

The contents of the report were shown to Sir Richard Peirse and his group commanders. Their attempts to explain the report's implications impressed neither the Air Ministry nor the War Cabinet. In his operations during the weeks after the report was issued, there is evidence that Peirse was no longer concentrating on the offensive against the priority targets which would cut off the transportation links from the Ruhr war industries. The bombers were sent instead to places of lesser importance in the hope that he could counter the adverse comments of the Butt Report by gaining successes on targets which were less well protected by Flak, searchlights and ground haze. There is also evidence, however, that the proportion of crews prepared to press on through difficult conditions and bomb even those secondary targets was declining. In short, Bomber Command was losing its confidence.

As far as the bomber crews were concerned it was that other part of the equation – the casualties incurred – which meant more to them than a Whitehall-produced report of which they had never heard. The latest round of operations – classified in this diary as 7/8 July to 10 November – had cost 414 night bombers and 112 day bombers lost over enemy territory, in the sea or shot down over England by German Intruders. This was approximately equivalent to the loss of Bomber Command's entire front-line strength of aircraft and crews in four months. The percentage loss of aircraft dispatched was 3·5 per cent by night and 7·1 per cent by day.

The views held by Bomber Command and Air Ministry on this dual state of affairs – results and losses – did not matter; it was the Prime Minister who decided the next move. Sir Richard Peirse was summoned to what must have been an uncomfortable meeting with Churchill at Chequers the evening after the heavy loss raid to Berlin of 7/8 November. The War Cabinet later discussed the situation at length and informed the Air Ministry of its decision. The bomber offensive, in its present form, was to be virtually halted to allow for the passage of the midwinter months and the formulation of a new policy. On 13 November the Air Ministry informed Sir Richard Peirse that only limited operations were to be carried out in the coming months while the whole future of Bomber Command was debated.

The squadrons would be subject to these orders for more than three months, a period which would see further world-shattering events. A British offensive in North Africa which commenced on 18 November made good progress and relieved the siege of Tobruk, but Rommel's Afrika Korps counter-attacked and would chase the Eighth Army back again in January. On 7 December the Japanese struck at Pearl Harbor and many other places and a new war flared across the Pacific and South-East Asia. Britain lost two capital ships, the *Prince of Wales* and the *Repulse*, off Malaya on 10 December and then the great base at Singapore surrendered in February. Those were grim days for Britain and her resources would be stretched to the limit, a factor that might affect the future of Bomber Command. There was one beacon in the darkness. Three days after the Japanese struck in the East, Hitler, although already locked in battle with the Russians, made the fateful decision to declare war on the United States. Having failed to knock Britain out of the war when she had no Allies, Hitler had now succeeded in bringing in on Britain's side the two most powerful nations in the world. Although there were dark days still to come, Hitler had now sealed his own fate. But what part would R.A.F. Bomber Command play in that process?

There were no Bomber Command operations from 10 to 15 November 1941.

15/16 November 1941

EMDEN

49 aircraft; bombing results were not observed because of cloud. 4 Wellingtons lost.

KIEL

47 aircraft; 4 Wellingtons lost. Only 8 aircraft reported bombing the target area. Kiel reports a cloudy night and no bombs.

Minor Operations: 9 Wellingtons to Boulogne, 5 Hampdens minelaying in the Frisians. No losses.

18/19 November 1941

Brest

6 Stirlings to bomb warships. Only 3 aircraft bombed the approximate position of the ships. No losses.

23/24 November 1941

LORIENT

51 Hampdens and 2 Manchesters. Fires were seen in the vicinity of the docks. No losses.

DUNKIRK

36 Wellingtons and 1 Stirling; only 7 aircraft bombed the primary target. No losses.

Minor Operations: 11 Stirlings to Brest, 4 O.T.U. sorties. No losses.

24 November 1941

4 Stirlings on cloud-cover raids to Germany but only 1 aircraft bombed ships off the Frisians. No losses.

25 November 1941

6 Blenheims bombed Morlaix airfield. 3 Stirlings to Germany turned back. No aircraft lost.

25/26 November 1941

Brest

11 Halifaxes and 7 Stirlings; smoke-screens concealed the German warships. No losses.

Cherbourg

17 Wellingtons and claimed a large fire in the dock area. No losses.

26/27 November 1941

EMDEN

80 Wellingtons and 20 Hampdens; only 55 aircraft bombed in cloudy conditions. 2 Wellingtons and 1 Hampden lost. No report is available from Emden.

Ostend

16 Wellingtons and 2 Stirlings; only 7 aircraft bombed. No losses.

27/28 November 1941

DÜSSELDORF

86 aircraft – 41 Wellingtons, 34 Hampdens, 6 Manchesters, 5 Stirlings. 1 Hampden and 1 Wellington lost.

52 aircraft claimed to have bombed the target and started large fires in the railway yards. Düsseldorf reports only 2 high-explosive bombs and 200 incendiaries, fire and damage at a water-purification plant, light damage to housing, no casualties.

Cologne reports bombs and damage to 119 properties, with 4 people killed and 15 injured.

Minor Operations: 6 Wellingtons and 1 Stirling to Ostend, 5 Hampdens minelaying off Wilhelmshaven. No losses.

30 November/1 December 1941

HAMBURG

181 aircraft – 92 Wellingtons, 48 Hampdens, 24 Whitleys, 11 Halifaxes, 4 Manchesters, 2 Stirlings – to bomb shipyards and 3 aiming points in the city. 13 aircraft – 6 Wellingtons, 4 Whitleys, 2 Hampdens, 1 Halifax – lost.

122 aircraft claimed good bombing results in moonlit conditions; 35 aircraft bombed alternative targets. Hamburg reports 22 fires – 2 large, 65 people killed, 176 injured and more than 2,500 bombed out.

Kiel reports bombs but no casualties and 4 bombers shot down in flames by the local Flak.

EMDEN

50 aircraft; good bombing results claimed. 1 Wellington and 1 Whitley lost.

Minor Operations: 3 aircraft to Ostend, 8 Hampdens minelaying in Baltic, 4 O.T.U. sorties. No losses.

Total effort for the night: 246 sorties, 15 aircraft (6·1 per cent) lost.

7/8 December 1941

AACHEN

130 aircraft dispatched with the headquarters building of the local Nazi party as their aiming point. This would have the same result as a general area attack on the centre of the town. 1 Halifax and 1 Hampden lost.

Only 64 aircraft claimed to have bombed Aachen, in difficult weather conditions. The Aachen report (incorrectly dated 8/9 December 1941) describes an attack by an estimated 16 aircraft, some of which flew as low as 400 metres to find the town. Only 5 high explosives – 2 of them duds – 9 incendiaries and a few leaflets – fell on Aachen itself. The Aachen-West railway goods yards were hit by 3 bombs, and 7 houses were slightly damaged by other bombs. There were no casualties. Many bombs fell in open ground north of Aachen.

BREST

23 Wellingtons and 7 Stirlings; only 3 aircraft bombed the approximate location of the warship targets. Stirlings of 7 and 15 Squadrons carried out the first operational trials of the *Oboe* device on this raid. Further trials would be carried out in other raids on Brest in December. (The characteristics of *Oboe* are described later.) There were no aircraft losses on this raid.

Minor Operations: 24 Wellingtons to Calais, 23 Blenheims to Ostend, 17 Whitleys and 5 Wellingtons to Dunkirk, 19 Wellingtons, Hampdens and Manchesters to Boulogne, 3 O.T.U. sorties. Losses: 1 Blenheim on the Ostend raid, 1 Manchester on the Boulogne raid, 1 Wellington on the Dunkirk raid.

Total effort for the night: 251 sorties, 5 aircraft (2·0 per cent) lost.

8/9 December 1941

6 O.T.U. Wellingtons dropped leaflets over Paris without loss.

---

9 December 1941

4 Stirlings to Germany but only 1 aircraft bombed ships off the Dutch coast. No aircraft lost.

10 December 1941

5 Hampdens to Dutch and German coasts all attacked targets such as ships, airfields and transport. 10 further Hampdens minelaying in the Frisians. No losses.

11 December 1941

6 Hampdens on coastal raids. Aurich and Leeuwarden airfields and a town, believed to be Borkum, were bombed. No aircraft lost.

11/12 December 1941
COLOGNE

60 aircraft. Only 23 aircraft reported bombing primary targets, starting a large fire, but Cologne has no record of bombs. The fire was probably a decoy. 1 Halifax lost.

Minor Operations: 34 aircraft to Le Havre, 21 to Brest, 5 Hampdens minelaying off Kiel. 2 Hampdens were lost, 1 each on the Le Havre and Kiel raids.

12 December 1941

6 Hampdens to Brest and 6 Hampdens on cloud-cover raids to Germany. The Brest raid was abandoned but 3 aircraft of the second force bombed targets in Germany. 1 Hampden sent to Gelsenkirchen was lost.

12/13 December 1941
BREST

18 Wellingtons and 6 Stirlings; bombing results were obscured by Flak and searchlights. No aircraft lost.

Dunkirk

6 Wellingtons and 3 Stirlings bombed Dunkirk without loss.

13 December 1941

16 Hampdens to Brest, 6 bombing and 10 minelaying. The bombing raid was abandoned. Of the minelaying force, 6 aircraft laid mines but 2 were lost.

14/15 December 1941

BREST

22 Hampdens and 6 Stirlings; only 1 aircraft claimed to have bombed the target. 1 Hampden lost.

Minor Operations: 3 Hampdens to Cherbourg, 2 Hampdens minelaying off Brest. 2 Hampdens lost on the Cherbourg raid.

15/16 December 1941

OSTEND

25 aircraft; 1 Hampden lost.

Brest

10 Wellingtons and 7 Stirlings. A large white explosion was seen but no other results were observed, because of cloud. No aircraft lost.

5 Hampdens laid mines in the Wilhelmshaven area without loss.

16/17 December 1941

WILHELMSHAVEN

83 aircraft – 57 Wellingtons, 14 Hampdens, 12 Whitleys – reported starting large fires throughout the target area but the Wilhelmshaven diary records only 'slight damage' and no casualties. No aircraft lost.

Minor Operations: 40 aircraft to Brest – 22 bombing and 18 minelaying, 32 aircraft to Ostend, 14 to Dunkirk, 4 O.T.U. sorties. 1 Whitley was lost from the Dunkirk raid.

17/18 December 1941

BREST

121 aircraft – 72 Wellingtons, 25 Hampdens, 24 Whitleys; 80 claimed to have bombed the approximate position of the German warships. 1 Hampden lost.

Minor Operations: 14 aircraft to Le Havre but only 1 aircraft bombed, 2 O.T.U. sorties. 1 Whitley lost from the Le Havre raid.

18 December 1941

BREST

47 aircraft – 18 Halifaxes, 18 Stirlings, 11 Manchesters – attempted a daylight raid on the German warships. Accurate bombing was claimed and black smoke was reported rising from the *Gneisenau*. 6 aircraft – 4 Stirlings, 1 Halifax, 1 Manchester – lost.

18/19 December 1941

Brest

19 Whitleys; no losses.

21 December 1941

12 Hampdens on what were recorded as 'Intruder operations' but the flights were all abandoned. 1 aircraft lost.

22 December 1941

3 Hampdens on 'rover patrols' did not proceed with their flights. No losses.

22/23 December 1941

WILHELMSHAVEN

12 Whitleys and 10 Wellingtons; cloud cover caused bombing difficulties. No aircraft lost. Wilhelmshaven reports bombs in 3 streets with several houses destroyed, 2 children killed and 8 people injured.

23/24 December 1941

COLOGNE

68 aircraft – 33 Wellingtons, 20 Hampdens, 15 Whitleys. The target was difficult to find. 29 crews claimed to have bombed at Cologne with a further 34 crews believing that they had bombed in the target area, but Cologne has no reports of any bombs. No aircraft were lost.

BREST

38 Wellingtons and 9 Stirlings. No losses.

Minor Operations: 9 Wellingtons to Ostend, 3 Wellingtons to Dunkirk, 17 Hampdens minelaying in the Frisians and off Kiel. No losses.

24 December 1941

6 Hampdens 'roving' in north-west Germany and 4 Hampdens to Brest; only 1 aircraft bombed, at Brest. No losses.

27 December 1941

THE VAAGSÖ RAID

The first Combined Operations raid of the war against German-held territory took place on this day when naval ships landed Commandos on the island of Vaagsö off the Norwegian coast. Bomber Command provided 19 Blenheims and 10 Hampdens for supporting operations.

6 Blenheims of 110 Squadron made an attack on shipping off the Norwegian coast in the Oberstad area to draw off German fighters from the Commando raid. A convoy was found and attacked but ships' defences and fighters caused the loss of 4 Blenheims. 13 Blenheims of 114 Squadron made a successful low-level raid on a German fighter airfield at Herdla but 2 Blenheims collided over the target and crashed. 7 Hampdens of 50 Squadron were sent to lay a smoke-screen at Vaagsö but 2 were shot down, probably by shore defences. 3 more Hampdens from the same squadron bombed a German gun position covering the approaches to Vaagsö.

The Vaagsö landing attained all its objectives and was regarded as a great success. The naval and army casualties were negligible but Bomber Command losses were 8 aircraft out of the 29 dispatched.

27/28 December 1941

DÜSSELDORF

132 aircraft – 66 Wellingtons, 30 Hampdens, 29 Whitleys, 7 Manchesters. 5 Whitleys and 2 Wellingtons lost.

96 aircraft claimed to have bombed Düsseldorf but the city reports only 32 high-explosive bombs and 3 batches of incendiaries. There was only very light damage and no casualties.

Minor Operations: 34 'freshmen' crews to Boulogne, 23 Wellingtons and 6 Stirlings to Brest, 6 Blenheims to Soesterberg airfield and 5 Hampdens minelaying off Kiel. There were no losses.

The Blenheims attacking Soesterberg were flying the first in a new series of Intruder raids against Luftwaffe airfields. Using far better intelligence on the identity of which airfields were likely to be active, this represents the start of a determined R.A.F. Intruder campaign which would be waged until the end of the war using aircraft of both Bomber and Fighter Commands. The Blenheims operating on this night, from 82 Squadron, dropped bombs on Soesterberg airfield and attacked 2 German bombers in the air with machine-guns.

Total effort for the night: 206 sorties, 7 aircraft (3·4 per cent) lost.

28/29 December 1941

WILHELMSHAVEN

86 Wellingtons, 1 lost.

The visibility was excellent and crews claimed good results. Wilhelmshaven records this as a heavy raid with widespread damage. Among the buildings mentioned as damaged were: the main railway station, the town library, 3 large business buildings, a naval clothing store, the naval fencing academy, the Christuskirche and much private housing. 10 people were killed and 75 injured.

HÜLS

81 Hampdens to attack the chemical works. Good bombing claimed. 4 aircraft lost.

EMDEN

40 aircraft – 25 Wellingtons, 14 Whitleys, 1 Stirling – claimed good results. 1 Whitley lost.

Minor Operations: 4 Wellingtons to Dunkirk, 6 Blenheim Intruders to Dutch airfields. There were no losses.

Total effort for the night: 217 sorties, 6 aircraft (2·8 per cent) lost.

---

30 December 1941

16 Halifaxes to attack warships in Brest harbour. 14 aircraft bombed in the correct area. 3 Halifaxes were lost and all those which returned were damaged by Flak.

---

2 January 1942

12 Hampdens on 'roving patrols' of Dutch and German coasts. Only 1 aircraft bombed, at Leeuwarden airfield. No Hampdens lost.

2/3 January 1942

BREST

22 Wellingtons and 9 Stirlings. Only 7 aircraft bombed the primary target. No aircraft lost.

ST-NAZAIRE

15 Whitleys and 12 Manchesters. Only 8 aircraft bombed the primary target. No aircraft lost.

Minor Operations: 36 Hampdens minelaying in the Frisians and off the French Biscay ports, 8 O.T.U. sorties. No losses.

3/4 January 1942

Brest, The Frisians

14 Wellingtons and 4 Stirlings to Brest, 10 Hampdens minelaying. 1 Wellington and 1 Hampden lost.

---

4 January 1942

12 Hampdens on roving patrols. Some minor attacks made. No aircraft lost.

5/6 January 1942

BREST

154 aircraft – 89 Wellingtons, 65 of other types – 87 aircraft being ordered to bomb the *Scharnhorst* and *Gneisenau*, the remainder being given the naval docks generally as their target. A smoke-screen prevented accurate bombing but large fires were claimed. No aircraft lost.

Minor Operations: 37 aircraft to Cherbourg, 5 Hampdens minelaying in Quiberon Bay, 5 O.T.U. sorties. No losses.

6/7 January 1942

Brest

31 Wellingtons of 1 Group attacked the German warships. 1 aircraft lost. No special bombing results were claimed but a bomb which fell alongside the *Gneisenau* holed the hull and flooded 2 compartments.

Minor Operations: 19 Hampdens on roving patrols over Northern Germany, 11 Whitleys to Stavanger airfield, 5 Wellingtons to Cherbourg, 16 O.T.U. sorties. No losses.

7/8 January 1942

FRENCH PORTS

68 Wellingtons to Brest and 27 aircraft to St-Nazaire. No losses.

8/9 January 1942

BREST

151 aircraft to Brest. 1 Manchester lost.

Minor Operations: 31 aircraft to Cherbourg, 5 Hampdens minelaying in the Frisians, 2 O.T.U. sorties. 1 Wellington lost on the Cherbourg raid.

9/10 January 1942

BREST

82 aircraft. No losses.

Minor Operations: 5 Hampdens minelaying off Brest, 1 Manchester on leaflet flight to France. 1 Hampden lost.

10/11 January 1942

WILHELMSHAVEN

124 aircraft; good bombing claimed but Wilhelmshaven records this only as a small raid with light damage and 6 people injured. 3 Wellingtons and 2 Hampdens lost.

Minor Operations: 29 aircraft to Emden, 2 Wellingtons to Boulogne, 5 Hampdens minelaying off Wilhelmshaven, 6 Blenheim Intruders to Holland, 1 Hampden on a leaflet flight to France. 1 Blenheim Intruder lost.

11/12 January 1942

BREST

23 Wellingtons and 3 Stirlings. No losses.

14/15 January 1942

HAMBURG

95 aircraft with shipyards and an airframe factory as targets. 2 Hampdens and 2 Wellingtons lost.

Only 48 aircraft claimed to have bombed Hamburg, which reports Altona station hit and 12 fires – 7 large, with 6 people killed and 22 injured – but no other major incidents.

Minor Operations: 18 aircraft to Emden, 11 aircraft to Rotterdam, 17 Blenheim Intruders to Dutch airfields, 5 Hampdens minelaying off Kiel and Warnemünde. 1 Intruder lost.

15/16 January 1942

HAMBURG

96 aircraft. 52 of them claimed to have bombed in difficult visibility. Hamburg reports 36 fires – 3 large, 3 people killed and 25 injured – but no major incidents. 3 Wellingtons and 1 Hampden were lost and 8 further aircraft crashed in England.

EMDEN

50 aircraft; claimed many fires. 1 Wellington and 1 Whitley lost.

Minor Operations: 5 Blenheims and 4 Wellingtons Intruding and bombing Dutch airfields, 3 Hampdens minelaying in the Frisians. No losses.

17/18 January 1942

BREMEN

83 aircraft; only 8 aircraft claimed to have bombed the primary target. Some of the aircraft attacking alternative targets reached Hamburg, which reports 11 fires and casualties of 5 dead and 12 injured. 3 Wellingtons were lost and 1 Stirling crashed in England after being fired at and damaged by a British convoy.

Minor Operations: 24 aircraft to Emden, 2 aircraft to Dunkirk, 2 to Soesterberg airfield, 8 Hampdens minelaying off Wilhelmshaven and Dunkirk. No losses.

20/21 January 1942

EMDEN

20 Wellingtons and 5 Hampdens. 3 Wellingtons and 1 Hampden lost.

21/22 January 1942

BREMEN

54 aircraft; only 28 claimed to have bombed the primary target. 2 Hampdens and 1 Wellington lost.

EMDEN

38 aircraft. 3 Hampdens and 1 Whitley lost.

Minor Operations: 7 Wellingtons to Boulogne, 8 Wellingtons attacking airfields in Holland, 1 Hampden minelaying in the Frisians, 9 Hampdens and 3 Manchesters on leaflet flights to France. No losses.

22/23 January 1942

MÜNSTER

47 aircraft on the first raid to inland Germany since 27/28 December 1941. Crews reported large fires in the railway-station area but the only report from Münster records the death of 5 people with no other details. 1 Wellington lost.

Minor Operations: 5 aircraft to Dunkirk, 6 Blenheim Intruders to Dutch airfields, 9 Hampdens minelaying in the Frisians and off Wilhelmshaven, 5 Hampdens on leaflets flights to France. 1 minelaying Hampden lost.

25/26 January 1942

BREST

61 aircraft dispatched but bombing results were not observed. No aircraft lost.

3 Hampdens were minelaying off French coast without loss.

26/27 January 1942

HANNOVER

71 aircraft; only 32 claimed to have found the target area, though many fires were believed to have been started. No aircraft lost.

EMDEN

31 aircraft. 2 Whitleys lost.

BREST

22 Wellingtons and 3 Stirlings. No losses.

Minor Operations: 6 Hampdens minelaying in the Frisians, 2 Whitleys to Germany and 2 Hampdens to France on leaflet flights. The Whitley leaflet flights were the first leaflet-only operations to Germany since April 1940. 1 Whitley lost.

28/29 January 1942

MÜNSTER

55 Wellingtons and 29 Hampdens. Visibility was very poor and no aircraft positively identified the target though many believed that they had bombed in the target area. Local records show that no bombs fell in Münster. 4 Hampdens and 1 Wellington lost.

BOULOGNE

48 aircraft. 1 Whitley was shot down into the sea by a British ship; there were no survivors.

Minor Operations: 29 Whitleys to Rotterdam, 16 Blenheim Intruders to French and Dutch airfields, 2 aircraft on leaflet flights to France. 1 Intruder lost.

29/30 January 1942

Tirpitz

9 Halifaxes and 7 Stirlings to bomb the battleship *Tirpitz* in Trondheim. Only 2 aircraft reached the Norwegian coast and bombed ships seen there. 1 Stirling lost.

---

31 January/1 February 1942

BREST

72 aircraft. 3 Manchesters and 2 Hampdens lost. The 3 Manchesters lost were all from 61 Squadron, which sent only 9 aircraft on the raid.

Minor Operations: 31 aircraft to St-Nazaire, 14 aircraft to Le Havre, 13 aircraft on leaflet flights to France. No losses.

4/5 February 1942

3 Manchesters to lay mines in the Frisians were recalled.

---

6 February 1942

33 Hampdens and 13 Manchesters carried out daylight minelaying operations in the Frisians. 1 Hampden lost.

6/7 February 1942

BREST

57 Wellingtons and 3 Stirlings; only 21 aircraft claimed to have bombed the primary target area, in thick cloud. 1 Wellington lost.

7 February 1942

32 Hampdens minelaying in the Frisians. German fighters attacked and 3 Hampdens were lost.

8/9 February 1942

4 Blenheim Intruders to Dutch airfields were recalled.

10/11 February 1942

BREMEN

55 aircraft. No losses.

Minor Operations: 12 Wellingtons and 8 Stirlings to Brest, where cloud completely covered the target, and 3 Whitleys to Emden. No losses.

11/12 February 1942

MANNHEIM

49 aircraft. No losses.

LE HAVRE

25 Wellingtons and 6 Whitleys. 1 Wellington lost.

Minor Operations: 18 Wellingtons to Brest, 1 Manchester minelaying in the Frisians, 5 aircraft on leaflet flights to France. 1 Wellington lost from the Brest raid.

12 February 1942

THE CHANNEL DASH

The German battle-cruisers *Scharnhorst* and *Gneisenau* and the lighter cruiser *Prinz Eugen* sailed from Brest to Germany through the English Channel in a carefully prepared and well-executed operation. News of the preparations did not reach Britain and the Germans chose a day when bad weather and low cloud gave their ships maximum concealment. A German fighter escort was provided throughout the voyage. The ships were not reported until late morning when a Spitfire of Fighter Command spotted them off Le Touquet. All available Royal Navy and R.A.F. units were ordered to attack the German ships before darkness closed in.

Most of Bomber Command was 'stood down' for the day; only 5 Group was at 4 hours' notice. The bomber squadrons made a frantic effort to prepare planes for attacks, which were mounted in 3 waves. Other aircraft of Coastal and Fighter Commands and of the Fleet Air Arm were also involved. The first Bomber Command aircraft were airborne at 1.30 p.m. and 242 sorties were flown by the squadrons before dark. Every type of aircraft available flew except the Whitleys which were stationed in the North of England. Bomber Command aircraft dispatched were: 92 Wellingtons, 64 Hampdens, 37 Blenheims, 15 Manchesters, 13 Halifaxes, 11 Stirlings and 10 of the new American-built Boston bombers with which some of the 2 Group squadrons were being equipped, although they were not yet officially ready for operations. It was the largest Bomber Command daylight operation of the war to date.

Most of the bombers were unable to find the German ships in the poor weather conditions and, of those aircraft which did bomb, no hits were scored on these fast-moving and heavily defended targets. None of the attacks by other forces caused any serious damage to the German ships but the two largest, the *Scharnhorst* and the *Gneisenau*, were both slowed down after striking mines laid by 5 Group Hampdens or Manchesters in the Frisian Islands during recent nights. *Scharnhorst* hit 2 mines and *Gneisenau* one. All the German ships reached the safety of ports in Germany before daybreak.

The sailing of these ships, although a successful operation for the Germans, finally released Bomber Command from the effort-consuming and costly requirement to bomb the ships while they had been in French ports. Bomber Command had dropped 3,413 tons of bombs on these 3 ships in recent months and lost 127 aircraft in doing so. But these raids had achieved some success. Both *Scharnhorst* and *Gneisenau* had been hit and badly damaged by bombs; this and the constant threat of further damage prevented the ships from sailing from Brest on another Atlantic shipping raid and persuaded the Germans that they should be brought back to the greater protection of German ports.

12/13 February 1942

12 Hampdens and 9 Manchesters were sent to lay further mines in the Frisians, although weather conditions were still unfavourable. Only 8 aircraft laid their mines but all returned without loss, but 1 Hampden crashed in England.

13/14 February 1942

COLOGNE, AACHEN, LE HAVRE

85 aircraft to these targets – 39 to Cologne, 28 to Le Havre, 18 to Aachen – but all encountered icing and thick cloud and only meagre bombing results were claimed. There were no losses.

14/15 February 1942

MANNHEIM

98 aircraft. 1 Hampden and 1 Whitley lost.

67 aircraft claimed to have bombed Mannheim in difficult conditions. The city reports only a light raid, with 2 buildings destroyed, 15 damaged, some railway damage and with 1 man (noted as being outside his shelter) wounded and 23 people bombed out. A machinery works employing 15 people had to close down until an unexploded bomb was cleared.

Minor Operations: 15 aircraft to Le Havre, 1 Manchester on a leaflet flight to France. No losses.

15/16 February 1942

ST-NAZAIRE

20 Whitleys and 6 Halifaxes; only 9 aircraft bombed, in cloudy conditions. No aircraft were lost but 3 crashed in England.

---

16 February 1942

8 Bostons, of 88 and 226 Squadrons, commenced the first regular operations with this new type of day bomber. They searched for German shipping off the Dutch coast without success or loss.

16/17 February 1942

MINELAYING

37 Hampdens and 12 Manchesters to the Frisian Islands. 1 Hampden and 1 Manchester lost.

Minor Operations: 28 Wellingtons on roving commissions to Northern Germany, 5 Blenheim Intruders over Dutch airfields, 22 aircraft on leaflet flights to France and Belgium. No losses.

---

17 February 1942

6 Bostons on an uneventful shipping search off the Dutch coast.

17/18 February 1942

Roving Commissions

10 Wellingtons and 3 Stirlings to Emden, Hamburg, Kassel and Aachen; visibility was poor and most bombing results were unobserved. Leaflet flights were carried out to Oslo by 1 Whitley and to France by 3 Hampdens. No aircraft were lost on this night.

18/19 February 1942

MINELAYING

25 Hampdens to lay mines in the Frisians and off Wilhelmshaven and Heligoland. 1 Hampden lost. 7 aircraft carried leaflets to France and Belgium without loss.

19/20 February 1942

Minor Operations

8 Wellingtons on roving commissions to Germany, 7 aircraft on leaflet flights to France and Belgium. No losses.

21/22 February 1942

ROVING COMMISSIONS

22 Wellingtons and 20 Hampdens to many areas of Germany. 2 Hampdens and 1 Wellington lost.

Norwegian Airfields

15 aircraft – 6 Halifaxes, 5 Manchesters, 4 Stirlings – attacked 4 airfields to provide a diversion for a proposed Fleet Air Arm strike from the aircraft carrier *Victorious* on the *Prinz Eugen*, which had taken shelter in a Norwegian fjord near Trondheim after being torpedoed and damaged by the submarine *Trident*. The Fleet Air Arm strike was not successful, because of poor weather conditions. 1 Manchester was lost in the Bomber Command diversion.

6 Manchesters minelaying off Wilhelmshaven without loss.

*Operational Statistics, 10/11 November 1941 to 22 February 1942
(104 days/nights)*

Number of days with operations: 20
Number of nights with operations: 54
Number of daylight sorties: 543, from which 40 aircraft (7·4 per cent) were lost
Number of night sorties: 5,001, from which 125 aircraft (2·5 per cent) were lost
Total sorties: 5,544, from which 165 aircraft (3·0 per cent) were lost
Approximate bomb tonnage in period: 5,322 tons
Averages per 24-hour period: 53·3 sorties, 1·6 aircraft lost, 51·2 tons of bombs dropped

10. NEW POLICY, NEW CHIEF

22/23 February to 30 May 1942

Air Marshal Sir Richard Peirse, the commander-in-Chief of Bomber Command since October 1940, was removed from that position on 8 January 1942. Because he eventually became Commander-in-Chief of Allied Air Forces in India and South-East Asia, it can hardly be said that Peirse was sacked, but his removal from the leadership of Bomber Command, at that time probably the most prestigious command in the R.A.F., was a judgement by the Air Ministry on Peirse's handling of the recent long period of poor bombing results combined with heavy casualties. In particular, Peirse was held responsible for the decision to send his bombers out on the night of 7/8 November 1941 when thirty-seven aircraft were lost in unfavourable weather conditions. Air Vice-Marshal J. E. A. Baldwin, the long-serving commander of 3 Group, acted as the temporary commander-in-chief from 9 January to 21 February until the Air Ministry appointed a more permanent successor.

During the restriction on operations imposed on Bomber Command after that heavy loss raid in November, the whole future of the R.A.F.'s strategic bombing campaign was debated at the highest level, with ideas and views being forcefully exchanged between the War Cabinet, the Air Ministry and other interested parties. Bomber Command could do little but carry out a few modest operations throughout the winter months and await the outcome of the debate. It would not be an exaggeration to say that Bomber Command stood at its second great crossroads in the war, with the whole future of the force being in doubt. The first occasion when the concept of the British strategic bomber might have been abandoned had been when Bomber Command was forced to discontinue daylight bombing and turn to the concealment of darkness early in the war. Now, with night bombing seemingly unable to hit the targets and incurring an increasing toll in aircraft casualties, the validity of retaining a large bomber force was again being considered.

There were many who wanted Bomber Command cut back to a modestly sized force of a more tactical nature, and their arguments had some merit. Britain's entire war effort was fully stretched. The continuing support of a large force of strategic bombers which was clearly a long way from playing the decisive role claimed for it by the bomber leaders was possibly a luxury that Britain could not afford at this stage of the war. The supporters of strategic bombing restated their old arguments. The only way to win the war was to defeat Germany. The bombing of Germany on a scale sufficiently great to cause a German domestic collapse was the only alternative to a costly invasion and a prolonged continental land campaign. The memories of the stalemated years and bogged-down offensives of the First World War haunted the minds of many leaders in this second war with Germany. Had not the Chiefs of Staff declared, in July 1941 after the Germans attacked Russia, 'We must first destroy the foundations upon which the German war machine runs – the economy which feeds it, the morale which sustains it, the supplies which nourish it and the hopes of victory which inspire it. Only then shall we be able to return to the continent and occupy and control portions of his territory and impose our will upon the enemy ... It is in bombing, on a scale undreamt of in the last war, that we find the new weapon on which we must principally depend for the destruction of German economic life and morale.'*

It would take time, but new aircraft of better performance and greater bomb-carrying capacity and revolutionary new navigational aids were now appearing. In the meantime, Bomber Command represented the only part of Britain's armed forces which could hit Germany in the West and bring some support to the Russians who were fighting so fiercely on the Eastern Front. In the last months of 1941, the Air Ministry produced a new plan backed by a mass of statistics. Forty-three leading German cities, all of industrial character and with a combined population of fifteen million people, were to be subjected to continuous air attack. A force of *4,000 bombers* would be required to complete this task satisfactorily. The new navigational devices would enable the targets to be found and hit. Although no one specifically said so in 1941, the attempts to bomb individual factory or military targets would have to be abandoned. The general destruction of the cities themselves would be Bomber Command's objective. Once the force of 4,000 bombers was provided, claimed Sir Charles Portal in a report to Churchill, Germany would collapse in six months.† This claim was too much for Churchill. He would continue to back Bomber Command at its present strength and in carrying out its present policies, but there could be no diversion of such a massive requirement of resources to provide and maintain a force of 4,000 bombers.

But Portal had achieved his primary objective. He had secured the support of Churchill – and hence of the War Cabinet which Churchill ruled – for the continuance of Bomber Command in a strategic role. What he needed now was a new tactical policy for Bomber Command and a new man to put that policy into practice. In this way did Bomber Command survive the crisis of that period and commence a new course of action that would occupy entirely the middle years of the Second World War.

The Air Ministry could now devote itself to the means by which the reprieved Bomber Command was to continue its campaign. The next decision was a momentous one. There had always been a body of opinion which believed that the general bombing of German cities, if on a large-enough scale, would produce such general dislocation and breakdown in civilian morale in the target cities that the German home front would collapse. With their cities and their own homes in ruins, the German civilians would be neither able nor willing to continue the war; so went the argument. The Butt Report had showed that accurate bombing of specific industrial premises could only rarely be achieved. The Air Ministry decided that such bombing should be virtually abandoned and most of Bomber Command's effort should now be devoted to the general bombing of the most densely built up areas of Germany's cities. The famous 'area bombing' directive was sent to Bomber Command on 14 February 1942:

---

*Official History, Vol. I, pp. 180–81.
† Letter from Portal to Churchill, 25 September 1941, quoted in the Official History, Vol. I, p. 182.

It has been decided that the primary objective of your operations should now be focussed on the morale of the enemy civil population and in particular of the industrial workers.*

Portal wrote a note the next day to Air Vice-Marshal Bottomley who had drafted the directive to Bomber Command:

Ref the new bombing directive: I suppose it is clear that the aiming points are to be the built-up areas, *not,* for instance, the dockyards or aircraft factories where these are mentioned in Appendix A.

This must be made quite clear if it is not already understood.†

The policy was not entirely new. Air Ministry directives had been encouraging Bomber Command since as early as October 1940 to devote a portion of its effort to just such a general attack on German cities, but only as a secondary task when weather conditions were unsuitable for selective industrial bombing. The bomber crews throughout 1941 had been aware of the gradual shift in emphasis and it is obvious from a study of raid results that, even though crews had been sent to attack industrial premises, bombs were increasingly dropped on the nearest built-up areas when difficulties were encountered. What was important about the new directive was that area bombing was now to be the primary type of bomber operation for the foreseeable future.

With the new policy came a new leader for Bomber Command. Air Chief Marshal Sir Arthur Harris was appointed on 22 February 1942, eight days after the arrival of the new directive. Harris would lead Bomber Command for the remainder of the war and his name would be linked irrevocably with its campaign during that period. However enthusiastically Harris prosecuted that new policy, it should be stated that he was not responsible for the formulation of it. Area bombing was the creation of Sir Charles Portal and the staff officers of the Air Ministry, with enthusiastic support being given by people such as Churchill and Trenchard, the veteran R.A.F. leader of the old school. There is no evidence that there had been any canvassing of the area-bombing policy by the staff of Bomber Command Headquarters.

As we are following all changes in command down to group level, it should be mentioned here that 2 Group had again changed its commander in December 1941 when Air Vice-Marshal A. Lees replaced Air Vice-Marshal Stevenson and 5 Group would lose Air Vice-Marshal Slessor in April 1942 (Slessor would soon become the successful commander of Coastal Command). The new 5 Group commander would be Air Vice-Marshal W. A. Coryton. A more significant event at this time was the arrival in England of the first officers of what would become the American Eighth Air Force; by coincidence, they arrived in England on the same day that Harris took over at Bomber Command.

Sir Arthur Harris inherited a force of aircraft no stronger in numbers than had been present a year earlier. The figures recorded in the Air Ministry War Room on 1 March 1942‡ are as shown in the table (see opposite page). The continuing drain of squadrons to Coastal Command and the Middle East and the heavy operational losses of 1941 had prevented any build-up in total strength.

---

*Official History, Vol. IV, p. 144.
†Official History, Vol. I, p. 324.
‡Public Record Office AIR 22/31–49.

Night Bombers		Day Bombers	
Wellingtons	221	Blenheims	56
Hampdens	112	Bostons	22
Whitleys	54		
Stirlings	29		
Halifaxes	29		
Manchesters	20		
Lancasters	4		
Total	469	Total	78

Within the overall figures, however, there were some significant trends. The reliable Lancaster had at last appeared and would increase its numbers rapidly. The Lancaster would soon replace the disappointing Manchester and eventually the ageing Hampden which had rendered such good service in 5 Group. Another old faithful which would disappear even earlier was the Whitley; the last Whitley squadron – 58 Squadron – would cease operating with Bomber Command at the end of April on transferring to Coastal Command. The other four-engined types, the Stirling and the Halifax, which had been so slow in developing their strengths would also make steady progress in the coming months. So, while Bomber Command's overall strength would not increase in 1942, its bomb-carrying capacity would.

Alongside the increase in bomb tonnage capable of being delivered, came the first major improvement in navigation. This was *Gee*, a device which enabled a bomber's navigator to fix his position by consulting an instrument – the Gee Box – which received pulse signals from three widely separated stations in England. *Gee* computed the difference between receipt of these signals and gave the navigator an instant 'fix'. As it was a line-of-sight device, its range depended on the aircraft's height and range. An aircraft flying at 20,000 feet 400 miles from England could just receive the signals; aircraft flying below that altitude or at greater ranges started to lose the *Gee* signals because of the curvature of the earth. *Gee* was thus a navigational device rather than a blind-bombing aid, although some attempts were made to use it for bombing when targets were found to be completely cloud-covered. The major benefit of *Gee* was in enabling crews to reach the general area of a target when winds encountered were not as forecast and might have taken the aircraft badly off course. The Ruhr, the Rhineland and some of the North Sea ports – Bremen, Emden and Wilhelmshaven – were all within *Gee* range but the device could still be of use in getting aircraft well started on raids to more distant targets and *Gee* always helped crews to find their way back to their bases in England. There were high hopes for this device, although it was realized that the Germans would eventually reassemble a set from a crashed bomber and produce a jamming device.

Sir Arthur Harris was fortunate in arriving at Bomber Command at the same time as *Gee* and the better types of aircraft but he also brought a lively and effective tactical mind and immediately introduced improvements in operational procedures. The first of these were the principle of concentration and the increased use of incendiary bombs. Gone were the days – or rather the nights – when Bomber Command would send its aircraft to two or three targets and spread its bombing over a period of several hours. Harris usually tackled only one main target on nights when operations were considered suitable, still using the moon period. The bombing at that main target was now to be concentrated into a period of two hours or less. The risk of collision was accepted in return for the better use of massed flares, the overwhelming effect of bombing upon a city's fire services and the reduction in the time during which the German Flak defences had the opportunity to engage bombers. The second of Harris's improvements, the use of incendiary bombs, supported the principle that it was easier to burn a city down than to blow it up. Bomber Command was soon to drop its first 8,000-pound blast bomb but, although this was a massive weapon, the more numerous 4,000-pound blast bombs were better for area bombing, especially when supported by a mass of the small 4-pound incendiaries. A standard raid would open with ordinary high-explosive bombs to crater and block roads with fallen masonry to prevent fire engines moving around the city and then the main raid, using blast bombs and incendiaries, would follow. The blast bombs blew off roofs and smashed windows; the incendiaries penetrated the roofs and started fires which were fed by air drawn in through the broken windows. Bomber Command was to become a great fire-raising force.

Harris realized there was little chance of a resumption in general day bombing and 2 Group would be left to languish in minor operations. For various technical reasons the American-built Flying Fortress had failed as a day bomber with the R.A.F., although the Americans would benefit from the R.A.F. experience and later use the Fortress with great success. The Blenheim's operational life with Bomber Command was almost finished but its replacements were never produced in large numbers and 2 Group's days of strength and glory, in Bomber Command at least, were past. Harris would try one small deep-penetration daylight raid by a small force of the new Lancaster aircraft but this experimental raid, to Augsburg, though pressed home with great gallantry, was in reality a costly failure and a sharp reminder that clear weather in daylight still meant death to unescorted bomber aircraft.

The directive on area bombing also released Bomber Command from the re-straint order of the previous November and the new commander-in-chief was now urged to make use of *Gee* in intensive operations. But Harris did not rush blindly into sending the bombers out too often. His first few months were characterized by long periods of steady development, interrupted by bursts of dramatic activity. The Renault works near Paris and the German cities of Essen, Lübeck and Rostock would be Harris's milestones in this first period of night operations. In particular, there would be a series of eight major raids on Essen in the hope that *Gee* could help to produce effective bombing results on this important but usually haze-concealed target. But there were also long gaps when the weather or the state of the moon was unfavourable. Harris was not prepared to waste effort in conditions which experience had shown to be almost without any hope of success. The overall level of operations and of bomb tonnage in the first three months of Harris's period of command were actually lower than in the equivalent period of the previous year.

The task would not be any easier. The casualty rate for night operations in the next few months would be slightly higher than any previous period of the war and the reports from Germany in this diary will show that there would be as many disappointments in bombing results as successes.

22/23 February 1942

WILHELMSHAVEN

31 Wellingtons and 19 Hampdens to bomb the floating dock which the Germans might be using to repair the *Scharnhorst* or *Gneisenau*. The area was cloud-covered

and bombs were mostly released on the estimated position of Wilhelmshaven. The local diary has no entry for this night.

Minor Operations: 7 aircraft to Emden, 5 to Ostend, 5 Manchesters minelaying off Wilhelmshaven, 2 Hampdens on leaflet flights to France.

There were no aircraft losses from the operations of this night.

23/24 February 1942

23 Hampdens minelaying off Wilhelmshaven and Heligoland. 1 aircraft lost.

24/25 February 1942

Minor Operations

42 Hampdens and 9 Manchesters minelaying in the Frisians and off Wilhelmshaven and Heligoland. 2 Hampdens lost. 5 aircraft on leaflet flights to France and Belgium without loss.

25/26 February 1942

KIEL

61 aircraft – 43 Wellingtons, 12 Manchesters, 6 Stirlings – to bomb the floating dock at Kiel. 3 Wellingtons lost.

Kiel records this as a 'revenge raid' by the R.A.F. after the British failure to prevent the sailing from Brest of the *Scharnhorst, Gneisenau* and *Prinz Eugen*. In the bombing of the harbour area, the accommodation ship *Monte Sarmiento* was hit and burnt out with the loss of 120–130 lives. 16 people were also killed and 39 injured in the town.

NORWAY

21 Whitleys to bomb aluminium factories at Heroya and Odda. These areas were cloud-covered and the Whitleys returned without bombing.

Minor Operations: 18 Hampdens and 1 Manchester minelaying off German ports, 3 aircraft on leaflet flights. No losses.

---

26 February 1942

4 Bostons of 226 Squadron commenced the first regular operations for this type of aircraft. Ships off the Hook of Holland were attacked without loss.

26/27 February 1942

KIEL

49 aircraft – 33 Wellingtons, 10 Hampdens, 6 Halifaxes – to attack the floating dock. 2 Wellingtons and 1 Halifax lost.

It was a night of mixed fortunes. Crews claimed good results in clear weather with bombs close to the floating dock. A high-explosive bomb scored a direct hit on the bows of the *Gneisenau*, causing severe damage and killing 116 men in the crew. This proved to be the end of *Gneisenau* as a fighting unit. Her guns were later removed for coastal defence work and she was taken to Gdynia but never repaired. Bombing in the town of Kiel destroyed several houses and killed 16 people.

A report from Denmark shows how some of the bomber crews failed to locate Kiel accurately and dropped their loads on towns on the islands and coast of east Denmark. Damage and casualties were caused in Vejle (3 killed, 6 injured) and Odense (1 killed, 7 injured). Vejle was 100 miles north of Kiel!

Minor Operations: 27 Hampdens minelaying off German ports, 5 Hampdens on leaflet flights. No losses.

27/28 February 1942

KIEL

68 aircraft – 33 Wellingtons, 17 Manchesters, 18 Hampdens – to bomb the floating dock. The area was completely cloud-covered. 47 aircraft bombed the approximate position of Kiel but, although Kiel reports hearing the planes, no bombs dropped in the town. No aircraft were lost.

WILHELMSHAVEN

33 aircraft of mixed types were sent to find and bomb the *Scharnhorst*, which was believed to be at Wilhelmshaven, but the cloud was present here also. Wilhelmshaven reports only 3 bombs exploding, in the water of the harbour. 3 Whitleys lost.

11 Hampdens and 4 Manchesters minelaying in the Frisians without loss.

---

28 February 1942

Ostend

6 Blenheims with a fighter escort bombed the harbour without loss.

---

2 March 1942

4 Bostons attacked ships off Den Helder without loss.

3/4 March 1942

THE BILLANCOURT RENAULT FACTORY

After a three-night rest, Bomber Command now carried out this most interesting operation.

The Air Ministry had asked Bomber Command to attempt a raid on one of the French factories known to be producing war material for the Germans. The Renault factory, in the town of Boulogne-Billancourt just west of the centre of Paris, was making an estimated 18,000 lorries a year for the German forces.

235 aircraft – 89 Wellingtons, 48 Hampdens, 29 Stirlings, 26 Manchesters, 23 Whitleys, 20 Halifaxes – were dispatched in 3 waves, the crews of the leading wave being selected for their experience. The plan called for the massed use of flares and a very low bombing level so that crews could hit the factory without too many bombs falling in the surrounding town. There were no Flak defences. 223 aircraft bombed the target, reporting excellent results. Only 1 Wellington was lost. The main raid lasted 1 hour and 50 minutes.

Many records were broken that night. The number of aircraft sent to this one target – 235 – was the greatest by the R.A.F. to a single target so far in the war; the previous record was 229 to Kiel on 7/8 April 1941. The concentration of bombers over the target – averaging 121 per hour – exceeded Bomber Command's previous best rate of 80 per hour; there were no collisions. A record tonnage of bombs was dropped, although the exact tonnage is in doubt, official records giving 412 and 470 tons. A significant tactical point was the mass use of flares and the selection of some experienced crews to open the raid, thus foreshadowing some of the 'pathfinding' methods to be used later in the war. *Gee* was not used, being not yet ready for operations. The raid was considered a great success and the destruction caused in the factory received much publicity.

The report from Billancourt says that 300 bombs fell on the factory, destroying 40 per cent of the buildings. Production was halted for 4 weeks and final repairs were not completed for several months. A post-war American estimate says that the production loss was nearly 2,300 lorries. Unfortunately, French civilian casualties were heavy. There were many blocks of workers' apartments very close to the factory. Few people had taken shelter when the sirens sounded; they had often sounded before when bombers were flying to and from Germany. 367 French people were killed; this too was a record, being more than double the death toll of any R.A.F. raid on a German city so far in the war. 72 people were killed in just one block of flats. A further 341 people were classed as badly injured and some of these would die later. 9,250 people lost their homes. A prominent Billancourt citizen, Georges Gorse, was serving with the Free French forces in London at the time and wrote as follows:

If we want the liberation of France, we have to clench our teeth and accept that the English bomb occupied Paris just as the Germans bombed London, that some French people perish under Allied bombs, just as much victims of Germany as the casualties of the 1940 campaign and the men shot at Nantes or Paris. The workers of Boulogne-Billancourt truly saw in the raids of March a promise of liberation. And those who died have also brought 'their own contribution to the coming of dawn'.

This well-publicized view must have been shared by the people of Billancourt because they elected M. Gorse as Mayor with a large majority after the war.

Minor Operations: 4 Wellingtons to Emden, 4 Blenheim Intruders to Dutch airfields but these were recalled. 4 Lancasters minelaying off the north-west German coast, 2 Whitleys on leaflet flights to France. 1 Wellington lost on the Emden raid.

Total effort for the night: 249 sorties, 2 aircraft (0·8 per cent) lost. The Lancaster mining sorties, flown by 44 Squadron, saw the introduction into operational service of this new type of aircraft.

7/8 March 1942

SUBMARINE BASES

17 aircraft bombed St-Nazaire and 17 Hampdens were sent minelaying off Lorient. 1 minelaying aircraft lost.

8 March 1942

BOSTON OPERATIONS

24 Bostons, with much support from Fighter Command, carried out a series of raids against targets in France. 12 Bostons of 88 and 226 Squadrons made a low-level attack on the Ford lorry factory at Poissy, near Paris, a target beyond the range of fighter cover. Two further formations, each of 6 Bostons, carried out *Circus* operations to Abbeville railway yards and Comines power-station at times which would divert German fighter attention from the Poissy raid.

All of these operations were carried out with much success. 8 Bostons bombed at Poissy, though 1 of them crashed soon afterwards. This was the first operational loss of a Boston aircraft. There were no other bomber losses.

8/9 March 1942

ESSEN

This was yet another major step forward, a heavy raid on the previously difficult target of Essen with leading aircraft now fitted with the *Gee* navigational aid.

211 aircraft – 115 Wellingtons, 37 Hampdens, 27 Stirlings, 22 Manchesters, 10 Halifaxes. 8 aircraft – 5 Wellingtons, 2 Manchesters, 1 Stirling – lost. It was a fine night but industrial haze over Essen prevented accurate bombing and the raid was a disappointment. *Gee* could only enable the aircraft to reach the approximate area of the target. Photographic evidence showed that the main target, the Krupps factories, was not hit but some bombs fell in the southern part of Essen.

Essen reports only a 'light' raid with a few houses and a church destroyed, 10 people killed and 19 'missing'. The most noticeable incident was the burning down of a well-known restaurant, the Blumenhof, in the Gruga Park, which was being used to house foreign workers.

Minor Operations: 13 Wellingtons and Stirlings to Le Havre, 6 Blenheims to Ostend, 6 Blenheim Intruders to Dutch airfields, 9 Hampdens minelaying in the Frisians, 3 Manchesters minelaying off Lorient, 1 Hampden on a leaflet flight to France. No losses.

Total effort for the night: 249 sorties, 8 aircraft (3.2 per cent) lost.

9 March 1942

6 Bostons on *Circus* raid to Mazingarbe fuel depot. All bombed; no losses.

9/10 March 1942

ESSEN

187 aircraft – 136 Wellingtons, 21 Stirlings, 15 Hampdens, 10 Manchesters, 5 Halifaxes – to continue the series of heavy *Gee*-guided raids to Essen. 2 Wellingtons and 1 Halifax lost.

Thick ground haze led to scattered bombing. Only 2 buildings were destroyed in Essen but 72 were damaged. Bombs also fell in 24 other Ruhr towns with particular damage in Hamborn and Duisburg. 10 people were killed, 19 were missing and 52 were injured in Essen; 74 people were killed and 284 injured in other towns.

Minor Operations: 9 Wellingtons and Stirlings to Boulogne, 5 Hampdens minelaying in the Frisians. No losses.

---

10 March 1942

4 Bostons on an uneventful shipping search off the Dutch coast.

10/11 March 1942

ESSEN

126 aircraft – 56 Wellingtons, 43 Hampdens, 13 Manchesters, 12 Stirlings, 2 Lancasters; this was the first participation by Lancasters in a raid on a German target. 4 aircraft – 2 Hampdens, 1 Stirling, 1 Wellington – lost.

This was another disappointing raid with unexpected cloud being the main cause of poor bombing. 62 crews claimed to have bombed Essen; 35 crews bombed alternative targets. The report from Essen shows that only 2 bombs fell on an industrial target – railway lines near the Krupps factory – and 1 house was destroyed and 2 damaged in residential areas. 5 Germans were killed and 12 injured and a Polish worker was killed by a Flak shell which descended and exploded on the ground.

Minor Operations: 23 'freshman' crews to Boulogne, 3 Hampdens minelaying off the French coast. No losses.

12/13 March 1942

KIEL

68 Wellingtons to attack the Deutsche Werke U-boat yard. 5 aircraft lost.

The report from Kiel indicates that the port area was successfully bombed, with damage in the Deutsche Werke and the Germania Werft, both building U-boats, and in the naval dockyard. The accommodation ship *Hamburg* was hit. There was also bombing in the town. Casualties are listed as 12 killed and 21 injured but it is not known whether service personnel were included. The Kiel report adds two unusual items, a siren which suffered a technical defect and 'howled' for an hour and a half, and a warning issued for people to watch out for spies being dropped by parachute during the raid.

EMDEN

20 Wellingtons and 20 Whitleys; 3 Whitleys lost. Bombing photographs indicated that the nearest bombs were 5 miles from the target.

Minor Operations: 26 Hampdens and 1 Manchester minelaying off German ports, 1 Hampden on a leaflet flight to France. No losses.

---

13 March 1942

11 Bostons to Hazebrouck railway yards. No losses.

13/14 March 1942

COLOGNE

135 aircraft of 6 different types. 1 Manchester lost.

This can be considered the first successful *Gee*-led raid. Although there was no moon, the leading crews carrying flares and incendiary-bomb loads located the target and much accurate bombing followed. It was later estimated that this raid was 5 times more effective than the average of recent raids on Cologne. This estimate is confirmed by the local report. In industrial areas, the Franz Cloud rubber works was seriously damaged, resulting in complete production loss for 1 month and 80 per cent loss for a further 11 months. The Land- und See-kabelwerke A.G. factory was also badly damaged and put out of action for a month. A further rubber factory and a large railway-repair workshop were also hit. All these industrial premises were in the Nippes section of the city. Non-industrial premises hit or damaged included 5 churches, the Tivoli cinema and more than 1,500 houses. There were 237 separate fires.

Casualties were 62 killed and 84 injured. 46 of the dead were in blocks of flats which were collapsed by two 4,000-lb bombs, one near the city centre and one in the northern suburb of Longerich. 2 children were rescued alive after 65 hours of digging in the city-centre incident.

Minor Operations: 20 aircraft to Boulogne, 19 to Dunkirk, 2 Blenheim Intruders to France and Holland, 5 Hampdens minelaying in the Frisians, 7 Hampdens on leaflet flights to France. 2 Wellingtons were lost from the Dunkirk raid and 1 Wellington from the Boulogne raid.

---

14 March 1942

6 Bostons on uneventful shipping sweeps off Le Havre.

---

15 March 1942

6 Bostons on uneventful shipping sweeps off Brittany.

15/16 March 1942

3 Blenheims on Intruder flights to Dutch airfields. Schiphol airfield was attacked. No losses.

17 March 1942

1 Wellington on a cloud-cover raid to Essen dropped its bombs somewhere in the Ruhr.

18 March 1942

5 Wellingtons to Essen returned because of lack of cloud.

19 March 1942

1 Wellington to Essen returned early because of lack of cloud.

20 March 1942

13 Manchesters and 6 Lancasters on daylight minelaying in the Frisians; only 11 aircraft reached the correct area. 2 Wellingtons to Essen returned because of lack of cloud. No losses.

21 March 1942

1 Wellington to Essen returned because of lack of cloud.

23/24 March 1942
Minelaying

12 Hampdens, 3 Stirlings and 2 Manchesters minelaying off Lorient without loss. This was the first time that Stirlings of 3 Group participated in the minelaying campaign.

24 March 1942

18 Bostons on escorted raids, 12 to Comines power-station and 6 to Abbeville railway yards. Bombing results were not observed. No Bostons lost.

24/25 March 1942
MINELAYING

35 aircraft of 3 and 5 Groups minelaying off Lorient. 1 Hampden and 1 Lancaster lost. These were the first Bomber Command losses for 11 days and nights and the

Lancaster lost, from 44 (Rhodesia) Squadron, was the first of its type to be lost on operations. The pilot, Flight Sergeant L. Warren-Smith, a South African, and his all-N.C.O. crew – 4 Englishmen, 2 Rhodesians, 1 Australian – all died.

---

25 March 1942

9 Bostons, with fighter escort, carried out accurate bombing at Le Trait shipyard. No Bostons lost.

25/26 March 1942

ESSEN

254 aircraft – 192 Wellingtons, 26 Stirlings, 20 Manchesters, 9 Hampdens, 7 Lancasters – in the largest force sent to 1 target so far. 9 aircraft – 5 Manchesters (out of the 20 dispatched), 3 Wellingtons, 1 Hampden – lost.

Visibility was good and 181 crews claimed to have bombed Essen, many claiming hits on the Krupps works, but bombing photographs showed that much of the effort was drawn off by the decoy fire site at Rheinberg, 18 miles west of Essen. Essen's report says that only 9 high-explosive bombs, 700 incendiaries and 1,627 leaflets were dropped there, the last figure being an example of German thoroughness. 1 house was destroyed and 2 seriously damaged. 5 people were killed and 11 injured.

Minor Operations: 27 aircraft to St-Nazaire, 38 aircraft minelaying off Lorient, 30 aircraft on leaflet flights to France. 1 Wellington on the St-Nazaire raid and 1 minelaying Hampden were lost.

Total effort for the night: 349 sorties, 11 aircraft (3·2 per cent) lost.

---

26 March 1942

24 Bostons to Le Havre. Hits were reported on ships in the harbour. 1 Boston lost.

26/27 March 1942

ESSEN

104 Wellingtons and 11 Stirlings. 10 Wellingtons and 1 Stirling lost.

The bombing force encountered heavy Flak at the target and many night fighters on the routes. Hits on the Krupps works and fires in Essen were claimed but the raid was actually another failure on this difficult target. Only 22 high-explosive bombs were counted in Essen, with 2 houses destroyed, 6 people killed and 14 injured. The bombers had suffered nearly 10 per cent casualties for this disappointing return.

Minor Operations: 8 aircraft to Le Havre, 11 Blenheims Intruding over Holland, 36 aircraft minelaying off Wilhelmshaven, in the Frisians and in the River Gironde, 15 aircraft on leaflet flights to France. 2 Blenheim Intruders and 2 Hampden minelayers lost.

27 March 1942

12 Bostons attacked Ostend power-station without loss but their bombs fell into fields short of the target.

27/28 March 1942

THE ST-NAZAIRE RAID

35 Whitleys and 27 Wellingtons to bomb German positions around St-Nazaire in support of the naval and Commando raid to destroy the dry-dock gates in the port. The aircraft were ordered to bomb only if the target had clear visibility. Conditions were bad, however, with 10/10ths cloud and icing, and only 4 aircraft bombed at St-Nazaire; 6 aircraft bombed elsewhere. 1 Whitley was lost in the sea.

Minor Operations: 8 Blenheims Intruding over Holland, 15 Hampdens minelaying off north-west German coasts. 1 Blenheim and 3 Hampdens lost.

28/29 March 1942

LÜBECK

234 aircraft – 146 Wellingtons, 41 Hampdens, 26 Stirlings, 21 Manchesters. 12 aircraft – 7 Wellingtons, 3 Stirlings, 1 Hampden, 1 Manchester – lost.

This famous raid took place on the night of Palm Sunday and was the first major success for Bomber Command against a German target. The attack was carried out in good visibility, with the help of an almost full moon and, because of the light defences of this target, from a low level, many crews coming down to 2,000 ft. The force was split into 3 waves, the leading one being composed of experienced crews with *Gee*-fitted aircraft; although Lübeck was beyond the range of *Gee*, the device helped with preliminary navigation. More than 400 tons of bombs were dropped; two thirds of this tonnage was incendiary. The aiming point was the centre of the *Altstadt*, which was built of narrow streets and old, half-timbered houses. It was a heavy, fire-raising attack on pure area-bombing lines.

191 crews claimed successful attacks. Aerial photographs and German reports confirmed the outstanding success of the raid. Information is available from many sources.* In Bomber Command's new terminology, approximately 190 acres of the old town were assessed on the basis of photographs as having been destroyed, mostly by fire; this was reckoned to be 30 per cent of Lübeck's built-up area. German sources show that 1,425 buildings in Lübeck were destroyed, 1,976 were seriously damaged and 8,411 were lightly damaged; these represented 62 per cent of all buildings in Lübeck. Of the 3,401 buildings classed as destroyed or seriously damaged, 3,070 were residential buildings, 70 were public buildings, 256 were industrial or commercial and 5 were agricultural. Among the public buildings destroyed were many of architectural

---

* The British Bombing Survey and the United States Strategic Bombing Survey are quoted in the British Official History, Vol. IV, p. 485, and Vol. I, pp. 483–4; Hans Brunswig's *Feuersturm über Hamburg* – Brunswig's fire unit was sent to help at Lübeck – op. cit., pp. 117–23, and Hans Rumpf's *The Bombing of Germany*, Muller, 1963, pp. 49–51, have also been consulted.

importance including the Rathaus and Marienkirche, described by Rumpf as the 'mother church of Northern Germany'. Among the industrial buildings destroyed was the Drägerwerke factory which made oxygen equipment for U-boats. Brunswig states that the cost of the damage caused was 200 million Reichsmarks (£20 million).

The casualties in Lübeck were 312 or 320 people killed (accounts conflict), 136 seriously and 648 slightly injured. This was the heaviest death toll in a German raid so far in the war, exceeding the 185 killed in Hamburg on 8/9 May 1941 but still less than the 367 French people killed at Billancourt earlier in this month.

Lübeck was not raided by the full strength of the R.A.F. again during the war. A Swiss diplomat who was president of the International Red Cross later negotiated an agreement with Britain that the port would not be bombed again because it was being used for the shipment of Red Cross supplies.

Minor Operations: 2 Blenheims Intruding over Holland, 7 Hampdens minelaying in the Frisians, 14 aircraft on leaflet flights to France. No losses.

Total effort for the night: 257 sorties, 12 aircraft (4·7 per cent) lost.

29/30 March 1942

18 Hampdens and 8 Manchesters minelaying in the Frisians and off Denmark, 6 aircraft on leaflet flights to France. 2 Manchester minelayers lost.

30/31 March 1942

TRONDHEIM

34 Halifaxes attempted to bomb the *Tirpitz* in a fjord near Trondheim. The *Tirpitz* was not located; 3 aircraft bombed Flak positions. 1 Halifax lost in the sea.

---

31 March 1942

11 Hampdens and 6 Wellingtons on cloud-cover raids to Germany. 6 aircraft found targets to bomb. No aircraft lost.

---

31 March/1 April 1942

4 Wellingtons, with selected crews, to Essen but only random targets were bombed by 2 aircraft. No losses.

---

1 April 1942

12 Bostons to Boulogne to attack an armed cargo ship. Cloud was encountered and the dock area was bombed instead. 1 Boston lost.

1/2 April 1942

LE HAVRE

34 Wellingtons and 22 Hampdens. Successful bombing was claimed. 1 Wellington lost.

HANAU, LOHR

35 Wellingtons and 14 Hampdens to carry out low-level attacks on railway targets, a new experiment which proved to be too costly. 22 aircraft reported that they had carried out this task but 12 Wellingtons – 34·3 per cent of the Wellingtons dispatched – and 1 Hampden were lost. 57 Squadron, based at Feltwell, a squadron which was often unlucky, lost 5 of the 12 Wellingtons it sent on this raid and 214 Squadron, from Stradishall, lost 7 of its 14 Wellingtons.

PARIS/POISSY

24 Whitleys and 17 Wellingtons to attack the Ford motor factory. Crews claimed accurate bombing but this was not confirmed by a later photographic flight. 1 Wellington lost.

Minor Operations: 3 Blenheim Intruder flights to Holland turned back, 15 aircraft minelaying off Lorient and in the mouth of the River Gironde, 5 aircraft on leaflet flights to France. No losses. This was the first night of minelaying by Wellingtons of 3 Group.

2/3 April 1942

PARIS/POISSY

40 Wellingtons and 10 Stirlings carried out successful bombing of the motor factory. 1 Wellington lost.

LE HAVRE

49 aircraft; crews claimed accurate bombing of harbour targets. No losses.

23 Hampdens and 7 Wellingtons minelaying in Quiberon Bay. 1 Hampden and 1 Wellington lost.

4 April 1942

ST-OMER

12 Bostons and 4 Wellingtons on escorted raid to St-Omer railway yards but their bombs fell in fields near the town. No losses.

CLOUD-COVER RAIDS

4 Wellingtons to Germany. 3 turned back early but 1 aircraft, although dispatched to Emden, turned south when its cloud cover ran out and dropped its bombs in the Essen area.

21 Hampdens attempted to use cloud cover to lay mines in the Frisians but only 2 aircraft did so successfully. There were no losses.

5/6 April 1942

COLOGNE

263 aircraft – 179 Wellingtons, 44 Hampdens, 29 Stirlings, 11 Manchesters – another new record for a force sent to a single target. 4 Wellingtons and 1 Hampden lost.

The main target allocated to crews was the Humboldt works, which was in the Deutz area of Cologne. 211 aircraft claimed good bombing results but the nearest bombing photographs developed were 5 miles from the Humboldt works. The Cologne report shows that bombing was scattered right across the city and lists just 1 industrial building hit, a mill in the Deutz area, with 90 houses destroyed or seriously damaged and other buildings, including a hospital, hit. 7 people were killed and 9 injured in the bombing but there were further casualties among a crowd of people who were watching a burning bomber – probably a Wellington – which had crashed in the middle of Cologne; the bomb load exploded killing 16 people and injuring 30 more. The bomber's crew, reported as being Canadians, had been killed in the original crash.

PARIS/GENNEVILLIERS

20 Whitleys to bomb the Gnome & Rhône engine factory. 14 aircraft bombed but the main target was not hit. Local records show 1 house destroyed and 4 damaged, with no casualties. No aircraft were lost.

Minor Operations: 18 aircraft to Le Havre, 6 Blenheims Intruding over Holland, 11 Hampdens and Wellingtons minelaying off the French coast. No losses.

Total effort for the night: 318 sorties, 5 aircraft (1·6 per cent) lost.

6/7 April 1942

ESSEN

The campaign against Essen continued, with 157 aircraft – 110 Wellingtons, 19 Stirlings, 18 Hampdens, 10 Manchesters. The crews encountered severe storms and icing and there was complete cloud cover over Essen. Only 49 aircraft claimed to have reached the target area. Essen reports only a few bombs, with light damage; no casualties are recorded. 5 aircraft – 2 Hampdens, 1 Manchester, 1 Stirling, 1 Wellington – lost.

---

8 April 1942

4 Bostons on a sweep off the Dutch coast. A ship was bombed but not hit. No aircraft were lost.

8/9 April 1942

HAMBURG

272 aircraft – 177 Wellingtons, 41 Hampdens, 22 Stirlings, 13 Manchesters, 12 Halifaxes, 7 Lancasters – on yet another record raid for aircraft numbers to 1 target. 4 Wellingtons and 1 Manchester lost.

Icing and electrical storms were again encountered. Although 188 aircraft reported bombing in the target area, the raid was a failure. According to Hamburg's records, bombs equivalent to only 14 aircraft loads fell on the city, causing 8 fires – 3 large; no particular incidents of property damage are mentioned. 17 people were killed and 119 injured.

Bremen reports a load of incendiaries dropped very accurately on the Vulkan shipyard where 4 U-boats under construction and several surrounding buildings were damaged by fire.

Minor Operations: 13 Wellingtons to Le Havre, 3 Blenheims Intruding over Holland, 24 aircraft minelaying near Heligoland, 16 aircraft on leaflet flights to Belgium and France. 1 Manchester on a leaflet flight was lost in the sea.

Total effort for the night: 328 sorties, 6 aircraft (1·8 per cent) lost.

---

9 April 1942

7 Wellingtons on cloud-cover raids to Essen; only 1 aircraft bombed, a village north of Essen. No aircraft lost.

10/11 April 1942

ESSEN

254 aircraft – 167 Wellingtons, 43 Hampdens, 18 Stirlings, 10 Manchesters, 8 Halifaxes, 8 Lancasters. 14 aircraft – 7 Wellingtons, 5 Hampdens, 1 Halifax, 1 Manchester – lost.

Crews were given a forecast of clear weather over Essen but cloud was met instead. The bombing force became scattered and suffered heavily from the Ruhr Flak defences. Bombing was poor. Essen reports 12 houses destroyed, no serious industrial damage, 7 people killed and 30 injured. Total bombs in Essen were approximately 6 aircraft loads from the 172 aircraft claiming to have bombed there.

Bomber Command's first 8,000-lb bomb was dropped during this raid by the 76 Squadron Halifax of Pilot Officer M. Renaut, whose aircraft was badly damaged by Flak. It is not known where Renaut's bomb fell.*

Minor Operations: 40 'freshmen' crews to Le Havre, 3 Blenheim Intruders to Holland, 3 aircraft minelaying off Heligoland, 5 leaflet flights to France. 1 Manchester on the Le Havre raid and 1 Hampden minelayer lost.

Total effort for the night: 305 sorties, 16 aircraft (5·2 per cent) lost.

---

*After the war Renaut wrote a book about his experiences, *Terror by Night*, Kimber, 1982.

12 April 1942

9 Bostons carried out accurate bombing at Hazebrouck railway yards but 1 aircraft was lost.

12/13 April 1942

ESSEN

251 aircraft – 171 Wellingtons, 31 Hampdens, 27 Stirlings, 13 Halifaxes, 9 Manchesters. 10 aircraft – 7 Wellingtons, 2 Hampdens, 1 Halifax – lost.

173 aircraft claimed to have bombed Essen but their bombing photographs showed many localities of the Ruhr. Essen's records show a slight improvement in the bombing. 5 high-explosive and 200 incendiary bombs hit the Krupps factory and a large fire was started there. 28 private dwellings were destroyed and 50 seriously damaged. 27 people were killed, 36 injured and 9 were missing.

This raid concluded a disappointing series of raids on this target, which was judged to be the heart of the German armaments industry. There had been 8 heavy raids since the first *Gee* raid on 8/9 March. These are the conclusions:

Aircraft dispatched	1,555
Crews reported bombing Essen	1,006
Aircraft lost	64
Aircraft bombing photographs showing ground detail	212
Aircraft bombing photographs within 5 miles of Essen	22

Essen's records show that industrial damage was caused on only 2 occasions – a fire in the Krupps factory and a few bombs on some nearby railway lines – that 63 civilians were killed and that a modest amount of residential property had been hit.

Minor Operations: 27 aircraft to Le Havre, 18 Whitleys to Genoa (the target was cloud-covered), 4 Blenheim Intruders to Holland, 20 aircraft minelaying in the German Bight, 7 leaflet flights to France. No losses.

Total effort for the night: 327 sorties, 10 aircraft (3·1 per cent) lost.

13/14 April 1942

Minor Operations

4 Wellingtons to Boulogne, 47 aircraft minelaying in the Frisians and the German Bight, 3 leaflet flights. 1 Stirling minelayer was lost.

---

14 April 1942

12 Bostons carried out accurate bombing at Mondeville power-station without loss.

14/15 April 1942

DORTMUND

208 aircraft – 142 Wellingtons, 34 Hampdens, 20 Stirlings, 8 Halifaxes, 4 Manchesters – a force which was several times greater than any previously sent to this city. 5 Wellingtons and 4 Hampdens lost.

132 aircraft claimed to have bombed Dortmund but bombing photographs showed that bombs fell across a 40-mile stretch of the Ruhr. Dortmund reports 1 unspecified industrial building destroyed, 1 military establishment severely damaged, 4 dwelling-houses destroyed and 31 damaged with 4 people killed and 27 injured. It is probable that other Ruhr cities and towns were hit but no details are available.

Minor Operations: 23 aircraft to Le Havre (all bombs fell in open country), 5 Blenheim Intruders to Soesterberg airfield, 1 Stirling minelaying near Heligoland. 1 Wellington lost on the Le Havre raid.

Total effort for the night: 237 sorties, 10 aircraft (4·8 per cent) lost.

---

15 April 1942

9 Bostons bombed harbour and railway targets at Cherbourg without loss.

15/16 April 1942

DORTMUND

152 aircraft – 111 Wellingtons, 19 Hampdens, 15 Stirlings, 7 Manchesters. 3 Wellingtons and 1 Stirling lost.

Thick cloud and icing were encountered. Only 88 aircraft claimed to have bombed Dortmund which reports 1 house destroyed and 13 seriously damaged, 2 people killed and 6 injured. Bombs falling in Dortmund were equivalent to eight aircraft loads.

Minor Operations: 18 Whitleys to St-Nazaire, 8 Wellingtons to Le Havre, 4 Blenheim Intruders, 11 aircraft minelaying off St-Nazaire, 4 leaflet flights to France. No aircraft lost.

---

16 April 1942

12 Bostons bombed Le Havre power-station and docks accurately and without loss.

16/17 April 1942

Minor Operations

21 aircraft to Le Havre and Lorient, 21 aircraft minelaying off French ports, 11 leaflet flights to France. 1 Manchester and 1 Wellington lost from the minelaying operation.

---

17 April 1942

THE AUGSBURG RAID

This was another of Sir Arthur Harris's experimental raids, an attempt to achieve accurate bombing of a vital target using a small force of the new Lancaster bombers flying at low level in daylight. The target selected by Bomber Command was the diesel-engine manufacturing workshop building in the M.A.N. factory at Augsburg, 500 miles from the French coast. Harris had earlier considered attacking one of the ball-bearing factories at Schweinfurt but preferred the Augsburg target for tactical reasons.

After a week of low-flying practice, 12 Lancasters – 6 each from 44 and 97 Squadrons – carried out this famous raid. 30 Bostons and a large Fighter Command effort were dispatched to targets in Northern France to divert German fighter attention from the Lancaster force but were not completely successful in this. 1 Boston was lost. 4 of the Lancasters were shot down *en route* to Augsburg and 3 more near the target. The 8 crews which did reach the target carried out accurate bombing but the casualties were too heavy and this type of operation was not repeated. Squadron Leader J. D. Nettleton of 44 Squadron, who returned in a badly damaged aircraft, was awarded the Victoria Cross for his leadership of the raid.

There was later some dispute over this raid. The British Official History contains the text of letters between the Ministry of Economic Warfare, the Prime Minister, the Air Ministry and Bomber Command over the selection of the diesel-engine factory at Augsburg for this raid. The Ministry of Economic Warfare protested that there were other, more vital, bottleneck targets in Southern Germany which they would have recommended for such a risky raid. Sir Arthur Harris defended his decision on tactical grounds and the correspondence ended on 2 May.

17/18 April 1942

HAMBURG

173 aircraft – 134 Wellingtons, 23 Stirlings, 11 Halifaxes, 5 Manchesters. 7 Wellingtons and 1 Manchester lost.

107 crews claimed to have bombed the target but the German estimate was that no more than 50 aircraft had attacked Hamburg. There were 75 fires in Hamburg – 33 classed as large – 23 people were killed and 66 injured. The largest fire was in the warehouse of a drinks manufacturer. 60,000 bottles of alcohol were lost, mainly because the heat of the fire forced the corks out of the bottles.

Minor Operations: 22 Whitleys to St-Nazaire, 4 aircraft to Le Havre, 6 Blenheim Intruders to Holland, 9 aircraft minelaying off Heligoland. 1 Intruder and 1 minelaying Manchester lost.

Total effort for the night: 214 sorties, 10 aircraft (4·7 per cent) lost.

19/20 April 1942

Minelaying

51 aircraft to the Frisian Islands; 1 Hampden and 1 Wellington lost.

22/23 April 1942

COLOGNE

64 Wellingtons and 5 Stirlings, all equipped with *Gee*, were dispatched on an experimental raid, with orders to use *Gee* as a blind-bombing aid. Some bombs were dropped accurately into Cologne but others were up to 10 miles from the target. 2 Wellingtons lost.

Cologne records show that 44 high-explosive and 1,200 incendiary bombs fell in the city, perhaps 12 to 15 aircraft loads. 4 people were killed and 8 injured and minor property damage was caused, although 6 industrial buildings are shown as having been damaged.

Minor Operations: 23 aircraft to Le Havre, 63 aircraft minelaying off Germany and Denmark, 1 leaflet flight to France. 1 Wellington on the Le Havre raid and 1 Hampden minelayer lost.

23/24 April 1942

ROSTOCK

161 aircraft – 93 Wellingtons, 31 Stirlings, 19 Whitleys, 11 Hampdens, 6 Manchesters, 1 Lancaster. 4 aircraft – 2 Wellingtons, 1 Manchester, 1 Whitley – lost.

This was the first of a series of 4 raids on this Baltic port town. These raids had many of the characteristics of the successful raid on nearby Lübeck 1 month earlier – a concentrated, incendiary, area-bombing attack on the narrow-street *Altstadt* of a town with only light defences. An added feature on each night, however, was the inclusion of a small force of bombers, from 5 Group on the first 3 nights, to attempt a precision attack on the Heinkel aircraft factory on the southern outskirts of Rostock.

On this first night, 143 aircraft were sent to bomb the town and 18 the Heinkel factory. Bombing conditions were good but the results of the raid were disappointing. The Heinkel factory was not hit and most of the main bombing intended for the *Altstadt* fell between 2 and 6 miles away. (Details of damage and casualties can only be given in combined totals for the series of raids; these are included in the fourth and last raid of the series, on 26/27 April 1942.)

24 April 1942

12 Bostons bombed Flushing docks; 6 further Bostons to Abbeville were recalled. No Bostons lost.

24/25 April 1942

ROSTOCK

125 aircraft of 6 types, 91 to the town and 34 to the Heinkel factory. 1 Hampden lost.

The centre of the town was bombed heavily on this night but the Heinkel factory buildings were not hit, although some bombs did fall in the general factory area.

Minor Operations: 39 aircraft to Dunkirk, 4 Blenheim Intruders, 3 leaflet flights. 1 Intruder lost.

25 April 1942

36 Bostons on *Circus* operations to Abbeville railway yards, Morlaix airfield and harbour targets at Cherbourg, Le Havre and Dunkirk. 29 aircraft bombed; 2 Bostons lost.

25/26 April 1942

ROSTOCK

128 aircraft of 6 types, 110 to the town and 18 to the Heinkel factory. No aircraft were lost although crews reported that Rostock's Flak defences had been strengthened.

Heavy bombing of the town and many fires were achieved. Some aircraft also hit the Heinkel factory for the first time; the crews achieving this were flying Manchesters from 106 Squadron, which was commanded by Wing Commander Guy Gibson.

Minor Operations: 6 Stirlings carried out a long-range attack on the Škoda armaments factory at Pilsen in Czechoslovakia (this target was found to be cloud-covered on arrival but at least 5 Stirlings bombed), 32 aircraft to Dunkirk, 2 Blenheim Intruders, 5 leaflet flights to France. 1 Stirling lost from the Pilsen raid.

26 April 1942

12 Bostons carried out accurate bombing of St-Omer and Hazebrouck railway yards without loss.

26/27 April 1942

ROSTOCK

106 or 109 aircraft (there are conflicting figures) of 7 different types, approximately half to the town and half to the Heinkel factory. 3 aircraft – 1 Stirling, 1 Wellington, 1 Whitley – lost. The Official History describes this raid as 'the masterpiece', with successful bombing by both parts of the force.*

---

* The Official History's description of the Rostock raids is in Vol. I, pp. 393-5.

The 4 raids in this series resulted in the destruction of 1,765 buildings and serious damage to 513 more buildings in Rostock. Bomber Command estimated that 130 acres were destroyed, 60 per cent of the main town area. Casualties were 204 people killed and 89 injured, figures which would have been much higher if large numbers of people had not fled after the first raids.

In reporting these raids, the Germans used the expression *'Terrorangriff'* ('terror raid') for the first time. Goebbels remarked in his diary that, 'community life in Rostock is practically at an end'.*

Minor Operations: 24 aircraft to Dunkirk, 2 Blenheim Intruders to Leeuwarden, 4 aircraft minelaying, 7 O.T.U. sorties. No losses.

---

27 April 1942

18 Bostons to Ostend and Lille; 1 Boston lost.

27/28 April 1942

COLOGNE

97 aircraft – 76 Wellingtons, 19 Stirlings, 2 Halifaxes. 6 Wellingtons and 1 Halifax lost.

Bombing conditions were favourable and this small force claimed good results. Cologne reports 9 industrial premises and 1,520 houses hit or damaged, and 19 other premises affected. 11 people were killed, 52 injured and 1,683 bombed out. A considerable number of bombs, however, fell outside the city to the east. Individual damage incidents recorded were: a technical school, a finance office, a telegraph office and 3 old churches all burnt out and 150 hectares of the Tannenwald destroyed by fire.

TRONDHEIM

31 Halifaxes and 12 Lancasters to attack the *Tirpitz* and other German warships in Trondheim Fjord. The *Tirpitz* was found and bombed but no hits were scored. 4 Halifaxes and 1 Lancaster lost.

One of the lost Halifaxes was piloted by Wing Commander D. C. T. Bennett, later the commander of the Pathfinders; Bennett escaped to neutral Sweden and returned to England 5 weeks later.

Another Halifax lost on this raid, W1048 of 35 Squadron, was damaged by Flak and its pilot, Pilot Officer Donald McIntyre, crash-landed it on the frozen surface of a nearby lake, Lake Hoklingen. The crew all survived and the Halifax, a new aircraft on its first operational flight, sank gently. In 1973 this aircraft was salvaged from the bed of the lake and, after restoration by airmen at R.A.F. Wyton, was placed on public display in the R.A.F. Museum at Hendon.

*The Goebbels Diaries, Hamish Hamilton, 1948, p. 146.

Minor Operations: 12 aircraft to Dunkirk, 8 aircraft minelaying off German coasts, 3 Lancasters from 5 Group and 5 O.T.U. Wellingtons on leaflet flights. 2 Halifaxes from the Dunkirk raid, 1 Stirling and 2 O.T.U. Wellingtons were lost to make the casualties for this night 17 aircraft, 10·1 per cent of the forces dispatched.

The 2 Whitleys dispatched by 58 Squadron to Dunkirk represent the last Whitley operations flown by a front-line Bomber Command squadron; their last operation to Germany had been by 5 aircraft against Rostock the previous night. O.T.U.s would continue to use small numbers of Whitleys on leaflet flights for some time.

---

28 April 1942

6 Bostons bombed St-Omer railway yards accurately and without loss.

28/29 April 1942

KIEL

88 aircraft – 62 Wellingtons, 15 Stirlings, 10 Hampdens, 1 Halifax. 5 Wellingtons and 1 Hampden lost.

54 aircraft claimed good bombing results in bright moonlight but against strong Flak and fighter defences. Post-raid photographs reported 'no new damage' but the Kiel records show that damage was caused at all 3 shipyards, to the hospital of the Naval Academy and to the university library as well as to private housing. 15 people were killed and 74 injured.

TRONDHEIM

23 Halifaxes and 11 Lancasters to attack the *Tirpitz*. Hits were claimed but these were not confirmed. 2 Halifaxes lost.

Minor Operations: 6 Blenheims to Langenbrugge power-station, 4 Blenheim Intruders, 6 aircraft minelaying off Kiel and Heligoland. 1 Blenheim lost from the Langenbrugge raid.

---

29 April 1942

6 Bostons bombed Dunkirk docks without loss.

29/30 April 1942

PARIS/GENNEVILLIERS

88 aircraft – 73 Wellingtons, 9 Hampdens, 6 Stirlings – to the Gnome & Rhône aero-engine factory. 3 Wellingtons lost.

The main factory was not hit but other industrial buildings in the nearby Port de Paris on the Seine were. The local report says that 1 industrial building was destroyed and 3 more damaged with no casualties being suffered by French people.

Minor Operations: 20 aircraft to Ostend, 6 Blenheim Intruders, 5 Manchesters minelaying off Kiel and the Danish coast. 1 Wellington and 1 Whitley from the 'freshmen' raid on Ostend and 1 minelaying Manchester were lost.

---

30 April 1942

24 Bostons on escorted raids to Le Havre and Flushing docks, Abbeville railway yards and Morlaix airfield. All targets were bombed without loss.

1 May 1942

12 Bostons attacked a parachute factory at Calais and the railway station at St-Omer, both of which were bombed. No Bostons lost.

2/3 May 1942

MINELAYING

96 aircraft of 3 and 5 Groups carried out extensive minelaying from Germany to Brittany. 2 Manchesters lost.

11 aircraft made leaflet flights to France without loss.

3 May 1942

6 Bostons bombed Dunkirk docks without loss.

3/4 May 1942

HAMBURG

On the 100th anniversary of a great fire in Hamburg, Bomber Command sent a comparatively small force of aircraft to attack this city after receiving an unfavourable weather forecast. 81 aircraft were dispatched: 43 Wellingtons, 20 Halifaxes, 13 Stirlings and 5 Hampdens. 3 Halifaxes and 2 Wellingtons were lost. The Bomber Command Operations Record Book contained no reference to the anniversary of the fire.

Hamburg was found to be completely cloud-covered and only 54 aircraft bombed on to its estimated position. Despite these unfavourable circumstances, a success out of all proportion to the numbers of aircraft involved was achieved. 113 fires were started in Hamburg, of which 57 were classed as large. Reported as completely burnt out were a large entertainment palace, a theatre and a cinema (all in the Reeperbahn area), and a dockside warehouse full of goods and vehicles. One 4,000-lb bomb lived up to its 'blockbuster' reputation when it exploded at a street junction in an old residential area near the city centre. 11 blocks of flats in the narrow streets were destroyed by blast, 11 more buildings were severely damaged and 352 slightly damaged. 59 people were killed here and 67 injured. The total casualty list in Hamburg on this night was 77 killed, 243 injured and 1,624 bombed out.

Minor Operations: 9 aircraft to St-Nazaire, 4 Blenheim Intruders, 2 aircraft minelaying off Heligoland, 8 aircraft on leaflet flights to France. No losses.

4 May 1942

6 Bostons to Le Havre power-station, but the only hits were on nearby buildings. No Bostons lost.

4/5 May 1942

STUTTGART

121 aircraft – 69 Wellingtons, 19 Hampdens, 14 Lancasters, 12 Stirlings, 7 Halifaxes – on the first large raid on this city. 1 Stirling lost.

As on the recent Rostock raids, a proportion of the force was detailed to attack a specific factory target, on this occasion the Robert Bosch factory, which made dynamos, injection pumps and magnetos. The Ministry of Economic Warfare judged this factory to be one of the most important in Germany. But Stuttgart, which straggled along a series of deep valleys, was a notoriously difficult target to find, even in conditions of good visibility. On this night, 10/10ths cloud covered the whole area and the raid was a failure. Bombs were scattered across a wide area of Stuttgart and the surrounding countryside. 13 people were killed and 37 injured in Stuttgart but 12 of the dead were the result of one 4,000-lb bomb in the north-western suburb of Zuffenhausen. The Bosch works were not hit. A decoy site near Lauffen, 15 miles north of Stuttgart, attracted many bombs. This clever decoy was 'defended' by up to 35 searchlights and 50 Flak guns and regularly attracted bombs when targets in Southern Germany were attacked. The town of Lauffen was bombed 37 times in the war because of the decoy; Stuttgart people were not popular there.

Minor Operations: 9 aircraft to Nantes, 5 Stirlings to Pilsen, 8 aircraft minelaying off Heligoland, 6 aircraft on leaflet flights to France. 1 Stirling lost on the Pilsen raid.

---

5 May 1942

12 Bostons to Zeebrugge coke ovens and Lille power-station; only the Zeebrugge target was bombed. No Bostons lost.

5/6 May 1942

STUTTGART

77 aircraft – 49 Wellingtons, 13 Stirlings, 11 Halifaxes, 4 Lancasters – to the city and the Bosch factory. 3 Wellingtons and 1 Stirling lost.

There was no cloud but the ground was haze-covered. The Lauffen decoy again attracted much of the bombing. The nearest bombs to Stuttgart fell in woods west of the city.

Minor Operations: 19 aircraft to Nantes, 4 Blenheim Intruders to Schiphol, 10 aircraft on leaflet flights to France. No losses.

---

6 May 1942

18 Bostons to Boulogne docks, Calais parachute factory and Caen power-station. All targets were bombed without loss to the Bostons.

6/7 May 1942

STUTTGART

97 aircraft – 55 Wellingtons, 15 Stirlings, 10 Hampdens, 10 Lancasters, 7 Halifaxes – to the city and the Bosch factory. 5 Wellingtons and 1 Halifax lost.

This third raid on Stuttgart was another failure, with crews again blaming ground haze for their inability to identify the city. Stuttgart's records show that no bombs fell in the city, though a few fell in woods to the west. The Lauffen decoy may have been responsible for a raid which developed on the large town of Heilbronn, only 5 miles from the decoy fire site but 20 miles from Stuttgart. More than 150 buildings were hit in Heilbronn and 7 people died there.

Minor Operations: 19 aircraft to Nantes, 4 Blenheim Intruders, 9 aircraft on leaflet flights to France. 1 Intruder lost.

---

7 May 1942

12 Bostons to Ostend power-station and Zeebrugge coke ovens; direct hits were scored at Zeebrugge, near misses at Ostend. No Bostons lost.

7/8 May 1942

MINELAYING

81 aircraft of 3 and 5 Groups to Copenhagen, the Great Belt, Kiel and Heligoland. 1 Hampden and 1 Wellington lost.

Minor Operations: 5 aircraft to St-Nazaire, 1 Halifax on leaflet flight to France. No losses.

---

8 May 1942

6 Bostons to Dieppe port and railway yards; none were lost.

8/9 May 1942

WARNEMÜNDE

193 aircraft – 98 Wellingtons, 27 Stirlings, 21 Lancasters, 19 Halifaxes, 19 Hampdens, 9 Manchesters – to the town and the nearby Heinkel aircraft factory. 19 aircraft – 8 Wellingtons, 4 Lancasters, 3 Hampdens, 2 Halifaxes, 1 Manchester, 1 Stirling – lost.

No details are available from Warnemünde but Bomber Command's own records say 'the attack was only moderately successful'.

Minor Operations: 3 Blenheim Intruders to Leeuwarden, 3 aircraft minelaying off Heligoland. No losses.

---

9 May 1942

12 Bostons to an oil depot at Bruges and railway yards at Hazebrouck. Only 'near misses' could be achieved at both targets. No Bostons lost.

9/10 May 1942

MINELAYING

20 aircraft to Danish coasts, Kiel and the German Bight. No losses.

---

13 May 1942

4 Wellingtons on cloud-cover raids to Essen but this target was not found. 3 aircraft bombed Mülheim and 2 unidentified places. No aircraft lost.

15/16 May 1942

MINELAYING

50 aircraft to the Western Baltic. 2 Hampdens and 2 Wellingtons lost.

---

17 May 1942

12 Bostons to Boulogne docks which were accurately bombed without loss to the Bostons.

16/17 May 1942

7 Lancasters and 7 Manchesters of 5 Group minelaying off Heligoland and Kiel without loss.

17/18 May 1942

MINELAYING

32 Stirlings and 28 Wellingtons of 3 Group to the Frisians and the Heligoland area. German night fighters were active and 5 Stirlings and 2 Wellingtons were lost.

Minor Operations: 27 aircraft to Boulogne, 1 Stirling on a leaflet flight to France. 1 Wellington lost on the Boulogne raid.

19/20 May 1942

MANNHEIM

197 aircraft – 105 Wellingtons, 31 Stirlings, 29 Halifaxes, 15 Hampdens, 13 Lancasters, 4 Manchesters. 11 aircraft – 4 Halifaxes, 4 Stirlings, 3 Wellingtons – lost.

155 aircraft reported hitting Mannheim but most of their bombing photographs showed forests or open country. The Mannheim report describes the long delay before the attack developed, with aircraft at greater heights than in previous raids passing to and fro searching for the target. When the raid did begin, bombs approximately equivalent to no more than 10 aircraft loads fell in the city. A concentrated group of about 600 incendiaries in the harbour area on the Rhine burnt out 4 small industrial concerns – a blanket factory, a mineral-water factory, a chemical wholesalers and a timber merchants. Only light damage was caused elsewhere in the city. The only fatal casualties were 2 firemen.

Minor Operations: 65 'freshmen' crews to St-Nazaire but bombing results were poor, 9 aircraft minelaying off Lorient and near Heligoland, 13 aircraft on leaflet flights to France. 1 Wellington lost on the St-Nazaire raid.

Total effort for the night: 284 sorties, 12 aircraft (4·2 per cent) lost.

21/22 May 1942

MINELAYING

33 Wellingtons and 15 Stirlings of 3 Group to the Biscay ports but poor weather allowed only 18 aircraft to lay mines. No aircraft lost.

22/23 May 1942

Minor Operations

27 Halifaxes to St-Nazaire but cloud prevented all but 3 from bombing, 31 aircraft minelaying to St-Nazaire and off German Baltic ports. No aircraft lost.

---

25 May 1942

4 Bostons on uneventful sweep off the Dutch coast.

26/27 May 1942

4 Lancasters minelaying in the Great Belt without loss.

29/30 May 1942

PARIS/GENNEVILLIERS

77 aircraft – 31 Wellingtons, 20 Halifaxes, 14 Lancasters, 9 Stirlings, 3 Hampdens – to the Gnome & Rhône factory. 4 Wellingtons and 1 Halifax lost.

Later photographic cover showed little or no damage to the factory. A local report says that 38 houses were destroyed and 49 damaged, with 34 French people being killed and 167 injured.

Minor Operations: 31 aircraft to Cherbourg, 17 aircraft to Dieppe, 21 aircraft minelaying in the Frisians and off Copenhagen. 3 aircraft on leaflet flights to France. 1 Stirling minelayer lost.

Operational Statistics, 22/23 February to 30 May 1942
(97 days/nights)

Number of days with operations: 46
Number of nights with operations: 60
Number of daylight sorties: 552, from which 15 aircraft (2·7 per cent) were lost
Number of night sorties: 8,019, from which 298 aircraft (3·7 per cent) were lost
Total sorties: 8,571, from which 313 aircraft (3·7 per cent) were lost
Approximate bomb tonnage in period: 9,253 tons
Averages per 24-hour period: 88·3 sorties, 3·2 aircraft lost, 95·4 tons of bombs dropped

11. THE THOUSAND RAIDS

30/31 May to 17 August 1942

Sir Arthur Harris was determined to capitalize on the undoubted successes against Lübeck and Rostock. He knew that the future of Bomber Command was still in doubt and he approached both Winston Churchill and Sir Charles Portal with the bold idea of assembling a force of 1,000 bombers and sending them out in one massive raid on a German city. Churchill and Portal were both impressed and they agreed. Although Harris had only a little over 400 aircraft with trained crews which were regularly used for front-line operational work, he did have a considerable number of further aircraft in the 'conversion units' attached to groups with four-engined aircraft and in Bomber Command's own operational training units 91 and 92 Groups. This secondary Bomber Command strength could be crewed by a combination of instructors, many of them ex-operational, and by men in the later stages of their training. To complete the 1,000 aircraft required, Harris asked for the help of his fellow commanders-in-chief in Coastal Command and Flying Training Command. Both officers were willing to help. Sir Philip Joubert of Coastal Command immediately offered to provide 250 bombers, many of them being from squadrons which had once served in Bomber Command. Flying Training Command offered fifty aircraft but many of these were later found to be insufficiently equipped for night bombing and only four Wellingtons were eventually provided from this source.

All now looked well. The target figure of 1,000 bombers was easily covered and detailed planning for the operation commenced. The tactics to be employed were of major concern, not only for the success of this unprecedented raid but as an experiment upon which future operations could be based. The tactics eventually adopted would form the basis for standard Bomber Command operations for the next two years and some elements would remain in use until the end of the war.

The major innovation was the introduction of a 'bomber stream' in which all aircraft would fly by a common route and at the same speed to and from the target, each aircraft being allotted a height band and a time slot in the stream to minimize the risk of collision. The recent introduction of *Gee* made it much easier for crews to navigate within the precise limits required for such flying, although there would always be wayward crews who would drift away from the stream. The hoped-for advantage from the bomber stream was that the bomber force could pass through the minimum number of German radar night-fighter boxes. The controller in each box could only direct a maximum of six potential interceptions per hour. The passage of the stream through the smallest number of boxes would, therefore, reduce the number of possible interceptions, particularly if the bomber stream could be kept as short as possible and pass through the belt of boxes quickly. This led on to the next decision, to reduce still further the time allowed for the actual bombing at the target. Where four hours had been allowed earlier in the war for a raid by 100 aircraft and two hours had been deemed a revolutionary concentration for 234 aircraft at Lübeck, only 90 minutes were allowed for 1,000 aircraft in this coming operation. The big fear in these matters was always that of collisions but, on this occasion, this was accepted in return for the opportunity to allow the bomber stream to pass through the night-fighter boxes quickly, to swamp the Flak defences at the target and, above all, to put down such a concentration of incendiary bombs in a short period that the fire services would be overwhelmed and large areas of the city would be consumed by conflagrations. As in previous raids, the coming operation would be led by experienced crews whose aircraft were equipped with *Gee*; 1 and 3 Groups were selected to provide these 'raid leaders' in the Thousand Plan.

But, as the planning period came to an end, potential disaster struck. The Admiralty refused to allow the Coastal Command aircraft to take part in the raid. This was obviously a step in the long-running battle between the R.A.F. and the Royal Navy over the control of maritime air power and the Admiralty realized that a success for this grandiose Bomber Command plan was not likely to help their prospects for building up a force of long-range aircraft for the war against the U-boat. They were quite correct in that belief. Harris now appeared to be falling well short of the dramatic figure of 1,000 aircraft with which he intended to carry out what was evidently a massive public-relations exercise; the word 'demonstration' is frequently used in histories of the air war.

Bomber Command redoubled its efforts. Every spare aircrew member and aircraft was gathered in by the operational squadrons but the decisive reinforcement came from Bomber Command's own training units, which committed more crews from the bottom half of their training courses. Every effort was made to provide the training crews with at least an experienced pilot but forty-nine aircraft out of the 208 provided by 91 Group would take off with pupil pilots. When the operation was eventually mounted, 1,047 bombers would be able to take off, all but the four from Training Command being provided by Bomber Command's own resources, in spite of the fearful risk of sending so many untrained crews. When Churchill and Harris discussed the possible casualty figures, Churchill said that he would be prepared for the loss of 100 aircraft. The force about to be dispatched was more than two and a half times greater than any previous single night's effort by Bomber Command. In addition to the bombers, forty-nine Blenheims of 2 Group reinforced by thirty-nine aircraft of Fighter Command and fifteen from Army Co-operation Command would carry out Intruder raids on German night-fighter airfields near the route of the bomber stream.

Final orders were ready on 26 May with the full moon approaching. The force stood ready, waiting for the weather. Harris hoped to use the 1,000-bomber force more than once if conditions permitted, before the extra aircraft gathered together were dispersed to their normal locations. His first choice of target was Hamburg, the second largest city in Germany, a great port and, an attraction for the Admiralty, builder of about 100 U-boats each year. But the weather over Germany was unfavourable for three days running and, on 30 May, Harris had to decide to send the bombers to his second target choice – Cologne, the third largest city in Germany. Soon after noon on that day, the order to attack Cologne went out to the groups and squadrons and the raid took place that night.

The first 1,000-bomber raid was a great success but a follow-up to Essen two nights later was not. The moon phase then passed and the training aircraft returned to their normal work, but they were recalled once more for a further massive raid on Bremen during the end of the June moon period, although the figure of 1,000 aircraft was not quite reached on that raid. Harris had originally hoped to assemble 1,000 aircraft for one or two raids in every moon period but he abandoned this idea and the full 'thousand' operation using so many training aircraft was not carried out again after the Bremen raid, although smaller numbers of training aircraft were called upon from time to time later in the year.

The 1,000-bomber raids certainly made their mark on history and were another great turning-point in Bomber Command's war. The new tactics were mainly successful; there were never any serious casualties through collision and the 'time over target' would progressively be shortened until 700 or 800 aircraft regularly passed over the city they were bombing in less than twenty minutes! The morale of Bomber Command was certainly uplifted by this great demonstration of air power and by the wide publicity which followed. That same publicity also confirmed Bomber Command's future as a major force and it can be said that, although there were bad as well as good times to come, Bomber Command never looked back after the 1,000-bomber raids. These events also placed Sir Arthur Harris firmly in the public eye where, as 'Bomber' Harris, he would remain for the rest of his life.

The rest of the midsummer weeks passed with the front-line squadrons being pressed hard when the weather and moon conditions were favourable – and sometimes when they were not so favourable. The shorter nights again restricted raids to the coastal targets, the Ruhr and the Rhineland. There was another concentration of sustained effort against Essen in June, but this important target remained elusive of Bomber Command success. A similar campaign against Duisburg fared little better. There were minor operational changes. Harris started to restrict the practice whereby 'freshmen' crews were introduced to operations gradually by being sent to lightly defended, close-range targets on the French coast. New crews were still allowed their one leaflet flight to France or Belgium but after that they were expected to go to any target in Europe. Harris was forced to agree to the temporary detachment of six more squadrons – even one of Lancasters – and one of his operational training units to Coastal Command to help with the U-boat war. There was a further draining away of operational effort when that unsatisfactory new aircraft, the Manchester, disappeared from 5 Group's order of battle at the end of June – although the Lancasters being sent to this group would soon more than replace the loss. There were only minor changes in 2 Group although one feature was to be the portent of a brilliant future for a new type of aircraft. In the early morning after the first 1,000-bomber raid, five small twin-engined bombers of wooden construction flew to the smoking city of Cologne to take photographs and throw a few more bombs into that unhappy place. The De Havilland Mosquito had arrived. By the time the war ended, this aircraft would perform an undreamt-of range of tasks for Bomber Command.

30/31 May 1942

THE THOUSAND-BOMBER RAID, COLOGNE

1,047 aircraft were dispatched, this number being made up as follows:

1 Group – 156 Wellingtons
3 Group – 134 Wellingtons, 88 Stirlings = 222 aircraft
4 Group – 131 Halifaxes, 9 Wellingtons, 7 Whitleys = 147 aircraft
5 Group – 73 Lancasters, 46 Manchesters, 34 Hampdens = 153 aircraft

91 (O.T.U.) Group – 236 Wellingtons, 21 Whitleys = 257 aircraft
92 (O.T.U.) Group – 63 Wellingtons, 45 Hampdens = 108 aircraft
Flying Training Command – 4 Wellingtons

Aircraft totals: 602 Wellingtons, 131 Halifaxes, 88 Stirlings, 79 Hampdens, 73 Lancasters, 46 Manchesters, 28 Whitleys = 1,047 aircraft

The exact number of aircraft claiming to have bombed Cologne is in doubt; the Official History says '898 aircraft bombed' but Bomber Command's Night Bombing Sheets indicate that 868 aircraft bombed the main target with 15 aircraft bombing other targets. The total tonnage of bombs was 1,455, two-thirds of this tonnage being incendiaries.

German records* show that 2,500 separate fires were started, of which the local fire brigade classed 1,700 as 'large' but there was no 'sea of fire' as had been experienced at Lübeck and Rostock because Cologne was mainly a modern city with wide streets. The local records contained an impressive list of property damaged: 3,330 buildings destroyed, 2,090 seriously damaged and 7,420 lightly damaged. More than 90 per cent of this damage was caused by fire rather than high-explosive bombs. Among the above total of 12,840 buildings were 2,560 industrial and commercial buildings, though many of these were small ones. However, 36 large firms suffered complete loss of production, 70 suffered 50–80 per cent loss and 222 up to 50 per cent. Among the buildings classed as totally destroyed were: 7 official administration buildings, 14 public buildings, 7 banks, 9 hospitals, 17 churches, 16 schools, 4 university buildings, 10 postal and railway buildings, 10 buildings of historic interest, 2 newspaper offices, 4 hotels, 2 cinemas and 6 department stores. Damage was also caused to 17 water mains, 5 gas mains, 32 main-electricity cables and 12 main-telephone routes. The only military installation mentioned is a Flak barracks. In domestic housing, the following 'dwelling units' (mainly flats/apartments) are listed: 13,010 destroyed, 6,360 seriously damaged, 22,270 lightly damaged. These details of physical damage in Cologne are a good example of the results of area bombing. Similar results can be expected in those of Bomber Command's raids which were successful during following years.

The estimates of casualties in Cologne are, unusually, quite precise. Figures quoted for deaths vary only between 469 and 486. The 469 figure comprises 411 civilians and 58 military casualties, mostly members of Flak units. This death toll was a new record for an R.A.F. raid. 5,027 people were listed as injured and 45,132 as bombed out. It was estimated that from 135,000 to 150,000 of Cologne's population of nearly 700,000 people fled the city after the raid.

The R.A.F. casualties were also a record high figure. 41 aircraft were lost, including 1 Wellington which was known to have crashed into the sea. The 41 lost aircraft were: 29 Wellingtons, 4 Manchesters, 3 Halifaxes, 2 Stirlings, 1 Hampden, 1 Lancaster, 1 Whitley. The total loss of aircraft exceeded the previous highest loss of 37 aircraft on the night of 7/8 November 1941 when a large force was sent out in bad weather conditions, but the proportion of the force lost in the Cologne raid – 3·9 per cent – though high, was deemed acceptable in view of the perfect weather conditions which not only led to the bombing success but also helped the German defences.

---

*Sources consulted are: our local 'consultant' in Cologne, Herr Erich Quadflieg, who in turn has had access to Cologne's civil records; the British Official History; and Hans Brunswig's *Feuersturm über Hamburg* (Brunswig had contact with the Cologne fire brigade).

Bomber Command later estimated that 22 aircraft were lost over or near Cologne – 16 shot down by Flak, 4 by night fighters and 2 in a collision; most of the other losses were due to night-fighter action in the radar boxes between the coast and Cologne. Bomber Command also calculated the losses suffered by each of the three waves of the attack – 4·8, 4·1 and 1·9 per cent – and assumed that the German defences were progressively overwhelmed by bombing and affected by smoke as the raid went on. Further calculations showed that the losses suffered by the operational training unit crews – 3·3 per cent – were lower than the 4·1 per cent casualties of the regular bomber groups and also that those training aircraft with pupil pilots suffered lower casualties than those with instructor pilots!

Another Victoria Cross was awarded for an action on this night. A Manchester of 50 Squadron, piloted by Flying Officer L. T. Manser, was caught in a searchlight cone and seriously damaged by Flak on the approaches to Cologne. Manser held the plane steady until his bomb load was released and, despite further damage, set course for England although he and his crew could have safely baled out after leaving the target area. But the Manchester steadily lost height and, when it became obvious that there was no hope of reaching England, Manser ordered his crew to bale out, which they all did safely. In holding the plane steady for the last man to leave, Manser lost the opportunity to save himself and was killed. He is buried at Heverlee War Cemetery in Belgium.

INTRUDER OPERATIONS

In a major effort to help the bomber force attacking Cologne, 34 Blenheims of 2 Group, 15 Blenheims of Army Co-Operation Command and 7 Havocs of Fighter Command attempted to attack German night-fighter airfields alongside the bomber route. No particular success was gained by these Intruders and 2 of the Blenheims were lost.

Total effort for the night: 1,103 sorties, 43 aircraft (3·9 per cent) lost. (The 7 Havoc sorties of Fighter Command are included in these figures but have not been added to the statistics at the end of the current period of the diary because they did not take place directly under Bomber Command control.)

---

31 May 1942

5 Mosquitoes of 105 Squadron were dispatched to take photographs of bomb damage at Cologne and drop a few more bombs there. These were Bomber Command's first Mosquito operations of the war but 1 aircraft was hit by Flak and later crashed into the North Sea; the bodies of the crew, Pilot Officers W. D. Kennard and E. R. Johnson, were washed up on the Belgian coast and buried at Antwerp.

---

31 May/1 June 1942

2 Wellingtons were dispatched to Cologne but the area was found to be cloud-covered and no bombing results were seen. The Wellingtons both returned safely.

---

1 June 1942

12 Bostons to Flushing docks and 2 Mosquitoes to Cologne. 1 Mosquito lost.

1/2 June 1942

ESSEN

This was the second raid carried out by the 'Thousand Force' although the full 1,000 aircraft could not be provided on this night. 956 aircraft were dispatched: 545 Wellingtons, 127 Halifaxes, 77 Stirlings, 74 Lancasters, 71 Hampdens, 33 Manchesters and 29 Whitleys.

The plan was similar to the recent raid on Cologne except that many more flares were dropped by the 'raid leaders' flying in Wellingtons of 3 Group. Despite a reasonable weather forecast, crews experienced great difficulty in finding the target; the ground was covered either by haze or a layer of low cloud. Bombing was very scattered.

Essen reports only 11 houses destroyed and 184 damaged, mostly in the south of the city, and one prisoner of war working camp burnt out. Casualties were 15 people killed and 91 injured. Bombs also fell on at least 11 other towns in or near the Ruhr. Particularly heavy bombing occurred in Oberhausen with 83 people killed, Duisburg with 52 killed, and Mülheim with 15 killed.

31 bombers were lost: 15 Wellingtons, 8 Halifaxes, 4 Lancasters, 1 Hampden, 1 Manchester, 1 Stirling, 1 Whitley. This was 3·2 per cent of the force dispatched.

INTRUDERS

48 Blenheims to German airfields. 10 aircraft made attacks; 3 were lost. Fighter and Army Co-Operation Command aircraft were also operating.

---

2 June 1942

6 Bostons to Dieppe and 2 Mosquitoes to Essen; no losses.

2/3 June 1942

ESSEN

195 aircraft – 97 Wellingtons, 38 Halifaxes, 27 Lancasters, 21 Stirlings, 12 Hampdens. 14 aircraft – 7 Wellingtons, 2 Halifaxes, 2 Lancasters, 2 Stirlings, 1 Hampden – lost.

This attack was also widely scattered. Essen records only 3 high-explosive and 300 incendiary bombs in the city, with no serious damage or casualties.

Minor Operations: 6 Wellingtons to Dieppe, 11 aircraft minelaying off Lorient and St-Nazaire, 4 Hampdens on leaflet flights to France. 1 Hampden minelayer was lost.

3 June 1942

12 Bostons to Cherbourg docks and a power-station at Le Havre. Bombing was poor at Cherbourg but better at Le Havre. No Bostons lost.

3/4 June 1942

BREMEN

170 aircraft of all standard types were dispatched on the first large raid to Bremen since October 1941. 11 aircraft – 4 Wellingtons, 2 Halifaxes, 2 Lancasters, 2 Stirlings, 1 Manchester – lost.

Crews reported only indifferent bombing results but Bremen recorded this as a heavy attack, the results of which exceeded all previous raids. Housing areas were heavily hit with 6 streets affected by serious fires. Damage to the U-boat construction yards and the Focke-Wulf factory is described as 'of no importance' but there were hits in the harbour area which damaged a pier, some warehouses and the destroyer Z-25. With 83 people dead, 29 seriously and 229 slightly injured, this would turn out to be Bremen's third heaviest casualty toll in the war and was nearly as great as the raid by the 'Thousand Force' later in June.

Minor Operations: 4 Wellingtons to Dieppe, 9 Blenheim Intruders to airfields, 7 aircraft mine-laying in the River Gironde and off St-Nazaire, 5 aircraft on leaflet flights to France. No losses.

4 June 1942

12 Bostons to Boulogne and Dunkirk docks with accurate bombing at both targets. 1 Boston lost.

4/5 June 1942

Minor Operations

20 aircraft to Dieppe, 13 Blenheims to Schiphol airfield, 2 aircraft on leaflet flights to France. No aircraft lost.

This night represents the exact mid-point of the war between Britain and Germany but, for Bomber Command, 82 per cent of its sorties, 77 per cent of its aircraft losses and 94 per cent of its bomb tonnage were still to come.

5 June 1942

24 Bostons to power-stations at Le Havre and Ostend and to Morlaix airfield. All targets were bombed without loss to the Bostons. 1 Mosquito photographed Schiphol airfield and returned safely.

5/6 June 1942

ESSEN

180 aircraft – 98 Wellingtons, 33 Halifaxes, 25 Stirlings, 13 Lancasters, 11 Hampdens. 12 aircraft – 8 Wellingtons, 2 Stirlings, 1 Halifax, 1 Lancaster – lost.

This was another failure, with bombing being scattered over a wide area. Essen suffered minor property damage, 10 people killed and 68 injured.

Minor Operations: 15 aircraft minelaying to the Frisians and Quiberon Bay, 3 aircraft on leaflet flights to France. No losses.

---

6 June 1942

11 Bostons to Fécamp harbour turned back.

6/7 June 1942

EMDEN

233 aircraft – 124 Wellingtons, 40 Stirlings, 27 Halifaxes, 20 Lancasters, 15 Hampdens, 7 Manchesters – on the first large raid on this target since November 1941. 9 aircraft – 3 Manchesters, 3 Wellingtons, 2 Stirlings, 1 Halifax – lost.

Crews reported good bombing results and this was confirmed by later photographic reconnaissance. Emden reports briefly that approximately 300 houses were destroyed and 200 seriously damaged and that 17 people were killed and 49 injured. Some unspecified damage was also experienced in the docks area.

6 Blenheims on Intruder operations to airfields without loss.

7/8 June 1942

Minor Operations

43 aircraft minelaying to unnamed locations, 3 aircraft on leaflet flights to France. No losses.

---

8 June 1942

12 Bostons bombed the port area of Bruges without loss.

8/9 June 1942

ESSEN

170 aircraft – 92 Wellingtons, 42 Halifaxes, 14 Stirlings, 13 Lancasters, 9 Hampdens. 19 aircraft – 7 Wellingtons, 7 Halifaxes, 3 Lancasters, 1 Hampden, 1 Stirling – lost.

Yet again, this target was not identified accurately and bombing was scattered over a wide area. Essen suffered further light housing damage, 13 people killed and 42 injured.

Minor Operations: 19 aircraft to Dieppe, 6 Blenheim Intruders, 1 Stirling on a leaflet flight. No losses.

9/10 June 1942

MINELAYING

54 aircraft to the Frisian Islands and off Swinemünde in the Baltic. No aircraft lost.

---

10 June 1942

23 Bostons to Lannion airfield but only 11 reached and bombed this target, the remainder of the force turning back. 1 Boston lost in the sea.

11/12 June 1942

MINELAYING

91 aircraft to the Frisian Islands and off Swinemünde. 4 aircraft – 2 Lancasters, 1 Stirling, 1 Wellington – lost.

---

12 June 1942

4 Wellingtons to Essen. 2 aircraft bombed there. No aircraft lost.

16/17 June 1942

ESSEN

106 aircraft – 40 Wellingtons, 39 Halifaxes, 15 Lancasters, 12 Stirlings. 8 aircraft – 4 Halifaxes, 3 Wellingtons, 1 Stirling – lost.

Only 16 crews reported that they had identified Essen; 56 bombed alternative targets, 45 of them attacking Bonn. Essen reports only 3 high-explosive and 400 incendiary bombs in the city with one person being wounded.

This raid concluded the present series of 5 raids on Essen in 16 nights. 1,607 sorties had been dispatched and 84 aircraft (5·2 per cent) lost. No industrial damage was caused in Essen on any of these raids; a few houses were destroyed and 38 civilians were killed. Bomber Command now temporarily abandoned its campaign against Essen which would not be visited in strength for 3 months.

Minor Operations: 12 Hampdens minelaying off Lorient, 9 aircraft on leaflet flights to France. No losses.

17/18 June 1942

Minor Operations

27 Stirlings and Wellingtons to St-Nazaire but only 6 aircraft bombed, in poor weather, 46 aircraft minelaying off St-Nazaire and in the Frisians, 2 Stirlings on leaflet flights. No losses.

---

18 June 1942

3 Mosquitoes to Bremen and Bremerhaven but the only places bombed were Wilhelmshaven and the island of Langeoog. No aircraft lost.

18/19 June 1942

MINELAYING

65 aircraft to Lorient and the Frisian Islands. 1 Hampden lost.

19/20 June 1942

EMDEN

194 aircraft – 112 Wellingtons, 37 Halifaxes, 25 Stirlings, 11 Hampdens, 9 Lancasters. 9 aircraft – 6 Wellingtons, 2 Stirlings, 1 Halifax – lost.

131 crews claimed to have bombed Emden. Bombing photographs showed that part of the flare force started a raid on Osnabrück, 80 miles from Emden, in which 29 aircraft eventually joined. Emden recorded only 5 high-explosive bombs and 200–300 incendiaries with no damage or casualties.

Minor Operations: 6 Blenheim Intruders, 5 aircraft on leaflet flights to France. No losses.

---

20 June 1942

12 Bostons to Le Havre power-station and 2 Mosquitoes to Emden, all without loss.

20/21 June 1942

EMDEN

185 aircraft of 5 types. 8 aircraft – 3 Wellingtons, 2 Stirlings, 1 Halifax, 1 Lancaster – lost.

Only part of the bomber force identified the target. Emden reports about 100 houses damaged and 1 person injured.

Minor Operations: 5 Blenheim Intruders, 3 aircraft on leaflet flights to France. No losses.

---

21 June 1942

12 Bostons attempted to bomb a cargo ship in Dunkirk harbour; the bombs fell on railway lines near the ship. No Bostons lost.

21/22 June 1942

Minor Operations

56 aircraft minelaying off St-Nazaire, 2 aircraft on leaflet flights to France. 1 Wellington minelayer lost.

22 June 1942

12 Bostons to Dunkirk. 6 aircraft bombed the docks; the other 6 bombed a nearby airfield. No Bostons lost.

22/23 June 1942

EMDEN

227 aircraft – 144 Wellingtons, 38 Stirlings, 26 Halifaxes, 11 Lancasters, 8 Hampdens. 6 aircraft – 4 Wellingtons, 1 Lancaster, 1 Stirling – lost.

196 crews claimed good bombing results but decoy fires are believed to have drawn off many bombs. Emden reports: 50 houses destroyed, 100 damaged, damage in the harbour (no details available), 6 people killed and 40 injured.

Minor Operations: 10 Blenheim Intruders, 2 Stirlings on leaflet flights. No losses.

23 June 1942

12 Bostons to Dunkirk docks and 6 to Morlaix airfield. Both targets were believed to have been accurately bombed. No Bostons lost.

23/24 June 1942

Minor Operations

14 Wellingtons and Stirlings to St-Nazaire but only 3 crews found and bombed the target, 52 aircraft minelaying off Lorient, Verdon and St-Nazaire and in the Frisians, 1 Lancaster on a leaflet flight. 2 Wellington minelayers lost.

24/25 June 1942

ST-NAZAIRE

21 aircraft. No losses.

25/26 June 1942

BREMEN

The 'Thousand Force' was reassembled for this raid, although only 960 aircraft became available for Bomber Command use. Every type of aircraft in Bomber Command was included, even the Bostons and Mosquitoes of 2 Group which, so far, had only been used for day operations. The force was composed as follows: 472 Wellingtons, 124 Halifaxes, 96 Lancasters, 69 Stirlings, 51 Blenheims, 50 Hampdens, 50 Whitleys, 24 Bostons, 20 Manchesters and 4 Mosquitoes. Bomber Command never before, or after, dispatched such a mixed force.

After Churchill had intervened and insisted that the Admiralty allow Coastal Command to participate in this raid, a further 102 Hudsons and Wellingtons of Coastal Command were sent to Bremen but official records class this effort as a separate raid, not under Bomber Command control. 5 further aircraft provided by Army Co-Operation Command were also added to the force. The final numbers dispatched, 1,067 aircraft, made this a larger raid than that on Cologne at the end of May.

Parts of the force were allocated to specific targets in Bremen. The entire 5 Group effort – 142 aircraft – was ordered to bomb the Focke-Wulf factory; 20 Blenheims were allocated to the A.G. Weser shipyard; the Coastal Command aircraft were to bomb the Deschimag shipyard; all other aircraft were to carry out an area attack on the town and docks.

The tactics were basically similar to the earlier 'Thousand' raids except that the bombing period was now cut to 65 minutes. Bremen, on the wide River Weser, should have been an easy target to find and the inland penetration of the German night-fighter belt was only a shallow one. There were doubts about a band of cloud which lay across the Bremen area during the day, but this was being pushed steadily eastwards by a strong wind. Unfortunately the wind dropped in the evening and the bomber crews found the target completely covered for the whole period of the raid. The limited success which was gained was entirely due to the use of *Gee*, which enabled the leading crews to start fires, on to the glow of which many aircraft of later waves bombed. 696 Bomber Command aircraft were able to claim attacks on Bremen.

The results in general terms were not as dramatic as at Cologne but much better than the second 'Thousand' raid to Essen. Bremen reports a strengthening wind at the time of the raid which fanned the many fires started throughout the town, increased the extent of the damage and, according to the diary provided by the Bremen Stadtarchiv, left whole areas of dwelling-houses in ruins. 572 houses were completely destroyed and 6,108 damaged. More than 90 per cent of these were in the southern and eastern quarters of the town's four air-raid areas. 85 people were killed, 497 injured and 2,378 bombed out.

On the industrial side, the diary stated that the R.A.F.'s plan to destroy the Focke-Wulf factory and the shipyards was not successful, although an assembly shop at the Focke-Wulf factory was completely flattened by a 4,000-lb bomb dropped by a 5 Group Lancaster. A further 6 buildings at this factory were seriously damaged and 11 buildings lightly so. Damage was also experienced by 4 important industrial firms – the Atlas Werke, the Vulkan shipyard, the Norddeutsche Hütte and the Korff refinery – and by 2 large dockside warehouses.

The Bremen report concludes with the estimate put forward by the senior local air-raid official at the time that only 80 R.A.F. bombers had attacked Bremen. The subsequent B.B.C. broadcast that over 1,000 bombers had been sent was judged to be a propaganda bluff and a device to explain away the heavy casualties suffered by the bombing force. The Germans claimed 52 bombers shot down. This figure, said the official, would not appear too serious to the British public if seen as part of a 1,000-bomber force.

The actual losses of the Bomber Command aircraft involved in the raid were 48 aircraft, including 4 which came down in the sea near England from which all but 2 crew members were rescued. This was a new record loss. It represented exactly 5 per cent of the Bomber Command aircraft dispatched. This time, heaviest casualties were suffered by the O.T.U.s of 91 Group, which lost 23 of the 198 Whitleys and Wellingtons provided by that group, a loss of 11·6 per cent. The relevant reasons for this may be the fact that O.T.U.s were usually equipped with old aircraft retired from front-line squadrons, that the Bremen raid involved a round trip 200 miles longer than the Cologne and Essen raids and that extra time had been taken up in searching for the target in the cloudy conditions of that night. The trainee crews of 91 Group suffered accordingly. 5 of the 102 Coastal Command aircraft were also lost.

INTRUDER OPERATIONS

56 aircraft of 2 Group – 31 Blenheims, 21 Bostons, 4 Mosquitoes – were dispatched to attack and harass 13 German airfields. 15 of the Blenheims were lent by Army Co-Operation Command and were operating under Bomber Command orders. The Boston and Mosquito sorties were the first Intruder flights by those aircraft types. Most of the Intruders bombed or machine-gunned the airfields to which they were allocated but there were no encounters with German aircraft. 2 of the Army Co-Operation Blenheims, attacking St-Trond and Venlo airfields, were lost.

Total Bomber Command effort for the night: 1,016 sorties, 50 aircraft (4·9 per cent) lost. *Total including Coastal Command:* 1,123 sorties, 55 aircraft (4·9 per cent) lost.

---

26 June 1942

12 Bostons attacked Le Havre power-station but the bombing fell outside the target area. 2 Mosquitoes photographed Bremen. 2 further Mosquitoes to Essen turned back. No aircraft lost.

26/27 June 1942

MINELAYING

29 Wellingtons and 10 Halifaxes off Lorient and St-Nazaire and in the Frisian Islands. No losses.

27/28 June 1942

BREMEN

144 aircraft – 55 Wellingtons, 39 Halifaxes, 26 Stirlings, 24 Lancasters. 9 aircraft – 4 Wellingtons, 2 Halifaxes, 2 Lancasters, 1 Stirling – lost.

119 aircraft bombed blindly through cloud after obtaining *Gee* fixes. Bomber Command believed the results were successful. Bremen records that two of the large firms hit in the recent 'Thousand' raid – the Atlas Werke and the Korff refinery – were damaged again, as well as several smaller firms and dockside warehouses. A hospital and an unrecorded number of dwelling-houses were also hit. 7 people were killed and 80 injured.

Minor Operations: 15 aircraft minelaying off St-Nazaire and Verdon, 6 Halifaxes on leaflet flights. No losses.

28/29 June 1942

Minor Operations

14 aircraft to St-Nazaire, 4 Lancasters minelaying in the River Gironde, 1 Stirling on leaflet flight. 1 Stirling on the St-Nazaire raid was lost.

29 June 1942

12 Bostons bombed railway yards at Hazebrouck without loss. 1 of the Bostons was manned by Captain Kegelman and his all-American crew, the first Americans of the Eighth Air Force to take part in a bomber operation. Their hosts were 226 Squadron at Swanton Morley.

29/30 June 1942

BREMEN

253 aircraft – 108 Wellingtons, 64 Lancasters, 47 Stirlings, 34 Halifaxes – dispatched, the first time that 4-engined bombers provided more than half of the force on a major raid. 11 aircraft – 4 Stirlings, 4 Wellingtons, 3 Halifaxes – were lost.

The Bremen report shows that 48 houses were destroyed and 934 damaged, mostly lightly, but the report devotes most of its space to details of 'extensive damage' in 5 important war industries, including the Focke-Wulf factory and the A.G. Weser U-boat construction yard, and at the local gasworks, a museum and a merchant-navy college. Most of this damage was caused by fire. The casualties in Bremen are not mentioned.

Minor Operations: 18 Blenheim Intruders, 7 Wellingtons minelaying off St-Nazaire, 5 leaflet flights. No losses.

1 July 1942

1 Mosquito bombed Kiel through cloud and returned safely. The Kiel diary has no entry.

1/2 July 1942

4 Lancasters laid mines in the Great Belt without loss.

2 July 1942

Flensburg

6 Mosquitoes were dispatched to carry out a low-level raid on a U-boat construction yard at Flensburg but were intercepted by German fighters which shot down into the sea the Mosquito of Wing Commander A. R. Oakeshott, commander of 139 Squadron, who, with his navigator Flying Officer V. F. E. Treherne, was killed. This was 139 Squadron's first Mosquito operation. The other Mosquitoes escaped from the German fighters by increasing speed and leaving the Germans behind but a second Mosquito was damaged by Flak over Flensburg and crashed in Germany. This second aircraft was piloted by Group Captain J. C. MacDonald, who became a prisoner of war.

These were the first Bomber Command daylight casualties for 3 weeks. Returning Mosquito crews claimed to have bombed the shipyard accurately.

2/3 July 1942

BREMEN

325 aircraft – 175 Wellingtons, 53 Lancasters, 35 Halifaxes, 34 Stirlings, 28 Hampdens. 13 aircraft – 8 Wellingtons, 2 Hampdens, 2 Stirlings, 1 Halifax – lost.

265 aircraft claimed to have bombed in good visibility but it is probable that much of the attack fell outside the southern borders of the town. A brief Bremen report says that more than 1,000 houses and 4 small industrial firms were damaged. 3 cranes and 7 ships in the port were also hit; 1 of the ships, the 1,736-ton steamer *Marieborg* sank and is recorded as having become a danger to navigation. Only 5 people were killed and 4 injured in a population which had probably become very air-raid-shelter conscious.

INTRUDERS

24 Blenheims were dispatched and attacked many airfields without loss.

3/4 July 1942

6 Lancasters minelaying in the Great Belt; 2 aircraft lost.

4 July 1942

12 Bostons were dispatched in 4 flights of 3 aircraft each, in low-level attacks on 4 Dutch airfields: De Kooy, Bergen, Haamstede and Valkenburg. As it was American Independence Day, 6 of the planes were crewed by members of the Eighth Air Force. Intense light Flak was encountered at the Dutch coast and at the targets and 3 Bostons were shot down, all of the aircraft lost being crewed by Americans; one of the crews lost was that of Captain Kegelman who had flown the first American bomber sortie a few days earlier.

5/6 July 1942

14 Wellingtons minelaying off St-Nazaire without loss.

6/7 July 1942

42 aircraft minelaying off Lorient and Verdon. 3 Wellingtons lost.

7/8 July 1942

MINELAYING

79 Wellingtons and 23 Stirlings of 1 and 3 Groups laid mines in the Frisian Islands without loss.

8/9 July 1942

WILHELMSHAVEN

285 aircraft – 137 Wellingtons, 52 Lancasters, 38 Halifaxes, 34 Stirlings, 24 Hampdens – to attack the dock areas. 5 aircraft – 3 Wellingtons, 1 Halifax, 1 Lancaster – lost.

Photographs showed that most of the bombing fell in open country west of the target. Wilhelmshaven reports damage to housing and a variety of other premises: the harbourmaster's residence and offices, a dockyard restaurant, a department store and a bus garage with 30 buses inside which were all destroyed. 25 people were killed and 170 injured.

5 Halifaxes made leaflet flights to France without loss.

9 July 1942

1 Mosquito to Wilhelmshaven bombed through cloud. The local diary has no entry.

9/10 July 1942

MINELAYING

59 aircraft to Heligoland and the Frisian Islands. 1 Wellington lost.

10 July 1942

8 Wellingtons on cloud-cover raids to Duisburg and Düsseldorf were recalled. 1 Wellington did not return.

11 July 1942

DANZIG

44 Lancasters were dispatched on another experimental raid. The plan called for the Lancasters to fly at low level and in formation over the North Sea, but then to split up and fly independently in cloud which was forecast to be present over Denmark and that part of the Baltic leading to Danzig (now Gdansk). The target was expected to be clear of cloud and the Lancasters were to bomb U-boat yards from normal bombing heights just before dusk and return to England during darkness. With a round trip of 1,500 miles, it was the most distant target Bomber Command had yet attempted to reach. It was also another attempt to utilize Lancasters in a semi-daylight role.

The plan worked well except that some of the Lancasters were late in identifying Danzig and had to bomb the general town area in the dark. 24 aircraft bombed at Danzig and returned; 2 more were shot down by Flak at the target. They were the only losses; the novel tactics and routeing prevented any German fighters making contact.

Minor Operations: 7 Hampdens flew 'roving commissions' in the Bremen area but only 1 of these dropped bombs. 6 Mosquitoes attacked a U-boat yard at Flensburg but 1 was lost, possibly crashing into the ground because of flying so low; a second aircraft struck the chimney of a house but returned safely with pieces of chimney pot in its cockpit. Both the Hampden and Mosquito operations were intended to divert German attention from the Lancasters flying to Danzig.

11/12 July 1942

41 Wellingtons and 8 Stirlings minelaying off Heligoland, in the Frisians and in the Langeland Belt. 2 Wellingtons lost.

---

12 July 1942

12 Bostons bombed an airfield near Abbeville but results were not seen because of cloud. No aircraft were lost.

American crews flew in 6 of the Bostons, their last introductory flight with the Bostons of 2 Group. The Americans, from the 15th (Light) Bomb Squadron, had flown 13 sorties with the R.A.F.'s 226 Squadron but had lost 3 crews.

12/13 July 1942

MINELAYING

55 aircraft to Lorient, St-Nazaire and the Frisians. 1 Hampden and 1 Wellington lost.

1 Lancaster made a leaflet flight to France and returned safely.

---

13 July 1942

12 Bostons bombed Boulogne railway yards without loss.

13/14 July 1942

DUISBURG

194 aircraft – 139 Wellingtons, 33 Halifaxes, 13 Lancasters, 9 Stirlings – on the first of a series of raids on this industrial city on the edge of the Ruhr. 6 aircraft – 3 Wellingtons, 2 Stirlings, 1 Lancaster – were lost and 4 more aircraft crashed in England.

The force encountered cloud and electrical storms and reported that their bombing was well scattered. Duisburg reports only housing damage – 11 houses destroyed, 68 seriously damaged – and 17 people killed.

Minor Operations: 10 Blenheim Intruders, 6 aircraft on leaflet flights. 1 Intruder lost.

14/15 July 1942

MINELAYING

52 aircraft to Lorient, St-Nazaire, Verdon, the Frisians and the River Elbe. No aircraft were lost.

4 aircraft made leaflet flights to France without loss.

---

16 July 1942

LÜBECK

21 Stirlings in a raid using similar tactics to the cloud-cover approach and dusk attack as had been used on the recent raid to Danzig. Only 8 aircraft reported bombing the main target; 2 Stirlings were lost.

Other Operations: 2 Wellingtons on cloud-cover raids to Essen, 4 Mosquitoes – 2 to Ijmuiden, 1 to Vegesack and 1 to Wilhelmshaven. The only loss was the Mosquito to Wilhelmshaven whose local diary says that it dropped 2 bombs in dockyard installations, wounding 4 people, but was then shot down.

---

17 July 1942

16 Wellingtons on cloud-cover raids to Emden (9 aircraft) and Essen (7 aircraft). Only 3 aircraft from the Essen force bombed and machine-gunned a convoy off the Dutch coast. Only near misses were achieved by the bombs. No aircraft lost.

---

18 July 1942

10 Lancasters to Essen but only 3 aircraft bombed, by *Gee*, through thick cloud and another aircraft attacked a ship in the East Scheldt river. No aircraft lost.

19 July 1942

20 Bostons in pairs to hunt for targets of opportunity at low level, a new form of operation. On this day some were frustrated by bad weather but 14 aircraft bombed various targets. 7 Wellingtons and 3 Lancasters were sent to Essen but none bombed and 5 Hampdens had 'roving commissions' over Germany. 4 aircraft – 2 Bostons, 1 Hampden, 1 Wellington – were lost.

19/20 July 1942

VEGESACK

99 4-engined aircraft – 40 Halifaxes, 31 Stirlings, 28 Lancasters. 3 Halifaxes lost.

The force had orders to bomb the Vulkan U-boat yard visually or, if that was not possible, to bomb the town by *Gee*. The target area was found to be cloud-covered and all the aircraft bombed by *Gee*. Later photographs showed that no bombs fell in Vegesack. A report from Bremen, a few miles up river from Vegesack, describes how 2 storehouses of military equipment were bombed and completely burnt out, the cost of the lost material being estimated at 1 million Reichsmarks (£100,000). Further damage in Bremen included a wooden-hutted military camp. The number of casualties is not mentioned.

19 Wellingtons were minelaying off Lorient, St-Nazaire and La Pallice. 1 aircraft lost.

20 July 1942

12 Wellingtons on a cloud-cover raid to Bremen; only 3 aircraft bombed scattered locations. 4 Bostons bombed targets at Lille. No aircraft lost.

20/21 July 1942

1 Stirling on a leaflet flight to Belgium returned safely.

21 July 1942

6 Mosquitoes were dispatched on single flights to different targets in the Ruhr and Northern Germany but only 3 aircraft bombed targets of opportunity seen through gaps in the cloud. One of the places bombed was believed to be the inland docks at Duisburg. No aircraft lost.

21/22 July 1942

DUISBURG

291 aircraft – 170 Wellingtons, 39 Halifaxes, 36 Stirlings, 29 Lancasters, 17 Hampdens. 12 aircraft – 10 Wellingtons, 1 Halifax, 1 Hampden – lost.

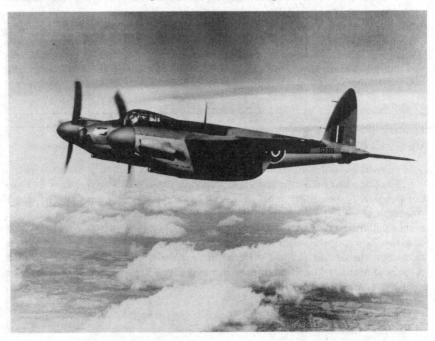

13. The Mosquito bomber, which operated so successfully in a variety of roles in Bomber Command. This is an early version, a Mark IV day bomber flying with 105 Squadron in 2 Group, which was only with the squadron for two months before it was shot down in a daylight raid to Northern Germany on 20 October 1942. It crashed near Wilhelmshaven and its crew – F/Sgt L. W. Deeth and W.O. F. E. M. Hicks – were killed.

253 returning crews reported that they had bombed and started many fires but photographs showed that the flares of the leading aircraft, dropped by *Gee*, were not accurate and part of the bombing fell in open country over the Rhine to the west.

This large raid was possibly sent on a moonless night to avoid the increasing casualties being inflicted on night-bomber forces by German night fighters. It is interesting to note that bombing results were better than on many moonlit raids but the bomber casualties, at 4·1 per cent, were heavier than normal. Returning crews reported that Duisburg's Flak and searchlight defences were not as fierce as in recent raids to that target because of the haze and most of the bomber losses were suffered in the coastal fighter belt.

Duisburg reports much damage in housing areas, 94 buildings being destroyed and 256 seriously damaged, with 49 people killed. What Bomber Command documents describe as 'ground sources' later stated that the Thyssen steelworks and 2 other important war industries were hit.

Minor Operations: 8 Blenheim Intruders to St-Trond, Venlo and Vechta airfields, 9 aircraft minelaying off Texel and in the Frisians, 6 aircraft on leaflet flights to France. 1 Intruder lost.

---

22 July 1942

8 Bostons in pairs attacked various targets. 2 aircraft bombed Sluiskil power-station and then machine-gunned barges near Ghent and 2 aircraft bombed Langenbrugge power-station. 1 Wellington was sent to Essen and 1 Mosquito to Münster but these aircraft turned back because of lack of cloud. No aircraft lost.

---

23 July 1942

4 Mosquitoes on cloud-cover raids to Germany. 3 turned back but 1 aircraft bombed a factory in the area south of Grevenbroich. No aircraft lost.

23/24 July 1942

DUISBURG

215 aircraft – 93 Wellingtons, 45 Lancasters, 39 Stirlings, 38 Halifaxes. 7 aircraft – 3 Wellingtons, 2 Lancasters, 2 Stirlings – lost.

Much cloud was present over the target and the flares dropped by the leading aircraft were scattered. Those bombs which did fall in Duisburg again caused some housing damage and 65 people were killed.

Minor Operations: 8 Blenheim Intruders, 13 aircraft minelaying. 2 Intruders lost.

---

25 July 1942

12 Bostons were dispatched in low-level pairs but only 2 aircraft bombed Sluiskil power-station. Later in the day, 12 further Bostons were sent out in an attempt to bomb an open air 'Quisling meeting' at Lunteren in Holland but they had to turn back because of lack of cloud cover. 2 Mosquitoes were dispatched and both reached and bombed their targets, Frankfurt and Mannheim. No aircraft lost.

25/26 July 1942

DUISBURG

313 aircraft – 177 Wellingtons, 48 Stirlings, 41 Halifaxes, 33 Lancasters, 14 Hampdens. 12 aircraft – 7 Wellingtons, 2 Halifaxes, 2 Lancasters, 1 Stirling – lost.

Thick cloud covered the target area. Duisburg again reports property damage, though not as heavy as on the last two raids. 6 people were killed.

Minor Operations: 21 Blenheim Intruders, 8 aircraft minelaying off St-Nazaire and Verdon, 7 Halifaxes on leaflet flights. 3 Intruders and 1 Lancaster minelayer lost.

Total effort for the night: 349 sorties, 16 aircraft (4·9 per cent) lost.

26 July 1942

3 Mosquitoes to Cologne, Duisburg and Essen all reached and bombed their targets without loss.

26/27 July 1942

HAMBURG

403 aircraft – 181 Wellingtons, 77 Lancasters, 73 Halifaxes, 39 Stirlings, 33 Hampdens – dispatched in what was probably a full 'maximum effort' for the regular Bomber Command squadrons. 29 aircraft – 15 Wellingtons, 8 Halifaxes, 2 Hampdens, 2 Lancasters, 2 Stirlings – were lost, 7·2 per cent of the force.

Crews encountered a mixture of cloud and icing at some places on the route but clear weather at the target. Good bombing results were claimed. Hamburg reports show that severe and widespread damage was caused, mostly in housing and semi-commercial districts rather than in the docks and industrial areas. At least 800 fires were dealt with, 523 being classed as large. For the first time, the strong Hamburg fire department was forced to call for extensive help from outside the city. 823 houses were destroyed and more than 5,000 damaged. Estimates of compensation for damage claimed ran to 250 million Reichsmarks (£25 million). More than 14,000 people were bombed out. 337 people were killed and 1,027 injured.

12 Bostons and 10 Blenheims carried out Intruder flights to airfields. 1 Boston of 226 Squadron was lost while attacking Jever; this was the first Boston Intruder casualty.

---

27 July 1942

8 Wellingtons on cloud-cover raids to Northern Germany bombed blindly through clouds in the Bremen and Emden areas. 2 aircraft lost.

---

28 July 1942

6 Mosquitoes on cloud-cover raids to widely separated targets. 5 aircraft bombed; 1 lost.

28/29 July 1942

HAMBURG

256 aircraft – 165 from 3 Group and 91 O.T.U. aircraft – dispatched. A much larger force had been detailed for this raid but bad weather over the bases of 1, 4 and 5 Groups prevented their participation. The force which took off comprised 161 Wellingtons, 71 Stirlings and 24 Whitleys.

The weather, both on the outward flight and over the English bases, worsened and the O.T.U. aircraft were recalled, although 3 of them went on to bomb Hamburg. That part of the bomber force which did proceed became very scattered; many more aircraft turned back and only 68 bombed in the target area. Hamburg suffered 13 people killed and 48 injured with 56 fires, 15 of them large. The worst incident was a direct hit on a ward of the Eppendorf Hospital where 12 patients and nurses were killed and 39 injured.

Bomber casualties were heavy. 16 Wellingtons and 9 Stirlings were lost from 3 Group, 15·2 per cent of those dispatched by the group. 4 O.T.U. Wellingtons were lost and a Whitley crashed in the sea.

30 Bostons and 13 Blenheim Intruders were dispatched. 2 Bostons and 1 Blenheim lost.

---

29 July 1942

3 Mosquitoes to Düsseldorf, Münster and the village of Oberlahnstein in the Westerwald where a railway traffic centre was the target. All 3 aircraft could only bomb approximate positions through cloud. No Mosquitoes lost.

29/30 July 1942

SAARBRÜCKEN

291 aircraft of 5 types on the first large raid to this target. 9 aircraft – 3 Wellingtons, 2 Halifaxes, 2 Lancasters, 2 Stirlings – lost.

The defences at the target were not expected to be strong and crews were urged to bomb at lower than normal altitudes. 248 aircraft reported accurate bombing, three quarters of them doing so from below 10,000 ft. Bomber Command claimed 'severe damage' to 2 industrial targets, an ironworks and an engineering works. Saarbrücken's records show severe damage and casualties in the centre and north-western districts. 396 buildings were destroyed and 324 seriously damaged, with 155 people being killed.

---

30 July 1942

6 Bostons sent to Abbeville had to turn back. 4 Mosquitoes on cloud-cover raids to Frankfurt, Hamborn, Hannover and Lübeck. No aircraft lost.

30/31 July 1942

6 Blenheims on Intruder flights were recalled but one did not hear the signal and went on to bomb Rheine airfield. There were no losses.

---

31 July 1942

24 Bostons to Abbeville airfield and St-Malo harbour; all bombed accurately and without loss. 1 Mosquito bombed the dock area of Duisburg.

---

31 July/1 August 1942

DÜSSELDORF

630 aircraft – 308 Wellingtons, 113 Lancasters, 70 Halifaxes, 61 Stirlings, 54 Hampdens, 24 Whitleys. This was another raid in which Bomber Command's training units provided aircraft, though it was not an attempt to reach the 1,000-aircraft figure. It was the first occasion when more than 100 Lancasters took part in a raid. 484 aircraft claimed successful bombing although their photographs showed that part of the force bombed open country. More than 900 tons of bombs were dropped.

Düsseldorf's records are very detailed (page 16 of the report gives details of a cow with an injured udder caused by a bomb splinter!). Most parts of the city and of Neuss, the suburb town over the Rhine, were hit. 453 buildings in Düsseldorf and Neuss were destroyed and more than 15,000 damaged (12,192 only 'lightly'). 954 fires were started, of which 67 were classed as large. (It is probable that different cities had different standards when classing fires as 'large'.) 279 people were killed – 245 in Düsseldorf and 34 in Neuss; 1,018 people were injured and 12,053 were bombed out. (The British Official History, p. 487, gives 379 deaths but this is believed to be an error.)

The casualties of the bomber force were again heavy. 29 aircraft – 16 Wellingtons, 5 Hampdens, 4 Halifaxes, 2 Lancasters, 2 Whitleys – were lost; this was 4·6 per cent of those dispatched. 92 (O.T.U.) Group lost 11 of its 105 aircraft on the raid, a casualty rate of 10·5 per cent.

6 Blenheim Intruder sorties were flown; 1 Blenheim lost.

---

1 August 1942

6 Bostons to Flushing docks; 2 aircraft lost. 5 Mosquitoes to widely separated German targets; 1 Mosquito lost.

---

3 August 1942

10 Halifaxes to Hamburg and 2 Mosquitoes to Hagen and Vegesack all turned back because of lack of cloud.

3/4 August 1942

8 Lancasters minelaying in Kiel Bay and off Denmark. No aircraft lost.

---

4 August 1942

3 Mosquitoes and 1 Wellington to the Ruhr, Stuttgart and Bremen all turned back.

4/5 August 1942

ESSEN

38 aircraft dispatched encountered severe icing and only 18 aircraft bombed in the Essen area. 1 Lancaster lost.

45 aircraft minelaying in the Frisians and off Brest, Lorient and St-Nazaire. 2 Wellingtons lost.

5 August 1942

3 Mosquitoes to Germany, only 1 bombed. No aircraft lost.

5/6 August 1942

THE RUHR

25 aircraft, 17 to Essen and 8 to Bochum. The intention was to reach the target area by *Gee* and then to bomb visually through gaps in the cloud. Only 3 aircraft bombed at Bochum and only 1 at Essen. 5 aircraft – 3 Halifaxes, 1 Lancaster and 1 Wellington – were lost and a further aircraft crashed in England.

Minor Operations: 57 aircraft minelaying off France, Holland and Germany, 14 aircraft on leaflet flights. 1 Wellington minelayer lost.

6 August 1942

3 Mosquitoes to Germany but only 1 aircraft bombed, at Hannover. No losses.

6/7 August 1942

DUISBURG

216 aircraft of 5 types. 5 aircraft – 2 Halifaxes, 2 Stirlings, 1 Wellington – lost.

Most of the bombs fell in open country west of the target. Duisburg reports 18 buildings destroyed, 66 seriously damaged and 24 people killed.

This was the last of a series of 5 raids on Duisburg in just over 3 weeks. Only one raid had resulted in significant industrial damage but 212 houses were destroyed, 741 damaged and 161 people were killed. Bomber Command lost 43 aircraft in these raids, 3·5 per cent of the 1,229 sorties dispatched.

Minor Operations: 5 aircraft to Le Havre but this force did not bomb, 3 Blenheim Intruders, 1 Lancaster minelaying in the Frisians. No losses.

7 August 1942

3 Mosquitoes to Germany but only 1 bombed, at Mannheim or Worms. No losses.

8/9 August 1942

12 Lancasters minelaying in Kiel Bay and off Denmark. No losses.

9 August 1942

3 Mosquitoes to Germany but only 1 bombed, at Frankfurt. No losses.

9/10 August 1942

OSNABRÜCK

192 aircraft – 91 Wellingtons, 42 Lancasters, 40 Stirlings, 19 Halifaxes. 3 Halifaxes and 3 Wellingtons lost.

Visibility was good but the initial flares were dropped over a wide area. Osnabrück's report shows that 206 houses and 1 military building were destroyed and nearly 4,000 other buildings were damaged, mostly lightly. Among industrial buildings hit were a vehicle works, a gas-meter factory, a textile factory and an iron foundry. The Herz Jesu church was hit. Much damage was also caused in the town's dock area where 10 canal barges were damaged. 62 people were killed – 40 civilians, 17 foreign workers, 5 service or air-raid men – and 107 injured.

Minor Operations: 18 aircraft to Le Havre, 13 Blenheim Intruders, 3 aircraft minelaying in the Frisians. No losses.

An important event which occurred on this night was the first effective jamming by the Germans of *Gee* signals.

10 August 1942

3 Mosquitoes to Germany but only 1 aircraft bombed at Cologne. No losses.

10/11 August 1942

MINELAYING

52 aircraft to Kiel Bay and the Danish coast. 1 Lancaster and 1 Stirling lost.

11/12 August 1942

MAINZ

154 aircraft – 68 Wellingtons, 33 Lancasters, 28 Stirlings, 25 Halifaxes – on the first large raid to this city. 6 aircraft – 3 Wellingtons, 2 Halifaxes, 1 Lancaster – lost.

Much damage was caused in the centre of Mainz, with some ancient cultural buildings being hit; the castle and its museum were burnt out. The number of people killed is believed to be 152 – 87 men, 64 women and 1 soldier – but there may be some doubt about this.

Minor Operations: 16 aircraft to Le Havre, 9 Blenheim Intruders, 9 Hampdens minelaying in the Elbe, 3 Lancasters on leaflet flights. 1 Halifax and 1 Lancaster lost on the Le Havre raid.

---

12 August 1942

1 Mosquito attacked a chemical factory at Wiesbaden but its bombs fell short. The aircraft returned safely.

12/13 August 1942

MAINZ

138 aircraft of 4 types followed up the previous night's raid. 5 aircraft – 2 Lancasters, 1 Hampden, 1 Stirling, 1 Wellington – were lost.

More damage was caused in the centre of Mainz and also in industrial areas. The main railway station was seriously damaged. Again there is some confusion over casualties; figures of 40 and 163 are quoted for numbers killed. Bomber Command estimated that 135 acres of Mainz were destroyed in the two raids. The roof of the cathedral and the bishop's palace were both burnt out but it is not known on which night these events happened.

The town of Bingen, 15 miles west of Mainz, recorded that the nearby villages of Kempten and Gaulsheim were each hit by a 4,000-lb bomb on this night. 130 houses were damaged in Kempten and 97 in Gaulsheim but only 1 person, in Kempten, was injured.

Minor Operations: 6 Blenheim Intruders, 9 aircraft minelaying in the Frisians, 2 Lancasters on leaflet flights. No losses.

---

13 August 1942

7 Bostons on a shipping sweep off the Frisian Islands claimed 1 ship sunk and 1 Mosquito bombed Essen. No aircraft lost.

13/14 August 1942

MINELAYING

36 aircraft to many locations along the German and Dutch coasts. 1 Stirling lost.

---

14 August 1942

1 Mosquito to Mannheim turned back.

---

15 August 1942

1 Mosquito to Mainz was lost.

15/16 August 1942

DÜSSELDORF

131 aircraft of 5 types. 4 aircraft – 2 Lancasters, 1 Hampden, 1 Wellington – lost.

Visibility was poor and the bombing was scattered. Düsseldorf and Neuss reports only a light raid, the most serious incident being in the centre of Neuss where a 4,000-lb bomb caused much blast damage to buildings, including the Rathaus, the police station, the telegraph office and the hospital at the Herz Jesu convent. 1 person was killed in Neuss, none in Düsseldorf; 13 people were injured. No industrial production of any kind was lost as a result of this raid.

9 aircraft laid mines in the Frisians. 1 Stirling lost.

16 August 1942

1 Mosquito bombed Vegesack and returned safely.

16/17 August 1942

MINELAYING

56 aircraft to the Frisian Islands. 2 Lancasters lost.

17 August 1942

1 Mosquito bombed the Kiel area and returned safely.

Operational Statistics, 30/31 May to 17 August 1942
(79 days/nights)

Number of days with operations: 54
Number of nights with operations: 60
Number of daylight sorties: 583, from which 27 aircraft (4·6 per cent) were lost
Number of night sorties: 11,139, from which 476 aircraft (4·3 per cent) were lost
Total sorties: 11,722, from which 503 aircraft (4·3 per cent) were lost
Approximate bomb tonnage in period: 17,095 tons
Averages per 24-hour period: 148·4 sorties, 6·4 aircraft lost, 216·4 tons of bombs dropped

12. PATHFINDER FORCE

17/18 August to 20 December 1942

The war was now half over, though none knew this at the time. Bomber Command's own main campaign, unleashed against the Germans in May 1940, was two and a half years old. The bomber force now had a dynamic commander who was receiving more powerful and effective aircraft, who had weathered a crisis of confidence and secured the political support required to press on with the strategic bombing offensive. And yet all was far from well. Sir Arthur Harris had produced the spectacular 1,000-bomber raids and had dealt some effective blows against a number of German cities and towns but the new device *Gee* had not produced any revolutionary improvement in target finding and bombing accuracy. For every success at places like Cologne, Lübeck and Rostock there were two or three failures at places like Essen and Duisburg. It is probable that between one half and three quarters of the bombs dropped at night were not even hitting the cities designated as the targets. And all the time the effectiveness of the German defences was increasing. The 4·3 per cent loss rate of the recent period was by far the highest of the night bombing war to date and the trend would continue upwards in the next period.

For some time Bomber Command had been using 'raid leaders' in attempts to improve target-finding. All groups and most squadrons contained a proportion of crews who, by survival and experience or by above-average skill, showed a consistent ability to find and bomb their targets. The obvious suggestion was made that these crews should be gathered together permanently into a 'Target Finding Force'. The concept of such a force had been floating around the Air Ministry since late in 1941. It was the brainchild of Group Captain S. O. Bufton, who had commanded Nos 10 and 76 Squadrons in 4 Group earlier in the war and who was now Director of Bomber Operations at the Air Ministry. While flying with 10 Squadron, Bufton had pioneered attempts by the best crews in his squadron to find the location of their target by the light of flares and attract other crews to it by firing a coloured Verey light. He had also helped to introduce more reliable flares. But this particular target-finding technique had not been attempted outside Bufton's own squadron. On his being posted to the Air Ministry, he vigorously set about convincing others that the Target Finding Force should be established for the use of the whole of Bomber Command.

Bufton gained the support of his fellow staff officers at the Air Ministry and the idea was put to Harris as soon as Harris took over at Bomber Command in February 1942. The idea was not accepted. Harris opposed the concept of an élite element in Bomber Command, preferring the more experienced men to remain with their squadrons in order to give day-to-day encouragement and inspiration to the newer crews. Harris was supported in this view by all of his group commanders. Bufton made a new suggestion: if the commander-in-chief of Bomber Command would not agree to the formation of a select force, would he allow six ordinary squadrons to be gathered together and to be stationed in close proximity to each other so that they could exchange ideas and develop target-finding tactics.

Sir Arthur Harris still resisted. He looked forward to the day, soon, when all crews would have *Gee* and bombing cameras; the spirit of competition to obtain the best bombing photographs, he said, would do the rest. A basic principle of the utmost importance to the bombing war was at stake here. It was a conflict between those on the one side who saw the current policy of general-area bombing as a temporary expedient until Bomber Command could develop new techniques to return to the pre-war ideals of the R.A.F. and move back to the bombing of selected individual targets. On the other side were those who saw area bombing as the only way forward, using the increasing weight of Bomber Command to bomb the German cities until the spirit of the industrial workers broke.

The arguments proceeded all through the summer of 1942. Sir Charles Portal had to chose between the advice given to him by his own staff and the wishes of his field commander but he eventually came down on the side of his staff officers and he ordered Harris to abandon his objections and prepare the new force. There was still a delay of several weeks until the Treasury agreed to the principle, requested by Harris, that the men of the new force should be promoted by one rank when they reached a certain standard of efficiency. This was to compensate them for the dangers of the longer tours of duty they would now be expected to fly and for the more rapid promotions they could have expected at their old squadrons. All was finally ready on 11 August 1942 and Sir Arthur Harris received the official instructions to establish a force of squadrons to help Bomber Command find its targets. Even then, Harris rejected the originally suggested name of 'Target Finding Force' and selected what was to become one of the air war's most famous titles – the 'Pathfinder Force'. The Pathfinders would not yet be given group status but were to work directly under the control of the Bomber Command Headquarters planning staff, although the orders would actually pass through the headquarters of 3 Group.

As the commander of this new force, Bufton had suggested Group Captain Basil Embry, who had earlier served in 2 Group and whose escape from behind German lines in France in 1940 was one of the war's early legends. It was thought that Embry could provide the necessary skill and inspiration to lead the Pathfinders but, although he was only serving as Station Commander at Wittering, a Fighter Command station, Embry was not released, for reasons which are not known. The man who had been suggested as Embry's Senior Air Staff Officer had an equally spectacular reputation in aviation although one gained in entirely different circumstances. This was the Australian Wing Commander D. C. T. Bennett, a distinguished pre-war pilot and navigation expert and holder of several long-distance flying records. Rejoining the R.A.F. – he had served as a junior officer in the early 1930s – Bennett had, like Bufton, commanded Halifax squadrons in 4 Group and was now preparing to take part of 10 Squadron to the Middle East. 10 Squadron can be said to have been the cradle of the Pathfinder Force. Donald Bennett's posting to the Middle East was cancelled and he became, not the number two man in the Pathfinders, but its first and only wartime leader. He formed his headquarters at Wyton airfield, in 1943 moving to Castle Hill House in nearby Huntingdon.

Each of the night-bombing groups was ordered to send one of its regular squadrons to the Pathfinders. It had been hoped by the supporters of the Pathfinder concept that the groups would select the best crews from all their squadrons and ask them to volunteer for transfer to the group's designated Pathfinder squadron, but Harris did not issue a firm order on this subject and a study of the records shows that there was hardly any transfer of crews. Four ordinary squadrons thus found themselves forming the new Pathfinder Force. 156 Squadron came from 1 Group, 7 Squadron from 3 Group, 35 Squadron from 4 Group and 83 Squadron from 5 Group. Each group was to remain responsible for supplying replacement crews for 'its' Pathfinder squadron, but there were often difficulties over this and it is recognized that the Pathfinders never received the pick of the best crews in the groups. The only group commander to give any consistent support to the Pathfinders was Air Vice-Marshal Carr of 4 Group and it is interesting to note that both Bufton and Bennett had served their operational tours in that group.

The squadrons of Pathfinder Force transferred to their new bases in Huntingdonshire and Cambridgeshire on 17 August. The hard-driving Harris warned them to be ready for operations in their new role *in the coming night.* Because of weather conditions over Germany, however, this first Pathfinder-led raid was cancelled and an ordinary raid to a minor target, Osnabrück, was substituted. The first raid for the Pathfinders was to Flensburg on the following night.

The new force had few advantages. It had no history or tradition. It was operating four different types of aircraft – Halifaxes, Lancasters, Stirlings and Wellingtons. It came into being at a time of increasing tactical difficulty: the growing Flak and searchlight defences at targets were forcing bombers to fly at ever increasing heights; the still growing effectiveness of the German night fighters was starting to force the use of moonless rather than moonlit nights; the winter weather was approaching; the Germans had just started to jam *Gee.* The early Pathfinders had no special bombs for marking targets and could attempt no more than the finding of a target and the illuminating of it with flares. Within weeks, however, a crude form of 'target marker bomb' was produced by packing the casing of 250- and 4,000-pound bombs with inflammable material and chemicals which would produce a distinctively coloured 'super incendiary' to burn on the ground, it was hoped at or near the centre of the target area, and act as a guide for what would become known as the Main Force. The first of these so-called 'Pink Pansies' were used in September and, although of only moderate assistance, they proved to be the start of a process of improvement which would serve Bomber Command well and justify the foundation of the Pathfinder Force.

The only command change at group level in Bomber Command during the next few months was the appointment of Air Vice-Marshal The Hon. R. A. Cochrane to relieve the long-serving and much respected Air Vice-Marshal Baldwin at 3 Group. Baldwin was the last of the pre-war group commanders to leave; he had served Bomber Command well. His departure coincided with the retirement of two more of the pre-war bombers. The last Blenheim sorties were flown on the night of the first Pathfinder raid and the last Hampden squadron would hand over its aircraft to training units in mid-September. Only the Wellingtons remained of the old types. The four-engined aircraft, particularly the Lancaster, on which so many of Bomber Command's future hopes rested, were now growing steadily in numbers. The only new type of aircraft to appear on the scene was another stop-gap purchase from the Americans; this was the Lockheed Ventura which was given to 2 Group, intended for use as a night Intruder, but the aircraft only operated in the day-bomber role.

It is time that something was said about the morale of the bomber crews serving in squadrons at that time. There had been some boost in spirits at the time of the first 1,000-bomber raid on Cologne, but later 'Thousand' raids had not been successful and all of these raids had incurred heavy casualties. There had also been serious losses in a disappointing run of raids on targets in the Ruhr, particularly Essen and Duisburg. Morale in Bomber Command usually held up at an amazingly high level, much of this being due to the leadership of Harris himself, but twice in the war it is recognized that morale sagged and this period, the middle and later months of 1942, was the first of those occasions.

Bomber Command eventually settled down to a system by which a man selected for aircrew duty in the command was expected to complete a first tour of thirty operations and then, after a rest, a second tour of twenty operations. He could not be forced to fly again in Bomber Command after those fifty raids, though some men did volunteer to continue. There were some variations but the fifty-operation rule is satisfactory for these comments. These were the mathematical chances of a member of a bomber crew surviving fifty operational flights at various rates of loss:

Casualty Rate (%)	Survivors from 100 Crews
1·0	60·5
1·5	47·0
2·0	36·4
2·5	28·2
3·0	21·8
3·5	16·8
4·0	13·0

The casualty rates for Bomber Command night operations during the recent periods of this diary were as follows:

10/11 November 1941 to 22 February 1942 (the winter-restraint period): 2·5 per cent

22/23 February to 30 May 1942 (Sir Arthur Harris takes command): 3·7 per cent

30/31 May to 17 August 1942 (the 1,000-bomber raids period): 4·3 per cent

The casualty rate during the coming period, that of the opening operations of the Pathfinder Force, would be 4·6 per cent! It is not surprising that some of the crews of the night squadrons were losing heart under such a relentlessly increasing casualty rate.

It was recognized that a loss rate exceeding 4 per cent would lead to the eventual decline of the force, with insufficient crews managing to survive a first tour of operations to provide the leadership and experience in squadrons for the increasing proportion of raw reinforcements. The situation in the Halifax squadrons of 4 Group at this time provides a good illustration. The Halifax was basically a sound aircraft but it experienced serious technical difficulties in its early models and was suffering heavy casualties. From March to August 1942, 109 Halifaxes were lost from 1,770 sorties, a casualty rate of 6·2 per cent. Morale in the Halifax units – 10, 35, 76, 78, 102, 158 and 405 Squadrons – fell and the whole of the Halifax force had to be rested from operations for nearly a month. It was against this background that the Pathfinder Force commenced its operations.

There was one other event of importance at this time. On 17 August 1942, the same day that the Pathfinder squadrons assembled at their new airfields, twelve B-17 Fortresses of the Eighth Air Force carried out the first American heavy-bomber operation when they attacked railway yards at Rouen. Bomber Command now had a daylight partner in what would become a combined strategic-bombing offensive.

17/18 August 1942

OSNABRÜCK

139 aircraft of 5 types. 5 aircraft – 3 Wellingtons, 1 Lancaster, 1 Stirling – lost, 3·6 per cent of the force.

111 crews reported accurate bombing. Osnabrück recorded a sharp attack on the north and north-western parts of the town with 77 dwelling-houses and 4 military buildings destroyed and 125 other buildings seriously damaged, including the town's main hospital, a paper-mill and a copper-wire factory. 7 people were killed and 15 were injured.

Minor Operations: 8 Blenheim Intruders, 4 aircraft minelaying in the Frisians and off Texel and Verdon. No aircraft lost.

The last operational flights in Bomber Command by Blenheims were carried out on this night when 18 Squadron, based at Wattisham, carried out the last Blenheim Intruder operation, attacking airfields at Leeuwarden, Rheine, Twente and Vechta.

18 August 1942

1 Mosquito bombed Hamburg, which reports 2 people killed, 32 injured and 31 bombed out.

18/19 August 1942

FLENSBURG

118 aircraft, including 31 Pathfinders. 4 aircraft – 2 Wellingtons, 1 Halifax, 1 Stirling – lost, 3·4 per cent of the force.

Flensburg, on an inlet of the Baltic, was in theory an easy target for the Pathfinders on their first operation but the winds encountered were not as forecast and the bomber force drifted north of the target to a part of Denmark whose coast also had many inlets. 16 Pathfinder crews claimed to have marked the target area and 78 Main Force crews also claimed to have bombed in the correct place. Flensburg reports that the town was not hit at all but a Danish report shows that the towns of Sønderborg and Abenra and a large area of Denmark up to 25 miles north of Flensburg were hit by scattered bombing. 26 houses were destroyed and 660 were damaged but only 4 Danish people were injured.

The Pathfinders lost their first aircraft on this night, Halifax W1226 of 35 Squadron captained by Sergeant J. W. Smith; the crew all became prisoners of war.

9 Wellingtons laid mines in the Frisian Islands without loss.

19 August 1942

THE DIEPPE RAID

2 Group flew 62 Boston smoke-laying and bombing sorties in support of the Canadian landing at Dieppe; some crews carried out more than 1 flight. 3 Bostons were lost.

1 Mosquito sent to bomb Bremen did not return.

20/21 August 1942

MINELAYING

57 aircraft laid mines at many places from Brest to Danzig. 3 Stirlings and 3 Wellingtons lost. 5 Halifaxes made leaflet flights to France without loss.

21 August 1942

1 Mosquito bombed Chocques power-station and returned safely.

22/23 August 1942

3 Halifaxes dropped leaflets over Paris without loss.

23 August 1942

6 Wellingtons on cloud-cover raids to Bremen but only 2 aircraft bombed, at Emden. 1 Mosquito to Flensburg. No aircraft lost.

24/25 August 1942

FRANKFURT

226 aircraft – 104 Wellingtons, 61 Lancasters, 53 Stirlings, 8 Halifaxes. 16 aircraft – 6 Lancasters, 5 Wellingtons, 4 Stirlings, 1 Halifax – lost, 7·1 per cent of the force. 5 Pathfinder aircraft, including that of the commanding officer of 7 Squadron, were among the aircraft lost.

This was the second Pathfinder-led raid and the Pathfinder crews again experienced great difficulty in locating the target in cloudy conditions; most of the bombing fell in open country north and west of Frankfurt. Local reports say that some bombs fell in the city, with 17 large and 53 small fires and with moderate property damage. 5 people were killed, including 2 Flak gunners, and 95 people were injured. The Frankfurt report describes an incident where a 4-engined bomber crashed on the edge of a metalworks and its bomb load exploded. The prisoners of war, whose nationality is not recorded, in the factory barracks nearby behaved 'splendidly'. The outlying villages of Schwalbach and Eschborn were heavily bombed.

3 Lancasters of 5 Group were sent to bomb specific targets in the towns of Bingen, Mayen and Bad Kreuznach, all on the approach route of the main bomber

force to Frankfurt. Bad Kreuznach was believed to be the location of the German Western Army Headquarters. All 3 Lancasters bombed and returned safely. The town records of Bingen describe the explosion of their Lancaster's 4,000-lb bomb near the famous Ehrenfels mountain overlooking the Rhine. 225 houses in Bingen were damaged by the blast!

6 Wellingtons minelaying in the Frisians without loss.

---

25 August 1942

4 Mosquitoes to Hannover, Brauweiler and Cologne. 3 aircraft bombed with unseen results; 1 was lost.

---

27 August 1942

12 Bostons bombed Abbeville airfield, 4 Mosquitoes to Holland and Germany. Bremen reports one Mosquito dropping 3 bombs and scoring a direct hit on the foundry of the Vulkan shipyard, which stopped production for several days. 1 Boston and 1 Mosquito lost.

27/28 August 1942

KASSEL

306 aircraft of 5 types. 31 aircraft – 21 Wellingtons, 5 Stirlings, 3 Lancasters, 1 Halifax, 1 Hampden – lost, 10·1 per cent of the force. 142 Squadron, based at Grimsby, lost 5 of its 15 Wellingtons taking part in the raid. Many of the casualties were attributed to night-fighter action.

There was only a little cloud over Kassel and the Pathfinders were able to illuminate the area well. Widespread damage was caused, particularly in the south-western parts of the city. Kassel reports that 144 buildings were destroyed and 317 seriously damaged. Several military establishments were hit and the number of dead soldiers, 28, exceeded the number of civilians killed, 15. 187 civilians and 64 soldiers were injured. Among the buildings severely damaged were all three of the factories of the Henschel aircraft company and the private wing of the city hospital. There were 73 large fires. The report also states that many bombs fell outside the town in fields and woods.

GDYNIA

9 Lancasters of 106 Squadron, 5 Group, were dispatched on a special operation. Each aircraft was loaded with a special 'Capital Ship' bomb which had been developed for attacks on large warships. It was believed that one direct hit could sink such a ship. The target on this night was the new German aircraft carrier *Graf Zeppelin*, which was reputed to be almost ready for sailing. 7 of the Lancasters reached Gdynia, 950 miles from their base, but could not locate the *Graf Zeppelin* because of haze and bombed the harbour area instead. If these aircraft had managed to sink the *Graf Zeppelin*, this raid would have ranked as one of the bombing war's epics. No Lancasters were lost. The Germans never did use the *Graf Zeppelin* as an aircraft carrier.

4 aircraft made leaflet flights to France without loss.

28/29 August 1942

NUREMBERG

159 aircraft – 71 Lancasters, 41 Wellingtons, 34 Stirlings, 13 Halifaxes. 23 aircraft – 14 Wellingtons, 4 Lancasters, 3 Stirlings, 2 Halifaxes – lost, 14·5 per cent of the force. The Wellington losses were 34 per cent of those dispatched!

Crews were ordered to attack Nuremberg from as low as possible. The Pathfinders found their aiming point and, for the first time, 'marked' it with 'target indicators' adapted from 250-lb bomb casings. Photographs showed that these were placed with great accuracy and the crews of the Main Force claimed to have carried out a good attack.

A report from Nuremberg does not quite confirm this. Bombs were dropped as far away as the town of Erlangen, nearly 10 miles to the north, and 4 people were killed there. In Nuremberg itself, the number of bombs recorded would indicate that approximately 50 aircraft hit the town. There was some damage in the *Altstadt*, where about 10 historic old houses were destroyed and the castle and imperial stables were damaged. In the south of the city, where the great pre-war Nazi rallies were held, the Kongresshalle and the wooden 'Kraft durch Freude' town (the Strength through Joy colony) were both destroyed by fire. 137 people were killed, 126 civilians and 11 foreigners. An express train halted during the raid on an open stretch of line in the south of Nuremberg and a bomb falling nearby damaged a sleeping car, killing 3 people including a general.

SAARBRÜCKEN

113 aircraft – 71 Wellingtons, 24 Halifaxes, 17 Hampdens, 1 Stirling. This was an experimental raid by a force of oddments – Halifaxes of 4 Group which were being rested from major operations, Hampdens of 5 Group and new crews from other groups. There were no Pathfinders. The moon was four fifths full and it was judged that this relatively undefended target, just inside Germany, could be successfully attacked while the main raid on Nuremberg was taking place.

The raid was not a success; bombing was scattered over a wide area. 15 houses were destroyed and 51 seriously damaged in Saarbrücken and one woman was killed. 7 aircraft – 4 Hampdens, 2 Halifaxes, 1 Wellington – lost, 6·2 per cent of the force.

3 Halifaxes made leaflet flights without loss.

Total effort for the night: 275 sorties, 30 aircraft (10·9 per cent) lost.

---

29 August 1942

18 Bostons – 12 to Ostend, 6 to Comines power-station; both targets were bombed. 2 Mosquitoes to Pont-à-Vendin power-station. 1 Boston and 1 Mosquito lost.

---

31 August/1 September 1942

5 Lancasters minelaying off Denmark without loss.

---

1 September 1942

8 Bostons on uneventful sweep off the Dutch coast.

1/2 September 1942

SAARBRÜCKEN

231 aircraft of 5 types. 4 aircraft – 1 Halifax, 1 Lancaster, 1 Stirling, 1 Wellington – lost, 1·7 per cent of the force.

The Pathfinders illuminated and marked a town which they believed to be Saarbrücken and the Main Force bombed that place vigorously. A total of 205 aircraft claimed good bombing results. But the town bombed was Saarlouis, 13 miles to the north-west and situated in a similar bend of the River Saar. The small, non-industrial town of Saarlouis and the villages immediately surrounding were heavily damaged. The exact extent of this damage was not recorded but 52 civilians were killed. The report from Saarlouis adds that the number of deaths would have been much higher if many people had not been able to take shelter in the unoccupied concrete positions of the *Westwall* (the Siegfried Line) which ran round Saarlouis. The report also says that this community was 'enraged' to be bombed so heavily. No bombs fell in Saarbrücken.

---

2 September 1942

8 Bostons in low-level pairs to Holland and Belgium and 6 Mosquitoes individually to Germany. Targets at Ghent, Ijmuiden, Sluiskil, Cologne, Essen and Osnabrück all attacked. No aircraft lost.

2/3 September 1942

KARLSRUHE

200 aircraft of 5 types with 4 Group Halifaxes now back on major operations. 8 aircraft – 4 Wellingtons, 2 Lancasters, 1 Halifax, 1 Stirling – lost, 4·0 per cent of the force.

The Pathfinders were accurate and this was a successful raid. An estimated 200 fires were seen burning at the same time. Reconnaissance photographs showed much residential and some industrial damage. A very short report from Karlsruhe says only that 73 people were killed and that 3 public buildings in the city centre were hit.

3 aircraft minelaying in the Frisians without loss.

3/4 September 1942

EMDEN

11 aircraft – 7 Wellingtons, 3 Stirlings, 1 Halifax – dispatched but could only bomb through cloud on dead-reckoning positions. 2 Wellingtons lost.

4 September 1942

6 Mosquitoes to Germany. 3 aircraft bombed the Cologne, Essen and Münster areas through thick cloud. No aircraft lost.

4/5 September 1942

BREMEN

251 aircraft – 98 Wellingtons, 76 Lancasters, 41 Halifaxes, 36 Stirlings. 12 aircraft – 7 Wellingtons, 3 Lancasters, 1 Halifax, 1 Stirling – lost, 4·8 per cent of the force.

The Pathfinders introduced new techniques on this night, splitting their aircraft into 3 forces: 'illuminators', who lit up the area with white flares; 'visual markers', who dropped coloured flares if they had identified the aiming point; then 'backers-up', who dropped all-incendiary bomb loads on to the coloured flares. This basic pattern – illuminating, marking and backing-up – would form the basis of most future Pathfinder operations with proper target-indicator bombs and various electronic bombing aids being employed as they became available.

The weather was clear and the Pathfinder plan worked well; heavy bombing of the target followed. Bremen confirms that this was a successful raid. Property was hit as follows:

| | | Damaged | |
	Destroyed	Seriously	Light
Large/medium industrial	6	6	50
Small industrial	15	29	64
Dwelling-houses	460	1,361	7,592

Approximately 6,000 further houses suffered broken windows. After the raid, the local authority telegraphed to Berlin, asking for 3 companies of men for glass, roof and other minor repair work and 1,000 tons of fuel and repair materials. Among the industrial buildings seriously hit were the Weser aircraft works and the Atlas shipyard. 4 dockside warehouses were destroyed and 3 oil-storage tanks were burnt out. Various public buildings together with 7 schools and 3 hospitals were hit. 124 people were killed and 470 injured. The local report adds, 'It was no comfort for the hard pressed population that one bomber was shot down by Flak. The people knew that the Flak could not protect the town effectively.'

3 Wellingtons laid mines in the Frisian Islands without loss.

6 September 1942

12 Bostons bombed ships in Boulogne harbour but scored no hits, 5 Mosquitoes flew to Germany but only Bremerhaven was bombed. 1 Mosquito lost.

6/7 September 1942

DUISBURG

207 aircraft of 6 types. 8 aircraft – 5 Wellingtons, 2 Halifaxes, 1 Stirling – lost, 3·9 per cent of the force.

Cloud and haze were present and the bombing was not concentrated. But Duisburg reports its heaviest raid to date, with 114 buildings destroyed and 316 seriously damaged; 86 people were killed.

Minor Operations: 9 aircraft minelaying off Heligoland and in the Frisians, 5 aircraft on leaflet flights. No losses.

7 September 1942

5 Mosquitoes bombed Bremerhaven, Cologne, Emden, Essen and Wilhelmshaven. The Cologne and Wilhelmshaven diaries have no records of bombs falling. No aircraft lost.

7/8 September 1942

MINOR OPERATIONS

16 aircraft dispatched to bomb the Heinkel works at Warnemünde were recalled, 43 aircraft minelaying off Biscay ports and in the Frisians. 1 Wellington minelayer lost.

8 September 1942

12 Bostons bombed Cherbourg and Le Havre docks without loss.

8/9 September 1942

FRANKFURT

249 aircraft of 5 types. 5 Wellingtons and 2 Halifaxes lost, 2·8 per cent of the force.

The Pathfinders were unable to locate Frankfurt accurately and most of the bombing fell south-west of the city and in the town of Rüsselsheim, 15 miles away. Frankfurt reports only a few bombs – approximately 6 aircraft loads – with minor damage, 1 person dead and 30 injured. No report is available from Rüsselsheim but Bomber Command documents state that the Opel tank factory and the Michelin tyre factory were damaged.

9 September 1942

6 Mosquitoes attacked Münster, Osnabrück and Bielefeld without loss.

9/10 September 1942

MINELAYING

34 aircraft to many places from Denmark to Biscay. 1 Lancaster lost.

10/11 September 1942

DÜSSELDORF

479 aircraft – 242 Wellingtons, 89 Lancasters, 59 Halifaxes, 47 Stirlings, 28 Hampdens, 14 Whitleys. Training aircraft of 91, 92 and 93 Groups took part in this raid. 33 aircraft – 20 Wellingtons, 5 Lancasters, 4 Stirlings, 3 Halifaxes, 1 Hampden – lost, 7·1 per cent of the force. 16 O.T.U., from Upper Heyford, lost 5 of its 13 Wellingtons on the raid.

The Pathfinders successfully marked the target, using 'Pink Pansies' in converted 4,000-lb bomb casings for the first time. (The actual weight of the Pink Pansy was 2,800 lb.) All parts of Düsseldorf except the north of the city were hit as well as the neighbouring town of Neuss. The local report, 20 pages long, gives many details. 39 industrial firms in Düsseldorf and 13 in Neuss were damaged so much that all production ceased for various periods. 8 public buildings were destroyed and 67 damaged. 911 houses were destroyed and 1,506 seriously and 8,340 lightly damaged. 132 people were killed, 120 in Düsseldorf and 12 in Neuss. 116 further people were still classed as missing 2 days later and 19,427 people were bombed out.

13/14 September 1942

BREMEN

Training aircraft from O.T.U.s were again included in the 446 aircraft dispatched. 21 aircraft – 15 Wellingtons, 2 Lancasters, 1 Halifax, 1 Hampden, 1 Stirling, 1 Whitley – were lost, 4·7 per cent of the force.

Bremen reports another heavy raid with 848 houses destroyed and 'Bremen's industry suffering further considerable damage'. The Lloyd dynamo works was put out of action for 2 weeks and various parts of the Focke-Wulf factory for from 2 to 8 days. 5 nearly completed aircraft were destroyed and 3 more damaged. The report also lists 7 cultural and historical buildings hit in the centre of the town as well as 6 schools and 2 hospitals. 70 people were killed and 371 injured.

Gauleiter Wegener announced in the local newspaper: 'The Führer has specifically instructed me to express to you all his admiration and appreciation for your bravery and disciplined behaviour.'* The report goes on to add, with some relief, that Bomber Command now left Bremen alone for the next 5 months.

---

* *Bremer Zeitung*, as quoted in the Bremen Stadtarchiv report, p. 44.

14 September 1942

5 Mosquitoes bombed ports in Northern Germany without loss. Wilhelmshaven reports 4 bombs falling in the town centre, with an old folks' home and several houses hit and 10 people injured. Kiel reports 4 bombs on a nearby village with no particular damage and no casualties.

14/15 September 1942

WILHELMSHAVEN

202 aircraft of 5 types. 2 Wellingtons were the only aircraft lost. The 4 aircraft of 408 (Canadian) Squadron on this raid represent the last operational effort by Hampden aircraft with front-line squadrons.

The Pathfinder marking was accurate and Wilhelmshaven reports its worst raid to date. Housing and city-centre type buildings are listed as being hit hardest. 77 people were killed and more than 50 injured.

15 September 1942

12 Bostons of 107 Squadron bombed the whaling factory ship *Solglint* in Cherbourg harbour; the ship was set on fire and gutted. No Bostons lost.

15/16 September 1942

MINELAYING

27 Wellingtons and 13 Stirlings of 1 and 3 Groups were minelaying in the Frisian Islands and off Verdon without loss.

16 September 1942

9 Bostons to Den Helder turned back, 4 of 6 Mosquitoes to Wiesbaden bombed a chemical factory without loss.

16/17 September 1942

ESSEN

369 aircraft, including aircraft from the training groups. 39 aircraft – 21 Wellingtons, 9 Lancasters, 5 Stirlings, 3 Halifaxes, 1 Whitley – lost, 10·6 per cent of the force.

Although much of the bombing was scattered, this was probably the most successful attack on this difficult target. There were 33 large and 80 'medium' fires. 8 industrial and 6 transport premises were hit. The Krupps works were hit by 15 high-explosive bombs and by a crashing bomber loaded with incendiaries. There was much housing damage. In Essen and its immediate surroundings, 47 people were killed and 92 injured.

Many other towns were hit, in particular Bochum with 50 fires and 4 people dead, Wuppertal with 13 dead, Herne with a large fire in a lorry garage and Cochem, a small town on the Moselle 90 miles south of Essen, which received 1 bomb load destroying 4 houses and killing 15 people.

17/18 September 1942

3 Halifaxes on leaflet flights to France without loss.

---

18 September 1942

3 Mosquitoes were dispatched to German ports but only 1 bombed the approximate position of Borkum. No aircraft lost.

18/19 September 1942

MINELAYING

115 aircraft to many locations between Lorient and Danzig. 5 aircraft – 2 Lancasters, 2 Stirlings, 1 Wellington – lost.

1 Halifax on leaflet flight to France returned safely.

---

19 September 1942

6 Mosquitoes of 105 Squadron attempted the first daylight bombing raid on Berlin. 2 aircraft had to turn back with mechanical trouble, 2 aircraft bombed Hamburg and 1 aircraft bombed the Berlin area through thick cloud. The remaining Mosquito was lost, believed shot down by a German fighter.

19/20 September 1942

SAARBRÜCKEN

118 aircraft – 72 Wellingtons, 41 Halifaxes, 5 Stirlings. 3 Wellingtons and 2 Halifaxes lost, 4·2 per cent of the force.

The Pathfinders had to mark 2 targets on this night and the Pathfinder crews allocated to this raid experienced difficulties with ground haze. Bombing was scattered to the west of the target. Saarbrücken reports on 13 houses destroyed, 27 seriously damaged and 1 man killed.

MUNICH

68 Lancasters and 21 Stirlings. 3 Lancasters and 3 Stirlings lost, 6·7 per cent of the force.

Approximately 40 per cent of the crews dropped bombs within 3 miles of the centre of Munich but most of the bombs fell in the western, southern and eastern suburbs of the city. It has not been possible to obtain a report from Munich.

Total effort for the night: 207 sorties, 11 aircraft (5·3 per cent) lost.

21/22 September 1942

17 aircraft minelaying in Kiel Bay and off Denmark. 3 Wellingtons lost.

22 September 1942

18 Bostons in low-level pairs attacked power-stations in France. 6 Mosquitoes were sent to Ijmuiden steelworks; 4 aircraft bombed there. 2 Bostons lost.

23/24 September 1942

During this prolonged period of bad weather, Bomber Command sent out 3 small raids without Pathfinders.

WISMAR

83 Lancasters of 5 Group; 4 lost.
    This was judged to be a successful attack on the Baltic coastal town and the nearby Dornier aircraft factory. Many crews came down to less than 2,000 ft. Numerous fires were seen including a large one in what was believed to be the aircraft factory. Wismar reports 32 houses and 8 industrial buildings seriously damaged, 67 people killed and 109 injured.

FLENSBURG

28 Halifaxes of 4 Group; 5 lost. Only 16 aircraft claimed to have bombed Flensburg.

VEGESACK

24 Stirlings of 3 Group; 1 lost.

25 Wellingtons and 8 Stirlings of 1 and 3 Groups minelaying at many places between Biscay and Denmark. 2 Wellingtons lost.

Total effort for the night: 168 sorties, 12 aircraft (7·1 per cent) lost.

24/25 September 1942

MINELAYING

51 aircraft to Texel, the Frisian Islands, Heligoland and the Baltic. 1 Lancaster lost.

25 September 1942

OSLO GESTAPO HEADQUARTERS

This raid was intended to be a morale raiser for the Norwegian people and was timed to coincide with a rally of Norwegians who supported the Germans.

4 Mosquitoes of 105 Squadron set off from Leuchars in Scotland but were intercepted by FW 190s on their low-level bombing run and 1 Mosquito was shot down. 4 bombs hit the Gestapo headquarters but 3 passed right through the building without exploding and the fourth, which remained inside the building, also failed to explode.

25/26 September 1942

10 Wellingtons minelaying in the Frisian Islands without loss.

26/27 September 1942

FLENSBURG

28 Halifaxes of 4 Group were recalled. 1 aircraft went on to bomb the target area and 1 aircraft was lost.

52 Wellingtons and 19 Stirlings minelaying in the Frisians and off Denmark. 1 Wellington lost.

---

28 September 1942

6 Wellingtons to Lingen, on the Dortmund–Ems Canal. Only 1 aircraft bombed ships, but missed. 1 Wellington lost.

29/30 September 1942

14 Lancasters minelaying in the Baltic off Bornholm, Sassnitz and Swinemünde. 1 aircraft was lost.

---

30 September/1 October 1942

20 Wellingtons and 5 Stirlings minelaying off Texel and in the Frisians. 1 Stirling and 1 Wellington lost.

---

1 October 1942

3 Mosquitoes; 2 aircraft attacked a chemical works at Sluiskil and an oil depot at Ghent. No aircraft lost.

1/2 October 1942

3 small raids were initiated in difficult weather conditions and without Pathfinders.

WISMAR

78 Lancasters of 5 Group. Bombing was scattered. 2 aircraft lost.

FLENSBURG

27 Halifaxes of 4 Group. Good bombing results were claimed by 12 crews but 12 aircraft were lost, nearly half of the force.

LÜBECK

25 Stirlings of 3 Group. Bombing was scattered. 3 aircraft lost.

Total effort for the night: 130 sorties, 17 aircraft (13·0 per cent) lost.

---

2 October 1942

6 Mosquitoes attacked a steelworks at Liège without loss.

2/3 October 1942

KREFELD

188 aircraft – 95 Wellingtons, 39 Halifaxes, 31 Lancasters, 23 Stirlings. 7 aircraft – 3 Halifaxes, 2 Wellingtons, 1 Lancaster, 1 Stirling – lost, 3·7 per cent of the force.

The Pathfinders encountered dense haze and their marking was late. The raid which developed was dispersed and not expected to cause much damage. Krefeld's rather general report on wartime bombing does not class this as a '*Grossangriff*' – a major raid; only 3 streets in the northern part of the town are mentioned as being hit but most of the 41 people recorded as being killed by raids in 1942 probably died on this night.

3 Wellingtons laid mines in the Frisians without loss.

---

5 October 1942

1 Mosquito to Frankfurt bombed a town believed to be Siegen and returned safely.

5/6 October 1942

AACHEN

257 aircraft – 101 Wellingtons, 74 Lancasters, 59 Halifaxes, 23 Stirlings. 10 aircraft – 5 Halifaxes, 2 Stirlings, 2 Wellingtons, 1 Lancaster – lost, 3·9 per cent of the force. A further 6 aircraft crashed in England, possibly in thunderstorms which were present when some squadrons took off for the raid.

The weather continued to be bad over Germany. There was little Pathfinder marking at Aachen and most of the bombing fell in other areas. Aachen reports that the raid on this night was carried out by an estimated 10 aircraft and that the centre of the attack appeared to be in the southern suburb of Burtscheid, where a 4,000-lb bomb severely damaged a hospital and 2 nearby churches. 34 fires were started, 5 of them being classified as large. A moderate amount of housing was hit and, rather surprisingly, 22 industrial buildings were damaged. 5 people were killed and 39 injured.

Many of the bombs intended for Aachen fell in the small Dutch town of Lutterade, 17 miles away from Aachen, and it seems that most of the Pathfinder marking was over this place. The Mayor of Geleen, the Dutch district in which Lutterade is now situated, reports heavy bombing and much damage in Lutterade on that night. More than 800 houses were seriously damaged; 83 people were killed, 22 were injured and 3,000 were made homeless.

---

6 October 1942

7 Mosquitoes to a diesel-engine works at Hengelo in Holland and to Bremen, Essen and Trier. All 7 aircraft bombed, though not always at their designated targets; none were lost.

6/7 October 1942

OSNABRÜCK

237 aircraft – 101 Wellingtons, 68 Lancasters, 38 Stirlings, 30 Halifaxes. 6 aircraft – 2 Halifaxes, 2 Lancasters, 2 Stirlings – were lost, 2·5 per cent of the force.

The Pathfinders succeeded in illuminating the Dummer See, a large lake northeast of the target which was used as a run-in point. The town of Osnabrück was then found and marked. The bombing was well concentrated, with most of the attack falling in the centre and the southern parts of the target. Osnabrück's report shows that 149 houses were destroyed, 530 were seriously damaged and 2,784 lightly damaged. 6 industrial premises were destroyed and 14 damaged. Other places hit were 6 public buildings, 5 churches, 4 schools, 1 hospital and the local gasworks. 65 people were killed – 45 civilians, 16 policemen or servicemen and 4 foreign workers – and 151 were injured.

---

8 October 1942

1 Mosquito to Saarbrücken bombed a factory believed to be in the nearby town of Bous.

8/9 October 1942

MINELAYING

57 aircraft to Lorient, St-Nazaire, Brest, Ostend, Texel and the Frisians. 2 Wellingtons lost.

---

9 October 1942

5 Mosquitoes to scattered targets in Germany. 1 aircraft lost.

9/10 October 1942

14 Wellingtons laid mines in the Frisian Islands without loss.

10/11 October 1942

MINELAYING

47 aircraft off Biscay ports and in the Frisians without loss.

11 October 1942

8 Mosquitoes to Sluiskil, Hannover and Saarbrücken. 1 aircraft lost.

11/12 October 1942

MINELAYING

80 aircraft to many locations. 2 Wellingtons and 1 Stirling lost.

12/13 October 1942

WISMAR

59 Lancasters of 5 Group encountered bad weather conditions but claimed to have started a large fire at the target. 2 aircraft lost.

13/14 October 1942

KIEL

288 aircraft – 100 Wellingtons, 82 Lancasters, 78 Halifaxes, 28 Stirlings. 8 aircraft – 5 Wellingtons, 1 each of other types – lost, 2·8 per cent of the force.

A decoy fire site was operating and at least half of the bombing was drawn away into open countryside, but the rest of the attack fell on Kiel and its immediate surroundings. The Kiel diarist records a now familiar list of area-bombing damage, the only items of particular interest being that 17 omnibuses were destroyed in their garage or parking area and that much of the bombing fell on the south-eastern suburbs of Elmschenhagen. He also refers to a constantly recurring theme in recent raids, the vast amount of roof damage and glass breakage with the increasing use by Bomber Command of high-capacity blast bombs. 250,000 square metres of roof tiling and 150,000 square metres of glass were blown away in Kiel on this night. Casualties were 41 killed and 101 injured. Finally, Herr Boelck writes: 'Amazingly, the Flak hardly opened fire for some time although the bombers were over the town.* This withholding of fire was a ploy which the German defences developed to hinder the identification of a target by the bombers, particularly when a nearby decoy site was being used. There were often disagreements between local party offi-

* *Kiel im Luftkrieg 1939–1945*, op. cit. p. 41.

cials, who wanted their people to see the Flak banging away vigorously, and the local Luftwaffe Flak commanders who were attempting this tactical deception.

Some of the bomber force attacked Hamburg, either as an alternative target or in error. 2 large fires were started; 8 people were killed and 43 injured. Hans Brunswig refers to this as the R.A.F.'s 'October raid', indicating perhaps that cities like Hamburg now expected to be attacked regularly once a month.

14/15 October 1942

5 Wellingtons minelaying in the Frisian Islands without loss.

---

15 October 1942

LE HAVRE

23 Bostons, with fighter escort, attempted to bomb a large German merchant ship recently seen in Le Havre docks. The intended target had moved from its berth but a 5,000-ton ship near by was bombed instead and so badly damaged that she was later seen aground and later still seen in dry dock. No Bostons lost.

4 Mosquitoes bombed a factory at Hengelo and 1 Mosquito bombed the docks at Den Helder, all without loss.

15/16 October 1942

COLOGNE

289 aircraft – 109 Wellingtons, 74 Halifaxes, 62 Lancasters, 44 Stirlings. 18 aircraft – 6 Wellingtons, 5 Halifaxes, 5 Lancasters, 2 Stirlings – lost, 6·2 per cent of the force.

This was not a successful raid. Winds were different from those forecast and the Pathfinders had difficulty in establishing their position and marking the target sufficiently to attract the Main Force away from a large decoy fire site which received most of the bombs. Cologne reports 1 '*Luftmine*' (out of 71 4,000-pounders carried by the bombing force), 3 other high-explosive bombs (out of 231) and 210 incendiary bombs (out of 68,590). 226 houses were damaged but only 2 of these received what was classed as 'serious damage'; 4 people were injured.

---

16 October 1942

6 Mosquitoes bombed a factory at Hengelo. 6 Bostons attempted to reach Le Havre but were turned back by bad weather. No aircraft lost.

16/17 October 1942

MINOR OPERATIONS

23 Wellingtons and 11 Stirlings minelaying off Biscay ports, 5 O.T.U. sorties. 2 Wellingtons and 2 Stirlings lost from the minelaying force.

---

17 October 1942

LE CREUSOT

This famous raid was carried out against the large Schneider factory at Le Creusot, situated more than 300 miles inside France. The factory was regarded as the French equivalent to Krupps and produced heavy guns, railway engines and, it was believed, tanks and armoured cars. A large workers' housing estate was situated at one end of the factory. Bomber Command had been given this as the highest priority target in France for a night attack but only in the most favourable of conditions. Harris decided to attack by day, at low level, despite the fate of the force sent to Augsburg exactly 6 months earlier, when 7 out of the 12 Lancasters dispatched were shot down. The task was given to Air Vice-Marshal Coryton's 5 Group and its 9 Lancaster squadrons carried out a series of low-level practice flights over England.*

After a favourable weather report, 94 Lancasters set out on the afternoon of 17 October. The force was led by Wing Commander L. C. Slee of 49 Squadron. 88 aircraft were to bomb the Schneider factory; the other 6 were to attack a nearby transformer station which supplied the factory with electricity. The Lancasters flew in a loose formation over the sea around Brittany, and crossed the coast of France between La Rochelle and St-Nazaire without any fighter escort. For 300 miles the Lancasters flew at tree-top level across France. No German fighters attacked the bombers during this flight. The greatest danger was from birds; 4 aircraft were damaged and 2 men injured in bird strikes.

After a fine piece of work by Wing Commander Slee's navigator, Pilot Officer A. S. Grant, the force reached its last turning-point near Nevers and gained height for bombing. There was practically no Flak at the target and bombing took place in clear conditions at heights of between 2,500 and 7,500 ft. Nearly 140 tons of bombs were dropped. The Lancasters returned home safely as darkness closed in. The only casualty was one aircraft of 61 Squadron which bombed the nearby transformer power-station at such a low level that it crashed into a building.

The 5 Group crews claimed a successful attack on the Schneider factory but photographs taken later showed that much of the bombing had fallen short and had struck the workers' housing estate near the factory. Some bombs had fallen into the factory area but damage there was not extensive. It has not been possible to obtain a report from France on the casualties suffered by the local people in this raid.

11 Bostons sent to Le Havre had to turn back but 6 other Bostons carried out a sweep to create a diversion for the Le Creusot force. No Bostons lost.

17/18 October 1942

7 Stirlings minelaying in the Baltic off Bornholm and Sassnitz without loss.

---

*As a 10-year-old boy, I was out in a field near my home in Boston, gathering blackberries, when the amazing and thrilling sight of nearly 100 Lancasters swept over my head carrying out one of those practice flights. – M.M.

20 October 1942

6 Mosquitoes to individual German targets; 2 aircraft bombed at Bremen and 1 at Minden. 1 Mosquito lost.

21 October 1942

3 Mosquitoes to Germany but only 2 were able to bomb targets in Holland, a factory at Hengelo and the airfield at Leeuwarden. No losses.

21/22 October 1942

7 Stirlings and 7 Wellingtons were dispatched to lay mines off Denmark and in the Frisians but the Wellingtons were recalled. 1 Stirling lost.

22 October 1942

22 Wellingtons on cloud-cover raids to Essen, the Ruhr and the Dortmund–Ems Canal at Lingen. 13 aircraft bombed estimated positions through cloud. One of the Wellingtons came down low and machine-gunned a train near Lingen, setting some of the carriages alight. No aircraft were lost.

22/23 October 1942

GENOA

112 Lancasters of 5 Group and the Pathfinders were dispatched to recommence the campaign against Italy to coincide with the opening of the Eighth Army offensive at El Alamein. It was a perfectly clear moonlight night and the Pathfinder marking was described as 'prompt and accurate'. The bombing by this comparatively small force of aircraft, carrying only 180 tons of bombs, could hardly have been carried out under more ideal conditions. No Lancasters were lost.

Details from Genoa are not precise but very heavy damage was caused in the city centre and in the eastern districts. Many old buildings, including the Palazzo Ducale and several museums and churches, were destroyed. Provisional estimates of casualties were 39 dead and 200 injured but the actual figures may have been higher. Local reports mention the severe effect on the morale of the people of Genoa.

12 Stirlings laid mines off the southern Biscay coast without loss.

23 October 1942

THE RUHR

26 Wellingtons, 15 to Krefeld and 11 to Essen. 11 aircraft bombed estimated positions through cloud without loss.

4 Mosquitoes to Hengelo and 1 to Oldenburg; 1 aircraft from the Hengelo force was lost.

23/24 October 1942

GENOA

122 aircraft – 53 Halifaxes, 51 Stirlings, 18 Wellingtons. These aircraft were provided by 3 and 4 Groups and the Pathfinders. 2 Halifaxes and 1 Stirling lost.

The target area was found to be almost completely cloud-covered and it was later discovered that the raid had actually fallen on the town of Savona, 30 miles along the coast from Genoa. It has not been possible to obtain a report from Savona. Several aircraft bombed Turin where 2 people were killed and 10 injured.

17 Wellingtons of 1 Group minelaying off La Pallice and the Danish coast. 1 aircraft lost.

24 October 1942

MILAN

88 Lancasters of 5 Group in another risky daylight operation. The aircraft proceeded independently by a direct route across France, using partial cloud cover, to a rendez-vous at Lake Annecy. The Alps were then crossed and Milan bombed in broad daylight. Anti-aircraft fire and Italian fighter defences were both weak. Accurate bombing took place.

The raid came as a complete surprise in Milan, where the warning sirens sounded after the first bombs exploded. 135 tons of bombs fell in 18 minutes. The Italians claimed that a Lancaster came down to roof-top level and machine-gunned people in streets near the church of St Christopher. 30 large fires were started. 441 houses were destroyed or damaged and the Italians admitted that the following public buildings were hit: the university, the prison, the offices of the local Fascist Party, 2 churches, 2 schools, 2 hospitals – one a maternity hospital. R.A.F. reconnaissance photographs later discovered that a number of commercial and industrial buildings were also hit, including the Caproni aircraft factory. At least 171 people were killed.

3 Lancasters were lost, 1 near Milan and 2 over Northern France and the Channel. A further Lancaster crashed in England and its crew were all killed.

24/25 October 1942

MILAN

71 aircraft of 1 and 3 Groups and the Pathfinders – 25 Halifaxes, 23 Stirlings, 23 Wellingtons – continued the attack on Milan. 4 Wellingtons and 2 Stirlings were lost, 8·5 per cent of the force.

Storms *en route* dispersed the bomber force; some aircraft flew over Switzerland and were 'warned' by anti-aircraft fire. Only 39 aircraft claimed to have bombed Milan and local reports say that little further damage was caused there.

Minor Operations: 25 Wellingtons of 1 Group minelaying in several areas between La Pallice and Denmark, 11 O.T.U. sorties. 2 Wellington minelayers lost.

25 October 1942

12 Bostons were again dispatched to Le Havre to attack the large merchant ship there but had to turn back because of lack of cloud cover. 3 Mosquitoes to Germany also turned back. There were no aircraft losses.

26/27 October 1942

MINELAYING

24 Stirlings and Wellingtons of 3 Group to the Frisian Islands and to Biscay ports without loss.

---

27 October 1942

8 Mosquitoes to Flensburg, Belgium and Holland. 2 Mosquitoes bombed a shipyard at Flensburg; 4 Mosquitoes bombed other unidentified targets. No aircraft lost.

27/28 October 1942

MINOR OPERATIONS

36 aircraft minelaying between St-Nazaire and the Frisians, 4 O.T.U. sorties. No losses.

28/29 October 1942

9 Wellingtons minelaying off St-Nazaire and Denmark. 1 aircraft lost.

---

29 October 1942

7 Mosquitoes to Holland and the German Frisian Islands, 6 Wellingtons on 'roving commissions' of the Ruhr. 6 Mosquitoes and 1 Wellington bombed various targets but 3 Wellingtons and 2 Mosquitoes were lost.

---

30 October 1942

9 Mosquitoes dispatched but none reached their designated targets. 7 aircraft bombed targets of opportunity at mostly unidentified places. 1 aircraft lost.

30/31 October 1942

4 Wellingtons minelaying in the Frisians without loss.

---

31 October 1942

17 Bostons in low-level cloud-cover raids on power-stations in France. Cover was sparse and 10 aircraft attacked mostly minor targets. 1 Boston lost.

8 Wellingtons to Emden and 6 to Essen. 9 aircraft bombed; 1 lost.

31 October/1 November 1942

MINELAYING

22 Wellingtons and Stirlings to Biscay ports. 1 Wellington lost.

1 November 1942

6 Bostons to St-Omer airfield, 3 bombed here and 3 bombed the docks at Calais as an alternative target. 1 Boston lost.

3 November 1942

3 Stirlings to Lingen; 2 of these aircraft bombed a factory. 3 Venturas of 21 Squadron commenced operations with this new type of day bomber; they were unable to find their primary target, a factory at Hengelo, and bombed railways in Holland instead. No aircraft lost on this day.

3/4 November 1942

MINELAYING

29 Wellingtons to Biscay ports. 1 aircraft lost.

6 November 1942

14 Wellingtons and 5 Lancasters on cloud-cover raids to Essen, Osnabrück and Wilhelmshaven. Only 6 aircraft bombed, through cloud, in the Osnabrück and Wilhelmshaven areas. No aircraft lost.

12 Bostons bombed an airfield near Caen without loss.

10 Venturas in fours and twos carried out low-level raids to Holland. 3 aircraft lost.

6/7 November 1942

GENOA

72 Lancasters of the Pathfinder Force and 5 Group. 2 Lancasters lost.

The attack was concentrated but most bombs fell in residential areas. No separate report for this raid is available from Genoa.

Minor Operations: 65 aircraft minelaying from Lorient to the Frisians, 4 O.T.U. sorties, 3 Stirling minelayers lost.

---

7 November 1942

6 Mosquitoes of 105 Squadron carried out a successful low-level attack on the 5,000-ton German ship *Elsa Essberger* which had just arrived in the mouth of the River Gironde from a blockade-running voyage from the Far East with scarce raw materials. The merchant ship was escorted by an armed naval vessel. The Mosquitoes claimed to have hit both ships but 1 Mosquito was shot down.

In other operations, 9 Bostons, 6 Venturas and 5 Wellingtons attempted raids to many places in Germany, Belgium and Holland but most only achieved attacks on minor targets of opportunity. 1 Boston and 1 Ventura lost.

7/8 November 1942

GENOA

175 aircraft – 85 Lancasters, 45 Halifaxes, 39 Stirlings, 6 Wellingtons. 6 aircraft – 4 Halifaxes, 1 Lancaster, 1 Wellington – lost, 3·4 per cent of the force.

Returning crews claimed a very successful and concentrated raid and this was confirmed by photographs. No report is available from Genoa.

36 Wellingtons of 1 Group minelaying in many areas from St-Nazaire to Denmark. 1 aircraft lost.

8/9 November 1942

MINELAYING

70 aircraft to many places from Brest to the Frisian Islands. 2 Halifaxes and 2 Wellingtons lost.

LEAFLETS

26 Stirlings of 3 Group carried out a special operation to drop leaflets over many towns in France giving news of the latest successes of the Allied forces in North Africa, following the successful invasion of the French territories there. No aircraft were lost.

---

9 November 1942

12 Bostons bombed Le Havre and scored a hit on the large German merchant ship which had been the objective of recent raids. The ship was put out of action for several months. No Bostons were lost.

9/10 November 1942

HAMBURG

213 aircraft – 74 Wellingtons, 72 Lancasters, 48 Halifaxes, 19 Stirlings. 15 aircraft – 5 Lancasters, 4 Stirlings, 4 Wellingtons, 2 Halifaxes – lost, 7·0 per cent of the force.

The bombers encountered cloud and icing and winds which had not been forecast. No clear identification or marking of Hamburg was made. 150 crews reported bombing, 133 believing themselves to be in the Hamburg area, 17 claiming attacks in other places. Hamburg reports thick cloud and heavy rain and says that many bombs fell in the Elbe or in open country. There were, however, 26 fires in Hamburg of which 3 were large ones. Casualties were 3 people killed and 16 injured. 1 bomber crashed in the city's main cemetery, in the Ohlsdorf district; this is where many R.A.F. men who died while raiding this part of Germany are buried in a Commonwealth War Graves Commission section.

15 Stirlings carried more leaflets to France without loss.

---

10 November 1942

18 Bostons attempted to continue attacks on the German ship at Le Havre but it had been moved. 15 aircraft bombed the dock area. 2 Bostons crashed in the sea.

10/11 November 1942

MINELAYING

42 aircraft to the southern Biscay coast of France and to the Frisian Islands. No aircraft were lost but 2 Lancasters crashed in England.

11/12 November 1942

MINELAYING

31 Wellingtons to Biscay ports and the Frisians. No losses.

---

13 November 1942

6 Wellingtons to Emden but only 1 aircraft dropped bombs, which hit fields. No losses.

The German merchant ship which had recently been damaged at Le Havre was now spotted at Flushing where it had been taken for repair. 2 Mosquitoes of 105 Squadron set out to Flushing but did not return. It is believed, however, that they did hit the ship again. 2 more Mosquitoes and 6 Bostons then took off to carry out a sea search for the crews of the 2 lost Mosquitoes. These were not found and 1 of the Bostons was then lost.

13/14 November 1942

GENOA

67 Lancasters and 9 Stirlings of the Pathfinder Force and 5 Group. More successful bombing was carried out but no details are available. No aircraft lost.

12 Wellingtons minelaying off Lorient and St-Nazaire without loss.

15/16 November 1942

GENOA

78 aircraft – 40 Halifaxes, 27 Lancasters, 11 Stirlings – continued the raids on Genoa with further accurate bombing. No aircraft lost.

22 Wellingtons of 1 Group minelaying off La Pallice, Lorient and St-Nazaire. 1 aircraft lost.

16 November 1942

6 Mosquitoes bombed targets in the small German towns of Emmerich, Jülich and Lingen without loss.

16/17 November 1942

MINOR OPERATIONS

65 aircraft minelaying to various places from Lorient to the Frisian Islands. 2 Wellingtons and 1 Stirling lost. 5 Halifaxes on leaflet flights to France without loss.

17/18 November 1942

MINOR OPERATIONS

43 aircraft minelaying from Lorient to the Frisian Islands, 14 aircraft on leaflet flights to France. 1 Halifax lost on the leaflet operation.

18/19 November 1942

TURIN

77 aircraft dispatched. Many fires were started in the city-centre area. Hits were also achieved on the Fiat motor factory. Turin records show that 42 people were killed and 72 injured.

No aircraft were lost but the 35 Squadron Halifax of Squadron Leader B. V. Robinson returned with only the pilot aboard. The load of flares in the aircraft had ignited and it appeared that the aircraft would crash. Robinson ordered his crew to bale out but, after they had done so, the rush of air from an escape hatch blew the fire out and the pilot was able to reach an airfield in England safely. The parachuting crew members would account for the claim of 1 aircraft shot down in the Turin records. (Later in the war, as Group Captain Robinson, D.S.O., D.F.C. and Bar, A.F.C., this officer was killed when his Halifax was shot down during a raid on Berlin on the night of 23/24 August 1943. He is buried in the Berlin War Cemetery.)

5 O.T.U. aircraft took leaflets to France without loss.

19/20 November 1942

11 Wellingtons of 1 Group minelaying off Lorient and St-Nazaire. 1 aircraft lost.

20/21 November 1942

TURIN

232 aircraft – 86 Lancasters, 54 Wellingtons, 47 Halifaxes, 45 Stirlings – on the largest raid to Italy during this period. 3 aircraft – 1 Halifax, 1 Stirling, 1 Wellington – lost.

This was another successful attack, with large fires being started. Dense smoke prevented further observations of the effects of the bombing but the casualty roll in Turin, 117 dead and 120 injured, confirms that many bombs fell in the city.

Minor Operations: 4 Stirlings minelaying in the River Gironde, 4 O.T.U. sorties. No losses.

21/22 November 1942

MINELAYING

30 aircraft to Biscay ports from Lorient to Bayonne without loss.

22/23 November 1942

STUTTGART

222 aircraft – 97 Lancasters, 59 Wellingtons, 39 Halifaxes, 27 Stirlings. 10 aircraft – 5 Lancasters, 3 Wellingtons, 2 Halifaxes – lost, 4·5 per cent of the force.

A thin layer of cloud and some ground haze concealed Stuttgart and the Pathfinders were not able to identify the centre of the city. Heavy bombing developed to the south-west and south and the outlying residential districts of Vaihingen, Rohr, Mohringen and Plieningen, all about 5 miles from the centre, were hit. 88 houses were destroyed and 334 seriously damaged; 28 people were killed and 71 injured. The Stuttgart report says that 2 bombers attacked the centre of the city at low level and dropped bombs on to the main railway station which caused severe damage to the wooden platforms and some trains in the station.

There was 1 O.T.U. leaflet sortie to France which returned safely.

14. Completely burnt-out railway station in Stuttgart on the night of 22/23 November 1942 (see diary entry).

23/24 November 1942

MINELAYING

35 aircraft to Biscay ports and the Frisian Islands without loss.

25 November 1942

In the first Bomber Command day operation for 10 days, 6 Wellingtons and 5 Lancasters were sent on cloud-cover raids to Essen and 5 smaller German tartgets. Most of these aircraft turned back because of insufficient cloud. 1 Wellington bombed ships off the Dutch coast. 1 Lancaster and 1 Wellington lost.

25/26 November 1942

22 Wellingtons and Halifaxes minelaying off St-Nazaire and in the Frisians without loss.

26/27 November 1942

30 aircraft minelaying off Lorient and St-Nazaire and in the Frisians and the Kattegat. No losses.

27 November 1942

6 Bostons in low-level pairs to Belgium and Holland. 3 aircraft bombed various targets. No losses.

27/28 November 1942

32 Lancasters and Stirlings were recalled from a raid to Stettin and jettisoned their bombs in the North Sea. 10 aircraft were sent minelaying in the River Gironde and off Texel, Gdynia and Danzig. The more distant locations were not reached. No aircraft lost.

28/29 November 1942

TURIN

228 aircraft – 117 Lancasters, 47 Stirlings, 45 Halifaxes, 19 Wellingtons. 2 Stirlings and 1 Wellington lost.

Part of the force bombed before the Pathfinders were ready but the remainder carried out very accurate bombing, some of it around the Royal Arsenal. Wing Commander G. P. Gibson and Flight Lieutenant W. N. Whamond of 106 Squadron dropped the first 8,000-lb bombs on Italy. Turin recorded 67 people killed and 83 injured.

During the raid on Turin, a Stirling of 149 Squadron came down to 2,000 ft in order to establish the exact position of its target. The Australian captain of the crew, Flight Sergeant R. H. Middleton, made 3 runs across the city and his aircraft was hit by light anti-aircraft fire, a shell exploding in the cockpit. The 2 pilots and the wireless operator were all seriously wounded. Flight Sergeant Middleton became unconscious temporarily, but the co-pilot, Flight Sergeant L. A. Hyder, managed to keep control and the bombs were released. The Stirling was hit again over Turin and also over France on the return flight.

The coast of England was reached but the captain decided there was little chance of landing safely, mainly because of a shortage of petrol but also because of the damaged state of the aircraft and the injuries of the 2 pilots. Flight Sergeant Middleton himself had been badly wounded in the head, was very weak and could hardly see or speak. He turned parallel with the coast and ordered his crew to bale out. 5 men did so and survived but Middleton and 2 other men were still in the plane when it crashed into the sea.

Flight Sergeant Middleton was awarded a posthumous Victoria Cross; he was the second Australian in Bomber Command to win the V.C. The co-pilot was awarded the D.F.M. and 4 other members of the crew were decorated. Middleton's body was washed up on the Kent coast and was buried at Beck Row, Mildenhall, near his home airfield of Lakenheath.

Minor Operations: 19 aircraft minelaying off Biscay ports, 5 O.T.U. sorties. No losses.

29/30 November 1942

TURIN

29 Stirlings and 7 Lancasters of 3 Group and the Pathfinder Force dispatched, with the Fiat works as their main target. Weather conditions were poor and only 18 aircraft – 14 Pathfinders and 4 Stirlings of 3 Group – are known to have definitely crossed the Alps and bombed Turin. 2 further Stirlings were lost. Turin can report only that 16 people were killed and 15 injured.

6 Mosquitoes to Belgium to seek targets of opportunity. This was the first Mosquito night operation of the war. Railway yards at 5 places in Belgium were bombed and the Mosquitoes all returned safely.

---

30 November/1 December 1942

6 Wellingtons of 3 Group laid mines at La Pallice without loss.

2/3 December 1942

FRANKFURT

112 aircraft – 48 Halifaxes, 27 Lancasters, 22 Stirlings, 15 Wellingtons. 6 aircraft – 3 Halifaxes, 1 each of the other types – lost, 5·4 per cent of the force.
     There was thick haze and the Pathfinders were unable to establish the location of Frankfurt. Most of the bombing fell in country areas south-west of the city; it is possible that a decoy fire site was operating.

4 O.T.U. sorties were flown without loss.

4/5 December 1942

MINOR OPERATIONS

29 aircraft minelaying in the Frisians and in the Baltic off Gdynia and Danzig, 3 O.T.U. sorties. No aircraft lost.

5/6 December 1942

6 O.T.U. sorties were flown to France without loss.

---

6 December 1942

EINDHOVEN

This was a special, and famous, raid carried out by all of the operational day-bomber squadrons in 2 Group. Their targets were the Philips radio and valve factories in the Dutch town of Eindhoven. These factories produced a large amount of important electrical material for the German armed forces. 93 aircraft took part in the raid – 47 Venturas, 36 Bostons and 10 Mosquitoes. 1 of the Mosquitoes was a photographic aircraft. A squadron equipped with the North American Mitchell bomber was withdrawn from the force during the training period because its crews had not gained enough experience on this new type of aircraft.* Eindhoven was situated 70 miles inland and well beyond the range of any available fighter escort. A large diversion to Lille was flown by 84 American B-17s escorted by Spitfires of Fighter Command and an R.A.F. Mustang squadron carried out a sweep along the Dutch coast to give indirect support. The raid was flown at low level and in clear weather conditions. Bombing was accurate and severe damage was caused to the factory, which was situated in the middle of the town. Because the raid was deliberately carried out on a Sunday, there were few casualties in the factory but several bombs fell in nearby streets and 148 Dutch people and 7 German soldiers were killed. Full production at the factory was not reached again until 6 months after the raid.

The bomber casualties were heavy: 9 Venturas, 4 Bostons and 1 Mosquito were lost over Holland or the sea. This was a loss rate of 15 per cent for the whole force; the Venturas, the aircraft with the poorest performance, suffered 19 per cent casualties. 3 more aircraft crashed or force-landed in England and most of the other aircraft were damaged – 23 by bird strikes!

6/7 December 1942

MANNHEIM

272 aircraft – 101 Lancasters, 65 Halifaxes, 57 Wellingtons, 49 Stirlings. 10 aircraft – 5 Wellingtons, 3 Halifaxes, 1 Lancaster, 1 Stirling – lost, 3·7 per cent of the force, and 4 more aircraft crashed in England.

The target area was found to be completely cloud-covered. Most of the Pathfinders withheld their flares and many of the 220 crews who bombed did so on dead-reckoning positions. Mannheim reports only 500 or so incendiary bombs and some leaflets. The only serious incident over the city was the destruction by fire of an old wooden building at the army 'Pioneer Water Exercise Centre' on the Neckar Canal; the lower part of the building was used by a local farmer who lost 25 sheep, 4 lambs, some turnips and some hay. The total claim for the building was 11,000 Reichsmarks (£1,100) and for the animals, etc. 3,000 Reichsmarks (£300). The roofs of a house and of the local canoe clubhouse were also set on fire but soon extinguished. There were no casualties in Mannheim.

14 Lancasters and Wellingtons laid mines in the Frisian Islands without loss.

---

* Michael J. F. Bowyer provides a good description of the preparations for this raid and the outcome of it on pp. 263–83 of his book *2 Group R.A.F.*, op. cit.

15 (a and b). The successful but costly raid by 2 Group on the Philips radio factory at Eindhoven in Holland. The aircraft over the target are Bostons.

7/8 December 1942

MINELAYING

36 aircraft were sent to a wide extent of coast from the southern Biscay to the Frisians. This appears to be the first night on which aircraft of 4 Group joined in the minelaying campaign.

---

8 December 1942

6 Mosquitoes carried out daylight Intruder patrols over Holland and just over the German frontier. 1 Mosquito lost.

8/9 December 1942

TURIN

133 aircraft of 5 Group and the Pathfinder Force – 108 Lancasters, 9 Halifaxes, 9 Wellingtons, 7 Stirlings; 1 Lancaster lost.

The Pathfinders illuminated the target well and bombing was very accurate. Residential and industrial areas were both extensively damaged. Turin reports 212 dead and 111 injured; this was the largest number of dead in all of the 1942 raids on this city, even though much larger forces of bombers were dispatched on 3 other raids. Fires from this raid were still burning the following night.

MINELAYING

80 aircraft of 1, 3 and 4 Groups to the German and Danish coasts; 5 aircraft – 3 Stirlings, 1 Halifax, 1 Lancaster – lost.

Total effort for the night: 213 sorties, 6 aircraft (2·8 per cent) lost.

---

9 December 1942

5 Mosquitoes on individual flights to France and Holland; all aircraft attacked targets, mostly trains. No losses.

9/10 December 1942

TURIN

227 aircraft – 115 Lancasters, 47 Halifaxes, 40 Wellingtons, 25 Stirlings. 2 Wellingtons and 1 Lancaster lost.

This was a disappointing raid with the Pathfinders not able to perform as efficiently as on the previous night. Smoke from old fires partially obscured the target area. Turin, however, records 73 more people killed and 99 injured.

Minor Operations: 2 Stirlings minelaying in the Frisians, 12 O.T.U. sorties. 1 O.T.U. Whitley lost.

11/12 December 1942

TURIN

82 aircraft of 1, 4 and 5 Groups and the Pathfinders – 48 Halifaxes, 20 Lancasters, 8 Stirlings, 6 Wellingtons – were dispatched but more than half of the force turned back before attempting to cross the Alps, because of severe icing conditions. 28 crews claimed to have bombed Turin but the city reports only 3 high-explosive bombs (2 of them duds) and a few incendiaries, with no casualties. 3 Halifaxes and 1 Stirling lost.

Minor Operations: 26 Wellingtons minelaying off Biscay ports and in the Frisians, 4 O.T.U. sorties. No losses.

12/13 December 1942

Because of bad weather, no major night raids were possible for the remainder of this diary period. On this night, 15 Wellingtons of 1 and 3 Groups were sent minelaying in the Frisian Islands without loss.

13 December 1942

4 Bostons and 4 Mosquitoes on railway attacks in France and Belgium but only 2 Mosquitoes bombed, at Laon and Criel. No aircraft lost.

13/14 December 1942

6 Wellingtons minelaying off Lorient and St-Nazaire without loss.

14 December 1942

4 Mosquitoes on railways attacks in Belgium and Holland but only 1 aircraft bombed at Ghent. No losses.

14/15 December 1942

MINELAYING

68 aircraft – 27 Halifaxes, 23 Lancasters, 18 Wellingtons – to Texel, Heligoland and the Frisians. The 5 Group Lancasters were recalled but most of the other types carried out their tasks. There were no losses.

15/16 December 1942

5 Wellingtons minelaying off Lorient and St-Nazaire without loss.

16/17 December 1942

Minor Operations

8 Wellingtons attempted to bomb a German aircraft depot at Diepholz; 3 aircraft bombed the general area of the target but 'with no evidence of success' and 1 Wellington was lost. 18 aircraft minelaying in the River Gironde and off Brest and Lorient; 1 Stirling lost.

17 December 1942

6 Wellingtons and 4 Mosquitoes on cloud-cover and railway attacks over a wide area. 5 aircraft attacked various targets. There were no losses.

17/18 December 1942

MINOR OPERATIONS

27 Lancasters of 5 Group were sent on raids to 8 small German towns and 16 Stirlings and 6 Wellingtons of 3 Group attempted to attack the Opel works at Fallersleben. This type of limited operation proved to be a costly failure. 9 of the 27 Lancasters were lost and, at Fallersleben, only 3 aircraft bombed the target, in cloud conditions, and 6 Stirlings and 2 Wellingtons were lost from this part of the night's operations. 75 (New Zealand) Squadron, based at Newmarket, lost 4 out of the 5 Stirlings sent on the Fallersleben raid, including the aircraft of its commanding officer, Wing Commander V. Mitchell, whose name is on the Runnymede Memorial to the Missing.

50 aircraft were dispatched to lay mines from Denmark to southern Biscay – 1 Lancaster was lost – and there were 5 O.T.U. sorties to France.

Total losses for the night: 18 aircraft out of 104 dispatched, 17·3 per cent.

19/20 December 1942

15 Wellingtons minelaying off Brest, Lorient and St-Nazaire without loss.

20 December 1942

11 Mosquitoes to north-west Germany. 9 aircraft attacked trains and rolling stock; 1 Mosquito lost.

Operational Statistics, 17/18 August to 20 December 1942
(125 days/nights)

Number of days with operations: 59
Number of nights with operations: 92
Number of daylight sorties: 948, from which 61 aircraft (6·4 per cent) were lost
Number of night sorties: 10,256, from which 465 aircraft (4·5 per cent) were lost
Total sorties: 11,204, from which 526 aircraft (4·7 per cent) were lost
Approximate bomb tonnage in period: 15,421 tons
Averages per 24-hour period: 89·6 sorties, 4·2 aircraft lost, 123·4 tons of bombs dropped

13. AN ACCESSION OF STRENGTH

20/21 December 1942 to 5 March 1943

Bomber Command had been struggling on now for more than three years, trying to keep its strength together in the face of urgent demands for help from other services and other fronts, trying to overcome the many obstacles to the successful bombing of German targets by night. But now, at the end of 1942, this steadfastness and patience was suddenly to be rewarded by a whole bonanza of improvements.

The first of these was called *Oboe*. This was a blind-bombing device fitted into an aircraft but controlled from ground stations in England. Two stations transmitted pulses which were picked up by the aircraft and retransmitted to the ground stations again. The aircraft receiving the *Oboe* signals used the pulses to keep itself on the correct track in order to pass over the target; the stations in England, by measuring the time taken to receive the pulses back again, calculated the aircraft's exact position and sent a short signal at the moment when its bombs should be released. An average bomb-aiming error of less than 300 yards could be achieved when all went well. The advantages of *Oboe* were self-evident, but there were three limitations. Firstly, it was a line-of-sight device whose signal could not be bent over the curvature of the earth; this limited the range of its use. Secondly, each station in England could only control six aircraft per hour, and as the maximum numbers of stations that could be used was three only eighteen aircraft per hour could thus use *Oboe*. Finally, the aircraft making the bomb run had to fly straight and level for several minutes and was likely to become an ideal target for German Flak or night fighters.

Although originally developed as a simple blind-bombing device – it had been tested as such by Stirlings against the German battle-cruisers of Brest – it was realized that the small number of *Oboe* aircraft that could be employed at any one time could best be used as marker aircraft in the Pathfinder Force. Eighteen aircraft per hour could not provide all the marking for a major raid but they could provide the primary marking for a raid, with non-*Oboe* Pathfinder aircraft of the heavy squadrons 'backing-up' with different coloured markers. In August 1942, a special *Oboe* marking squadron, 109 Squadron, commenced *Oboe* trials using Wellingtons, the type of aircraft originally intended for this work. A second squadron, No. 105, using Mosquitoes, was to be employed later. There was a delay but it was a delay which was to have a beneficial outcome. The new light bomber, the Mosquito, was found to have an operational ceiling of 30,000 feet or more, well above the altitude that could be reached by a Wellington or any other of Bomber Command's types. The Mosquito, as an *Oboe* bomber, would thus extend the range at which the device could be used and could cover all of the Ruhr area. The superior speed of the

Mosquito would also reduce the time on the bomb run when it was vulnerable to the German defences.

The first *Oboe* Mosquitoes were ready for operations on 20 December 1942. The way in which the device was introduced to operations is described in the relevant diary entries. On nights when the *Oboe* aircraft were not required for Pathfinder marking, they could be used in the bombing role; although they could never deliver a huge tonnage, their accuracy was amazing. Individual factory buildings could be attacked and were frequently hit. The Germans never managed to jam *Oboe* properly, one of their greatest failures of the bombing war.

Although the *Oboe* transmissions could be directed to intersect above any target within their range, most of the remainder of Germany would be free from the attentions of that device, at least until after the invasion of 1944 when mobile *Oboe* stations could move to France. But hard on the heels of *Oboe* came a second Bomber Command device which had no limitations to the range of its usefulness. This was *H2S*, the forerunner of the simple airborne ground-scanning radar set which most aircraft now have and whose presence and reliability are now taken so much for granted. Not so those early *H2S* sets which were delivered to Bomber Command at the end of 1942. A flickering, often indeterminate picture was all that the *H2S* operator in the bomber crew had, even when his set was working properly. Coast-lines and wide rivers could usually be distinguished, city outlines sometimes, other features not often. But the device was a boon to a force which until then had to rely on dead-reckoning navigation and the *Gee* device, which the Germans were now jamming regularly from the North Sea onwards. In the hands of a skilled operator, *H2S* could be an invaluable navigational aid and could even be used as a rough-and-ready aiming device when no better means were available, not as accurate as *Oboe* but of unlimited range because the set was carried in the aircraft.

The Pathfinder Force received the first *H2S* sets to be issued to Bomber Command. Thirteen Stirlings of 7 Squadron and ten Halifaxes of 35 Squadron were ready for the first operational use by the end of January 1943. *H2S* would enable the leading Pathfinder crews to find the target city more quickly and drop illuminating flares or markers. Every Pathfinder aircraft would have its own *H2S* set in 1943 and by early 1944 there would be enough sets for the whole of the Main Force.

To round off these two major technological advances, we should mention the first developments in Bomber Command to counter the Germans' own radar and radio devices. *Mandrel* was a ground device in England for jamming the Germans' own ground radar stations, the same stations which directed the German night fighters in controlled interceptions. *Tinsel* was a small microphone near one of an R.A.F. bomber's engines which could be tuned by the aircraft's wireless operator to any frequency on which he heard instructions being broadcast to German pilots. These two devices both became operational in December 1942, the same month in which *Oboe* was first used. *Mandrel* and *Tinsel* did not cause major disruptions to the German night-fighter system – they were a minor but steady irritant – but they were the forerunners of a vast radio-countermeasures effort eventually mounted in Bomber Command. Everything that could help reduce casualties was needed. The recent period had seen the highest casualty rates so far in the war; fortunately the coming period would show an improvement, partly because greater numbers of bombers were starting to swamp the German night-fighter box system and partly because Bomber Command – with the help of its blind-marking and bombing devices *Oboe* and *H2S* – was beginning to restrict its operations on moonlight nights.

The scientists and engineers were still not finished. The initial operations of the

Pathfinder Force had been hampered by lack of an effective 'marker bomb'. Now a purpose-built marker was produced for Pathfinder use, most of the work being done by the pre-war firework industry. A standard Pathfinder marker called the 'target indicator' was now produced and it would last until the end of the war. It was a 250-pound bomb casing packed with pyrotechnic candles which could be ejected at various heights by a barometric fuze and cascade slowly to the ground in a mass of bright colour; red, green and yellow were the standard Pathfinder variations. The target indicator was reliable, vivid, distinctive and not easily copied by German decoys; around it, the Pathfinders developed marking techniques which would also stand until the end of the war. The first target indicators were ready for use in mid-January 1943. So, after years of operating with virtually no technical aids, Bomber Command received *Oboe, H2S*, the target-indicator bomb and its first radio-counter-measures devices all in less than two months.

And the story of Bomber Command's resurgence did not end with that catalogue of technology. The force of aircraft available for operations was at last increasing in number. The days were gone when new squadrons were formed and trained, only to be sent away to Coastal Command or the Middle East. The new four-engined types were pouring out of the factories. 1 Group had become the second group to start equipping with Lancasters, after a brief false start with Halifaxes. 3 Group was now an almost entirely Stirling force; this group had only one Wellington squadron left. The Halifax had overcome most of its early problems and three quarters of the aircraft in 4 Group were now of this type, the remainder of its aircraft being Welling-tons. 5 Group was entirely equipped with the Lancaster and was now capable of delivering a greater tonnage of bombs in one night than the whole of Bomber Command of a year earlier.

There was a completely new group – No. 6 (Canadian) Group – based in North Yorkshire and Durham. This group had existed on paper since October 1942 but did not become operational until New Year's Day of 1943. In the interval, 4 Group had performed a valuable task in gathering together the existing Canadian squadrons in Bomber Command and forming further new squadrons. Thus nine squadrons – six of Wellingtons and three of Halifaxes – were handed over to 6 Group, most of them ready for immediate operations. Air Vice-Marshal G. E. Brooks, a Canadian officer, was the first commander, with his headquarters at Allerton Park Castle near Knares-borough. The Canadian Government would pay the full costs of the group for the remainder of the war and nearly all the ground staff and many of the aircrew were Canadians. (Canadians also served in other groups; there was never any completely national unit in Bomber Command.)

The Pathfinders were also promoted to group status, becoming No. 8 Group on 8 January 1943. When 8 Group was formed, Sir Arthur Harris resisted Air Ministry pressure to take in a senior regular R.A.F. officer, preferring to retain the junior Group Captain Donald Bennett, who was promoted to air commodore at once and who would be an air vice-marshal before 1943 was out, having risen from wing commander to air vice-marshal in a year!

The overall result of this recent expansion and reorganization was that Bomber Command had suddenly become a more powerful and more effective force. If one ignores the 1,000-bomber raids, which were carried out by temporarily assembled forces artificially boosted in number, 250 bombers had, until now, been considered a major effort for a night raid. During the coming period, in the middle of February, the figure suddenly leapt to 450 bombers for a raid to Lorient. Nor was that all. The average bomb load per aircraft so far in the war had rarely exceeded one ton, but the growing proportion of four-engined types, particularly the Lancaster, would produce an average bomb load of two and a quarter tons for that Lorient raid. The hitting power of Bomber Command at least doubled within a few weeks.

None of these comments apply to the ever languishing 2 Group. The group received yet another new day bomber, the North American Mitchell, and a new commander when Air Vice-Marshall J. H. D'Albiac took over from Air Vice-Marshal Lees at the end of December. This was the fifth commander for 2 Group so far in the war. But the group had now little part to play in Bomber Command's main plans. Not many knew it, but the units which flew by day with 2 Group had only a few months remaining in Bomber Command.

Sir Arthur Harris, in his post-war dispatch, described 1942 as 'the preliminary phase' during which he developed his bombing techniques and awaited the arrival of the new devices and the necessary increase in strength required for his main offensive. In theory, all was now ready for this to start and Harris had developed his ideas on how it should be conducted. But Bomber Command was to suffer yet again the frustration of being pulled away from the campaign against Germany by the needs of another theatre of war. It was the U-boat danger again. On 14 January 1943, a new directive was issued. One aspect of it was startling. This is the relevant passage:*

As a result of the recent serious increase in the menace of the enemy U-boat operations, the War Cabinet has given approval to a policy of area bombing against the U-boat operational bases on the west coast of France.

A decision has accordingly been made to subject the following bases to a maximum scale of attack by your command at night with the object of effectively devastating the whole area in which are located the submarines, their maintenance facilities and the services, power, water, light, communications, etc. and other resources upon which their operation depend. The order of priority of importance of the bases is as follows:

> Lorient
> St-Nazaire
> Brest
> La Pallice.

To give effect to this decision, I am to request that you will initially undertake such an operation on the heaviest scale against Lorient.

The startling aspect of these orders was that Bomber Command was deliberately to 'area bomb' French towns. The need to do this instead of attempting the precise attacks on the actual U-boat base facilities is a measure of the ruthlessness with which this three-year-old war was now being prosecuted and the danger posed at that time by the German U-boat force in the Atlantic. The tragedy in store for the French ports was obvious but it was compounded by a major error which had already been committed. After Bomber Command's last major 'naval diversion' in 1941, the Germans had commenced the construction of huge U-boat 'pens', shelters covered by concrete roofs which were easily proof against the explosion of any conventional bomb. This work was now complete, having been uninterrupted by any serious

*Official History, Vol. IV, pp. 152–3.

bombing. The construction of these shelters must have been one of the finest investments the Germans made during the war, the failure to bomb them during the vulnerable stages of construction a major British failure. The Germans concentrated all their essential services into these shelters and, when this new round of bombing commenced in early 1943, they quickly moved all their non-essential services out of the port towns to outlying villages. Former U-boat men described how, by evening, everything and everyone connected with the U-boat service was either in the bomb-proof shelters or out in the safety of the countryside. The next round of bombing would cause irritation to the Germans but no serious disruption of U-boat operations and no loss of U-boats. The French towns were reduced to ruins and many of the townspeople killed in what proved to be one of the most ineffective and tragic episodes of the bombing war.

Lorient and St-Nazaire were repeatedly attacked but Brest and La Pallice were spared when the campaign was later abandoned after the realization came that the bombing was causing little harm to the Germans. A further directive, however, issued late in January, added the U-boat construction yards in German ports to the list of targets. Bomber Command made a start on these but this campaign, too, would be short-lived. The coming weeks also saw a dissipation of the effort available against Germany when the Prime Minister personally urged that attacks on Italy should continue. So, at a time when Bomber Command was far better equipped to attack Germany than ever before, the coming period of nearly three months would prove to be one of the quietest periods of the war for most of the German cities.

But it was only a temporary respite. Things were turning sour for Germany. Their army at Stalingrad was forced to surrender on 2 February 1943; their troops in North Africa would march off to prison camps soon afterwards. Come the spring and Bomber Command would be back to the German cities.

20/21 December 1942

DUISBURG

232 aircraft – 111 Lancasters, 56 Halifaxes, 39 Wellingtons, 26 Stirlings. 12 aircraft – 6 Lancasters, 4 Wellingtons, 2 Halifaxes – lost, 5·2 per cent of the force.

The bombing force found that the target area was clear and claimed much damage. It has not been possible to obtain a report from Duisburg.

LUTTERADE *OBOE* TRIAL

6 Mosquitoes of 109 Squadron were dispatched to bomb a power-station at Lutterade, a small town in Holland near the German frontier. The first *Oboe*-aimed bombs were dropped by Squadron Leader H. E. Bufton and his navigator Flight Lieutenant E. L. Ifould. 2 other crews bombed on *Oboe* but the equipment in the remaining 3 aircraft did not function properly and they bombed elsewhere. The Mosquitoes all returned safely.

Daylight photographs taken after the raid showed so many old bomb craters from an earlier raid when the Pathfinder mistook Lutterade for Aachen that it was impossible to identify the *Oboe* results reliably. A local report, however, states that 9 bombs fell together in open ground 2 km from the power-station, fortunately just missing a large area of housing situated between the power-station and the place where the bombs fell. It is surprising that the target for this first *Oboe* trial should have been a location in friendly Holland which had so much housing near by.

4 O.T.U. Wellingtons on leaflet flights to France without loss.

---

21 December 1942

9 Venturas and 6 Bostons to attack railway targets in France, Belgium and Holland but only 2 Venturas found targets, at Monceau and Valenciennes. No aircraft lost.

21/22 December 1942

MUNICH

137 aircraft of 1 and 5 Groups and the Pathfinder Force – 119 Lancasters, 9 Stirlings, 9 Wellingtons. 12 aircraft – 8 Lancasters, 3 Stirlings, 1 Wellington – lost, 8·8 per cent of the force.

110 aircraft claimed to have bombed Munich and started fires but their photographs showed that all or most of the bombs fell in open country, possibly attracted by a decoy site.

---

22 December 1942

6 Wellingtons on a cloud-cover raid to Emden; 4 aircraft bombed estimated positions through cloud. 6 Mosquitoes on Intruder raids to Belgium, Holland and north-west Germany; only 2 aircraft attacked railway targets and 1 Mosquito was lost.

22/23 December 1942

Minor Operations

4 *Oboe* Mosquitoes to Hamborn and Rheinhausen, 4 O.T.U. sorties. No losses.

---

23 December 1942

18 Bostons bombed St-Malo docks and 6 Venturas bombed naval installations at Den Helder. The Den Helder bombing was particularly accurate and serious damage was caused to a torpedo workshop and other buildings. No aircraft lost.

23/24 December 1942

5 *Oboe* Mosquitoes attacked industrial targets in Essen, Hamborn, Meiderich and Rheinhausen. No results could be observed, because of haze, and later daylight photographs could not distinguish craters caused by these attacks from those of other raids but a map from Essen shows accurate bomb bursts in the middle of the main Krupps factory on this night. No Mosquitoes lost.

24/25 December 1942

3 *Oboe* Mosquitoes attacked Essen and Meiderich without loss. The Essen bombs fell on the northern parts of the Krupps factory.

28/29 December 1942

5 Wellingtons and 1 Stirling laid mines in the Frisian Islands without loss.

29 December 1942

6 Mosquitoes attacked various targets in France without loss.

29/30 December 1942

Minor Operations

3 *Oboe* Mosquitoes attacked Essen and Meiderich in 10/10ths cloud conditions. The Essen bombs fell 500 metres east of the Krupps factory. 14 Lancasters minelaying in the River Gironde. No aircraft lost.

31 December 1942

6 Mosquitoes attacked various targets in Belgium and France without loss.

31 December 1942/1 January 1943

OBOE TRIALS

8 Lancasters and 2 *Oboe* Mosquitoes of the Pathfinder Force to Düsseldorf. 1 Lancaster lost.

This was a trial raid, with the Mosquitoes dropping target markers by *Oboe* for the small Lancaster force. Only 1 Mosquito was able to use *Oboe*. The Düsseldorf report shows that, out of 9 recorded bombing incidents, 6 were at industrial premises, though no serious damage was caused. 10 civilians and 2 Flak soldiers were killed, 34 people were injured and 7 more were classified as 'missing'. 2 barrage balloons broke away from their moorings during the raid.

Later in the night, 3 more *Oboe* Mosquitoes were sent to attack the German night-fighter control room at Florennes airfield in Belgium. 2 Mosquitoes operated their *Oboe* equipment satisfactorily and dropped 6 high-explosive bombs from 28,000 ft through 10/10ths cloud. The results are not known. No aircraft lost.

Minor Operations: 29 aircraft minelaying off Biscay ports, 8 O.T.U. sorties. 1 Wellington minelayer lost.

2 January 1943

12 Bostons and 1 Mosquito, all or most to attack a whaling factory ship at Cherbourg but all aircraft recalled.

2/3 January 1943

MINOR OPERATIONS

24 Wellingtons and 18 Lancasters minelaying off Biscay ports, 2 O.T.U. sorties. No losses.

3 January 1943

11 Bostons to Cherbourg were recalled, 6 Mosquitoes attacked railway targets in the Amiens and Tergnier areas. No aircraft lost.

3/4 January 1943

ESSEN

3 Pathfinder Mosquitoes and 19 Lancasters of 5 Group continued the *Oboe*-marking experimental raids. 3 Lancasters lost.

Essen reports bombing in the city centre with property damaged and 6 people killed.

Minor Operations: 39 Wellingtons and 6 Lancasters minelaying off the French and Dutch coasts, 3 O.T.U. sorties. No losses.

The first operational sorties by the new 6 (Canadian) Group were flown on this night by 6 Wellingtons of 427 Squadron taking part in the minelaying operation; 3 of these laid mines in the Frisian Islands but the other 3 aircraft had to return early with mechanical difficulties.

4/5 January 1943

ESSEN

4 Pathfinder Mosquitoes and 29 Lancasters of 5 Group. 2 Lancasters lost.

'Skymarker' flares were dropped on *Oboe*. Essen reports concentrated bombing in the Borbeck suburb, north of the centre, with 42 buildings destroyed, 64 seriously damaged and 14 people killed.

7/8 January 1943

ESSEN

3 Pathfinder Mosquitoes and 19 Lancasters of 5 Group. No aircraft lost.

This raid was not as effective as earlier *Oboe* trials. Only incendiary bombs were recorded in Essen but 9 buildings were destroyed, 34 seriously damaged and 10 people were killed.

8/9 January 1943

DUISBURG

3 Mosquitoes of the Pathfinders, now officially designated as 8 Group, and 38 Lancasters of 5 Group. (It can be assumed that all Mosquitoes on night-bombing operations were from 8 Group until otherwise stated and, in other operations, the terms '8 Group' and 'Pathfinders' will both be used; they are quite interchangeable.) 3 Lancasters were lost. No report is available from Duisburg.

Minor Operations: 73 aircraft minelaying off the Danish and German coasts, 2 O.T.U. sorties. 2 minelaying Lancasters were lost.

9 January 1943

12 Venturas dispatched to Ijmuiden steelworks, 12 Bostons to Abbeville airfields and 7 Mosquitoes to railway targets at Mons and Rouen. The Abbeville force was recalled but all other targets were bombed. 1 Mosquito lost.

9/10 January 1943

ESSEN

2 Pathfinder Mosquitoes and 50 Lancasters of 5 Group. 3 Lancasters lost.
    Essen reports concentrated bombing in or near the centre with 127 buildings destroyed or seriously damaged and 28 people killed.

MINELAYING

121 aircraft – 78 Halifaxes, 41 Wellingtons, 2 Stirlings – on a large minelaying operation in the Frisians, the German Bight and the Kattegat. 97 aircraft reported laying mines in the designated areas. 4 Halifaxes lost.

11/12 January 1943

ESSEN

4 Pathfinder Mosquitoes and 72 Lancasters of 1 and 5 Groups. 1 Lancaster lost.
    Essen's records have no report for this night but it is not known whether bombs did not fall in the city or whether the local officials did not retain the report.

12/13 January 1943

ESSEN

4 Pathfinder Mosquitoes and 55 Lancasters of 1 and 5 Groups. 1 Lancaster lost.
    The *Oboe* equipment of the first Mosquito to arrive failed and the other 3 Mosquitoes were all late. Because of this, many of the Lancasters bombed on dead reckoning. Some bombs did fall in Essen, where 20 houses were destroyed or seriously

damaged and 9 people were killed, but other bombs fell in Neviges, Remscheid, Solingen and Wuppertal, a group of towns 12–20 miles south of Essen. 19 people were killed in Remscheid.

Minor Operations: 32 aircraft minelaying off Biscay ports, 5 O.T.U. sorties. No losses.

---

13 January 1943

36 aircraft of 2 Group – 18 Venturas, 12 Bostons, 6 Mosquitoes – attacked airfield and railway targets in France. 6 Wellingtons laid mines in the Frisian Islands. No aircraft lost.

13/14 January 1943

ESSEN

3 Mosquitoes and 66 Lancasters. 4 Lancasters lost.

The *Oboe* Mosquitoes were again in trouble. 2 aircraft had to return without marking and the sky-markers of the third aircraft failed to ignite above the cloud. German aircraft also appeared to have dropped decoy flares to distract the Lancasters. Despite all this, Essen reports a sharp raid with 52 buildings destroyed and 67 seriously damaged. 20 of the buildings destroyed were wooden hutments for workers. 63 people were killed, including 11 French prisoners of war and 6 other foreigners, and 113 people were injured.

This raid concluded the recent series of *Oboe* Mosquito trials.

---

14 January 1943

6 Halifaxes on a cloud-cover raid to Leer but only 1 aircraft bombed, through a gap in the clouds. 7 Wellingtons of 4 Group minelaying in the Frisians; 1 aircraft lost.

14/15 January 1943

LORIENT

122 aircraft – 63 Halifaxes, 33 Wellingtons, 20 Stirlings, 6 Lancasters – in the first of 8 area attacks on this French port being used as a U-boat base. 2 Wellingtons lost. This was 6 Group's first bombing operation, with 9 Wellingtons and 6 Halifaxes being sent to Lorient. Wellington BK165 of 426 Squadron was the group's first loss; Pilot Officer George Milne and his crew – 5 Canadians and 1 Englishman – all died when the Wellington was lost in the sea.

The Pathfinder marking of the target was accurate but later bombing by the Main Force was described as 'wild'. Lorient's scanty report shows a minimum of 12 people killed in the centre of the town and 120 buildings, including 2 churches, destroyed.

Minor Operations: 41 aircraft minelaying off Lorient and Brest, 13 O.T.U. flights. 1 Wellington of 91 O.T.U. lost.

---

15 January 1943

10 Bostons attacked a whaling factory ship at Cherbourg but scored no hits. 6 Wellingtons attempted a cloud-cover raid to Norden but only 1 aircraft bombed. No aircraft lost on this day.

15/16 January 1943

LORIENT

157 aircraft – 65 Wellingtons, 48 Halifaxes, 40 Stirlings, 4 Lancasters. 1 Stirling and 1 Wellington lost.

Bombing was more accurate than on the previous night. At least 800 buildings were destroyed and 12 civilians killed. Most of the inhabitants had fled the town during the previous day.

Minor Operations: 2 Mosquitoes to Aachen, 9 Wellingtons minelaying off Lorient and St-Nazaire, 3 O.T.U. sorties. No losses. The 2 Mosquitoes raiding Aachen used *Oboe* when bombing; it can be assumed that most attacks by small numbers of Mosquitoes in and around the Ruhr area will now be *Oboe* raids.

16/17 January 1943

BERLIN

201 aircraft – 190 Lancasters, 11 Halifaxes – from the Pathfinders and 1, 4 and 5 Groups were dispatched on this interesting raid – the first attack on Berlin for 14 months, the first use of proper 'target indicators' and the use of an all 4-engined bombing force. Stirlings were withdrawn from an original plan so that only the higher-flying Lancasters and Halifaxes would participate. Most of the force was provided by 5 Group.

The raid was a disappointment. Berlin was well beyond the range of *Gee* and *Oboe*, and *H2S* radar was not yet ready. Thick cloud which was encountered on the way to the target hindered navigation and Berlin was found to be covered by haze. Bombing was scattered, mostly in the southern areas, with the greatest concentration in the Tempelhof district. The report from Berlin contains some interesting items among the usual details of buildings destroyed, etc. The German air-raid warning system failed to report the approach of a large bomber force, only of a few single aircraft. The Lancasters and Halifaxes thus arrived over Berlin in the evening when a lot of people were away from their homes. The first bombs coincided with the sounding of the sirens and there were many scenes of panic until the police could control the crowds attempting to find shelter. Goebbels, the Gauleiter of Berlin, is reported as having been most angry and he ordered an overhaul of the procedure. Because of the failure, an unusually high number of people were killed, considering the weakness of the bombing: 198; but this figure includes 53 prisoners of war – 52 Frenchmen and 1 Englishman – and 6 foreign workers. Another event was that about half of the personnel of the Berlin Flak units were away from the city, taking part in a course; this resulted in a very much lighter barrage than normal.

The next day, the whole of Berlin was talking of a 'miracle' which had occurred at the Deutschlandhalle, the largest covered hall in Europe, with 10,000 seats. The raid had started in the middle of the evening show of the yearly circus in the hall, a

16 (a and b). The huge Deutschlandhalle in Berlin before and after bombing from which 10,000 people escaped just before it was bombed on 16/17 January 1943.

major event in Berlin's social life. The air-raid police and the fire brigade managed to supervise the evacuation of every person and all the circus animals to open ground in parks around the hall. 21 people were slightly injured in the crush as the crowds left the building. Just after the last person had left, a large number of incendiary bombs fell on to the hall and it was completely burned out, becoming the largest ruin in Berlin so far in the war. None of the 10,000 people in the open near by were hurt!

The R.A.F. casualties were also light. Only 1 Lancaster, from 5 Group, was lost. The Bomber Command report mentions the lightness of the Berlin Flak defences and assumed that the greater altitude of the bomber force surprised the German gunners.

2 Mosquitoes attacked Duisburg and Essen without loss.

17/18 January 1943

BERLIN

170 Lancasters and 17 Halifaxes repeated the raid on Berlin. The weather was better than on the previous night but the Pathfinders were again unable to mark the centre of the city and again the bombing fell mainly in the southern areas. The Bomber Command report stated that the Daimler-Benz factory was hit, either during this night or during the raid of the previous night, but this is not confirmed by the German report; however, a B.M.W. aero-engine factory at Spandau was hit by incendiaries and slightly damaged. There was no important damage in any part of Berlin on this raid; the city records did not classify a single building in the 'destroyed' or 'seriously damaged' sections, only in the lightly damaged section. 8 people were killed and 41 were injured.

The routes taken by the bombers to and from Berlin were the same as those followed on the previous night and German night fighters were able to find the bomber stream. 19 Lancasters and 3 Halifaxes were lost, 11·8 per cent of the force. The experiments with this Lancaster/Halifax force, using target indicators against Berlin, now ceased until *H2S* became available.

An observer of this raid was Richard Dimbleby, the B.B.C. broadcaster, who flew in a 106 Squadron Lancaster piloted by Wing Commander Guy Gibson.

---

18 January 1943

21 Venturas and 14 Bostons to Caen and Cherbourg were all recalled because of unfavourable weather.

18/19 January 1943

MINELAYING

22 Stirlings and 7 Wellingtons of 3 Group to the Frisian Islands without loss.

---

20 January 1943

8 Mosquitoes made a low-level attack on the Stork engineering works at Hengelo. 6 aircraft bombed successfully and there were no losses.

20/21 January 1943

8 Wellingtons minelaying in the Frisians without loss.

21 January 1943

36 Bostons and 15 Venturas attempted to attack the docks at Flushing and Cherbourg and an airfield near Caen. Cloud spoiled most of the bombing. There were no losses.

21/22 January 1943

ESSEN

79 Lancasters and 3 Mosquitoes encountered 10/10ths cloud and bombs were dropped blindly on estimated positions. 4 Lancasters lost.

MINELAYING

70 aircraft on a large operation in the Frisian Islands; 4 Wellingtons and 2 Halifaxes lost.

22 January 1943

23 Bostons and 18 Venturas attacked airfields in France while 12 Mitchells of 98 and 180 Squadrons carried out the first raid by this new type of aircraft on oil targets at Terneuzen near Ghent. 2 Venturas and 3 Mitchells were lost, including the aircraft of Wing Commander C. C. Hodder, commander of 180 Squadron.

22/23 January 1943

2 Mosquitoes attacked Cologne without loss. This was the first *Oboe* attack on Cologne, which reports 55 houses damaged, 5 people killed and 22 injured. These details of damage and casualties in a minor raid have been included because they show that a few aircraft using modern aids could sometimes cause as much damage as the forces of up to 100 bombers which had often been sent to Cologne in marginal weather conditions in 1941 and 1942.

23 January 1943

6 Wellingtons of 6 Group on a cloud-cover raid to a target near Wilhelmshaven; all found somewhere to bomb without loss. 4 Mosquitoes bombed Osnabrück railway yards; 1 Mosquito lost.

23/24 January 1943

LORIENT

121 aircraft – 75 Halifaxes, 33 Stirlings, 8 Lancasters, 5 Wellingtons – dispatched and claimed successful bombing of the target area in good visibility. 1 Stirling lost.

DÜSSELDORF

80 Lancasters and 3 Mosquitoes of 1, 5 and 8 Groups dispatched and bombed through complete cloud cover. A brief report from Düsseldorf says that some bombs fell in the south of the city. 2 Lancasters lost.

4 O.T.U. Whitleys dropped leaflets on French towns without loss.

25 January 1943

12 Bostons bombed Flushing docks; 1 Boston lost.

26 January 1943

24 Venturas and 12 Bostons to railway targets in France and Belgium but only 12 Venturas reached their targets. No aircraft lost.

26/27 January 1943

LORIENT

157 aircraft – 139 Wellingtons, 11 Lancasters, 4 Halifaxes, 3 Stirlings – dispatched and bombed in poor visibility. 2 Wellingtons and 1 Lancaster lost.

Minor Operations: 9 Halifaxes of 6 Group attempted to bomb shipping in the River Gironde; only 3 aircraft bombed, Bordeaux docks. 18 O.T.U. sorties were flown. There were no losses from these operations.

27 January 1943

9 Mosquitoes made a successful low-level attack on a diesel engine factory at Copenhagen. 1 aircraft lost.

27/28 January 1943

DÜSSELDORF

162 aircraft – 124 Lancasters, 33 Halifaxes, 5 Mosquitoes. 3 Halifaxes and 3 Lancasters lost, 3·7 per cent of the force.

This was the first occasion when *Oboe* Mosquitoes carried out 'ground marking' for the Pathfinders. ('Ground markers' were the now standard target indicators set to burst and cascade just above the ground. They were far more accurate than the 'sky-marker' parachute flares previously used by Mosquitoes when marking targets.) Pathfinder Lancasters 'backed-up' the *Oboe*-aimed markers. There was a thin sheet of cloud over the target and, without *Oboe* and the new target indicators, this raid would have almost certainly been another typical Ruhr area failure. Bombing was well concentrated on the southern part of Düsseldorf. The local report lists damage at a wide variety of property: 10 industrial firms destroyed or seriously damaged, 21 lightly damaged; 9 public buildings or amenities destroyed or seriously damaged, 7 lightly damaged; 456 houses destroyed or seriously damaged, 2,400 lightly damaged. The opera house was destroyed. 66 people were killed and 225 injured; 23 of the dead and 169 of the injured were members of the Wehrmacht who were in a train at the main railway station when it was hit by high-explosive bombs.

MINELAYING

54 aircraft to Texel and the Frisians; 1 Stirling lost.

---

29 January 1943

12 Bostons bombed a railway viaduct at Morlaix and 2 of 12 Venturas dispatched bombed a steelworks at Ijmuiden. 1 Boston lost.

29/30 January 1943

LORIENT

75 Wellingtons and 41 Halifaxes of 1, 4 and 6 Groups. 2 Halifaxes and 2 Wellingtons lost.

Crews encountered thick cloud and icing and, with no Pathfinder marking, the bombing was well scattered.

Minor Operations: 17 Wellingtons minelaying off Biscay ports and 5 O.T.U. sorties to France also encountered bad weather. 1 aircraft from each operation was lost.

---

30 January 1943

BERLIN

2 formations, each of 3 Mosquitoes, made dramatic attemps to interrupt large rallies being addressed by Nazi leaders in Berlin on this day. These raids would be the first time the German capital was bombed in daylight.

3 Mosquitoes of 105 Squadron successfully reached Berlin and bombed in mid-morning at the exact time that Goering was due to speak. The speech was postponed for an hour. These 3 Mosquitoes returned safely.

In the afternoon, 3 Mosquitoes of 139 Squadron arrived at the time Goebbels was due to speak and again bombed at the correct time but the German defences were alerted and the aircraft of Squadron Leader D. F. Darling was shot down. Darling and his navigator,. Flying Officer W. Wright, were both killed and are now buried in Berlin.

---

30 January 1943

19 Wellingtons of 4 Group and 17 Bostons to many places in Germany and Holland but only 5 Wellingtons and 1 Boston found targets to bomb. 4 Wellingtons lost.

30/31 January 1943

HAMBURG

148 aircraft – 135 Lancasters, 7 Stirlings, 6 Halifaxes – or 1, 5 and 8 Groups carried out the first *H2S* attack of the war, with Pathfinder Stirlings and Halifaxes using the new device to mark the target. 5 Lancasters were lost, 3·4 per cent of the force.

Although *H2S* would later become a more effective device, its use was not successful on this night even though Hamburg, close to a coastline and on a prominent river, was the best type of *H2S* target. Bombing was scattered over a wide area and the local historian, Hans Brunswig, commenting on the R.A.F. figure of 315 tons of bombs dropped in the Hamburg area, suggests that most of the bombs must have fallen in the River Elbe or in the surrounding marshes.* However, 119 fires – 71 large – were started; 58 people were killed and 164 injured. The only incident mentioned by Brunswig is the destruction of a railway bridge, which blocked the entire Hamburg network for 2 days.

Minor Operations: 4 Mosquitoes to targets in the Ruhr, 17 aircraft minelaying off St-Nazaire and in the Frisians. No losses.

---

2 February 1943

36 Venturas bombed railway targets at Abbeville and Bruges without loss.

2/3 February 1943

COLOGNE

161 aircraft – 116 Lancasters, 35 Halifaxes, 8 Stirlings, 2 Mosquitoes. 5 aircraft – 3 Lancasters, 1 Halifax, 1 Stirling – lost, 3·1 per cent of the force.

This was a further experiment using a 4-engined bombing force with various forms of Pathfinder techniques. On this cloudy night, markers were dropped by both the *Oboe* Mosquitoes and the *H2S* heavy marker aircraft. Again the results were disappointing, with no clear concentration of markers being achieved and with subsequent bombing being well scattered.

The report from Cologne shows that damage was caused right across the city but was nowhere serious. No industrial premises were hit but the military airfield at Butzweiler Hof was struck by 6 4,000-lb bombs, causing 'medium to serious' damage. 65 houses were destroyed and nearly 1,600 were damaged but the report says that most of this was caused by blast from the 15 4,000-pounders which fell in the city. 14 people were killed and 63 injured.

---

* *Feuersturm über Hamburg*, op. cit., pp. 157–8.

A Pathfinder aircraft on this raid, Stirling R9264 of 7 Squadron, was shot down by a night fighter and crashed in Holland. It was unfortunate for the Pathfinders that the Germans thus obtained an example of the *H2S* set on only the second night that this new device was used. The set was damaged but the German firm of Telefunken was able to reassemble it. This gave the Germans an early indication of the operational use of *H2S* and eventually led to the development of a device, 'Naxos', which would enable German night fighters to home on to a bomber which was using its *H2S* set.

Minor Operations: 13 Halifaxes of 6 Group minelaying in the Kattegat but bad weather was encountered and only 5 aircraft laid their mines; there was 1 O.T.U. sortie. No aircraft lost.

---

3 February 1943

60 Venturas to various targets in France, Belgium and Holland but only 15 aircraft bombed railway yards at Abbeville and at St-Omer airfield. 2 Venturas lost.

3/4 February 1943

HAMBURG

263 aircraft – 84 Halifaxes, 66 Stirlings, 62 Lancasters, 51 Wellingtons – provided by all groups on the first 200-plus raid for more than 2 weeks.

Icing conditions in cloud over the North Sea caused many aircraft to return early. The Pathfinders were unable to produce concentrated and sustained marking on *H2S* and the bombing of the Main Force was scattered. The results in Hamburg were no better than the attack by a much smaller force a few nights earlier. 45 fires classed as 'large' were started, including 2 in various oil depots and 1 in a warehouse near the Elbe waterfront. 55 people were killed and 40 injured.

The German night fighters operated effectively, despite the bad weather, and 16 bombers were lost – 8 Stirlings, 4 Halifaxes, 3 Wellingtons and 1 Lancaster, 6·1 per cent of the force.

Minor Operations: 8 Wellingtons minelaying off Lorient and St-Nazaire, 4 O.T.U. sorties. 1 Wellington minelayer lost.

4/5 February 1943

TURIN

188 aircraft – 77 Lancasters, 55 Halifaxes, 50 Stirlings, 6 Wellingtons. 3 Lancasters lost.

156 aircraft reached and bombed Turin, causing serious and widespread damage. The brief local report states that 29 people were killed and 53 injured.

LA SPEZIA

4 Pathfinder Lancasters were sent to this Italian port to try out a new type of 'proximity fuzed' 4,000-lb bomb which exploded between 200 and 600 ft above the ground to widen the effects of the resulting blast. 3 aircraft dropped their bombs

successfully, but this type of weapon does not seem to have come into general use. The Lancasters all returned safely.

LORIENT

128 aircraft – 103 Wellingtons, 16 Halifaxes, 9 Lancasters. 1 Wellington lost.

This was an all-incendiary attack without the Pathfinders. Bombing was concentrated and large areas of fire were started.

Minor Operations: 2 Mosquitoes bombed Bochum and Ruhrort, 1 Wellington laid mines off Lorient. No aircraft lost.

Total effort for the night: 323 sorties, 4 aircraft (1·2 per cent) lost.

5/6 February 1943

19 Stirlings of 3 Group were sent minelaying in the Frisian Islands; 2 aircraft lost.

6/7 February 1943

MINOR OPERATIONS

52 Wellingtons and 20 Halifaxes minelaying between St-Nazaire and Texel, 2 Mosquitoes to Düsseldorf, 3 O.T.U. sorties. 3 minelaying Wellingtons lost.

7/8 February 1943

LORIENT

323 aircraft – 100 Wellingtons, 81 Halifaxes, 80 Lancasters, 62 Stirlings. 7 aircraft – 3 Lancasters, 2 Halifaxes, 2 Wellingtons – lost.

The Pathfinder marking plan worked well and the two Main Force waves produced a devastating attack.

2 Mosquitoes bombed Essen and Hamborn without loss.

8/9 February 1943

6 Lancasters laid mines in Baltic areas without loss.

9/10 February 1943

MINOR OPERATIONS

21 Wellingtons minelaying between Brest and Texel, 2 Mosquitoes to Essen and Ruhrort. No losses. A map from Essen shows that the *Oboe* Mosquito's bomb load fell just north of the Krupps factory.

---

10 February 1943

12 Venturas bombed Caen railway yards without loss but the escorting Spitfires had a fierce fight with German fighters.

11 February 1943

19 Bostons attempted attacks on railway targets over a wide area. 8 aircraft bombed various locations; 1 Boston lost.

11/12 February 1943

WILHELMSHAVEN

This was an interesting and important raid. 177 aircraft – 129 Lancasters, 40 Halifaxes and 8 Stirlings – dispatched. 3 Lancasters lost, 1·7 per cent of the force.

The Pathfinders found that the Wilhelmshaven area was completely covered by cloud and they had to employ their least reliable marking method, sky-marking by parachute flares using *H2S*. The marking was carried out with great accuracy and the Main Force bombing was very effective. Crews saw through the clouds a huge explosion on the ground, the glow of which lingered for nearly 10 minutes. This was caused by bombs blowing up the naval ammunition depot at Mariensiel to the south of Wilhelmshaven. The resulting explosion devastated an area of nearly 120 acres and caused widespread damage in the naval dockyard and in the town. Much damage was also caused by other bombs. It has not been possible to obtain details of the casualties from Wilhelmshaven.

This raid represented the first blind-bombing success for the *H2S* radar device.

Minor Operations: 2 Mosquitoes to Bochum and Hamborn, 36 aircraft minelaying from La Pallice to the Frisians, 5 O.T.U. sorties. No losses.

Total effort for the night: 220 sorties, 3 aircraft (1·4 per cent) lost.

12 February 1943

16 Mosquitoes attacked targets in Eastern Belgium and over the German border without loss.

12/13 February 1943

MINOR OPERATIONS

2 Mosquitoes bombed Düsseldorf and Rheinhausen, 38 aircraft minelaying off Heligoland and in the Frisians, 2 O.T.U. sorties. There were no losses.

13 February 1943

34 Venturas and 22 Bostons were sent in 5 different raids to attack Ijmuiden steelworks (the

Venturas) and ships at Boulogne and the lock gates at St-Malo (the Bostons). 41 aircraft bombed successfully and none were lost.

13/14 February 1943

LORIENT

466 aircraft – 164 Lancasters, 140 Wellingtons, 96 Halifaxes, 66 Stirlings – carried out Bomber Command's heaviest attack on Lorient during the war. The ordinary squadrons of Bomber Command, not reinforced for a 1,000-bomber type raid, dropped more than 1,000 tons of bombs on a target for the first time.

The raid was carried out in clear visibility and considerable further damage was caused to the already battered town of Lorient. 7 aircraft – 3 Wellingtons, 2 Lancasters, 1 Halifax, 1 Stirling – were lost, 1·5 per cent of the force.

Minor Operations: 2 Mosquitoes to Duisburg and Essen, 17 O.T.U. sorties. No losses.

---

14 February 1943

10 Mosquitoes to Tours railway yards, which were accurately bombed by 6 aircraft without loss.

14/15 February 1943

COLOGNE

243 aircraft – 90 Halifaxes, 85 Wellingtons, 68 Stirlings. 9 aircraft – 3 of each type – lost, 3·7 per cent of the force.

The Pathfinder marking was again based on sky-markers dropped by *H2S* but it was only of limited success. 218 aircraft claimed to have bombed Cologne but local records suggest that less than 50 aircraft hit the target, mostly in the western districts. 2 industrial, 2 agricultural and 97 domestic premises were destroyed. 51 civilians were killed and 135 injured and 25 French workers died when their barracks at an old fort on the western outskirts of Cologne were bombed.

MILAN

142 Lancasters of 1, 5 and 8 Groups attacked Milan and carried out concentrated bombing in good visibility. Fires could be seen from 100 miles away on the return flight. No report is available from Milan.

Italian defences were usually weak and only 2 Lancasters were lost on this raid. An unusual story is available, however, about a Lancaster of 101 Squadron, which was attacked by an Italian C R 42 fighter just after bombing the target. The Lancaster was set on fire and the two gunners were both seriously injured, although they claimed to have shot down the fighter. The pilot, Sergeant I. H. Hazard, had to dive 8,000 ft to put out the fire and 1 member of the crew mistook instructions and baled out. The remainder of the crew completed the extinguishing of the fire, tended the wounded and eventually reached England. The only officer in the crew, Pilot Officer F. W. Gates the wireless operator, was awarded the Distinguished Service Order and Sergeant Hazard and the other members of the crew who helped to bring the Lancaster home all received Conspicuous Gallantry Medals, an unusually high number of awards of this decoration.

Sergeant Hazard died with his flight engineer and navigator when their Lancaster crashed in a flying accident in Yorkshire less than a month after the Milan incident, and Pilot Officer Gates died when the Lancaster in which he was flying, with another crew, crashed when returning from Dortmund on 5 May 1943; the two air gunners in the crew appear to have survived the war.

4 Pathfinder Lancasters bombed La Spezia docks without loss.

Total effort for the night: 389 sorties, 11 aircraft (2·8 per cent) lost.

The quantity of bombs carried by Bomber Command so far in the war reached 100,000 tons during this night's operations.

---

15 February 1943

23 Bostons attacked Dunkirk harbour, claiming hits on ships, and 12 Mosquitoes bombed railway workshops at Tours. No aircraft lost.

15/16 February 1943

Minor Operations

6 *Oboe* Mosquitoes bombed Essen, Rheinhausen and the German night-fighter airfield at St-Trond; a map from Essen shows that bombs were dropped on the southern part of the Krupps factory. 4 Stirlings laid mines in the River Gironde and 2 O.T.U. Wellingtons dropped leaflets over France. No aircraft lost.

16/17 February 1943

LORIENT

377 aircraft – 131 Lancasters, 103 Halifaxes, 99 Wellingtons, 44 Stirlings – carried out the last large raid in this series on Lorient. 363 aircraft dropped mainly incendiary loads in clear visibility. 1 Lancaster lost.

Bomber Command had flown 1,853 sorties in 8 'area' raids in response to direct instructions from the Air Ministry. 1,675 aircraft claimed to have bombed Lorient during these raids, dropping nearly 4,000 tons of bombs. 24 aircraft – 1·3 per cent of those dispatched – were lost. Few records are available from Lorient but it is known that the town was now almost completely ruined and deserted.

Minor Operations: 32 aircraft minelaying off Brest and St-Nazaire, 4 O.T.U. sorties. No losses.

Total effort for the night: 413 sorties, 1 aircraft (0·2 per cent) lost.

---

17 February 1943

12 Venturas to Dunkirk but the target was not reached, 6 Wellingtons on cloud-cover raids to Emden which was bombed by 3 aircraft. There were no losses.

17/18 February 1943

Minor Operations

2 Mosquitoes to Bochum and Hamborn, 12 Stirlings minelaying in southern Biscay. No aircraft lost.

---

18 February 1943

26 Mosquitoes to Tours railway yards, 12 Venturas sent to Dunkirk did not reach their target. 1 Mosquito lost.

18/19 February 1943

WILHELMSHAVEN

195 aircraft – 127 Lancasters, 59 Halifaxes, 9 Stirlings. 4 Lancasters lost, 2·0 per cent of the force.

The Pathfinders claimed accurate marking in clear visibility but bombing photographs showed that most of the attack fell in open country west of the target. Wilhelmshaven's report says that the bombs which did fall in the town killed 5 people and injured 47 and caused damage to a variety of buildings including 'Heine's Hotel'.

MINELAYING

89 aircraft carried out widespread minelaying operations from St-Nazaire to the Frisians. 2 Halifaxes lost.

9 O.T.U. aircraft on leaflet flights. 1 Wellington lost.

Total effort for the night: 293 sorties, 7 aircraft (2·4 per cent) lost.

---

19 February 1943

12 Venturas attacked German naval torpedo workshops at Den Helder without loss.

19/20 February 1943

WILHELMSHAVEN

338 aircraft – 120 Wellingtons, 110 Halifaxes, 56 Stirlings, 52 Lancasters. 12 aircraft – 5 Stirlings, 4 Lancasters, 3 Wellingtons – lost, 3·6 per cent of the force.

This raid was another failure, with the Pathfinder marking causing the Main

Force bombing to fall north of Wilhelmshaven. The local report says that only 3 people were slightly injured. After this raid it was found that the Pathfinders had been issued with out-of-date maps which did not show recent town developments. A general updating of maps now took place.

2 Mosquitoes bombed Dortmund and Essen without loss. The Essen bombs just missed the Krupps works.

20/21 February 1943

20 Wellingtons laid mines in the Frisian Islands. 1 aircraft lost.

21/22 February 1943
BREMEN

143 aircraft – 130 Lancasters, 7 Stirlings, 6 Halifaxes – dispatched and 129 crews bombed, through cloud. No photographs were brought back because of the cloud and no report is available from Bremen.

No aircraft were lost from this medium- to large-sized raid.

24/25 February 1943
WILHELMSHAVEN

115 aircraft of 6 and 8 Groups – 71 Wellingtons, 27 Halifaxes, 9 Stirlings, 8 Lancasters. Bomber Command documents make no comment on the outcome of this raid. Wilhelmshaven's report calls it a 'small raid' with 'a little damage in the town' and makes no mention of casualties. Once again, the bomber force returned without losing any aircraft.

This was the last raid on the much-bombed town of Wilhelmshaven until October 1944.

4 Mosquitoes bombed Brauweiler and Düsseldorf without loss.

25/26 February 1943
NUREMBERG

337 aircraft – 169 Lancasters, 104 Halifaxes, 64 Stirlings. 9 aircraft – 6 Lancasters, 2 Stirlings, 1 Halifax – lost, 2·7 per cent of the force.

Weather conditions were poor and the Pathfinders were late with their marking. Nuremberg's report shows that the bombing fell on the northern edges of Nuremberg and on the neighbouring town of Fürth and in the countryside up to 12 km further north. However, more than 300 buildings were damaged in Nuremberg, including a historic military chapel which was burnt out. 12 civilians, 1 soldier on leave and 1 prisoner of war were killed in Nuremberg; 26 people were killed in Fürth and there may have been further casualties in the villages to the north.

Minor Operations: 6 Mosquitoes to the Ruhr (13 people were killed in Cologne), 54 aircraft minelaying off Brittany and in the Frisians, 20 O.T.U. sorties. No losses.

Total effort for the night: 417 sorties, 9 aircraft (2·2 per cent) lost.

---

26 February 1943

DUNKIRK

60 Venturas. 33 aircraft bombed; none lost.

RENNES

20 Mosquitoes were sent to attack a naval stores depot. 17 aircraft bombed and an ammunition dump was seen to explode. 3 Mosquitoes were lost including 2 which collided.

26/27 February 1943

COLOGNE

427 aircraft – 145 Lancasters, 126 Wellingtons, 106 Halifaxes, 46 Stirlings, 4 Mosquitoes. 10 aircraft – 4 Wellingtons, 3 Lancasters, 2 Halifaxes, 1 Stirling – lost, 2·3 per cent of the force.

Most of the bombs from this large raid fell to the south-west of Cologne. Figures from Cologne itself suggest that only a quarter of the force hit the city. An increasingly familiar list of destroyed and damaged buildings was provided – much housing, minor industry, churches, historic buildings, public utilities and offices. The worst incident was when 40 to 50 people were trapped in several blocks of flats hit by a 4,000-lb bomb in the Einhardstrasse. The wreckage began to burn before the rescue workers could free the trapped people and most of them died. The total casualty list in Cologne was 109 people dead, more than 150 injured and 6,322 bombed out.

Minor Operations: 2 Mosquitoes to Aachen, 21 aircraft minelaying in the Frisians, 4 O.T.U. sorties. No losses.

Total effort for the night: 454 sorties, 10 aircraft (2·2 per cent) lost.

---

27 February 1943

24 Venturas attacked ships at Dunkirk without loss.

27/28 February 1943

MINELAYING

91 aircraft to the Frisian Islands and Texel. 1 Halifax was lost.

Minor Operations: 6 Mosquitoes to the Ruhr, 2 O.T.U. sorties. No losses.

---

28 February 1943

10 Mosquitoes to targets in Holland without loss.

28 February/1 March 1943

ST-NAZAIRE

Having destroyed Lorient, Bomber Command was now ready to start on the second target on the list of French U-boat base ports which the directive of 14 January had ordered to be destroyed. 437 aircraft – 152 Lancasters, 119 Wellingtons, 100 Halifaxes, 62 Stirlings, 4 Mosquitoes – were dispatched. 5 aircraft – 2 Lancasters, 2 Wellingtons, 1 Stirling – were lost, 1·1 per cent of the force.

This initial raid caused widespread destruction. Local reports say that many bombs fell into the port area and that 60 per cent of the town was destroyed. 29 people are reported as being killed and 12 injured; it is presumed that most of the local population had left the town.

Minor Operations: 3 Mosquitoes to the Ruhr, 5 Wellingtons minelaying off St-Nazaire, 2 O.T.U. sorties. No losses.

1/2 March 1943

BERLIN

302 aircraft – 156 Lancasters, 86 Halifaxes, 60 Stirlings. 17 aircraft – 7 Lancasters, 6 Halifaxes, 4 Stirlings – lost, 5·6 per cent of the force.

The Pathfinders experienced difficulty in producing concentrated marking because individual parts of the extensive built-up city area of Berlin could not be distinguished on the *H2S* screens. Bombing photographs showed that the attack was spread over more than 100 square miles with the main emphasis in the south-west of the city. However, because larger numbers of aircraft were now being used and because those aircraft were now carrying a greater average bomb load, the proportion of the force which did hit Berlin caused more damage than any previous raid to this target. This type of result – with significant damage still being caused by only partially successful attacks – was becoming a regular feature of Bomber Command raids.

Much damage was caused in the south and west of Berlin. 22 acres of workshops were burnt out at the railway repair works at Tempelhof and 20 factories were badly damaged and 875 buildings – mostly houses – were destroyed. 191 people were killed.

Some bombs hit the Telefunken works at which the *H2S* set taken from the Stirling shot down near Rotterdam was being reassembled. The set was completely destroyed in the bombing but a Halifax of 35 Squadron with an almost intact set crashed in Holland on this night and the Germans were able to resume their research into *H2S* immediately.

Minor Operations: 6 Mosquitoes to the Ruhr, 49 Wellingtons and Halifaxes minelaying off French and German coasts, 4 O.T.U. sorties. 2 Wellington minelayers lost.

Total effort for the night: 361 sorties, 19 aircraft (5·3 per cent) lost.

2/3 March 1943
MINELAYING

60 aircraft to coastal areas between Texel and the River Gironde. 2 Wellingtons and
1 Lancaster lost.

6 Mosquitoes to the Ruhr without loss. The aircraft which bombed Essen scored direct hits in
the middle of the main Krupps factory.

---

3 March 1943

10 Mosquitoes of 139 Squadron carried out a long-range raid on the important molybdenum
mine at Knaben in Norway. The target was successfully bombed but 1 Mosquito was shot down
by FW 190s.

3/4 March 1943
HAMBURG

417 aircraft – 149 Lancasters, 123 Wellingtons, 83 Halifaxes, 62 Stirlings. 10 aircraft
– 4 Lancasters, 2 Wellingtons, 2 Halifaxes, 2 Stirlings – lost, 2·4 per cent of the force.
     Visibility was clear over the target but the Pathfinders made a mistake, possibly
thinking that the *H2S* indications of mudbanks in the Elbe which had been uncovered
by the low tides were sections of the Hamburg docks. Most of the Main Force
bombing thus fell 13 miles downstream from the centre of Hamburg, around the
small town of Wedel. Even so, a proportion of the bombing force did hit Hamburg
which suffered 27 people killed and 95 injured and whose fire brigade had to put out
100 fires before devoting all its energies to helping the town of Wedel, which suffered
so heavily. The damage at Wedel included a large naval-clothing store burnt out as
well as several important industrial concerns destroyed in Wedel's harbour area and
this illustrated another Bomber Command view: that bombing could usually be
useful even if the wrong target was hit.

Minor Operations: 5 Mosquitoes to the Ruhr, with more direct hits on Krupps, 14 aircraft
minelaying in the Frisians, 5 O.T.U. sorties. 1 Stirling minelayer lost.

Total effort for the night: 441 sorties, 11 aircraft (2·5 per cent) lost.

---

4 March 1943

12 Mosquitoes attacked railway targets at Arnage and Aulnoye without loss.

4/5 March 1943
Minor Operations

6 Mosquitoes to the Ruhr, 27 aircraft minelaying in areas as far south as Bayonne and as far
north as Gydnia, 16 O.T.U. sorties. 1 Lancaster minelayer and 1 O.T.U. Wellington lost.

Operational Statistics, 20/21 December 1942 to 5 March 1943
(75 days/nights)

Number of days with operations: 38
Number of nights with operations: 58
Number of daylight sorties: 923, from which 25 aircraft (2·7 per cent) were lost
Number of night sorties: 9,057, from which 251 aircraft (2·8 per cent) were lost
Total sorties: 9,980 sorties, from which 276 aircraft (2·8 per cent) were lost
Approximate bomb tonnage in period: 17,834 tons
Averages per 24-hour period: 133·1 sorties, 3·7 aircraft lost, 237·8 tons of bombs dropped

14. THE BATTLE OF THE RUHR

5/6 March to 24 July 1943

Sir Arthur Harris called the period from the spring of 1943 until the spring of 1944 his 'main offensive'. He had steered Bomber Command through the recent winter with great skill, recognizing that the time was not yet ripe for an all-out effort, conserving and building up his force, yet constantly experimenting with new tactics and the introduction of new devices. But now, in the early March of 1943, all was ready for a sustained and major effort against Germany and Harris decided that he would commence what he called at the time the Battle of the Ruhr. History would confirm the suitability of that title.

The 'battle' concept was a reflection of the principle of concentration, with the main strength of Bomber Command's night force being directed as much as was tactically possible against one target system until that target system was destroyed. It is probable that Harris had Berlin in mind as his ultimate battle; to destroy Berlin would surely force Germany out of the war. But Harris knew that Berlin was too difficult a target for Bomber Command at that time. The vital considerations were the need for further development of target-finding methods and the duration of darkness. Berlin required the increasing nights of autumn and winter, not the shortening ones of the coming spring. The Ruhr was the logical place to fight Bomber Command's first pitched battle. The whole of the Ruhr area, with its huge spread of industrial cities, was within range of the blind-marking device *Oboe* and any target in that area could easily be reached in the shorter nights of spring and summer.

There were two aspects of the coming offensive which should be mentioned. Firstly, none of Bomber Command's battles could ever concentrate exclusively on one target area. Such a course of action would have allowed the Germans to concentrate their night-fighter and Flak defences and defeat the bombers. The main Battle of the Ruhr would last for four months, during which forty-three major raids were mounted. Two thirds of these raids were on the Ruhr but the remainder were scattered across widely spread areas of Europe – to Stettin on the Baltic, to Pilsen in Czechoslovakia, to Munich deep in Bavaria, to Turin in Italy. It was a good example of the flexibility of air power and the Germans were never allowed to concentrate all their defences at the Ruhr. The second point, however, is that the Flak and searchlight defences around the Ruhr cities were already the most powerful in Germany and the night-fighter units manning the boxes on the routes between the coast of Europe and the Ruhr were already the most experienced and best equipped in the Luftwaffe. Despite the dispatch of some raids to distant points, the Germans were bound to reinforce both their ground and air defences around the Ruhr as the battle developed. The coming period was going to be a major test between the skill, determination and courage of the participants. On the one side stood the commander-in-chief of Bomber Command and the men of his squadrons; on the other side stood the German city civilians and the personnel of the Flak and night-fighter units which were attempting to defend the cities. The levels of death and destruction were about to mount dramatically.

Two major factors were on the side of the British. The first was the continuing increase in Bomber Command's striking power. At the opening of the Battle of the Ruhr there were nearly 600 bombers available and, at the peak of the battle, towards the end of May, the city of Dortmund would be attacked by more than 800 aircraft. *Four fifths of these were four-engined aircraft.* One set of statistics can illustrate this point. On the night of 13/14 February 1943, the ordinary squadrons of Bomber Command dropped 1,000 tons of bombs for the first time. The target was Lorient. Within a little more than three months of that night, more than 2,000 tons of bombs would be dropped on Dortmund. There had been times before, however, when Bomber Command had seemed to be on the verge of a new and favourable phase in its offensive against its main objectives only to be pulled back by orders to help out elsewhere. This was not to happen now. The only directive received by Bomber Command during the main part of the Battle of the Ruhr would be one which released Bomber Command from the need for further attacks on the U-boat bases in France. Sir Arthur Harris would be left with complete freedom to concentrate his forces on the Battle of the Ruhr until that battle had run its full course.

The second favourable factor was the ability of the Pathfinders to find and mark the Ruhr cities accurately. Earlier diary entries have shown how painfully and with so many setbacks the Pathfinders developed their tactics. Over the Ruhr would come almost complete success, a success dependent entirely upon *Oboe*. The *Oboe* beams would be set up to cross with near complete reliability over target after target and guide the Mosquito Pathfinder aircraft to that point in the sky where their target indicators were released with an accuracy undreamt of in the early years of bombing. The Pathfinder heavy squadrons also played a major role. The small numbers of Mosquitoes which the *Oboe* system could handle were only able to provide the primary marking, always the Pathfinder backers-up had to come in, straight and level through the searchlights and Flak, to drop their markers of a different colour. The Main Force had orders to bomb the Mosquito markers if visible, the backing-up markers if not. Very rarely did the crews of the Pathfinder heavies leave a gap in the marking. It was during this period that 8 Group received important reinforcements. 97 Squadron came in as the second squadron provided by 5 Group and the newly formed 6 (Canadian) Group sent 405 Squadron. A further significant addition to the Pathfinders was the creation of 1409 (Meteorological) Flight which, directly under 8 Group control, carried out daylight weather reconnaissance flights in preparation for nearly every Bomber Command raid to Germany until the end of the war, as well as a large number of flights for the bomber units of the American Eighth Air Force. All these additions to the Pathfinders took place in April. But the Pathfinder unit without which the Battle of the Ruhr could not have been fought so successfully was 109 Squadron and its handful of *Oboe*-equipped Mosquitoes. The contribution of the fast, high-flying, safe Mosquito cannot be overestimated. To all this should be added the degree of perseverance and courage shown by the men of the Main Force squadrons who fought this battle, sustaining heavy losses over a long period. Their morale never wavered and the old dictum was proved that heavy casualties can be sustained by a force as long as successful results are being visibly achieved.

17. Aircrew from the Empire and the United States at a Bomber Command station in 'the north of England'.

But, outside the Ruhr and beyond the range of *Oboe*, success continued to elude Bomber Command on many occasions. The Pathfinders had to struggle with inadequate technical devices to probe the darkness of the non-moon periods and place their target indicators exactly over a certain point hundreds of miles from their bases. It was a task that was frequently not achieved and the diary entries for individual raids outside the Ruhr area show that this continued to be Bomber Command's main problem for many months to come. This leads to mention of the famous Dams Raid carried out by 617 Squadron, which was formed in 5 Group to tackle particularly important small targets. The 617 Squadron raid on the dams near the Ruhr was quite independent of the main Battle of the Ruhr operations. The historical relevance of the Dams Raid, and of a lesser known but equally significant raid by other squadrons of 5 Group on a factory at Friedrichshafen, was that such operations reflected the aspirations of that small body of opinion which hoped that Bomber Command would develop tactics of more finesse than the methods of mass and tonnage that were now Bomber Command's almost exclusively chosen instruments. There is no need to go into more detail on this here; this section of the diary properly belongs to the success of the methods used in the Battle of the Ruhr, but the subject would become more relevant as the war progressed and the contrast became apparent between the almost simple ease with which *Oboe* marking could be used to smash German cities within the range of that device and the sometimes insurmountable difficulties of finding and marking the multitude of targets in other parts of Germany.

A series of major changes took place in the top ranks of Bomber Command just before the Battle of the Ruhr opened. The movement of senior officers started with Sir Robert Saundby, Senior Air Staff Officer at Bomber Command Headquarters, being raised to the newly created position of Deputy Commander-in-Chief, and a number of further changes left Bomber Command and the Groups with a team that would see the command through the war almost to the end. The line-up established by the end of February 1943 was:

Commander-in-Chief – Air Chief Marshal Sir Arthur Harris

Deputy Commander-in-Chief – Air Marshal Sir Robert Saundby
1 Group – Air Vice-Marshal E. A. B. Rice
3 Group – Air Vice-Marshal R. Harrison
4 Group – Air Vice-Marshal C. R. Carr
5 Group – Air Vice-Marshal The Hon. R. Cochrane
6 (Canadian) Group – Air Vice-Marshal G. E. Brookes
8 (Pathfinder) Group – Air Vice-Marshal D. C. T. Bennett

The only other change which would occur before 1945 would be the replacement of Air Vice-Marshal Brooks by Air Vice-Marshal C. M. McEwen in February 1944.

2 Group has not been included in the above list because this day-bombing organization left Bomber Command completely during this period. The capabilities of this courageous group had not fitted in with the main operations of Bomber Command since the switch to the night offensive in 1940. Although the group several times tried to join in the night battle, its equipment was never suited to this task and the diary has shown how the group's squadrons were forced to become an almost independent force, often experiencing difficulty in finding a viable role, frequently thrust into a type of operation which brought little success and fearful casualties. Now, with the invasion of Europe being planned for 1944, 2 Group left Bomber Command at the end of May 1943, temporarily to join Fighter Command which provided the escort cover for most of the group's operations but eventually to form the core of the R.A.F.'s Second Tactical Air Force which would achieve success and glory in providing close support to the British invasion forces in 1944 and 1945. From 1 June 1943 until the end of the war, 2 Group would be commanded by Air Vice-Marshal Basil Embry, who had once come so close to becoming the commander of the Pathfinders. (2 Group remained in Germany until it was disbanded in 1958 but the Second Tactical Air Force is still there!) But when 2 Group left Bomber Command in 1943, Sir Arthur Harris did not let all of its squadrons go with it. He insisted on keeping the two Mosquito squadrons – 105 and 139 – and transferred them to the Pathfinders. 105 Squadron was fitted out as a second *Oboe* squadron but 139 became the first unit of a unique force within 8 Group. This was the Light Night Striking Force which eventually grew to a strength of eight Mosquito squadrons and performed a host of useful duties for Bomber Command, mostly flying diversionary raids in support of major operations or carrying out independent harassing raids on German cities.

5/6 March 1943

ESSEN

442 aircraft – 157 Lancasters, 131 Wellingtons, 94 Halifaxes, 52 Stirlings, 8 Mosquitoes. It was on this night that Bomber Command's 100,000th sortie of the war was flown. 14 aircraft – 4 Lancasters, 4 Wellingtons, 3 Halifaxes, 3 Stirlings – lost, 3·2 per cent of the force.

The only tactical setback to this raid was that 56 aircraft – nearly 13 per cent of the force – turned back early because of technical defects and other causes. 3 of the 'early returns' were from the 8 *Oboe* Mosquito marker aircraft upon which the success of the raid depended but the 5 Mosquitoes which did reach the target area opened the attack on time and marked the centre of Essen perfectly. The Pathfinder backers-up also arrived in good time and carried out their part of the plan. The whole of the marking was 'blind', so that the ground haze which normally concealed

Essen did not affect the outcome of the raid. The Main Force bombed in 3 waves – Halifaxes in the first wave, Wellingtons and Stirlings in the second, Lancasters in the third. Two thirds of the bomb tonnage was incendiary; one third of the high-explosive bombs were fuzed for long delay. The attack lasted for 40 minutes and 362 aircraft claimed to have bombed the main target. These tactics would be typical of many other raids on the Ruhr area in the next 4 months.

Reconnaissance photographs showed 160 acres of destruction with 53 separate buildings within the Krupps works hit by bombs. A map from Essen shows the main area of damage to have been between the Krupps works and the city centre. The local report states that 3,018 houses were destroyed and 2,166 were seriously damaged. The number of people killed is given in various reports as between 457 and 482; at least 10 of these were firemen. If the higher figure is correct, the previous record number of people killed in an air raid on Germany – 469 in the 1000-bomber raid on Cologne in May 1942 – was exceeded.

Small numbers of bombs fell in 6 other Ruhr cities.

7 aircraft of 4 Group were sent minelaying in the Frisian Islands without loss.

7/8 March 1943

Minor Operations
14 Wellingtons and 6 Halifaxes of 4 Group minelaying in the Frisians, 2 O.T.U. sorties. 1 Halifax and 1 Wellington of the minelaying force lost.

---

8 March 1943

16 Mosquitoes to railway centres at Tergnier and Aulnoye in France and at Lingen in Germany. All targets were bombed; 1 Mosquito lost.

8/9 March 1943

NUREMBERG

335 aircraft – 170 Lancasters, 103 Halifaxes, 62 Stirlings. 8 aircraft – 4 Stirlings, 2 Halifaxes, 2 Lancasters – lost, 2·4 per cent of the force.

This distant raid had to be marked by a combination of $H2S$ and visual means. The Pathfinders had no moon to help them and, although there was no cloud, they found that haze prevented accurate visual identification of the target area. The result was that both marking and bombing spread over more than 10 miles along the line of the attack, with more than half of the bombs falling outside the city boundaries. This result would be typical of raids carried out beyond the range of *Oboe* during this period. Nuremberg reports that more than 600 buildings were destroyed and nearly 1,400 were damaged, including the M.A.N. and Siemens factories. Railway installations were also hit. Figures given for the dead vary from 284 to 343.

Sergeant D. R. Spanton, a mid-upper gunner in a 7 Squadron Stirling, had a fortunate escape on this night. After his aircraft crossed the English coast on the return flight, Spanton realized that he was the only man still in the plane. The remainder of the crew, a new crew in this Pathfinder squadron, had baled out earlier, possibly because of suspected fuel shortage, and the pilot left the plane flying on automatic pilot. Spanton had not heard the order. He parachuted safely over Kent and the empty Stirling later crashed into the Thames estuary. The remainder of the crew, presumably thinking they were parachuting over France, had actually come down in the sea and were all drowned. Sergeant Spanton went on to fly a further 12 operations but his plane was lost on the night of 24/25 June 1943 in a raid on Wuppertal and the presence of his name on the Runnymede Memorial probably indicates that he died in the sea on that occasion.

Minor Operations: 4 Mosquitoes to the Ruhr, 16 Wellingtons minelaying in the Frisians. No losses.

---

9 March 1943

15 Mosquitoes bombed the Renault works at Le Mans and scored direct hits. 1 Mosquito lost.

9/10 March 1943

MUNICH

264 aircraft – 142 Lancasters, 81 Halifaxes, 41 Stirlings. 8 aircraft – 5 Lancasters, 2 Halifaxes, 1 Stirling – lost, 3·0 per cent of the force.

The wind caused this raid to be concentrated on the western half of Munich rather than on the centre of the city, but much damage was caused. 291 buildings were destroyed, 660 severely damaged and 2,134 less seriously damaged; these included many public buildings – 11 hospitals, the cathedral, 4 churches and 14 'cultural' buildings for example – but also 3 wholesale and 22 retail business premises were completely destroyed and no less than 294 military buildings were hit, including the headquarters of the local Flak brigade, which was burnt out. The most serious industrial damage was at the B.M.W. factory where the aero-engine assembly shop was put out of action for 6 weeks. Many other industrial concerns were hit, including 141 small, back-street-type workshops which were destroyed.

The detailed Munich reports show that 208 people were killed and 425 injured. The dead included: 2 party officials on duty, 10 soldiers, 1 Hitler Youth boy serving at a Flak site, 2 policemen and 4 foreigners. The local Flak fired 14,234 rounds of ammunition – 2,314 of 105 mm, 8,328 of 88 mm, 3,592 of 20 mm – and 7 night fighters were reported as being on duty in the Munich area but only 1 bomber, unidentified because of its explosion in the air, was shot down over the city.

Minor Operations: 8 Mosquitoes to the Ruhr, 62 aircraft minelaying off Kiel and in the Frisians, 4 O.T.U. sorties. 3 Wellington minelayers lost.

Total effort for the night: 338 sorties, 11 aircraft (3·3 per cent) lost.

10/11 March 1943

MINOR OPERATIONS

2 Mosquitoes to Essen and Mulheim, 20 Lancasters and 15 Stirlings minelaying over a wide area from Biscay to Swinemünde in the Baltic, 5 O.T.U. sorties. 2 Lancaster minelayers lost.

11/12 March 1943

STUTTGART

314 aircraft – 152 Lancasters, 109 Halifaxes, 53 Stirlings. 11 aircraft – 6 Halifaxes, 3 Stirlings, 2 Lancasters – lost, 3·5 per cent of the force.

This raid was not successful. The Pathfinders claimed to have marked Stuttgart accurately but the Main Force is reported to have been late arriving. The first use by the Germans of dummy target indicators is also reported. Most of the bombing fell in open country but the south-western suburbs of Vaihingen and Kaltental were hit. 118 buildings – nearly all houses – were destroyed, 112 people were killed and 386 were injured. The only industrial damage reported was to a small packing store at the Bosch factory.

11 Stirlings and 3 Lancasters laid mines in the Frisians and the River Gironde without loss.

---

12 March 1943

12 Mosquitoes bombed an armaments factory at Liège and scored direct hits. 1 Mosquito lost.

12/13 March 1943

ESSEN

457 aircraft – 158 Wellingtons, 156 Lancasters, 91 Halifaxes, 42 Stirlings, 10 Mosquitoes. 23 aircraft – 8 Lancasters, 7 Halifaxes, 6 Wellingtons, 2 Stirlings lost, 5·0 per cent of the force.

This was another very successful *Oboe*-marked raid. The centre of the bombing area was right across the giant Krupps factory, just west of the city centre, with later bombing drifting back to the north-western outskirts. Photographic interpretation assessed that Krupps received 30 per cent more damage on this night than on the earlier successful raid of 5/6 March. Nearly 500 houses were also destroyed in the raid. The number of people killed is variously reported between 169 and 322, with 198 probably being the most accurate figure, made up of 64 men, 45 women, 19 children, 4 soldiers, 61 foreign workers and 5 prisoners of war.

German records say that one third of the bombs dropped on this night did not hit Essen and that 39 people were killed in other towns with Bottrop, just north of Essen, being the worst hit, but these towns were all close to Essen and there was often no clear division between overlapping built-up areas.

Minor Operations: 9 Stirlings minelaying in the Frisians, 7 O.T.U. sorties. No losses.

13/14 March 1943

MINELAYING

51 Wellingtons and 17 Lancasters to areas between Lorient and the Kattegat. 2 Wellingtons and 1 Lancaster lost.

14/15 March 1943

13 Wellingtons minelaying in the Frisians without loss.

15 March 1943

11 Venturas bombed La Pleine airfield in Brittany. 1 Ventura lost in the sea.

16 March 1943

16 Mosquitoes attacked railway workshops at Paderborn, nearly 200 miles inland from the coast, and scored direct hits. 1 Mosquito lost.

16/17 March 1943

12 Wellingtons of 1 Group minelaying in the Frisian Islands without loss.

18 March 1943

12 Venturas attacked an oil refinery at Maasluis but their bombs just missed the target; 12 further Venturas turned back from raids to targets in France. No aircraft lost.

20 March 1943

12 Mosquitoes to Louvain and Malines railway yards but only Louvain was reached.

    1 Lancaster bombed Leer, near Emden. This flight was carried out by Squadron Leader C. O'Donoghue of 103 Squadron, 1 Group. O'Donoghue decided to make this lone flight after a major Bomber Command effort planned for the previous night was cancelled. The Lancaster attacked Leer soon after dawn and its bombs fell close to the railway station. (See diary entry for 1 April 1943.)

20/21 March 1943

12 Wellingtons and 4 Lancasters minelaying off Biscay ports but the Wellingtons were recalled. No aircraft lost.

22 March 1943

12 Venturas attacked Maasluis oil refinery but again failed to hit the target. 12 further Venturas turned back from French targets. No aircraft lost.

22/23 March 1943

ST-NAZAIRE

357 aircraft – 189 Lancasters, 99 Halifaxes, 63 Stirlings, 6 Mosquitoes. 1 Lancaster lost.

3 Group sent out a recall order to its Stirlings and only 8 carried on to bomb the target. Accurate marking led to a concentrated attack by 283 aircraft on the port area of St-Nazaire.

6 Wellingtons laid mines off Texel without loss.

---

23 March 1943

15 Mosquitoes to railway-engine works at Nantes. Direct hits were scored and no aircraft were lost.

23/24 March 1943

MINOR OPERATIONS

45 aircraft laid mines in the Frisian Islands and south of Texel, 21 O.T.U. aircraft dropped leaflets over French towns. 2 Wellingtons lost, one each from the minelaying and O.T.U. forces.

---

24 March 1943

3 Mosquitoes shot up trains in areas east of the Ruhr without loss.

26/27 March 1943

DUISBURG

455 aircraft – 173 Wellingtons, 157 Lancasters, 114 Halifaxes, 9 Mosquitoes, 2 Stirlings. 6 aircraft – 3 Wellingtons, 1 Halifax, 1 Lancaster, 1 Mosquito – lost, 1·3 per cent of the force. The Mosquito lost was the first *Oboe* Mosquito casualty. A message was received from the pilot, Flight Lieutenant L. J. Ackland, that he was having to ditch in the North Sea. His body was never found but his navigator, Warrant Officer F. S. Sprouts, is believed to have survived.

This raid was one of the few failures of this series of attacks on Ruhr targets. It was a cloudy night and, for once, accurate *Oboe* sky-marking was lacking because 5 *Oboe* Mosquitoes were forced to return early with technical difficulties and a sixth was lost. The result was a widely scattered raid. The only details reported from Duisburg were 15 houses destroyed and 70 damaged, with 11 people killed and 36 injured.

5 O.T.U. aircraft carried leaflets to France without loss.

27 March 1943

5 Mosquitoes reached and bombed an engineering factory at Hengelo but 7 other Mosquitoes did not reach their targets. No aircraft lost.

27/28 March 1943

BERLIN

396 aircraft – 191 Lancasters, 124 Halifaxes, 81 Stirlings. 9 aircraft – 4 Halifaxes, 3 Lancasters, 2 Stirlings – lost, 2·3 per cent of the force.

This raid was basically a failure. The bombing force approached the target from the south-west and the Pathfinders established two separate marking areas, but both well short of the city. No bombing photographs were plotted within 5 miles of the aiming point in the centre of Berlin and most of the bombing fell from 7 to 17 miles short of the aiming point.

The Berlin report confirms that damage in the city was not heavy, although the bombing was slightly more widespread than the bombing photographs indicated. The local report, however, contains several interesting aspects. Only 16 houses were classed as completely destroyed but many further buildings, including public utilities and factories, suffered light damage. These were typical results in a scattered raid; the local fire services were able to contain fires quickly. But 102 people were killed and 260 injured. The majority of these casualties occurred when two bombs at the An- halter Station hit a military train bringing men on leave from the Russian Front; 80 soldiers were killed and 63 injured. Our researcher in Berlin, Arno Abendroth, states that the damage in Berlin would have been heavier if approximately one quarter of the bombs dropped had not turned out to be 'duds'. 'The English factories must have been under some stress,' he writes. Further out from the city centre, stray bombs hit several Luftwaffe establishments. 3 planes were destroyed and a Flak position was hit at Tempelhof airfield; the flying school at Staaken airfield was damaged and a further 70 service personnel were killed or wounded. These casualties are in addition to those in Berlin.

But the most interesting story concerns a secret Luftwaffe stores depot in the woods at Teltow, 11 miles south-west of the centre of Berlin. By chance, this was in the middle of the main concentration of bombs and a large quantity of valuable radio, radar and other technical stores was destroyed. The Luftwaffe decided that this depot was the true target for the R.A.F. raid on this night and were full of admiration for the special unit which had found and bombed it so accurately. The Gestapo investigated houses near by because someone reported that light signals had been flashed to the bombers. This theory was still current when our research into this raid was carried out in 1983!

Minor Operations: 24 aircraft minelaying in the Frisians and off Texel, 4 O.T.U. sorties. No losses.

Total effort for the night: 424 sorties, 9 aircraft (2·1 per cent) lost.

28 March 1943

24 Venturas, escorted by fighters, bombed Rotterdam docks and hit at least 6 ships and started a fire in a dockside warehouse. No Venturas were lost.

6 Mosquitoes were dispatched to attack a railway yard near Liège but 2 aircraft were shot down and the remaining 4 bombed an alternative target.

28/29 March 1943

ST-NAZAIRE

323 aircraft – 179 Wellingtons, 52 Halifaxes, 50 Lancasters, 35 Stirlings, 7 Mosquitoes. 1 Halifax and 1 Lancaster lost.

This *Oboe*-marked attack fell mainly in the port area.

Minor Operations: 7 aircraft minelaying off St-Nazaire, 5 O.T.U. sorties. No losses.

---

29 March 1943

61 Venturas flew 2 raids to Rotterdam docks and 1 to a railway target at Abbeville but the weather was unfavourable and only the bombing on the second raid to Rotterdam was accurate. No Venturas lost.

29/30 March 1943

BERLIN

329 aircraft – 162 Lancasters, 103 Halifaxes, 64 Stirlings. 21 aircraft – 11 Lancasters, 7 Halifaxes, 3 Stirlings – lost, 6·4 per cent of the force.

Weather conditions were difficult, with icing and inaccurately forecast winds. The marking for the raid appeared to be concentrated but in a position which was too far south and the Main Force arrived late. Most of the bombs fell in open country 6 miles south-east of Berlin. German records say that 148 people were killed in Berlin and 148 buildings were totally destroyed but there is some doubt about the accuracy of these figures.

BOCHUM

8 *Oboe* Mosquitoes and a 'Main Force' composed of 149 Wellingtons to Bochum. 12 Wellingtons lost, 8·0 per cent of the Wellington force.

This raid was another failure. The night was moonless and cloudy. The Mosquitoes were not able to adhere to their timetable and there were long gaps in the sky-marking. Local records say that only 4 buildings in Bochum were destroyed and 35 were damaged, with 28 people being killed.

Minor Operations: 1 Mosquito to Dortmund and 7 Stirlings minelaying in the Frisians without loss.

Total effort for the night: 494 sorties, 33 aircraft (6·9 per cent) lost.

30 March 1943

10 Mosquitoes bombed the Philips works at Eindhoven but could only hit the corner of the factory. No aircraft lost.

1 April 1943

12 Mosquitoes bombed a power-station and railway yards at Trier. Both targets were hit. A local report says that 21 people were killed in the attack but gives no other detail. No Mosquitoes were lost.

A lone Lancaster of 103 Squadron, again piloted by Squadron Leader C. O'Donoghue, set out to bomb the town of Emmerich just over the German border, but the Lancaster was shot down over Holland and the crew were all killed.

2 April 1943

The only Bomber Command operation on this day was the first sortie of the newly formed 1409 (Meteorological) Flight, based at Oakington. One Mosquito, crewed by Flight Lieutenant P. Cunliffe-Lister and Sergeant J. Boyle, made a weather reconnaissance flight to Brittany in preparation for the Bomber Command raids to be carried out in the coming night. The Mosquito returned safely.

1409 Flight operated until the end of the war, flying 1,364 sorties on 632 days. Only 3 Mosquitoes were lost during this period. Although all these sorties were under Bomber Command control, it will not be practicable to list every sortie in this diary or to include them in the periodic statistical summaries.

2/3 April 1943

ST-NAZAIRE/LORIENT

55 mixed aircraft to St-Nazaire and 47 to Lorient in the last raids on these French ports. Bomber Command was released from the obligation to bomb these targets 3 days later. 1 Lancaster was lost from the St-Nazaire raid.

The only report available from France says that the local fire-brigade headquarters at St-Nazaire was hit and 1 person was wounded. Both towns were now largely deserted by their former civilian populations.

33 aircraft laid mines off the southern part of the Biscay coast. 1 Lancaster lost.

3 April 1943

12 Venturas bombed shipping at Brest and 8 Mosquitoes attacked railway targets in Belgium and France. 1 Mosquito lost.

3/4 April 1943

ESSEN

348 aircraft – 225 Lancasters, 113 Halifaxes, 10 Mosquitoes; this was the first raid in which more than 200 Lancasters had taken part. 12 Halifaxes and 9 Lancasters lost – 6·0 per cent of the force – and 2 further Halifaxes crashed in England.

The weather forecast was not entirely favourable for this raid and the Pathfinders prepared a plan both for sky-marking and ground-marking the target. In the event, there was no cloud over Essen and the Main Force crews were somewhat confused to find two kinds of marking taking place. The resultant bombing, however, was accurate and a higher proportion of aircraft produced good bombing photographs than on any of the earlier successful raids on Essen.

Local reports showed that there was widespread damage in the centre and in the western half of Essen. 635 buildings were destroyed and 526 seriously damaged. 118 people – 88 civilians, 10 Flak gunners, 2 railwaymen, 2 policemen and 16 French workers – were killed and 458 people were injured.

Minor Operations: 16 Wellingtons minelaying off Brittany ports, 9 O.T.U. sorties. 1 minelaying aircraft lost.

Total effort for the night: 377 sorties, 23 aircraft (6·1 per cent) lost.

---

4 April 1943

60 Venturas attacked an airfield near Caen (24 aircraft), a shipyard at Rotterdam (24 aircraft) and a railway target as St-Brieuc (12 aircraft). All targets were successfully bombed but 2 aircraft from the Rotterdam raid were lost.

4/5 April 1943

KIEL

577 aircraft – 203 Lancasters, 168 Wellingtons, 116 Halifaxes, 90 Stirlings – on the largest raid so far to Kiel, more than twice as many aircraft as on any previous raid taking part. This was also the largest 'non-1,000' bombing force of the war so far. 12 aircraft – 5 Lancasters, 4 Halifaxes, 2 Stirlings, 1 Wellington – lost, 2·1 per cent of the force.

The Pathfinders encountered thick cloud and strong winds over the target so that accurate marking became very difficult. It was reported that decoy fire sites may also have drawn off some of the bombing. Kiel reports only a few bombs in the town with 11 buildings destroyed, 46 damaged and 26 people being killed. No commercial premises were hit; the only building hit apart from houses was a Catholic church.

---

5 April 1943

12 Venturas attacked a tanker at Brest. The ship was not hit but nearby dock installations were. 3 Venturas were lost.

6 April 1943

8 Mosquitoes attacked Namur railway workshops accurately and without loss.

6/7 April 1943

MINELAYING

47 aircraft to lay mines off the Biscay ports. 1 Halifax and 1 Wellington lost.

8/9 April 1943

DUISBURG

392 aircraft – 156 Lancasters, 97 Wellingtons, 73 Halifaxes, 56 Stirlings, 10 Mosquitoes. 19 aircraft – 7 Wellingtons, 6 Lancasters, 3 Halifaxes, 3 Stirlings – lost, 4·8 per cent of the force.

Thick cloud again ruined the Pathfinder marking and the resultant bombing was widely scattered. Duisburg experienced only moderate damage, with 40 buildings destroyed, 72 seriously damaged and 36 people killed. Bombs fell on at least 15 other towns in the Ruhr.

27 aircraft sent minelaying off the Biscay coast. 1 Wellington lost.

---

9 April 1943

4 Mosquitoes attacked various targets just over the German border but a raid by 4 more Mosquitoes to a railway target at Orléans was abortive. No aircraft lost.

9/10 April 1943

DUISBURG

5 Mosquitoes and 104 Lancasters were dispatched but thick cloud again caused a scattered attack. 50 houses were destroyed and 27 people were killed in Duisburg. Other bombs fell over a wide area of the Ruhr. 8 Lancasters lost.

5 O.T.U. Wellingtons carried leaflets to France without loss.

10/11 April 1943

FRANKFURT

502 aircraft – 144 Wellingtons, 136 Lancasters, 124 Halifaxes, 98 Stirlings. 21 aircraft – 8 Wellingtons, 5 Lancasters, 5 Stirlings, 3 Halifaxes – lost, 4·2 per cent of the force.

Complete cloud cover in the target area again led to a failure. The bombing photographs of every aircraft showed nothing but cloud and Bomber Command had no idea where bombs had fallen. Frankfurt reports only a few in the suburbs of the city south of the River Main. The only damage listed was fires in a paper-goods store and in the rafters of a few neighbouring houses. The Frankfurt report says that there were no casualties in the city, but another report says that 18 people died, presumably in country areas.

Minor Operations: 7 Stirlings minelaying in the Frisians, 4 O.T.U. sorties. No losses.

---

11 April 1943

8 Mosquitoes bombed an engineering factory at Hengelo and railway workshops at Malines. 2 Mosquitoes lost.

11/12 April 1943

MINELAYING

46 aircraft were sent to lay mines off Texel, Brittany and the Biscay ports. 1 Stirling and 1 Wellington lost.

---

13 April 1943

24 Venturas bombed railway targets at Abbeville and Caen but most of the bombs missed their targets. No Venturas lost.

13/14 April 1943

LA SPEZIA

208 Lancasters and 3 Halifaxes bombed the dock area of La Spezia and caused heavy damage. 4 Lancasters were lost and 3 more, either damaged or in mechanical difficulty, flew on to land at Allied airfields in North Africa. It is believed that this was the first occasion that the recently captured North African airfields were used for Bomber Command aircraft in distress. The 3 Lancasters flew back to England later.

MOSQUITO NUISANCE RAID

6 Mosquitoes of 105 Squadron, 2 Group, carried out nuisance raids to Bremen, Hamburg and Wilhelmshaven, 2 aircraft being sent to each target. These were the first non-*Oboe* Mosquito night raids and were the forerunners of Light Night Striking Force operations; the Germans hated the nuisance and harassing effect of the Mosquito raids and could rarely shoot down any of these fast, high-flying aircraft. The Mosquito was later modified to carry a 4,000-lb bomb as far as Berlin – a favourite Mosquito target – and, in winter, individual Mosquitoes were sometimes able to make 2 flights to Berlin under the cover of darkness in the same night, changing crews after the first landing.

Minor Operations: 10 Lancasters minelaying off Germany, 18 O.T.U. sorties. 1 O.T.U. Wellington was lost in the sea.

14/15 April 1943

STUTTGART

462 aircraft – 146 Wellingtons, 135 Halifaxes, 98 Lancasters, 83 Stirlings. 23 aircraft – 8 Stirlings, 8 Wellingtons, 4 Halifaxes, 3 Lancasters – lost, 5·0 per cent of the force.

The Pathfinders claimed to have marked the centre of this normally difficult target accurately but the main bombing area developed to the north-east, along the line of approach of the bombing force. This was an example of the 'creepback', a feature of large raids which occurred when Main Force crews – and some Pathfinder backers-up – failed to press through to the centre of the marking area but bombed – or re-marked – the earliest markers visible. Bomber Command was never able to eliminate the creepback tendency and much bombing fell outside city areas because of it.

On this night the creepback extended over the suburb of Bad Canstatt, which was of an industrial nature, and some useful damage was caused, particularly in the large railway-repair workshops situated there. The neighbouring districts of Münster and Mühlhausen were also hit and the majority of the 393 buildings destroyed and 942 severely damaged and the 200-plus civilian casualties were in these northern areas.

Only a few bombs fell in the centre of Stuttgart but the old Gedächtnis church was destroyed. In the district of Gaisburg, just east of the centre, 1 bomb scored a direct hit on an air-raid shelter packed with French and Russian prisoners of war. 257 Frenchmen and 143 Russians were killed. This tragedy brought the total death roll in Stuttgart to 619, a new record for raids to Germany.

---

15 April 1943

13 Venturas bombed a whaling factory ship in dry dock at Cherbourg. Bomb bursts were seen to straddle the target. No Venturas lost.

15/16 April 1943

Minor Operations

23 aircraft minelaying from Brest to Lorient, 5 O.T.U. sorties. No aircraft lost.

---

16 April 1943

25 Venturas bombed a chemical factory at Ostend and railway yards at Haarlem without loss.

The bombing at Ostend was accurate but the Haarlem raid hit housing near the railway causing many casualties. 85 Dutch people were killed and 160 injured and the old Town Hall was damaged by fire.*

---

* Details from Bowyer, op. cit., pp. 296–7.

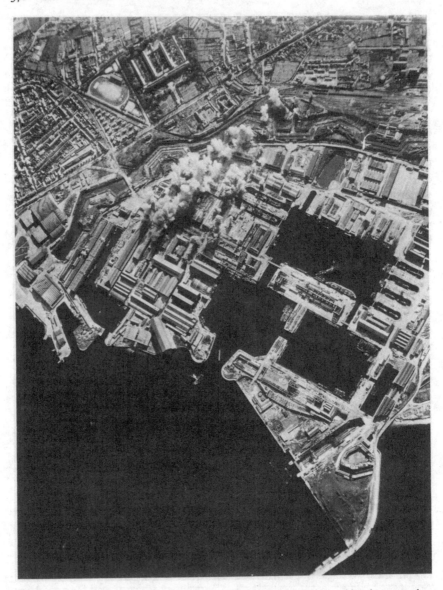

18. The bombing results of thirteen Venturas which were attempting to hit a large merchant ship recently spotted at Cherbourg.

16/17 April 1943

PILSEN

327 aircraft – 197 Lancasters and 130 Halifaxes. 18 Lancasters and 18 Halifaxes lost, 11·0 per cent of the force. The Canadian 408 Squadron lost 4 of its 12 Halifaxes dispatched.

This raid, on the Škoda armaments factory, took place by the light of a full moon but was not a success. In a complicated plan, the Main Force was ordered to confirm the position of the Škoda factory visually; the Pathfinder markers were only intended as a general guide. In the event, a large asylum building 7 miles away was mistaken for the factory and only 6 crews brought back bombing photographs which were within 3 miles of the real target. The Škoda factory was not hit. One report says that 200 German soldiers were killed when their barracks near the asylum was bombed.

MANNHEIM

271 aircraft – 159 Wellingtons, 95 Stirlings, 17 Halifaxes. 18 aircraft – 9 Wellingtons, 7 Stirlings, 2 Halifaxes – lost, 6·6 per cent of the force.

The Pathfinders marked this target accurately and an effective attack followed. 130 buildings were totally destroyed and nearly 3,000 damaged. Production was stopped or reduced at 41 industrial premises. 130 people were killed, 269 injured and 6,954 bombed out of their homes.

11 O.T.U. aircraft dropped leaflets over France without loss.

Total effort for the night: 609 sorties, 54 aircraft (8·9 per cent) lost. The aircraft losses on this night were the highest so far in the war, exceeding the 50 lost on the 1,000-bomber-type raid on Bremen on 25/26 June 1942, but 14 of the aircraft lost from the Pilsen and Mannheim raids came down in the sea and a proportion of their crews were rescued.

---

17 April 1943

37 Venturas bombed railway targets at Abbeville and Caen and a power-station at Zeebrugge. All targets were hit and no aircraft were lost.

17/18 April 1943

Minelaying

24 aircraft laid mines off the Biscay ports without loss.

---

18 April 1943

12 Venturas attacked shipping and dock installations at Dieppe without loss.

18/19 April 1943

LA SPEZIA

173 Lancasters and 5 Halifaxes were dispatched to bomb the dockyard but the centre of the bombing was north-west of the aiming point. The main railway station and many public buildings were hit. 1 Lancaster was lost. 8 further Lancasters laid mines off La Spezia harbour.

Minor Operations: 10 Stirlings minelaying in southern Biscay, 5 O.T.U. sorties. No losses.

---

19 April 1943

6 Mosquitoes to bomb railway workshops at Namur could not locate the target in bad visibility. No aircraft lost.

---

20 April 1943

36 Venturas bombed railway yards at Boulogne, shipping at Cherbourg and the power-station at Zeebrugge. No Venturas lost.

20/21 April 1943

STETTIN

339 aircraft – 194 Lancasters, 134 Halifaxes, 11 Stirlings. 21 aircraft – 13 Lancasters, 7 Halifaxes, 1 Stirling – lost, 6·2 per cent of the force.

This raid, on a target more than 600 miles from England, proved to be the most successful attack beyond the range of *Oboe* during the Battle of the Ruhr. Visibility was good and the Pathfinder marking was carried out perfectly. 24 fires were still burning when a photographic reconnaissance aircraft flew over Stettin a day and a half later. Approximately 100 acres in the centre of the town were claimed as devastated; much of this area comprised industrial buildings. German reports show that 13 industrial premises and 380 houses were completely destroyed. A large chemical factory was among the places where production was completely halted. 586 people were killed in Stettin.

ROSTOCK

86 Stirlings were dispatched to attack the Heinkel factory near Rostock but a smoke-screen concealed this target and bombing was scattered. 8 Stirlings were lost.

Minor Operations: 11 Mosquitoes carried out a raid to Berlin as a diversion for the forces attacking Stettin and Rostock; 18 Wellingtons were minelaying off Brittany ports and there were 3 O.T.U. sorties. 1 Mosquito was lost from the Berlin raid.

Total effort for the night: 457 sorties, 30 aircraft (6·6 per cent) lost.

---

21 April 1943

11 Venturas bombed railway yards at Abbeville. 3 Venturas lost.

22/23 April 1943

MINOR OPERATIONS

32 aircraft minelaying off Biscay ports, 5 O.T.U. sorties. 1 Lancaster and 1 Wellington from the minelaying force were lost.

---

24 April 1943

5 Mosquitoes attacked railway targets at Tours, Paderborn and Trier without loss.

---

26 April 1943

6 Mosquitoes attacked railway targets at Tours, Jülich and Lingen without loss.

26/27 April 1943

DUISBURG

561 aircraft – 215 Lancasters, 135 Wellingtons, 119 Halifaxes, 78 Stirlings, 14 Mosquitoes. 17 aircraft – 7 Halifaxes, 5 Wellingtons, 3 Lancasters, 2 Stirlings – lost, 3·0 per cent of the force.

This heavy raid was a partial failure. The Pathfinders claimed to have marked the target accurately but daylight reconnaissance showed that most of the bombing had fallen to the north-east of Duisburg; the Main Force may have bombed too early or they may have been lured by early fires short of the target. However, Duisburg had more than 300 buildings destroyed and a death roll of between 130 and 207 (reports vary). 4 of the Mosquitoes taking part in this raid were from 2 Group; they bombed Duisburg 3 hours after the main raid, then dived hard and flew back to England at low level.

Bombs hit 6 other towns in the Ruhr.

8 O.T.U. aircraft dropped leaflets over France without loss.

---

27 April 1943

12 Venturas dispatched to attack a railway target at St-Brieuc turned back because of 10/10ths cloud.

27/28 April 1943

MINELAYING

160 aircraft – 58 Halifaxes, 46 Lancasters, 31 Wellingtons, 25 Stirlings – in the biggest minelaying operation so far mounted. 123 aircraft carried out their flights successfully, laying 458 mines off the Biscay and Brittany ports and in the Frisian Islands. 1 Lancaster lost.

4 O.T.U. Wellingtons carried leaflets to France without loss.

28/29 April 1943

MINELAYING

207 aircraft – 68 Lancasters, 60 Halifaxes, 47 Wellingtons, 32 Stirlings – carried out another large minelaying operation. 167 aircraft laid 593 mines off Heligoland, in the River Elbe and in the Great and Little Belts. Low cloud over the German and Danish coasts forced the minelayers to fly low in order to establish their positions before laying their mines and much German light Flak activity was seen. 22 aircraft – 7 Lancasters, 7 Stirlings, 6 Wellingtons, 2 Halifaxes – were lost. This was the heaviest loss of aircraft while minelaying in the war, but the number of mines laid was the highest in one night.

6 Mosquitoes carried out a raid to Wilhelmshaven, dropping many flares to divert attention from that part of the minelaying force which was operating near by. No Mosquitoes lost.

---

30 April/1 May 1943

ESSEN

305 aircraft – 190 Lancasters, 105 Halifaxes, 10 Mosquitoes. 6 Halifaxes and 6 Lancasters lost, 3·9 per cent of the force.

Cloud was expected over the target so a Pathfinder technique based solely on *Oboe* Mosquito sky-markers was planned. This was not expected to give such good results as ground-marking but the plan worked well and 238 crews reported that they had bombed Essen. Because of the cloud, no bombing photographs were produced. A map from Essen shows that this modest attack did produce new damage areas all over the city, although there was no major concentration. 189 buildings were destroyed and 237 severely damaged. The Krupps factory was hit again. 53 people were killed and 218 injured.

Bombs also fell on 10 other Ruhr towns, particularly in Bottrop just to the north of Essen, which was hit by 86 high-explosive bombs.

8 Stirlings and 4 Halifaxes of the Pathfinders carried out *H2S* training attacks on Bocholt. 1 Stirling lost.

---

1 May 1943

12 Bostons to a railway target at Caen and 6 Mosquitoes to the Philips factory at Eindhoven; both raids were abandoned because of cloud.

1/2 May 1943

MINELAYING

18 Wellingtons and 12 Stirlings laid mines off the Brittany and Biscay coasts. 1 Stirling lost.

---

2 May 1943

12 Bostons and 12 Venturas attacked a steelworks at Ijmuiden; the Venturas hit the target but not the Bostons. 7 Mosquitoes bombed railway workshops at Thionville. No aircraft lost.

3 May 1943

12 Venturas of 487 (New Zealand) Squadron were dispatched to attack a power-station on the northern outskirts of Amsterdam. 1 aircraft returned early; the remaining 11 proceeded with an escort of 3 squadrons of Spitfires. Unfortunately, an earlier Spitfire sweep alerted the German defences while the Ventura force was still flying at low level over the North Sea. Unfortunately, too, an exceptional number of experienced German fighter pilots were present at Schiphol airfield for a conference. 69 German fighters were thus up in the air near Amsterdam when the Ventura force crossed the Dutch coast. Some of the German fighters engaged the Spitfires while the remainder attacked the bombers. 9 Venturas were shot down before reaching the target and a tenth was badly damaged but it managed to turn back and reach England. The only remaining Ventura from the formation was that of Squadron Leader L. H. Trent, a New Zealander. His Ventura, completely alone, pressed on to the target and bombed it. The bombs just missed but some blast damage was caused. This last Ventura was then immediately shot down. Squadron Leader Trent and his navigator were the only survivors and became prisoners of war. The story of this action, in which 10 out of 11 Venturas were shot down, was reconstructed after the war and Squadron Leader Trent was awarded the Victoria Cross in 1946.*

6 Bostons successfully bombed the steelworks at Ijmuiden but 1 aircraft crashed into the sea.

Total Bomber Command effort for the day: 18 sorties, 11 aircraft (61 per cent) lost.

3/4 May 1943

4 O.T.U. Whitleys dropped leaflets over France without loss.

4 May 1943

12 Venturas attacked railway yards at Abbeville. 3 Mosquitoes out of 6 dispatched bombed power-stations at Haarlem and The Hague. No aircraft lost.

4/5 May 1943

DORTMUND

596 aircraft – 255 Lancasters, 141 Halifaxes, 110 Wellingtons, 80 Stirlings, 10 Mosquitoes – on the largest 'non-1,000' raid of the war to date and the first major attack

*A more detailed account of the action is given in Michael Bowyer's *2 Group R.A.F.*, op. cit., pp. 309–14.

on Dortmund. 31 aircraft – 12 Halifaxes, 7 Stirlings, 6 Lancasters, 6 Wellingtons – lost, 5·2 per cent of the force. A further 7 aircraft crashed in bad weather at the bomber bases.

The initial Pathfinder marking was accurate but some of the backing-up marking fell short. A decoy fire site also attracted many bombs. But half of the large force did bomb within 3 miles of the aiming point and severe damage was caused in central and northern parts of Dortmund. The city's report states that 1,218 buildings were destroyed and 2,141 seriously damaged, including the Hoesch and the Dortmunder Union steel factories and many facilities in the dock area. The old Rathaus was among 7 buildings of a cultural nature which were destroyed. At least 693 people were killed, including 200 prisoners of war, and 1,075 people were injured. The number of dead in this raid was a new record.

Minor Operations: 6 Stirlings and 2 Halifaxes on an *H2S* training raid to Rheine, 24 O.T.U. sorties. No losses.

Total effort for the night: 628 sorties, 31 aircraft (4·9 per cent) lost.

---

5 May 1943

5 Mosquitoes to attack a railway works south of Brussels. Only one aircraft is believed to have hit this target. No aircraft lost.

5/6 May 1943

21 Stirlings minelaying in the Frisian Islands; 1 aircraft lost.

---

7 May 1943

6 Mitchells to a railway target at Boulogne were recalled.

9/10 May 1943

21 Stirlings minelaying off La Pallice and in the River Gironde without loss.

---

11 May 1943

6 Mitchells to a railway target at Boulogne were recalled.

12/13 May 1943

DUISBURG

572 aircraft – 238 Lancasters, 142 Halifaxes, 112 Wellingtons, 70 Stirlings, 10 Mosquitoes. 34 aircraft – 10 Lancasters, 10 Wellingtons, 9 Halifaxes, 5 Stirlings – lost, 5·9 per cent of the force.

This was the fourth raid on Duisburg so far during the Battle of the Ruhr, the first 3 raids having been only partially successful. The Pathfinder marking on this night, however, was near perfect and the Main Force bombing was particularly well concentrated. The centre of Duisburg and the port area just off the River Rhine, the largest inland port in Germany, suffered severe damage. 1,596 buildings were totally destroyed and 273 people were killed. 4 of the August Thyssen steel factories were damaged. Nearly 2,000 prisoners of war and forced workers were drafted into Duisburg to repair windows, roofs and other bomb damage. In the port area, 21 barges and 13 other ships totalling 18,921 tons were sunk and 60 further ships of 41,000 tons were damaged. It was not deemed necessary to attack Duisburg again during this period.

---

13 May 1943

12 Bostons attacked Cherbourg docks and 6 Mitchells attacked railway targets at Boulogne. 1 Mitchell lost.

13/14 May 1943

BOCHUM

442 aircraft – 135 Halifaxes, 104 Wellingtons, 98 Lancasters, 95 Stirlings, 10 Mosquitoes; 5 Group did not take part in this raid. 24 aircraft – 13 Halifaxes, 6 Wellingtons, 4 Stirlings, 1 Lancaster – lost, 5·4 per cent of the force.

This raid started well but, after 15 minutes, what were believed to be German decoy markers drew much of the bombing away from the target. The only information available from Germany is that 394 buildings in Bochum were destroyed, 716 were seriously damaged and 302 people were killed.

PILSEN

156 Lancasters and 12 Halifaxes were dispatched in a further attempt to bomb the Škoda armaments factory. 120 aircraft from this force were from 5 Group; the remainder were Pathfinders. 9 aircraft were lost.

This target again proved to be a difficult one to find and mark accurately and nearly all the bombs fell in open country north of the Škoda works.

Minor Operations: 12 Mosquitoes to Berlin, 8 aircraft minelaying in the Frisians, 12 O.T.U. flights. 1 Mosquito on the Berlin raid was lost.

Total effort for the night: 642 sorties, 34 aircraft (5·3 per cent) lost.

---

14 May 1943

6 Mitchells sent to the steelworks at Ijmuiden were recalled.

14/15 May 1943

5 O.T.U. Wellingtons dropped leaflets over France without loss.

---

15 May 1943

24 Bostons and 12 Mitchells to various targets. 12 Bostons and 6 Mitchells were recalled but 12 Bostons bombed Poix airfield and 6 Mitchells attacked an industrial target at Caen. No aircraft lost.

15/16 May 1943

Minor Operations

3 Mosquitoes to Berlin, 16 O.T.U. sorties. No aircraft lost.

16 May 1943

12 Venturas bombed Morlaix airfield and 5 Mitchells bombed Caen airfield but 7 further Mitchells could not locate their airfield target. No aircraft lost.

16/17 May 1943

THE DAMS RAID

617 Squadron was formed by Wing Commander Guy Gibson on 21 March 1943 from selected crews in 5 Group and the squadron trained for 6 weeks for this special operation. 19 Lancasters were dispatched in 3 waves, each aircraft armed with the special 'bouncing bomb' developed by Barnes Wallis for attacking German dams. The entire operation was to be carried out at low level to escape attack from German night fighters and to release the bombs just above the water in the dams.

One aircraft had to return early after it struck the sea a glancing blow which tore off its bomb. 5 further aircraft were shot down or crashed before reaching their targets and 1 was so badly damaged by Flak that it had to turn back. This left 12 Lancasters available to bomb the dams. Wing Commander Gibson's aircraft and 4 other crews bombed the Möhne Dam and breached it despite intense fire from light Flak defending the dam. 3 aircraft went on to bomb the Eder Dam, which was also breached. 2 aircraft bombed the Sorpe Dam and 1 the Schwelme Dam but without causing breaches in their walls. The twelfth surviving aircraft could not find its target in misty conditions and returned to England without dropping its bomb. 3 further Lancasters were shot down after they had bombed.

Total casualties were 8 aircraft out of the 19 dispatched. It is estimated that 4 were shot down by light Flak, 1 crashed after being damaged by the explosion of its own bomb, 2 crashed after hitting electricity cables and 1 after striking a tree when its pilot was dazzled by a searchlight. Of the 56 crew members in these planes, 53 were killed and only 3 became prisoners of war, 2 of them being badly injured. For his leadership of this amazing operation and for his courage in attacking Flak positions at the Möhne Dam after having carried out his own bombing run, Wing Commander Gibson was awarded the Victoria Cross. 34 other men received decorations.

The breaching of the Möhne and Eder Dams were major achievements. The Möhne reservoir contained nearly 140 million tons of water and was the major source of supply for the industrial Ruhr 20 miles away. The water released caused

19 (a and b). The breach in the Möhne Dam caused by 617 Squadron. The conical shapes on the wall are dummy fir trees; the flotation balls visible on the far side of the lower water are the remains of the anti-torpedo netting which had been inside the dam before the raid.

(below) The flood of water beating against a rail bridge.

widespread flooding and disruption of rail, road and canal communications and of the supply of electricity and water. The water-supply network was particularly affected by the silting up of pumping stations by the flood water. It is not possible to state the effect of all this upon industrial production in precise terms but there was certainly some disruption and water rationing was in force until the winter rains came and filled the reservoirs again.

The Eder was even larger than the Möhne, containing 210 million tons of water, but it was 60 miles from the Ruhr. The city of Kassel, 25 miles away, and the inland waterway system in the Kassel area, were more affected by the attack on the Eder than was the Ruhr area. The German view is that, if the aircraft which were allocated to the Eder had been switched to the Sorpe Dam, the effect upon the Ruhr's industrial production would have been extremely serious, but the Sorpe's construction was of a nature which made it a difficult target for the Wallis bomb, hence its low priority in the raid. The Sorpe reservoir just managed to keep the Ruhr supplied with water until the Möhne Dam was repaired.

The number of people drowned has been calculated at 1,294,* most of them near the Möhne Dam. The town of Neheim-Hüsten, which was situated 5 miles downstream of the Möhne Dam, took the full impact of the flood and at least 859 people died there. By one of those tragedies which periodically struck foreign workers and prisoners of war whose camps were near targets in Germany, 493 foreigners – mostly Ukrainian women landworkers – died in their camp at Neheim-Hüsten. It is believed that 58 or more of the dead were around the Eder Dam. The total number of dead – as quoted at 1,294 – was a new record for a raid on Germany, easily exceeding the 693 people killed at Dortmund in a raid earlier in May in which 596 aircraft took part!

Minor Operations: 9 Mosquitoes to Berlin, Cologne, Düsseldorf and Münster, 54 aircraft minelaying off Biscay ports and in the Frisians, 4 O.T.U. sorties. 1 Wellington minelayer lost.

---

17 May 1943

13 Venturas bombed Caen airfield without loss.

17/18 May 1943

Minor Operations

3 Mosquitoes to Munich, 6 aircraft minelaying off La Pallice. 1 Stirling minelayer lost.

---

18 May 1943

13 Bostons bombed Abbeville airfield without loss.

---

*The casualty calculation is in John Sweetman's *Operation Chastise*, Jane's, 1982, p. 153. Other sources which have been consulted are Alan W. Cooper's *The Men Who Breached the Dams*, Kimber, 1982; Hans Rumpf's *The Bombing of Germany*, op. cit., pp. 64–77; and the British Official History, Vol. I, pp. 168–78 and 289–92, and Vol. IV, pp. 375 and 392.

18/19 May 1943

13 Lancasters and 4 Wellingtons minelaying off Brest and in the southern part of Biscay. No losses.

19 May 1943

12 Venturas to Morlaix airfield were recalled.

19/20 May 1943
Minor Operations

6 Mosquitoes to Berlin – only 2 bombed there, 5 O.T.U. sorties. No losses.

20 May 1943

2 Mosquitoes bombed locomotive sheds at Tergnier without loss.

20/21 May 1943
MINOR OPERATIONS

3 Mosquitoes to Berlin, 23 aircraft minelaying in southern Biscay, 5 O.T.U. sorties. No losses.

21 May 1943

4 Mosquitoes bombed a railway target at Orleans; 1 aircraft lost. 12 Mitchells to Abbeville airfield were recalled.

21/22 May 1943
MINELAYING

104 aircraft – 64 Wellingtons, 36 Stirlings, 4 Lancasters – carried out extensive minelaying in the Frisians and the River Gironde, and off La Pallice. 3 Wellingtons and 1 Stirling lost.

4 Mosquitoes attacked Berlin without loss.

22 May 1943

7 Mosquitoes to attack railway workshops at Nantes turned back because of fighter opposition. No aircraft lost.

23 May 1943

12 Venturas of 487 Squadron bombed a power-station at Zeebrugge in the first operation for the squadron since its heavy losses on the Amsterdam raid 3 weeks earlier. The formation's bombs fell on to railway yards near the power-station. No aircraft were lost.

23/24 May 1943

DORTMUND

After a 9-day break in major operations, Bomber Command dispatched 826 aircraft on this raid, the greatest number in a 'non-1,000' raid so far in the war and the largest raid of the Battle of the Ruhr. The force comprised: 343 Lancasters, 199 Halifaxes, 151 Wellingtons, 120 Stirlings and 13 Mosquitoes. 38 aircraft – 18 Halifaxes, 8 Lancasters, 6 Stirlings, 6 Wellingtons – were lost, 4·6 per cent of the force.

The Pathfinders marked the target accurately in clear weather conditions and the ensuing attack proceeded according to plan. It was a very successful raid. Large areas in the centre, the north and the east of Dortmund were devastated. Nearly 2,000 buildings were completely destroyed. Many industrial premises were hit, particularly the large Hoesch steelworks, which ceased production. 599 people were killed, 1,275 were injured and the bodies of about 25 other people were never found.

20. The increasing strength of Bomber Command. A Halifax Mark II of 408 (Canadian) Squadron at Linton-on-Ouse in 1943 being loaded with high-explosive and incendiary bombs.

Dortmund was not attacked in strength again by Bomber Command until exactly 1 year after this raid.

There is an interesting story to tell about a Wellington of 431 Squadron which took part in this raid. Just after leaving the target, the Wellington was coned by searchlights and hit several times by fragments of Flak. The rear gunner reported

21 (a and b). The collection and identification of the dead in Dortmund during the Battle of the Ruhr.

that he thought the aircraft was on fire. The pilot twice put the aircraft into a steep dive to evade the searchlights but was not able to do so. There was some confusion over whether an order to bale out was given by the pilot and the pilot actually did leave the aircraft. The bomb aimer, Sergeant S. N. Sloan, an Englishman, took over the controls and eventually was able to shake off the searchlights. The navigator and wireless operator were still aboard and Sergeant Sloan flew the aircraft back to England and made a perfect landing at Cranwell. He was immediately awarded the Conspicuous Gallantry Medal, commissioned and posted to a pilot training course. The wireless operator, Flying Officer J. B. G. Bailey, and the navigator, Sergeant G. C. W. Parslow, received immediate awards of the D.F.C. and the D.F.M. respectively. They later became part of the crew of Wing Commander J. Coverdale, the squadron commander, but were killed with Coverdale on the night of 21/22 June 1943 on a raid to Krefeld.

Sergeant (later Flight Lieutenant) Sloan came back to Bomber Command as a Halifax pilot with 158 Squadron and flew on operations from January 1945 until the end of the war. In the post-war years he served with the King's Flight.

15 O.T.U. aircraft carried out leaflet flights to France. 1 Wellington lost.

---

25 May 1943

12 Mitchells attempted to raid Abbeville airfield but cloud over the target and Flak disrupted the attack and only 5 aircraft bombed dispersal buildings near the airfield. 2 Mitchells were lost. 12 Bostons on a raid to Cherbourg abandoned the operation.

25/26 May 1943

DÜSSELDORF

759 aircraft – 323 Lancasters, 169 Halifaxes, 142 Wellingtons, 113 Stirlings, 12 Mosquitoes. 27 aircraft – 9 Lancasters, 8 Stirlings, 6 Wellingtons, 4 Halifaxes – lost, 3·6 per cent of the force.

This raid was a failure. There were two layers of cloud over the target and the Pathfinders experienced great difficulty in marking it. It is believed that the Germans were also operating decoy markers and fire sites. The result was that the Main Force bombing was scattered over a wide area. There was no concentration in Düsseldorf which recorded only 50 to 100 buildings destroyed and some 30 people killed.

---

27 May 1943

Jena

14 Mosquitoes of 105 and 139 Squadrons were dispatched to fly at low level and attack a glassworks and the Zeiss optical-instruments factory at Jena. These were the last operations flown by the two squadrons with 2 Group before the coming transfer to 8 Group.

The round flight from the Dutch coast was more than 500 miles. 2 Mosquitoes of 139 Squadron collided on the outward flight near Paderborn and crashed; another Mosquito of 105 Squadron was also lost. 11 aircraft bombed the 2 targets with great accuracy. On the return to England, 2 more Mosquitoes – 1 from each squadron – crashed in Norfolk and the crews were all killed.

27/28 May 1943

ESSEN

518 aircraft – 274 Lancasters, 151 Halifaxes, 81 Wellingtons, 12 Mosquitoes. 23 aircraft – 11 Halifaxes, 6 Lancasters, 5 Wellingtons, 1 Mosquito – lost, 4·4 per cent of the force.

22. Essen, 1943. The damaged Fire Brigade Headquarters carries on and, in the distance on the left, smoking factory chimneys show that some factories survive.

The weather was cloudy and sky-marking had to be used. The main bombing was scattered, with many aircraft undershooting. The limited damage caused in Essen was mainly in the central and northern districts. 488 buildings were destroyed. 196 people were killed and 547 injured. Bombs fell in 10 surrounding Ruhr towns.

Minor Operations: 23 aircraft minelaying in the Frisians, 19 O.T.U. sorties. 1 Stirling minelayer lost.

23. A Party funeral in Essen.

28 May 1943

12 Venturas bombed a power-station at Zeebrugge. 1 Ventura lost.

28/29 May 1943

MINOR OPERATIONS

34 aircraft minelaying in the Frisians, off Brittany ports and in the River Gironde, 5 O.T.U. sorties. No aircraft lost.

29 May 1943

12 Venturas bombed Caen airfield without loss.

29/30 May 1943

WUPPERTAL

719 aircraft – 292 Lancasters, 185 Halifaxes, 118 Stirlings, 113 Wellingtons, 11 Mosquitoes. 33 aircraft – 10 Halifaxes, 8 Stirlings, 8 Wellingtons, 7 Lancasters – lost, 4·6 per cent of the force.

    This attack was aimed at the Barmen half of the long and narrow town of Wuppertal and was the outstanding success of the Battle of the Ruhr. Both Pathfinder marking and Main Force bombing was particularly accurate and a large fire area developed in the narrow streets of the old centre of the town. It is probable that this fire was so severe that the first, small form of what would later become known as a 'firestorm' developed. Because it was a Saturday night, many of the town's fire and air-raid officials were not present, having gone to their country homes for the weekend, and the fire services of the town – in their first raid – were not able to control the fires.

Approximately 1,000 acres – possibly 80 per cent of Barmen's built-up area – was destroyed by fire. 5 out of the town's 6 largest factories, 211 other industrial premises and nearly 4,000 houses were completely destroyed. The number of buildings classed as seriously damaged – 71 industrial and 1,800 domestic – indicates the high proportion of complete destruction. Various figures were given for the number of people killed but our expert on Ruhr raids, Norbert Krüger, advises that the figure of 'approximately 3,400' is the nearest reasonable estimate.

The above figures indicate that the property damage in this raid was about twice as severe as any previous raid on a German city, while the number of people killed in this comparatively unprepared backwater of the Ruhr was about 5 times greater than any previous city raid.

3 O.T.U. aircraft on leaflet flights to France were recalled.

30/31 May 1943

MINOR OPERATIONS

27 aircraft minelaying off Biscay ports, 14 O.T.U. sorties. No losses.

---

31 May 1943

LAST 2 GROUP RAIDS

The squadrons of 2 Group dispatched 54 aircraft on 5 raids on this, the last day before the group left Bomber Command.

30 Venturas were dispatched: 12 to attack Zeebrugge power-station, 12 to Caen airfield and 6 to Cherbourg docks. 12 Mitchells bombed a shipyard at Flushing. All of these raids were successful. The only casualty was a Mitchell of 180 Squadron which ditched in the sea; 3 of its crew were picked up safely, but Flight Sergeant A. W. Wood, the New Zealand wireless operator/air gunner, died – the last casualty suffered by 2 Group with Bomber Command. 12 Bostons sent to attack a power-station in France were not able to reach their target.

1/2 June 1943

MINELAYING

23 Wellingtons and 10 Stirlings laid mines in the Frisians, off Texel and off the Biscay ports without loss.

2/3 June 1943

MINELAYING

21 Wellingtons and 14 Stirlings laid mines off the Biscay ports without loss.

3/4 June 1943

MINOR OPERATIONS

24 Wellingtons and 15 Stirlings minelaying off the Biscay ports, 16 O.T.U. leaflet flights. 1 O.T.U. Wellington was lost in the sea.

5/6 June 1943

Minor Operations

12 aircraft minelaying in the Frisians, 5 O.T.U. sorties to the Vichy-controlled area of France. No aircraft lost.

9/10 June 1943

8 O.T.U. Wellingtons on leaflet flights to France. 1 aircraft crashed in England.

10/11 June 1943

5 Whitleys and 1 Wellington from O.T.U.s on leaflet flights to France. 1 Whitley lost.

(The operations since the end of May are a good example of the way in which Bomber Command now curtailed its operations during the moon period.)

11/12 June 1943

DÜSSELDORF

783 aircraft – 326 Lancasters, 202 Halifaxes, 143 Wellingtons, 99 Stirlings, 13 Mosquitoes. This was the first night that more than 200 Halifaxes took part in a raid. 38 aircraft – 14 Lancasters, 12 Halifaxes, 10 Wellingtons, 2 Stirlings – lost, 4·9 per cent of the force.

The Pathfinder marking plan proceeded excellently until an *Oboe* Mosquito inadvertently released a load of target indicators 14 miles north-east of Düsseldorf. This caused part of the Main Force to waste its bombs on open country. But the main bombing caused extensive damage in the centre of Düsseldorf, where 130 acres were claimed as destroyed, and this proved to be the most damaging raid of the war for this city.

Düsseldorf reports that the fire area measured 8 km by 5 km, covering the city centre – both the old and new parts, the Derendorf district and the south of the city. No less than 8,882 separate fire incidents were recorded of which 1,444 were classified as large. 1,292 people were killed. 140,000 people were bombed out of their homes. The list of destroyed and seriously damaged industrial and public buildings covers 4 typed pages in the Düsseldorf report! 42 industries connected with the war effort suffered complete stoppages of production and 35 more suffered a partial reduction. 20 military establishments were hit. 8 ships were sunk or damaged. The *Gau* (province) local government headquarters was destroyed.

MÜNSTER

72 aircraft – 29 Lancasters, 22 Halifaxes, 21 Stirlings – were dispatched on an interesting raid. All the aircraft were provided by 8 Group and it was really a mass *H2S* trial. 33 of the aircraft carried markers or flares, the remaining aircraft acting as the bombing force, although the marker aircraft also bombed. The marking and bombing were very accurate and the whole raid lasted less than 10 minutes. Photographic reconnaissance showed that much damage was done to railway installations in Münster as well as to housing areas. Münster's report is very brief, stating only that 132 buildings were destroyed, 317 were seriously damaged and 52 people were killed.

Unfortunately the raid was expensive for the small force involved; 5 aircraft – 2 Halifaxes, 2 Lancasters and 1 Stirling – were lost, 6·9 per cent of the aircraft involved.

Minor Operations: 3 Mosquitoes to Duisburg and 2 to Cologne, 23 O.T.U. sorties to France. 1 O.T.U. Wellington was lost.

Total effort for the night: 883 sorties, 44 aircraft (5·0 per cent) lost. The number of aircraft dispatched on this night represented a new record for a 'non-1,000' raid.

12/13 June 1943

BOCHUM

503 aircraft – 323 Lancasters, 167 Halifaxes, 11 Mosquitoes. 14 Lancasters and 10 Halifaxes lost, 4·8 per cent of the force.

This raid took place over a completely cloud-covered target but accurate *Oboe* sky-marking enabled the all Lancaster/Halifax Main Force to cause severe damage to the centre of Bochum. After daylight photographs had been taken, 130 acres of destruction were claimed. The only report from Germany says that 449 buildings were destroyed and 916 severely damaged and that 312 people were killed.

MINELAYING

34 Wellingtons to the Frisians, Lorient and St-Nazaire. No losses.

13/14 June 1943

MINOR OPERATIONS

13 Mosquitoes – 6 to Berlin, 4 to Düsseldorf and 3 to Cologne – but all targets were cloud-covered and only estimated positions were bombed. 18 Wellingtons and 12 Stirlings were sent minelaying off the Biscay ports and there were 8 O.T.U. sorties. 1 Wellington minelayer lost.

14/15 June 1943

OBERHAUSEN

197 Lancasters and 6 Mosquitoes; 17 Lancasters lost, 8·4 per cent of the force.

This target was also cloud-covered but once again the *Oboe* sky-marking was accurate. The report from Oberhausen says that the Germans noted the markers right over the top of the *Altstadt*. 267 buildings were destroyed and 584 seriously damaged. 85 people were killed and 258 were injured.

Minor Operations: 2 Mosquitoes to Cologne, 29 aircraft minelaying off Brittany and in the River Gironde. 1 Stirling minelayer lost.

15/16 June 1943

6 Mosquitoes carried out a nuisance raid to Berlin without loss.

16/17 June 1943

COLOGNE

202 Lancasters and 10 Halifaxes of 1, 5 and 8 Groups. 14 Lancasters lost.

The marking for this raid was not by *Oboe* but by 16 heavy bombers of the Pathfinders fitted with *H2S*. The target was cloud-covered and some of the Pathfinder aircraft had trouble with their *H2S* sets. The sky-marking was late and sparse, and the bombing of the all-Lancaster Main Force was thus scattered. The local report believed that several hundred planes approached Cologne but, because of bad weather, only the first 100 bombed, the remainder turning back. Most of the damage in Cologne was to housing areas; 401 houses were destroyed and nearly 13,000 suffered varying degrees of damage. 16 industrial premises were hit, including the Kalk Chemical Works which, according to R.A.F. photographic reconnaissance, was burnt out. Other buildings destroyed or damaged included 9 railway stations, 2 railway stores, 1 telephone exchange, 2 district town halls (at Ehrenfeld and Spanischer Bau), 5 churches, 5 hospitals, 3 cinemas and 2 schools. 147 people were killed and 213 were injured.

Minor Operations: 3 Mosquitoes to Berlin, 4 O.T.U. sorties. No losses.

17/18 June 1943

7 Mosquitoes, 4 to Berlin and 3 to Cologne and the Ruhr. No aircraft lost.

19/20 June 1943

LE CREUSOT

290 aircraft of 3, 4, 6 and 8 Groups – 181 Halifaxes, 107 Stirlings, 2 Lancasters – to bomb the Schneider armaments factory and the Breuil steelworks. 2 Halifaxes lost.

The tactics for this raid were that the Pathfinders would only drop flares and that each crew of the Main Force was to identify their part of the target by the light of these flares. The Main Force crews were then to make 2 runs over the target area, dropping a short stick of bombs on each run from altitudes between 5,000 and 10,000 ft. By this stage of the war, however, Main Force crews were used to bombing target indicators and many had difficulty in making a visual identification of their target. Lingering smoke from the large number of flares was blamed for most of the difficulty. Bombing photographs showed that all crews bombed within 3 miles of the centre of the target but only about one fifth managed to hit the factories. Many bombs fell on nearby residential property but no report could be obtained from France to give details of casualties.

MONTCHANIN

26 of the $H2S$-equipped Pathfinders who had released flares at Le Creusot were intended to fly on to drop flares over the electrical-transformer station at Montchanin. By the light of these flares, a further 26 Lancaster bombers of 8 Group were to attack this second target. Most of the attacking crews, however, mistook a small metal factory for the transformer station and bombed that target instead. A few aircraft did identify the correct target but their bombs scored no hits on it.

Minor Operations: 6 Mosquitoes to Cologne, Duisburg and Düsseldorf, 12 Lancasters of 3 Group minelaying in the River Gironde. 1 Lancaster was lost.

Total effort for the night: 334 sorties, 3 aircraft (0·9 per cent) lost.

20/21 June 1943

FRIEDRICHSHAFEN

60 Lancasters to attack the Zeppelin works at Friedrichshafen, on the shores of Lake Constance (the Bodensee). This factory made *Würzburg* radar sets which were an important part of the German-fighter interception boxes through which Bomber Command had to fly every time they attacked a target in Germany.

This was a special raid with interesting and novel tactics. Like the recent Dams Raid, the attack was to be 'controlled' by the pilot of one of the Lancasters. This feature would later be known as 'the Master Bomber' technique. The plan was formulated by 5 Group which provided the Master Bomber – Group Captain L. C. Slee – and nearly all of the aircraft involved; the Pathfinders sent 4 Lancasters of 97 Squadron. Group Captain Slee's aircraft developed engine trouble and he handed over to his deputy, Wing Commander G. L. Gomm of 467 Squadron. The attack, like the recent raid on Le Creusot, was intended to be carried out from 5,000 to 10,000 ft in bright moonlight, but the Flak and searchlight defences were very active and Wing Commander Gomm ordered the bombing force to climb a further 5,000 ft. Unfortunately the wind at the new height was stronger than anticipated and this caused difficulties.

The bombing was in 2 parts. The first bombs were aimed at target indicators dropped by one of the Pathfinder aircraft. The second phase was a 'time-and-distance' bombing run from a point on the shores of the lake to the estimated position of the factory. This was a technique which 5 Group was developing. Photographic reconnaissance showed that nearly 10 per cent of the bombs hit the small factory and that much damage was caused there. Nearby factories were also hit. 44 people are known to have been killed in Friedrichshafen.

The bomber force confused the German night fighters waiting for the return over France by flying on in the first shuttle raid to North Africa. No Lancasters were lost.

Minor Operations: 4 Mosquitoes to Berlin and 1 to Düsseldorf, 15 aircraft minelaying off La Pallice and in the River Gironde. 3 O.T.U. sorties. No losses.

21/22 June 1943

KREFELD

705 aircraft – 262 Lancasters, 209 Halifaxes, 117 Stirlings, 105 Wellingtons, 12 Mosquitoes. 44 aircraft – 17 Halifaxes, 9 Lancasters, 9 Wellingtons, 9 Stirlings – were lost, 6·2 per cent of the force. This raid was carried out before the moon period was over and the heavy casualties were mostly caused by night fighters. 12 of the aircraft lost were from the Pathfinders; 35 Squadron lost 6 out of its 19 Halifaxes taking part in the raid.

The raid took place in good visibility and the Pathfinders produced an almost perfect marking effort, ground-markers dropped by *Oboe* Mosquitoes being well backed up by the Pathfinder heavies. 619 aircraft bombed these markers, more than three quarters of them achieving bombing photographs within 3 miles of the centre of Krefeld. 2,306 tons of bombs were dropped. A large area of fire became established and this raged, out of control, for several hours. The whole centre of the city – approximately 47 per cent of the build-up area – was burnt out. The total of 5,517 houses destroyed, quoted in Krefeld's records, was the largest figure so far in the war. 1,056 people were killed and 4,550 were injured. 72,000 people lost their homes; 20,000 of these were billeted upon families in suburbs, 30,000 moved in with relatives or friends and 20,000 were evacuated to other towns.

Minor Operations: 1 Mosquito to Hamborn, 15 O.T.U. sorties. No losses.

22/23 June 1943

MÜLHEIM

557 aircraft – 242 Lancasters, 155 Halifaxes, 93 Stirlings, 55 Wellingtons, 12 Mosquitoes. 35 aircraft – 12 Halifaxes, 11 Stirlings, 8 Lancasters, 4 Wellingtons – lost, 6·3 per cent of the force.

The Pathfinders had to mark this target through a thin layer of stratus cloud but Mülheim's records contain reference to the accuracy of the markers over this medium-sized town and to the ferocity of the ensuing bombing. The now familiar area of fire and temporary breakdown of the fire and rescue services followed. In later stages of the raid, the Pathfinder markers and the bombing moved slightly, into the northern part of the town; this had the effect of cutting all road and telephone communications with the neighbouring town of Oberhausen, with which Mülheim was linked for air-raid purposes. Not even cyclists or motor-cyclists were able to get out of Mülheim; only messengers on foot could get through. The centre and north of Mülheim and the eastern parts of Oberhausen were severely damaged. 578 people were killed and 1,174 were injured in the 2 towns. 1,135 houses were destroyed and 12,637 damaged. Other buildings hit were 41 public buildings, 27 schools, 17 churches and 6 hospitals. The only reference to industry is a general note: 'a large proportion of industries were severely affected'. The post-war British Bombing Survey Unit estimated that this single raid destroyed 64 per cent of the town of Mülheim.

Minor Operations: 4 Mosquitoes each to Berlin and Cologne, 26 O.T.U. sorties. 1 O.T.U. Wellington lost.

Total effort for the night: 591 sorties, 36 aircraft (6·1 per cent) lost.

23/24 June 1943

LA SPEZIA

52 Lancasters from the force which bombed Friedrichshafen 3 nights earlier flew from North Africa, bombed La Spezia, and then flew on to England without loss. Bomber Command claimed damage to an armaments store and an oil depot at La Spezia.

Minor Operations: 3 Mosquitoes each to Cologne and Duisburg, 30 aircraft minelaying off Brittany and Biscay ports. No aircraft lost.

24/25 June 1943

WUPPERTAL

630 aircraft – 251 Lancasters, 171 Halifaxes, 101 Wellingtons, 98 Stirlings, 9 Mosquitoes. 34 aircraft – 10 Halifaxes, 10 Stirlings, 8 Lancasters, 6 Wellingtons – lost, 5·4 per cent of the force.

This attack was aimed at the Elberfeld half of Wuppertal, the Barmen half of the town having been devastated at the end of May. The Pathfinder marking was accurate and the Main Force bombing started well but the creepback became more pronounced than usual. 30 aircraft bombed targets in more western parts of the Ruhr; Wuppertal was at the eastern end of the area. These bombing failures were probably a result of the recent run of intensive operations incurring casualties at a high level. However, much serious damage was again caused to this medium-sized Ruhr town. The post-war British survey estimated that 94 per cent of the Elberfeld part of Wuppertal was destroyed on this night and Wuppertal's own records show that more bombs fell in Elberfeld than had fallen in Barmen on the last raid. 171 industrial premises and approximately 3,000 houses were destroyed; 53 industrial premises and 2,500 houses were severely damaged. Approximately 1,800 people were killed and 2,400 injured.

There was a dramatic incident in Gelsenkirchen, 20 miles north of Wuppertal, when an R.A.F. 4-engined bomber crashed into the hall of a building which had been taken over by the Wehrmacht. The bomber blew up 'with a terrific explosion'. A German officer, 13 soldiers, the caretaker of the building and 5 Dutch trainee postal workers were killed and 2 more soldiers died later.

24 (a and b). A shot-down Wellington on a hillside above Hagen, in the Ruhr, with the bodies of at least two crew members trapped in the wreckage.

Minor Operations: 4 Mosquitoes to Duisburg, 4 Stirlings minelaying in the River Gironde, 7 O.T.U. sorties. No losses.

25/26 June 1943

GELSENKIRCHEN

473 aircraft – 214 Lancasters, 134 Halifaxes, 73 Stirlings, 40 Wellingtons, 12 Mosquitoes. This was the first raid to Gelsenkirchen since 1941, when it had been one of Bomber Command's regular 'oil targets', although, being in the middle of the Ruhr, this town had often been hit when other targets were attacked. 30 aircraft – 13 Lancasters, 7 Halifaxes, 6 Stirlings, 4 Wellingtons – were lost, 6·3 per cent of the force.

The target was obscured by cloud and the *Oboe* Mosquitoes, for once, failed to produce regular and accurate marking since 5 of the 12 *Oboe* aircraft found that their equipment was unserviceable. The raid was not a success. Düsseldorf reports 24 buildings destroyed and 3,285 damaged but 2,937 of these suffered only superficial blast damage. 20 industrial premises were hit and 4 of them suffered total production loss but no large fires were involved and the loss in production lasted for no longer than 2 weeks. 16 people were killed.

Bombs probably fell on many other Ruhr towns. Solingen, nearly 30 miles from Gelsenkirchen, recorded 21 people killed and 58 injured on this night.

33 aircraft were sent minelaying in the Frisians and off French ports. 1 Lancaster lost.

26/27 June 1943

MINOR OPERATIONS

4 Mosquitoes to Hamburg, 3 Mosquitoes to Duisburg, 16 Wellingtons minelaying off Lorient and Brest, 14 O.T.U. sorties. 1 Wellington minelayer lost.

27/28 June 1943

MINOR OPERATIONS

15 Lancasters and 15 Stirlings minelaying in the Frisians, off La Pallice and in the River Gironde, 4 O.T.U. sorties. 1 Lancaster minelayer lost.

28/29 June 1943

COLOGNE

608 aircraft – 267 Lancasters, 169 Halifaxes, 85 Wellingtons, 75 Stirlings, 12 Mosquitoes. 25 aircraft – 10 Halifaxes, 8 Lancasters, 5 Stirlings, 2 Wellingtons – lost, 4·1 per cent of the force.

The circumstances of this raid did not seem promising. The weather forecast said that Cologne would probably be cloud-covered although there might be a break; the Pathfinders had to prepare a dual plan. The target was cloud-covered and the less reliable sky-marking system had to be employed. Only 7 of the 12 *Oboe* Mosquitoes reached the target and only 6 of these were able to drop their markers. The marking was 7 minutes late in starting and proceeded only intermittently. Despite all these setbacks, the Main Force delivered its most powerful blow of the Battle of the Ruhr. The result was Cologne's worst raid of the war. 43 industrial, 6 military and 6,368 other buildings were destroyed; nearly 15,000 other buildings were damaged. Listed as 'completely destroyed' were: 24 schools, 16 churches, 15 major administrative buildings, 11 hotels, 8 cinemas, 7 post offices, 6 large banks, 2 hospitals and 2 theatres. The cathedral was seriously damaged by high-explosive bombs.

The casualties in Cologne were 4,377 people killed, approximately 10,000 injured and 230,000 forced to leave their damaged homes. The number of dead was greater than in any previous Bomber Command raid of the war on any target. The 'number of dead' record had thus increased nearly tenfold since the opening of the Battle of the Ruhr 3½ months earlier.

Minor Operations: 4 Mosquitoes to Hamburg, 6 Stirlings minelaying in the River Gironde. No losses.

29/30 June 1943

16 Wellingtons were sent to lay mines off Lorient and St-Nazaire. 1 aircraft lost.

1/2 July 1943

MINOR OPERATIONS

12 Lancasters minelaying in the Frisian Islands, 25 O.T.U. sorties. No aircraft lost.

2/3 July 1943

MINOR OPERATIONS

3 Mosquitoes to Cologne, 2 Mosquitoes to Duisburg, 32 aircraft minelaying in the Frisians and off Brittany ports. No aircraft lost.

3/4 July 1943

COLOGNE

653 aircraft – 293 Lancasters, 182 Halifaxes, 89 Wellingtons, 76 Stirlings, 13 Mosquitoes. 30 aircraft – 9 Halifaxes, 8 Lancasters, 8 Wellingtons, 5 Stirlings – lost, 4·6 per cent of the force.

The aiming point for this raid was that part of Cologne situated on the east bank of the Rhine. Much industry was located there. Pathfinder ground marking was accurately maintained by both the Mosquito *Oboe* aircraft and the backers-up, allowing the Main Force to carry out another heavy attack on Cologne. 20 industrial premises and 2,200 houses were completely destroyed. 588 people were killed, approximately 1,000 were injured and 72,000 bombed out.

This night saw the first operations of a new German unit, *Jagdgeschwader* 300, equipped with single-engined fighters using the *Wilde Sau* (Wild Boar) technique. In this, a German pilot used any form of illumination available over a city being bombed – searchlights, target indicators, the glow of fires on the ground – to pick out a bomber for attack. Liaison with the local Flak defences was supposed to ensure that the Flak was limited to a certain height above which the Wild Boar fighter was free to operate. R.A.F. crews were not used to meeting German fighters over a target city and it was some time before the presence of the new danger was realized. The reports on this night from 4 bombers that they had been fired on over the target by other bombers were almost certainly the result of Wild Boar attacks. The new German unit claimed 12 bombers shot down over Cologne but had to share the 12 available aircraft found to have crashed with the local Flak, who also claimed 12 successes.

Minor Operations: 4 Mosquitoes to Duisburg and 4 to Hamburg, 14 Stirlings minelaying in the Frisians. 2 Stirlings lost.

4/5 July 1943

MINOR OPERATIONS

3 Mosquitoes to Duisburg, 13 Stirlings minelaying off La Pallice and in the River Gironde, 4 O.T.U. sorties. No aircraft lost.

5/6 July 1943

MINOR OPERATIONS

4 Mosquitoes to Cologne and 4 to Hamburg, 34 aircraft minelaying off French ports and in the Frisians, 18 O.T.U. sorties. 1 Stirling and 1 Wellington lost from the minelaying force.

6/7 July 1943

MINOR OPERATIONS

4 Mosquitoes to Cologne and 3 to Düsseldorf, 36 aircraft minelaying off Biscay ports. 1 Lancaster minelayer lost.

7/8 July 1943

4 Mosquitoes to Cologne and 4 Mosquitoes to Düsseldorf. No losses.

8/9 July 1943

COLOGNE

282 Lancasters and 6 Mosquitoes of 1, 5 and 8 Groups. 7 Lancasters lost, 2·5 per cent of the force.

The *Oboe* sky-marking was accurate and another successful raid followed, the north-western and south-western sections of the city being the worst hit. 19 industrial and 2,381 domestic buildings were destroyed in areas which had not been severely bombed until now. 502 civilians were killed but the fatalities at a prisoner-of-war camp and an artillery barracks which were both heavily bombed are not known. A further 48,000 people were bombed out, making a total of 350,000 people losing their homes during this series of 3 raids in 1 week.

Minor Operations: 8 Mosquitoes to Duisburg, 46 aircraft minelaying off Texel, Brittany and the Biscay coast, 27 O.T.U. sorties. 1 Wellington minelayer lost.

Total effort for the night: 364 sorties, 8 aircraft (2·2 per cent) lost.

9/10 July 1943

GELSENKIRCHEN

418 aircraft – 218 Lancasters, 190 Halifaxes, 10 Mosquitoes. 12 aircraft – 7 Halifaxes and 5 Lancasters – lost, 2·9 per cent of the force.

This raid was not successful. The *Oboe* equipment failed to operate in 5 of the Mosquitoes and a 6th Mosquito dropped sky-markers in error 10 miles north of the target. Gelsenkirchen reports that its southern districts were bombed and assumed that the main raid was on the neighbouring towns of Bochum and Wattenscheid, also to the south, which received many more bombs than did Gelsenkirchen. Gelsenkirchen itself suffered 10 industrial firms hit, including the all-important synthetic-oil refinery at Scholven, but damage in all places was only light. 41 people died in Gelsenkirchen.

Minor Operations: 4 Mosquitoes to Nordstern, 18 aircraft minelaying in the Frisians and off Texel. No losses.

12/13 July 1943

TURIN

295 Lancasters of 1, 5 and 8 Groups. 13 Lancasters lost, 4·4 per cent of the force.

The main weight of this raid fell just north of the centre of Turin in clear weather conditions. The only report obtainable from Italy states that 792 people were killed and 914 injured. This was Turin's highest number of air-raid fatalities during the 10 raids made on the city by Bomber Command during the war.

Among the R.A.F. casualties on this night was Wing Commander J. D. Nettleton, commander of 44 (Rhodesia) Squadron, who had won the Victoria Cross for the low-level daylight raid on Augsburg in April 1942. Nettleton's Lancaster was shot down by a German night fighter over the Channel while returning from Turin. He and his crew all died and their names are on the Runnymede Memorial.

Minor Operations: 22 Wellingtons minelaying off Brest, Lorient and St-Nazaire, 19 O.T.U. sorties. No losses.

13/14 July 1943

AACHEN

374 aircraft – 214 Halifaxes, 76 Wellingtons, 55 Stirlings, 18 Lancasters, 11 Mosquitoes; 5 Group did not take part in this raid. 20 aircraft – 15 Halifaxes, 2 Lancasters, 2 Wellingtons, 1 Stirling – lost, 5·3 per cent of the force.

A strong tail wind brought the first waves of the Main Force into the target area before Zero Hour with the result that, when the first Pathfinder markers were released, an unusually large number of aircraft bombed in the first minutes of the raid. The visibility was good and large areas of Aachen appeared to burst into flame at once. In the words of the report from Aachen, 'A *Terrorangriff* of the most severe scale was delivered.'* 2,927 individual buildings were destroyed. These contained 16,828 flats/apartments and there was the familiar list of public and cultural buildings hit. Among those classed as severely damaged were the cathedral, the Rathaus, the town theatre, the police headquarters, the local prison, the main post office, two infantry barracks and an army food depot, and 8 large industrial premises including an aero-engine factory, a rubber factory, a tyre factory and a wagon works. 294 people were killed and 745 injured and 28,500 people appear to have fled the town and were still absent when new ration cards were issued nearly 7 weeks later.

Minor Operations: 2 *Oboe* Mosquitoes carried out a diversion for the Aachen raid by dropping target indicators over Cologne. 8 O.T.U. Wellingtons carried out leaflet flights to France. 1 Wellington crashed in the sea.

14/15 July 1943

8 Mosquitoes carried out a nuisance raid on Berlin. 1 aircraft crashed in the sea.

15/16 July 1943

MONTBÉLIARD

165 Halifaxes – 134 from 4 Group and 31 from 8 Group – to attack the Peugeot motor factory in the Montbéliard suburb of the French town of Sochaux, near the Swiss border. 5 Halifaxes were lost, 3·0 per cent of the force.

The outcome of this raid illustrates again the difficulties of hitting relatively small targets in the occupied countries and the danger to surrounding civilians. The night was clear, the target was only lightly defended and the attack altitude was 6,000 to 10,000 ft, but the centre of the group of markers dropped by the Pathfinder crews of 35 Squadron was 700 yards beyond the factory. The local report says that approximately 30 bombs fell in the factory but 600 fell in the town. 123 civilians were killed and 336 injured. The factory was classed as 5 per cent damaged; the production was normal immediately after the raid.

617 Squadron carried out its first operation since the Dams Raid in May. It had been decided to keep the squadron in being and to use it for independent precision raids

* Report from Hubert Beckers, private archivist in Aachen.

25 (a and b). An early night raid on a target in France, the Peugeot motor factory at Montbéliard. Most of the bombs missed the factory and the French dead are taken to their funeral on new trucks from the factory.

on small targets. It remained in 5 Group and most of its replacement crews came from the squadrons of that group.

The targets on this night were two electrical-transformer stations in Northern Italy – one near Bologna and the other near Genoa. The intention was to disrupt the supply of electricity to the railways carrying German troops and supplies to the battle front in Sicily. 12 Lancasters of 617 Squadron were joined by 12 further 5 Group Lancasters for these attacks, which were not successful. No flares or markers were carried and the targets were partially hidden by mist. After bombing, the Lancasters flew on to North Africa. 2 Lancasters of the supporting force were lost.

6 Mosquitoes flew on a nuisance raid to Munich but only 2 aircraft actually reached the target. No aircraft lost.

16/17 July 1943

MINOR OPERATIONS

18 Lancasters of 5 Group attempted raids on two more transformer stations in Northern Italy. 7 aircraft bombed the Cislago station accurately but the second target was not located and an alternative target was bombed instead. 1 Lancaster lost. 6 Mosquitoes bombed Munich and 7 O.T.U. Wellingtons dropped leaflets over French towns without loss.

17/18 July 1943

4 O.T.U. Wellingtons dropped leaflets over France without loss.

18/19 July 1943

16 Wellingtons of 1 Group laid mines off Lorient and St-Nazaire without loss.

23/24 July 1945

7 O.T.U. Wellingtons dropped leaflets over France without loss.

Operational Statistics, 5/6 March to 24 July 1943
(141 days/nights)

Number of nights with operations: 99
Number of days with operations: 55 (there were no day operations after 2 Group left Bomber Command on 31 May)
Number of night sorties: 23,401, from which 1,000 aircraft (4·3 per cent) were lost
Number of daylight sorties: 954, from which 38 aircraft (4·0 per cent) were lost
Total sorties: 24,355, from which 1,038 aircraft (4·3 per cent) were lost
Approximate bomb tonnage in period: 57,034 tons
Averages per 24-hour period: 172·7 sorties, 7·4 aircraft lost, 404·5 tons of bombs dropped

15. THE BATTLE OF HAMBURG

24/25 July to 3 August 1943

Sir Arthur Harris had decided upon his next step well before the Battle of the Ruhr was over. As early as 27 May, he had circulated an order* to his group commanders to start preparing for a series of heavy raids on Hamburg – Europe's largest port and the second largest city in Germany, with one and three-quarter million people. Bomber Command had attacked this target ninety-eight times so far in the war. But Hamburg had twice missed being the target for 1,000-bomber raids in 1942 and it had never been seriously hit as had Cologne and many of the Ruhr communities. Harris felt that the time was now ripe for this target to receive the full attentions of Bomber Command.

Hamburg was well beyond the range of *Oboe* but the city was theoretically a good *H2S* target. The important factors were a distinctively shaped coastline only 60 miles away on which the Pathfinders could make accurate landfalls after their long sea crossing, and the wide River Elbe and Hamburg's dock basins which should show up well on the *H2S* screens. The aiming points and approach routes for the coming raids would all be chosen so that the now familiar creepback would fall across various sections of the main residential areas of this huge city which were on the north bank of the Elbe. Hamburg was a famous shipyard city; the battleship *Bismarck* – now at the bottom of the Atlantic – and at least 200 U-boats had already been built there. But the port and shipbuilding areas, which were on the south bank of the Elbe, were not to be targets in the coming raids. It was hoped to slow down production by the indirect means of crippling the general life of the city.

For the first time, the heavy daylight bombers of the American Eighth Air Force were invited to join directly in with a Bomber Command 'battle'. B-17 Fortresses would fly 252 sorties in the two days immediately following the first R.A.F. night raid. The American targets were all industrial and included the U-boat yards. But the American effort would run into difficulties, mainly caused by the dense smoke from the fires started by the R.A.F. bombing still obscuring their targets. The Americans quickly withdrew from the Battle of Hamburg and were not keen to follow immediately on the heels of R.A.F. raids, in future, because of the smoke problem.

This diary shows that Sir Arthur Harris directed four major raids on Hamburg in the space of ten nights. A total of 3,091 sorties were flown and nearly 10,000 tons of bombs dropped, though not all of these would hit Hamburg. Because of the firestorm which developed in the city on the second R.A.F. raid, it is often suggested

*Public Record Office A I R 24/257.

that Bomber Command carried an unusually high proportion of incendiary bombs in these attacks and was launching 'firestorm raids'. This was not true. Just under half the total tonnage dropped on Hamburg was incendiary, a proportion which was actually lower than on many of the recent Ruhr raids. It cannot be stressed too strongly that the raids to be carried out against Hamburg at this time were no more than Bomber Command's normal area attacks for this period of the bombing war. The Hamburg firestorm was caused by other, unexpected, factors which will be described later.

There was, however, one major tactical innovation in the Battle of Hamburg – a device which enabled the bombers to pass through the German defences and to reach Hamburg in greater safety and numbers. This was *Window*, strips of coarse black paper exactly 27 centimetres long and 2 centimetres wide with thin aluminium foil stuck to one side of the strips. It had been proved in trials that, if sufficient of these were released by a force of bombers, the German *Würzburg* radar sets on the ground which controlled both the night-fighter interceptions and the radar-laid Flak guns, as well as the smaller airborne *Lichtenstein* radar sets which the night-fighter crews used for their final part of the bomber interception process, would be swamped by false echoes and rendered virtually useless. *Window* had been ready since April 1942 but Bomber Command had not been allowed to use it for fear that the Luftwaffe would copy it and use it in raids against England. It was a bad decision. The Luftwaffe was mainly in Russia at this time and the weak German raids on England had been of only the most minor nature compared with the Bomber Command night offensive against Germany. Bomber Command lost 2,200 aircraft during the *Window* embargo period, a large proportion of them to German radar-assisted defences. *Window* was released in time for Bomber Command to use it for the Battle of Hamburg and would be carried by R.A.F. bombers for the remainder of the war. It can be estimated that, in the six major raids carried out in the ten nights of operations which comprised the Battle of Hamburg, *Window* saved 100–130 Bomber Command aircraft which would otherwise have been lost. The German defensive system was rendered obsolete at a stroke, although they started to recover and reorganize remarkably quickly and it will be shown later that, in one respect, the introduction of *Window* would be beneficial for the Germans.*

24/25 July 1943

HAMBURG

791 aircraft – 347 Lancasters, 246 Halifaxes, 125 Stirlings, 73 Wellingtons. 12 aircraft – 4 Halifaxes, 4 Lancasters, 3 Stirlings, 1 Wellington – lost, 1·5 per cent of the force.

Window was used for the first time on this night. Conditions over Hamburg were clear with only a gentle wind. The marking – a mixture of *H2S* and visual – was a little scattered but most of the target indicators fell near enough to the centre of Hamburg for a concentrated raid to develop quickly. 728 aircraft dropped 2,284 tons of bombs in 50 minutes. Bombing photographs showed that less than half of the

* A full description of the four R.A.F. and two U.S.A.A.F. raids on Hamburg, and of the introduction of *Window* and its effect upon the German defences, is contained in Martin Middlebrook's *The Battle of Hamburg*, London, Allen Lane, 1980; New York, Scribner's, 1981; and, as *Hamburg Juli '43*, Berlin, Ullstein, 1983.

force bombed within 3 miles of the centre of Hamburg and a creepback 6 miles long developed. But, because Hamburg was such a large city, severe damage was caused in the central and north-western districts, particularly in Altona, Eimsbüttel and Hohe-luft. The Rathaus, the Nikolaikirche, the main police station, the main telephone exchange and the Hagenbeck Zoo (where 140 animals died) were among the well-known Hamburg landmarks to be hit. Approximately 1,500 people were killed. This was the greatest number of people killed so far in a raid outside the area in which *Oboe* could be used.

26. The women of Hamburg after a raid.

LEGHORN

33 Lancasters of 5 Group returning from North Africa bombed Leghorn docks but the target was covered by haze and bombing was scattered. No aircraft lost.

Minor Operations: 13 Mosquitoes carried out diversionary and nuisance raids to Bremen, Kiel, Lübeck and Duisburg; 6 Wellingtons laid mines in the River Elbe while the Hamburg raid was in progress and there were 7 O.T.U. sorties. No aircraft lost.

25/26 July 1943

ESSEN

705 aircraft – 294 Lancasters, 221 Halifaxes, 104 Stirlings, 67 Wellingtons, 19 Mosquitoes. 26 aircraft – 10 Halifaxes, 7 Stirlings, 5 Lancasters, 4 Wellingtons – lost, 3·7 per cent of the force. The commander of the American VIII Bomber Command, Brigadier-General Fred Anderson, observed this raid as a passenger in an 83 Squadron Lancaster.

This was an attempt to achieve a good raid on this major target while the effects of *Window* were still fresh. The raid was successful, with particular damage being recorded in Essen's industrial areas in the eastern half of the city. The Krupps works suffered what was probably its most damaging raid of the war. The next morning, Doktor Gustav Krupp had a stroke from which he never recovered; this saved him from being charged with war crimes after the war.* 51 other industrial buildings were destroyed and 83 seriously damaged. 2,852 houses were destroyed. 500 people were killed, 12 were missing and 1,208 were injured. The 500 dead are recorded as follows: 165 civilian men, 118 women, 22 children, 22 servicemen, 131 foreign workers and 42 prisoners of war.

Minor Operations: 6 Mosquitoes to Hamburg and 3 each to Cologne and Gelsenkirchen, 17 aircraft minelaying in the Frisians, 7 O.T.U. sorties. No losses.

26/27 July 1943

Minor Operations

6 Mosquitoes to Hamburg, 3 O.T.U. sorties. No losses.

27/28 July 1943

HAMBURG

787 aircraft – 353 Lancasters, 244 Halifaxes, 116 Stirlings, 74 Wellingtons. 17 aircraft – 11 Lancasters, 4 Halifaxes, 1 Stirling, 1 Wellington – lost, 2·2 per cent of the force. The American commander, Brigadier-General Anderson, again flew in a Lancaster and watched this raid.

The centre of the Pathfinder marking – all carried out by *H2S* on this night – was about 2 miles east of the planned aiming point in the centre of the city, but the marking was particularly well concentrated and the Main Force bombing 'crept back' only slightly. 729 aircraft dropped 2,326 tons of bombs.

This was the night of the firestorm, which started through an unusual and unexpected chain of events. The temperature was particularly high (30° centigrade at 6 o'clock in the evening) and the humidity was only 30 per cent, compared with an average of 40–50 per cent for this time of the year. There had been no rain for some time and everything was very dry. The concentrated bombing caused a large number of fires in the densely built-up working-class districts of Hammerbrook, Hamm and Borgfeld. Most of Hamburg's fire vehicles had been in the western parts of the city, damping down the fires still smouldering there from the raid of 3 nights earlier, and only a few units were able to pass through roads which were blocked by the rubble of buildings destroyed by high-explosive bombs early in this raid. About half-way through the raid, the fires in Hammerbrook started joining together and competing with each other for the oxygen in the surrounding air. Suddenly, the whole area became one big fire with air being drawn into it with the force of a storm. The bombing continued for another half hour, spreading the firestorm area gradually eastwards. It is estimated that 550–600 bomb loads fell into an area measuring only 2 miles by 1 mile. The firestorm raged for about 3 hours and only subsided when all burnable material was consumed.

---

*The Doktor Krupps incident is taken from Philip Moyes's *Bomber Squadrons of the R.A.F. and Their Aircraft*, Macdonald, 1964, p. 348.

27. Hamburg. Some of the dead, caught in the open street during the firestorm.

The burnt-out area was almost entirely residential. Approximately 16,000 multi-storeyed apartment buildings were destroyed. There were few survivors from the firestorm area and approximately 40,000 people died, most of them by carbon monoxide poisoning when all the air was drawn out of their basement shelters. In the period immediately following this raid, approximately 1,200,000 people – two thirds of Hamburg's population – fled the city in fear of further raids.

Minor Operations: 3 Mosquitoes to Duisburg, 6 Wellingtons minelaying in the River Elbe, 11 O.T.U. sorties. 1 Mosquito lost.

28/29 July 1943

MINOR OPERATIONS

4 Mosquitoes to Hamburg and 3 to Düsseldorf, 17 aircraft minelaying in the Frisian Islands, 4 O.T.U. sorties. No aircraft lost.

29/30 July 1943

HAMBURG

777 aircraft – 340 Lancasters, 244 Halifaxes, 119 Stirlings, 70 Wellingtons, 4 Mosquitoes. 28 aircraft – 11 Halifaxes, 11 Lancasters, 4 Stirlings, 2 Wellingtons – lost, 3·6 per cent of the force.

The marking for this raid was again all by *H2S*. The intention was to approach Hamburg from almost due north and bomb those northern and north-eastern districts which had so far not been bombed. The Pathfinders actually came in more than 2 miles too far to the east and marked an area just south of the devastated firestorm area. The Main Force bombing crept back about 4 miles, through the devastated area, but then produced very heavy bombing in the Wandsbek and Barmbek districts and parts of the Uhlenhorst and Winterhude districts. These were all residential areas. 707 aircraft dropped 2,318 tons of bombs. There was a widespread fire area – though no firestorm – which the exhausted Hamburg fire units could do little to check. The worst incident was in the shelter of a large department store in Wandsbek. The building collapsed and blocked the exits from the shelter which was in the basement of the store. 370 people died, poisoned by carbon monoxide fumes from a burning coke store near by.

Minor Operations: 4 Mosquitoes to Düsseldorf, 6 Wellingtons minelaying in the River Elbe, 9 Lancasters of 617 Squadron dropping leaflets over Italian cities, 3 O.T.U. sorties. No aircraft lost.

30/31 July 1943

REMSCHEID

273 aircraft – 95 Halifaxes, 87 Stirlings, 82 Lancasters, 9 Mosquitoes – were dispatched to this previously unbombed town on the southern edge of the Ruhr; only 26 people had been killed in Remscheid, by stray bombs, in the last 3 years. This raid marks the true end of the Battle of the Ruhr. 15 aircraft – 8 Stirlings, 5 Halifaxes, 2 Lancasters – were lost, 5·5 per cent of the force.

The *Oboe* ground-marking and the bombing of the comparatively small Main Force were exceptionally accurate and this was a most successful raid. Only 871 tons of bombs were dropped but the post-war British Bombing Survey estimated that 83 per cent of the town was devastated. 107 industrial buildings were destroyed; the town's industry, generally, lost 3 months' production and never fully regained previous levels. 3,115 houses were destroyed. 1,120 people were killed and 6,700 were injured.

8 aircraft laid mines in the Frisian Islands without loss.

1/2 August 1943

15 Stirlings and 14 Wellingtons laid mines off French Biscay ports without loss.

2/3 August 1943

HAMBURG

740 aircraft – 329 Lancasters, 235 Halifaxes, 105 Stirlings, 66 Wellingtons, 5 Mosquitoes. 30 aircraft – 13 Lancasters, 10 Halifaxes, 4 Wellingtons, 3 Stirlings – lost, 4·1 per cent of the force.

The bombing force encountered a large thunderstorm area over Germany and the raid was a failure. Many crews turned back early or bombed alternative targets. At least 4 aircraft, probably more, were lost because of icing, turbulence or were struck by lightning. No Pathfinder marking was possible at Hamburg and only scattered bombing took place there. Many other towns in a 100-mile area of Northern Germany received a few bombs. A sizeable raid developed on the small town of Elmshorn, 12 miles from Hamburg. It is believed that a flash of lightning set a house on fire here and bomber crews saw this through a gap in the storm clouds and started to bomb the fire. 254 houses were destroyed in Elmshorn and 57 people were killed, some of them refugees from recent raids on Hamburg.

Minor Operations: 5 Mosquitoes to Duisburg, 6 Wellingtons minelaying in the River Elbe, 12 O.T.U. sorties. 1 Wellington minelayer lost.

Operational Statistics, 24/25 July to 3 August 1943
(10 days/nights)

Number of nights with operations: 9
Number of night sorties: 4,307, from which 130 aircraft (3·0 per cent) were lost
Approximate bomb tonnage in period: 10,815 tons
Averages per 24-hour period: 430·7 sorties, 13·0 aircraft lost, 1,081·5 tons of bombs dropped

16. THE ROAD TO BERLIN

3/4 August to 18 November 1943

Bomber Command pressed on vigorously during the remainder of August and that month would prove to be the most active in 1943. There was a period of good weather and every advantage was taken of the shattering effect *Window* had on the German defences. Much of the month was taken up with a series of raids which Bomber Command was ordered to carry out against Italian cities in order to hasten the exit of Italy from the war. This policy succeeded and Italy surrendered to the Allies on 8 September, although the Germans remained in Italy and contested the Allied landings in the south which started on 3 September. It should not be forgotten that the bombing of the Italian cities was a major factor in forcing this enemy country out of the war.

There was a respite for the bomber squadrons during the moon period in the third week of August, although Sir Arthur Harris took advantage of the moon to risk the special raid on the German rocket-research establishment at Peenemünde which he had been ordered to make. Then, at the end of the month, Harris launched what was probably intended to be the opening of his next battle – the Battle of Berlin. He was prepared to devote several months to this next offensive. He started with three raids in the twelve nights between 23 August and 4 September. But this opening effort produced disappointing results. The concentration of bombing was not comparable with the recent results in Hamburg and bomber casualties were heavy. From the 1,669 sorties dispatched 125 aircraft were lost, a rate of 7·5 per cent. Inland Berlin did not prove to be a good *H2S* target and the German defences were clearly recovering from the setback of *Window*.

Harris decided to draw back from Berlin. An improved version of *H2S* was in the pipeline and should reach the Pathfinders in a few weeks and another navigational aid called the Ground Position Indicator was also due to come into use soon. The arrival of these aids later in the year would also coincide with the nights of deeper and longer darkness. There followed a two-month period in which the bombers were still sent out whenever possible, but to what might be termed intermediate targets in Germany – important cities, usually beyond the range of *Oboe*, but not as fiercely defended as Berlin. In particular, there was a substantial effort against Hannover, which was raided four times, as many aircraft being used as had been dispatched on the first three raids which had devastated Hamburg. But Hannover was another inland target which did not show up well on the *H2S* sets and only one of the raids achieved a limited success. Altogether 110 bombers were lost in these raids to Hannover.

There was a major change in the shape of Bomber Command during this period. That veteran pre-war aircraft, the Wellington, finally disappeared from the Main Force. This dependable and much-loved aircraft had flown continually on Bomber

Command operations since the first day of the war four years earlier. Its contribution to the command's offensive cannot be praised too highly. Some of the Wellington squadrons would remain in Bomber Command until well into 1944 but only flying limited operations, mainly minelaying.

Bomber Command's overall strength remained static during this period; the heady days of expansion earlier in 1943 were over. There was some gradual progress in modernization. 3 Group and 6 Group started to equip some of their Stirling and Halifax squadrons with the Hercules-engined Mark II version of the Lancaster (115 Squadron of 3 Group had actually received their Lancasters earlier in the year), but production of this version was only limited. The more popular Merlin-engined Lancasters were still pouring off the assembly lines but the need to replace battle casualties and worn-out aircraft in the existing Lancaster squadrons meant that the conversion of other squadrons proceeded only slowly.

A number of new devices were introduced during the period but none of them were of a revolutionary nature. The operational trials of a promising new blind-bombing device called *G-H* were carried out by Mosquitoes in October and by Lancasters in November. These trials were successful and the device was withdrawn until enough sets could be provided to equip a larger force. This would not be until 1944 and a description of the device will be left until a later section of the diary. Two new radio-countermeasures systems came into operation. *Corona* was the code-name for the ground listening and broadcasting stations in England from which R.A.F. men and women who were fluent German speakers attempted, often successfully, to imitate the German fighter controllers and broadcast false instructions to the night fighters. *A.B.C.* (*Airborne Cigar*) was a jamming device fitted into the Lancasters of 101 Squadron, 1 Group, with which an extra German-speaking crew member attempted to jam the German voice transmissions. The *A.B.C.* aircraft also carried bomb loads and they formed part of the normal bomber stream to targets. Both devices were introduced in October and they were further illustrations of the growing complexity of the bombing war.

Yet another sign of this was an extension of the 'diversion raid' tactic. Mosquitoes of 8 Group had been carrying out this type of operation for some weeks, attempting to draw the Luftwaffe's attention away from Bomber Command's main target by dropping flares and target indicators over other cities. But there were too few Mosquitoes available for this task and it was apparent that the Germans were rarely fooled. With the growing mobility of the German night-fighter force, after *Window* had rendered the box system obsolete, it was becoming important to conceal the identity of the main target for as long as possible. For this reason, Bomber Command now started flying diversionary raids – sometimes called 'spoofs' – by small forces of ordinary bombers in an attempt to deceive the German controllers. This was an escalation of a trend which was drawing Bomber Command planners away from the principle of concentration that had served so well in the past year and a half. The coming year of the bombing war would see a steady weakening of the main effort in this way.

There was one more innovation. On the night of 8/9 September, five B-17 Fortresses of the 422nd Bomb Squadron, part of the 305th Bombardment Group of the American Eighth Air Force, joined in a Bomber Command night raid on German gun positions near Boulogne. This was undoubtedly an experiment initiated by Brigadier-General Fred Anderson, the American bomber commander who had recently taken part in R.A.F. raids to Essen and Hamburg, flying in a Lancaster. The Eighth Air Force had suffered severe losses in their first deep penetration raids into Germany and Anderson was allowing a handful of his B-17s to experiment with night-bombing operations, perhaps with a view to devoting a part of his force to the night offensive in which the British had always urged the Americans to join. The 422nd Squadron participated in seven further raids with Bomber Command, five of them to German cities; thirty-five B-17 sorties were dispatched altogether and two aircraft were lost. These flights ended early in October and, although 422nd Squadron continued to fly leaflet operations by night until the end of the war, it never returned to night bombing and was not joined by other American bomber units.

3/4 August 1943

12 Wellingtons of 6 Group minelaying off Lorient and St-Nazaire without loss.

4/5 August 1943

5 Mosquitoes bombed the estimated positions of Cologne and Duisburg through cloud. No losses.

5/6 August 1943

5 Mosquitoes, out of 8 dispatched, bombed Duisburg and Düsseldorf without loss.

6/7 August 1943

MINOR OPERATIONS

8 Mosquitoes to Cologne and Duisburg, 20 Stirlings and 14 Wellingtons minelaying south of Texel and off Brest and the Biscay ports, 13 O.T.U. sorties. 2 Stirling minelayers were lost.

7/8 August 1943

ITALY

In response to urgent political orders, 197 Lancasters of 1, 5 and 8 Groups were dispatched to attack Genoa, Milan and Turin. It is believed that every aircraft reached the target area; 195 crews returned and reported bombing; 2 aircraft were lost. Group Captain J. H. Searby, of 83 Squadron, acted as Master Bomber for the bombing at Turin but with only limited success. This was a trial in preparation for the role he would play in the raid on Peenemünde later in the month.

The only report available from Italy says that 20 people were killed and 79 were injured in Turin.

4 Mosquitoes bombed Cologne and 1 bombed Düsseldorf. No losses.

9/10 August 1943

MANNHEIM

457 aircraft – 286 Lancasters and 171 Halifaxes. 9 aircraft – 6 Halifaxes and 3 Lancasters – lost, 2·0 per cent of the force.

The target area was mainly cloud-covered and the Pathfinder plan did not work well. The resulting bombing appeared to be scattered. Mannheim, whose wartime officials must have produced some of the best air-raid reports in Germany, sent 37 typed pages of details which showed that this raid caused considerable damage in and around the city. 1,316 buildings were classed as 'totally destroyed' or 'seriously damaged'. 42 industrial concerns, some of them being quite large ones, suffered loss of production. The compensation claims for 9 of the factories totalled 43,815,000 Reichsmarks (£4,381,500). 269 people were killed and 1,210 were injured. There were 1,528 fires: 133 large, 417 medium-sized and 978 small fires. 8 railway engines, 146 passenger carriages and 40 goods wagons were damaged. 144 farm animals were killed: 96 pigs, 18 goats, 15 cows, 12 horses, 2 oxen and a calf.

It is a measure of the increased striking power of Bomber Command that all of the damage and casualties quoted above was caused by a medium-sized raid which is described in the Bomber Command Operations Record Book as 'a scattered attack'.

Minor Operations: 6 Mosquitoes to Duisburg, 10 Stirlings minelaying in the Frisians, 14 O.T.U. sorties. No aircraft lost.

10/11 August 1943

NUREMBERG

653 aircraft – 318 Lancasters, 216 Halifaxes, 119 Stirlings. 16 aircraft – 7 Halifaxes, 6 Lancasters, 3 Stirlings – lost, 2·5 per cent of the force.

The Pathfinders attempted to ground-mark the city and, although their markers were mostly obscured by cloud, a useful attack developed in the central and southern parts of Nuremberg. The Lorenzkirche, the largest of the city's old churches, was badly damaged and about 50 of the houses in the preserved *Altstadt* were destroyed. There was a large 'fire area' in the Wöhrd district. Serious property damage – both housing and industrial – was caused and 577 people were killed.

Minor Operations: 9 Mosquitoes to the Ruhr, 18 Wellingtons minelaying off Texel and in the Frisians. No losses.

11/12 August 1943

MINOR OPERATIONS

8 Mosquitoes to Cologne and Duisburg, 23 Wellingtons minelaying off Brest, Lorient and St-Nazaire, 19 O.T.U. sorties. 1 Wellington minelayer was lost and 1 O.T.U. Wellington came down in the sea.

12/13 August 1943

MILAN

504 aircraft – 321 Lancasters and 183 Halifaxes. 2 Halifaxes and 1 Lancaster lost.

Bomber Command considered that this was a successful raid. Milan only provided a general report which stated that, during August 1943, 4 major factories – including the Alfa-Romeo motor works – the main railway station and the La Scala opera house were all badly hit and that 1,174 people died in air raids during 1943. Most of these results probably occurred on this night.

TURIN

152 aircraft of 3 and 8 Groups – 112 Stirlings, 34 Halifaxes, 6 Lancasters. 2 Stirlings lost.

The raid was described by the crews involved as 'heavy and concentrated'. Turin can report only 18 people killed and 83 injured.

Minor Operations: 7 Mosquitoes to Berlin, 24 Wellingtons minelaying off Brittany ports, 9 O.T.U. sorties. 1 Mosquito and 2 Wellington minelayers lost.

Total effort for the night: 696 sorties, 8 aircraft (1·1 per cent) lost.

One of the bravest Victoria Crosses was won on this night. A Stirling of 218 Squadron was badly damaged by a burst of fire while approaching Turin. The navigator was killed and several members of the crew were wounded, including the pilot, Flight Sergeant Arthur Louis Aaron, who was struck in the face by a bullet which shattered his jaw and tore part of his face away; he was also injured in the chest and his right arm could not be used. The flight engineer and the bomb aimer took over the controls of the aircraft and set course for North Africa although one engine was useless, the pilot was out of action, having been dosed with morphia, and the navigator was dead.

The Stirling reached the cost of Africa and Flight Sergeant Aaron insisted on returning to his seat in the cockpit to help prepare for the landing. Twice he tried to take over the controls and, although he had to give up this attempt, he continued to help by writing down instructions for landing with his left hand. He could not speak. Under Aaron's guidance, given in great pain and at the limits of exhaustion, the Stirling landed safely at its fifth attempt at Bône airfield with its wheels up.

Flight Sergeant Aaron died 9 hours later. It was considered that he might have survived if he had rested after having been wounded instead of insisting on helping his crew. The wireless operator, Sergeant T. Guy, and the flight engineer, Sergeant M. Mitcham, were each awarded the Distinguished Flying Medal. It was later established that the machine-gun fire which struck the Stirling was fired by a nervous tail gunner in another bomber. Flight Sergeant Aaron was 21 years old and came from Leeds.

14/15 August 1943

MILAN

140 Lancasters of 1, 5 and 8 Groups carried out another attack on Milan, claiming much further damage. 1 Lancaster lost.

7 Mosquitoes carried out a nuisance raid on Berlin without loss.

15/16 August 1943

MILAN

199 Lancasters continued the offensive against Milan, claiming particularly concentrated bombing. 7 aircraft were lost, mostly to German fighters which were awaiting the bombers' return over France.

Minor Operations: 8 Mosquitoes to Berlin, 63 aircraft minelaying in the Frisians and off Texel and off all the main Brittany and Biscay ports, 16 O.T.U. sorties. 2 Wellingtons and 1 Stirling from the minelaying force were lost.

16/17 August 1943

TURIN

154 aircraft of 3 and 8 Groups – 103 Stirlings, 37 Halifaxes, 14 Lancasters. 4 aircraft – 2 Halifaxes, 1 Lancaster, 1 Stirling – lost.

Crews claimed a concentrated attack on Turin, including damage to the Fiat motor works but the city's casualties were much lower than in recent raids, only 5 dead and 56 injured.

This raid concluded the Bomber Command attacks on Italian cities which had commenced in June 1940.

17/18 August 1943

PEENEMÜNDE

596 aircraft – 324 Lancasters, 218 Halifaxes, 54 Stirlings. This was the first raid in which 6 (Canadian) Group operated Lancaster aircraft. 426 Squadron dispatched 9 Mark II Lancasters, losing 2 aircraft including that of the squadron commander, Wing Commander L. Crooks, D.S.O., D.F.C., an Englishman, who was killed.

This was a special raid which Bomber Command was ordered to carry out against the German research establishment on the Baltic coast where V-2 rockets were being built and tested. The raid was carried out in moonlight to increase the chances of success. There were several novel features. It was the only occasion in the second half of the war when the whole of Bomber Command attempted a precision raid by night on such a small target. For the first time, there was a Master Bomber controlling a full-scale Bomber Command raid; Group Captain J. H. Searby, of 83 Squadron, 8 Group, carried out this task. There were three aiming points – the scientists' and workers' living quarters, the rocket factory and the experimental station – and the Pathfinders employed a special plan with crews designated as 'shifters', who attempted to move the marking from one part of the target to another as the raid progressed. Crews of 5 Group, bombing in the last wave of the attack, had practised the 'time-and-distance' bombing method as an alternative method for their part in the raid.

The Pathfinders found Peenemünde without difficulty in the moonlight and the

28 (a and b). Precision bombing. The V-2 rocket assembly hall and the workers' housing area at Peenemünde.

Master Bomber controlled the raid successfully throughout. A Mosquito diversion to Berlin drew off most of the German night-fighters for the first 2 of the raid's 3 phases. Unfortunately, the initial marking and bombing fell on a labour camp for forced workers which was situated 1½ miles south of the first aiming point, but the Master Bomber and the Pathfinders quickly brought the bombing back to the main targets, which were all bombed successfully. 560 aircraft dropped nearly 1,800 tons of bombs; 85 per cent of this tonnage was high-explosive. The estimate has appeared in many sources that this raid set back the V-2 experimental programme by at least 2 months and reduced the scale of the eventual rocket attack. Approximately 180 Germans were killed at Peenemünde, nearly all in the workers' housing estate, and 500–600 foreigners, mostly Polish, were killed in the workers' camp, where there were only flimsy wooden barracks and no proper air-raid shelters.

Bomber Command's losses were 40 aircraft – 23 Lancasters, 15 Halifaxes and 2 Stirlings. This represents 6·7 per cent of the force dispatched but was judged an acceptable cost for the successful attack on this important target on a moonlit night. Most of the casualties were suffered by the aircraft of the last wave when the German night fighters arrived in force; the groups involved in this were 5 Group, which lost 17 of its 109 aircraft on the raid (14·5 per cent) and the Canadian 6 Group which lost 12 out of 57 aircraft (19·7 per cent). This was the first night on which the Germans used their new *schräge Musik* weapons; these were twin upward-firing cannons fitted in the cockpit of Me 110s. Two *schräge Musik* aircraft found the bomber stream flying home from Peenemünde and are believed to have shot down 6 of the bombers lost on the raid.*

8 Mosquitoes carried out a successful diversion raid on Berlin. 1 aircraft lost.

18/19 August 1943
30 O.T.U. Wellingtons on leaflet raids to France without loss.

19/20 August 1943
8 Mosquitoes to Berlin. 1 aircraft lost.

22/23 August 1943

LEVERKUSEN

462 aircraft – 257 Lancasters, 192 Halifaxes, 13 Mosquitoes. 3 Lancasters and 2 Halifaxes lost, 1·1 per cent of the force.

The I.G. Farben factory at Leverkusen was chosen as the aiming point for this raid and it was hoped that some of the bombs would hit this important place. But the raid was not successful. There was thick cloud over the target area and there was a partial failure of the *Oboe* signals. Bombs fell over a wide area; at least 12 other towns in and near the Ruhr recorded bomb damage. Düsseldorf was the hardest hit of these other places; 132 buildings were destroyed and 644 seriously damaged. Solingen reported 40 people killed and 65 injured.

*For further details on the Peenemünde raid see *The Peenemünde Raid* by Martin Middlebrook, London, Allen Lane, 1982; New York, Bobbs-Merrill, 1983.

Only a few bombs fell in Leverkusen, where 4 people were killed. The I.G. Farben factory received only superficial damage, in the acid department; 5 Germans were injured in the factory and 1 foreign worker was killed.

Minor Operations: 12 Mosquitoes to the Ruhr and 6 to Hamburg, 47 aircraft minelaying in the Frisians and off Texel, 7 O.T.U. sorties. No losses.

23/24 August 1943

BERLIN

727 aircraft – 335 Lancasters, 251 Halifaxes, 124 Stirlings, 17 Mosquitoes. The Mosquitoes were used to mark various points on the route to Berlin in order to help keep the Main Force on the correct track. A Master Bomber was used; he was Wing Commander J. E. Fauquier, the Commanding Officer of 405 (Canadian) Squadron. (The famous 'Johnny' Fauquier later commanded 617 Squadron.) 56 aircraft – 23 Halifaxes, 17 Lancasters, 16 Stirlings – were lost, 7·9 per cent of the heavy bomber force. This was Bomber Command's greatest loss of aircraft in one night so far in the war.

The raid was only partially successful. The Pathfinders were not able to identify the centre of Berlin by *H2S* and marked an area in the southern outskirts of the city. The Main Force arrived late and many aircraft cut a corner and approached from the south-west instead of using the planned south-south-east approach; this resulted in more bombs falling in open country than would otherwise have been the case. The German defences – both Flak and night fighters – were extremely fierce.

Much of the attack fell outside Berlin – 25 villages reported bombs, with 6 people killed there – and in the sparsely populated southern suburbs of the city. Despite this, Berlin reports the most serious raid of the war so far, with a wide range of industrial, housing and public properties being hit. 2,611 individual buildings were destroyed or seriously damaged. The worst damage was in the residential areas of Lankwitz and Lichterfelde and the worst industrial damage was in Mariendorf and Marienfelde; these districts are all well south of the city centre. More industrial damage was caused in the Tempelhof area, nearer the centre, and some of those bombs which actually hit the centre of the city fell by chance in the 'government quarter', where the Wilhelmstrasse was recorded as having not a building undamaged. 20 ships on the city's canals were sunk.

Casualties in Berlin were heavy considering the relatively inaccurate bombing. 854 people were killed: 684 civilians, 60 service personnel, 6 air-raid workers, 102 foreign workers (89 of them women) and 2 prisoners of war. 83 more civilians were classified as missing. The city officials who compiled the reports found out that this high death rate was caused by an unusually high proportion of the dead not having taken shelter, as ordered, in their allocated air-raid shelters. Our excellent adviser from Berlin, Arno Abendroth, who was living in the city at this time until evacuated in September 1943, says that when Doktor Goebbels, who as well as being Minister of Propaganda was also Berlin's Gauleiter, received the report on the number of people killed outside the shelters, Goebbels 'nearly went nuts'.

Minor Operations: 40 Wellingtons minelaying in the Frisians and off Lorient and St-Nazaire, 22 O.T.U. sorties. No losses.

24/25 August 1943

MINOR OPERATIONS

8 Mosquitoes to Berlin, 66 aircraft minelaying in the Heligoland, Frisian and Texel areas. No aircraft lost.

25/26 August 1943

MINOR OPERATIONS

6 Mosquitoes to Berlin, 42 aircraft minelaying off Brest and the Biscay ports, 7 O.T.U. sorties. 1 O.T.U. Wellington lost.

26/27 August 1943

MINOR OPERATIONS

32 aircraft minelaying off Brest and the Biscay ports, 1 O.T.U. sortie. No aircraft lost.

27/28 August 1943

NUREMBERG

674 aircraft – 349 Lancasters, 221 Halifaxes, 104 Stirlings. 33 aircraft – 11 of each type on the raid – lost, 4·9 per cent of the force.

The marking for this raid was based mainly on *H2S*. 47 of the Pathfinder *H2S* aircraft were ordered to check their equipment by dropping a 1,000-lb bomb on Heilbronn while flying to Nuremberg. 28 Pathfinder aircraft were able to carry out this order. Heilbronn reports that several bombs did drop in the north of the town soon after midnight. The local officials assumed that the bombs were aimed at the industrial zone; several bombs did fall around the factory area and other bombs fell further away. No industrial buildings were hit; one house was destroyed but there were no casualties.

Nuremberg was found to be free of cloud but it was very dark. The initial Pathfinder markers were accurate but a creepback quickly developed which could not be stopped because so many Pathfinder aircraft had difficulties with their *H2S* sets. The Master Bomber (whose name is not recorded) could do little to persuade the Main Force to move their bombing forward; only a quarter of the crews could hear his broadcasts. Bomber Command estimated that most of the bombing fell in open country south-south-west of the city but the local reports say that bombs were scattered across the south-eastern and eastern suburbs. The only location mentioned by name is the Zoo, which was hit by several bombs. 65 people were killed.

Minor Operations: 47 aircraft minelaying in the Frisians and off La Pallice, Lorient and St-Nazaire, 10 O.T.U. sorties. 1 Wellington minelayer lost.

29/30 August 1943

4 *Oboe* Mosquitoes to Cologne and 4 to Duisburg. 1 aircraft lost.

30/31 August 1943

MÖNCHENGLADBACH/RHEYDT

660 aircraft – 297 Lancasters, 185 Halifaxes, 107 Stirlings, 57 Wellingtons, 14 Mosquitoes. 25 aircraft – 8 Halifaxes, 7 Lancasters, 6 Stirlings, 4 Wellingtons – lost, 3·8 per cent of the force.

This was a 'double' attack, with a 2-minute pause after the first phase while the Pathfinders transferred the marking from Mönchengladbach to the neighbouring town of Rheydt. It was the first serious attack on both towns. The visibility was good and the *Oboe*-assisted marking of both targets was described in Bomber Command's records as 'a model' of good Pathfinder marking. The bombing was very concentrated with little creepback. Approximately half of the built-up area in each town was destroyed.

Only short reports are available from Germany. Mönchengladbach recorded 1,059 buildings destroyed – 171 industrial, 19 military and 869 domestic, with 117 people killed. The town's telegraph office is the only building mentioned by name. The number of buildings destroyed in Rheydt is given as 1,280 with damage to the main railway station and many rail facilities being stressed, and with 253 people being killed. A further 2,152 people were injured and 12 were missing but these last figures are combined ones for the two towns.

ST-OMER

This was the first of a series of small raids in which O.T.U. crews bombed ammunition dumps located in various forests of Northern France. A handful of Pathfinder aircraft marked each target and one of the purposes of the raids was to accustom O.T.U. crews to bombing on to markers before being posted to front-line squadrons.

This raid was carried out by 33 O.T.U. Wellingtons, with the Pathfinders providing 6 *Oboe* Mosquitoes and 6 Halifaxes. The target was a dump in the Forêt d'Eperlecques, just north of St-Omer. The bombing was successful and a large explosion was seen. 2 Wellingtons were lost.

Minor Operations: 12 Mosquitoes to Duisburg, 9 Stirlings minelaying in the Frisians. 1 Mosquito lost.

31 August/1 September 1943

BERLIN

622 aircraft – 331 Lancasters, 176 Halifaxes, 106 Stirlings, 9 Mosquitoes. 47 aircraft – 20 Halifaxes, 17 Stirlings, 10 Lancasters – lost, 7·6 per cent of the force. The Stirling casualties were 16·0 per cent! Approximately two thirds of the bombers lost were shot down by German fighters operating over or near Berlin. The use of 'fighter flares', dropped by German aircraft to 'mark' the bomber routes into and away from the target, was noted for the first time in Bomber Command records.

This raid was not successful. There was some cloud in the target area; this, together with difficulties with *H2S* equipment and probably the ferocity of the German defences, all combined to cause the Pathfinder markers to be dropped well south of the centre of the target area and the Main Force bombing to be even further away. The main bombing area eventually extended 30 miles back along the bombers' approach route. 85 dwelling-houses were destroyed in Berlin but the only industrial buildings hit were classed as damaged – 4 severely and 3 lightly. The only important public buildings hit were the headquarters of the Berlin inland canal and harbour system, the state police hospital and some market halls. 66 civilians and 2 soldiers were killed, 109 people were injured and 2,784 bombed out.

After this raid, Gauleiter Goebbels ordered the evacuation from Berlin of all children and all adults not engaged in war work to country areas or to towns in Eastern Germany where air raids were not expected.

Minor Operations: 30 O.T.U. Wellingtons with 6 Mosquitoes and 5 Halifaxes of the Pathfinders bombed an ammunition dump in the Forêt de Hesdin and 6 Mosquitoes were sent to Brauweiler. No aircraft lost.

2/3 September 1943

MINOR OPERATIONS

30 O.T.U. Wellingtons with 6 Mosquitoes and 5 Lancasters of the Pathfinders successfully bombed an ammunition dump in the Forêt de Mormal, 8 Mosquitoes were sent to Cologne and Duisburg, 89 aircraft were minelaying in the Frisians, near Texel and off Brittany and Biscay ports. 1 Stirling minelayer lost.

3/4 September 1943

BERLIN

316 Lancasters and 4 Mosquitoes; because of the high casualty rates among Halifaxes and Stirlings in recent Berlin raids the heavy force was composed only of Lancasters. 22 Lancasters were lost, nearly 7·0 per cent of the Lancaster force. The Mosquitoes were used to drop 'spoof' flares well away from the bombers' route to attract German night fighters.

This raid approached Berlin from the north-east but the marking and bombing were, once again, mostly short of the target. That part of the bombing which did reach Berlin's built-up area fell in residential parts of Charlottenburg and Moabit and in the industrial area called Siemensstadt. Several factories were hit and suffered serious loss of production and among 'utilities' put out of action were major water and electricity works and one of Berlin's largest breweries. 422 people were listed as killed – 225 civilians, 24 servicemen, 18 men and 2 women of the air-raid services, 123 foreign workers – 92 women and 31 men. 170 further civilians were 'missing'. The Berlin records also mention the deaths of another soldier and 7 'criminal' assistants when the 2 delayed-action bombs on which they were working exploded; these 'criminals' could earn remission of their sentences by volunteering for this work on unexploded and delayed-action bombs.

Minor Operations: 32 O.T.U. Wellingtons, 6 Mosquitoes and 6 Halifaxes to an ammunition dump in the Forêt de Raismes, near Valenciennes; 44 Stirlings and 12 Halifaxes minelaying off Denmark, in the Frisians and off the Biscay coast; 4 Mosquitoes to Düsseldorf and 7 O.T.U. Whitleys on leaflet raids. 1 Wellington, 1 Stirling and 1 Whitley were lost.

4/5 September 1943

MINOR OPERATIONS

8 Mosquitoes to Cologne and Duisburg, 25 Wellingtons and 13 Stirlings minelaying in the Frisians, in the River Gironde and off Lorient and St-Nazaire. No aircraft lost.

5/6 September 1943

MANNHEIM/LUDWIGSHAFEN

605 aircraft – 299 Lancasters, 195 Halifaxes, 111 Stirlings. 34 aircraft – 13 Halifaxes, 13 Lancasters, 8 Stirlings – lost, 5·6 per cent of the force.

The target area for this double attack was clear of cloud and the Pathfinder marking plan worked perfectly. Ground-markers were placed on the eastern side of Mannheim so that the bombing of the Main Force – approaching from the west – could move back across Mannheim and then into Ludwigshafen on the western bank of the Rhine. The creepback did not become excessive and severe destruction was caused in both targets.

Mannheim's normally detailed air-raid report does not give any specific details of property damage or casualties. It is probable that the raid was so severe that the normal report gathering and recording process broke down. The Mannheim records speak only of 'a catastrophe' and give general comments on the activities of the air-raid services and the behaviour of the population which are both described as '*vor-bildlich*' (exemplary).

More detail is available from Ludwigshafen where the central and southern parts of the town were devastated. The fire department recorded 1,993 separate fires including 3 classed as 'fire areas' and 986 as large fires; 139 of the fires were in industrial premises. 1,080 houses, 6 military and 4 industrial buildings were destroyed and 8 more industrial buildings were seriously damaged, including the I.G. Farben works. 127 people were killed and 568 were injured; 10 of the dead were Flak troops. A further 1,605 people are described as suffering from eye injuries. The relatively small number of deaths may be an indication that many of the German cities were evacuating parts of their population after the recent firestorm disaster at Hamburg and other heavy raids.

Minor Operations: 4 Mosquitoes to Düsseldorf, 25 aircraft minelaying in the German Bight, near Texel and off Brest and Lorient. No aircraft lost.

6/7 September 1943

MUNICH

257 Lancasters and 147 Halifaxes. 16 aircraft – 13 Halifaxes, 3 Lancasters – lost, 4·0 per cent of the force.

The Pathfinders found that Munich was mostly covered by cloud and neither their ground-markers nor their sky-markers were very effective. Most of the Main Force crews could do no more than bomb on a timed run from the Ammersee, a lake situated 21 miles south-west of the target. The bombing was mostly scattered over the southern and western parts of the city.

No report is available from Munich.

8/9 September 1943

BOULOGNE GUN POSITIONS

257 aircraft – 119 Wellingtons, 112 Stirlings, 16 Mosquitoes, 10 Halifaxes. O.T.U. aircraft formed part of this force and 5 B-17s also flew the first American night-bombing sorties of the war with Bomber Command. Nos. 4 and 5 Groups did not take part in the raid. No aircraft lost.

The target was the site of a German long-range gun battery and the marking was mainly provided by *Oboe* Mosquitoes, some of whom were experimenting with a new technique. But the raid was not successful; the marking and the bombing were not accurate and the battery does not appear to have been damaged.

13/14 September 1943

5 *Oboe* Mosquitoes to Cologne and 5 to Duisburg. No losses.

14/15 September 1943

Minor Operations

8 Lancasters of 617 Squadron set out with the new 12,000-lb bomb (not the 12,000-lb *Tallboy* 'earthquake' bomb developed later) to attack the banks of the Dortmund–Ems Canal near Ladbergen. While the force was over the North Sea, however, a weather reconnaissance Mosquito reported that there was fog in the target area and the Lancasters were recalled. The aircraft of Flight Lieutenant D. J. H. Maltby, one of the original members of the squadron that had attacked the Ruhr dams, crashed into the sea and the crew were all killed. Maltby's body was washed ashore and is buried at Wickhambreux, near Canterbury in Kent; the names of the other 6 crew members are on the Runnymede Memorial for the Missing.

8 Mosquitoes made a nuisance raid on Berlin. 1 aircraft lost.

15/16 September 1943

MONTLUÇON

369 aircraft of 3, 4, 6 and 8 Groups – 209 Halifaxes, 120 Stirlings, 40 Lancasters. 5 American B-17s also took part. 2 Halifaxes and 1 Stirling lost.

This was a moonlit raid on the Dunlop rubber factory at Montluçon in Central France. The Pathfinders marked the target accurately and the Master Bomber, Wing Commander D. F. E. C. Deane, brought the Main Force in well to carry out some accurate bombing. Every building in the factory was hit and a large fire was started. This appears to be the last occasion on which the Pathfinders used the Master Bomber technique until the spring of 1944.

No report of the raid is available from France.

Dortmund–Ems Canal

8 Lancasters of 617 Squadron took off to carry out the postponed raid on the banks of the canal but the area was misty and 5 aircraft were lost, including those of Pilot Officer L. G. Knight, another of the Dams Raid survivors, and the new squadron commander, Squadron Leader G. Holden. These heavy losses, and the losses of the Dams Raid, confirmed that low-level attacks on German targets, even when away from major defended areas, were not viable with heavy bombers and this type of operation was not repeated. 617 Squadron now started retraining as a specialist high-altitude-bombing unit.

16/17 September 1943

MODANE

340 aircraft of 3, 4, 6 and 8 Groups – 170 Halifaxes, 127 Stirlings, 43 Lancasters – to attack the important railway yards at Modane on the main railway route from France to Italy. 5 American B-17s also took part. The marking of the target, situated in a steep valley, was not successful and the bombing was not accurate. No report is available from France. 2 Halifaxes and 1 Stirling lost.

Anthéor Viaduct

12 Lancasters – 8 from 617 Squadron and 4 from 619 Squadron – attempted to bomb the railway viaduct near Cannes on the coastal railway line leading to Italy, but no direct hits were scored. 1 Lancaster of 619 Squadron was lost; it came down in the sea off Portugal, possibly while trying to reach Gibraltar.

Minor Operations: 5 Mosquitoes to Berlin, 3 O.T.U. sorties. No losses.

17/18 September 1943

Minor Operations

6 Mosquitoes to Berlin, 8 Wellingtons minelaying off Brest. No losses.

18/19 September 1943

MINOR OPERATIONS

5 Mosquitoes to Cologne, 49 aircraft minelaying in the Frisians and off Biscay ports. No losses.

20/21 September 1943

MINOR OPERATIONS

8 Mosquitoes to Berlin, 20 Wellingtons minelaying off Brest, Lorient and St-Nazaire, 21 O.T.U. sorties. No losses.

21/22 September 1943

Minor Operations

26 aircraft minelaying in the Frisians and off Brest, 3 O.T.U. sorties. No losses.

22/23 September 1943

HANNOVER

711 aircraft – 322 Lancasters, 226 Halifaxes, 137 Stirlings, 26 Wellingtons – on the first major raid to Hannover for 2 years; this was the first of a series of 4 heavy raids on this target. 5 American B-17s also took part in the raid, their first night raid on Germany. 26 aircraft – 12 Halifaxes, 7 Lancasters, 5 Stirlings, 2 Wellingtons – lost, 3·7 per cent of the force.

Visibility in the target area was good but stronger winds than forecast caused the marking and the bombing to be concentrated between 2 and 5 miles south-south-east of the city centre. It has not been possible to obtain a German report but it is unlikely that serious damage was caused.

OLDENBURG

21 Lancasters and 8 Mosquitoes of 8 Group carried out a diversionary raid, dropping much *Window* and many flares and target indicators to simulate the arrival of a larger force. The losses on the Hannover raid, lower than the recent average, may indicate that this tactic was partially successful. No aircraft were lost on the diversionary raid.

Minor Operations: 12 Mosquitoes on a further diversion to Emden, 4 Stirlings minelaying in the Frisians, 7 O.T.U. sorties. No losses.

23/24 September 1943

MANNHEIM

628 aircraft – 312 Lancasters, 193 Halifaxes, 115 Stirlings, 8 Mosquitoes. 5 B-17s also took part. 32 aircraft – 18 Lancasters, 7 Halifaxes, 7 Wellingtons – lost, 5·1 per cent of the force.

This raid was intended to destroy the northern part of Mannheim, which had not been so severely hit in the successful raid earlier in the month. The Pathfinder plan worked well and concentrated bombing fell on the intended area, although later stages of the raid crept back across the northern edge of Ludwigshafen and out into the open country. The following buildings were destroyed in Mannheim: 927 houses, 20 industrial premises, 11 schools, 6 public buildings and a church. A large number of other buildings were damaged and approximately 25,000 people were bombed out of their homes. 102 people were killed and 418 were injured. There were more than 2,000 fires.

Local records (provided on this night by Herr Erwin Folz and not from the local authorities) show that the later stages of the bombing crept back across the Rhine to the northern part of Ludwigshafen, where the I.G. Farben factory was severely damaged, and then to the smaller outlying towns of Oppau and Frankenthal. Ludwigshafen suffered 47 people killed and 260 injured. A further 8,000 people were bombed out, of whom 4,289 were foreign workers. The centre of the small town of Frankenthal was completely burnt out and 38 people were killed there.

DARMSTADT

21 Lancasters and 8 Mosquitoes of 8 Group carried out a diversionary raid on Darmstadt without loss.

The diversionary purpose of this raid was not achieved because Darmstadt was too close to Mannheim and the German night fighters could see the main attack only 20 miles away quite clearly. But the small force of bombers caused much damage in this university town which had little industry and which had not been seriously bombed before. 273 buildings were damaged and 147 people were killed.

Minor Operations: 6 Mosquitoes to Aachen, 28 O.T.U. sorties. 1 O.T.U. Wellington lost.

24/25 September 1943

MINOR OPERATIONS

4 Mosquitoes to Duisburg, 39 aircraft minelaying in the Frisians and south of Texel, 2 O.T.U. sorties. 1 Stirling minelayer lost.

25/26 September 1943

Minor Operations

8 Mosquitoes to Cologne and Düsseldorf, 10 Stirlings minelaying in the Frisians, 11 O.T.U. sorties. No losses.

26/27 September 1943

Minor Operations

5 Mosquitoes to Aachen and 4 each to Cologne and Hamborn, 4 O.T.U. sorties. No losses.

The 5 Mosquitoes attacking Aachen were carrying out the first trials of Mark II *Oboe* but the equipment failed and bombs were released visually or on dead reckoning.

27/28 September 1943

HANNOVER

678 aircraft – 312 Lancasters, 231 Halifaxes, 111 Stirlings, 24 Wellingtons. 5 B-17s also took part. 38 Bomber Command aircraft – 17 Halifaxes, 10 Lancasters, 10 Stirlings, 1 Wellington – lost, 5·6 per cent of the force, and 1 B-17 also lost.

The use by the Pathfinders of faulty forecast winds again saved the centre of Hannover. The bombing was very concentrated but fell on an area 5 miles north of the city centre. No details are available from Germany but R.A.F. photographic evidence showed that most of the bombs fell in open country or villages north of the city.

BRUNSWICK

21 Lancasters and 6 Mosquitoes of 8 Group carried out a diversionary raid on Brunswick which was successful in drawing off some night fighters. 218 people were killed in Brunswick – 51 Germans and 167 foreigners. 1 Lancaster lost.

Minor Operations: 9 Mosquitoes on another diversion to Emden, 5 Mosquitoes on *Oboe* tests to Aachen (3 were successful), 19 aircraft minelaying in the Kattegat and the Frisian Islands, 4 O.T.U. sorties. No losses.

28/29 September 1943

8 Mosquitoes attacked Cologne and Gelsenkirchen without loss.

29/30 September 1943

BOCHUM

352 aircraft – 213 Lancasters, 130 Halifaxes, 9 Mosquitoes. 9 aircraft – 5 Halifaxes and 4 Lancasters – lost, 2·6 per cent of the force.

The *Oboe*-assisted Pathfinder plan worked perfectly and led to accurate and concentrated bombing. In the Bochum air-raid area – which included 3 small towns near by – 527 houses were destroyed and 742 were seriously damaged. The *Altstadt* is mentioned as having been particularly hard-hit. 161 people were killed, including 33 foreign workers and prisoners of war, and 337 people were injured.

Minor Operations: 11 Mosquitoes to Gelsenkirchen, 14 Lancasters minelaying off Danzig, Gdynia and Pillau in the Baltic. No aircraft lost.

1/2 October 1943

HAGEN

243 Lancasters and 8 Mosquitoes of 1, 5 and 8 Groups. 2 Lancasters lost, 0·8 per cent of the force.

This raid was a complete success achieved on a completely cloud-covered target of small size, with only a moderate bomber effort and at trifling cost. The *Oboe* sky-marking was perfect and severe damage was caused in Hagen. There was the usual housing damage but 2 of the town's 4 industrial areas were severely hit and a third suffered lesser damage. Hagen reports that 46 industrial firms (not individual buildings) were destroyed and 166 were damaged. In his post-war interrogation, Albert Speer stated that the destruction in Hagen of an important factory making accumulator batteries slowed down the output of U-boats considerably. Speer did not mention this raid specifically but Hagen was not heavily attacked again until December 1944.

29. Hagen, a Ruhr town not seriously bombed until late 1943. This scene, of smoking ruins and workers having to walk to work because of disrupted bus and suburban rail services, was typical on the mornings after R.A.F raids.

Other details from the Hagen report: 3,480 fires of which 100 were large and 715 medium-sized, 241 Germans and 25 foreigners killed, 2,386 Germans and 135 foreigners wounded, 30,000 people bombed out.

At the same time as the main attack on Hagen was ending, 12 *Oboe* Mosquitoes were dispatched to attack a steelworks at Witten, north-west of Hagen, for training purposes. 8 Mosquitoes bombed at Witten and 2, whose *Oboe* equipment failed, dropped their bombs on the fires burning in Hagen. No aircraft lost.

2/3 October 1943

MUNICH

294 Lancasters of 1, 5 and 8 Groups and 2 B-17s. 8 Lancasters lost, 2·7 per cent of the force.

Visibility over the target was clear but the initial marking was scattered. Heavy bombing developed over the southern and south-eastern districts of Munich but later stages of the raid fell up to 15 miles back along the approach route. Most of this inaccurate bombing was carried out by 5 Group aircraft, which were again attempting their 'time-and-distance' bombing method independently of the Pathfinder marking. The 5 Group crews were not able to pick out the Wurmsee lake, which was the starting-point for their timed run.

Brief reports from Germany state that 339 buildings were destroyed, 191 people were killed and 748 were injured. No other details are available.

Minor Operations: 8 Mosquitoes to Cologne and Gelsenkirchen, 117 aircraft minelaying at various places from Lorient to Heligoland, 21 O.T.U. sorties. 1 Halifax minelayer lost.

3/4 October 1943

KASSEL

547 aircraft – 223 Halifaxes, 204 Lancasters, 113 Stirlings, 7 Mosquitoes. 24 aircraft – 14 Halifaxes, 6 Stirlings, 4 Lancasters – lost, 4·4 per cent of the force.

This raid did not proceed according to plan. The *H2S* 'blind marker' aircraft overshot the aiming point badly and the 'visual markers' could not correct this because their view of the ground was restricted by thick haze. German decoy markers may also have been present. The main weight of the attack thus fell on the western suburbs and outlying towns and villages. But, even so, large fires were started at both the Henschel and Fieseler aircraft factories, at the city's main hospital and at several other important buildings. The eastern suburb of Wolfshanger was devastated. Kassel's casualties were 118 dead – 68 civilians, 12 military and 38 foreigners – and 304 injured. Musgrove, in his excellent book *Pathfinder Force*,* records that a large ammunition dump at Ihringshausen, just north of Wolfshanger, was hit by a chance bomb load and the resulting explosions attracted further bombs; photographs taken later showed 84 buildings at the military location destroyed and a great mass of craters. The outlying townships of Bettenhausen and Sandershausen were also severely hit but details for these places are not available.

Mosquito Operations

10 aircraft on a diversion to Hannover, 12 *Oboe* aircraft to Knapsack power-station near Cologne, 4 aircraft on Mark II *Oboe* trials to Aachen. No losses.

Minor Operations: 7 Stirlings minelaying in the Frisians, 7 O.T.U. sorties. No losses.

4/5 October 1943

FRANKFURT

406 aircraft – 162 Lancasters, 170 Halifaxes, 70 Stirlings, 4 Mosquitoes. 3 B-17s also took part. 10 aircraft – 5 Halifaxes, 3 Lancasters, 2 Stirlings – lost, 2·5 per cent of the force. 1 B-17 was also lost. This was the last R.A.F. night-bombing raid in which American aircraft took part, but individual B-17s occasionally carried out bombing flights in following weeks.

Clear weather and good Pathfinder marking produced the first serious blow on Frankfurt so far in the war, with extensive destruction being caused in the eastern half of the city and in the inland docks on the River Main; both of these areas are described in the Frankfurt report as having been a 'sea of flames'. Many city-centre-type buildings are also mentioned as being hit; the new Rathaus had its roof burnt out. No overall figures are given for casualties, the only mention being a tragedy at an orphanage housed in the former Jewish hospital, where a bomb scored a direct hit on the basement shelter killing 90 children, 14 nuns and other members of the staff. In the following days, the main railway station was packed with people trying to leave Frankfurt.

*London, Macdonald & Janes', 1976, p. 80.

LUDWIGSHAFEN

66 Lancasters of 1 and 8 Groups carried out a diversionary raid without loss but the marking and bombing were scattered.

Minor Operations: 12 Mosquitoes to Knapsack power-station, 1 Mosquito to Aachen, 5 Stirlings minelaying in the River Gironde, 8 O.T.U. sorties. No aircraft lost.

The Mosquito attacking Aachen was carrying out the first operational trial of the *G-H* blind bombing equipment but the trial was not successful.

7/8 October 1943

STUTTGART

343 Lancasters of 1, 3, 5, 6 and 8 Groups. The first aircraft to be equipped with *A.B.C.* (night-fighter communications jamming), from 101 Squadron, 1 Group, operated on this night. The German night-fighter controller was confused by the Mosquito diversion on Munich and only a few night fighters reached Stuttgart at the end of the attack; 4 Lancasters were lost, 1·2 per cent of the force.

The target area was cloud-covered and the *H2S* Pathfinder marking developed in 2 areas. Many bombs fell in various parts of Stuttgart where 344 buildings – mostly dwelling-houses – were destroyed and 4,586 buildings were damaged. In the city centre, 4 hospitals, a museum (the Lindenmuseum) and the garrison church were hit, and 36 people were drowned in an underground air-raid shelter at the main railway station when a water main was damaged by a bomb and burst. Total casualties in Stuttgart were 104 killed and missing, 300 injured. The town of Böblingen, 10 miles to the south-west, must have been under the second group of markers. 350 houses were hit and 60 people were killed here.

Friedrichshafen

16 Lancasters of 8 Group carried out a diversionary raid without loss and claimed hits on the Zeppelin factory.

Minor Operations: 10 Mosquitoes to Munich, 7 to Emden, 5 to Aachen, 79 aircraft minelaying from Brest to Heligoland, 14 O.T.U. sorties. 1 Stirling minelayer lost.

8/9 October 1943

HANNOVER

504 aircraft – 282 Lancasters, 188 Halifaxes, 26 Wellingtons, 8 Mosquitoes. This was the last Bomber Command raid in which Wellingtons took part. 300 (Polish) and 432 (Canadian) Squadrons provided the 26 Wellingtons which operated on this night; they all returned safely. The German controller guessed correctly that Hannover was the target and many night fighters arrived before the attack was over. 27 aircraft – 14 Lancasters and 13 Halifaxes – were lost, 5·4 per cent of the force.

Conditions over Hannover were clear and the Pathfinders were finally able to mark the centre of the city accurately; a most concentrated attack followed with a creepback of only 2 miles, all within the built-up area. This was probably Hannover's worst attack of the war. The local report describes extensive damage in the centre of the city and in many other parts except the west. The telephone system and electricity supply failed at the beginning of the raid and many water mains were quickly broken. A large area of fire quickly developed in the centre and south-central districts. Acting upon instructions from the Party Headquarters and from district air-raid posts, the population were shepherded to collecting places in open areas between the fires. This action is believed to have saved many lives but 1,200 people were killed and 3,345 were injured, 449 seriously so. A further 6,000–8,000 people received eye injuries because of smoke and heat. 3,932 buildings were completely destroyed and more than 30,000 were damaged in varying degree, but no individual buildings are named. R.A.F. reconnaissance, however, showed that the important Continental rubber factory and the Hanomag machine works were badly hit.

BREMEN

119 aircraft – 95 Stirlings, 17 Halifaxes, 7 Lancasters of 3 and 8 Groups. This was a diversionary raid on a larger scale than ever before. The bombing was scattered but this was a subsidiary aim of the operation. 3 Stirlings were lost, 2·5 per cent of the force.

Minor Operations: 10 Mosquitoes to Castrop-Rauxel, 7 to Berlin, 1 to Düren, 17 Stirlings minelaying in the River Gironde and off La Pallice, 2 O.T.U. sorties. No losses.

Total effort for the night: 660 sorties, 30 aircraft (4·5 per cent) lost.

9/10 October 1943

6 Mosquitoes attacked Berlin without loss.

13/14 October 1943

4 Mosquitoes to Cologne and 4 to Duisburg without loss.

16/17 October 1943

Minor Operations

9 Mosquitoes to Dortmund, 11 O.T.U. sorties. No losses.
    One of the Mosquitoes was carrying out a *G-H* trial but its equipment failed and it had to bomb by dead reckoning.

17/18 October 1943

MINOR OPERATIONS

8 Mosquitoes to Berlin, 2 to Aachen, 2 to Hamborn, 54 Stirlings and Wellingtons minelaying in the Frisians and off Biscay ports, 16 O.T.U. sorties. No aircraft lost.

18/19 October 1943

HANNOVER

360 Lancasters. 18 Lancasters lost, 5·0 per cent of the force.

The target area was covered by cloud and the Pathfinders were not successful in marking the position of Hannover. The raid was scattered, with most bombs falling in open country north and north-west of the city.

This raid concluded the current series of raids on Hannover. Bomber Command had dispatched 2,253 sorties in 4 raids and 10 American B-17 sorties had also been flown. 1,976 aircraft claimed to have bombed in the target area. Only 1 raid had been completely successful but that had caused severe damage. 110 bombers were lost on the raids, 4·9 per cent of those dispatched.

Minor Operations: 30 Mosquitoes to Duisburg (11 aircraft), Berlin (8 aircraft) and to 4 other targets, 6 Wellingtons minelaying off Texel, 12 O.T.U. sorties. No aircraft lost.

One of the Lancasters lost on the Hannover raid was the 5,000th Bomber Command aircraft lost on operations since the start of the war. By the end of this night, the bombers had flown approximately 144,500 sorties – 90 per cent of them by night – and lost 5,004 aircraft – 4,365 by night and 639 by day – over enemy territory, crashed in the sea or shot down over England by German Intruders or 'friendly' defences. The average number of sorties flown in each 24-hour period since the outbreak of war was 96 – 87 in each night, only 9 in each day – and the average operational loss rate was 3·5 per cent of all sorties dispatched. (The reader may like to compare these statistics with those presented after the last diary entry of the war, on page 707.)

20/21 October 1943

LEIPZIG

358 Lancasters of 1, 5, 6 and 8 Groups. 16 Lancasters lost, 4·5 per cent of the force.

This was the first serious attack on this distant German city. Weather conditions were very difficult – Bomber Command records describe them as 'appalling' – and the bombing was very scattered. No report is available from Leipzig but it is unlikely that much damage was caused by the 271 aircraft which bombed in that area.

Minor Operations: 28 Mosquitoes to Berlin, Cologne, Brauweiler and Emden, 12 Stirlings minelaying in the Frisians, 26 O.T.U. sorties. 2 Mosquitoes lost.

21/22 October 1943

11 Mosquitoes to Emden, the Bruderich steelworks at Düsseldorf and Dortmund. All targets bombed without loss.

22/23 October 1943

KASSEL

569 aircraft – 322 Lancasters, 247 Halifaxes. The German controller was again successful in assessing the target and 43 aircraft – 25 Halifaxes, 18 Lancasters – were lost, 7·6 per cent of the force.

The initial 'blind' *H2S* marking overshot the target but 8 out of the 9 'visual' markers correctly identified the centre of Kassel and placed their markers accurately. Although German decoy markers may have drawn off part of the bomber force, the main raid was exceptionally accurate and concentrated. The result was the most devastating attack on a German city since the firestorm raid on Hamburg in July and the results at Kassel would not be exceeded again until well into 1944. The fires were so concentrated that there was a firestorm, although not as extensive as the Hamburg one.

It is impossible to list all the damage. 4,349 separate dwelling blocks containing 26,782 family living units (flats/apartments) were destroyed and 6,743 more blocks with 26,463 'units' were damaged. 63 per cent of all Kassel's living accommodation became unusable and 100,000–120,000 people had to leave their homes. The fire services dealt with 3,600 separate fires. The intensity of the destruction is illustrated by the fact that more buildings were completely destroyed than those classed as 'lightly damaged' and there were more 'large' fires (1,600) than small ones (1,000); in most raids the lightly damaged buildings and small fires outnumbered serious incidents several times over.

In addition to dwelling-houses, the following properties were destroyed or badly damaged: 155 industrial buildings, 78 public buildings, 38 schools, 25 churches, 16 police and military buildings (including the local Gestapo), 11 hospitals. The Kassel records do not provide any further detail about the industrial damage caused but R.A.F. photographic reconnaissance showed that the Kassel railway system and its installations were severely hit and all 3 Henschel aircraft factories seriously damaged; as these were making V-1 flying bombs at the time, this was a most useful result of the raid and had a major effect upon the eventual opening and scale of the V-1 campaign, comparable to the recent raid on Peenemünde which set back the V-2 rocket programme.

The Kassel records give the number of dead recovered up to the end of November as 5,599, of which 1,817 bodies were unidentifiable and the records go on to add that the 'Missing Department' (the Vermisstensuchstelle) was still trying to trace 3,300 people. 459 survivors, however, had been recovered from ruined houses 'after many days of heavy work'. 3,587 people were injured – 800 seriously – and a further 8,084 people were treated for smoke and heat injury to their eyes.

FRANKFURT

28 Lancasters and 8 Mosquitoes of 8 Group carried out a diversionary raid. Bombing was scattered. 1 Lancaster lost.

Minor Operations: 12 *Oboe* Mosquitoes to Knapsack power-station and 1 to Dortmund, 17 aircraft minelaying in the Frisians and off Texel, 10 O.T.U. sorties. 1 Mosquito lost.

Total effort for the night: 645 sorties, 45 aircraft (7·0 per cent) lost.

It was on this night that an R.A.F. ground radio station in England, probably the one at Kingsdown in Kent, started its broadcasts with the intention of interrupting and confusing the German controllers' orders to their night fighters. The Official History (Vol. IV, p. 23n.) describes how, at one stage, the German controller broke into vigorous swearing, whereupon the R.A.F. voice remarked, 'The Englishman is now swearing'. To this, the German retorted, 'It is not the Englishman who is swearing, it is me'.

24/25 October 1943

MINOR OPERATIONS

13 Mosquitoes to 5 targets in the Ruhr area and 6 Mosquitoes to Emden, 30 Stirlings and Wellingtons minelaying in the Frisians and off Texel. No aircraft lost.

25/26 October 1943

23 Stirlings minelaying in the Kattegat without loss.

27/28 October 1943

22 O.T.U. Wellingtons on leaflet flights to France without loss.

---

31 October/1 November 1943

11 Mosquitoes to the Ruhr and 6 Mosquitoes to Emden. All targets were bombed but 1 aircraft was lost from its sortie to the Ruhr.

3/4 November 1943

DÜSSELDORF

589 aircraft – 344 Lancasters, 233 Halifaxes, 12 Mosquitoes. 18 aircraft – 11 Lancasters, 7 Halifaxes – lost, 3·1 per cent of the force.

The main weight of the raid fell in the centre and south of the city but it is difficult to obtain precise results of the outcome; like some other German cities, Düsseldorf's records start to show a deterioration under the pressure of the severe raids of 1943. There was certainly extensive damage both to housing and to industrial premises but a detailed résumé is not possible. The same problem exists with casualties. An early local report says that 23 people died but this appears to have been altered to 118 at a later date. The United States Bombing Survey* gives a figure of 622 dead and 942 injured for the whole month of November; there were no more other attacks on Düsseldorf in that month.

38 Mark II Lancasters – 13 from 3 Group and 25 from 6 Group – which took

---

* *Report of Effects of Area Bombing, Düsseldorf*, p. 12b.

part in this raid made the first large-scale test of the *G-H* blind-bombing device and attempted to bomb the Mannesmann tubular-steel works on the northern outskirts of Düsseldorf while the main raid was taking place. 5 of the *G-H* Lancasters had to return early and 2 more were lost; the equipment in 16 other aircraft failed to function leaving only 15 aircraft to bomb the factory on *G-H*. The Düsseldorf records do mention this factory, stating that 'several assembly halls were burnt out'; *G-H* later became a most useful blind-bombing device when it was produced in sufficient numbers for a major part of Bomber Command to be fitted with it.

COLOGNE

52 Lancasters and 10 Mosquitoes of 8 Group carried out a diversionary raid without loss.

A report from Cologne shows the extreme accuracy with which some of the bombs hit the centre of the city. The cathedral was hit several times, one heavy bomb blowing a 10-metre hole in the north-west tower. The Cathedral Hotel, another hotel near by and the ramp to the Hohenzollern Bridge were all severely damaged by high-explosive bombs. 7 people were killed in the city.

Minor Operations: 13 *Oboe* Mosquitoes to a Krupps foundry at Rheinhausen and 2 Mosquitoes to Dortmund, 23 aircraft of 3 Group minelaying in the Frisians, 27 O.T.U. sorties. 1 O.T.U. Whitley lost. *H2S* was used for the first time to assist the minelaying force and is an indication that a start had been made in equipping Main Force squadrons with *H2S*.

Total effort for the night: 716 sorties, 19 aircraft (2·7 per cent) lost.

A further Victoria Cross was awarded for an action during the Düsseldorf raid. The Lancaster of Flight Lieutenant William Reid, 61 Squadron, was twice attacked by night fighters before the target was reached. The aircraft suffered extensive damage, which put most of its guns out of action; the navigator was killed and the wireless operator fatally injured. Flight Lieutenant Reid was wounded in both attacks and his flight engineer was also hurt but Reid pressed on for the remaining 200 miles to the target and his bomb aimer, Sergeant L. G. Rolton, obtained an 'aiming point photograph'. The return flight was full of problems. The cockpit windscreen was shattered and the oxygen supply failed. The pilot lapsed into semi-consciousness and the injured flight engineer, Sergeant J. W. Norris, had to do some of the flying. Flight Lieutenant Reid recovered to take over for the emergency landing in misty conditions which took place at Shipdham in Norfolk, even though he could not see properly for blood running into his eyes from a head wound. One leg of the Lancaster's under-carriage collapsed but the landing was otherwise successful.

Flight Lieutenant Reid was awarded the Victoria Cross but the 61 Squadron Operations Record Book, not one of Bomber Command's best, does not say whether other crew members were decorated.

4/5 November 1943

MINOR OPERATIONS

24 Mosquitoes attacked a chemical works at Leverkusen, causing fires and a large explosion, 4 Mosquitoes to Aachen, 36 aircraft minelaying at various places from Lorient to the Kattegat. 4 minelaying Stirlings lost.

5/6 November 1943

MINOR OPERATIONS

26 Mosquitoes made small attacks on Bochum, Dortmund, Düsseldorf, Hamburg and Hannover. 27 O.T.U. Wellingtons carried leaflets to France. No aircraft lost.

6/7 November 1943

MINOR OPERATIONS

19 Mosquitoes to Bochum, Duisburg and Düsseldorf, 16 Wellingtons minelaying off Texel, Brest, Lorient and St-Nazaire, 8 O.T.U. sorties. No aircraft lost.

7/8 November 1943

MINOR OPERATIONS

6 Mosquitoes to Essen, 35 aircraft minelaying off the French coast from Brest to southern Biscay, 7 O.T.U. sorties. 1 Stirling minelayer lost.

8/9 November 1943

7 *Oboe* Mosquitoes bombed Cologne and Duisburg without loss.

9/10 November 1943

18 *Oboe* Mosquitoes bombed blast furnaces at Bochum and a steelworks at Duisburg. No aircraft lost.

10/11 November 1943

MODANE

313 Lancasters of 5 and 8 Groups to attack the railway yards on the main line to Italy. The Pathfinder marking, in difficult conditions, was slightly beyond the target but 200 aircraft brought back photographs to show that their bombs fell within 1 mile of the target and the railway system was seriously damaged. No report is available from France.

Minor Operations: 2 Mosquitoes to Dortmund, 7 Stirlings minelaying in the River Gironde and off La Pallice, 20 O.T.U. flights.

No aircraft were lost from the 342 sorties flown on this night.

11/12 November 1943

CANNES

124 Halifaxes and 10 Lancasters of 4, 6 and 8 Groups to bomb the marshalling yards and railway installations on the main coastal line to Italy. 4 Halifaxes lost.

The night was clear and the Pathfinders marked the target from 5,000 ft but the railway yards were not hit at all and the railway workshops suffered only blast damage. A report from Cannes states that the local people were at first thrilled to see the 'firework display' of the Pathfinders and could even see the R.A.F. aircraft in the moonlight, but the bombing, 'like a typhoon', mainly fell in the working-class suburb of La Bocca, where 39 people were killed, and in the village of d'Agay, where the casualties were not recorded. A local newspaper,* under German control, writes of the resentment of the local French people at the inaccurate bombing, particularly as the British had been such popular pre-war visitors to Cannes. The British were, writes the newspaper, 'pure savages' and the raid was 'nothing but murder for British glory ... too much like a sport'.

Anthéor Viaduct

617 Squadron resumed operations after its period of high-level training with the new 'Stabilizing Automatic Bomb Sight'. 10 Lancasters each dropped one 12,000-lb bomb but could not hit the viaduct. No aircraft lost.

Minor Operations: 29 Mosquitoes to Berlin, Hannover and the Ruhr, 45 aircraft minelaying from Brest to the Frisian Islands, 6 O.T.U. sorties. 1 Halifax and 1 Wellington lost from the minelaying force.

12/13 November 1943

7 Mosquitoes attacked Düsseldorf, Essen and Krefeld without loss.

13/14 November 1943

9 Mosquitoes to Berlin, 8 *Oboe* Mosquitoes to blast furnaces at Bochum. No losses.

15/16 November 1943

10 Mosquitoes to Düsseldorf and 2 to Bonn. 2 aircraft lost, one from each target.

16/17 November 1943

MINOR OPERATIONS

21 Mosquitoes to Cologne, Gelsenkirchen and Krefeld, 8 O.T.U. Wellingtons on leaflet flights to France. No losses.

---

* *L'Éclaireur de Nice et du Sud-Est*, 15 November 1943.

17/18 November 1943

LUDWIGSHAFEN

66 Lancasters and 17 Halifaxes of 8 Group on a purely *H2S* blind-bombing raid without any target indicators being dropped. Few details are available about the results of the bombing but it is believed that the attack was accurate and the I.G. Farben factory was hit. Because of misleading instructions broadcast from England to the German night-fighter pilots, most of the fighter force landed early and only 1 Lancaster was lost.

Minor Operations: 21 Mosquitoes to Berlin, Bochum, Bonn and Duisburg, 4 O.T.U. sorties. No losses.

Operational Statistics, 3/4 August to 18 November 1943
(107 days/nights)

Number of nights with operations: 79. There were no day operations
Number of night sorties: 18,878, from which 661 aircraft (3·5 per cent) were lost
Approximate bomb tonnage in period: 52,377 tons
Averages per 24-hour period: 176·4 sorties, 6·2 aircraft lost, 489·5 tons of bombs dropped

17. BERLIN – THE MAIN BATTLE

18/19 November 1943 to 31 March 1944

Bomber Command was now ready for what would prove to be its greatest test of the war. The all-out assault on Berlin began on the night of 18/19 November and Sir Arthur Harris would be allowed – with only small exceptions – a completely free hand in pursuing his main aim for the next four and a half months. Bomber Command would mount thirty-two major raids on Germany during this period, sixteen on Berlin and sixteen on other large cities. Nearly all of these raids would be to distant targets and the bomber crews would have to contend both with a succession of long flights in wintry weather conditions and with a succession of fierce battles against a reorganized German night-fighter force. On the technical devices front, it would be a major test for the new models of *H2S* now being fitted to the Pathfinder aircraft; only one of the thirty-two major raids of the Battle of Berlin period would be to a target within the range of *Oboe*.

The main battle against Berlin was not a week old before the German defences forced a major part of Harris's bomber force to be withdrawn from the front line of operations. The Stirlings, with which most of the 3 Group squadrons were equipped, had never been able to achieve the altitude performance which the other types of bombers could attain and had suffered heavier casualties accordingly because they had never received the full protective cover of the bomber stream. The Lancasters and Halifaxes were often ordered to come down lower and share the more dangerous lower height bands with the Stirlings but, when the night fighters struck, most of the Lancaster and Halifax crews quickly climbed again. In the period from August to the third week in November, the Stirlings lost 109 aircraft in raids on Germany, a loss rate of 6·4 per cent. As their bomb load was not as good as the other types, it was decided that the Main Force would operate without the Stirlings from then onwards. The Stirlings never flew again to Germany. This was a sad period for 3 Group, which had borne its full share of Bomber Command operations since the beginning of the war, but most of its squadrons were now relegated to secondary work during the long period in which a very slow conversion to Lancasters took place.

A similar fate was soon to befall those squadrons of 4 and 6 Groups which were equipped with the Mark II and V versions of the Halifax bomber. These aircraft, too, suffered from having inferior performance and, after the Stirlings left, their casualties soared. In an eleven-week period from the beginning of December to mid-February, no less than 9·8 per cent of Halifax II and V sorties to Germany were lost. (These figures do *not* include aircraft which signalled that they were coming down in the sea, and the losses quoted are expressed as a percentage of those which took off. The true losses on operations would be much higher than the 9·8 per cent quoted because up to 10 per cent of a force often turned back before crossing the enemy coast.) The Halifax squadrons with the heaviest losses in January 1944 – the worst month – were 434 Squadron with a 24·2 per cent loss rate, 102 Squadron with 18·7 per cent, 76 Squadron with 16·7 per cent, 77 Squadron with 15·0 per cent and 427 Squadron with 13·9 per cent. 427 and 434 Squadrons were Canadian. After a bad raid to Leipzig on the night of 19/20 February, when the Halifax IIs and Vs suffered more than 16·0 per cent casualties, Sir Arthur Harris felt that he could not ask the crews of these aircraft to face the German defences again and ten more squadrons disappeared from Bomber Command's front line, although a few Halifax IIs continued to fly with one of the Pathfinder squadrons.

These two depletions cost Harris approximately 250 aircraft, about one third of his total strength of heavy bombers and at least 20 per cent of his bomb-carrying capacity. This serious reduction of strength at the time of Bomber Command's greatest test was only partly compensated for in a steady increase in numbers of Lancasters and of the more reliable Mark III version of the Halifax, but most of the new production of these aircraft was required to replace casualty losses.

The period covered by the Battle of Berlin was to be the high tide of success for the German night-fighter force, rather surprisingly and disappointingly so for Bomber Command after the obvious setback caused to the German night defence by the introduction of *Window* only a few weeks earlier. Before this new device destroyed the German reliance on their box system, it had been the German practice to place their best crews in the most favourable boxes. These crews quickly built up their score of successes and became the much publicized and decorated *'Experten'* of the night-fighter force. This force had been expanding all through 1942 and 1943 but, until the introduction of *Window*, the newer crews were usually stand-bys or reserves, rarely given a chance in the best boxes. So, when *Window* rendered the box system obsolete by blinding the radar sets upon which the system depended, the unknown mass of more junior German crews did not regard *Window* as a setback; to these men, *Window* was the liberating force which gave them as much chance of finding and shooting down R.A.F. bombers as the *Experten*. There are many ex-Luftwaffe night-fighter aircrew who believe that *Window* was the finest gift that could have been given to the German defences. It forced the Germans to send their fighters 'freelancing' on the bomber routes into and away from the cities being attacked, each German crew using its own initiative to find the bombers. The single-engined Wild Boar fighters had already been doing this in the target area for some weeks but, although the Wild Boar force was expanded and played an important part in the Battle of Berlin, these fighters were not to become the dominant factor. Attrition to the single-seater fighters, flying by night, with few navigational aids, in wintry weather, was high; landing accidents in particular were numerous. It was a slightly different tactic, called by the Germans *Zahme Sau* or Tame Boar – which was to cause the destruction of so many R.A.F. bombers. The whole essence of Tame Boar was to provide the twin-engined night fighters with every possible assistance to find the bomber stream, either on the way to the target or on the return flight of the stream to England, and then leave it to the skill of the individual fighter crews to find and engage the bombers. The Germans would have nearly 400 such fighters in action before the Battle of Berlin was over, each with radio and navigational equipment, a good flying endurance and a radar set which would soon be improved to allow it to penetrate *Window*. Every night-fighter crew now had the same chance of success.

They did not all become experts but, after the first few shaky flights, many developed a flair for this type of action and scored steadily. The effect was cumulative. The German crews gained both in numbers and skill; the bomber losses mounted steadily. The heaviest Bomber Command loss of the war would come on the last night operation of the Battle of Berlin.

A typical Tame Boar operation would start even before the bombers took off. A sophisticated radio-listening service could tell the approximate number of bombers being prepared for operations by monitoring the short signals produced when each aircraft's radio set was tested. The approach of the bombers over the North Sea could be plotted by radar, with the radar not plotting individual aircraft but following the image of the *Window* cloud – the whole essence of the German use of radar in this period was to plot the location and course of the bomber stream as represented by the cloud of *Window*. The night fighters were ordered up and they used a network of radio beacons to find their way across Germany and were often held over certain beacons until the future course of the bombers became clear. There were special German reconnaissance units whose Junkers 88s attempted to find the bomber stream at an early stage and fly alongside the stream without attacking, sending back to the German control rooms a steady stream of information instead. Other special units of 'illuminators', Junkers 88s again, flew above the bomber stream dropping strings of flares to attract the main night-fighter force to the scene of battle. And all the time, the German control rooms were gathering information and broadcasting a 'running commentary' to the night fighters, describing every move made by the bomber stream and attempting to forecast its future movements.

Bomber Command followed every German development and attempted to fight back. The Stirlings and old Halifaxes which no longer flew on major raids carried out major minelaying operations, dropping masses of *Window* as they flew across the North Sea to simulate the approach of a large force. Sometimes the training groups flew a large exercise operation over the sea, turning away before reaching the German coast. The main bomber force was sent by increasingly indirect routes, with frequent course changes; the neutrality of Sweden was sometimes ignored in wide sweeps to the north on the route to Berlin. The duration of the bombing period over the target was cut again and again until 800 aircraft could pass over the target in less than twenty minutes! The bomber stream which, when first established in 1942, was considered to be a great risk when it was 300 miles long, was now only 70 miles long. The radio-countermeasures force was increased, the main object being to jam the German running commentary. Fighter Command was asked to send more and more Intruders to German airfields. A new group was formed, 100 (Bomber Support) Group under Air Commodore E. B. Addison, a signals expert. It was the last group to be formed in Bomber Command and to it were posted the radio-countermeasures squadrons and several Mosquito fighter squadrons so that Bomber Command could directly control the Intruder and *Serrate* effort. All these tactical developments took place during the Battle of Berlin.

(Because, tactically, this was such an interesting period, more detail than normal on the Bomber Command planning and the German defence reaction is included in the diary entries of major raids.)

The story of the Battle of Berlin is of a steady deterioration of effectiveness by the bomber force at increasing cost. The main offensive against Berlin was fought between 18/19 November 1943 and the end of January 1944, a period which saw fourteen large raids on the city employing 7,403 sorties and losing 384 aircraft. Some of the raids caused serious damage in Berlin; the local reports sent for the use of this diary show that more destruction was caused than Bomber Command suspected at the time. (Our expert in Berlin, Arno Abendroth, studied six different wartime reports for each of his raid reports. He stresses that much of the information sent on this series of raids was secret at the time and has never been published. 'Hope you use it!', he writes.) But the overwhelming success sought by Harris proved to be elusive. Berlin was not reduced to ruins at the end of the battle and the Germans were nowhere near surrender by April 1944 as Harris had forecast. In February and March the main weight of the campaign turned to lesser German cities, although Berlin was raided twice more before the end of March. The first raids of the pre-invasion periods against railway targets in France and Belgium started in March, but these raids mostly used the under-employed Stirlings and Halifax IIs and Vs.

Much has been written about the morale of the bomber crews and the degree by which it fell during the Battle of Berlin. The main strain fell on the men who flew Lancasters and Halifax IIIs, the latter having the most severe test to face because, when the fighters struck and bomber pilots made for altitude, whatever their orders, the Halifax IIIs were now left at the lower altitudes and the Germans found them first. There were no 'freshman' raids for the Lancaster and Halifax men; a new crew could arrive at a squadron from a training unit and a flight to Berlin in midwinter could be their first operation. Aircrew morale was undoubtedly put to a severe test. There is evidence that some Halifax squadrons had a consistently higher rate of early returns than other squadrons. The attempt to increase the Lancaster's bomb tonnage also affected the willingness of crews to comply fully with orders. No. 1 Group was

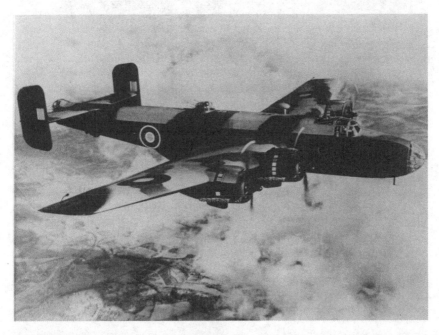

30. This fine photograph shows a Mark III Halifax, the version used extensively in 4 and 6 Groups during the final years of the war. This aircraft was used briefly by 51 Squadron at Snaith until shot down on the way to Nuremberg on 30/31 March 1944, its all-N.C.O. crew being all killed.

31. A Lancaster of 101 Squadron at Ludford Magna and a typical area-bombing load: one 4,000-pound 'Blockbuster', four general-purpose high-explosive bombs and containers of 4-pound incendiaries.

the most enthusiastic in loading its aircraft with extra bombs and, whenever 1 Group aircraft were flying across the North Sea, a succession of explosions below would show how some crews were anonymously making their aircraft more manoeuvrable by jettisoning part of their loads. Bomber Command documents of this period several times contain written exhortations to 1 Group crews to cease this practice. Around the targets, too, there were the so-called 'fringe merchants' who dropped their loads a little too early and caused the creepback to extend for many miles out into the country from the target city.

But these comments must be kept in perspective. Most crews did not abort unnecessarily, did not drop bombs in the sea and did their utmost to reach the centre of the target. What Bomber Command suffered from in the Battle of Berlin was not a widespread drop in morale but a deterioration of efficiency caused by adverse weather, the longer routes which had to be employed and which forced more fuel to be carried at the expense of bomb tonnage, and steadily increasing casualties which led to an ever greater reliance on inexperienced crews. All these factors applied to the Pathfinders as well as to the Main Force squadrons. There was also a steady dilution of effort. In the closing phases of the battle, up to 20 per cent of the aircraft dispatched by Bomber Command were employed on diversionary and supporting raids and, although it must be said that some of those aircraft were not suitable for Main Force raids, the German defences had forced a departure from the principle of concentration. Finally, the electronic aids which had ensured victory in the Battle of the Ruhr were not available over Berlin. The limiting range at which *Oboe* could be used was the supremely vital factor in the outcome of the Battle of Berlin.

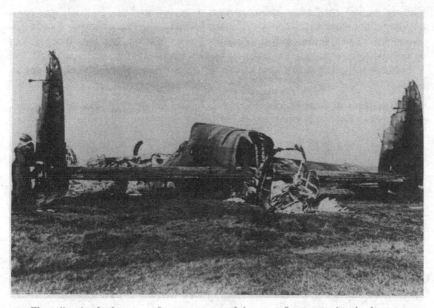

32. The tail unit of a burnt-out Lancaster, one of the 3,431 Lancasters lost in the war.

18/19 November 1943

BERLIN

440 Lancasters and 4 Mosquitoes were dispatched. Few German fighters intercepted the force. 9 Lancasters were lost, 2·0 per cent of the force.

Berlin was completely cloud-covered and both marking and bombing were carried out blindly; Bomber Command could make no assessment of the results. The local Berlin report shows that bombs fell in most parts of the city and no main concentration ('*Schwerpunkt*') could be detected, although more southern districts are mentioned than others. 4 industrial premises were totally destroyed and 28 damaged; 11 'explosive' works and 4 chemical plants were among these figures. 169 houses were destroyed and 476 seriously damaged. Casualties were: 131 people killed, 14 missing and 391 injured; 27 of the killed were foreign workers or prisoners of war.

MANNHEIM/LUDWIGSHAFEN

395 aircraft – 248 Halifaxes, 114 Stirlings, 33 Lancasters – of 3, 4, 6 and 8 Groups were on this major diversionary raid. German fighters successfully engaged the bomber force and 23 aircraft – 12 Halifaxes, 9 Stirlings, 2 Lancasters – were lost, 5·8 per cent of the force.

Cloud was present over the target area and much of the bombing was scattered. Mannheim reports that the majority of the damage was in the north of the city. 4 industrial buildings were destroyed and 11 seriously damaged, the most serious being the Daimler-Benz car factory which suffered a 90 per cent production loss for 'an unknown period'. 325 other buildings were destroyed and 335 seriously damaged, including 2 churches and 3 schools. 4 army barracks and the airfield at Sandhofen were all hit. 21 people were killed, 154 injured and 7,500 bombed out. Many bombs fell outside the city and the local report lists much damage and loss at farms.

This was the last major raid on the much-bombed city of Mannheim for 15 months.

Minor Operations: 10 Mosquitoes to Essen, 6 to Aachen and 6 to Frankfurt, 16 Wellingtons minelaying from Texel to St-Nazaire, 7 O.T.U. sorties. No losses.

Total effort for the night: 884 sorties, 32 aircraft (3·6 per cent) lost. The total number of aircraft dispatched was a new record for a non-1,000 raid night, but only by 1 sortie.

19/20 November 1943

LEVERKUSEN

266 aircraft – 170 Halifaxes, 86 Stirlings, 10 Mosquitoes – of 3, 4, 6 and 8 Groups. Only 4 Halifaxes and 1 Stirling – 1·9 per cent of the force – lost; very few German fighters were operating, probably because of bad weather at their airfields.

Failures of equipment prevented most of the *Oboe* marking being carried out and other Pathfinder aircraft were unable to mark the target properly in difficult weather conditions, leading to bombs being scattered over a wide area. At least 27 towns, mostly well to the north of Leverkusen, recorded bombs. Leverkusen's own records show only one high-explosive bomb in the town!

Minor Operations: 6 Mosquitoes to Duisburg and 2 to Rheinhausen, 25 aircraft minelaying off Biscay ports, 11 O.T.U. sorties. No losses.

Many of the aircraft returning from operations encountered fog conditions on reaching England and 2 Halifaxes and 1 Stirling crashed, but 4 Halifaxes of 35 Squadron landed safely at Graveley when the first operational use was made of the oil-burning fog-dispersal equipment called FIDO (Fog Investigation Dispersal Operation), which was installed at Graveley airfield. Several other airfields were soon fitted with this useful device.

22/23 November 1943

BERLIN

764 aircraft – 469 Lancasters, 234 Halifaxes, 50 Stirlings, 11 Mosquitoes. This was the greatest force sent to Berlin so far but it was also the last raid in which Stirlings were sent to Germany. Bad weather again kept most of the German fighters on the ground and the bomber force was able to take a relatively 'straight in, straight out' route to the target without suffering undue loss. 26 aircraft – 11 Lancasters, 10 Halifaxes, 5 Stirlings – were lost, 3·4 per cent of the force.

Berlin was again completely cloud-covered and returning crews could only estimate that the marking and bombing were believed to be accurate. In fact, this was the most effective raid on Berlin of the war. A vast area of destruction stretched from the central districts westwards across the mainly residential areas of Tiergarten and Charlottenburg to the separate suburb city of Spandau. Because of the dry weather conditions, several 'firestorm' areas were reported and a German plane next day measured the height of the smoke cloud as 6,000 metres (nearly 19,000 ft).

It is impossible to give anything like full details of the damage or to separate completely details from this raid and a smaller one on the next night. At least 3,000 houses and 23 industrial premises were completely destroyed, with several thousands of other buildings damaged. It was estimated that 175,000 people were bombed out. More than 50,000 soldiers were brought in to help from garrisons up to 100 km distant; these were equivalent to nearly 3 army divisions taken from their normal duties. Interesting entries among the lists of buildings destroyed or severely damaged are: the Kaiser-Wilhelm-Gedächtniskirche (the Kaiser Wilhelm Memorial Church which is now, half ruined, half restored, a major attraction in West Berlin), the Charlottenburg Castle, the Berlin Zoo, much of the Unter den Linden, the British, French, Italian and Japanese embassies, the Ministry of Weapons and Munitions, the Waffen S.S. Administrative College, the barracks of the Imperial Guard at Spandau and, among many industrial premises, 5 factories of the Siemens electrical group and the Alkett tank works which had recently moved from the Ruhr.

It is difficult to give exact casualty figures: an estimated 2,000 people were killed, including 500 in a large shelter in Wilmersdorf which received a direct hit, and 105 people were killed in another shelter which was next to the Neuköln gasworks, where there was a huge explosion.

Minor Operations: 12 Mosquitoes to Leverkusen, 14 Wellingtons minelaying in the Frisians and off Texel, 12 O.T.U. sorties. No losses.

Total effort for the night: 802 sorties, 26 aircraft (3·2 per cent) lost.

23/24 November 1943

BERLIN

383 aircraft – 365 Lancasters, 10 Halifaxes, 8 Mosquitoes – to continue the attack on Berlin. The bombing force used the same direct route as had been employed on the previous night. The German controllers made an early identification of Berlin as the probable target; their single-engined fighters were gathered over the city by Zero Hour and other fighters arrived a few minutes later. Fake instructions broadcast from England caused much annoyance to the German who was giving the 'running commentary'; the Germans started using a female commentator but this was promptly countered by a female voice from England ordering the German pilots to land because of fog at their bases. 'Spoof' fighter flares dropped by Mosquitoes north of the bomber stream also caused some diversion of German effort. Bomber crews noticed that Flak over the target was unusually restrained, with the German fighters obviously being given priority. 20 aircraft – all Lancasters – were lost, 5·2 per cent of the bomber force.

The target was again cloud-covered and the Pathfinders carried out sky-marking, but many of the Main Force crews aimed their bombs through the cloud at the glow of 11 major fires still burning from the previous night. Much further destruction was caused in Berlin but, because many of the details of the 2 raids were recorded together by the Germans, it is only possible to say that more than 2,000 further houses, 94 wooden barracks buildings, 8 industrial premises and 1 military establishment were destroyed, with many other buildings damaged. Approximately 1,400–1,500 people were killed on this night.

6 *Oboe* Mosquitoes attacked the Knapsack power-station near Cologne without loss.

24/25 November 1943

Minor Operations

6 Mosquitoes bombed Berlin through cloud and 9 O.T.U. Wellingtons took leaflets to France. 1 Mosquito lost.

25/26 November 1943

FRANKFURT

262 aircraft – 236 Halifaxes and 26 Lancasters – of 4, 6 and 8 Groups. As on the previous night, there were no major diversions and the bomber force took a relatively direct route to the target. The German controller did not, at first, know whether Mannheim or Frankfurt was the real objective but he eventually chose Frankfurt, where the Flak was restricted to 15,000 ft. 12 bombers – 11 Halifaxes and 1 Lancaster – lost, 4·6 per cent of the force.

Cloud covered the target area and the bombing appeared to be scattered. Frankfurt's report confirms this, the number of bombs recorded suggesting that fewer than 100 aircraft managed to hit the city. A moderate amount of housing was destroyed, 80 people were killed and 3,500 were bombed out. The report states that some fires in granaries and cattle sheds in outlying farms were blamed, not on the bombing but on sabotage, presumably by foreign workers.

Minor Operations: 3 Mosquitoes to Berlin, 48 aircraft minelaying off Brest and Texel and in the Frisians, 28 O.T.U. sorties. 1 Stirling minelayer lost.

Total effort for the night: 341 sorties, 13 aircraft (3·8 per cent) lost.

26/27 November 1943

BERLIN

443 Lancasters and 7 Mosquitoes. The Berlin force and the Stuttgart diversionary force (see details later) flew a common route over Northern France and on nearly to Frankfurt before diverging. The German controllers thought that Frankfurt was the main target until a late stage and several bombers were shot down as they flew past Frankfurt. Only a few fighters appeared over Berlin, where Flak was the main danger, but the scattered condition of the bomber stream at Berlin meant that bombers were caught by fighters off track on the return flight and the casualties mounted. 28 Lancasters were lost, 6·2 per cent of the force, and 14 more Lancasters crashed in England.

The weather was clear over Berlin but, after their long approach flight from the south, the Pathfinders marked an area 6–7 miles north-west of the city centre and most aircraft bombed there. Because of Berlin's size, however, most of the bombing still fell within the city boundaries and particularly on the semi-industrial suburb of Reinickendorf; smaller amounts of bombing fell in the centre and in the Siemensstadt (with many electrical factories) and Tegel districts. 38 war-industry factories were destroyed and many more damaged. The now routine destruction of housing and public buildings also took place but not on as great a scale as on the 2 previous raids to Berlin. The Berlin Zoo was heavily bombed on this night. Many of the animals had been evacuated to zoos in other parts of Germany but the bombing killed most of the remainder. Several large and dangerous animals – leopards, panthers, jaguars, apes – escaped and had to be hunted and shot in the streets.

Because of the confusion caused by so many raids in a short period, it was only possible for the Germans to record an approximate number of people killed, on this night, of about 700–800. The local officials did, however, produce a report in January 1944 giving details of the combined casualties of the three raids of 22/23, 23/24 and 26/27 November. 4,330 people were killed, of whom the bodies of 574 were never recovered. The districts with the most deaths were: Tiergarten, 793; Charlottenburg, 735; and Wedding, 548. 157 of the dead were foreign workers and 26 were prisoners of war. The property damage was extensive, with 8,701 dwelling buildings containing 104,613 flats/apartments destroyed, and several times that number damaged. 417,665 people lost their homes for more than a month and 36,391 for up to a month.

STUTTGART

157 Halifaxes and 21 Lancasters on a diversionary raid. 6 Halifaxes lost, 3·4 per cent of the force.

The bombing was very scattered and caused little damage but part of the night-fighter force was drawn off from the Berlin operation.

Minor Operations: 19 Stirlings and 14 Wellingtons minelaying off Texel and in the Frisians, 5 O.T.U. sorties. No losses.

Total effort for the night: 666 sorties, 34 aircraft (5·1 per cent) lost.

28/29 November 1943

Minor Operations

10 Mosquitoes to Essen and 1 to Duisburg, 10 aircraft minelaying off Brest and Cherbourg, 7 O.T.U. sorties. No losses.

29/30 November 1943

Minor Operations

21 Mosquitoes to Bochum, Cologne and Düsseldorf, 9 O.T.U. sorties. No losses.

30 November/1 December 1943

100 Group Operations

192 Squadron, flying from Foulsham, inaugurated 100 Group's operations by dispatching 4 Wellingtons on radio-countermeasures flights. (These operations are recorded as 'R.C.M. sorties' in subsequent diary entries. The loose term 'R.C.M.' covered a variety of operations and some R.C.M. aircraft also carried bombs which were dropped on main or decoy targets.) No aircraft lost.

Minor Operations: 4 Mosquitoes to Essen, 29 Stirlings and 15 Wellingtons minelaying from Brest to Bayonne, 7 O.T.U. sorties. No losses.

1/2 December 1943

MINELAYING

19 Stirlings and 12 Halifaxes were sent to the Frisians and to the east coast of Denmark. 2 Stirlings lost.

2/3 December 1943

BERLIN

458 aircraft – 425 Lancasters, 18 Mosquitoes, 15 Halifaxes. There were no major diversions and the bombers took an absolutely direct route across the North Sea and Holland and then on to Berlin. The Germans identified Berlin as the target 19 minutes before Zero Hour and many fighters were waiting there. Incorrectly forecast winds scattered the bomber stream, particularly on the return flight, and German fighters scored further victories here. A total of 40 bombers – 37 Lancasters, 2 Halifaxes, 1 Mosquito – were lost, 8·7 per cent of the force. 460 (Australian) Squadron lost 5 of its 25 Lancasters on this raid, including the aircraft in which two newspaper reporters were flying. These were Captain Grieg of the *Daily Mail* and Norman Stockton of the *Sydney Sun*. The body of Mr Stockton is buried in the Berlin War Cemetery.

The inaccurate wind forecast caused great difficulties for the Pathfinders, who were not able to establish their positions correctly. The bombing photographs of the Main Force suggested that the attack was scattered over a wide area of southern Berlin and the countryside south of the city. The Berlin report confirms this but adds that some useful damage was caused in industrial areas of the eastern and western districts, with two more of the Siemens factories, a ball-bearing factory and several railway installations being badly hit. Damage elsewhere was light, only 136 buildings being destroyed. 36 people were killed and a further 105 were classed as 'missing'. (It is noticed again and again that, as the war progressed, German reports become more erratic or incomplete. The 'final report' – *Schlussbericht* –for this raid is missing from the Berlin archives.)

Minor Operations: 6 Mosquitoes to Bochum and 1 to Witten, 3 R.C.M. sorties, 25 O.T.U. sorties. 1 Mosquito lost from the Bochum raid.

3/4 December 1943

LEIPZIG

527 aircraft – 307 Lancasters, 220 Halifaxes. Despite the loss of two pressmen on the previous night, the well-known American broadcaster, Ed Murrow, flew on the raid with a 619 Squadron Lancaster crew. He returned safely.

The bomber force took another direct route towards Berlin before turning off to bomb Leipzig. German fighters were in the bomber stream and scoring successes before the turn was made but most of them were then directed to Berlin when the Mosquito diversion opened there. There were few fighters over Leipzig and only 3 bombers are believed to have been lost in the target area, 2 of them being shot down by Flak. A relatively successful raid, from the point of view of bomber casualties, was spoiled when many aircraft flew by mistake into the Frankfurt defended area on the long southern withdrawal route and more than half of the bombers shot down on this night were lost there. 24 aircraft – 15 Halifaxes, 9 Lancasters – were lost, 4·6 per cent of the force.

The Pathfinders found and marked this distant inland target accurately and the bombing was very effective; this was the most successful raid on Leipzig during the war. A large area of housing and many industrial premises were severely damaged. One place which was hit by a large number of bombs was the former World Fair exhibition site, whose spacious buildings had been converted to become war factories, the largest buildings being taken over by the Junkers aircraft company. The British Official History (Vol. IV, p. 267) quotes the Leipzig city records as giving a figure of 1,182 people killed but a German local police report compiled a week after the raid gives a different figure, 614 people killed and 464 injured. It is not known which report is correct.

Minor Operations: 9 Mosquitoes in feint attack on Berlin, 3 R.C.M. sorties, 12 Halifaxes minelaying in the Frisians. No losses.

4/5 December 1943

MINOR OPERATIONS

9 Mosquitoes to Duisburg, 48 aircraft minelaying in the Frisians, 9 O.T.U. sorties. 1 Stirling minelayer and 1 O.T.U. Whitley lost.

5/6 December 1943

3 Wellingtons flew R.C.M. sorties without loss.

9/10 December 1943

3 Wellingtons flew R.C.M. sorties without loss.

10/11 December 1943

MINOR OPERATIONS

25 Mosquitoes to Leverkusen and 2 to Krefeld, 4 O.T.U. sorties. No losses.

11/12 December 1943

18 Mosquitoes attacked Duisburg and 1 Wellington flew an R.C.M. sortie without loss.

12/13 December 1943

MINOR OPERATIONS

Mosquitoes: 20 to Essen, 9 to Düsseldorf, 1 to Osnabrück, 4 R.C.M. sorties, 4 O.T.U. sorties. 1 Mosquito lost on the Essen raid.

13/14 December 1943

MINOR OPERATIONS

16 Mosquitoes to Düsseldorf, 1 to Bonn, 25 O.T.U. sorties. No losses.

15/16 December 1943

4 Mosquitoes to Bochum and 4 to Leverkusen, 3 R.C.M. sorties. No losses.

16/17 December 1943

BERLIN

483 Lancasters and 10 Mosquitoes on the main raid and 5 further Mosquitoes dropped decoy fighter flares south of Berlin.

The bomber route again led directly to Berlin across Holland and Northern Germany and there were no major diversions. The German controllers plotted the course of the bombers with great accuracy; many German fighters were met at the coast of Holland and further fighters were guided on to the bomber stream throughout the approach to the target. More fighters were waiting at the target and there were many combats. The bombers shook off the opposition on the return flight by taking a northerly route over Denmark. 25 Lancasters, 5·2 per cent of the Lancaster force, were lost. Many further aircraft were lost on returning to England (see later paragraph).

Berlin was cloud-covered but the Pathfinder sky-marking was reasonably accurate and much of the bombing fell in the city. The local report says that the raid had no identifiable aiming point but the central and eastern districts were hit more than other areas. Little industrial damage was caused; most of the bombing hit housing and railways. Conflicting figures on the number of dead are given; the overall total may be 720, of which 279 were foreign workers – 186 women, 65 men and 28 youths. 70 of these foreigners – all from the East – were killed when the train in which they were travelling was bombed at the Halensee Station. In the city centre, the National Theatre and the building housing Germany's military and political archives were both destroyed. The damage to the Berlin railway system and to rolling stock, and the large numbers of people still leaving the city, were having a cumulative effect upon the transportation of supplies to the Russian Front; 1,000 wagon-loads of war material were held up for 6 days. The sustained bombing had now made more than a quarter of Berlin's total living accommodation unusable.

On their return to England, many of the bombers encountered very low cloud at their bases. The squadrons of 1, 6 and 8 Groups were particularly badly affected. 29 Lancasters (and a Stirling from the minelaying operation) either crashed or were abandoned when their crews parachuted. The group with heaviest losses was 1 Group with 13 aircraft lost; the squadron with heaviest losses was 97 Squadron, 8 Group, with 7 aircraft lost. There is a little confusion in Bomber Command records over aircrew casualties but it is probable that 148 men were killed in the crashes, 39 were injured and 6 presumed lost in the sea.

FLYING-BOMB SITES

47 aircraft – 26 Stirlings, 12 Mosquitoes, 9 Lancasters – carried out raids on 2 sites near Abbeville. No aircraft lost.

Neither raid was successful. The larger raid, by the Stirlings on the Tilley-le-Haut site, failed because the *Oboe* Mosquito markers could not get any closer than 450 yards from the small target. The 9 Lancasters of 617 Squadron which attacked the second site, in a wood at Flixecourt, dropped their 12,000-lb bombs accurately on the markers placed by the only *Oboe* Mosquito operating at this target but the markers were 350 yards from the flying-bomb site and none of the 617 Squadron bombs were more than 100 yards from the markers.

Serrate Operations

2 Beaufighters and 2 Mosquitoes of 141 Squadron, recently transferred from Fighter Command to 100 Group, inaugurated Bomber Command's *Serrate* operations in patrols near the routes of the Berlin raid. (*Serrate* was a device which homed on to the radar emissions of a German night fighter.) 1 Mosquito made contact with an Me 110 and damaged it with cannon-fire. The crew of this first successful Bomber Command *Serrate* patrol was Squadron Leader F. F. Lambert and Flying Officer K. Dear. (Freddie Lambert was for many years after the war a very helpful official at the Public Record Office.)

Minor Operations: 5 Mosquitoes to Duisburg, 35 aircraft minelaying in the Frisians and off Biscay ports. No losses.

Total effort for the night: 589 sorties, with 25 aircraft missing and 30 crashed in or near England, a total casualty rate of 9·3 per cent.

19/20 December 1943

6 O.T.U. Wellingtons dropped leaflets over French towns without loss.

20/21 December 1943

FRANKFURT

650 aircraft – 390 Lancasters, 257 Halifaxes, 3 Mosquitoes. The German control rooms were able to plot the bomber force as soon as it left the English coast and were able to continue plotting it all the way to Frankfurt. There were many combats on the route to the target. The Mannheim diversion did not draw fighters away from the main attack until after the raid was over but the return flight was quieter. 41 aircraft – 27 Halifaxes, 14 Lancasters – lost, 6·3 per cent of the force.

The bombing at Frankfurt did not go according to plan. The Pathfinders had prepared a ground-marking plan on the basis of a forecast giving clear weather but they found up to 8/10ths cloud. The Germans lit a decoy fire site 5 miles south-east of the city and also used dummy target indicators. Some of the bombing fell around the decoy but part of the creepback fell on Frankfurt causing more damage than Bomber Command realized at the time. 466 houses were completely destroyed and 1,948 seriously damaged in Frankfurt and in the outlying townships of Sachsenhausen and Offenbach. 117 bombs hit various industrial premises but no important factories are mentioned. The report stresses the large number of cultural, historical and public buildings hit, including the cathedral, the city library, the city hospital and no fewer than 69 schools. The Wehrmacht suffered damaged to 4 Flak positions, a clothing store, a veterinary depot and the Army Music School. 64 people were killed and 111 were missing or still covered by wreckage. 23,000 people were bombed out. A train standing 6 miles south of Frankfurt was hit by a 4,000-lb bomb and 13 people in it were killed.

Part of the bombing somehow fell on Mainz, 17 miles to the west, and many houses along the Rhine waterfront and in southern suburbs were hit. 14 people were killed.

MANNHEIM

44 Lancasters and 10 Mosquitoes of 1 and 8 Groups carried out a diversionary raid on this target but most of the bombing fell outside Mannheim. No aircraft lost.

Minor Operations: 8 Lancasters of 617 Squadron and 8 Pathfinder Mosquitoes attempted to bomb an armaments factory near Liège but the Mosquito marking was not visible below the clouds and the Lancasters did not bomb; 1 Lancaster lost. 6 Mosquitoes to Rheinhausen and 5 to Leverkusen, 8 R.C.M. sorties, 2 Beaufighters on *Serrate* patrol, 23 Stirlings minelaying in the Frisians, 38 O.T.U. sorties. 1 Stirling minelayer lost.

Total effort for the night: 802 sorties, 43 aircraft (5·4 per cent) lost.

21/22 December 1943

Minor Operations

9 *Oboe* Mosquitoes to the Mannesmann factory at Düsseldorf and 4 to the Knapsack power station, 4 O.T.U. sorties. No losses.

22/23 December 1943

FLYING-BOMB SITES

51 aircraft – 29 Stirlings, 11 Lancasters, 8 Mosquitoes, 3 Halifaxes – to attack 2 sites between Abbeville and Amiens. 1 site was bombed accurately but the other could not be located. No aircraft lost.

Minor Operations: 9 Mosquitoes to Frankfurt and 2 to Bonn, 2 R.C.M. sorties, 16 aircraft minelaying off Biscay ports, 21 O.T.U. sorties. No losses.

23/24 December 1943

BERLIN

379 aircraft – 364 Lancasters, 8 Mosquitoes, 7 Halifaxes. The bomber casualties were not as heavy as on recent raids, partly because German fighters encountered difficulty with the weather and partly because the German controller was temporarily deceived by the Mosquito diversion at Leipzig. The main force of fighters only appeared in the target area at the end of the raid and could not catch the main bomber stream. 16 Lancasters were lost, 4·2 per cent of the force.

The Berlin area was covered by cloud and more than half of the early Pathfinder aircraft had trouble with their *H2S* sets. The markers were scattered and sparse. The Berlin report shows that only the south-eastern suburbs of Köpenick and Treptow received any serious number of bombs. 287 houses and other mixed property were destroyed. 1 canal cargo ship was sunk and 3 seriously damaged. 178 people were killed: 157 civilians, 11 police and soldiers, 10 foreign workers.

Minor Operations: 12 Mosquitoes to Aachen, 9 to Duisburg and 7 to Leipzig, 4 R.C.M. sorties, 3 Beaufighters on *Serrate* patrols, 7 O.T.U. sorties. 1 Beaufighter lost.

24/25 December 1943

No bombing raids were carried out on Christmas Eve but 35 Halifaxes were sent minelaying in the Frisians and returned without loss.

28/29 December 1943

MINOR OPERATIONS

Mosquitoes: 10 to Duisburg, 9 to Düsseldorf, 1 to Cologne, 11 O.T.U. sorties. No losses.

29/30 December 1943

BERLIN

712 aircraft – 457 Lancasters, 252 Halifaxes, 3 Mosquitoes. A long approach route from the south, passing south of the Ruhr and then within 20 miles of Leipzig, together with Mosquito diversions at Düsseldorf, Leipzig and Magdeburg, caused the German controller great difficulties and there were few fighters over Berlin. Bad weather on the outward route also kept down the number of German fighters finding the bomber stream. 20 aircraft – 11 Lancasters, 9 Halifaxes – were lost, 2·8 per cent of the force.

Berlin was again cloud-covered. The Bomber Command report claiming a concentrated attack on sky-markers is not confirmed by the local report. The heaviest bombing was in the southern and south-eastern districts but many bombs also fell to the east of the city. 388 houses and other mixed property were destroyed but no item of major interest is mentioned. 182 people were killed, more than 600 were injured and over 10,000 were bombed out.

Minor Operations: 8 Mosquitoes to Magdeburg, 6 to Düsseldorf, 5 to Leipzig, 4 to Bristillerie – a suspected V-weapon site near Cherbourg – and 3 to Leverkusen, 6 R.C.M. sorties, 2 Beaufighters on *Serrate* patrols, 5 Stirlings minelaying in the Frisians and off French ports, 4 O.T.U. sorties. No losses.

30/31 December 1943

Flying-Bomb Site

10 Lancasters of 617 Squadron and 6 Pathfinder Mosquitoes attempted to destroy a site which had been missed on an earlier raid, but the markers were 200 yards from the target and, with the Lancasters' bombs well grouped around these, the site was again undamaged. No aircraft lost.

Minor Operations: 10 Mosquitoes to Cologne, 8 to Duisburg and 3 to Bochum, 6 R.C.M. sorties, 26 aircraft minelaying off Texel and French ports, 28 O.T.U. sorties. No losses.

---

31 December 1943/1 January 1944

There were no bomber operations on New Year's Eve; 2 Stirlings laid mines off the Dutch coast and returned safely.

1/2 January 1944

BERLIN

421 Lancasters. German fighters were directed on to the bomber stream at an early stage and were particularly active between 2 route-markers on the way to Berlin. The German controller was not deceived by the Mosquito feint at Hamburg but his fighters were not very effective over Berlin, only 2 bombers being shot down by fighters there, and the local Flak was probably restricted to the height at which it could fire and the guns only shot down 2 bombers over the target. 28 Lancasters were lost, 6·7 per cent of the force.

The target area was covered in cloud and the accuracy of the sky-marking soon deteriorated. The Berlin report says that there was scattered bombing, mainly in the southern parts of the city. A large number of bombs fell in the Grunewald, an extensive wooded area in the south-west of Berlin. Only 21 houses and 1 industrial building were destroyed, with 79 people being killed. A high-explosive bomb hit a lock on an important canal and stopped shipping at that area for several days.

Minor Operations: 15 Mosquitoes to Hamburg, 11 to Witten, 7 to Duisburg, 4 to Bristillerie and 1 to Cologne, 6 R.C.M. sorties, 14 O.T.U. sorties. No losses.

2/3 January 1944

BERLIN

383 aircraft – 362 Lancasters, 12 Mosquitoes, 9 Halifaxes. The German control rooms followed the bombers all the way to Berlin, which was assessed as the target 40 minutes before Zero Hour. Night fighters were sent to a radio beacon between Hannover and Bremen but these fighters missed the bomber stream and did not come into action until they were directed to Berlin. Most of the bomber casualties were in the Berlin area. 27 Lancasters were lost, 7·0 per cent of the force. The casualties included 10 Pathfinder aircraft; 156 Squadron, from Warboys, lost 5 of its 14 aircraft taking part in the raid.

This was another ineffective raid. Bombs were scattered over all parts of Berlin, with the local reports stressing that there were no large fires; the fire services were able to contain all fires soon after they started. 82 houses were destroyed and 36 people were killed. Industrial damage was insignificant.

Minor Operations: 8 Mosquitoes to Duisburg and 3 to Bristillerie, 2 Beaufighters on *Serrate* patrols, 26 aircraft minelaying in the Frisians and off French ports, 25 O.T.U. sorties. No losses.

3/4 January 1944

6 Mosquitoes to Solingen and 2 to Essen. No losses.

4/5 January 1944

FLYING-BOMB SITES

80 aircraft – 57 Stirlings, 12 Mosquitoes, 11 Lancasters – to two sites, one in the Pas de Calais and one at Bristillerie, near Cherbourg. Both targets were attacked effectively and no aircraft were lost.

SPECIAL OPERATIONS: SUPPLIES AND AGENTS FOR RESISTANCE FORCES

Bomber Command's records for this night contain their first mention of this type of operation, although 138 and 161 Squadrons had been carrying out such operations for 2 years under nominal Bomber Command control. 18 Halifaxes and 1 Hudson of 138 and 161 Squadrons made flights on this night and 6 Stirlings from 214 Squadron also operated. No aircraft were lost. The Stirling flights represented a new type of work for the Stirling squadrons, which had recently been relieved from bombing raids to Germany.

This type of flight was always referred to as 'special operations' in wartime records, but the term 'Resistance operations' is preferred here.

Minor Operations: 13 Mosquitoes to Berlin, 3 to Krefeld and 2 to Cologne, 4 R.C.M. sorties, 40 aircraft minelaying off Lorient and Brest, 8 O.T.U. sorties. No aircraft lost.

5/6 January 1944

STETTIN

348 Lancasters and 10 Halifaxes in the first large raid on this target since September 1941. The Mosquito diversion at Berlin successfully kept most of the German fighters away from the main force of bombers. 16 aircraft – 14 Lancasters, 2 Halifaxes – lost, 4·5 per cent of the force.

The raid on Stettin started accurately and the central districts suffered heavily from fire, but later phases of the bombing drifted to the west. 504 houses and 20 industrial buildings were destroyed and 1,148 houses and 29 industrial buildings were seriously damaged. 8 ships were sunk in the harbour. 244 people were killed and 1,016 were injured.

Minor Operations: 13 Mosquitoes to Berlin and 25 to four other targets, 1 Mosquito R.C.M. sortie, 1 Beaufighter *Serrate* patrol, 6 Lancasters minelaying off Swinemünde. No losses.

The Beaufighter sortie on this night was the last *Serrate* flight by this type of aircraft; all later *Serrate* patrols were carried out by Mosquitoes.

6/7 January 1944

MINOR OPERATIONS

Mosquitoes: 16 to Duisburg, 2 to Bristillerie and 1 each to Dortmund and Solingen, 57 aircraft minelaying off Biscay ports, 10 O.T.U. sorties. No losses.

7/8 January 1944

MINOR OPERATIONS

6 Mosquitoes to Krefeld and 5 to Duisburg, 1 aircraft on a Resistance operation, 28 O.T.U. sorties. The Resistance operation aircraft – a 138 Squadron Halifax – crashed in England soon after taking off, killing all 10 men on board, probably 7 crew and 3 passengers.

8/9 January 1944

23 Mosquitoes: 10 to Frankfurt, 8 to Solingen, 3 to Aachen, 2 to Dortmund. 2 aircraft lost.

10/11 January 1944

20 Mosquitoes: 10 to Berlin, 7 to Solingen, 2 to Koblenz, 1 to Krefeld. No losses.

13/14 January 1944

25 Mosquitoes: 12 to Essen, 9 to Duisburg, 2 to Aachen, 2 to Koblenz. 1 aircraft lost.

14/15 January 1944

BRUNSWICK

496 Lancasters and 2 Halifaxes on the first major raid to Brunswick of the war. 38 Lancasters lost, 7·6 per cent of the force. The German running commentary was heard following the progress of the bomber force from a position only 40 miles from the English coast and many German fighters entered the bomber stream soon after the German frontier was crossed near Bremen. The German fighters scored steadily until the Dutch coast was crossed on the return flight. 11 of the lost aircraft were Pathfinders.

Brunswick was smaller than Bomber Command's usual targets and this raid was not a success. The city report describes this only as a 'light' raid, with bombs in the south of the city which had only 10 houses destroyed and 14 people killed. Most of the attack fell either in the countryside or in Wolfenbüttel and other small towns and villages well to the south of Brunswick.

FLYING-BOMB SITES

82 aircraft – 59 Stirlings, 13 Halifaxes, 10 Mosquitoes – attacked sites at Ailly, Bonneton and Bristillerie without loss.

Minor Operations: 11 Mosquitoes to Magdeburg and 6 to Berlin, 9 R.C.M. sorties, 2 *Serrate* patrols, 29 aircraft minelaying off Brest and in the Frisians, 36 O.T.U. sorties. No losses.

Total effort for the night: 673 sorties, 38 aircraft (5·6 per cent) lost.

20/21 January 1944

BERLIN

769 aircraft – 495 Lancasters, 264 Halifaxes, 10 Mosquitoes. 35 aircraft – 22 Halifaxes, 13 Lancasters – lost, 4·6 per cent of the force. 102 Squadron, from Pocklington, lost 5 of its 16 Halifaxes on this raid, 2 more crashed in England and the squadron would lose 4 more aircraft in the next night's raid. The bomber approach route took a wide swing to the north but, once again, the German controller managed to feed his fighters into the bomber stream early and the fighters scored steadily until the force was well on the way home. The diversions were not large enough to deceive the Germans.

The Berlin area was, as so often, completely cloud-covered and what happened to the bombing is a mystery. The Pathfinder sky-marking appeared to go according to plan and crews who were scanning the ground with their *H2S* sets believed that the attack fell on eastern districts of Berlin. No major navigational problems were experienced. No photographic reconnaissance was possible until after a further 4 raids on Berlin were carried out but the various sources from which the Berlin reports are normally drawn all show a complete blank for this night. It is not known whether this is because of some order issued by the German authorities to conceal the extent of the damage or whether the entire raid missed Berlin.

Minor Operations: 12 Mosquitoes to Düsseldorf, 4 to Kiel and 3 to Hannover, 6 R.C.M. sorties, 5 *Serrate* patrols, 29 aircraft minelaying in the Frisians and off French ports, 20 O.T.U. sorties. No losses.

Total effort for the night: 848 sorties, 35 aircraft (4·1 per cent) lost.

21/22 January 1944

MAGDEBURG

648 aircraft – 421 Lancasters, 224 Halifaxes, 3 Mosquitoes – on the first major raid to this target. The German controller again followed the progress of the bomber stream across the North Sea and many night fighters were in the stream before it crossed the German coast. The controller was very slow to identify Magdeburg as the target but this did not matter too much because most of the night fighters were able to stay in the bomber stream, a good example of the way the Tame Boar tactics were developing. 57 aircraft – 35 Halifaxes, 22 Lancasters – were lost, 8·8 per cent of the force; it is probable that three quarters of the losses were caused by German night fighters. The Halifax loss rate was 15·6 per cent!

The heavy bomber casualties were not rewarded with a successful attack. Some of the Main Force aircraft now had *H2S* and winds which were stronger than forecast brought some of these into the target area before the Pathfinders' Zero Hour. The crews of 27 Main Force aircraft were anxious to bomb and did so before Zero Hour. The Pathfinders blamed the fires started by this early bombing, together with some very effective German decoy markers, for their failure to concentrate the marking. No details are available from Magdeburg but it is believed that most of the bombing fell outside the city. An R.A.F. man who was in hospital at Magdeburg at the time reports only, 'bangs far away'.

BERLIN

22 Lancasters and 12 Mosquitoes of 5 and 8 Groups carried out a diversionary raid; 1 Lancaster lost.

FLYING-BOMB SITES

111 aircraft – 89 Stirlings, 12 Lancasters, 10 Mosquitoes – carried out raids on 6 sites in France without loss.

Minor Operations: 8 Mosquitoes to Oberhausen and 5 to Rheinhausen, 8 R.C.M. sorties, 5 *Serrate* patrols, 8 Wellingtons minelaying off St-Nazaire, 16 O.T.U. sorties. No aircraft lost.

Total effort for the night: 843 sorties, 58 aircraft (6·9 per cent) were lost. The number of aircraft lost was the heaviest in any night of the war so far, but only by 2 aircraft.

23/24 January 1944

MINOR OPERATIONS

37 Mosquitoes dispatched to 6 different targets, 3 R.C.M. sorties, 9 aircraft minelaying off Cherbourg, Brest and Le Havre. No aircraft lost.

25/26 January 1944

FLYING-BOMB SITES

76 aircraft – 56 Stirlings, 12 Lancasters, 8 Mosquitoes – attacked sites in the Pas de Calais and near Cherbourg without loss.

Minor Operations: 14 Mosquitoes to Aachen, 18 O.T.U. sorties. 1 O.T.U. Wellington lost.

27/28 January 1944

BERLIN

515 Lancasters and 15 Mosquitoes. The German fighters were committed to action earlier than normal, some being sent out 75 miles over the North Sea from the Dutch coast. But the elaborate feints and diversions had some effect. Half of the German fighters were lured north by the Heligoland mining diversion and action in the main bomber stream was less intense than on recent nights. 33 Lancasters lost, 6·4 per cent of the heavy force.

33. German dead in the Battle of Berlin.

The target was cloud-covered again and sky-marking had to be used. Bomber Command was not able to make any assessment of the raid except to state that the bombing appeared to have been spread well up and down wind. Local reports confirm that the bombing was spread over a wide area, although many bombs fell in the southern half of the city, less in the north, but 61 small towns and villages outside the city limits were also hit with 28 people being killed in those places. Details of houses destroyed in Berlin are not available but it is known that nearly 20,000 people were bombed out. 50 industrial premises were hit and several important war industries suffered serious damage. 567 people were killed, including 132 foreign workers.

DIVERSIONARY AND SUPPORT OPERATIONS

Extensive operations were carried out in support of the Berlin raid. 80 Stirlings and Wellingtons flew to the Dutch coast and laid mines there, 21 Halifaxes did the same near Heligoland, both hoping to draw the German fighters up early. 9 aircraft flew R.C.M. sorties and 12 Mosquitoes flew *Serrate* patrols. 18 Mosquito-bomber aircraft dropped imitation 'fighter flares' away from the main bomber routes to and from the target. 140 aircraft were thus engaged in various operations in support of the main raid. 1 Stirling minelayer lost.

Minor Operations: 9 Mosquitoes bombed a flying-bomb site at Herbouville, 8 Halifaxes flew Resistance operations sorties, 10 O.T.U. aircraft dropped leaflets over France. No aircraft lost.

Total effort for the night: 697 sorties, 34 aircraft (4·9 per cent) lost.

28/29 January 1944

BERLIN

677 aircraft – 432 Lancasters, 241 Halifaxes, 4 Mosquitoes. Part of the German fighter force was drawn up by the early diversions and the bomber approach route over Northern Denmark proved too distant for some of the other German fighters. The German controller was, however, able to concentrate his fighters over the target and many aircraft were shot down there. 46 aircraft – 26 Halifaxes, 20 Lancasters – lost, 6·8 per cent of the force.

The cloud over Berlin was broken and some ground-marking was possible but the Bomber Command claim that this was the most concentrated attack of this period is not quite fully confirmed by German records. The western and southern districts were hit but so too were 77 places outside the city. The Berlin recording system was now showing an increasing deterioration. No overall figure for property damage was recorded; approximately 180,000 people were bombed out on this night. Although many industrial firms were again hit, the feature of this night is the unusually high proportion of administrative and public buildings appearing in the lists of buildings hit: the new Chancellery, 4 theatres, the 'French' cathedral, 6 hospitals, 5 embassies, the State Patent Office, etc. The report concludes with this entry: 'The casualties are still not known but they are bound to be considerable. It is reported that a vast amount of wreckage must still be cleared; rescue workers are among the mountains of it.' *

---

* Report of Technischen Nothilfe, Gau III – Berlin and Brandenburg, in Berlin city archives.

DIVERSION AND SUPPORT OPERATIONS

63 Stirlings and 4 Pathfinder Halifaxes carried out minelaying in Kiel Bay 5 hours before the main Berlin operation; this was the first time that Pathfinder aircraft helped a minelaying operation. 6 Mosquitoes bombed Berlin 4 hours before the main attack and 18 Mosquitoes bombed night-fighter airfields at Deelen, Leeuwarden and Venlo. 4 Mosquitoes carried out a diversionary raid to Hannover and 6 more Mosquitoes flew *Serrate* patrols at the same time as the main raid. 2 Stirling minelayers and 1 *Serrate* Mosquito were lost from these operations.

16 O.T.U. Wellingtons carried out leaflet flights to France without loss.

Total effort for the night: 794 sorties, 49 aircraft (6·2 per cent) lost.

29/30 January 1944

Minor Operations

22 Mosquitoes – 12 to Duisburg and 10 to Herbouville flying-bomb site – 6 O.T.U. sorties. No losses.

30/31 January 1944

BERLIN

534 aircraft – 440 Lancasters, 82 Halifaxes, 12 Mosquitoes. There were no preliminary diversions on this night and the attempt by the German controllers to intercept the bomber stream over the sea failed. The bombers were, therefore, well on the way to Berlin before meeting any fighters but the Germans were then able to follow the bomber stream until well into the return flight. 33 aircraft – 32 Lancasters and 1 Halifax – lost, 6·2 per cent of the force.

The raid took place through complete cloud cover but Bomber Command claimed another concentrated attack. The local report repeats a recent trend – heavy damage in the city at the same time as widespread bombing in the country areas outside. 79 towns and villages reported various numbers of bombs but most of these fell in open country; 17 people were killed and 28 injured outside Berlin.

The main concentration of damage in the city was in the centre and in the south-western quarter, though many other districts were also hit. The seriousness of fire damage on this night is stressed. Once again, overall figures for domestic property damage and casualties are not available but, by a process of deduction from an overall report for this period, it is certain that at least 1,000 people died. Some details of individual property damage were recorded: 2 industrial premises were completely destroyed and 15 were seriously damaged; many public buildings are mentioned, including Goebbels's Propaganda Ministry; the Berlin transport system suffered, not only by the destruction of 94 U-Bahn carriages at the Kreuzberg depot.

SUPPORT AND MINOR OPERATIONS

22 Mosquitoes to Elberfeld and 5 to Brunswick, 8 R.C.M. sorties, 7 *Serrate* patrols, 12 Stirlings minelaying in the River Gironde, 22 O.T.U. sorties. No losses.

Total effort for the night: 610 sorties, 33 aircraft (5·4 per cent) lost.

1/2 February 1944

MINOR OPERATIONS

12 Mosquitoes to Berlin, 3 to Aachen and 3 to Krefeld, 3 *Serrate* patrols. 1 Mosquito lost on the Berlin raid.

2/3 February 1944

MINOR OPERATIONS

7 Mosquitoes to Rheinhausen and 6 to Elberfeld, 2 R.C.M. sorties, 5 *Serrate* patrols, 50 Halifaxes minelaying in Kiel Bay. The Kiel Bay mining operation was a ploy to draw up German fighters, even though no major bombing raid was planned. No aircraft were lost from these operations.

3/4 February 1944

MINOR OPERATIONS

7 Mosquitoes to Krefeld, 4 to Dortmund and 3 to Cologne, 6 R.C.M. sorties, 1 *Serrate* patrol, 35 aircraft minelaying off French Channel and Atlantic ports, 4 O.T.U. sorties. No aircraft lost.

4/5 February 1944

MINOR OPERATIONS

9 Mosquitoes to Frankfurt, 5 to Elberfeld and 1 to Aachen, 2 *Serrate* patrols, 28 aircraft minelaying in the Bay of Biscay, 49 aircraft – 27 Stirlings, 17 Halifaxes, 3 Lysanders, 2 Hudsons – on Resistance operations. This was the first widespread use of the 3 Group Stirling squadrons for Resistance operations work. No aircraft lost.

5/6 February 1944

MINOR OPERATIONS

18 Mosquitoes to Berlin, 7 to Duisburg and 1 to Hannover, 3 *Serrate* patrols, 29 Stirlings and 17 Halifaxes on Resistance operations, 19 Halifaxes minelaying off Oslo and Fredrijkstad in Norway, 15 O.T.U. sorties. 1 Stirling lost on Resistance operations work.

7/8 February 1944

MINOR OPERATIONS

19 Mosquitoes to Frankfurt, 8 to Elberfeld, 5 to Krefeld, 2 to Aachen and 1 to Mannheim, 4 *Serrate* patrols. No losses.

8/9 February 1944

Limoges

12 Lancasters of 617 Squadron, led by its new commanding officer Wing Commander Leonard Cheshire, attacked the Gnome & Rhône aero-engine factory.

This was a very important raid. 617 Squadron had been experiencing difficulty in finding a useful role after the Dams Raid nearly 9 months earlier. Low-level precision raids on targets in Germany had been too costly. High-level precision bombing on small targets in France and Belgium had been unsatisfactory, not because 617 Squadron's bombing was inaccurate but because the *Oboe* marking provided by Pathfinder Mosquitoes was not quite accurate enough for extremely small targets like flying-bomb sites or individual factory buildings with civilian housing near by. Wing Commander Cheshire wanted to try his own marking, flying at very low level; he had unofficially experimented with this already. For the Limoges attack, Cheshire was given official permission to attempt low-level marking of this target, which had many French civilian houses near by.

The factory was undefended, except for 2 machine-guns, and Cheshire made 3 low-level runs in bright moonlight to warn the French factory workers to escape. On his 4th run, he dropped a load of 30-lb incendiaries from between 50 and 100 ft. Each of 11 other Lancasters then dropped a 12,000-lb bomb with great accuracy; 10 bombs hit the factory and the remaining one fell in the river alongside. The factory was severely damaged and production almost completely ceased. There were few if any casualties among the French people. No Lancasters were lost.

The tactical importance of this raid was that a method appeared to have been found of marking and bombing small targets accurately, although fears were expressed that the method would be prohibitively costly against defended targets. In the following weeks and months, 617 Squadron would show that low-level marking was reliable and did not incur heavy casualties, particularly when Mosquito aircraft were used for the marking. This type of marking was eventually employed for most 617 Squadron operations and was later extended to larger raids carried out by the whole of 5 Group, sometimes with a further group being added to the bombing force. But 8 Group, the regular Pathfinders for Bomber Command, resisted the introduction of the low-level marking method and it was never used for full-scale raids even though 8 Group operated several squadrons of Mosquitoes. It was a controversial subject then and continued so long after the war.

Minor Operations: 11 Mosquitoes to Brunswick and 8 to Elberfeld, 2 *Serrate* patrols, 39 aircraft on Resistance operations, 19 O.T.U. sorties. No losses.

9/10 February 1944

16 Mosquitoes dispatched – 8 to Elberfeld, 7 to Krefeld and 1 to Aachen. 1 aircraft lost on the Krefeld raid.

10/11 February 1944

MINOR OPERATIONS

21 Mosquitoes to Berlin and 4 to Aachen, 2 Wellingtons on R.C.M. flights, 21 aircraft minelaying off Brittany and Biscay ports, 26 aircraft on Resistance operations. No aircraft lost.

11/12 February 1944

MINOR OPERATIONS

11 Mosquitoes to Brunswick, 8 to Elberfeld, 4 to Aachen and 4 to Duisburg, 2 R.C.M. sorties, 5 *Serrate* patrols, 52 aircraft minelaying off French Channel and Atlantic ports, 27 aircraft on Resistance operations, 6 O.T.U. sorties. No aircraft lost.

12/13 February 1944

Anthéor Viaduct

10 Lancasters of 617 Squadron attempted to bomb this important railway link between France and Italy but, as on two earlier raids, were not successful despite low-level runs by Wing Commander Cheshire and Squadron Leader Martin. The sides of the valley were very steep and the target was defended by guns which damaged both of the low-level aircraft. Flight Lieutenant R. C. Hay, the bomb aimer in Martin's aircraft and the Squadron Bombing Leader since 617's formation, was killed.

Minor Operations: 8 Mosquitoes to Elberfeld and 4 to Duisburg, 3 *Serrate* patrols, 25 Halifaxes and Stirlings minelaying in the Frisians and off Cherbourg. 1 Halifax minelayer lost.

15/16 February 1944

BERLIN

After a rest of more than 2 weeks for the regular bomber squadrons, 891 aircraft – 561 Lancasters, 314 Halifaxes, 16 Mosquitoes – were dispatched. This was the largest force sent to Berlin and the largest non-1,000 bomber force sent to any target, exceeding the previous record of 826 aircraft (which included Stirlings and Wellingtons) sent to Dortmund on the night of 23/24 May 1943. It was also the first time that more than 500 Lancasters and more than 300 Halifaxes were dispatched. The quantity of bombs dropped, 2,642 tons, was also a record.

The German controllers were able to plot the bomber stream soon after it left the English coast but the swing north over Denmark for the approach flight proved too far distant for many of the German fighters. The German controller ordered the fighters not to fly over Berlin, leaving the target area free for the Flak, but many fighters ignored him and attacked bombers over the city. The diversion to Frankfurt-on-Oder failed to draw any fighters. 43 aircraft – 26 Lancasters, 17 Halifaxes – were lost, 4·8 per cent of the force.

Berlin was covered by cloud for most of the raid. Heavy bombing fell on the centre and south-western districts but many places out in the country again recorded bombs, with 59 people being killed there. Damage in Berlin was extensive with 599 large and 572 medium fires and nearly 1,000 houses and 526 temporary wooden barracks, of which there were now a large number in Berlin, destroyed. Some of Berlin's most important war industries were hit, including the large Siemensstadt area. 320 people were killed – 196 civilians, 34 service personnel, 9 air-raid workers, 80 foreign workers and 1 prisoner of war. The diminishing proportion of civilian casualties reflects the large-scale evacuation which had now taken place but a further 260 civilians were recorded as being 'buried alive' and it is not known how many of these survived.

This was really the end of the true 'Battle of Berlin'; only one more raid took place on the city in this period and that was not for more than a month.

DIVERSION AND SUPPORT OPERATIONS

23 *Oboe* Mosquitoes attacked 5 night-fighter airfields in Holland, 43 Stirlings and 4 Pathfinder Halifaxes carried out minelaying in Kiel Bay, 24 Lancasters of 8 Group made a diversion raid on Frankfurt-on-Oder (where 147 buildings were damaged, 25 people were killed and 34 were seriously injured), 9 aircraft made R.C.M. flights and 14 Mosquitoes carried out *Serrate* patrols. A *Serrate* Mosquito was the only aircraft lost.

MINOR OPERATIONS

2 Mosquitoes to Aachen, 6 Stirlings and 6 Wellingtons minelaying off Bayonne and Lorient, 48 aircraft on Resistance operations. 1 Stirling lost from a Resistance flight.

Total effort for the night: 1,070 sorties, 45 aircraft (4·2 per cent) lost.

19/20 February 1944

LEIPZIG

823 aircraft – 561 Lancasters, 255 Halifaxes, 7 Mosquitoes. 78 aircraft – 44 Lancasters and 34 Halifaxes – lost, 9·5 per cent of the force. The Halifax loss rate was 13·3 per cent of those dispatched and 14·9 per cent of those Halifaxes which reached the enemy coast after 'early returns' had turned back. The Halifax IIs and Vs were permanently withdrawn from operations to Germany after this raid.

This was an unhappy raid for Bomber Command. The German controllers only sent part of their force of fighters to the Kiel minelaying diversion. When the main bomber force crossed the Dutch coast, they were met by a further part of the German fighter force and those German fighters which had been sent north to Kiel hurriedly returned. The bomber stream was thus under attack all the way to the target. There were further difficulties at the target because winds were not as forecast and many aircraft reached the Leipzig area too early and had to orbit and await the Pathfinders. 4 aircraft were lost by collision and approximately 20 were shot down by Flak.

Leipzig was cloud-covered and the Pathfinders had to use sky-marking. The raid appeared to be concentrated in its early stages but scattered later. There are few details of the effects of the bombing. No report is available from Germany and there was no immediate post-raid reconnaissance flight. When photographs were eventually taken, they included the results of an American raid which took place on the following day.

DIVERSION AND SUPPORT OPERATIONS

45 Stirlings and 4 Pathfinder Halifaxes minelaying in Kiel Bay, 16 *Oboe* Mosquitoes bombing night-fighter airfields in Holland, 15 Mosquitoes on a diversion raid to Berlin, 12 *Serrate* patrols. 1 Mosquito lost from the Berlin raid.

3 Mosquitoes attacked Aachen and 3 more bombed flying-bomb sites in France without loss.

Total effort for the night: 921 sorties, 79 aircraft (8·6 per cent) lost. This was the heaviest Bomber Command loss of the war so far, easily exceeding the 58 aircraft lost on 21/22 January 1943 when Magdeburg was the main target.

20/21 February 1944

STUTTGART

598 aircraft – 460 Lancasters, 126 Halifaxes, 12 Mosquitoes. The North Sea sweep and the Munich diversion successfully drew the German fighters up 2 hours before the main bomber force flew inland and only 9 aircraft – 7 Lancasters and 2 Halifaxes – were lost, 1·5 per cent of the force. 4 further Lancasters and 1 Halifax crashed in England.

Stuttgart was cloud-covered and the bombing became scattered. The local report states that considerable damage was caused in the centre of the city and in the north-eastern and north-western suburbs of Bad Canstatt and Feuerbach. Several important cultural buildings in the centre of the city were badly damaged – the Neues Schloss, the Landtag (regional parliament building), the state picture gallery, the state archives, the state theatre and two old churches. In the Feuerbach suburb, however, the Bosch factory, which produced dynamos, injection pumps and magnetos and was considered to be one of the most important factories in Germany, was heavily damaged. 125 people were killed and 510 injured.

DIVERSION AND SUPPORT OPERATIONS

156 aircraft – 132 from training units and 24 from squadrons – flew a large training exercise across the North Sea as a preliminary feint; 24 Mosquitoes attacked airfields in Holland; 7 Mosquitoes made a diversionary raid on Munich and there were 7 *Serrate* patrols. No aircraft lost.

28 Stirlings and 6 Wellingtons laid mines off French ports. 1 Wellington lost.

Total effort for the night: 826 sorties, 10 aircraft (1·2 per cent) lost.

21/22 February 1944

MINOR OPERATIONS

17 Mosquitoes to Duisburg, Stuttgart and 2 flying-bomb sites, 1 *Serrate* patrol, 41 aircraft minelaying in the Frisians and off French ports, 10 O.T.U. sorties. 1 Stirling minelayer lost.

22/23 February 1944

MINOR OPERATIONS

Mosquitoes: 10 to Stuttgart, 8 to Duisburg and 3 to Aachen, 71 Halifaxes and 40 Stirlings sent minelaying off North German coast recalled because of bad weather at bases, 2 R.C.M. sorties, 2 *Serrate* patrols. No aircraft lost.

23/24 February 1944

MINOR OPERATIONS

17 Mosquitoes to Düsseldorf, 2 *Serrate* patrols, 3 O.T.U. sorties. No aircraft lost. A Mosquito of 692 Squadron on the Düsseldorf raid was the first Mosquito to drop a 4,000-lb bomb. The Mosquitoes of the Light Night Striking Force regularly carried such heavy bombs during the remaining months of the war to targets as far distant as Berlin.

24/25 February 1944

SCHWEINFURT

734 aircraft – 554 Lancasters, 169 Halifaxes, 11 Mosquitoes – carried out the first Bomber Command raid on this target, home of Germany's main ball-bearing factories. 266 American B-17s had raided the factories the previous day.

34. Crashed Halifax in Schweinfurt; a burning gas main has consumed most of the fuselage. This is probably one of the seven Halifaxes lost on the night of 24/25 February 1944.

Bomber Command introduced a novel tactic on this night. The Schweinfurt force was split into two parts – 392 aircraft and 342 aircraft, separated by a 2-hour interval. Part of the German fighter force was drawn up by earlier diversions. The first wave of the Schweinfurt bombers lost 22 aircraft, 5·6 per cent; the second wave lost only 11 aircraft, 3·2 per cent, and it is believed that only 4 bombers from the second wave were shot down by night fighters. Total losses were 33 aircraft – 26 Lancasters, 7 Halifaxes – 4·5 per cent of the force.

Both phases of the bombing suffered from undershooting by some of the Pathfinder backers-up and by many of the Main Force crews. Schweinfurt records refer to 'nominal damage' in the R.A.F. night raid and give a combined figure of 362 people killed by the American raid the previous day and by this R.A.F. raid No breakdown of this figure is available.

DIVERSION AND SUPPORT OPERATIONS

179 training aircraft on a diversionary sweep over the North Sea, 60 Halifaxes and 50 Stirlings minelaying in Kiel Bay and the Kattegat, 15 Mosquitoes to airfields in Holland, 8 Mosquitoes to Kiel and 7 to Aachen, 12 *Serrate* patrols. 2 Stirlings were lost from the minelaying operation and 1 *Serrate* Mosquito of 141 Squadron was lost, the first *Serrate* aircraft to be lost under Bomber Command control.

5 Wellingtons laid mines off Lorient without loss.

Total effort for the night: 1,070 sorties, 36 aircraft (3·4 per cent) lost.

25/26 February 1944

AUGSBURG

594 aircraft – 461 Lancasters, 123 Halifaxes, 10 Mosquitoes – on the first large raid to this target. The various diversions and the splitting of the main bomber force into 2 waves again reduced casualties still further. 21 aircraft – 16 Lancasters, 5 Halifaxes – lost, 3·6 per cent of the force; at least 4 of these casualties were due to collision.

The bombing at Augsburg was outstandingly successful in clear weather conditions and against this 'virgin' target with only weak Flak defences. The Pathfinder ground-marking was accurate and more than 2,000 tons of bombs were dropped by the 2 waves of the force.

The R.A.F. night raid became controversial because of the effects of its outstanding accuracy. The beautiful old centre of Augsburg was completely destroyed by high explosive and fire, with much less than the usual spread of bombing to the more modern outer areas, where some industry was located. 2,920 houses were destroyed and more than 5,000 were damaged; 85,000–90,000 people were bombed out. Among the main public and cultural buildings destroyed or seriously damaged were the old Rathaus (completely destroyed), 16 churches and 11 hospitals, but all patients in the hospitals were safely evacuated except for 2 women foreign workers. The total value of lost works of art was estimated to be 800 million Reichsmarks (£80 millon). Among the buildings destroyed was the famous puppet threatre – Heimbühne Puppenschrein – of Walter Oehmichen. Oehmichen re-created his puppets and, exactly 4 years later, opened the 'Augsburger Puppenkiste' (packing-case puppet theatre) now well known in Germany and often seen on television. There were 246 large or medium fires and 820 small ones; the temperature was so cold (minus 18° Celsius) that the River Lech was frozen over and many of the water hoses also froze. Between 678 and 762 people were killed and approximately 2,500 were injured. The Germans publicized it as an extreme example of 'terror bombing'.

Part of the bombing of the second wave of aircraft did spread to the northern and eastern parts of Augsburg and damage was caused to an important aircraft component factory and to some former paper and cotton mills which had been taken over by the M.A.N. engineering company.

DIVERSION AND SUPPORT OPERATIONS

131 aircraft minelaying in Kiel Bay, 22 Mosquitoes to airfields in Holland, 15 Mosquitoes on diversionary raids to 4 towns to the north of the Augsburg routes, 5 R.C.M. sorties, 10 *Serrate* patrols. 3 Halifaxes and 1 Stirling lost from the minelaying operation.

Total effort for the night: 777 sorties, 25 aircraft (3·2 per cent) lost.

28/29 February 1944

8 O.T.U. Wellingtons carried out leaflet operations to France without loss.

---

29 February/1 March 1944

MINOR OPERATIONS

15 Mosquitoes to Düsseldorf and 1 to a flying-bomb site at Sottevaast, 20 O.T.U. sorties. 1 O.T.U. Whitley lost.

Day Operations, 1–16 March 1944

On 5 days during this period, 2 Bomber Command *Oboe* Mosquitoes acted as 'formation leaders' for bomber units of the Second Tactical Air Force attacking flying-bomb sites. The formation bombed as soon as it saw the bombs of the *Oboe* Mosquito being released. There were no losses from the 10 Bomber Command sorties flown in this period.

1/2 March 1944

STUTTGART

557 aircraft – 415 Lancasters, 129 Halifaxes, 13 Mosquitoes. Thick cloud on the routes to and from Stuttgart made it difficult for the German fighters to get into the bomber stream and only 4 aircraft – 3 Lancasters and 1 Halifax – were lost, 0·7 per cent of the force.

The same cloud was present over the target and the Pathfinder markers quickly disappeared into it. Returning crews were unable to judge how successful the raid had been but the local report shows that much new damage was caused in the central, western and northern parts of Stuttgart. Several more historic buildings in the centre were hit, including the Kronprinzenpalais and the Altes Schloss. The Neues Schloss, severely damaged 10 nights earlier, was now totally destroyed. Much housing was hit and 125 people were killed and 510 injured. Several important industrial premises were seriously damaged, including the Bosch works and the Daimler-Benz motor factory, and 'the remains' of the main railway station, hit in earlier raids, were further damaged.

DIVERSION AND SUPPORT OPERATIONS

18 Mosquitoes to airfields in Holland, 11 Mosquitoes on a diversion raid to Munich, 6 R.C.M. sorties, 10 *Serrate* patrols. No aircraft lost.

Minor Operations: 1 Mosquito to a flying-bomb site, 10 Halifaxes and 1 Stirling on Resistance operations, 16 O.T.U. sorties. No losses.

Total effort for the night: 630 sorties, 4 aircraft (0·6 per cent) lost.

2/3 March 1944

MEULAN-LES-MEUREAUX

117 Halifaxes and 6 Mosquitoes of 4, 6 and 8 Groups to attack the S.N.C.A. aircraft factory, 15 miles outside Paris. The *Oboe* marking was accurate and the Halifaxes seriously damaged the factory buildings. No aircraft lost.

Minor Operations: 15 Lancasters of 617 Squadron in successful raid on aircraft factory at Albert in France, 13 Mosquitoes to 3 targets in Germany and a flying-bomb site, 2 R.C.M. sorties, 8 *Serrate* patrols, 8 Stirlings minelaying off French Channel ports, 44 aircraft on Resistance operations, 10 O.T.U. sorties.

Total effort for the night: 223 sorties with no aircraft lost.

3/4 March 1944

MINOR OPERATIONS

16 Mosquitoes to Berlin, 10 to Düsseldorf, 1 to Krefeld and 2 to Sottevaast flying-bomb site, 45 aircraft minelaying off French ports, 9 O.T.U. sorties. No losses.

3 Wellington minelaying sorties flown on this night by 300 (Polish) Squadron, based at Ingham, were the last Wellington operations flown by a normal Bomber Command squadron; R.C.M. squadrons of 100 Group would continue to use Wellingtons in small numbers for several months and the O.T.U.s would use Wellingtons until the end of the war.

4/5 March 1944

MINOR OPERATIONS

Mosquitoes: 15 to Berlin, 6 to Duisburg, 1 to Aachen and 1 to Sottevaast, 10 Halifaxes minelaying off Brest, 76 aircraft on Resistance operations. 15 Lancasters of 617 Squadron were unable to locate their target, the La Ricamerie needle-bearing factory near Lyons, because of cloud, and returned without bombing. No aircraft lost.

5/6 March 1944

MINOR OPERATIONS

9 Mosquitoes to Duisburg and 1 to Aachen, 4 R.C.M. sorties, 4 *Serrate* patrols, 49 Stirlings and 17 Halifaxes on Resistance operations. 1 aircraft, believed to be a Halifax, was lost on one of the Resistance flights.

6/7 March 1944

TRAPPES

261 Halifaxes and 6 Mosquitoes of 4, 6 and 8 Groups on the first of a series of raids on railway targets in France and Belgium in preparation for the invasion. No aircraft lost.

The attack took place in good visibility and later photographs showed 'enormous damage' to railway tracks, rolling stock and installations.

Minor Operations: 15 Mosquitoes to Hannover, 6 to Kiel and 1 to Krefeld, 1 R.C.M. sortie, 30 aircraft on Resistance operations. No losses.

7/8 March 1944

LE MANS

304 aircraft – 242 Halifaxes, 56 Lancasters, 6 Mosquitoes – of 3, 4, 6 and 8 Groups. No aircraft lost. The target was cloud-covered but heavy damage to the railway yards was believed to have been caused.

A report from Le Mans shows that the attack was successful. Approximately 300 bombs fell in the railway yards; 250 wagons were destroyed, many railway lines were cut, a turntable was put out of action and 6 locomotives were hit. A store of railway sleepers was burnt out. It was impossible for Bomber Command to place every bomb inside these railway targets and inevitably some bombs fell among French civilian areas. This was the great anxiety for Allied commanders in ordering these raids. On this occasion, only 30 bombs fell outside the immediate target area, killing 31 French people and injuring 45. Anti-British slogans which appeared on walls in Le Mans may have been sincere, written in the immediate aftermath of the raid, or may have been inspired by the Germans.

Minor Operations: 15 Mosquitoes to 4 German targets, 6 R.C.M. sorties, 1 *Serrate* patrol, 51 aircraft on Resistance operations, 6 O.T.U. sorties. No losses.

9/10 March 1944

MARIGNANE

44 Lancasters of 5 Group attacked an aircraft factory at Marignane near Marseilles and carried out an accurate raid in bright moonlight. No aircraft lost.

Minor Operations: 8 Mosquitoes to Düsseldorf, 2 *Serrate* patrols. No losses.

10/11 March 1944

5 GROUP RAIDS

102 Lancasters of 5 Group carried out moonlight raids on 4 factories in France – 33 aircraft to the Michelin works at Clermont-Ferrand, 30 to an aircraft factory at Châteauroux, 23 to Ossun and 16 (from 617 Squadron) to the La Ricamerie factory. All targets were successfully bombed. 1 Lancaster lost from the Clermont-Ferrand raid.

Minor Operations: 29 Mosquitoes to Duisburg, 93 aircraft on Resistance operations. No losses.

11/12 March 1944

MINOR OPERATIONS

47 Mosquitoes to 6 German cities, with the largest raid being by 20 aircraft to Hamburg, 4 *Serrate* patrols, 43 aircraft minelaying in the Frisians and off Brest and Biscay ports, 22 aircraft on Resistance operations, 21 O.T.U. sorties. 1 Stirling minelayer lost.

12/13 March 1944

14 Mosquitoes, 11 to Aachen and 3 to Duisburg; none lost.

13/14 March 1944

LE MANS

213 Halifaxes and 9 Mosquitoes of 4, 6 and 8 Groups. 1 Halifax lost. The local report shows that the Maroc Station and two nearby factories were severely damaged, with many lines being cut and 15 locomotives and 800 wagons being destroyed. 48 civilians were killed and 57 injured and many Germans were killed but no figure is available.

Minor Operations: 39 Mosquitoes to 5 German targets, with the largest raid being by 26 aircraft to Frankfurt, 4 R.C.M. sorties, 4 *Serrate* patrols, 25 Stirlings and 10 Halifaxes minelaying off French Channel ports, 19 aircraft on Resistance operations, 21 O.T.U. sorties. 1 Stirling minelayer lost.

14/15 March 1944

MINOR OPERATIONS

30 Mosquitoes to Düsseldorf, 2 Mosquitoes on R.C.M. sorties, 3 Halifaxes on Resistance operations. No losses.

Bomber Command had carried out operations on 15 nights since 29 February, flying 2,699 sorties but only losing 10 aircraft, 0·4 per cent of the forces involved. This was a most unusual run of light losses for this period of the war but the operations contained only 1 major raid to Germany.

15/16 March 1944

STUTTGART

863 aircraft – 617 Lancasters, 230 Halifaxes, 16 Mosquitoes. The German fighter controller split his forces into 2 parts. The bomber force flew over France nearly as far as the Swiss frontier before turning north-east to approach Stuttgart. This delayed the German fighters contacting the bomber stream but, when the German fighters did arrive, just before Stuttgart was reached, the usual fierce combats ensued. 37 aircraft – 27 Lancasters, 10 Halifaxes – were lost, 4·3 per cent of the force. 2 of the Lancasters force-landed in Switzerland.

Adverse winds delayed the opening of the attack and the same winds may have been the cause of the Pathfinder marking falling back well short of the target, despite the clear weather conditions. Some of the early bombing fell in the centre of Stuttgart but most of it fell in open country south-west of the city. The Akademie was damaged in the centre of Stuttgart and some housing was destroyed in the south-western suburbs. 88 people were killed and 203 injured.

AMIENS

140 aircraft – 94 Halifaxes, 38 Stirlings, 8 Mosquitoes. 2 Halifaxes and 1 Stirling lost. The Bomber Command report claims much damage to the railway yards but few details are available from Amiens, where 18 French civilians were killed.

WOIPPY

22 Lancasters of 5 Group to an aero-engine factory at Woippy, near Metz. 10/10ths cloud caused the attack to be abandoned before any bombs were dropped. No aircraft lost.

SUPPORT AND MINOR OPERATIONS

17 Mosquitoes to 5 German targets and 10 Mosquitoes to airfields in Holland, 2 R.C.M. sorties, 11 *Serrate* patrols, 2 Stirlings minelaying off Texel, 31 aircraft on Resistance operations, 18 O.T.U. sorties. 1 *Serrate* Mosquito lost.

Total effort for the night: 1,116 sorties, 41 aircraft (3·7 per cent) lost. The number of sorties flown on this night was a new record.

16/17 March 1944

AMIENS

130 aircraft – 81 Halifaxes, 41 Stirlings, 8 Mosquitoes. No aircraft lost. The Bomber Command report again reported sucessful bombing. Amiens suffered 18 civilians killed and at least 14 injured.

Clermont-Ferrand

21 Lancasters of 5 Group, mostly from 617 Squadron, carried out a successful precision attack on the Michelin tyre factory. No aircraft lost.

Minor Operations: 8 Mosquitoes to Cologne and 1 to Duisburg (only Cologne was bombed), 2 R.C.M. sorties, 2 *Serrate* patrols, 3 Stirlings minelaying off the Dutch coast. No losses.

17/18 March 1944

MINOR OPERATIONS

28 Mosquitoes to Cologne and 2 to Aachen, 1 Mosquito on R.C.M. sortie. No losses.

18/19 March 1944

FRANKFURT

846 aircraft – 620 Lancasters, 209 Halifaxes, 17 Mosquitoes. The German fighter force was again split. One part was lured north by the Heligoland mining operation but the second part waited in Germany and met the bomber stream just before the target was reached, although cloud made it difficult for these fighters to achieve much success. 22 aircraft – 12 Halifaxes, 10 Lancasters – were lost, 2·6 per cent of the force.

The Pathfinders marked the target accurately and this led to heavy bombing of eastern, central and western districts of Frankfurt. The later phases of the bombing were scattered but this was almost inevitable with such a large force; new crews were usually allocated to the final waves. Extensive destruction was caused in Frankfurt. The local report gives a long list of 'cultural buildings', including the Opera House and the preserved medieval quarter, destroyed. Most of the report consists of statistics: 5,495 houses, 99 industrial firms, 412 small businesses, 56 public buildings – all destroyed or seriously damaged; many other buildings were lightly damaged. 421 civilians were killed and 55,500 were bombed out. A military train was hit and 20 soldiers in it were killed and 80 wounded but this may have been by the action of a Fighter Command Intruder aircraft; the Frankfurt report says that the train was shot up by cannon-fire.

DIVERSION AND SUPPORT OPERATIONS

17 Mosquitoes to airfields in Holland, Belgium and France, 98 aircraft on minelaying diversion in the Heligoland area, 11 Mosquitoes on a diversion raid to Kassel, 4 R.C.M. sorties, 13 *Serrate* patrols. No aircraft were lost and the *Serrate* Mosquitoes claimed 3 Ju 88s destroyed.

Minor Operations: 19 Lancasters of 5 Group (including 13 aircraft from 617 Squadron) on an accurate raid of an explosives factory at Bergerac in France, 12 Mosquitoes to Aachen, Dortmund and Duisburg, 8 aircraft on Resistance operations, 18 O.T.U. sorties. No aircraft lost.

Total effort for the night: 1,046 sorties, 22 aircraft (2·1 per cent) lost.

19/20 March 1944

MINOR OPERATIONS

21 Mosquitoes – 9 to Berlin, 8 to Düsseldorf and 4 to Aachen, 4 R.C.M. sorties, 3 *Serrate* patrols, 19 Stirlings minelaying off Dutch and French coasts, 6 O.T.U. sorties. 1 R.C.M. Wellington lost.

20/21 March 1944

MINOR OPERATIONS

20 Lancasters of 5 Group – 14 from 617 Squadron – bombed an explosives factory at Angoulême; 25 Mosquitoes attacked 5 targets in Germany, the largest raid being by 12 aircraft to Munich, and 9 aircraft flew on Resistance operations. No aircraft lost.

21/22 March 1944

MINOR OPERATIONS

Mosquitoes: 27 to Cologne, 6 to Aachen and 3 to Oberhausen, 1 R.C.M. sortie, 3 *Serrate* patrols, 18 aircraft minelaying off Channel and Biscay coasts, 4 O.T.U. sorties. No losses.

22/23 March 1944

FRANKFURT

816 aircraft – 620 Lancasters, 184 Halifaxes, 12 Mosquitoes. Again, an indirect route was employed, this time crossing the Dutch coast north of the Zuider Zee and then flying almost due south to Frankfurt. This, and the Kiel minelaying diversion, confused the Germans for some time; Hannover was forecast as the main target. Only a few fighters eventually found the bomber stream. 33 aircraft – 26 Lancasters, 7 Halifaxes – were lost, 4·0 per cent of the force.

The marking and bombing were accurate and Frankfurt suffered another heavy blow; the city's records show that the damage was even more severe than in the raid carried out 4 nights earlier. Half of the city was without gas, water and electricity 'for a long period'. All parts of the city were hit but the greatest weight of the attack fell in the western districts. The report particularly mentions severe damage to the industrial areas along the main road to Mainz. The report also has long lists of historic buildings, churches and hospitals destroyed and statistics for the destruction of property. Mention is made of 5 important and 26 lesser Nazi Party buildings hit. 948 people were killed, 346 seriously injured and 120,000 bombed out.

162 B-17s of the Eighth Air Force used Frankfurt as a secondary target when they could not reach Schweinfurt 36 hours after this R.A.F. raid and caused further damage. The Frankfurt diary has this entry:

The three air raids of 18th, 22nd and 24th March were carried out by a combined plan of the British and American air forces and their combined effect was to deal the worst and most fateful blow of the war to Frankfurt, a blow which simply ended the existence of the Frankfurt which had been built up since the Middle Ages.*

One result of these heavy raids was that recently captured R.A.F. men often had to be protected by their guards from the assaults of angry civilians when they passed through Frankfurt to reach the nearby Oberursel interrogation and transit camp.

---

* Stadtarchiv Frankfurt am Main, Chroniken S5/140, Vol. 6, p. 988.

DIVERSION AND SUPPORT OPERATIONS

20 Mosquitoes bombing night-fighter airfields, 128 Halifaxes and 18 Stirlings mine-laying in Kiel Bay and off Denmark, 22 Mosquitoes on diversion and harassing raids to Berlin, Dortmund, Hannover and Oberhausen, 16 R.C.M. sorties and 16 *Serrate* patrols. 1 Halifax minelayer lost.

20 O.T.U. Wellingtons carried out leaflet flights to France without loss.

Total effort for the night: 1,056 sorties, 34 aircraft (3·2 per cent) lost.

23/24 March 1944

LAON

143 aircraft – 83 Halifaxes, 48 Stirlings, 12 Mosquitoes – of 3, 4, 6 and 8 Groups. 2 Halifaxes lost.

The weather in the target area was clear but the Master Bomber ordered the attack to be stopped after 72 aircraft had bombed. The local report states that about half of the bombs hit the railway yards but the remainder were scattered in an area up to 3 km from the target. The bombing did cut the through lines but these were repaired the following day. 83 houses around the station were hit but only 7 civilians were killed and 9 injured because most of the people who lived near the station moved to other parts of Laon at night.

Lyons

20 Lancasters of 5 Group, including 617 Squadron, bombed an aero-engine factory near Lyons without loss.

Minor Operations: 13 Mosquitoes to Dortmund and 2 to Oberhausen, 5 R.C.M. sorties, 4 *Serrate* patrols, 2 Stirlings minelaying off Brittany, 6 O.T.U. sorties. No losses.

24/25 March 1944

BERLIN

811 aircraft – 577 Lancasters, 216 Halifaxes, 18 Mosquitoes. 72 aircraft – 44 Lancasters, 28 Halifaxes – lost, 8·9 per cent of the force.

This night became known in Bomber Command as 'the night of the strong winds'. A powerful wind from the north carried the bombers south at every stage of the flight. Not only was this wind not forecast accurately but it was so strong that the various methods available to warn crews of wind changes during the flight failed to detect the full strength of it. The bomber stream became very scattered, particularly on the homeward flight and radar-predicted Flak batteries at many places were able to score successes. Part of the bomber force even strayed over the Ruhr defences on the return flight. It is believed that approximately 50 of the 72 aircraft lost were destroyed by Flak; most of the remainder were victims of night fighters. The Berlin report says that 14 bombers were shot down by fighters in the target area.

The strong winds caused difficulties in the marking at Berlin with, unusually, markers being carried beyond the target and well out to the south-west of the city.

126 small towns and villages outside Berlin recorded bombs and 30 people were killed in those places. The majority of the damage in Berlin was in the south-western districts. As usual, much housing was destroyed and about 20,000 people were bombed out. Approximately 150 people were killed. No industrial concerns were classed as destroyed but several important ones were damaged. 5 military establishments were badly hit including the depot of the Waffen-S.S. Leibstandarte Adolf Hitler Division in Lichterfelde.

This was the last major R.A.F. raid on Berlin during the war, although the city would be bombed many times by small forces of Mosquitoes.

DIVERSION AND SUPPORT OPERATIONS

147 aircraft from training units carried out a diversionary sweep west of Paris; 27 Mosquitoes bombed night-fighter airfields and 15 Mosquitoes bombed Duisburg, Kiel and Münster; aircraft of 100 Group flew 4 R.C.M. sorties and 10 *Serrate* patrols. 1 *Serrate* Mosquito lost.

9 aircraft dropped supplies to the Resistance without loss.

Total effort for the night: 1,023 sorties, 73 aircraft (7·1 per cent) lost.

25/26 March 1944

AULNOYE

192 aircraft – 92 Halifaxes, 47 Lancasters, 37 Stirlings, 16 Mosquitoes. No aircraft lost.

The weather was clear but the Pathfinders were not able to mark the railway yards accurately. Most bombs fell wide of the target but no report is available from France.

Minor Operations: 22 Lancasters of 5 Group to an aero-engine factory at Lyons, 10 Mosquitoes to Berlin and 2 to Hamm, 7 *Serrate* patrols, 14 Stirlings minelaying in Brittany to the Frisians, 5 O.T.U. sorties. No losses.

26/27 March 1944

ESSEN

705 aircraft – 476 Lancasters, 207 Halifaxes, 22 Mosquitoes. The sudden switch by Bomber Command to a Ruhr target just across the German frontier caught the German fighter controllers by surprise and only 9 aircraft – 6 Lancasters, 3 Halifaxes – were lost, 1·3 per cent of the force.

Essen was covered by cloud but the *Oboe* Mosquitoes marked the target well and this was a successful attack. 48 industrial buildings were seriously damaged and 1,756 houses destroyed. 550 people were killed, 49 missing and 1,569 were injured. The figures for killed and missing are broken down in the Essen report as follows: Germans – 192 women, 155 men, 27 children, 6 soldiers, 4 policemen and 2 Hitler Youth. Foreigners – 74 forced workers and 1 prisoner of war. The remaining 138 victims were mixed German and foreign concentration-camp prisoners, large numbers of whom were now providing the labour forces in German factories.

COURTRAI

109 aircraft – 70 Halifaxes, 32 Stirlings, 7 Mosquitoes – of 3, 4, 6 and 8 Groups. No aircraft lost.

A detailed report is available from Courtrai (from local historian José Vanbossele). It is obvious that the bombing spread to many built-up areas beyond the railway targets. 313 buildings in the town were destroyed, including the gaol, where 5 prisoners were killed, and a Catholic school, where 9 nuns died. When the gaol was hit, several prisoners escaped including a local butcher who had been caught helping airmen to evade capture. The total number of civilians killed was 252; 79 of these people were not local inhabitants but visitors who had come to Courtrai for the celebration of a religious feast. Many fires developed in the town and Hauptmann Schüller, from a nearby airfield, is noted as having been most helpful in sending men to put out the fires.

Details on damage to the railways are limited. The Germans called in 450 unemployed civilians and 1,200 other local men to repair the damage and the railway line was open 3 days later.

Minor Operations: 22 Mosquitoes to Hannover, 3 to Aachen and 3 to Julianadorp, 8 R.C.M. sorties, 13 *Serrate* patrols, 20 Stirlings minelaying off French ports, 4 aircraft on Resistance operations, 12 O.T.U. sorties. No aircraft lost.

Total effort for the night: 899 sorties, 9 aircraft (1·0 per cent) lost.

27/28 March 1944

14 Mosquitoes to Duisburg and 3 to Krefeld. No losses.

29/30 March 1944

VAIRES

76 Halifaxes and 8 Mosquitoes of 4, 6 and 8 Groups attacked the railway yards at Vaires, near Paris, in bright moonlight. The bombing was very accurate and 2 ammunition trains which were present blew up; it is reported that 1,270 German troops were killed. 1 Halifax lost.

Minor Operations: 19 Lancasters of 5 Group to the aero-engine factory at Lyons, which was bombed accurately. Mosquitoes: 32 to Kiel, where 47 people were killed and 134 were injured, 11 to Krefeld, 5 to Aachen and 4 to Cologne. No losses.

30/31 March 1944

NUREMBERG

This would normally have been the moon stand-down period for the Main Force, but a raid to the distant target of Nuremberg was planned on the basis of an early forecast that there would be protective high cloud on the outward route, when the moon would be up, but that the target area would be clear for ground-marked bombing. A Meteorological Flight Mosquito carried out a reconnaissance and reported that the protective cloud was unlikely to be present and that there could be cloud over the target, but the raid was not cancelled.

35. Squadron Leader Peter Hill briefs Halifax crews of 51 Squadron at Snaith for the Nuremberg raid of 30/31 March 1944, when Bomber Command suffered its greatest loss of the war. On this night 51 Squadron lost six aircraft out of seventeen dispatched; Squadron Leader Hill and thirty-four more of the men in this picture would be killed and seven would become prisoners of war.

795 aircraft were dispatched – 572 Lancasters, 214 Halifaxes and 9 Mosquitoes. The German controller ignored all the diversions and assembled his fighters at 2 radio beacons which happened to be astride the route to Nuremberg. The first fighters appeared just before the bombers reached the Belgian border and a fierce battle in the moonlight lasted for the next hour. 82 bombers were lost on the outward route and near the target. The action was much reduced on the return flight, when most of the German fighters had to land, but 95 bombers were lost in all – 64 Lancasters and 31 Halifaxes, 11·9 per cent of the force dispatched. It was the biggest Bomber Command loss of the war.

Most of the returning crews reported that they had bombed Nuremberg but subsequent research showed that approximately 120 aircraft had bombed Schweinfurt, 50 miles north-west of Nuremberg. This mistake was a result of badly forecast winds causing navigational difficulties. 2 Pathfinder aircraft dropped markers at Schweinfurt. Much of the bombing in the Schweinfurt area fell outside the town and only 2 people were killed in that area.

The main raid at Nuremberg was a failure.* The city was covered by thick cloud and a fierce cross-wind which developed on the final approach to the target caused many of the Pathfinder aircraft to mark too far to the east. A 10-mile-long creepback also developed into the countryside north of Nuremberg. Both Pathfinders and

---

*Readers might like to consult Martin Middlebrook's *The Nuremberg Raid*, London, Allen Lane, 1973, 1980; New York, Morrow, 1974; and, as *Die Nacht in der die Bomber Starben*, Berlin, Ullstein, 1975.

Main Force aircraft were under heavy fighter attack throughout the raid. Little damage was caused in Nuremberg; 69 people were killed in the city and the surrounding villages.

DIVERSION AND SUPPORT OPERATIONS

49 Halifaxes minelaying in the Heligoland area, 13 Mosquitoes to night-fighter airfields, 34 Mosquitoes on diversions to Aachen, Cologne and Kassel, 5 R.C.M. sorties, 19 *Serrate* patrols. No aircraft lost.

Minor Operations: 3 *Oboe* Mosquitoes to Oberhausen (where 23 Germans waiting to go into a public shelter were killed by a bomb) and 1 Mosquito to Dortmund, 6 Stirlings minelaying off Texel and Le Havre, 17 aircraft on Resistance operations, 8 O.T.U. sorties. 1 Halifax shot down dropping Resistance agents over Belgium.

Total effort for the night: 950 sorties, 96 aircraft (10·1 per cent) lost.

Pilot Officer C. J. Barton, a Halifax pilot of 578 Squadron, was awarded a posthumous Victoria Cross for carrying on to the target in the Nuremberg operation after his bomber was badly damaged in a fighter attack and 3 members of his crew baled out through a communication misunderstanding. Although the navigator and wireless operator were among the men who had parachuted, Barton decided to attempt the return flight to England in spite of the fact that only 3 engines were running. An unexpected wind took the Halifax steadily up the North Sea and it was short of fuel when the English coast was reached near Sunderland. Barton had to make a hurried forced landing when his engines failed through lack of fuel and he died in the crash, but his 3 remaining crew members were only slightly hurt.

Pilot Officer Barton's Victoria Cross was the only one awarded during the Battle of Berlin, which had now officially ended.

Operational Statistics, 18/19 November 1943 to 31 March 1944 (134 days/nights)

Number of nights with operations: 100
Number of days with operations: 5
Number of night sorties: 29,449, from which 1,117 aircraft (3·8 per cent) were lost; a further 113
    aircraft crashed in England while setting out for or returning from operational flights
Number of daylight sorties: 10, from which no aircraft were lost
Total sorties: 29,459, from which 1,117 aircraft (3·8 per cent) were lost
Approximate bomb tonnage in period: 78,477 tons
Averages per 24-hour period: 219·8 sorties, 8·3 aircraft lost, 585·6 tons of bombs dropped

18. INVASION PREPARATIONS

31 March/1 April to 5 June 1944

The invasion of Normandy by Allied ground forces would commence in less than ten weeks' time. Most of Bomber Command's efforts in recent years had been weakening the general capacity of Germany to resist an invasion of Europe but now the efforts of Sir Arthur Harris's squadrons were to be directed in far more precise manner against targets in the hinterland of the invasion coast. Despite his reservations about the new role, mainly over the ability of his force to hit the many small targets allocated to it without killing too many friendly civilians, Harris gave full and loyal support to the directions he received, both in the preparations for the invasion and in support of the first weeks of the land battle.

The official date for the transference of the main Bomber Command effort to pre-invasion targets was 14 April, but that date was almost meaningless. Harris had already made a modest start on the new list of targets in March. For historical purposes, 1 April 1944 is a more realistic date to mark the opening of the new phase. So, after a pause following the disastrous Nuremberg raid, the bomber crews found themselves flying a series of raids on railway targets in France and Belgium with a view to isolating the German forces in Normany from any form of railway-born reinforcement. There were also raids on military camps, ammunition depots and explosives and armament factories in France and Belgium and, just before the invasion, on radio and radar stations and coastal gun batteries. There was one aspect of the bombing of which the bomber crews were unaware. A massive Allied deception plan was in operation to persuade the Germans that the main landing would be in the Pas de Calais area, 150 miles further up the coast from Normandy and the same distance nearer to Germany. Bomber Command played a full part in this deception. For every bomb which needed to be dropped on the French railway system leading to Normandy, almost as many bombs were dropped further north. Bomber Command shared these duties with the American Eighth Air Force heavy bombers and with the Allied tactical day-bomber forces. On a few nights, when Bomber Command was not required for the invasion targets, cities in Germany were attacked, but only in the most favourable of conditions. Few risks were taken.

Bomber Command was more successful in attacking the small, sensitive targets in France and Belgium than anyone had ever hoped. The use of a Master Bomber became a standard feature of these raids, the crews of such men often becoming casualties as they remained flying over the target area throughout a raid. Much of the credit for the success also goes to the dedication shown by the bomber crews concerned; they were delighted to be associated with the invasion and liberation of Europe, one of the great events of the war, and happy to be attacking targets of an obviously more military nature than the German cities. There was relief too that the long winter of costly and often disappointing raids to Germany was over. There was, however, one very sad aspect about the raids in France and Belgium; however dedicated the crews and accurate the bombing, reports from these places will show that many civilians who had already endured long years of German occupation would die by Allied bombs and never see the dawn of liberation of their homes.

One tactical factor in the comparative success of the pre-invasion raids should be mentioned. On the night of 5/6 April, 144 Lancasters of 5 Group attacked and, with unusual accuracy, destroyed an aircraft factory at Toulouse. The marking for this raid was carried out by 617 Squadron, not by Pathfinder aircraft. In the first low-level Mosquito marking flight of the war, Wing Commander Leonard Cheshire dropped his markers on his third pass over the factory building. The target was well defended but the Mosquito was so fast that it was not hit. Two Lancasters of 617 Squadron dropped further markers which were so reliably placed that the resultant bombing was of near perfect concentration. The crews carrying out this bombing were from ordinary squadrons of 5 Group, mostly without any special training. Within hours of the Toulouse operation, Sir Arthur Harris informed Air Vice-Marshal Cochrane that 5 Group could now operate as an independent force using its own marking techniques. The two Pathfinder Lancaster squadrons in 8 Group – 83 and 97 Squadrons – which had originally served in 5 Group and whose crews were largely drawn from 5 Group, were returned to Cochrane. More Mosquitoes were provided for 617 Squadron and 8 Group was also ordered to release a Mosquito squadron, 627 Squadron, to 5 Group. Air Vice-Marshal Cochrane now had available: twelve ordinary Lancaster squadrons, two squadrons of Pathfinder Lancasters, a squadron of Mosquitoes and the specialist 617 Squadron. A '5 Group marking technique' was quickly developed, based on low-level identification of the target and marking by Mosquitoes, with the Lancasters of 83 and 97 Squadrons providing flare forces and backing-up marking which could be assessed and corrected by the Mosquitoes. The 5 Group method was used with much success over several targets in France as well as over some of the German cities. The 5 Group method was not perfect and there were disadvantages. The weather had to be clear; 5 Group could not penetrate cloud any better than 8 Group could. The delay in calling in the main force of 5 Group bombers sometimes allowed the arrival of German fighters and led to heavy bomber losses. But the average 5 Group bombing error during the next few months was 380 yards, compared to the average error of 680 yards when the marking was based on *Oboe*, the method employed as a basis of most other attacks on French and Belgian targets. This reduction of error was of vital importance in attacking small targets.

The establishment of 5 Group as a semi-independent force was the only major change at this time. The Mosquito growth in 8 Group continued and there was a modest increase of strength in most other groups. The Lancaster expansion proceeded only slowly after this type had been forced to shoulder the main burden in recent operations to Germany. The same factor led to the slow phasing out of the Stirlings in 3 Group, whose squadrons were waiting for Lancaster replacements, but the process of replacing the less satisfactory version of the Halifax by the Mark III version was completed just before the invasion; all of 4 Group and part of 6 Group would then use the Mark IIIs until the end of the war in Europe. The first Free French squadrons in Bomber Command – 346 and 347 – were formed in 4 Group just before the invasion. It is ironic that their first raids should have been on targets in their mother country; the Frenchmen would fly nearly 3,000 sorties before the war in Europe ended.

The average casualty rate fell. The Luftwaffe night-fighter force was still powerful but the shorter raids did not allow the German Tame Boar fighter tactics to be developed fully. The introduction of long-range fighter escorts for the American daylight raids, particularly the provision of the P-51 Mustang fighter, often drew the German night fighters into battle by day or caused the night fighters to be strafed on the ground. A decline started which would never be reversed and history would look back on January to March of 1944 as the zenith of the German night-fighter fortunes, with their successes at Magdeburg, Leipzig, Berlin and Nuremberg never being repeated. There would continue to be some setbacks and the diary will identify the raids when the German fighters caused heavy loss to part of the bomber force, but such nights were not frequent and the fighters never caught the whole of Bomber Command at once.

---

31 March/1 April 1944

MINOR OPERATIONS

3 *Oboe* Mosquitoes to Essen, 28 aircraft on Resistance operations, 15 O.T.U. sorties. 1 Halifax on a Resistance supply-dropping operation was lost.

1/2 April 1944

HANNOVER

35 Mosquitoes bombed the city through thin cloud. No aircraft lost.

Minor Operations: Mosquitoes – 7 to Aachen, 6 to Krefeld and 2 to La Glacerie flying-bomb site, 1 R.C.M. sortie, 4 *Serrate* patrols, 34 Halifaxes minelaying off the Dutch coast, 9 aircraft on Resistance operations. No aircraft lost.

4/5 April 1944

COLOGNE

41 Mosquitoes dispatched; none lost. Cologne reports several bombs in and around the main railway station and in other parts of the city. 19 people were killed.

16 other Mosquitoes were dispatched: 5 to Aachen, 4 to Essen, 3 to Duisburg, 2 to Krefeld and 2 to La Glacerie. No losses.

5/6 April 1944

TOULOUSE

144 Lancasters and 1 Mosquito of 5 Group. 1 Lancaster exploded in the air over the target.

This was the successful attack on the aircraft factory which was described in the introduction to this period of the diary. A report from Toulouse confirms that the factory was severely damaged. Most of the people living nearby had time to take shelter or run into fields but 22 people were killed and 45 were injured when about 100 houses near the factory were hit.

Minor Operations: 24 Stirlings minelaying off Biscay ports, 37 aircraft on Resistance operations. No losses.

6/7 April 1944

HAMBURG

35 Mosquitoes; 1 aircraft lost. Hamburg reports 39 people dead and 161 injured (Hamburg's first air-raid casualties since October 1943), 7 fires and 322 people bombed out.

Minor Operations: 14 Mosquitoes bombed 7 targets in the Ruhr and the Rhineland, and 3 aircraft flew R.C.M. sorties. No losses.

7/8 April 1944

Minor Operations

1 R.C.M. sortie, 4 Mosquitoes on *Serrate* patrols, 12 Halifaxes minelaying off the Dutch coast. No aircraft lost.

8/9 April 1944

ESSEN

40 Mosquitoes attacked the Krupps works area without loss.

Minor Operations: 3 Mosquitoes to Duisburg and 3 to Osnabrück, 2 R.C.M. sorties, 8 Halifaxes minelaying off Texel and Den Helder. No losses.

9/10 April 1944

LILLE

239 aircraft – 166 Halifaxes, 40 Lancasters, 22 Stirlings, 11 Mosquitoes – of 3, 4, 6 and 8 Groups. 1 Lancaster lost.

A full description of this raid is available from our French researcher, Philippe Lerat, who lives near Lille. The target was the Lille-Délivrance goods station, which was hit by 49 bombs. Much damage was caused to buildings and tracks and 2,124 of the 2,959 goods wagons in the yards were destroyed. Unfortunately for the local people, much of the attack fell outside the railway area and 456 French people were killed. More than 90 per cent of these casualties were in the suburb of Lomme, where more than 5,000 houses were destroyed or damaged. M. Lerat's report continues: 'The Cité des Cheminots, the housing area in Lomme where all the railwaymen lived in pleasant but frail houses, was completely destroyed. Fortunately the full moon permitted the search for wounded. The inhabitants were very resentful towards the British at the time. My own bookseller was living near by and remembers Frenchmen and women walking as lost among the bomb holes and shouting "bastards, bastards!" They had lost everything. Many inhabitants of other suburbs felt they were living their last hour, such was the intensity of the bombing.'

VILLENEUVE-ST-GEORGES

225 aircraft – 166 Lancasters, 49 Halifaxes, 10 Mosquitoes – of all groups. No aircraft lost.

Bomber Command claimed a successful attack on these railway yards near Paris. The local report does not contain details of damage to the railways but states that more than 400 houses were damaged or destroyed and that 93 people were killed and 167 injured.

Minor Operations: 36 Mosquitoes to Mannheim and 8 to four other targets, 16 *Serrate* patrols, 103 Lancasters of 1 and 5 Groups minelaying off Danzig, Gdynia and Pillau in the Baltic, 61 aircraft on Resistance operations, 9 O.T.U. sorties. 9 Lancasters from the minelaying force and 1 *Serrate* Mosquito were lost.

Total effort for the night: 697 sorties, 11 aircraft (1·6 per cent) lost.

10/11 April 1944

TOURS

180 Lancasters of 5 Group. 1 aircraft lost. The railway yards were seriously damaged.

TERGNIER

157 Halifaxes of 4 Group and 10 Pathfinder Mosquitoes. 10 Halifaxes lost. The railway yards were seriously damaged.

LAON

148 Lancasters and 15 Mosquitoes of 3, 6 and 8 Groups. 1 Lancaster lost. The marking was not completely accurate and only a corner of the railway yards was hit.

AULNOYE

132 Lancasters of 1 Group and 15 Pathfinder Mosquitoes. 7 Lancasters lost. The attack was successful; a later examination showed that 287 bombs hit the railway yards. The local report says that many bombs fell in fields near the railway but the engine-shed was hit and 30 locomotives were put out of action. 340 houses were destroyed or damaged and 14 civilians were killed.

GHENT

122 Halifaxes of 6 Group and 10 Pathfinder Mosquitoes. No aircraft lost.

Ghent was the only target of this night to provide a report. The raid caused much damage at the Merelbeke-Melle railway yards, on the main line to Brussels, but surrounding housing areas were also hit. 428 Belgians were killed and 300 injured. 584 buildings were destroyed – including 7 schools, 2 convents and an orphanage – and 1,009 other buildings were damaged.

Minor Operations: 36 Mosquitoes to Hannover and 2 to Duisburg, 17 Lancasters and 1 Mosquito of 617 Squadron to St-Cyr signals depot, 8 R.C.M. sorties, 9 *Serrate* patrols, 8 Stirlings minelaying off La Pallice, 46 aircraft on Resistance operations, 17 O.T.U. sorties. No aircraft lost.

Total effort for the night: 908 sorties, 19 aircraft (2·1 per cent) lost. (25 Mosquitoes each marked two targets; only 25 sorties have been counted for these aircraft.)

11/12 April 1944

AACHEN

341 Lancasters and 11 Mosquitoes of 1, 3, 5 and 8 Groups. 9 Lancasters lost, 2·6 per cent of the force.

This raid was accurate and caused widespread damage and fires in the centre of Aachen and in the southern part of the town, particularly in the suburb of Burtscheid. This was Aachen's most serious raid of the war.

Control of the air-raid services was quickly lost when one of the first salvoes of bombs cut communications between the main operations centre and outlying posts. The 5th and 6th Air Raid posts were both destroyed. In the 5th, in the Burtscheid district, the local leader, 15 of his men and several Hitler Youth messengers were all killed. The police headquarters was also hit. The local officials did not make a count of buildings destroyed and no details of industrial damage are given but 6 hospitals were listed as being hit. 80 patients and 11 staff were killed in the town hospital. Much damage was caused to railway and road communications and to power supplies. 1,525 people were killed, this number being broken down as follows: 758 women, 454 male civilians, 212 children, 49 service personnel, 21 police and air-raid workers, 13 prisoners of war, 10 foreign workers and 8 unidentified.

SUPPORT AND MINOR OPERATIONS

7 Mosquitoes to bomb night-fighter airfields, 36 Mosquitoes on diversion raid to Hannover and 3 each to Duisburg and Osnabrück, 7 R.C.M. sorties, 7 *Serrate* patrols, 35 Halifaxes and 8 Stirlings minelaying off Brest and in the Kattegat, 26 aircraft on Resistance operations, 8 O.T.U. sorties. No aircraft lost.

Total effort for the night: 492 sorties, 9 aircraft (1·8 per cent) lost.

12/13 April 1944

OSNABRÜCK

39 Mosquitoes carried out a harassing raid without loss.

Minor Operations: 2 Mosquitoes on *Serrate* patrols, 40 Halifaxes and 10 Stirlings minelaying in the Frisians and off Heligoland, 21 aircraft on Resistance operations, 11 O.T.U. sorties. 2 Stirlings lost on Resistance operations.

13/14 April 1944

BERLIN

29 Mosquitoes were dispatched but observation of bombing results was not possible because of the glare of massed searchlights. No aircraft lost.

Minor Operations: 6 Mosquitoes to Düren and 3 to Dortmund, 10 Stirlings and 6 Halifaxes minelaying off Cherbourg, Le Havre and La Pallice. No losses.

17/18 April 1944

COLOGNE

26 Mosquitoes; none lost.

Minor Operations: 2 Mosquitoes to Le Mans railway yards, 2 *Serrate* patrols, 14 Halifaxes and 6 Stirlings minelaying in Kiel Bay and the Frisians, 4 O.T.U. sorties. 1 Halifax minelayer lost.

18/19 April 1944

ROUEN

273 Lancasters and 16 Mosquitoes of 1, 3 and 8 Groups. No aircraft lost. Bomber Command claimed a concentrated attack on the railway yards, with much destruction.

JUVISY

202 Lancasters and 4 Mosquitoes of 5 Group, with 3 *Oboe* Mosquitoes of 8 Group. 1 Lancaster lost. The attack appeared to be completely successful.

NOISY-LE-SEC

181 aircraft – 112 Halifaxes, 61 Lancasters, 8 Mosquitoes – of 6 and 8 Groups. The Mosquitoes also operated against Tergnier. 4 Halifaxes lost.

The local report describes results which were typical of these railway-target raids. The marshalling yards, the engine-sheds and the railway workshops suffered great damage. Approximately 200 delayed-action bombs continued to explode in the week after the raid. A through line was established several days later but the marshalling yards were not completely repaired until 6 years after the war. In addition to this railway damage, however, the bombing area was measured as 6 km long and 3 km wide. 750 houses were destroyed and more than 2,000 damaged. 464 French people were killed and 370 injured.

TERGNIER

171 aircraft – 139 Halifaxes, 24 Lancasters, 8 Mosquitoes – of 3, 4 and 8 Groups. 6 Halifaxes lost. 50 railway lines were blocked but most of the bombing fell on housing areas south-west of the railway yards. French casualties are not known.

MINELAYING OPERATION

168 aircraft – 88 Halifaxes, 44 Stirlings, 36 Lancasters – to Swinemünde, Kiel Bay and to the Danish coast. 2 Stirlings and 1 Halifax lost.

Minor Operations: Mosquitoes – 24 to Berlin, 2 to Osnabrück and 2 to Le Mans, 9 R.C.M. sorties, 32 *Serrate* patrols, 46 O.T.U. sorties. No aircraft lost.

Total effort for the night: 1,125 sorties, 14 aircraft (1·2 per cent) lost. The total number of sorties on this night was a new Bomber Command record.

20/21 April 1944

COLOGNE

357 Lancasters and 22 Mosquitoes of 1, 3, 6 and 8 Groups. 4 Lancasters lost.

This concentrated attack fell into areas of Cologne which were north and west of the city centre and partly industrial in nature. 192 industrial premises suffered various degrees of damage, together with 725 buildings described as 'dwelling-houses with commercial premises attached'. 7 railway stations or yards were also severely damaged.

But more general city buildings were also heavily bombed: 46 churches and chapels, the Opera House (partly burnt out), the city market halls, etc. The Capitol cinema, the largest in Cologne, was destroyed by fire. 1,861 houses or apartments were destroyed and more than 20,000 damaged. There were 1,290 separate fires. 664 people were killed and 1,067 were injured. The Cologne report mentions 'high-explosive bombs of new calibre which penetrated the normally safe basement shelters'; 80 per cent of the dead were in those shelters.

LA CHAPELLE

The raid on this railway target just north of Paris was the first major test for the new 5 Group marking method, with the group employing not only 617 Squadron's low-level markers but the three Pathfinder squadrons recently transferred from 8 Group. A few regular 8 Group Mosquitoes were also used to drop markers by *Oboe* to provide a first indication of the target's location for the main 5 Group marking force. 247 Lancasters of 5 Group and 22 Mosquitoes from 5 and 8 Groups dispatched. 6 Lancasters lost.

The bombing force was split into two parts, with an interval between them of 1 hour, and each part of the force aimed at different halves of the railway yards. There were a few difficulties at the opening of the attack, with the markers of the *Oboe* Mosquitoes being a fraction late and with communications between the various controlling aircraft being faulty, but these difficulties were soon overcome and both parts of the bombing force achieved extremely accurate and concentrated bombing. Unfortunately, no report is available from La Chapelle.

OTTIGNIES

196 aircraft – 175 Halifaxes, 14 Lancasters, 7 Mosquitoes – from 4 and 8 Groups. No aircraft lost. The southern half of the railway yards was severely damaged.

LENS

175 aircraft – 154 Halifaxes, 14 Lancasters, 7 Mosquitoes – of 6 and 8 Groups. 1 Halifax lost. The railway yards were accurately bombed, with particular damage being caused to the engine-sheds and the carriage-repair workshop.

Chambly

14 Stirlings, using the *G-H* blind-bombing device, to bomb a railway depot but only 4 aircraft bombed and 1 was lost.

Minor Operations: 8 Mosquitoes to Berlin, 14 R.C.M. sorties, 25 *Serrate* and 8 Intruder patrols, 30 Stirlings and 8 Halifaxes minelaying off French ports, 2 aircraft on Resistance operations, 27 O.T.U. sorties. 2 *Serrate* Mosquitoes and 1 O.T.U. Wellington lost.

Total effort for the night: 1,155 sorties, 15 aircraft (1·3 per cent) lost. The number of sorties flown was a new record. Small jumps in record efforts will no longer be recorded in the diary.

21/22 April 1944

COLOGNE

24 Mosquitoes bombed the Cologne area through complete cloud cover. No aircraft lost.

Minor Operations: 4 R.C.M. sorties, 40 Halifaxes and 18 Stirlings minelaying off Brest and Lorient and in the Frisians, 9 aircraft on Resistance operations, 11 O.T.U. aircraft and 4 Stirlings on leaflet flights to France. No aircraft lost.

22/23 April 1944

DÜSSELDORF

596 aircraft – 323 Lancasters, 254 Halifaxes, 19 Mosquitoes – of all groups except 5 Group. 29 aircraft – 16 Halifaxes and 13 Lancasters – lost, 4·9 per cent of the force.

2,150 tons of bombs were dropped in this old-style heavy attack on a German city which caused much destruction but also allowed the German night-fighter force to penetrate the bomber stream. The attack fell mostly in the northern districts of Düsseldorf. Widespread damage was caused. Among the mass of statistics in the local report are: 56 large industrial premises hit (of which 7 were completely destroyed), more than 2,000 houses destroyed or badly damaged. Casualties recorded by 2.0 p.m. on 25 April were 883 people killed, 593 injured and 403 still to be dug out of wrecked buildings; at least three quarters of this last figure would have been dead.

BRUNSWICK

238 Lancasters and 17 Mosquitoes of 5 Group and 10 Lancasters of 1 Group. Few German fighters were attracted to this raid and only 4 Lancasters were lost, 1·5 per cent of the force.

This raid is of importance to the history of the bombing war because it was the first time that the 5 Group low-level marking method was used over a heavily defended German city. The raid was not successful. The initial marking by 617 Squadron Mosquitoes was accurate but many of the main force of bombers did not bomb these, partly because of a thin layer of cloud which hampered visibility and partly because of faulty communications between the various bomber controllers. Many bombs were dropped in the centre of the city but the remainder of the force bombed reserve *H2S*-aimed target indicators which were well to the south. Brunswick's records contain little information on this raid and the fact that only 44 people were killed shows that the damage caused was not extensive.

LAON

181 aircraft – 69 Halifaxes, 52 Lancasters, 48 Stirlings, 12 Mosquitoes – of 3, 4, 6 and 8 Groups. 9 aircraft – 4 Lancasters, 3 Stirlings, 2 Halifaxes – lost, 5·0 per cent of the force.

The attack on the railway yards was carried out in 2 waves and severe damage was caused. The aircraft of one of the Master Bombers, Wing Commander A. G. S. Cousens of 635 Squadron, was shot down; Wing Commander Cousens was killed.

Minor Operations: 17 Mosquitoes on diversion raid to Mannheim and 2 more to a flying-bomb store at Wissant, 10 R.C.M. sorties, 19 *Serrate* and 7 Intruder patrols, 19 aircraft on leaflet flights. No aircraft lost.

Total effort for the night: 1,116 sorties, 42 aircraft (3·8 per cent) lost.

23/24 April 1944

MINELAYING

114 aircraft – 70 Halifaxes, 30 Stirlings, 14 Lancasters – to lay mines in 5 areas of the Baltic. 4 Halifaxes and 1 Stirling lost.

MANNHEIM

25 Mosquitoes carried out a harassing raid without loss.

Brussels

12 *G-H* Stirlings bombed a signals depot without loss.

Minor Operations: 2 R.C.M. sorties, 4 *Serrate* patrols, 10 aircraft on Resistance operations, 6 O.T.U. sorties. No aircraft lost.

24/25 April 1944

KARLSRUHE

637 aircraft – 369 Lancasters, 259 Halifaxes, 9 Mosquitoes – of all groups except 5 Group. 19 aircraft – 11 Lancasters, 8 Halifaxes – lost, 3·0 per cent of the force.

Cloud over the target and a strong wind which pushed the Pathfinders too far north spoiled this attack. Only the northern part of Karlsruhe was seriously damaged and most of the bombs fell outside the city. It has been difficult to obtain details from this target. One report says that 23 people were killed, 133 were injured and more than 900 houses were destroyed or badly damaged, but another report gives the number of people killed as 118. Mannheim, 30 miles to the north, recorded a raid by approximately 100 aircraft on this night and Darmstadt, Ludwigshafen and Heidelberg were also hit by aircraft which failed to find the main target. It must be assumed that many bombs fell in open country between Karlsruhe and Mannheim; another German report says that bombs fell in 120 parishes.

MUNICH

234 Lancasters and 16 Mosquitoes of 5 Group and 10 Lancasters of 1 Group in another 5 Group method raid on a major German target. 9 Lancasters were lost, 3·5 per cent of the force.

The marking and controlling plan worked well and accurate bombing fell in the centre of Munich. The intense Flak and searchlight defences did not prevent the low-flying Mosquito markers from carrying out their task properly and none was seriously damaged.

A German report * details much property damage, mostly of a public and domestic nature rather than industrial, though much damage was caused to railway installations. 1,104 buildings were completely destroyed and 1,367 were badly damaged, including 48 public buildings, 30 schools, 24 police and air-raid posts, 18 military buildings, 13 churches and 7 hospitals. Casualties were: 88 killed, 2,945 injured and 30,000 bombed out, with 24 more people or bodies still trapped in wreckage when the report was completed. It is not known why the proportion of dead should have been so low.

DIVERSION AND SUPPORT OPERATIONS

165 O.T.U. aircraft carried out a diversionary sweep over the North Sea to a point 75 miles off the German coast. 23 Mosquitoes bombed Düsseldorf; 6 Lancasters of 617 Squadron dropped flares and target indicators over Milan as a diversion for the Munich raid; 100 Group flew 11 R.C.M., 21 *Serrate* and 8 Intruder sorties. 2 Wellingtons were lost from the O.T.U. sweep.

Minor Operations: 4 *G-H* Stirlings to Chambly railway depot, 18 Halifaxes minelaying off Channel ports and in the Frisians, 7 aircraft on Resistance operations. No aircraft lost.

Total effort for the night: 1,160 sorties, 30 aircraft (2·6 per cent) lost.

25/26 April 1944

MINOR OPERATIONS

4 Mosquitoes to Cologne, 25 Stirlings minelaying off the French coast, 9 O.T.U. sorties. No losses.

---

* The report is *Luftgaukommando VII, München*, from the Bundesarchiv, Freiburg.

26/27 April 1944

ESSEN

493 aircraft – 342 Lancasters, 133 Halifaxes, 18 Mosquitoes – from all groups except 5 Group. 7 aircraft – 6 Lancasters, 1 Halifax – lost, 1·4 per cent of the force. The Bomber Command report states that this was an accurate attack, based on good Pathfinder ground-marking. The only report available from Essen states that 313 people were killed and 1,224 injured.

SCHWEINFURT

206 Lancasters and 11 Mosquitoes of 5 Group and 9 Lancasters of 1 Group. 21 Lancasters lost, 9·3 per cent of the force.

This raid was a failure. The low-level marking provided for the first time by Mosquitoes of 627 Squadron was not accurate. Unexpectedly strong head winds delayed the Lancaster marker aircraft and the main force of bombers. German night fighters were carrying out fierce attacks throughout the period of the raid. The bombing was not accurate and much of it fell outside Schweinfurt. Only 2 people were killed in Schweinfurt.

A Victoria Cross was awarded after the war to Sergeant Norman Jackson, a flight engineer in a Lancaster of 106 Squadron which was shot down near Schweinfurt. The Lancaster was hit by a German night fighter and a fire started in a fuel tank in the wing near the fuselage. Sergeant Jackson climbed out of a hatch with a fire extinguisher, with another crew member holding the rigging lines of Jackson's parachute which had opened in the aircraft. Sergeant Jackson lost the fire extinguisher and, as both he and his parachute rigging were being affected by the fire, the men in the aircraft let the parachute go. Sergeant Jackson survived, though with serious burns and a broken ankle received on landing with his partially burnt parachute. The remainder of the crew baled out soon afterwards.

VILLENEUVE-ST-GEORGES

217 aircraft – 183 Halifaxes, 20 Lancasters, 14 Mosquitoes – of 4, 6 and 8 Groups. 1 Halifax lost.

Bomber Command claims that the southern end of the railway yards was successfully bombed. The local report states that this raid was more accurate than the one earlier in the month, although civilian areas were again hit and 29 people were killed and 52 were injured.

Support and Minor Operations: 16 Mosquitoes to Hamburg (which reports no casualties, 1 fire and 50 people bombed out), 10 Stirlings to Chambly, 12 R.C.M. sorties, 20 *Serrate* and 13 Intruder patrols, 16 Halifaxes and 6 Stirlings minelaying off the Dutch coast and in the Frisians, 10 aircraft on Resistance operations, 21 O.T.U. flights. 1 *Serrate* Mosquito lost.

Total effort for the night: 1,060 sorties, 30 aircraft (2·8 per cent) lost.

27/28 April 1944

FRIEDRICHSHAFEN

322 Lancasters and 1 Mosquito of 1, 3, 6 and 8 Groups. This was a raid with some

interesting aspects. The Air Ministry had urged Bomber Command to attack this relatively small town in moonlight because it contained important factories making engines and gearboxes for German tanks. But the flight to this target, deep in Southern Germany on a moonlit night, was potentially very dangerous; the disastrous attack on Nuremberg had taken place only 4 weeks previously in similar conditions. However, Friedrichshafen was further south and on the fringe of the German night-fighter defences; because of this and the various diversions which confused the German controllers, the bombers reached the target without being intercepted. However, the German fighters arrived at the target while the raid was taking place and 18 Lancasters were lost, 5·6 per cent of the force.

1,234 tons of bombs were dropped in an outstandingly successful attack based on good Pathfinder marking; Bomber Command later estimated that 99 acres of Friedrichshafen, 67 per cent of the town's built-up area, were devastated. Several factories were badly damaged and the tank gearbox factory was destroyed. When the American bombing survey team investigated this raid after the war, German officials said that this was the most damaging raid on tank production of the war. A civil report states that 136 people were killed and 375 injured in Friedrichshafen, and that 656 houses were destroyed and 421 severely damaged.

AULNOYE

223 aircraft – 191 Halifaxes, 16 Lancasters, 16 Mosquitoes – of 4, 6 and 8 Groups. 1 Halifax lost. Bombing was concentrated and much damage was caused to the railway yards.

MONTZEN

144 aircraft – 120 Halifaxes, 16 Lancasters, 8 Mosquitoes – of 4, 6 and 8 Groups. The bombing force, particularly the second of the 2 waves, was intercepted by German fighters and 14 Halifaxes and 1 Lancaster were shot down. Only one part of the railway yards was hit by the bombing.

The only Lancaster lost was that of Squadron Leader E. M. Blenkinsopp, a Canadian pilot of 405 Squadron who was acting as Deputy Master Bomber. Blenkinsopp managed to team up with a Belgian Resistance group and remained with them until captured by the Germans in December 1944. He was taken to Hamburg to work as a forced labourer and later died in Belsen concentration camp 'of heart failure'. He has no known grave.

SUPPORT AND MINOR OPERATIONS

159 O.T.U. aircraft on a diversionary sweep over the North Sea, 24 Mosquitoes on diversion raid to Stuttgart, 11 R.C.M. sorties, 19 *Serrate* and 6 Intruder patrols, 8 Halifaxes minelaying off Brest and Cherbourg, 44 aircraft on Resistance operations. 1 *Serrate* Mosquito lost.

Total effort for the night: 961 sorties, 35 aircraft (3·6 per cent) lost.

28/29 April 1944

ST-MÉDARD-EN-JALLES

88 Lancasters and 4 Mosquitoes of 5 Group to attack this explosives factory near

Bordeaux. Only 26 aircraft bombed the target. Because of haze and smoke from fires started by flares in woods near the factory, the Master Bomber ordered the remainder of the force to retain their bombs. No aircraft lost.

OSLO

51 Lancasters and 4 Mosquitoes of 5 Group were dispatched and bombed an airframe factory near Oslo. Visibility was clear; the bombing was accurate and no aircraft were lost.

Minor Operations: 26 Mosquitoes to Hamburg (3 small fires, 2 people killed, 97 bombed out), 2 R.C.M. sorties, 40 aircraft on Resistance operations. No aircraft lost.

29/30 April 1944

ST-MÉDARD-EN-JALLES

68 Lancasters and 5 Mosquitoes of 5 Group returned to the explosives factory and carried out concentrated bombing on it without loss.

CLERMONT-FERRAND

54 Lancasters and 5 Mosquitoes of 5 Group attacked the Michelin tyre factory accurately and without loss.

Minor Operations: 8 Mosquitoes to Oberhausen and 4 to Achères railway yards, 5 R.C.M. sorties, 6 *Serrate* patrols, 34 Halifaxes and 4 Stirlings minelaying off French ports and in the Frisians. 20 aircraft on Resistance operations, 9 O.T.U. sorties. No aircraft lost.

---

30 April/1 May 1944

SOMAIN

143 aircraft – 114 Halifaxes, 20 Lancasters, 9 Mosquitoes – of 6 and 8 Groups. 1 Halifax lost.

The initial *Oboe* marking was inaccurate and the Master Bomber ordered the bombing force to wait. Most of the Halifaxes making up the Main Force either did not hear or ignored his orders and their bombs missed the target. Some damage was caused to the railway yards by the remainder of the force. A report from the French Railways (S.N.C.F., Région de Lille) says that some of the bombing fell into the local Cité de Cheminots (railwaymen's housing), although no casualties there are mentioned in the report. 3 railwaymen were killed inside the railway yards. It is probable that much of the bombing fell in open country.

ACHÈRES

128 aircraft – 107 Halifaxes, 13 Lancasters, 8 Mosquitoes – of 4 and 8 Groups attacked the railway yards without loss.

The Mayor of the small town of Achères reports that the bombing completely destroyed the railway yards and that there were no civilian victims, the Mayor attributing this to the fact that the bombers flew at comparatively low level.

MAINTENON

116 Lancasters of 1 Group attacked the largest Luftwaffe bomb and ammunition dump in Northern France. The marking for this raid appears to have been provided by the 1 Group Marking Flight, based at Binbrook; the Bomber Command records do not mention any other group taking part. The raid was entirely successful and a spectacular series of explosions were seen on the ground. French houses near by were not hit.

Minor Operations: 28 Mosquitoes to Saarbrücken and 5 to Düren, 14 R.C.M. sorties, 9 *Serrate* and 5 Intruder patrols, 48 Halifaxes minelaying off the French coast, 36 aircraft on Resistance operations. No aircraft lost.

Total effort for the night: 532 sorties, 1 aircraft (0·2 per cent) lost.

Day Operations, 1–21 May 1944

On 6 days during this period, Bomber Command *Oboe* Mosquitoes flew as 'formation leaders' in Second Tactical Air Force attacks on small targets in Northern France. There were no losses from the 12 Bomber Command sorties flown.

1/2 May 1944

TOULOUSE

131 Lancasters and 8 Mosquitoes of 5 Group attacked the aircraft assembly factory and an explosives factory. Both targets were hit and no aircraft were lost.

ST-GHISLAIN

137 aircraft – 89 Halifaxes, 40 Lancasters, 8 Mosquitoes – of 6 and 8 Groups attacked the railway yards with great accuracy. 1 Halifax and 1 Lancaster lost.

MALINES

132 aircraft – 110 Halifaxes, 14 Lancasters, 8 Mosquitoes – of 4 and 8 Groups. 1 Halifax lost.

The bombing was scattered, although the locomotive sheds were damaged. A report from Malines shows that extensive damage was caused to civilian areas; 1,355 buildings were destroyed or seriously damaged and 2,365 were slightly damaged and there were many Belgian casualties – 171 killed, 123 injured.

CHAMBLY

120 aircraft – 96 Lancasters, 16 Stirlings, 8 Mosquitoes – of 3 and 8 Groups. 3 Lancasters and 2 Stirlings lost.

Chambly was the main railway stores and repair depot for the Northern French system which the Allied bombers were trying to put out of action. The local report (provided by the office of the present Chief Engineer at Chambly) shows that the raid

36 (a and b). The results of a successful raid on a French railway stores and repair depot at Chambly during the communications campaign before D-Day. Most of this damage was caused by aircraft of 3 Group.

was extremely successful. Approximately 500 high-explosive bombs fell inside the railway depot area and serious damage was caused to all departments. The depot was completely out of action for 10 days. There were no casualties in the depot, nor in Chambly, but the wind took some of the markers eastwards towards the village of Persan and 5 people were killed there.

LYONS

75 Lancasters of 1 Group attacked the Berliet motor works. The factory was badly damaged and nearby railways and factories were also hit. There is no local report to say whether civilian casualties were caused. No aircraft were lost.

TOURS

46 Lancasters and 4 Mosquitoes of 5 Group carried out an accurate attack on aircraft-repair workshops. The main buildings were completely destroyed. No aircraft lost.

Minor Operations: 28 Mosquitoes to Ludwigshafen and 2 to Achères, 9 R.C.M. sorties, 16 *Serrate* and 18 Intruder patrols, 32 Halifaxes and 3 Stirlings minelaying off the French coast and in the Frisians, 40 aircraft on Resistance operations. 1 *Serrate* Mosquito lost.

Total effort for the night: 801 sorties in 14 separate operations, 9 aircraft (1·1 per cent) lost.

2/3 May 1944

MINOR OPERATIONS

29 Mosquitoes to Leverkusen and 7 to Achères, 2 R.C.M. sorties, 9 Stirlings minelaying in the Frisian Islands. No losses.

3/4 May 1944

MAILLY-LE-CAMP

346 Lancasters and 14 Mosquitoes of 1 and 5 Groups and 2 Pathfinder Mosquitoes to bomb a German military camp situated close to the French village of Mailly. 42 Lancasters lost, 11·6 per cent of the force.

The control of this raid in the target area failed to operate according to plan. The initial low-level markers were accurate and were well backed up by Lancaster marker aircraft. The 'Marker Leader', Wind Commander Cheshire, ordered the Main Force to come in and bomb but the 'Main Force Controller', Wing Commander L. C. Deane, could not transmit the order to do so to the waiting Lancasters because his V.H.F. radio set was being drowned by an American forces broadcast and his wireless transmitter was wrongly tuned. German fighters arrived during the delay and bomber casualties were heavy.

The main attack eventually started when the Deputy Controller, Squadron Leader E. N. M. Sparks, took over. Approximately 1,500 tons of bombs were dropped with great accuracy. 114 barrack buildings, 47 transport sheds and some ammunition buildings in the camp were hit; 102 vehicles, including 37 tanks, were destroyed. 218 German soldiers were killed and 156 were injured. Most of the casualties were *Panzer* N.C.O.s. There were no French casualties through bombing but some people were killed when a Lancaster crashed on their house.

The night-fighter attacks continued over the target and on the return route. Among the aircraft shot down was that of Squadron Leader Sparks, who had stayed over the target to the end. Sparks evaded capture and soon returned to England. The squadrons of 1 Group, which made up the second wave of the attack, suffered the most casualties – 28 aircraft out of their 173 dispatched. 460 (Australian) Squadron, from Binbrook, lost 5 out of its 17 Lancasters on the raid.

MONTDIDIER

84 Lancasters and 8 Mosquitoes attacked a Luftwaffe airfield and caused much damage among buildings and installations on the northern part of the airfield. 4 Lancasters lost.

Minor Operations: 27 Mosquitoes to Ludwigshafen and 14 to an ammunition dump at Châteaudun, 3 R.C.M. sorties, 7 Intruder and 6 *Serrate* patrols, 32 Halifaxes minelaying off the French coast and in the Frisians, 23 aircraft on Resistance operations, 34 O.T.U. sorties. 4 aircraft lost: 1 R.C.M. Halifax, 1 *Serrate* Mosquito, 1 Resistance operation Lysander and 1 O.T.U. Wellington.

Total effort for the night: 598 sorties, 50 aircraft (8·3 per cent) lost.

4/5 May 1944

MINOR OPERATIONS

28 Mosquitoes to Ludwigshafen and 4 to Leverkusen, 20 Halifaxes minelaying off Channel and Biscay ports. No losses.

5/6 May 1944

MINOR OPERATIONS

16 Halifaxes and 12 Stirlings minelaying off Channel and Biscay ports, 30 aircraft on Resistance operations, 6 O.T.U. sorties. No losses.

6/7 May 1944

MANTES-LA-JOLIE

149 aircraft – 77 Halifaxes, 64 Lancasters, 8 Mosquitoes – of 4 and 8 Groups attacked railway installations in the Gassicourt suburb. 2 Lancasters and 1 Halifax lost.

Bomber Command's records state that 'stores depots and locomotive sheds' were severely damaged but the local report shows that some of the bombing fell outside the railway objective. The western part of the town – including 'old Mantes', the suburb of Gassicourt and the hamlet of Dennemont – were all bombed. The church, the old town hall and the school at Gassicourt were destroyed, together with 128 houses. 740 other houses were damaged. 54 civilians were killed.

SABLE-SUR-SARTHE

64 Lancasters and 4 Mosquitoes of 5 Group attacked an ammunition dump which was destroyed by 'enormous explosions'. No aircraft lost.

AUBIGNE

52 Lancasters of 1 Group attacked an ammunition dump accurately and the entire target was destroyed. 1 aircraft lost.

The only Lancaster shot down on this raid, from 576 Squadron, contained a senior officer who was flying as second pilot. This was Air Commodore R. Ivelaw-Chapman, who was commanding a 'base' (usually 3 airfields) in 1 Group. Ivelaw-Chapman had only just taken up this position after a staff job in which he had had access to details of the coming invasion. There was great anxiety in England that, if Ivelaw-Chapman became a prisoner of war, the Germans might hand him over to the Gestapo for questioning. He was taken prisoner but the Germans never realized his importance and he was treated in the normal manner.

Minor Operations: 28 Mosquitoes to Ludwigshafen, 5 to Leverkusen and 2 to Châteaudun, 9 R.C.M. sorties, 9 *Serrate* and 5 Intruder patrols, 8 Halifaxes and 6 Stirlings minelaying off Biscay ports. 33 aircraft on Resistance operations, 6 O.T.U. sorties. 1 Mosquito lost from the Leverkusen raid.

Total effort for the night: 380 sorties, 5 aircraft (1·3 per cent) lost.

7/8 May 1944

NANTES

93 Lancasters and 6 Mosquitoes of 3 and 8 Groups to bomb the airfield. 1 Lancaster lost. Accurate bombing hit runways and hangars.

ST-VALÉRY

56 Halifaxes of 6 Group and 8 Pathfinder Mosquitoes attempted to bomb a coastal gun position but just missed the target. No aircraft lost.

SALBRIS

58 Lancasters and 4 Mosquitoes of 5 Group attacked an ammunition dump. The bombing was accurate and much damage was caused but 7 Lancasters were lost.

TOURS

53 Lancasters and 8 Mosquitoes of 5 Group bombed the airfield and caused much damage. 1 Lancaster and 1 Mosquito lost.

RENNES

55 Lancasters of 1 Group bombed the airfield and an ammunition dump. The force was not able to locate and mark the target adequately and most of the bombs fell on a nearby village, but no details are available. No aircraft lost.

Minor Operations: 28 Mosquitoes to Leverkusen and 4 to Châteaudun, 5 R.C.M. sorties, 12 Intruder patrols, 42 aircraft minelaying in the Frisians and in the River Gironde, 39 aircraft on Resistance operations. 2 Halifaxes lost dropping supplies to the Resistance.

Total effort for the night: 471 sorties, 12 aircraft (2·5 per cent) lost.

8/9 May 1944

HAINE-ST-PIERRE

123 aircraft – 62 Halifaxes, 53 Lancasters, 8 Mosquitoes – of 6 and 8 Groups. 6 Halifaxes and 3 Lancasters lost. Severe damage was caused to half of the railway yards and to locomotive sheds.

BREST

58 Lancasters and 6 Mosquitoes of 5 Group attacked the airfield and seaplane base at Lanveoc-Poulmic with great accuracy. 1 Lancaster lost.

MORSALINES

31 Halifaxes of 4 Group and 8 Pathfinder Mosquitoes scored direct hits on a coastal gun position. 1 Halifax lost.

BERNEVAL

32 Halifaxes of 4 Group and 7 Pathfinder Mosquitoes attacked a gun position but only 1 aircraft hit the target. Most of the bombing was 600–700 yards from the gun position. No aircraft lost.

CAP GRIZ NEZ

30 Lancasters of 3 Group and 8 Pathfinder Mosquitoes located the gun position but no hits were scored. No aircraft lost.

Minor Operations: 28 Mosquitoes to Osnabrück and 2 to Oberhausen, 4 R.C.M. sorties, 10 *Serrate* patrols, 30 Halifaxes and 8 Stirlings minelaying off the Dutch and French coasts, 41 aircraft on Resistance operations, 26 O.T.U. sorties. 1 Stirling lost on Resistance supply work.

Total effort for the night: 452 sorties, 12 aircraft (2·7 per cent) lost.

9/10 May 1944

COASTAL BATTERIES

414 aircraft – 206 Halifaxes, 180 Lancasters, 28 Mosquitoes – attacked 7 coastal gun

batteries in the Pas de Calais area. Four of the positions were claimed to have been hit. 1 Lancaster lost while bombing the Mardyck position.

GENNEVILLIERS

56 Lancasters and 8 Mosquitoes of 5 Group attacked the Gnome & Rhône factory and another factory near by. A local report confirms the Bomber Command claim that both targets were hit, but 24 French people were killed and 107 injured. 5 Lancasters lost.

ANNECY

39 Lancasters and 4 Mosquitoes of 5 Group to a small ball-bearing factory. Weather *en route* was very bad and only 2 Mosquito marker aircraft reached the target, but the factory was accurately bombed. No aircraft lost.

Minor Operations: 30 Mosquitoes to Berlin and 6 to Châteaudun, 10 R.C.M. sorties, 11 *Serrate* and 24 Intruder patrols, 20 Halifaxes and 5 Stirlings minelaying off Dutch and French coasts, 43 aircraft on Resistance operations, 12 O.T.U. sorties. 2 Stirlings and 1 Halifax on Resistance operations and 1 O.T.U. Wellington were lost.

Total effort for the night: 682 sorties in 18 separate operations, 10 aircraft (1·5 per cent) lost.

10/11 May 1944

RAILWAY TARGETS

506 aircraft – 291 Lancasters, 187 Halifaxes, 28 Mosquitoes – to bomb railway yards at Courtrai, Dieppe, Ghent, Lens and Lille. No post-raid reconnaissance was carried out at Dieppe and results of the raid there are not known. All other raids were successful, although some bombs fell on nearby civilian housing. At Ghent, 48 Belgian civilians were killed and 58 were injured but no other details are available. 12 Lancasters lost from the 5 Group raid to Lille and 1 Lancaster lost from the Dieppe raid.

Minor Operations: 29 Mosquitoes to Ludwigshafen and 2 to Châteaudun, 5 R.C.M. sorties, 9 Intruder and 3 *Serrate* patrols, 26 aircraft minelaying off Brest and Heligoland, 28 aircraft on Resistance operations, 10 O.T.U. sorties. 1 Halifax minelayer lost.

Total effort for the night: 618 sorties, 14 aircraft (2·3 per cent) lost.

11/12 May 1944

BOURG-LÉOPOLD

190 Lancasters and 8 Mosquitoes of 5 Group, with 3 Mosquitoes of 8 Group, were dispatched to attack this large military camp in Belgium. Haze hampered the marking of the target and the Master Bomber ordered the raid to be abandoned, for fear of hitting the nearby civilian housing, after 94 Lancasters had bombed. 5 Lancasters lost.

BOULOGNE

135 aircraft – 80 Halifaxes, 47 Lancasters, 8 Mosquitoes – of 6 and 8 Groups. 2 Halifaxes lost.

Some bombs fell in the railway yards but the main weight of the raid missed the target and fell on nearby civilian housing. 128 civilians were killed.

HASSELT

126 Lancasters and 6 Mosquitoes of 1 and 8 Groups. The target was marked and 39 aircraft bombed, but all missed the railway yards because of thick haze and the Master Bomber ordered the bombing to stop. 5 Lancasters lost.

LOUVAIN

105 Lancasters and 5 Mosquitoes of 3 and 8 Groups attacked the railway yards but the main weight of the bombing hit the railway workshops and nearby storage buildings. 4 Lancasters lost. (See Louvain raid in next night for local details.)

TROUVILLE

53 Halifaxes of 4 Group and 6 Pathfinder Mosquitoes attacked railway yards. The bombing was accurate and a large explosion was seen. No aircraft lost.

COLLINE BEAUMONT

53 Halifaxes of 4 Group and 6 Pathfinder Mosquitoes attacked a gun position. The target proved difficult to mark and no results were established. No aircraft lost.

Minor Operations: 8 R.C.M. sorties, 6 *Serrate* patrols, 12 aircraft minelaying off French ports, 3 aircraft on Resistance operations. No aircraft lost.

Total effort for the night: 725 sorties, 16 aircraft (2·2 per cent) lost.

12/13 May 1944

LOUVAIN

120 aircraft – 96 Halifaxes, 20 Lancasters, 4 Mosquitoes – of 6 and 8 Groups. 3 Halifaxes and 2 Lancasters lost.

The bombing was more accurate than on the previous night and considerable damage was caused in the railways yards. The local report, which consolidates the 2 raids, confirms that the railways were badly damaged and says that parts of the system were still being repaired 6 months later. But civilian casualties were also heavy, with 160 people being killed and 208 injured in Louvain and its suburbs of Herent and Wilsele. Building damage in Louvain included 5 blocks of the university, 8 factories, 4 convents and a church.

HASSELT

111 aircraft – 100 Halifaxes, 7 Lancasters, 4 Mosquitoes – of 4 and 8 Groups. 6

Halifaxes and 1 Lancaster lost. Most of the attack fell in open fields and only a few bombs hit the railway yards.

SPECIAL MINELAYING OPERATION

22 Mosquitoes of 8 Group attempted to block the Kiel Canal by laying mines from low level. Intelligence sources had said that the Flak defences on part of the canal had been removed. 20 Mosquitoes laid their mines in this stretch; 1 aircraft lost.

Minor Operations: 12 Mosquitoes to Brunsbüttel (as a diversion for the Kiel Canal mining operation) and 8 to Châteaudun, 10 R.C.M. sorties, 12 *Serrate* and 9 Intruder patrols, 43 aircraft minelaying off the French coast and in the Frisians. 8 O.T.U. sorties. 1 Intruder Mosquito lost.

Total effort for the night: 355 sorties, 14 aircraft (3·9 per cent) lost.

14/15 May 1944

MINOR OPERATIONS

41 Mosquitoes – 29 to Cologne, 5 to Courtrai, 4 to Châteaudun and 3 to Leverkusen, 1 R.C.M. sortie, 10 Halifaxes and 2 Stirlings minelaying off Channel and Biscay ports, 10 O.T.U. sorties. No aircraft lost.

15/16 May 1944

MINOR OPERATIONS

43 Mosquitoes – 30 to Ludwigshafen, 10 to Carpiquet airfield near Caen and 3 to Leverkusen, 1 R.C.M. sortie, 2 *Serrate* patrols, 43 aircraft minelaying from Kiel to Biscay, 6 aircraft on Resistance operations, 24 O.T.U. sorties. 3 Lancaster minelayers and 1 O.T.U. Wellington lost.

16/17 May 1944

29 Mosquitoes attacked Berlin; none were lost.

18/19 May 1944

Oboe Tests

17 Mosquitoes on calibration tests to targets in France. 4 aircraft bombed Mondeville and 2 bombed Orly; others did not bomb. 7 R.C.M. aircraft also operated on this night. No aircraft lost.

19/20 May 1944

BOULOGNE

143 aircraft – 106 Halifaxes, 32 Lancasters, 5 Mosquitoes – of 4 and 8 Groups

attacked the railway yards. Only 1 of the *Oboe* Mosquitoes was able to mark the target but the bombing was accurate. The local report says that the main station was badly damaged; 33 civilians were killed. No aircraft lost.

ORLÉANS

118 Lancasters and 4 Mosquitoes of 1 and 8 Groups carried out a particularly accurate attack on the railway yards. 1 Lancaster lost.

AMIENS

112 Lancasters and 9 Mosquitoes of 5 and 8 Groups found that their railway target was cloud-covered and the Master Bomber ordered the attack to stop after 37 Lancasters had bombed. 1 Lancaster lost.

TOURS

113 Lancasters and 4 Mosquitoes of 5 Group to attempt the difficult task of attacking the railway installations in the centre of Tours. A previous 5 Group raid had destroyed the yards on the outskirts of the town. Both the marking and the bombing force were ordered to carry out their tasks with particular care and to be prepared to wait until the Master Bomber was satisfied that the surrounding housing areas were not hit. The raid continued until well after the planned period but no fighters appeared and no aircraft were lost. Much damage was caused to the railways but some bombs did fall to the west of the target. No local report is available.

LE MANS

112 Lancasters and 4 Mosquitoes of 3 and 8 Groups. The majority of the bombs hit the railway yards and caused serious damage. The local report says that the locomotive sheds were destroyed, an ammunition train (or some ammunition wagons) blew up, 2 main lines were destroyed and all other lines blocked because overhead power lines were brought down across the tracks. Civilian casualties are recorded as only 9 people killed (of whom 2 were railwaymen) and 5 injured.

Unfortunately the Lancasters of the Master Bomber and his deputy collided over the target and crashed. The Master Bomber was a brilliant young New Zealander, Wing Commander J. F. Barron, D.S.O. and Bar, D.F.C., D.F.M., and the Deputy Master Bomber was Squadron Leader J. M. Dennis, D.S.O., D.F.C. They were both killed; both were from 7 Squadron. 1 other Lancaster was lost.

LE CLIPON

58 Halifaxes of 6 Group and 6 Pathfinder Mosquitoes attacked a coastal gun position but there was haze and the results are not known. No aircraft lost.

MERVILLE

63 aircraft – 42 Halifaxes, 15 Lancasters, 6 Mosquitoes – of 6 and 8 Groups bombed the gun position. Some bombs did fall in the battery position despite the presence of haze. No aircraft were lost.

MONT COUPLE

39 Lancasters and 5 Mosquitoes of 8 Group to attack a radar station. The Mosquitoes were not able to use their *Oboe* equipment but 31 Lancasters used their *H2S* sets to make a timed run from the coast and bomb the approximate position of the target. 1 Lancaster shot down by Flak.

Minor Operations: 29 Mosquitoes to Cologne, 10 R.C.M. sorties, 8 *Serrate* and 23 Intruder patrols, 24 Halifaxes and 4 Stirlings minelaying off the French coast, 12 O.T.U. sorties. 1 O.T.U. Wellington lost.

Total effort for the night: 900 sorties, 7 aircraft (0·8 per cent) lost.

20/21 May 1944

DÜSSELDORF

30 Mosquitoes. The target area was cloud-covered and the *Oboe* markers quickly disappeared into the cloud. Most aircraft bombed on dead reckoning but this must have been inaccurate; Wuppertal, 17 miles east of Düsseldorf, reports 71 people killed on this night. No Mosquitoes lost.

Minor Operations: 14 Mosquitoes to Reisholz, 5 *Serrate* and 4 Intruder patrols, 12 Halifaxes and 4 Stirlings minelaying off French Atlantic ports, 7 O.T.U. sorties. No aircraft lost.

21/22 May 1944

DUISBURG

510 Lancasters and 22 Mosquitoes of 1, 3, 5 and 8 Groups carried out the first large raid on this target for a year. 29 Lancasters were lost, 5·5 per cent of the force.

The target was covered by cloud but the *Oboe* sky-marking was accurate and much damage was caused in the southern areas of the city. 350 buildings were destroyed and 665 seriously damaged but no other details of material damage are available. 124 people were killed.

MINELAYING

70 Lancasters and 37 Halifaxes to the Frisians, Heligoland, the Kattegat and Kiel Bay. 3 Lancasters lost.

Minor Operations: 25 Mosquitoes to Hannover and 8 to Courtrai, 9 R.C.M. sorties, 28 *Serrate* and 7 Intruder patrols. No aircraft lost.

Total effort for the night: 716 sorties, 32 aircraft (4·5 per cent) lost.

22/23 May 1944

DORTMUND

361 Lancasters and 14 Mosquitoes of 1, 3, 6 and 8 Groups carried out the first large raid on this target for a year. 18 Lancasters were lost, 4·8 per cent of the force.

The attack fell mainly in the south-eastern districts of Dortmund, mostly in residential areas. 852 houses and 6 industrial buildings were destroyed; 788 houses were seriously damaged. 335 Germans and 26 prisoners of war were killed and 1,697 people were injured.

BRUNSWICK

225 Lancasters and 10 Mosquitoes of 1 and 5 Groups. 13 Lancasters lost, 5·5 per cent of the force.

This raid was a failure. The weather forecast had predicted a clear target but the marker aircraft found a complete covering of cloud. There was also interference on the Master Bomber's radio communications. The 5 Group method could not cope with these conditions and most of the bombing fell in the country areas around Brunswick. The city records show only a few bombs and there were no casualties. A reconnaissance aircraft flying through this area an hour later found it completely free of cloud.

LE MANS

133 aircraft – 112 Halifaxes, 13 Lancasters, 8 Mosquitoes – of 6 and 8 Groups again attacked the railway yards. The local report confirms that the bombing was accurate, with much damage to the railways and the nearby Gnome & Rhône factory. Only 2 French people were injured. 1 Halifax lost.

ORLÉANS

128 aircraft – 108 Halifaxes, 12 Lancasters, 8 Mosquitoes – of 4 and 8 Groups. 1 Halifax lost. Most of the bombs fell on the passenger station and the railway-repair workshops.

Minor Operations: 26 Mosquitoes to Ludwigshafen and 9 to Courtrai, 9 R.C.M. sorties, 21 Serrate and 8 Intruder patrols, 54 aircraft minelaying in the Frisians and off the French coast, 25 O.T.U. sorties. 1 O.T.U. Whitley was lost, probably the last Whitley to be lost on operations.

Total effort for the night: 1,023 sorties, 34 aircraft (3·3 per cent) lost. The raids on Dortmund and Brunswick were the last major Bomber Command raids on German cities until after the invasion forces were firmly established in Normandy.

23/24 May 1944

MINOR OPERATIONS

46 Mosquitoes – 24 to Dortmund, 16 to Berlin and 6 to a railway junction at Lison in France, 2 R.C.M. sorties, 2 Serrate patrols, 30 aircraft minelaying off various coasts, 4 aircraft on Resistance operations, 8 O.T.U. sorties. No aircraft lost.

24/25 May 1944

AACHEN

442 aircraft – 264 Lancasters, 162 Halifaxes, 16 Mosquitoes – of all groups except 5 Group to attack 2 railway yards at Aachen – Aachen-West and Rothe Erde (east of

the town). These were important links in the railway system between Germany and France. 18 Halifaxes and 7 Lancasters lost, 5·7 per cent of the force.

The Aachen report duly records that the 2 railway yards were the targets attacked, with the railways to the east of Aachen being particularly hard hit. But, because this was a German town, Bomber Command sent more aircraft than normal for railway raids and many bombs fell in Aachen itself and in villages near the railway yards. The Monheim war-industry factory and the town's gasworks were among many buildings destroyed. 207 people were killed in Aachen and 121 were seriously injured. 14,800 people were bombed out. Several villages near the railway yards also incurred casualties; Eilendorf, near the Rothe Erde yards, had 52 people killed.

The Aachen report comments on the great number of high-explosive bombs and the small number of incendiaries dropped. There were only 6 large fires. 288 high-explosive bombs were found to be duds, approximately 10 per cent of those dropped.

EINDHOVEN

59 Lancasters and 4 Mosquitoes of 5 Group were dispatched to attack the Philips factory but the Master Bomber ordered the force not to bomb because of bad visibility. 1 aircraft did not hear the order and released its load. No aircraft lost.

COASTAL BATTERIES

106 Halifaxes, 102 Lancasters and 16 Mosquitoes, split into small forces, attacked coastal gun positions at Boulogne, Colline Beaumont, Le Clipon and Trouville without loss.

ANTWERP

44 Lancasters and 7 Mosquitoes of 5 and 8 Groups to attack the Ford motor factory but the bombing missed the target. Some bombs fell on nearby dockside buildings. No aircraft lost.

Minor Operations: 15 Mosquitoes to Berlin, 6 R.C.M. sorties, 31 *Serrate* and 8 Intruder patrols, 18 Halifaxes and 7 Stirlings minelaying in the Frisians and off Brest, 23 O.T.U. sorties. 1 R.C.M. Halifax lost.

Total effort for the night: 888 sorties, 26 aircraft (2·9 per cent) lost.

26/27 May 1944

MINOR OPERATIONS

30 Mosquitoes to Ludwigshafen, 11 to railway yards at Aachen and 8 to Lison, 7 *Serrate* patrols, 42 aircraft minelaying off Dutch, Belgian and French coasts. 2 Mosquitoes were lost from the Ludwigshafen raid.

27/28 May 1944

BOURG-LÉOPOLD

331 aircraft – 267 Halifaxes, 56 Lancasters, 8 Mosquitoes – to attack the military camp. 9 Halifaxes and 1 Lancaster lost, 3·0 per cent of the force.

1 *Oboe*-aimed target indicator fell right on the target and the bombing which followed caused severe damage to the camp. No further details are available.

AACHEN

162 Lancasters and 8 Mosquitoes of 1, 3 and 8 Groups to attack the Rothe Erde railway yards. 12 Lancasters lost, 7·0 per cent of the force.

The railway lines at the yards, which were not seriously hit in the raid of 2 nights earlier, were now severely damaged and all through traffic was halted. A large proportion of delayed-action bombs were dropped. The bombing also hit the nearby Aachen suburb of Forst which, in the words of our local expert Hubert Beckers, 'was razed to the ground'. The local hospital, an army barracks, an army-stores office, 2 police posts and 21 industrial buildings were hit, as well as 603 houses. 167 people were killed and 164 injured. The local people were impressed that the whole raid only lasted 12 minutes.

NANTES

100 Lancasters and 4 Mosquitoes of 5 Group to attack a railway junction and workshops. The first 50 Lancasters bombed so accurately that the Master Bomber ordered the remainder of the force to retain their bombs. 1 Lancaster lost.

RENNES

78 Lancasters and 5 Mosquitoes of 8 Group attacked the airfield in good visibility. The marking was good and the bombing was very accurate. Much damage to the airfield installations was caused and there was a large explosion, probably in the bomb dump.

COASTAL BATTERIES

272 aircraft – 208 Lancasters, 49 Halifaxes, 15 Mosquitoes – carried out raids on 5 coastal-battery positions on the French coast. All of the targets were bombed satisfactorily. 1 Lancaster and 1 Mosquito lost.

Minor Operations: 23 Mosquitoes to Berlin and 6 to Düsseldorf, 7 R.C.M. sorties, 28 *Serrate* and 10 Intruder patrols, 60 aircraft minelaying from Le Havre to the River Gironde, 10 aircraft on Resistance operations, 7 O.T.U. sorties. 3 Mosquitoes – 2 Intruders and 1 *Serrate* – lost.

Total effort for the night: 1,111 sorties in 17 separate operations, 28 aircraft (2·5 per cent) lost.

28/29 May 1944

ANGERS

118 Lancasters and 8 Mosquitoes of 3 and 8 Groups attacked the railway yards and junction. 1 Lancaster lost.

The Bomber Command report describes this as 'a good, concentrated attack' with the tracks and rolling stock very seriously damaged. A brief report from Angers, however, shows that much of the bombing must have fallen outside the target. 800 buildings were destroyed and 6,819 were damaged; 254 French people were killed and 220 injured.

COASTAL BATTERIES

181 Lancasters and 20 Mosquitoes bombed 3 coastal gun positions. 1 Lancaster lost.

Minor Operations: 31 Mosquitoes to Ludwigshafen and 6 to a railway junction at Laval, 3 R.C.M. sorties, 6 Intruder patrols, 10 Halifaxes and 6 Stirlings minelaying off Dutch, Belgian and French coasts, 24 aircraft on Resistance operations, 14 O.T.U. sorties. 2 O.T.U. Wellingtons shot down in error by anti-aircraft guns on the Dorset coast.

Total effort for the night: 427 sorties, 4 aircraft (0·9 per cent) lost.

29/30 May 1944

MINOR OPERATIONS

31 Mosquitoes to Hannover, 11 to Xanten ammunition dump and 4 to a coastal battery at Mardyck, 6 Halifaxes minelaying off Ijmuiden, Dunkirk and Brest. No aircraft lost.

30/31 May 1944

BOULOGNE

50 Lancasters and 4 Mosquitoes of 3 and 8 Groups attacked a coastal gun position without loss.

Minor Operations: 30 Mosquitoes to Leverkusen, 12 Stirlings minelaying off the Dutch and French coasts, 11 Stirlings on Resistance operations. No aircraft lost.

---

31 May/1 June 1944

TRAPPES

219 aircraft – 125 Lancasters, 86 Halifaxes, 8 Mosquitoes – of all groups except 5 Group successfully attacked the railway yards in 2 waves. 4 Lancasters lost.

AU FÈVRE

129 aircraft – 109 Halifaxes, 16 Lancasters, 4 Mosquitoes – of 6 and 8 Groups bombed a coastal wireless transmitting station and destroyed 4 of the 6 masts. No aircraft lost.

MONT COUPLE

115 aircraft – 60 Lancasters, 51 Halifaxes, 4 Mosquitoes – of 6 and 8 Groups bombed a radio jamming station which was 'rendered completely unserviceable'. No aircraft lost.

TERGNIER

111 Lancasters and 4 Mosquitoes of 1 and 8 Groups attacked the railway yards. The sidings and workshops were 'squarely hit'. 2 Lancasters lost.

SAUMUR

82 Lancasters and 4 Mosquitoes of 5 Group attacked and destroyed a railway junction without loss.

MAISY

68 Lancasters of 5 Group raiding a coastal gun battery found it covered by cloud and only 6 aircraft bombed. No aircraft lost.

Minor Operations: 14 R.C.M. sorties, 16 *Serrate* and 9 Intruder patrols, 28 aircraft minelaying off the Dutch and French coasts, 9 aircraft on Resistance operations, 12 O.T.U. sorties. 5 aircraft were lost – 2 Halifaxes and 1 Hudson on Resistance operations, 1 Stirling minelayer and 1 Intruder Mosquito.

Total effort for the night: 820 sorties, 11 aircraft (1·3 per cent) lost.

1/2 June 1944

FERME-D'URVILLE

101 Halifaxes of 4 Group and 8 Pathfinder Mosquitoes attacked the main German radio-listening station near the coast chosen for the invasion, but cloud and haze prevented accurate bombing. No aircraft lost.

SAUMUR

58 Lancasters of 5 Group attacked a railway junction. Photographic reconnaissance showed 'severe damage to junction, main lines torn up'. No aircraft lost.

Minor Operations: 6 Mosquitoes to the port of Aarhus in Denmark, 3 *Serrate* patrols, 18 aircraft minelaying in the Kattegat and off Dunkirk, 40 aircraft on Resistance operations. 1 Halifax on Resistance operations lost.

2/3 June 1944

TRAPPES

128 aircraft – 105 Halifaxes, 19 Lancasters, 4 Mosquitoes – of 1, 4 and 8 Groups attacked the railway yards. Most of the bombing fell in the eastern half of the target area. 15 Halifaxes and 1 Lancaster lost, 12·5 per cent of the force.

BERNEVAL

103 Lancasters and 4 Mosquitoes of 1 and 8 Groups attacked a radar-jamming station with great accuracy and without loss.

COASTAL BATTERIES

271 aircraft – 136 Lancasters, 119 Halifaxes, 16 Mosquitoes – attacked 4 coastal gun positions with the loss of 1 Lancaster. In only 1 raid was the bombing accurate but this was not too serious because these raids were part of the invasion deception plan. None of the targets were in the Normandy area; all were on the Pas de Calais coast.

Further raids in the next 2 nights would continue the deception and the Normandy batteries would only be bombed on the last night before the invasion.

Minor Operations: 23 Mosquitoes to Leverkusen, 4 to Laval and 3 to Lison, 16 R.C.M. sorties, 9 *Serrate* and 6 Intruder patrols, 53 aircraft minelaying from Dunkirk to Brest, 36 aircraft on Resistance operations, 11 O.T.U. sorties. 1 Stirling lost on a Resistance operation.

Total effort for the night: 667 sorties, 17 aircraft (2·5 per cent) lost.

3/4 June 1944

FERME-D'URVILLE

96 Lancasters of 5 Group and 4 Pathfinder Mosquitoes to attack the important German signals station which had escaped serious damage in bombing 2 nights earlier. 3 of the *Oboe* Mosquitoes placed their markers perfectly and the Lancasters wiped out the station. No aircraft lost.

COASTAL BATTERIES

127 Lancasters and 8 Mosquitoes of 1, 3 and 8 Groups continued the deception raids on coastal batteries at Calais and Wimereux. The bombing was accurate; no aircraft lost.

Minor Operations: 20 Mosquitoes to Ludwigshafen and 5 to Argentan, 4 R.C.M. sorties, 6 *Serrate* and 3 Intruder patrols, 57 aircraft minelaying from the River Scheldt to Dunkirk. No aircraft lost.

Total effort for the night: 330 sorties with no aircraft losses.

4/5 June 1944

COASTAL BATTERIES

259 aircraft – 125 Lancasters, 118 Halifaxes, 16 Mosquitoes – of 1, 4, 5, 6 and 8 Groups to bomb 4 gun positions; 3 of these were deception targets in the Pas de Calais but the fourth battery, at Maisy, was in Normandy between what would soon be known as Omaha and Utah Beaches, where American troops would land in less than 36 hours' time. Unfortunately, Maisy was covered by cloud and could only be marked by *Oboe* sky-markers, but it was then bombed by 52 Lancasters of 5 Group. 2 of the 3 gun positions in the Pas de Calais were also affected by bad weather and could only be bombed through cloud but the position at Calais itself was clear and was accurately marked by the Mosquitoes and well bombed by Halifaxes and Lancasters of 6 Group.

No aircraft lost on these operations.

Minor Operations: 20 Mosquitoes to Cologne and 6 to Argentan, 4 R.C.M. sorties, 6 *Serrate* patrols, 4 Halifaxes and 3 Lancasters minelaying from the Scheldt to Dunkirk, 17 aircraft on Resistance operations. No aircraft lost.

Total effort for the night: 319 sorties with no aircraft losses.

Operational Statistics, 31 March/1 April to 5 June 1944 (66 days/nights)

Number of nights with operations: 57
Number of days with operations: 6
Number of night sorties: 24,060, from which 525 aircraft (2·2 per cent) were lost
Number of daylight sorties: 12, from which no aircraft were lost
Total sorties: 24,072, from which 525 aircraft (2·2 per cent) were lost
Approximate bomb tonnage in period: 75,748 tons
Averages per 24-hour period: 364·7 sorties, 8·0 aircraft lost, 1,147·7 tons of bombs dropped

19. THE BATTLE OF NORMANDY

5/6 June to 16 August 1944

The Allied armies made their historic landings on five beaches on the Normandy coast at dawn on 6 June, but they would remain locked in battle with a determined German defence for ten weeks before breaking out to sweep forward towards Germany. On the night before the landings, Bomber Command flew 1,211 sorties, its greatest total yet in one night; nearly all were in direct support of the invasion forces. Bad weather for much of the first two weeks restricted some air operations but the bomber crews became full partners in the invasion, a fact that would be a matter of great pride to the Bomber Command survivors. Their main invasion tasks would be the direct bombing of German troop and gun positions, ammunition and oil dumps, the continuing attack on German rail and road communications to the battle front, and the bombing of French ports where E-boats and other light-attack vessels were gathering to threaten the Allied supply ships off the invasion beaches.

But these tasks only required a part of Bomber Command's great strength and there was a variety of other operations during this period. One of the most important of these was a renewal of the attack on the German synthetic-oil industry, which had been tried in the early years of the bombing war but had failed because of the chronic target-finding difficulties of those years. The effects of a successful attack on the German oil industry upon the outcome of the Battle of Normandy were obvious. The American day bombers had started bombing the oil plants in May and General Eisenhower, the supreme Allied commander, asked Bomber Command to join in as soon as the Allied ground forces were safely established ashore in Normandy. Bomber Command was allocated the oil targets in and around the Ruhr; the R.A.F. night attacks would save the American bombers having to face the fierce Ruhr Flak defences by day. The R.A.F. bombers duly tackled these difficult targets with much success, though with some setbacks and the occasional heavy casualties caused by night fighters.

But, as had happened so often in earlier years, there came a call to divert the bomber effort from the main task. The Germans launched the first V-1 flying bombs against London six days after the invasion. The prolonged V-1 campaign was a nuisance rather than a major military threat because the Germans directed most of the V-1s against London, as a 'revenge weapon' for R.A.F. bombing, rather than against the invasion supply ports. But the damage and casualties in London were heavy and everything possible had to be done to knock out the multitude of small launching ramps which were hidden in the countryside of the Pas de Calais area. The Allied air forces had to turn their attention to the V-1 launching sites and stores, although more important invasion tasks always took priority. The V-1 campaign would last until late August, when advancing Allied troops captured most of the sites; the last ground-launched V-1 was dispatched by the Germans on 3 September.

A smaller diversion forced on Bomber Command by the V-1s was the need to send at least two Mosquito fighter squadrons of 100 Group back to Fighter Command (now called Air Defence of Great Britain) for the interception of V-1s, but there were few major raids on Germany at this time and the 100 Group Mosquitoes could easily be spared. These squadrons are believed to have shot down eighteen flying bombs and they returned to Bomber Command when the V-1 threat ended. (The 100 Group Mosquito anti-flying-bomb operations were flown under the control of Air Defence of Great Britain Headquarters – Fighter Command under a new title – but they are also recorded in the Bomber Command records; because of the difficulty which would be experienced in separating details of these operations from other 100 Group Mosquito operations, the anti-flying-bomb sorties are included in the diaries here.)

So the men of Bomber Command played their part in the events of those historic weeks. For the bomber crews it was a time of almost unbelievable intensity, variety and interest. There were no major raids in Germany in June but time was found to make five attacks on German cities during the non-moon period in July. Day raids were reintroduced, though with some reluctance, by Harris with his memories of heavy daylight losses earlier in the war, but all went well as long as the bombers operated within the limits of the range of the vast Allied fighter-escort force available. The benefits accruing from the return to daylight operations were the virtual doubling of Bomber Command's potential strength at a stroke and the elimination of some of the problems of target-finding, at least on days of good visibility. The need for accurate bombing was greater than ever, particularly when the targets being attacked were near Allied troops, French communities or were the small flying-bomb sites. In the early daylight raids of this period, Bomber Command simply pretended that day was still night and used Pathfinder markers in the long established manner, but more sophisticated means were quickly developed. The most important of these were the *Oboe*-leader and the *G-H* formation methods, in which aircraft fitted with these devices led small formations of heavy bombers which released their bombs when the leading aircraft bombed. The '*Oboe*-leader' method proved to be the most accurate of all daylight methods but *G-H* was more flexible because there was no limit to the number of aircraft which could eventually be fitted with the *G-H* blind-bombing device and hence to the force of ordinary bombers which could be employed.

Operations during this period consisted of a multitude of small or medium-sized raids. The planners never worked harder, nor did the aircrew and the ground staffs. Sometimes aircrews flew two sorties in twenty-four hours. By day, they might be bombing targets only a few yards from the battle lines in Normandy; a few hours later they could be bombing an oil refinery in the Ruhr. Bomber Command flew approximately the same number of sorties in an average week during this period – more than 5,000 sorties – as in the first nine months of the war! No one who flew in those weeks and survived will ever forget them.

5/6 June 1944

NORMANDY COASTAL BATTERIES

1,012 aircraft – 551 Lancasters, 412 Halifaxes, 49 Mosquitoes – to bomb coastal batteries at Fontenay, Houlgate, La Pernelle, Longues, Maisy, Merville, Mont Fleury, Pointe-du-Hoc, Ouisterham and St-Martin-de-Varreville. 946 aircraft carried out their bombing tasks. 3 aircraft were lost – 2 Halifaxes of 4 Group on the Mont Fleury raid and 1 Lancaster of 6 Group on the Longues raid. Only two of the targets – La Pernelle and Ouisterham – were free of cloud; all other bombing was entirely based on *Oboe* marking. At least 5,000 tons of bombs were dropped, the greatest tonnage in one night so far in the war.

SUPPORT OPERATIONS

110 aircraft of 1 and 100 Groups carried out extensive bomber-support operations: 24 *A.B.C.*-equipped Lancasters of 101 Squadron patrolled all likely night-fighter approaches, so that their German-speaking operators could jam the German controllers' instructions; 100 Group flew 34 R.C.M. sorties and 27 *Serrate* and 25 Intruder Mosquito patrols. 2 Intruders and 1 *A.B.C.* Lancaster were lost.

DIVERSION OPERATIONS

58 aircraft of 3 and 5 Groups carried out a variety of operations to conceal the true location of the invasion for as long as possible. 16 Lancasters of 617 Squadron and 6 *G-H* fitted Stirlings of 218 Squadron dropped a dense screen of *Window*, which advanced slowly across the Channel, to simulate a large convoy of ships approaching the French coast between Boulogne and Le Havre, north of the real invasion coast. These flights required exact navigation; both squadrons had been practising for this operation for more than a month. The second diversion was carried out by 36 Halifaxes and Stirlings of 90, 138, 149 and 161 Squadrons. These aircraft dropped dummy parachutists and explosive devices to simulate airborne landings over areas not being invaded. 2 Stirlings of 149 Squadron were lost while carrying out this duty.

Osnabrück

31 Mosquitoes bombed Osnabrück without loss.

Total Bomber Command effort for the night: 1,211 sorties, 8 aircraft (0·7 per cent) lost. The number of sorties flown was a new record. British, American and Canadian divisions landed on five Normandy beaches early the next morning.

6/7 June 1944

COMMUNICATIONS

1,065 aircraft – 589 Lancasters, 418 Halifaxes, 58 Mosquitoes – to bomb railway and road centres on the lines of communication behind the Normandy battle area. All of the targets were in or near French towns. 3,488 tons of bombs were dropped on targets at Achères, Argentan, Caen, Châteaudun, Condé-sur-Noireau, Coutances, St-Lô, Lisieux and Vire. Every effort was made to bomb accurately but casualties to the French civilians were inevitable. Cloud affected the accuracy of the bombing at many of the targets and, at Achères, the Master Bomber ordered the raid to be abandoned because of cloud and no bombs were dropped.

10 Lancasters and 1 Halifax were lost in these raids; 6 of the Lancasters were lost

in the 5 Group raid at Caen, where the main force of bombers had to wait for the target to be properly marked and then fly over an area full of German units and guns at bombing heights below 3,000 ft.

Some details are available of the effects of the bombing. At Argentan, Châteaudun and Lisieux, much damage was done to railways, although the towns, Lisieux in particular, were hit by many bombs. Important bridges at Coutances were badly damaged but the town was hit and set on fire; approximately 65 per cent of the buildings were destroyed and 312 civilians were killed. The town centres of Caen, Condé-sur-Noireau, St-Lô and Vire were all badly bombed and most of the roads through those towns were blocked.

Minor Operations: 32 Mosquitoes to Ludwigshafen, 18 *Serrate* patrols, 19 aircraft minelaying in the Brest area, 26 aircraft on Resistance operations. No aircraft lost.

Total effort for the night: 1,160 sorties, 11 aircraft (0·9 per cent) lost.

7/8 June 1944

COMMUNICATIONS

337 aircraft – 195 Halifaxes, 122 Lancasters, 20 Mosquitoes – attacked railway targets at Achères, Juvisy, Massey-Palaiseau and Versailles. Bombing conditions were better than on the previous night. All targets were accurately bombed and, although no details are available, it is probable that fewer civilians were killed. The targets were mostly more distant from the battle front than those recently attacked and German night fighters had more time to intercept the bomber forces. 17 Lancasters and 11 Halifaxes were lost, 8·3 per cent of the forces involved.

FORÊT DE CERISY

112 Lancasters and 10 Mosquitoes of 1, 5 and 8 Groups carried out an accurate attack on an important 6-way road junction half-way between Bayeux and St-Lô. The surrounding woods were believed to contain fuel dumps and German tank units preparing to counter-attack the Allied landing forces. The nearest French village was several kilometres away. 2 Lancasters lost.

Minor Operations: 32 Mosquitoes to Cologne, 10 R.C.M. sorties, 18 *Serrate* and 18 Intruder patrols, 22 Halifaxes and 3 Stirlings minelaying off Lorient and Brest, 24 aircraft on Resistance operations. No aircraft lost.

Total effort for the night: 586 sorties, 30 aircraft (5·1 per cent) lost.

8/9 June 1944

COMMUNICATIONS

483 aircraft – 286 Lancasters, 169 Halifaxes, 28 Mosquitoes – attacked railways at Alençon, Fougères, Mayenne, Pontabault and Rennes to prevent German reinforcements from the south reaching Normandy. All of the raids appear to have been successful. 4 aircraft were lost, 2 Lancasters from the Pontabault raid and 1 Lancaster and 1 Mosquito from the Rennes raid.

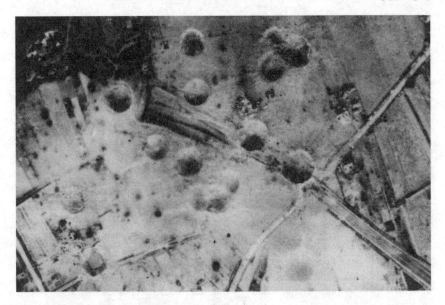

37. Precision bombing. The huge craters caused by 617 Squadron's 12,000-pound bombs, which blocked the Saumur railway tunnel and held up a Panzer division moving towards the Normandy battlefield.

The first 12,000-lb *Tallboy* bombs developed by Barnes Wallis were used on this night by 617 Squadron in a raid on a railway tunnel near Saumur, 125 miles south of the battle area. The raid was prepared in great haste because a German Panzer unit was expected to move by train through the tunnel. The target area was illuminated with flares by 4 Lancasters of 83 Squadron and marked at low level by 3 Mosquitoes. 25 Lancasters of 617 Squadron then dropped their *Tallboys* with great accuracy. The huge bombs exploded under the ground to create miniature 'earthquakes'; one actually pierced the roof of the tunnel and brought down a huge quantity of rock and soil. The tunnel was blocked for a considerable period and the Panzer unit was badly delayed. No aircraft were lost from this raid.

Minor Operations: 17 *Serrate* and 19 Intruder patrols, 34 aircraft minelaying from the Scheldt to Lorient. No aircraft lost.

Total effort for the night: 585 sorties, 4 aircraft (0·7 per cent) lost.

9/10 June 1944

AIRFIELDS

401 aircraft – 206 Lancasters, 175 Halifaxes, 20 Mosquitoes – of 1, 4, 6 and 8 Groups bombed airfields at Flers, Le Mans, Laval and Rennes, all situated south of the Normandy battle area. Bomber Command documents do not give any reason for these raids; it is possible that the intention was to prevent these airfields being used for German reinforcements being brought in by air because the railways were blocked. All the attacks were successful. 2 Halifaxes were lost on the Laval raid.

ÉTAMPES

108 Lancasters and 4 Mosquitoes of 5 Group, with 5 Pathfinder Mosquitoes, attempted to bomb a railway junction at Étampes, south of Paris. 6 Lancasters lost. The marking was accurate but late and the bombing spread from the railway junction into the town. The local report states that a quarter of the small town was affected by the bombing; between 400 and 500 houses were destroyed and 133 people were killed and 51 injured.

Minor Operations: 36 Mosquitoes to Berlin, 13 R.C.M. sorties, 2 *Serrate* patrols, 24 Halifaxes and 4 Stirlings minelaying off Brest. No aircraft lost.

Total effort for the night: 597 sorties, 8 aircraft (1·3 per cent) lost.

10/11 June 1944

RAILWAYS

432 aircraft – 323 Lancasters, 90 Halifaxes, 19 Mosquitoes – attacked railway targets at Achères, Dreux, Orléans and Versailles. All targets were believed to have been hit but few further details are available. 15 Lancasters and 3 Halifaxes lost.

Minor Operations: 32 Mosquitoes to Berlin, 13 R.C.M. sorties, 7 *Serrate* and 18 Intruder patrols, 30 aircraft minelaying off France on the flanks of the invasion area. 2 Mosquitoes lost from the Berlin raid.

Total effort for the night: 532 sorties, 20 aircraft (3·8 per cent) lost.

11/12 June 1944

RAILWAYS

329 aircraft – 225 Lancasters, 86 Halifaxes, 18 Mosquitoes – of 1, 3, 4 and 8 Groups attacked railway targets at Évreux, Massey-Palaiseau, Nantes and Tours. All of the raids appeared to be successful. 3 Lancasters and 1 Halifax – 1 aircraft from each raid – were lost.

Minor Operations: 33 Mosquitoes to Berlin, 30 *Serrate* patrols, 13 Halifaxes minelaying on the flanks of the invasion coast. 2 Mosquitoes lost from the Berlin raid.

Total effort for the night: 405 sorties, 6 aircraft (1·5 per cent) lost.

12/13 June 1944

COMMUNICATIONS

671 aircraft – 348 Halifaxes, 285 Lancasters, 38 Mosquitoes – of 4, 5, 6 and 8 Groups to attack communications, mostly railways, at Amiens/St-Roch, Amiens/Longueau, Arras, Caen, Cambrai and Poitiers. (It is interesting to note that, with the exception of Caen, all of these targets were the sites of well-known battles of earlier wars and Caen was soon to be the scene of fierce fighting.)

Bomber Command's records state that the Poitiers attack, by 5 Group, was the most accurate of the night and that the 2 raids at Amiens and the raid at Arras were of reasonable accuracy. The target at Cambrai was hit but many bombs also fell in the town. The most scattered attack (also by 5 Group) was at Caen.

23 aircraft – 17 Halifaxes and 6 Lancasters – were lost from these raids; all of these losses were from 4 and 6 Groups. A Canadian airman, Pilot Officer Andrew Charles Mynarski from Winnipeg, was awarded a posthumous Victoria Cross for his bravery on the Cambrai raid. His Lancaster, of 419 Squadron, was attacked by a night fighter and set on fire and the crew were ordered to abandon the aircraft. Mynarski was about to jump when he saw that the tail gunner was trapped in his turret and he went through fierce flames to help. The rear turret was so badly jammed that it could not be freed and the trapped gunner eventually waved Mynarski away. By the time he left the aircraft, Mynarski's clothing and parachute were on fire and he died while being cared for by French civilians soon after he landed. The tail gunner was fortunate to survive the crash and his report on Mynarski's courage led to the award of the Victoria Cross. Pilot Officer Mynarski is buried in the small village cemetery at Meharicourt, east of Amiens.

GELSENKIRCHEN

303 aircraft – 286 Lancasters and 17 Mosquitoes of 1, 3 and 8 Groups – carried out the first raid of the new oil campaign; the target was the Nordstern synthetic-oil plant (the Germans called the plant Gelsenberg A.G.). 17 Lancasters were lost, 6·1 per cent of the Lancaster force.

The attack opened with exceptional accuracy owing to good work by the Path-finders and to improved versions of *Oboe* sets now available. Later phases of the bombing were spoiled by the clouds of smoke from the burning target and by a rogue target indicator which fell 10 miles short of the target and was bombed by 35 aircraft. A German industrial report * shows that all production at the oil plant ceased, with a loss of 1,000 tons of aviation fuel a day for several weeks, as well as the loss of other fuels. Gelsenkirchen's civil records also pay tribute to the accuracy of the attack; 1,500 bombs fell inside the oil-plant area. The civil records also describe the extensive damage in the nearby working-class district of Horst. A total of 270 people were killed, including 24 workers in the oil plant at the time of the attack, 23 foreign workers who were killed when their wooden barracks near by were hit, and 6 school-boy *'Flakhilfers'*.

Minor Operations: 27 Mosquitoes to Cologne, 3 R.C.M. sorties, 39 *Serrate* and 13 Intruder patrols, 9 Halifaxes and 5 Stirlings minelaying off Brest and St-Nazaire, 13 aircraft on Resistance operations. No aircraft lost.

Total effort for the night: 1,083 sorties, 40 aircraft (3·7 per cent) lost.

13/14 June 1944

MINOR OPERATIONS

8 Mosquitoes to Mönchengladbach and 3 to Düren, 15 *Serrate* patrols, 8 Stirlings and 4

---

* Quoted in the Official History, Vol. IV, p. 322.

Lancasters minelaying off Brest and St-Nazaire, 2 Halifaxes on Resistance operations. No aircraft lost.

---

14 June 1944

LE HAVRE

221 Lancasters and 13 Mosquitoes of 1, 3, 5 and 8 Groups carried out Bomber Command's first daylight raid since the departure of 2 Group at the end of May 1943. The objectives were the fast German motor-torpedo boats (E-boats) and other light naval forces which were threatening Allied shipping off the Normandy beaches only 30 miles away.

The raid took place in 2 waves, one during the evening and the second at dusk. Most of the aircraft in the first wave were from 1 Group and in the second wave from 3 Group. Pathfinder aircraft provided marking by their normal methods for both raids. No unexpected difficulties were encountered; the naval port area was accurately bombed by both waves with 1,230 tons of bombs and few E-boats remained undamaged. 617 Squadron sent 22 Lancasters, each loaded with a 12,000-lb *Tallboy* bomb, and 3 Mosquito marker aircraft to attack the concrete-covered E-boat pens just before the first wave bombed. Several hits were scored on the pens and one bomb penetrated the roof.

This raid was regarded as an experiment by Sir Arthur Harris, who was still reluctant to risk his squadrons to the dangers of daylight operations but both waves of the attack were escorted by Spitfires of 11 Group and only 1 Lancaster was lost.

Two reports are available from Le Havre (from the local press and the report of the Défense Passive); they give no details of damage to the naval vessels or facilities, except to mention the *'ravages considérables'* caused in the port area by 617 Squadron's bombs. Both reports stress the courage of the local civil and French naval fire brigades which continued to fight the fires caused by the first wave of bombing when the second wave attacked. The Nôtre-Dame district, near the port, was devastated but the people there had fortunately been evacuated at an earlier date. Other districts were also hit, with 700 houses and a tobacco factory being destroyed and the local gaol damaged. 76 civilians were killed and 150 injured. These details of damage and casualties in the town area should not obscure the fact that most of the bombing fell into the harbour area and that the E-boat threat to the invasion beaches from this port was almost completely removed by this raid.

14/15 June 1944

TROOP POSITIONS

337 aircraft – 223 Lancasters, 100 Halifaxes, 14 Mosquitoes – of 4, 5 and 8 Groups attacked German troop and vehicle positions at Aunay-sur-Odon and Évrecy, near Caen. These raids were prepared and executed in great haste, in response to an army report giving details of the presence of major German units. The weather was clear and both targets were successfully bombed. The target at Aunay, where the marking was shared by 5 and 8 Groups, was particularly accurate. No aircraft were lost.

RAILWAYS

330 aircraft – 61 Lancasters, 255 Halifaxes, 14 Mosquitoes – of 4, 6 and 8 Groups attacked railways at Cambrai, Douai and St-Pol. All of the targets were either partially cloud-covered or affected by haze and the bombing was not completely concentrated or accurate. 3 Halifaxes and 1 Lancaster were lost, the Lancaster being the Master Bomber's aircraft at Douai.

SCHOLVEN/BUER

35 Mosquitoes to attack the Scholven/Buer oil plant. A short German report says that 3 bombs fell into the plant area and that 3 civilians outside the factory – a farmer, a lorry-driver and a housewife – were killed. No Mosquitoes lost.

Minor Operations: 8 R.C.M. sorties, 19 *Serrate* and 18 Intruder patrols, 12 Stirlings minelaying off French ports, 10 aircraft on Resistance operations. No aircraft lost.

Total effort for the night: 769 sorties, 4 aircraft (0·5 per cent) lost.

---

15 June 1944

BOULOGNE

297 aircraft – 155 Lancasters, 130 Halifaxes, 12 Mosquitoes – of 1, 4, 5, 6 and 8 Groups carried out attacks on German light naval vessels now gathering in Boulogne harbour. The tactics employed and the bombing results were similar to those at Le Havre the previous evening, although the visibility was not so clear. 1 Halifax lost. The only details from France are in a short civil report which describes this as the worst raid of the war on Boulogne, with great destruction in the port and the surrounding areas and with approximately 200 people being killed.

15/16 June 1944

AMMUNITION AND FUEL DUMPS

227 aircraft – 119 Lancasters, 99 Halifaxes, 9 Mosquitoes – of 4, 5 and 8 Groups attacked an ammunition dump at Fouillard and a fuel dump at Châtellerault. The raid at Fouillard, carried out by 4 Group with Pathfinder marking, hit the north-western section of the target and the all-5 Group raid at Châtellerault destroyed 8 fuel sites out of 35 in the target area. No aircraft lost.

RAILWAYS

224 aircraft – 184 Lancasters, 30 Stirlings, 10 Mosquitoes – of 3 and 8 Groups attacked railway yards at Lens and Valenciennes. The raids took place in clear visibility and both targets were accurately bombed. 6 Lancasters were lost from the Lens raid and 5 Lancasters from Valenciennes.

Minor Operations: 31 Mosquitoes to Gelsenkirchen, 13 *Serrate* and 21 Intruder patrols, 7 Stirlings and 4 Halifaxes minelaying off Channel ports. 1 Mosquito lost from the Gelsenkirchen raid.

Total effort for the night: 527 sorties, 12 aircraft (2·3 per cent) lost.

---

16 June 1944

2 Mosquitoes of 100 Group carried out uneventful daylight Intruder patrols to Leeuwarden airfield.

16/17 June 1944

FLYING-BOMB SITES

405 aircraft – 236 Lancasters, 149 Halifaxes, 20 Mosquitoes – of 1, 4, 5, 6 and 8 Groups commenced the new campaign against flying-bomb launching sites with raids on 4 sites in the Pas de Calais area. All targets were accurately marked by *Oboe* Mosquitoes and successfully bombed. No aircraft lost.

STERKRADE/HOLTEN

321 aircraft – 162 Halifaxes, 147 Lancasters, 12 Mosquitoes – of 1, 4, 6 and 8 Groups to attack the synthetic-oil plant despite a poor weather forecast.

The target was found to be covered by thick cloud and the Pathfinder markers quickly disappeared. The Main Force crews could do little but bomb on to the diminishing glow of the markers in the cloud. R.A.F. photographic reconnaissance and German reports agree that most of the bombing was scattered, although some bombs did fall in the plant area, but with little effect upon production. 21 Germans and 6 foreigners were killed and 18 houses in the vicinity were destroyed.

Unfortunately, the route of the bomber stream passed near a German night-fighter beacon at Bocholt, only 30 miles from Sterkrade. The German controller had chosen this beacon as the holding point for his night fighters. Approximately 21 bombers were shot down by fighters and a further 10 by Flak. 22 of the lost aircraft were Halifaxes, these losses being 13·6 per cent of the 162 Halifaxes on the raid. 77 Squadron, from Full Sutton near York, lost 7 of its 23 Halifaxes taking part in the raid.

Minor Operations: 25 Mosquitoes and 1 Lancaster of 8 Group to Berlin, 12 R.C.M. sorties (the airborne *Mandrel* jamming screen was used for the first time on this night), 53 *Serrate*, Intruder and flying-bomb patrols, 8 Stirlings and 4 Halifaxes minelaying in the Frisians and off the Biscay coast. 1 Stirling R.C.M. aircraft lost.

Total effort for the night: 829 sorties, 32 aircraft (3·9 per cent) lost.

17/18 June 1944

RAILWAYS

317 aircraft – 196 Lancasters, 90 Halifaxes, 19 Mosquitoes, 12 Stirlings – of 1, 3, 4 and 8 Groups attacked railway targets at Aulnoye, Montdidier and St-Martin-l'Hortier. 1 Lancaster was lost on the Montdidier raid. All targets were covered by cloud and the Master Bombers at Aulnoye and Montdidier ordered their forces to stop bombing after only 7 and 12 aircraft had bombed respectively. 87 aircraft of 4 Group bombed their target at St-Martin-l'Hortier but no results were seen.

FLYING-BOMB SITE

114 aircraft – 90 Halifaxes, 19 Lancasters, 5 Mosquitoes – of 6 and 8 Groups bombed a site at Oisemont, near Abbeville. No results were observed and no aircraft were lost.

Minor Operations: 30 Mosquitoes to Berlin and 4 to the Scholven/Buer oil plant, 10 R.C.M. sorties, 54 Mosquitoes on *Serrate*, Intruder and flying bomb patrols, 8 Stirlings and 4 Halifaxes minelaying in the Channel Islands, 12 Halifaxes on Resistance operations. No aircraft lost.

Total effort for the night: 553 sorties, 1 aircraft (0·2 per cent) lost.

18/19 June 1944

Watten

In a period of bad flying weather, only 10 Mosquitoes could be sent to attack a large concrete flying-bomb storage building in the woods at Watten, near St-Omer. 9 aircraft bombed but no details of the results are available. No aircraft lost.

5 Halifaxes and 2 Stirlings laid mines off Brest and St-Malo.

---

19 June 1944

WATTEN

After standing by for 3 days waiting for cloud over the Pas de Calais to clear, 19 Lancasters and 2 Mosquitoes of 617 Squadron, with 9 Mosquitoes of 8 Group providing preliminary marking, attacked the flying-bomb store, but the conditions were too difficult for accurate marking and the nearest *Tallboy* bomb was 50 yards from the concrete store.

---

20 June 1944

Wizernes

17 Lancasters and 3 Mosquitoes of 617 Squadron attempted to attack a large, concrete-covered V-weapon site in a quarry at Wizernes, but the target was cloud-covered and no bombs were dropped.

---

21 June 1944

FLYING-BOMB SITES

322 aircraft – 165 Halifaxes, 142 Lancasters, 15 Mosquitoes – of 3, 6 and 8 Groups attacked 3 sites. Because of cloud, 2 of the raids were abandoned after only 17 aircraft had bombed; the third target, at St-Martin-l'Hortier, was bombed through 10/10ths cloud. No aircraft lost.

3 Mosquitoes of 100 Group flew Ranger patrols and claimed an Me 110 shot down. No Mosquitoes lost.

21/22 June 1944

WESSELING

133 Lancasters and 6 Mosquitoes to attack the synthetic-oil plant at Wesseling; all the aircraft in this force were from 5 Group except for 5 Lancasters provided by 1 Group.

The weather forecast for the target area (and for the attack on Scholven/Buer which took place at the same time) predicted clear conditions but the bombing force encountered 10/10ths low cloud. The planned 5 Group low-level marking method could not be used and the reserve method, in which the Lancasters bombed on *H2S*, was used instead. German night fighters made contact with the bomber force and 37 Lancasters were lost, 44, 49 and 619 Squadrons each losing 6 aircraft. The casualty rate represented 27·8 per cent of the Lancaster force.

Post-raid reconnaissance showed that only slight damage was caused to the oil plant and this is borne out by a local German report which adds the information that 15 Germans, 5 foreign workers and 1 prisoner of war were killed in the nearby town of Wesseling. But a secret German report quoted in the British Official History* records a 40 per cent production loss at Wesseling after this raid. It is possible that the loss was only of short duration.

SCHOLVEN/BUER

123 Lancasters and 9 Mosquitoes of 1, 5 and 8 Groups (124 aircraft from 5 Group) to attack the synthetic-oil plant. 8 Lancasters lost.

This target was also cloud-covered and the 5 Group marking method could not be used, the Pathfinder aircraft present providing *Oboe*-based sky-marking instead. Again there is a contradiction in reports on the effect of the bombing. Post-raid photographs appeared to show no new damage but the German secret reports indicate a 20 per cent production loss.

Minor Operations: 32 Mosquitoes to Berlin, 41 Mosquito patrols, 13 Stirlings minelaying off Guernsey, St-Malo and St-Nazaire, 10 Halifaxes on Resistance operations. 1 Mosquito of 100 Group lost.

Total effort for the night: 361 sorties, 46 aircraft (12·7 per cent) lost.

---

22 June 1944

V-WEAPON SITES

234 aircraft – 119 Lancasters, 102 Halifaxes, 13 Mosquitoes – of 1, 4, 5 and 8 Groups to special V-weapon sites and stores. The sites at Mimoyecques and Siracourt were accurately bombed by 1 and 4 Group forces with Pathfinder marking but the 617 Squadron force attacking Wizernes failed to find its target because of cloud and returned without dropping its bombs. 1 Halifax lost from the Siracourt raid.

2 Mosquitoes flew uneventful Ranger patrols.

---

* Vol. IV, p. 323.

22/23 June 1944

RAILWAYS

221 aircraft – 111 Lancasters, 100 Halifaxes, 10 Mosquitoes – of 1, 4 and 8 Groups attacked railway yards at Laon and Rheims. 4 Halifaxes lost from the Laon raid and 4 Lancasters from the Rheims raid. The bombing at both targets was successful.

Minor Operations: 29 Mosquitoes to Hamburg and 8 to Rouen, 15 R.C.M. sorties, 35 Mosquito patrols, 6 Halifaxes and 4 Stirlings minelaying off French ports. No aircraft lost.

23 June 1944

2 Mosquitoes on uneventful Ranger patrols.

23/24 June 1944

FLYING-BOMB SITES

412 aircraft – 226 Lancasters, 164 Halifaxes, 22 Mosquitoes – of 3, 4, 6 and 8 Groups attacked 4 flying-bomb sites, which were all hit. 5 Lancasters lost.

RAILWAYS

203 Lancasters and 4 Mosquitoes of 1 and 5 Groups attacked railway yards at Limoges and Saintes. Both targets were bombed with great accuracy. 2 Lancasters of 1 Group were lost from the Saintes raid.

Minor Operations: 32 Mosquitoes to Bremen and 10 to a railway junction at Boves near Amiens, 14 R.C.M. sorties, 27 Mosquito patrols, 12 aircraft minelaying off French ports. 1 Stirling lost from the minelaying force.

Total effort for the night: 714 sorties, 8 aircraft (1·1 per cent) lost.

24 June 1944

FLYING-BOMB SITES

321 aircraft – 200 Halifaxes, 106 Lancasters, 15 Mosquitoes – of 1, 4, 6 and 8 Groups attacked 3 sites in clear weather conditions. All targets were accurately bombed; no aircraft lost.

16 Lancasters and 2 Mosquitoes of 617 Squadron bombed the Wizernes site and scored several hits with their *Tallboy* bombs. 1 Lancaster was shot down by Flak, the first loss by the squadron for exactly 2 months.

24/25 June 1944

FLYING-BOMB SITES

739 aircraft – 535 Lancasters, 165 Halifaxes, 39 Mosquitoes – from all groups attacked 7 sites, causing fresh damage at most of the targets. (The flying-bomb sites were now

becoming so cratered by R.A.F., 8th Air Force and 2nd Tactical Air Force bombing that results for individual raids were becoming difficult to determine.)

22 Lancasters were lost from these raids; it was a clear, moonlit night and most of the bomber casualties were caused by German night fighters, often operating with the help of searchlights. It is not known why all of the casualties were Lancasters.

Minor Operations: 27 Mosquitoes to Berlin, 7 R.C.M. sorties, 34 Mosquito patrols, 13 aircraft minelaying off French ports and in the Kattegat. 1 Mosquito lost from the Berlin raid.

Total effort for the night: 820 sorties, 23 aircraft (2·8 per cent) lost.

---

25 June 1944

FLYING-BOMB SITES

323 aircraft – 202 Halifaxes, 106 Lancasters, 15 Mosquitoes – of 1, 4, 6 and 8 Groups attacked 3 sites. The weather was clear and it was believed that all 3 raids were accurate. 2 Halifaxes of 4 Group were lost from the raid on the Montorgueil site.

617 Squadron sent 17 Lancasters, 2 Mosquitoes and 1 Mustang to bomb the Siracourt flying-bomb store. The Mustang was flown by Wing Commander Cheshire and used as a low-level marker aircraft. The Mustang had only arrived at Woodhall Spa that afternoon, by courtesy of the Eighth Air Force, and this was Cheshire's first flight in it. The Lancasters scored 3 direct hits on the concrete store with *Tallboy* bombs and no aircraft were lost. Cheshire had to make his first landing in the unfamiliar Mustang when he returned to his home airfield after dark.

25/26 June 1944

HOMBERG

42 Mosquitoes of 8 Group to bomb the Rheinpreussen synthetic-oil plant at Homberg/ Meerbeck; photographs showed that no new damage was caused. No aircraft lost.

Minor Operations: 8 Mosquitoes flew R.C.M. sorties and 16 Mosquitoes carried out *Serrate* patrols. No aircraft lost.

---

26 June 1944

2 Mosquitoes on uneventful Ranger patrols.

26/27 June 1944

GÖTTINGEN

35 Mosquitoes of 8 Group attacked Göttingen with the intention of hitting the railway workshops. The raid was carried out from medium altitude – 4,000 to 10,000 ft – but the marker aircraft experienced difficulties in locating the target and the bombing was scattered. 1 Mosquito lost.

This may have been an experimental raid, to try out the 8 Group Mosquitoes in a precision bombing role, but this type of operation was not repeated.

8 Halifaxes of 6 Group laid mines off French ports without loss.

27 June 1944

MIMOYECQUES

104 Halifaxes of 4 Group with 5 Mosquitoes and 2 Lancasters of the Pathfinders attacked the V-weapon site without loss. Bombing conditions were good and two large explosions were seen on the ground.

27/28 June 1944

FLYING-BOMB SITES

721 aircraft – 477 Lancasters, 207 Halifaxes, 37 Mosquitoes – attacked 6 sites. All raids were believed to have been successful. 3 Lancasters lost.

RAILWAYS

214 Lancasters and 9 Mosquitoes of 1, 5 and 8 Groups attacked Vaires and Vitry railway yards. The 8 Group raid on Vaires was particularly accurate; the Vitry yards were hit only at the western end. 4 Lancasters lost, 2 from each raid.

Minor Operations: 22 R.C.M. sorties, 61 Mosquito patrols, 8 Halifaxes minelaying off Biscay ports, 14 Halifaxes on Resistance operations. 2 Mosquitoes were lost but other Mosquitoes claimed 6 German night fighters destroyed.

Total effort for the night: 1,049 sorties, 9 aircraft (0·9 per cent) lost.

28 June 1944

WIZERNES

103 Halifaxes of 4 Group with 5 Mosquitoes and 2 Lancasters of the Pathfinders attacked the V-weapon site without loss. No report of the bombing results was filed.

2 Mosquitoes flew uneventful Ranger patrols.

28/29 June 1944

RAILWAYS

202 Halifaxes of 4 and 6 Groups with 28 Pathfinder Lancasters attacked yards at Blainville and Metz. Both targets were hit. 20 aircraft were lost, 11 Halifaxes of 4 Group and 1 Lancaster from the Blainville raid and 7 Halifaxes of 6 Group and 1 Lancaster from Metz. The combined loss rate was 8·7 per cent.

Minor Operations: 33 Mosquitoes to Saarbrücken and 10 to Scholven/Buer oil plant, 21 R.C.M. sorties, 35 Mosquito patrols, 8 Halifaxes and 4 Stirlings minelaying off Lorient and St-Malo. No aircraft lost.

29 June 1944

FLYING-BOMB SITES

286 Lancasters and 19 Mosquitoes of 1, 5 and 8 Groups attacked 2 flying-bomb launching sites and a store. There was partial cloud cover over all the targets; some bombing was accurate but some was scattered. 5 aircraft – 3 Lancasters and 2 Mosquitoes – lost, including the aircraft of the Master Bomber on the raid to the Siracourt site, Flight Lieutenant S. E. C. Clarke of 7 Squadron, but Clarke survived.

2 Mosquitoes carried out Ranger patrols and 1 shot up an E-boat while flying back to England. No aircraft lost.

29/30 June 1944

MINOR OPERATIONS

2 Fortresses on R.C.M. sorties, 14 Mosquitoes on flying-bomb patrols, 8 Stirlings minelaying off Biscay coasts, 16 aircraft on Resistance operations. 1 Mosquito shot down a flying bomb, probably the first 100 Group Mosquito success against the flying bombs. No Bomber Command aircraft lost.

30 June 1944

VILLERS-BOCAGE

266 aircraft – 151 Lancasters, 105 Halifaxes, 10 Mosquitoes – of 3, 4 and 8 Groups to bomb a road junction through which the tanks of two German Panzer divisions, the 2nd and 9th, would have to pass in order to carry out a planned attack on the junction of the British and American armies in Normandy that night. The raid was controlled with great care by the Master Bomber, who ordered the bombing force to come down to 4,000 ft in order to be sure of seeing the markers in the smoke and dust of the exploding bombs. 1,100 tons of bombs were dropped with great accuracy and the planned German attack did not take place. 1 Halifax and 1 Lancaster lost.

OISEMONT

102 Lancasters and 5 Mosquitoes of 1 and 8 Groups bombed a flying-bomb launching site. The attack took place through 10/10ths cloud and results were not observed. No aircraft were lost.

6 Mosquitoes flew uneventful Ranger patrols.

30 June/1 July 1944

VIERZON

118 Lancasters of 1 Group attacked railway yards at this small town south of Orléans and bombed with great accuracy, a success for 1 Group's own marking flight. 14 Lancasters were lost, nearly 12 per cent of the force.

Minor Operations: 40 Mosquitoes to Homberg oil plant, 6 R.C.M. sorties, 29 Mosquitoes on fighter patrols, 6 Stirlings minelaying in the River Scheldt. 1 Mosquito lost from the Homberg raid.

---

1 July 1944

FLYING-BOMB SITES

307 Halifaxes of 4 and 6 Groups with 15 Mosquitoes and 6 Lancasters of the Pathfinders attacked 2 launching sites and a stores site. All targets were completely or almost completely cloud-covered; bombing was on *Oboe* markers and no results could be seen. 1 Halifax of 4 Group was lost from the raid on the St-Martin-l'Hortier site.

2 Mosquitoes carried out uneventful Ranger patrols to airfields in Northern Holland.

1/2 July 1944

Minor Operations

6 Mosquitoes to Scholven/Buer and 4 to Homberg – both targets were oil plants – 6 Lancasters minelaying off Horn's Reef, 2 Mosquitoes on flying-bomb patrols. No aircraft lost.

---

2 July 1944

FLYING-BOMB SITES

374 Lancasters and 10 Mosquitoes of 1, 3 and 8 Groups attacked 3 sites. Cloud affected all of the raids but good concentrations of bombs were believed to have been dropped at all targets. No aircraft lost.

4 Mosquitoes on uneventful Ranger patrols.

3/4 July 1944

MINOR OPERATIONS

6 Mosquitoes to Scholven/Buer and 4 to Homberg, 4 Stirlings minelaying off Brest, 24 aircraft on Resistance operations, 11 Mosquitoes on flying-bomb patrols. No aircraft lost.

---

4 July 1944

FLYING-BOMB SITES

328 aircraft – 307 Halifaxes, 15 Mosquitoes, 6 Lancasters – of 4, 6 and 8 Groups to 3 launching sites. Some cloud was present but at least 2 of the attacks were assessed as accurate. No aircraft lost.

17 Lancasters, 1 Mosquito and 1 Mustang of 617 Squadron attacked a flying-bomb store in a large cave at St-Leu-d'Esserent, north of Paris, and bombed the site

accurately and without loss. (Aircraft of 5 Group, with some Pathfinders, attacked St-Leu-d'Esserent immediately after the 617 Squadron attack but Bomber Command records show the 617 Squadron operation as a day raid and the later operation as a night raid.)

4 Mosquitoes carried out uneventful Ranger patrols.

4/5 July 1944

ST-LEU-D'ESSERENT

231 Lancasters and 15 Mosquitoes, mostly from 5 Group but with some Pathfinder aircraft, continued the attack on the underground flying-bomb store with 1,000-lb bombs, in order to cut all communications to the store. The bombing was accurate but 13 Lancasters were lost when German fighters engaged the force.

RAILWAYS

282 Lancasters and 5 Mosquitoes of 1, 6 and 8 Groups attacked railway yards at Orléans and Villeneuve. Both targets were accurately bombed. 14 Lancasters were lost, 11 from the Villeneuve raid and 3 from Orléans.

Minor Operations: 36 Mosquitoes to Scholven/Buer, 25 R.C.M. sorties, 61 Mosquito patrols, 6 Stirlings and 5 Halifaxes minelaying off Brest and St-Nazaire, 16 aircraft on Resistance operations, 30 O.T.U. sorties. 1 Halifax R.C.M. aircraft lost.

Total effort for the night: 712 sorties, 28 aircraft (3·9 per cent) lost.

5/6 July 1944

FLYING-BOMB SITES

542 aircraft – 321 Lancasters, 201 Halifaxes, 20 Mosquitoes – of 3, 4, 6 and 8 Groups attacked 2 launching and 2 storage sites. The night was clear with a bright moon and all targets were hit. 4 Lancasters lost.

DIJON

154 Lancasters of 1 Group to the main railway area, which was heavily bombed. No aircraft lost.

Minor Operations: 35 Mosquitoes to Scholven/Buer and 10 to Düren, 9 R.C.M. sorties, 50 Mosquito patrols, 6 Halifaxes minelaying off Brest and St-Nazaire, 29 aircraft on Resistance operations, 3 O.T.U. sorties. 3 Mosquitoes were lost – 1 from the Scholven raid, 1 R.C.M. aircraft and 1 *Serrate* aircraft.

Total effort for the night: 838 sorties, 7 aircraft (0·8 per cent) lost.

---

6 July 1944

V-WEAPON SITES

551 aircraft – 314 Halifaxes, 210 Lancasters, 26 Mosquitoes, 1 Mustang – attacked 5 targets. Only 1 aircraft was lost, a 6 Group Halifax from a raid on Siracourt flying-bomb store. Four of the targets were clear of cloud and were believed to have been bombed accurately but no results were seen at the Forêt-de-Croc launching site.

On his return from leading 617 Squadron's attack on the Mimoyecques site, Wing Commander Leonard Cheshire was ordered by the commander of 5 Group to leave the squadron and rest. Cheshire had completed 4 tours and flown 100 operations. Squadron Leaders J. C. McCarthy, K. L. Munro and D. J. Shannon, the three 617 Squadron flight commanders – all survivors of the Dams Raid – were also ordered to rest. 2 months later, Cheshire was awarded the Victoria Cross for his 4 tours and for his courage and skill in developing low-level marking. He did not fly on operations again.

6/7 July 1944

MINOR OPERATIONS

33 Mosquitoes to Scholven/Buer and 3 to Mézières railway junction, 6 Intruder and 16 flying-bomb patrols, 4 Stirlings minelaying off the Belgian and Dutch coasts. No aircraft lost; Mosquitoes shot down 6 flying bombs, their best success of the war.

7 July 1944

NORMANDY BATTLE AREA

467 aircraft – 283 Lancasters, 164 Halifaxes, 20 Mosquitoes – of 1, 4, 6 and 8 Groups in a major effort to assist in the Normany land battle.

The Canadian 1st and British 2nd Armies were held up by a series of fortified village strongpoints north of Caen. The first plan was for Bomber Command to bomb these villages but, because of the proximity of friendly troops and the possibility of bombing error, the bombing area was moved back nearer to Caen, covering a stretch of open ground and the northern edge of the city. The weather was clear for the raid, which took place in the evening, and two aiming points were well marked by *Oboe* Mosquitoes and other Pathfinder aircraft. The Master Bomber, Wing Commander S. P. (Pat) Daniels of 35 Squadron, then controlled a very accurate raid. Dust and smoke soon obscured the markers but the bombing always remained concentrated. 2,276 tons of bombs were dropped.

It was afterwards judged that the bombing should have been aimed at the original targets. Few Germans were killed in the area actually bombed, although units near by were considerably shaken. The northern suburbs of Caen were ruined. No German fighters appeared and only 1 Lancaster, of 166 Squadron, was shot down by Flak. 2 further Lancasters and 1 Mosquito crashed behind the Allied lines in France. (For statistical purposes, Bomber Command aircraft which were recorded as having *crashed* in France, and later in other reoccupied countries in Europe, will be considered as 'lost', as it was unlikely that the aircraft would be salvaged for later use, although the crews often returned safely to England.)

7/8 July 1944

ST-LEU-D'ESSERENT

208 Lancasters and 13 Mosquitoes, mainly from 5 Group but with some Pathfinder aircraft, attacked a flying-bomb storage dump in a group of tunnels (formerly used for growing mushrooms). The bombing was accurately directed on to the mouths of the tunnels and on to the approach roads, thus blocking access to the flying bombs stored there.

German night fighters intercepted the bombing force and 29 Lancasters and 2 Mosquitoes were lost, 14·0 per cent of the force. 106 Squadron, from Metheringham, lost 5 of its 16 Lancasters on the raid and 630 Squadron, from East Kirkby, lost its commanding officer, Wing Commander W. I. Deas, who was flying his 69th operation. Wing Commander Deas was killed and is buried in a small cemetery at Omerville, north-west of Versailles.

VAIRES

123 Lancasters and 5 Mosquitoes of 1 and 8 Groups carried out an accurate raid on the railway yards without the loss of any aircraft.

SUPPORT AND MINOR OPERATIONS

106 aircraft of 1, 3, 5 and 93 Groups on a diversionary sweep almost to the coast of Holland, 7 Mosquitoes of 5 Group dropping 'spoof' markers in support of the St-Leu-d'Esserent raid, 32 Mosquitoes to Berlin and 9 to Scholven/Buer, 48 aircraft on R.C.M. sorties or Resistance operations (no breakdown available), 83 Mosquito patrols. 2 Mosquitoes were lost from the Berlin raid and 1 aircraft (type not recorded) was lost from a Resistance flight.

Total effort for the night: 634 sorties, 34 aircraft (5·3 per cent) lost.

8/9 July 1944

MINOR OPERATIONS

10 Mosquitoes to Scholven/Buer, 8 Halifaxes and 4 Stirlings minelaying off Biscay coasts, 7 aircraft on Resistance operations, 8 Mosquitoes on flying-bomb patrols. No aircraft lost.

---

9 July 1944

FLYING-BOMB SITES

347 aircraft – 197 Halifaxes, 120 Lancasters, 30 Mosquitoes – of 3, 4, 6 and 8 Groups bombed 6 launching sites but most of the targets were cloud-covered and some of the bombing was scattered. 1 Halifax and 1 Lancaster lost.

9/10 July 1944

MINOR OPERATIONS

8 Mosquitoes to Scholven/Buer, 14 R.C.M. sorties, 9 *Serrate* patrols, 8 Halifaxes and 4 Stirlings minelaying off Biscay ports, 19 aircraft on Resistance operations, 4 O.T.U. sorties. No aircraft lost.

---

10 July 1944

NUCOURT

213 Lancasters and 10 Mosquitoes of 1, 3 and 8 Groups attacked a flying-bomb storage dump but the target was covered by cloud and the bombing was not concentrated. No aircraft lost.

6 Mosquitoes carried out Ranger patrols without loss. 1 Ju 88 was claimed destroyed near Oldenburg.

10/11 July 1944

MINOR OPERATIONS

35 Mosquitoes to Berlin, 8 Halifaxes and 6 Lancasters minelaying in the Kattegat and in the Frisians, 13 Halifaxes and 9 Stirlings on Resistance operations, 4 O.T.U. sorties. 1 Mosquito lost on the Berlin raid.

11 July 1944

GAPENNES

26 Lancasters and 6 Mosquitoes of 8 Group made two separate raids on this flying-bomb site. The Lancasters made the first 'heavy *Oboe*' attack of the war. A Lancaster of 582 Squadron had been fitted with *Oboe* equipment and Wing Commander G. F. Grant, from 109 Squadron, one of the *Oboe* Mosquito squadrons, flew in the Lancaster and directed the bombing. When Grant released his bombs, other Lancasters flying in formation did the same. This method allowed a greater tonnage of bombs to be dropped directly on the *Oboe* signals and it became one of Bomber Command's most accurate bombing methods and enabled small targets like the flying-bomb sites to be bombed accurately in cloudy conditions. No aircraft were lost on this raid.

2 Mosquitoes flew Ranger patrols. 1 aircraft attacked a tanker with cannon-fire. The Mosquitoes returned safely.

11/12 July 1944

MINOR OPERATIONS

8 Mosquitoes to Homberg oil plant, 3 *Serrate* patrols, 21 aircraft on Resistance operations. No aircraft lost.

12 July 1944

FLYING-BOMB SITES

222 aircraft – 168 Halifaxes, 46 Lancasters, 8 Mosquitoes – of 4, 6 and 8 Groups bombed a storage dump at Thiverny but the target was cloud-covered and no results were seen. 18 Lancasters and 5 Mosquitoes of 8 Group used *Oboe* to bomb the Rollez launching site. No aircraft lost.

VAIRES

153 Lancasters and 6 Mosquitoes of 1, 3 and 8 Groups to attack the important railway yards on the outskirts of Paris; the target area was covered by cloud and the Master Bomber ordered the attack to be abandoned after 2 Mosquitoes had marked and 12 Lancasters had bombed. No aircraft lost.

12/13 July 1944

RAILWAYS

378 Lancasters and 7 Mosquitoes of 1, 5 and 8 Groups attacked railway targets at Culmont, Revigny and Tours. Culmont and Tours were accurately bombed but cloud interfered with the all-1 Group raid at Revigny and only half of the force bombed. 10 Lancasters were lost on the Revigny raid and 2 on the Culmont raid.

FLYING-BOMB SITES

230 aircraft – 196 Halifaxes, 17 Lancasters, 17 Mosquitoes – of 4, 6 and 8 Groups attacked 4 launching sites. All targets were hit, the raid on the Bremont-les-Hautes site being particularly accurate. No aircraft were lost.

SUPPORT AND MINOR OPERATIONS

168 aircraft of all Main Force groups and 92 and 93 (O.T.U.) Groups on a diversionary sweep over the North Sea, 8 Mosquitoes to Homberg, 32 R.C.M. sorties, 32 Mosquito patrols, 12 Halifaxes minelaying off Heligoland, 14 O.T.U. sorties. No aircraft lost.

Total effort for the night: 881 sorties, 12 aircraft (1·4 per cent) lost.

---

13 July 1944

13 Lancasters of 8 Group to attack a flying-bomb site and 2 Mosquitoes on Ranger patrols but thick cloud prevented all aircraft from operating.

13/14 July 1944

Minor Operations

4 Mosquitoes to Homberg and Scholven/Buer, 4 *Serrate* patrols over Denmark, 6 Stirlings minelaying off Brest, 3 Halifaxes on Resistance operations. No aircraft lost.

---

14 July 1944

Minor Operations

19 Lancasters of 8 Group attacked the flying-bomb site at St-Philibert-Ferme through thick cloud and 4 Mosquitoes flew Ranger patrols to Northern Germany and Denmark. No aircraft lost.

14/15 July 1944

RAILWAYS

242 Lancasters and 11 Mosquitoes of 1, 5 and 8 Groups to attack the railway yards at Revigny and Villeneuve. The raid on Villeneuve was carried out and the railways were hit, though much of the bombing fell to the east of the target. The raid to Revigny was abandoned because the railway yards could not be identified. 7 Lancasters lost from the Revigny raid.

FLYING-BOMB SITES

115 aircraft – 101 Halifaxes, 10 Mosquitoes, 4 Lancasters – of 4, 6 and 8 Groups attacked launching sites at Anderbelck and Les Landes. Anderbelck was accurately bombed in good visibility but the bombing at Les Landes was through 10/10ths cloud.

SUPPORT AND MINOR OPERATIONS

132 aircraft on a diversionary sweep over the North Sea, 42 Mosquitoes to Hannover, 35 R.C.M. sorties, 56 Mosquito patrols, 8 Stirlings minelaying off Biscay ports. 1 Mosquito of 100 Group lost.

Total effort for the night: 641 sorties, 8 aircraft (1·3 per cent) lost.

15 July 1944

NUCOURT

47 Lancasters and 6 Mosquitoes carried out an '*Oboe* leader' attack on the flying-bomb supply dump. No bombing results were seen, because of poor weather conditions. No aircraft lost.

15/16 July 1944

FLYING-BOMB SITES

234 aircraft – 162 Halifaxes, 58 Lancasters, 14 Mosquitoes – carried out accurate attacks in the Bois-des-Jardins launching site and the Nucourt supply dump. 1 Halifax lost.

RAILWAYS

222 Lancasters and 7 Mosquitoes attacked railway yards at Châlons-sur-Marne and Nevers. Both raids were successful. 3 aircraft lost, 2 Lancasters from the Nevers raid and 1 Lancaster from Châlons.

SUPPORT AND MINOR OPERATIONS

162 aircraft from 7 different groups on a diversionary sweep over the North Sea, 36 Mosquitoes to Berlin, 25 R.C.M. sorties, 45 Mosquito patrols, 6 Lancasters minelaying off Denmark, 11 aircraft on Resistance operations. 1 minelaying Lancaster lost.

Total effort for the night: 748 sorties, 5 aircraft (0·7 per cent) lost.

---

16 July 1944

ST-PHILIBERT-FERME

30 Lancasters and 3 Mosquitoes of 8 Group bombed the flying-bomb launching site through thick cloud. No aircraft lost.

16/17 July 1944

HOMBERG

38 Mosquitoes attacked the synthetic-oil plant without loss.

Minor Operations: 4 Stirlings minelaying off Brest, 5 O.T.U. sorties, 8 Mosquitoes on flying-bomb patrols. No aircraft lost.

---

17 July 1944

FLYING-BOMB SITES

132 aircraft – 72 Halifaxes, 28 Stirlings, 20 Lancasters, 11 Mosquitoes, 1 Mustang – attacked 3 sites without loss. Few details of bombing results were recorded.

17/18 July 1944

MINOR OPERATIONS

23 Stirlings and 11 Halifaxes from Heavy Conversion Units of 1 and 5 Groups on a diversion flight over the North Sea without loss, although no major operation took place elsewhere, 31 Mosquitoes to Berlin, 24 R.C.M. sorties, 38 Mosquito patrols, 8 Halifaxes minelaying off Heligoland and the Frisians, 16 aircraft on Resistance operations. No aircraft lost.

---

18 July 1944

NORMANDY BATTLE AREA

942 aircraft – 667 Lancasters, 260 Halifaxes, 15 Mosquitoes – to bomb 5 fortified villages in the area east of Caen through which British Second Army troops were about to make an armoured attack, Operation *Goodwood*.

The raids took place at dawn in clear conditions. 4 of the targets were satisfactorily marked by *Oboe* and, at the target where *Oboe* failed, the Master Bomber, Squadron Leader E. K. Creswell, and other Pathfinder crews used visual methods. American bombers also attacked these targets and a total of 6,800 tons of bombs were dropped, of which Bomber Command dropped more than 5,000 tons. Elements of two German divisions, the 16th Luftwaffe Field Division and the 21st Panzer Division, were badly affected by the bombing, the Luftwaffe Division particularly so. Operation *Goodwood* made a good start. This raid was either the most useful or one of the most useful of the operations carried out by Bomber Command in direct support of the Allied armies.*

The aircraft bombed from medium heights, 5,000–9,000 ft, but army artillery and naval gunfire subdued many of the Flak batteries and only 6 aircraft – 5 Halifaxes and 1 Lancaster – were shot down. No German fighters appeared; Allied air superiority over the battlefield by day was complete.

VAIRES

110 aircraft – 99 Halifaxes, 6 Lancasters, 5 Mosquitoes – of 4, 6 and 8 Groups attacked the railway yards but no report on the bombing results was filed. 2 Halifaxes lost.

Total effort for the day: 1,052 sorties, 8 aircraft (0·8 per cent) lost.

18/19 July 1944

WESSELING

194 aircraft – 111 Halifaxes, 77 Lancasters, 6 Mosquitoes – of 1, 6 and 8 Groups to attack the synthetic-oil plant. 1 Halifax lost.

A useful German report from Wesseling shows that this was a very successful raid and a credit to the Pathfinder marking. Approximately 1,000 high-explosive bombs fell inside the area of the plant in 20 minutes. 20 per cent of the installations were destroyed but, because some important buildings were particularly hard-hit, the loss of production was greater than this figure. 600 workmen were present on the night shift but they had good air-raid shelters and only 3 were killed. The nearby town was also hit and 151 houses were destroyed, many of them being in the estate for the oil-plant workers. The people here must also have been provided with good shelters because only 8 German people were killed. The local report stresses that no children of school age were among the casualties; the local school had been evacuated to Silesia a few weeks earlier. Foreign workers and prisoners of war in a nearby camp probably had poorer air-raid shelters; 22 foreign workers and 9 prisoners of war died.

SCHOLVEN/BUER

157 Lancasters and 13 Mosquitoes of 1 and 8 Groups attacked the oil plant. 4 Lancasters lost.

This was also a successful raid. The local report says that 550 bombs fell in the plant area, although 233 of them did not explode. Production came to 'a complete standstill for a long period'. 5 people were killed in the plant and a further 25 died in nearby houses which were hit. One of the fatal casualties committed suicide by shooting himself during the raid and another man drowned when he fell into an emergency water tank in the darkness and confusion.

*Some of the details from the 18 July report come from John Keegan's *Six Armies in Normandy*, Cape, 1982.

RAILWAYS

253 Lancasters and 10 Mosquitoes of 1, 3, 5 and 8 Groups attacked railway junctions at Aulnoye and Revigny. Both targets were hit and the railway lines to the battle front were cut. 2 Lancasters were lost on the Aulnoye raid but the 5 Group raid to Revigny was caught by German fighters and 24 Lancasters were shot down, nearly 22 per cent of the Lancasters involved. 619 Squadron, from Dunholme Lodge, lost 5 of its 13 aircraft taking part in the raid.

ACQUET

62 aircraft – 51 Halifaxes, 9 Mosquitoes, 2 Lancasters – of 4 and 8 Groups bombed a flying-bomb launching site but photographs indicated that no new damage was caused. 2 Halifaxes lost.

SUPPORT AND MINOR OPERATIONS

115 aircraft – 86 Wellingtons, 19 Stirlings, 10 Halifaxes – from Heavy Conversion and Operational Training Units on a diversionary sweep over the North Sea, 22 Mosquitoes to Berlin and 6 to Cologne, 20 R.C.M. sorties, 76 Mosquito patrols, 8 Halifaxes minelaying in the Frisians, 36 aircraft on Resistance operations. 3 aircraft lost: 1 Mosquito from the Berlin raid and 2 Halifaxes from Resistance operations.

Total effort for the night: 972 sorties, 36 aircraft (3·7 per cent) lost.

---

19 July 1944

FLYING-BOMB SITES

132 Lancasters and 12 Mosquitoes of 5 and 8 Groups attacked two launching sites and a supply dump. All target areas were partially cloud-covered but the targets were believed to have been hit. No aircraft lost.

19/20 July 1944

MINOR OPERATIONS

36 Mosquitoes to Bremen, 9 R.C.M. sorties, 29 Mosquito patrols, 6 Halifaxes minelaying off Heligoland, 8 O.T.U. sorties. No aircraft lost.

---

20 July 1944

V-WEAPON SITES

369 aircraft – 174 Lancasters, 165 Halifaxes, 30 Mosquitoes – attacked 6 flying-bomb launching sites and the V-weapon site at Wizernes. All raids were successful except the small raid by 20 aircraft on the Forêt-de-Croc site where the *Oboe* leader Lancaster was shot down on the bombing run and the bombs of this force all missed the target. This was the only aircraft lost.

8 Mosquitoes flew uneventful Ranger patrols.

The unsuccessful attempt on Hitler's life at his headquarters in East Prussia took place on this day.

20/21 July 1944

COURTRAI

302 Lancasters and 15 Mosquitoes of 1, 5 and 8 Groups attacked the railway yards and a 'triangle' rail junction at Courtrai. The Bomber Command report states that both targets 'were devastated'. 9 Lancasters lost.

BOTTROP

166 aircraft – 149 Halifaxes, 13 Mosquitoes, 4 Lancasters – of 4 and 8 Groups attacked the synthetic-oil refinery. The northern part of the target was badly damaged. 7 Halifaxes and 1 Lancaster lost.

HOMBERG

147 Lancasters and 11 Mosquitoes of 1, 3 and 8 Groups attacked the oil plant and caused severe damage. German documents show that the production of aviation fuel, which had stood at nearly 6,000 tons per day at the end of April, was now fluctuating between 120 and 970 tons per day, following Bomber Command and American Eighth Air Force raids. But German night fighters caught the Homberg bomber force and 20 Lancasters were lost. 75 (New Zealand) Squadron, from Mepal, lost 7 of its 25 aircraft on the raid.

V-WEAPON SITES

87 aircraft – 54 Halifaxes, 23 Lancasters, 10 Mosquitoes – of 4, 5 and 8 Groups attacked sites at Ardouval and Wizernes without loss but only 23 aircraft bombed at Ardouval and none at Wizernes.

SUPPORT AND MINOR OPERATIONS

106 aircraft from training units on a diversionary sweep over the North Sea, 6 Lancasters and 5 Mosquitoes on a 'spoof' raid to Alost, 26 Mosquitoes to Hamburg, 33 R.C.M. sorties, 42 Mosquito patrols, 8 Stirlings minelaying off Lorient, 17 aircraft on Resistance operations. 1 Mosquito lost from the Hamburg raid.

Total effort for the night: 971 sorties, 38 aircraft (3·9 per cent) lost.

---

21 July 1944

ANDERBECK

52 aircraft – 45 Halifaxes, 5 Mosquitoes, 2 Lancasters – of 6 and 8 Groups attacked a flying-bomb site. No results were recorded. No aircraft were lost.

2 Mosquitoes flew Ranger patrols to Aalborg, Grove and Jagel airfields; German aircraft seen on the ground were attacked. The Mosquitoes returned safely.

21/22 July 1944

MINOR OPERATIONS

33 Mosquitoes to Berlin, 20 R.C.M. sorties, 18 Mosquito patrols, 6 Halifaxes and 6 Lancasters minelaying in the Frisians and the Kattegat. 1 Mosquito Intruder lost.

---

22 July 1944

FLYING-BOMB SITES

48 Lancasters and 12 Mosquitoes of 8 Group carried out '*Oboe* leader' bombing of 4 sites through 10/10ths cloud. No aircraft lost.

2 Mosquitoes on Ranger patrols to Holland and Germany shot up trains without loss.

22/23 July 1944

MINOR OPERATIONS

6 Lancasters minelaying in the Kattegat, 10 Halifaxes on Resistance operations, 5 O.T.U. sorties. No aircraft lost.

---

23 July 1944

FLYING-BOMB SITES

48 Lancasters and 12 Mosquitoes of 3 and 8 Groups bombed sites at Forêt-de-Croc and Mont-Candon through thick cloud. No aircraft lost.

23/24 July 1944

KIEL

This was the first major raid on a German city for two months. 629 aircraft – 519 Lancasters, 100 Halifaxes, 10 Mosquitoes – were dispatched. The elaborate deception and R.C.M. operations combined with the surprise return to a German target completely confused the German fighter force and only 4 aircraft – all Lancasters – were lost, a rate of 0·6 per cent.

Kiel suffered heavily in this first R.A.F. raid since April 1943 and its heaviest R.A.F. raid of the war. The bombing force appeared suddenly from behind a *Mandrel* jamming screen and the local radio warning system only reported it as being a force of minelaying aircraft. 612 aircraft then bombed in a raid lasting only 25 minutes. All parts of Kiel were hit but the bombing was particularly heavy in the port areas and all of the important U-boat yards and naval facilities were hit. 315 people were killed and 439 injured. The presence of around 500 delayed-action bombs or unexploded duds caused severe problems for the rescue and repair services. There was no water for 3 days; trains and buses did not run for 8 days and there was no gas for cooking for 3 weeks.

DONGES

119 aircraft – 100 Halifaxes, 14 Lancasters, 5 Mosquitoes – of 6 and 8 Groups attacked an oil refinery and storage depot at Donges, near the mouth of the River Loire. This was the start of a new campaign against oil targets in the occupied countries. The bombing took place in good visibility. The target was severely damaged and a tanker was hit and capsized. No aircraft lost.

FLYING-BOMB SITES

116 aircraft – 102 Halifaxes, 12 Mosquitoes, 2 Lancasters – of 4 and 8 Groups attacked 2 sites with accurate bombing. 1 Halifax lost from the raid on the Les Hauts Buissons site.

SUPPORT AND MINOR OPERATIONS

180 aircraft of training units on diversionary sweep over the North Sea, 27 Mosquitoes to Berlin and 5 to Düren, 39 R.C.M. sorties, 45 Mosquito patrols, 6 Lancasters minelaying off Kiel and 2 Stirlings off Brest, 12 aircraft on Resistance operations, 8 O.T.U. sorties. 1 Lancaster lost while minelaying near Kiel.

Total effort for the night: 1,188 sorties, 5 aircraft (0·4 per cent) lost.

---

24 July 1944

FLYING-BOMB SITES

28 Lancasters and 8 Mosquitoes of 3 and 8 Groups bombed sites at Acquet and Prouville without loss.

3 Mosquitoes flew Ranger patrols to Northern Germany and attacked trains but 1 Mosquito was lost.

24/25 July 1944

STUTTGART

461 Lancasters and 153 Halifaxes. 17 Lancasters and 4 Halifaxes lost, 4·6 per cent of the force.

This was the first of 3 heavy raids on Stuttgart in 5 nights and the only report available is a composite one for the 3 raids. The 3 raids caused the most serious damage of the war in the central districts of Stuttgart which, being situated in a series of narrow valleys, had eluded Bomber Command for several years. They were now devastated and most of Stuttgart's public and cultural buildings were destroyed. The second of the 3 raids, on the night of 25/26 July, was the most successful. Total casualties in Stuttgart during this series of raids were 1,171 people killed and 1,600 injured.

DONGES

104 Lancasters and 9 Mosquitoes of 5 and 8 Groups attacked the oil depot again and, according to reports, the target was 'devastated'. 3 Lancasters lost.

FERFAY

112 aircraft – 100 Halifaxes, 10 Mosquitoes, 2 Lancasters – of 6 and 8 Groups attacked a flying-bomb site but the Master Bomber allowed only 73 aircraft to bomb. 1 Halifax lost.

SUPPORT AND MINOR OPERATIONS

107 aircraft from training units on diversionary sweep, 27 Mosquitoes to Berlin, 8 to Frankfurt and 5 to Aachen, 36 R.C.M. sorties, 46 Mosquito patrols, 4 Halifaxes minelaying off Brest and Lorient, 12 aircraft on Resistance operations, 4 O.T.U. sorties. No aircraft lost.

Total effort for the night: 1,088 sorties, 25 aircraft (2·3 per cent) lost.

---

25 July 1944

ST-CYR

94 Lancasters and 6 Mosquitoes of 5 Group attacked an airfield and signals depot. Bombing was accurate. 1 Lancaster lost.

FLYING-BOMB SITES

93 aircraft – 81 Lancasters, 11 Mosquitoes, 1 Mustang – of 5 and 8 Groups attacked 2 launching sites and the Watten storage site. All raids were successful and no aircraft were lost.

25/26 July 1944

STUTTGART

412 Lancasters and 138 Halifaxes to continue the attack on Stuttgart. 8 Lancasters and 4 Halifaxes lost, 2·2 per cent of the force.

WANNE-EICKEL

135 aircraft – 114 Halifaxes, 11 Lancasters, 10 Mosquitoes – of 1, 4 and 8 Groups attacked the Krupp oil refinery. No aircraft lost.

Only a few bombs hit a corner of the oil refinery and production was not seriously affected. Other bombs hit the south-eastern part of Eickel, destroying 14 houses and killed 29 civilians, 4 foreign workers and 3 prisoners of war and causing production at the Hannibal coal mine to cease.

FLYING-BOMB SITES

36 Lancasters and 15 Mosquitoes of 1 and 8 Groups bombed 3 launching sites and succeeded in destroying the launching ramp at the Bois-des-Jardins site. No aircraft lost.

38. Lancasters and Halifaxes finally destroy Stuttgart in the raid of 25/26 July 1944. The city on fire.

Minor Operations: 21 Mosquitoes to Berlin, 15 to Mannheim and 6 to Somain, 28 R.C.M. sorties, 37 Mosquito patrols, 4 Halifaxes minelaying off Brest, 5 Halifaxes on Resistance operations. 1 Mosquito of 100 Group lost.

Total effort for the night: 852 sorties, 13 aircraft (1·5 per cent) lost.

26/27 July 1944

GIVORS

178 Lancasters and 9 Mosquitoes of 5 Group carried out an accurate attack on the railway yards. 4 Lancasters and 2 Mosquitoes lost.

Minor Operations: 30 Mosquitoes to Hamburg, 11 to Somain and 2 to Saarbrücken, 6 R.C.M. sorties, 23 Mosquito patrols, 6 Lancasters minelaying off Heligoland, 6 aircraft on Resistance operations. 1 Mosquito lost from the Hamburg raid.

27 July 1944

FLYING-BOMB SITES

72 aircraft – 36 Lancasters, 24 Stirlings, 12 Mosquitoes – of 3 and 8 Groups attacked 5 sites without loss. All targets were cloud-covered and most of the bombing was 'confused and scattered'.

Some of the Stirlings on this raid, from 218 Squadron, were fitted with the *G-H* blind-bombing device and they used this in the attack on one of the sites; this was the first use of the '*G-H* leader' technique.

27/28 July 1944

MINOR OPERATIONS

30 Mosquitoes to Stuttgart and 12 aircraft on Resistance operations. No aircraft lost.

---

28 July 1944

PAS DE CALAIS

199 aircraft – 159 Halifaxes, 20 Mosquitoes, 20 Stirlings – of 3, 4 and 8 Groups attacked two launching sites and made two further separate raids on the Forêt de Nieppe storage site. All bombing was through cloud but the various methods used were believed to have led to accurate results. 1 Halifax lost from one of the Forêt de Nieppe raids.

28/29 July 1944

STUTTGART

494 Lancasters and 2 Mosquitoes of 1, 3, 5 and 8 Groups in the last raid of the current series on this target. German fighters intercepted the bomber stream while over France on the outward flight; there was a bright moon and 39 Lancasters were shot down, 7·9 per cent of the force.

HAMBURG

307 aircraft – 187 Halifaxes, 106 Lancasters, 14 Mosquitoes – from 1, 6 and 8 Groups. German fighters again appeared, this time on the homeward flight, and 18 Halifaxes and 4 Lancasters were lost, 7·2 per cent of the force. The Halifax casualties were 9·6 per cent; 431 (Canadian) Squadron, flying from Croft airfield in Co. Durham, lost 5 of its 17 aircraft on the raid.

This was the first heavy raid on Hamburg since the Battle of Hamburg just a year earlier. The bombing on this raid was not well concentrated. The Germans estimated that only 120 aircraft bombed in the city area, with no recognizable aiming point, though western and harbour areas received the most bombs. A large proportion of the attack fell on areas devastated in 1943 but 265 people were killed and more than 17,000 had to be evacuated from homes damaged in this raid, many of which were probably only temporary wooden accommodation at this stage of the war. Brunswig (p. 339) describes how a panic developed at the large Reeperbahn air-raid shelter when a lone aircraft came in to bomb after the all clear had sounded and nearby Flak guns opened fire. 2 women were trampled to death and others were badly hurt.

FORÊT DE NIEPPE

119 aircraft of 1, 4 and 8 Groups attacked the stores area again. No aircraft lost.

SUPPORT AND MINOR OPERATIONS

95 training aircraft on a diversionary sweep over the North Sea, 13 Mosquitoes to Frankfurt, 41 R.C.M. sorties, 50 Mosquito patrols, 5 Halifaxes minelaying in the River Elbe. No aircraft lost.

Total effort for the night: 1,126 sorties, 61 aircraft (5·4 per cent) lost.

---

29 July 1944

FORÊT DE NIEPPE

76 aircraft – 50 Halifaxes, 16 Stirlings, 10 Mosquitoes – of 3, 4 and 8 Groups attacked the stores dump in the forest without loss.

29/30 July 1944

MINOR OPERATIONS

30 Mosquitoes to Frankfurt (though some bombs fell in Mainz 20 miles away, killing 8 people), 9 to St-Trond and 4 to Coulommiers (these last 2 targets were German night-fighter airfields), 13 R.C.M. sorties, 6 Mosquito patrols, 9 O.T.U. sorties. No aircraft lost.

---

30 July 1944

NORMANDY BATTLE AREA

692 aircraft – 462 Lancasters, 200 Halifaxes, 30 Mosquitoes – were sent to bomb 6 German positions in front of a mainly American ground attack in the Villers Bocage-Caumont area. The presence of cloud caused many difficulties and only 377 aircraft were able to bomb, on to *Oboe* markers, and only 2 of the 6 targets were effectively hit. 4 Lancasters lost.

2 Mosquitoes carried out uneventful Ranger patrols.

30/31 July 1944

Minor Operations

20 Halifaxes on Resistance operations, 6 O.T.U. sorties. No aircraft lost.

---

31 July 1944

JOIGNY-LA-ROCHE

127 Lancasters and 4 Mosquitoes of 1 and 5 Groups carried out an accurate raid on the railway yards in clear conditions. 1 Lancaster lost.

RILLY-LA-MONTAGE

97 Lancasters and 6 Mosquitoes of 5 and 8 Groups attacked the ends of a railway tunnel being used as a flying-bomb store. 617 Squadron caved in both ends of the

tunnel with their *Tallboy* bombs and the other part of the bombing force cratered all the approach areas. 2 Lancasters were lost, including the 617 Squadron aircraft of Flight Lieutenant William Reid, who had won a Victoria Cross in 1943 in a raid on Düsseldorf while flying with 61 Squadron. Flight Lieutenant Reid survived.

LE HAVRE

52 Lancasters and 5 Mosquitoes of 1 and 8 Groups bombed the port area but the target soon became smoke-covered and results were uncertain, though one U-boat was believed to have been hit. 1 Lancaster lost.

---

31 July/1 August 1944

FLYING-BOMB SITES

202 aircraft – 104 Lancasters, 76 Halifaxes, 22 Mosquitoes – of 1, 6 and 8 Groups attacked two launching and two storage sites, but only at the Forêt de Nieppe storage site was effective damage caused. 1 Halifax and 1 Lancaster lost.

Minor Operations: 4 *Serrate* patrols, 4 Halifaxes minelaying off Brest.

---

1 August 1944

FLYING-BOMB SITES

777 aircraft – 385 Lancasters, 324 Halifaxes, 67 Mosquitoes, 1 Lightning – to attack numerous targets but only 79 aircraft were able to bomb; Bomber Command records do not state why the remaining sorties were abortive but poor weather conditions were the probable cause. No aircraft lost.

The Warsaw uprising by the Polish Home Army began on this day; the Poles fought until 3 October before being defeated.

---

2 August 1944

FLYING-BOMB SITES

394 aircraft – 234 Lancasters, 99 Halifaxes, 40 Mosquitoes, 20 Stirlings, 1 Lightning – attacked 1 launching site and 3 supply sites. Visibility was clear at all targets and good bombing results were claimed. 2 Lancasters of 5 Group lost from the raid on the Bois de Cassan supply site.

LE HAVRE

54 Lancasters of 1 and 8 Groups attacked German naval vessels in the port area in good visibility conditions and without loss.

---

3 August 1944

FLYING-BOMB STORAGE SITES

1,114 aircraft – 601 Lancasters, 492 Halifaxes, 21 Mosquitoes – carried out major raids on the Bois de Cassan, Forêt de Nieppe and Trossy-St-Maxim (sometimes spelt 'Maximin') flying-bomb stores. The weather was clear and all raids were successful. 6 Lancasters lost, 5 from the Trossy-St-Maxim raid and 1 from the Bois de Cassan raid. 1 Lightning and 1 R.C.M. aircraft accompanied the raids.

---

4 August 1944

FLYING-BOMB STORAGE SITES

291 aircraft – 169 Halifaxes, 112 Lancasters, 10 Mosquitoes – of 6 and 8 Groups attacked the Bois de Cassan and Trossy-St-Maxim sites in clear visibility. 2 Halifaxes of 6 Group were lost on the Bois de Cassan raid and 2 Lancasters on the Trossy-St-Maxim raid.

A posthumous Victoria Cross was later awarded to Squadron Leader I. W. Bazalgette of 635 Squadron, captain of one of the aircraft lost on the all-8 Group raid on Trossy-St-Maxim. Bazalgette's Lancaster was hit by Flak and set on fire while approaching the target but the pilot carried on to release his markers and bombs on the target. (The statement in the V.C. citation that Bazalgette was Master Bomber for this raid is not correct, although he had acted as Master Bomber on earlier raids.) On leaving the target, the Lancaster dived steeply, almost out of control, but the pilot was able to recover from this and 4 members of his crew were able to bale out. Bazalgette then made a good crash-landing in an attempt to save his wounded bomb aimer and the mid-upper gunner who was overcome by fumes or smoke, but the Lancaster exploded and all 3 men still inside were killed.

Squadron Leader Bazalgette and his 2 comrades are buried at the small village of Senantes.

OIL-STORAGE DEPOTS

288 Lancasters of 1, 3 and 8 Groups attacked Bec-d'Ambes and Pauillac in clear conditions and without loss. 27 *Serrate* Mosquitoes were used as escorts to the bombers attacking these 2 targets; this was the first use of 100 Group Mosquito fighters in this way. They did not encounter any German fighters.

ÉTAPLES

27 Lancasters, 2 Mosquitoes and 1 Mustang of 617 Squadron attacked a railway bridge at Étaples. Some hits were scored but the 1,000-lb bombs used failed to destroy the bridge. No aircraft lost.

3 Mosquitoes attacked the Forêt de Nieppe storage site without loss.

4/5 August 1944

MINOR OPERATIONS

12 Halifaxes minelaying off Brest, 29 aircraft on Resistance operations, 11 O.T.U. sorties. 1 Halifax and 1 Lysander lost on Resistance operations.

---

5 August 1944

FLYING-BOMB SITES

742 aircraft – 469 Halifaxes, 257 Lancasters, 16 Mosquitoes – of 4, 5, 6 and 8 Groups attacked the Forêt de Nieppe and St-Leu-d'Esserent storage sites. Bombing conditions were good. 1 Halifax lost from the St-Leu-d'Esserent raid.

31 Lancasters and 8 Mosquitoes of 8 Group attempted to carry out small '*Oboe* leader' raids on 4 launching sites but only 9 aircraft succeeded in bombing. None lost.

OIL-STORAGE DEPOTS

306 Lancasters of 1, 3 and 8 Groups attacked targets on the River Gironde at Blaye, Bordeaux and Pauillac with excellent results. 1 Lancaster was lost from the Pauillac raid. 30 Mosquitoes of 100 Group escorted these forces without loss.

Brest

15 Lancasters and 2 Mosquitoes of 617 Squadron attacked the U-boat pens and scored 6 direct hits with *Tallboys*. 1 Lancaster shot down by Flak.

Étaples

14 Lancasters of 5 Group attacked the railway bridge but the target was soon obscured by smoke and dust and no results could be seen. No aircraft lost.

Total effort for the day: 1,148 sorties, 3 aircraft (0·3 per cent) lost.

5/6 August 1944

WANNE-EICKEL

35 Mosquitoes attacked the synthetic-oil plant without loss. The markers appeared to be well placed and 2 fires were observed.

Minor Operations: 2 R.C.M. sorties, 3 Halifaxes minelaying off Brest, 6 aircraft on Resistance operations, 5 O.T.U. sorties. No losses.

---

6 August 1944

FLYING-BOMB SUPPLY SITES

222 aircraft – 107 Lancasters, 105 Halifaxes, 10 Mosquitoes – of 4, 5 and 8 Groups attacked the Bois de Cassan and Forêt de Nieppe sites. 1 Lightning accompanied the Bois de Cassan operation. The bombing at both targets was scattered. Some markers at Forêt de Nieppe were not accurate and some of the Master Bomber's instructions at Bois de Cassan were misunderstood, resulting in more than half of the bombing force there retaining their bombs. 3 Lancasters were lost on the Bois de Cassan raid.

HAZEBROUCK

62 aircraft – 51 Halifaxes, 6 Lancasters, 5 Mosquitoes – of 4 and 8 Groups bombed the railway centre. The attack opened well but the target became obscured by smoke. 1 Halifax lost.

Lorient

12 Lancasters and 3 Mosquitoes of 617 Squadron bombed the U-boat pens without loss. 2 direct hits were scored.

6/7 August 1944

CASTROP-RAUXEL

40 Mosquitoes attacked the synthetic-oil plant; a large fire was seen. 1 Mosquito lost.

Minor Operations: 7 Mosquitoes to Cologne and 4 to the Forêt de Nieppe, 14 R.C.M. sorties, 10 Lancasters of 8 Group on a special operation in support of ground troops, described as 'a recce of target marking by ground forces in the battle area', 10 Mosquito patrols, 12 Stirlings minelaying off Brest, 22 aircraft on Resistance operations. 1 Stirling minelayer lost.

---

7 August 1944

Minor Operations

25 Lancasters and 2 Mosquitoes of 5 Group recalled from a raid on U-boat pens at Lorient without bombing; 1 Wellington flew an R.C.M. sortie. No aircraft lost.

7/8 August 1944

NORMANDY BATTLE AREA

1,019 aircraft – 614 Lancasters, 392 Halifaxes, 13 Mosquitoes – attacked five aiming points in front of Allied ground troops. The attacks were carefully controlled – only 660 aircraft bombed – and German strong points and the roads around them were well cratered. 10 aircraft – all Lancasters – were lost, 7 to German fighters, 2 to Flak and 1 to an unknown cause.

Minor Operations: 4 Mosquitoes to Coulommiers airfield, 48 R.C.M. sorties, 11 Mosquito patrols, 18 Halifaxes and 11 Stirlings minelaying off Brest, 6 aircraft on Resistance operations. No aircraft lost.

Total effort for the night: 1,117 sorties, 10 aircraft (0·9 per cent) lost.

---

8 August 1944

FORÊT DE CHANTILLY

202 aircraft – 148 Halifaxes, 49 Lancasters, 5 Mosquitoes – of 6 and 8 Groups attacked an oil-storage dump which was hit and fires were started. 1 Halifax lost in the sea.

FLYING-BOMB SITES

58 Halifaxes and 20 Mosquitoes of 4 and 8 Groups attacked 4 launching sites; the bombing was accurate. 1 Halifax lost.

8/9 August 1944

OIL TARGETS

170 Lancasters and 10 Mosquitoes of 1, 3 and 8 Groups attacked depots and storage dumps at Aire-sur-Lys and the Forêt de Lucheux. Both raids were successful. 1 Lancaster lost from the Forêt de Lucheux raid.

Minor Operations: 34 Mosquitoes to Cologne, 11 R.C.M. sorties, 18 Mosquito patrols, 24 aircraft minelaying off Brittany ports, 15 aircraft on Resistance operations. 2 aircraft, probably Halifaxes, lost from the Resistance operations.

---

9 August 1944

FLYING-BOMB SITES

172 aircraft – 114 Halifaxes, 35 Mosquitoes, 23 Lancasters – of 4 and 8 Groups attacked 7 launching sites. Visibility was clear and all raids were successful. 3 Halifaxes lost.

FORÊT DE MORMAL

160 aircraft – 147 Halifaxes, 8 Lancasters, 5 Mosquitoes – of 4 and 8 Groups attacked a fuel-storage dump. A large column of thick smoke was rising from the target at the end of the raid. No aircraft lost.

LA PALLICE

29 Lancasters and 2 Mosquitoes of 5 Group. 17 Lancasters and 1 Mosquito attacked an oil depot and 12 Lancasters of 617 Squadron and 1 Mosquito attacked the U-boat pens but smoke and haze prevented observation of results at both targets. No aircraft lost.

2 Halifaxes and 2 Wellingtons flew R.C.M. sorties without loss.

9/10 August 1944

FLYING-BOMB SITES

311 aircraft – 171 Lancasters, 115 Halifaxes, 25 Mosquitoes – of 1, 3, 6 and 8 Groups attacked 4 launching sites and the Fort-d'Englos storage site. All targets were accurately bombed and no aircraft were lost.

FORÊT DE CHÂTELLERAULT

176 Lancasters and 14 Mosquitoes of 1 and 5 Groups successfully attacked an oil-storage dump. 2 Lancasters lost.

Minor Operations: 3 Mosquitoes to Osnabrück, 21 R.C.M. sorties, 40 Mosquito patrols, 16 Mosquitoes minelaying in the Dortmund–Ems Canal and 10 Lancasters minelaying off Biscay ports, 20 aircraft on Resistance operations, 15 O.T.U. sorties. No aircraft lost.

10 August 1944

DUGNY

98 Lancasters and 5 Mosquitoes of 1 and 8 Groups attacked aviation-fuel storage tanks at Dugny, near Paris. The bombing started badly but then became concentrated. No aircraft lost.

FERME-DU-FORESTAL

60 Lancasters of 1 Group and 20 Pathfinder Mosquitoes attempted to bomb a flying-bomb site but cloud caused difficulties and only 17 Mosquitoes and 13 Lancasters attacked, possibly because the 1 Group aircraft were unused to the *Oboe*-leader technique. No aircraft lost.

4 Wellingtons flew R.C.M. sorties without loss.

10/11 August 1944

OIL DEPOTS

215 aircraft – 109 Lancasters, 101 Halifaxes, 5 Mosquitoes – of 5, 6 and 8 Groups attacked depots at Bordeaux and La Pallice successfully and without loss.

DIJON

104 Halifaxes of 4 Group and 20 Lancasters of 1 and 8 Groups attacked a railway junction and the railway yards; much damage was caused. 2 Halifaxes were lost and a further Halifax crashed or crash-landed in the liberated part of Normandy.

Minor Operations: 32 Mosquitoes to Berlin, 3 Lancasters of 8 Group to Bremen, 8 R.C.M. sorties, 37 Mosquito patrols, 12 Lancasters minelaying off Biscay ports, 8 aircraft on Resistance operations. No aircraft lost. The 3 Pathfinder Lancasters which bombed Bremen were the first Lancaster Mark VIs flown on operations by Bomber Command and they dropped the command's first 10,000-lb bombs.

11 August 1944

RAILWAY TARGETS

459 aircraft – 270 Lancasters, 169 Halifaxes, 20 Mosquitoes – of 1, 3, 4 and 8 Groups attacked 3 railway yards and 1 bridge. Forces of between 133 and 142 aircraft attacked Douai, Lens and Somain; the bombing at these targets started well but ground features rapidly became covered by smoke and dust. 1 Halifax lost on the Somain raid. 49 aircraft attacked the Étaples railway bridge without loss and claimed direct hits on the bridge.

U-BOAT PENS

53 Lancasters and 3 Mosquitoes of 5 Group attacked pens at Bordeaux and La Pallice with 2,000-lb armour-piercing bombs, but examination of the pens after their capture a few weeks later showed that these bombs could not penetrate the roofs. 6 Mosquito fighters of 100 Group provided a partial escort cover for the Bordeaux raid but no German fighters were encountered. No aircraft lost.

FLYING-BOMB SITES

40 Halifaxes of 4 Group and 20 Pathfinder Mosquitoes attacked 4 launching sites. Visibility was clear; the bombing was accurate and no aircraft were lost.

11/12 August 1944

GIVORS

179 Lancasters and 10 Mosquitoes of 1 and 8 Groups carried out an exceptionally accurate attack on the railway yards. No aircraft lost.

Minor Operations: 33 Mosquitoes to Berlin and 2 to Trossy-St-Maxim, 9 R.C.M. sorties, 28 Mosquito patrols, 8 Stirlings and 6 Lancasters minelaying off Biscay ports, 14 aircraft on Resistance operations. 1 Mosquito lost from the Berlin raid.

---

12 August 1944

FORÊT DE MONTRICHARD

117 aircraft – 95 Halifaxes, 16 Lancasters, 6 Mosquitoes – of 6 and 8 Groups attacked a fuel dump, which was soon covered by a thick pall of smoke. No aircraft lost.

U-BOAT PENS

68 Lancasters of 1 Group and 2 Mosquitoes of 5 Group attacked pens at Brest, La Pallice and Bordeaux without loss. A U-boat was believed to have been hit at La Pallice. 8 Mosquitoes of 100 Group provided a fighter escort.

1 Wellington flew an R.C.M. sortie.

12/13 August 1944

BRUNSWICK

242 Lancasters and 137 Halifaxes. 17 Lancasters and 10 Halifaxes lost, 7·1 per cent of the force.

This was an experimental raid. No Pathfinder aircraft took part and there was no marking. The intention was to discover how successfully a force of aircraft could carry out a raid with each crew bombing on the indications of its own *H2S* set. The raid was not successful and there was no concentration of bombing. The Brunswick report calls it a 'heavy raid' but only states that bombs fell in the central and

Stadtpark areas and that 99 people were killed. Other towns, up to 20 miles distant, were mistaken for Brunswick and were also bombed.

RÜSSELSHEIM

297 aircraft – 191 Lancasters, 96 Halifaxes, 10 Mosquitoes. 13 Lancasters and 7 Halifaxes lost, 6·7 per cent of the force. The target for this raid was the Opel motor factory and normal Pathfinder marking methods were used. The motor factory was only slightly damaged; the local report states that the tyre and dispatch departments and the powerhouse were hit but most of the bombs fell in open countryside south of the target. 9 people were killed and 31 injured.

FALAISE

144 aircraft – 91 Lancasters, 36 Halifaxes, 12 Stirlings, 5 Mosquitoes – bombed a German troop concentration and a road junction north of Falaise. The bombing was believed to have been very effective. No aircraft lost.

FLYING-BOMB SITES

40 Halifaxes and 12 Mosquitoes bombed 2 launching sites and a storage depot. No aircraft lost.

SUPPORT AND MINOR OPERATIONS

143 training aircraft on a diversionary sweep over the English Channel, 21 Mosquitoes to Kiel, 10 to Frankfurt and 3 each to Coulommiers and Juvincourt airfields, 33 R.C.M. sorties, 47 Mosquito patrols, 10 Lancasters and 4 Halifaxes minelaying off Biscay ports, 21 O.T.U. sorties. 2 Mosquitoes lost – 1 from the Frankfurt raid and 1 Mosquito of 100 Group, probably a *Serrate* aircraft.

Total effort for the night: 1,167 sorties, 49 aircraft (4·2 per cent) lost. The bombs dropped during this night brought Bomber Command's total for the war so far to approximately 500,000 tons.

---

13 August 1944

Brest

28 Lancasters and 1 Mosquito of 5 Group attacked the U-boat pens and shipping. Hits were claimed on the pens, on the hulk of an old French battleship, the *Clémenceau*, and on a medium-sized tanker. The object of the attacks on ships was to prevent the Germans using any of the large ships in Brest to block the harbour just before its capture by American troops. 1 Lancaster lost.

Bordeaux

15 Lancasters of 5 Group bombed an oil depot accurately. 1 Lancaster lost.

8 Mosquito fighters and 1 R.C.M. Wellington of 100 Group flew operations without loss.

13/14 August 1944

MINOR OPERATIONS

30 Mosquitoes to Hannover, 22 R.C.M. sorties, 15 Mosquito patrols, 10 Halifaxes and 5 Lancasters minelaying off Biscay ports, 4 Halifaxes on Resistance operations, 9 O.T.U. sorties. No aircraft lost.

---

14 August 1944

NORMANDY BATTLE AREA

805 aircraft – 411 Lancasters, 352 Halifaxes, 42 Mosquitoes – to attack 7 German troop positions facing the 3rd Canadian Division, which was advancing on Falaise. 2 Lancasters lost.

A careful plan was prepared with *Oboe* and visual marking, and with a Master Bomber and a deputy at each of the 7 targets. Most of the bombing was accurate and effective but, about half-way through the raids, some aircraft started to bomb a large quarry in which parts of the 12th Canadian Field Regiment were positioned. This mistake may have been caused by the yellow identification flares which were ignited by the Canadians. It was unfortunate that the target indicators being used by the Pathfinders were also yellow. Bomber Command crews claimed that the Canadians used the yellow flares before any bombs fell in the quarry; the history of the Canadian units says the bombs fell first. The Master Bombers tried hard to stop further crews bombing in the wrong area but approximately 70 aircraft bombed the quarry and other nearby Allied positions over a 70-minute period. The Canadians took shelter in their slit trenches and most emerged unscathed though shaken, but 13 men were killed and 53 were injured and a large number of vehicles and guns were hit.

This was believed to have been the first occasion on which Bomber Command aircraft had hit friendly troops during the Battle of Normandy. The Canadian artillery regiment was machine-gunned by R.A.F. Spitfires and U.S.A.A.F. Mustangs the following day! *

BREST

155 Lancasters and 4 Mosquitoes of 5 Group made two separate attacks on ships in Brest harbour. The *Clémenceau* and the cruiser *Gueydon* were both hit and were believed left sinking in 'safe' positions which would not hinder Allied use of the port when American troops took possession. The Allied forces were anxious to capture a good port to which supplies and reinforcements for the land battle could be brought in directly from the United States. 2 Lancasters were lost.

---

* Details of the Canadian side of the bombing come from *Into Action with the 12th Field* by Captain T. J. Bell (published privately in Canada) and from the personal reminiscences of former Lance-Corporal George R. Carter of the 12th Canadian Field Regiment. George Carter's brother, Flying Officer Roy E. Carter of 431 Squadron, was a Bomber Command navigator whose Halifax had been shot down over Holland on the Sterkrade raid of 16/17 June 1944. Roy Carter baled out successfully but, while he was being hidden by Dutch civilians in a house at Tilburg, he was discovered by Germans on 8 July and shot, together with a Pathfinder pilot and an Australian airman. The bloodstained Dutch flag which covered the bodies after their death was brought to England in 1983 and placed in the 83 Squadron Memorial Chapel in Coningsby parish church.

1 Wellington flew an R.C.M. sortie.

Total effort for the day: 965 sorties, 4 aircraft (0·4 per cent) lost.

14/15 August 1944

MINOR OPERATIONS

32 Mosquitoes to Berlin, 2 to Sterkrade oil plant and 2 to St-Trond airfield, 1 R.C.M. sortie, 8 Halifaxes and 6 Lancasters minelaying off Biscay ports, 4 aircraft on Resistance operations, 7 O.T.U. sorties. No losses.

---

15 August 1944

LUFTWAFFE NIGHT-FIGHTER AIRFIELDS

1,004 aircraft – 599 Lancasters, 385 Halifaxes, 19 Mosquitoes, 1 Lightning – attacked 9 airfields in Holland and Belgium in preparation for a renewed night offensive against Germany. Visibility was perfect and all raids were considered successful. 3 Lancasters lost.

1 Wellington flew an R.C.M. sortie.

The invasion of Southern France started in the early hours of this day. The landings were only lightly opposed and the Allied troops advanced rapidly. The Allied break-out from Normandy was also taking place at this time.

15/16 August 1944

MINOR OPERATIONS

32 Mosquitoes to Berlin, 8 to Venlo airfield and 9 to various Ruhr targets, 1 R.C.M. sortie, 7 Mosquito patrols, 6 Halifaxes minelaying off La Pallice. No aircraft lost.

---

16 August 1944

La Pallice

25 Lancasters and 1 Mosquito of 5 Group to attack the U-boat pens found the target was cloud-covered and only 3 aircraft bombed. 1 Wellington R.C.M. sortie was flown. No aircraft lost.

Operational Statistics, 5/6 June to 16 August 1944
(72 days/nights)

Number of nights with operations: 66
Number of days with operations: 58

Number of night sorties: 29,264, from which 668 aircraft (2·3 per cent) were lost
Number of day sorties: 17,580, from which 59 aircraft (0·3 per cent) were lost
Total sorties: 46,844 from which 727 aircraft (1·6 per cent) were lost
Approximate bomb tonnage in period: 125,882 tons
Averages per 24-hour period: 650·6 sorties, 10·1 aircraft lost, 1,748·4 tons of bombs dropped

The number of daylight sorties in this period exceeded the total number of Bomber Command's daylight sorties flown between September 1939 and the departure of 2 Group in May 1943 – at about one tenth the cost in aircraft casualties.

20. THE RETURN TO GERMANY

16/17 August to 31 December 1944/1 January 1945

The Allied armies finally broke through the German defences in Normandy and, led by their armoured divisions, raced across France in all directions. A link was quickly made with the Allied units which had recently landed in Southern France. Paris was liberated on 24 August. Belgium was entered early in September – with the vital port of Antwerp being seized almost intact – and most of that small country was completely liberated within a few days. The first American troops reached the German border near Aachen and Trier on 10 September but their headlong dash was then held in front of Germany's old frontier fortifications, the Siegfried Line. Holland was reached on 15 September but then the bold plan to take a series of vital road bridges across the Rhine, Waal and Maas rivers by British and American airborne troops just failed, when relieving ground forces were not able to reach the British troops at the furthest bridge at Arnhem. Most of Holland would have to endure further months of German occupation.

The breaking of the German armies in Normandy and the swift advance to the German frontier completely altered the war situation. Many people had hoped that the advancing troops could continue unchecked on into Germany, to meet the Russian troops advancing from the East and end the war in Europe before the winter. But there was no chance of this happening; the hard facts of logistics and the need to bring fresh divisions in from the United States to man the huge new front line imposed themselves on the situation. The Allied commanders were seriously handicapped by lack of port facilities. Brest had fallen and was a useful port of direct entry from America, but it was now 500 miles from the new battle lines. The Germans had left do-or-die garrisons in all the Channel ports and, although the Allies held the perfectly placed port of Antwerp, the Germans still controlled the banks of its forty-mile river approach. The armies were forced to halt after Arnhem and wait for the clearance of the Channel ports and Antwerp.

Bomber Command had played little part in the great advance, though they had contributed greatly to the preliminary weakening of the German defence. Sir Arthur Harris was formally released from his control by Supreme Headquarters Allied Expeditionary Force in mid-September and Bomber Command reverted to Air Ministry control, although all future operations were still intended to fit into overall Allied planning. This was the last of Bomber Command's historic turning-points. Which path was the R.A.F. heavy-bomber offensive now to take, with the circumstances of the war so vastly altered? Firstly, Bomber Command was ordered to remain ready to answer any calls for direct assistance to the ground forces. No one argued about that and Harris thus devoted whatever part of his force was necessary to bombing the

German garrisons in the Channel ports, to clearing the approaches to Antwerp and, later, to bombing German towns facing Allied ground attacks. But the army demands required only a small proportion of Bomber Command's huge strength. How to employ the great potential remaining was the subject of much debate and, as usual, some controversy.

Two schools of thought favoured two different target systems – synthetic-oil production and the German transportation system; a smaller number of people favoured a third option, the continued general bombing of German industrial cities. A successful all-out attack on oil would produce obvious benefits; the Germans would be robbed of the ability to wage any form of mobile war on land and the Luftwaffe would be grounded. This was believed to be the best way to end the war by many of what might be termed 'the senior strategists', the men who held the highest positions in the direction of the Allied war effort. As far as the R.A.F. was concerned, this was the preferred policy of Sir Charles Portal and the Air Ministry. The second option – the attack on communications – was supported by the senior Allied commanders fighting in Europe; their success in Normandy and the recent advance to Germany owed much to the successful interdiction campaign by the British and American heavy bombers. Air Chief Marshal Sir Arthur Tedder, Eisenhower's deputy commander, was the main R.A.F. supporter of this policy.

An important directive issued both to R.A.F. Bomber Command and to the American Eighth Air Force on 25 September showed that the oil school of thought had won. A clear first priority was given to both air forces – 'the petroleum industry, with special emphasis on petrol (gasoline) including storage'.[*] Joint second priorities were the German rail and waterway transport system, tank production and motor-vehicle production. German cities were mentioned much later in the directive for general attack 'when weather and tactical conditions are unsuitable for operations against specific primary objectives'. These clear instructions were reinforced on 1 November by a directive addressed to Bomber Command alone:

Sir,
I am directed ... to inform you that, in view of the great contribution which the strategic bomber forces are making by their attacks on the enemy petroleum industry and his oil supplies, it has been decided that the maximum effort is to be made to maintain and, if possible, intensify pressure on this target system.[†]

Sir Arthur Harris scribbled a comment alongside this: 'Here we go round the mulberry bush.'

Harris made it quite clear to his superiors during the war and is perfectly open in his post-war writings that he did not hold with the bombing of particular target systems, 'panacea targets' he called them.[‡] He believed that, because of weather and tactical limitations, Bomber Command would be best employed in continuing to wear down the industrial production of large cities and the spirit of their inhabitants. Harris also still believed that Germany could collapse from within and the Allied armies could be spared the final task of storming the German frontier defences. His interpretations of the tactical latitude allowed to him in day-to-day (or night-to-

---

[*] The directive is printed in the British Official History, Vol. IV, pp. 172–3.
[†] ibid., Vol. IV, pp. 177–8.
[‡] See Chapter Ten of Harris's *Bomber Offensive* (Collins, 1947), for his detailed views on this subject.

39. Civilians hurrying to a substantial air-raid shelter in Münster.

40. Inside the air-raid shelters in which German civilians spent so much of their lives in the last year of the war. These people are a typical cross-section of wartime German city-dwellers – women, children and old men; the younger men are all at the front and the middle-aged men are either at the front or on air-raid duty.

night) target selection continued to lean generously towards area attacks on German cities, although many of those cities were associated with the oil industry.

Bomber Command's strength was now increasing steadily. The numbers of front-line aircraft rose by 50 per cent in 1944, most of the increase coming in the second half of the year, with a particular rush of new Lancaster squadrons being formed in the autumn. Expansion took place in every group. 1 and 5 Groups, equipped with Lancasters, were each able to drop as many bombs as had the whole of Bomber Command two years earlier. 6 (Canadian) Group became a mixed Halifax and Lancaster force and could, when required, provide nearly 300 aircraft for operations. 4 Group remained an all-Halifax force to the end, receiving the improved Mark VI version to add to the IIIs which had served them so well. The biggest change in the regular groups was the resurgence of 3 Group, which had borne the brunt of Bomber Command's early war years with the Wellington but had then suffered and more recently languished in near idleness with the Stirling. 3 Group's last Stirlings were transferred to 38 Group, in Transport Command, and soon not only would 3 Group be fully equipped with Lancasters, but many of its aircraft would be fitted with the *G-H* blind-bombing device. *G-H* enabled the 3 Group aircraft to bomb accurately in any weather, provided the cloud tops did not reach to the Lancasters' operational height. 3 Group was then permitted to operate on its own on most occasions. With 5 Group also acting in an independent role, the standard Main Force was now composed of 1, 4, 6 and 8 Groups but still able to provide up to 1,000 aircraft for a maximum effort. 8 Group received an improved Mark III version of *H2S* and an increase in the number of Mosquito squadrons in the Light Night Striking Force. Finally, 100 Group was steadily increasing both in strength and in its technical ability to outwit the Germans.

The scene was now set for Bomber Command's operational climax. The German night-fighter force was declining. Bomber casualties were falling. Bombing accuracy was improving. Daylight raids on Germany were resumed before the month was out. Several German cities which had so far defied all of Bomber Command's efforts were now destroyed; Brunswick (in October) and Nuremberg (in early 1945) come to mind. Old targets were attacked again; there was a second Battle of the Ruhr that autumn, mentioned under that title in the Official History but not as well remembered as the 1943 campaign. Much of the German war industry disappeared underground or to distant locations. Bomber Command then began to run out of large cities to attack and started to strike at smaller, less industrial communities, places like Darmstadt, Bremerhaven, Bonn, Freiburg, Heilbronn, Ulm; many more narrow streets of medieval houses and other cultural landmarks disappeared as well as a vast quantity of ordinary housing. And all the time Harris was sending smaller forces to attack the synthetic-oil refineries and the transportation targets. The bomber crews of that period certainly had variety. They could fly by night or by day; their log-books might contain details of raids on gun batteries near Calais or Boulogne, old faithfuls like Essen and Cologne, the dykes on Walcheren island, oil refineries, the Dortmund–Ems Canal or the railway yards in some German town they had never heard of – all in rapid succession.

Approximately 46 per cent of the total tonnage of bombs dropped by Bomber Command in five and a half years of war would be dropped in the remaining nine months.

16/17 August 1944

STETTIN

461 Lancasters to attack the port and industrial areas. 5 Lancasters lost.*

Bomber Command claimed an accurate attack, with much damage in the port and factory area. A German report states that 1,508 houses and 29 industrial premises were destroyed and 1,000 houses and 26 industrial premises badly damaged. 5 ships in the harbour (totalling 5,000 tons) were sunk and 8 ships (15,000 tons) were seriously damaged. 1,150 people were killed and 1,654 were injured; 33 of the dead and 72 of the injured were German soldiers.

KIEL

348 aircraft – 195 Lancasters, 144 Halifaxes, 9 Mosquitoes. 3 Halifaxes and 2 Lancasters lost.

This raid was only partially successful. The local report shows that serious damage was caused to the docks area and to many of the local shipbuilding firms, but it also stated that a large number of bombs fell outside the town, particularly in the Suchsdorf area to the north-west. 6 people were killed and 33 injured.

SUPPORT AND MINOR OPERATIONS

145 aircraft from training units on diversionary sweep over the North Sea, 23 Mosquitoes to Berlin, 5 to Deelen airfield and 3 each to Dortmund, Kamen and Sterkrade, 33 R.C.M. sorties, 47 Mosquito patrols, 89 aircraft minelaying in the Baltic and in Kiel Bay and 4 in the River Gironde, 24 O.T.U. sorties. 6 aircraft lost – 3 Halifaxes minelaying in Kiel Bay and 2 Lancasters off Swinemünde, and 1 O.T.U. Wellington.

Total effort for the night: 1,188 sorties, 16 aircraft (1·3 per cent) lost.

---

17 August 1944

BREST

79 Halifaxes of 4 Group were sent to bomb shipping in the port area of Brest but the target area was covered by 7–10/10ths cloud. Only 54 aircraft bombed and no results were observed. No aircraft lost.

17/18 August 1944

DIVERSIONARY SWEEP

55 O.T.U. Wellingtons and 14 R.C.M. aircraft carried out a sweep over the North Sea without loss. This type of operation was now being flown on some nights when no major raid was being carried out, in order to draw up the German fighters and cause them to waste fuel. These sweeps were, therefore, part diversionary to con-

---

*Because of the declining bomber-casualty rate, percentage losses for individual raids are no longer recorded unless of particular interest.

fuse the German controllers but also part of the campaign against German oil supplies.

Minor Operations: 37 Mosquitoes to Mannheim and 3 each to Dortmund, Kamen and Sterkrade, 15 R.C.M. sorties, 14 Mosquito patrols, 12 Halifaxes minelaying off Biscay coasts, 4 aircraft on Resistance operations, 2 O.T.U. leaflet sorties. No aircraft lost.

---

18 August 1944

L'ISLE-ADAM

158 Lancasters and 11 Mosquitoes of 5 Group attacked a German supply depot near Paris. 2 Lancasters lost.

Minor Operations: 64 Lancasters and 5 Mosquitoes to oil-storage depots at Bordeaux and Ertvelde-Rieme, near Ghent, 16 Halifaxes and 16 Lancasters to 7 small flying-bomb sites, 23 Lancasters to La Pallice U-boat pens. 2 Lancasters lost on the flying-bomb site raid.

18/19 August 1944

BREMEN

288 aircraft – 216 Lancasters, 65 Halifaxes, 7 Mosquitoes. 1 Lancaster lost.

Visibility over the target was clear and the Pathfinders provided perfect marking throughout the raid. Bremen's own records show this to have been the most destructive raid of the war, although only 274 aircraft attacked, dropping just over 1,100 tons of bombs. The whole of the centre and the north-western parts of Bremen, including the port area, were devastated. The 10-page report from Bremen is a more emotive and erratic document than normal, much of it describing the effect of the fierce fires (described as a firestorm), the condition of the packed bodies of victims later found in shelters (300 bodies were found in the Lesmona public shelter), the distress of the rescue workers and the sufferings of the bombed-out people. At least 1,058 bodies were recovered, of which 375 bodies could not be identified. The number of people classed as 'missing' far exceeded the 375 unidentified bodies.

8,635 'dwelling-houses', as usual in German cities, many of them being blocks of flats, were burnt out and 611 were severely damaged. The official who compiled the report made no attempt to list the commercial and industrial buildings hit, 'it would be endless', he wrote, but he did stress the severe damage caused to the port area, mentioning that 18 ships were sunk in the harbour and 61 seriously damaged alongside wharves.

Special ration cards were issued to the civilian population after this raid to help restore morale – 100 grammes of real bean coffee and 2 half bottles of spirits, 250 grammes of sweets for the children.

STERKRADE

234 aircraft – 210 Halifaxes, 14 Mosquitoes, 10 Lancasters – mainly from 4 Group, to attack the synthetic oil plant. 1 Halifax and 1 Lancaster lost. Bomber Command documents state that the raid was successful and that the plant was seriously damaged.

CONNANTRE

144 aircraft – 122 Halifaxes, 18 Lancasters, 4 Mosquitoes – of 6 and 8 Groups. No aircraft lost.

The target here was a railway station and yards 70 miles east of Paris. The Pathfinder marking was accurate and much damage was caused. This raid marked the end of the long series of attacks on the French and Belgian railway systems.

ERTVELDE RIEME

108 Lancasters and 5 Mosquitoes of 1 and 8 Groups attacked and caused severe damage to the oil depot and storage tanks. No aircraft lost.

SUPPORT AND MINOR OPERATIONS

139 training aircraft on a diversionary sweep to the Normandy area, 21 Mosquitoes to Berlin and 19 to five other targets, 33 R.C.M. sorties, 62 Mosquito patrols, 11 Halifaxes minelaying off Biscay ports, 5 aircraft on Resistance operations. 1 Mosquito lost on a raid to Harburg.

Total effort for the night: 1,069 sorties, 4 aircraft (0·4 per cent) lost.

---

19 August 1944

LA PALLICE

52 Lancasters of 5 Group attempted to bomb two groups of oil-storage tanks but the targets were difficult to identify and the effects of the bombing could not be seen. No aircraft lost.

1 Wellington of 100 Group carried out a 'signals watch' flight.

---

20 August 1944

3 Mosquitoes on Ranger patrols and 1 Wellington on 'signals watch'. No aircraft lost.

20/21 August 1944

7 aircraft minelaying off La Pallice without loss.

23/24 August 1944

MOSQUITO OPERATIONS

46 Mosquitoes attacked Cologne, whose local report mentions the heavy damage caused by 13 4,000-lb bombs which fell in residential areas with 721 domestic and 64 commercial or industrial buildings being destroyed or damaged, though 571 of them were only slightly damaged. 1 gasometer was blown up. 24 people were killed and 15 were injured.

8 other Mosquitoes attacked Homberg, Castrop-Rauxel and Venlo airfield. No aircraft lost.

---

24 August 1944

PORTS

53 Halifaxes of 4 Group attacked shipping in Brest harbour. 22 Lancasters and 1 Mosquito of 5 Group bombed E-boat pens at Ijmuiden. Both raids were successful and no aircraft were lost.

24/25 August 1944

6 Halifaxes minelaying off La Pallice without loss.

---

25 August 1944

FLYING-BOMB SITES

161 aircraft – 140 Halifaxes, 16 Lancasters, 5 Mosquitoes – attacked 5 launching or storage sites in the Pas de Calais with varying results. 2 Halifaxes and 1 Lancaster lost.

25/26 August 1944

RÜSSELSHEIM

412 Lancasters of 1, 3, 6 and 8 Groups attacked the Opel motor factory. 15 Lancasters were lost, 3·6 per cent of the force.

The Pathfinder marking was accurate and the raid was successfully completed in 10 minutes. An official German report * says that the forge and the gearbox assembly departments were put out of action for several weeks, but 90 per cent of the machine tools in other departments escaped damage. The assembly line and part of the pressworks were able to recommence work 2 days later and lorry assembly was unaffected because of considerable stocks of ready-made parts. 179 people were killed in the raid but their nationalities were not recorded.

DARMSTADT

190 Lancasters and 6 Mosquitoes of 5 Group to this target which had not been seriously attacked by Bomber Command before. 7 Lancasters lost.

This '5 Group method' raid was a failure. The Master Bomber had to return early; his 2 deputies were shot down; the flares were dropped too far west and the low-level Mosquito marker aircraft could not locate the target. 95 buildings were hit and 8 people were killed by the scattered bombs which did hit Darmstadt. 33 of the Lancasters bombed other targets, including at least 13 aircraft which joined in the successful raid on nearby Rüsselsheim.

---

* KTB Luftgaukommando VII, Bundesarchiv.

BREST

334 aircraft – 284 Halifaxes, 32 Lancasters, 18 Mosquitoes – of 4, 6 and 8 Groups attacked 8 coastal battery positions near Brest. Most of the bombing was accurate. 1 Halifax and 1 Lancaster lost.

SUPPORT AND MINOR OPERATIONS

2 Mosquitoes in preliminary reconnaissance of targets, 182 training aircraft on a diversionary sweep over the North Sea, 36 Mosquitoes to Berlin and 22 to five other targets, 47 R.C.M. sorties, 68 Mosquito patrols, 6 Halifaxes minelaying off La Pallice, 6 aircraft on Resistance operations. This was the first occasion on which 100 Group dispatched more than 100 aircraft. 1 R.C.M. Fortress lost.

Total effort for the night: 1,311 sorties, 25 aircraft (1·9 per cent) lost and 8 more aircraft crashed in England, including 3 O.T.U. Wellingtons from the diversionary sweep. The total effort for this night was a new record for Bomber Command, exceeding by exactly 100 the number of aircraft dispatched on 5/6 June, the eve of D-Day.

26/27 August 1944

KIEL

372 Lancasters and 10 Mosquitoes of 1, 3 and 8 Groups. 17 Lancasters lost, 4·6 per cent of the Lancaster force.

The Pathfinder marking was hampered by smoke-screens but the local report tells of a very serious raid with heavy bombing in the town centre and surrounding districts and widespread fires fanned by a strong wind. The Rathaus was completely burnt out and many other public buildings were destroyed or seriously damaged. A large public shelter, the Waisenhofbunker, was cut off by fire but the report does not say whether the people inside were eventually rescued. 134 people were killed and 1,002 were injured.

KÖNIGSBERG

174 Lancasters of 5 Group to this target, which was an important supply port for the German Eastern Front. The route to the target was 950 miles from the 5 Group bases. Photographic reconnaissance showed that the bombing fell in the eastern part of the town but no report is available from the target, now Kaliningrad in Russian Lithuania. 4 Lancasters lost.

SUPPORT AND MINOR OPERATIONS

108 training aircraft on a diversionary sweep to Normandy, 21 Mosquitoes to Berlin, 13 to Hamburg and 12 to five other targets, 19 R.C.M. sorties, 70 Mosquito patrols, 30 Lancasters and 15 Halifaxes minelaying off Danzig and Kiel. 7 aircraft lost – 5 Lancaster minelayers, 1 Mosquito R.C.M. aircraft and 1 Mosquito *Serrate* aircraft.

Total effort for the night: 844 sorties, 28 aircraft (3·3 per cent) lost.

---

27 August 1944

HOMBERG

243 aircraft – 216 Halifaxes of 4 Group and 14 Mosquitoes and 13 Lancasters of 8 Group – were dispatched on this historic raid, the first major raid by Bomber Command to Germany in daylight since 12 August 1941, when 54 Blenheims had attacked power-stations near Cologne for the loss of 10 aircraft.

This raid was escorted by 9 squadrons of Spitfires on the outward flight and 7 squadrons on the withdrawal. 1 Me 110 was seen; the Spitfires drove it off. There was intense Flak over the target but no bombers were lost. The target was the Rhein-preussen synthetic-oil refinery at Meerbeck. The bombing was based on *Oboe* marking but 5–8/10ths cloud produced difficult conditions, though some accurate bombing was claimed through gaps in the clouds.

MIMOYECQUES

226 aircraft – 176 Halifaxes, 40 Lancasters, 10 Mosquitoes – of 6 and 8 Groups carried out an accurate attack on a flying-bomb site without loss.

Brest

24 Lancasters and 1 Mosquito of 5 Group bombed 2 ships in the harbour and claimed hits on both. No aircraft lost.

27/28 August 1944

MINOR OPERATIONS

30 Mosquitoes to Mannheim, 66 O.T.U. Wellingtons on a diversionary sweep, 19 R.C.M. sorties, 26 Mosquito patrols, 7 aircraft on Resistance operations. 2 Mosquitoes from the Mannheim raid and 1 Intruder Mosquito lost.

---

28 August 1944

FLYING-BOMB SITES

150 aircraft – 77 Halifaxes, 48 Lancasters, 25 Mosquitoes – carried out small '*Oboe* leader' raids on 12 sites. Most of the targets were satisfactorily hit. This was the last of the long series of raids on the German flying-bomb launching and storage sites in the Pas de Calais area, which was captured by Allied ground troops a few days later.

There was 1 aircraft casualty. A 550 Squadron Lancaster, which had just bombed the Wemars/Cappel launching site near Amiens, received a direct hit from a Flak battery near Dunkirk. The Lancaster went down in flames and exploded. The pilot, Pilot Officer S. C. Beeson, and 3 other members of the crew escaped by parachute, but the wireless operator and the 2 gunners were killed. Sergeants J. K. Norgate, H. S. Picton and J. A. Trayhorn were thus the last fatal casualties in Bomber Command's campaign against the V-1 flying bomb.

Minor Operations: 30 aircraft of 6 and 8 Groups bombed a German battery on the Île de Cezembre, near St-Malo, and 23 Halifaxes of 6 Group bombed ships in Brest harbour. No aircraft lost.

28/29 August 1944

MINOR OPERATIONS

35 Mosquitoes to Essen, 4 to Leverkusen, 3 each to Le Culot and Venlo and 2 to Cologne, 13 Mosquito patrols, 6 Halifaxes minelaying off La Pallice, 19 aircraft on Resistance operations. 1 Halifax lost flying on a Resistance operation.

29/30 August 1944

STETTIN

402 Lancasters and 1 Mosquito of 1, 3, 6 and 8 Groups. 23 Lancasters lost, 5·7 per cent of the force.

This was a successful raid, hitting parts of Stettin which had escaped damage in previous attacks. A German report states that 1,569 houses and 32 industrial premises were destroyed and that 565 houses and 23 industrial premises were badly damaged. A ship of 2,000 tons was sunk and 7 other ships (totalling 31,000 tons) were damaged. 1,033 people were killed and 1,034 people were injured.

KÖNIGSBERG

189 Lancasters of 5 Group carried out one of the most successful 5 Group attacks of the war on this target at extreme range. Only 480 tons of bombs could be carried because of the range of the target but severe damage was caused around the 4 separate aiming points selected. This success was achieved despite a 20-minute delay in opening the attack because of the presence of low cloud; the bombing force waited patiently, using up precious fuel, until the marker aircraft found a break in the clouds and the Master Bomber, Wing Commander J. Woodroffe, probably 5 Group's most skilled Master Bomber, allowed the attack to commence. Bomber Command estimated that 41 per cent of all the housing and 20 per cent of all the industry in Königsberg were destroyed. There was heavy fighter opposition over the target and 15 Lancasters, 7·9 per cent of the force, were lost.

SUPPORT AND MINOR OPERATIONS

93 training aircraft on a diversionary sweep over the North Sea, 53 Mosquitoes bombing Berlin, Hamburg and 4 other targets, 35 R.C.M. sorties, 49 Mosquito patrols, 31 Lancasters and 12 Halifaxes minelaying off Baltic ports, 8 aircraft on Resistance operations. 2 O.T.U. Wellingtons from the sweep and 1 Lancaster minelayer lost.

Total effort for the night: 873 sorties, 41 aircraft (4·7 per cent) lost.

30/31 August 1944

MINOR OPERATIONS

36 Mosquitoes to Frankfurt, 6 R.C.M. sorties, 6 Mosquito patrols, 4 Halifaxes minelaying off La Pallice. No aircraft lost.

31 August 1944

V-2 ROCKET STORES

601 aircraft – 418 Lancasters, 147 Halifaxes, 36 Mosquitoes – to attack 9 sites in Northern France where the Germans were believed to be storing V-2 rockets. 8 of the sites were found and bombed. 6 Lancasters lost.

COASTAL BATTERY

165 Halifaxes of 6 Group and 5 Pathfinder Mosquitoes bombed the Île de Cezembre battery near St-Malo. 1 photographic Mosquito accompanied the raid. The bombing force flew at 3,000 ft or less over the undefended targets and achieved a good bombing concentration. 1 Halifax lost.

31 August/1 September 1944

MINOR OPERATIONS

42 Mosquitoes to Düsseldorf, 6 to Cologne and 6 to Leverkusen, 3 R.C.M. sorties, 21 Mosquito patrols, 24 aircraft on Resistance operations. 2 Mosquitoes lost, 1 each from the Cologne and Leverkusen raids.

1 September 1944

V-2 ROCKET STORES

121 aircraft – 97 Halifaxes, 15 Mosquitoes, 9 Lancasters – of 4 and 8 Groups bombed storage sites at Lumbres and La Pourchinte without loss. Both raids were successful, the Lumbres attack particularly so.

1 R.C.M. radio listening sortie was flown.

1/2 September 1944

MINOR OPERATIONS

35 Mosquitoes to Bremen, 4 R.C.M. sorties, 39 Mosquito patrols, 7 aircraft on Resistance operations. No aircraft lost.

2 September 1944

BREST

67 Lancasters of 5 Group bombed ships in Brest harbour in clear visibility. No aircraft lost.

3 September 1944

AIRFIELDS

675 aircraft – 348 Lancasters, 315 Halifaxes, 12 Mosquitoes – carried out heavy raids

on 6 airfields in Southern Holland. All raids were successful and only 1 Halifax was lost from the Venlo raid.

2 Mosquito Ranger patrols and 1 R.C.M. sortie were flown without loss.

---

4 September 1944

5 Mosquitoes of 100 Group flew Ranger patrols. 2 trains were attacked but 2 Mosquitoes were lost.

4/5 September 1944

MINOR OPERATIONS

43 Mosquitoes to Karlsruhe and 14 to Steenwijk airfield, 6 *Serrate* patrols. No losses.

---

5 September 1944

LE HAVRE

348 aircraft – 313 Lancasters, 30 Mosquitoes, 5 Stirlings – 1, 3 and 8 Groups carried out the first of a series of heavy raids on the German positions around Le Havre which were still holding out after being bypassed by the Allied advance. This was an accurate raid in good visibility. No aircraft lost.

BREST

60 Lancasters and 6 Mosquitoes of 5 Group bombed gun positions outside Brest, whose garrison was also still holding out. No aircraft lost.

5/6 September 1944

MINOR OPERATIONS

43 Mosquitoes to Hannover and 12 to Steenwijk, 8 R.C.M. sorties, 23 Mosquito patrols, 19 aircraft on Resistance operations. No aircraft lost.

---

6 September 1944

LE HAVRE

344 aircraft – 311 Lancasters, 30 Mosquitoes, 3 Stirlings – bombed German fortifications and transport without loss.

EMDEN

105 Halifaxes and 76 Lancasters of 6 and 8 Groups on the first large raid to this target since June 1942; it was also the last Bomber Command raid of the war on Emden. The force was provided with an escort, first of Spitfires and then of American Mustangs. Only 1 Lancaster, that of the deputy Master Bomber, Flight Lieutenant

Granville Wilson, D.S.O., D.F.C., D.F.M., of 7 Squadron, a 23-year-old Northern Irishman, was lost. Wilson's aircraft received a direct hit from a Flak shell and he was killed instantly, together with his navigator and bomb aimer, Sergeants D. Jones and E. R. Brunsdon. The 5 other members of the crew escaped by parachute. Flight Lieutenant Wilson is now buried in the Sage War Cemetery, near Oldenburg; the names of the 2 sergeants are on the Runnymede Memorial to the Missing.

The bombing was accurate and Emden was seen to be a mass of flames, but no local report is available other than a brief note which states that several small ships in the harbour were sunk.

6/7 September 1944

MINOR OPERATIONS

32 Mosquitoes to Hamburg and 6 to Emden, 17 R.C.M. sorties, 33 Mosquito patrols, 8 Halifaxes minelaying in the River Ems and off Texel, 6 Stirlings on Resistance operations. 1 *Serrate* Mosquito lost.

The bombing in the Mosquito raid to Hamburg was entirely on estimated positions through 10/10ths cloud but 68 people in Hamburg were killed and 73 were injured, some of them when Fire Station No. 13 in the harbour area received a direct hit.

7/8 September 1944

MINOR OPERATIONS

41 Mosquitoes to Karlsruhe, 12 to Steenwijk and 6 to Emden, 16 Stirlings on Resistance operations. No aircraft lost.

---

8 September 1944

LE HAVRE

333 aircraft – 304 Lancasters, 25 Mosquitoes, 4 Stirlings – of 1, 3 and 8 Groups attempted to bomb German positions but the weather was bad, with a low cloud base, and only 109 aircraft bombed, with indifferent results. 2 Lancasters lost.

The 4 Stirlings on this raid, all from 149 Squadron based at Methwold, were the last Bomber Command Stirlings to carry out a bombing operation. It is believed that Stirling LK 396, piloted by Flying Officer J. J. McKee, an Australian, was the last Stirling to bomb the target.

2 Hudsons carried out Resistance operations without loss.

8/9 September 1944

MINOR OPERATIONS

45 Mosquitoes to Nuremberg, 6 to Emden and 3 to Steenwijk, 13 R.C.M. sorties, 13 aircraft on Resistance operations. 1 Stirling on a Resistance flight was lost.

---

9 September 1944

LE HAVRE

272 aircraft – 230 Halifaxes, 22 Lancasters, 20 Mosquitoes – of 4, 6 and 8 Groups were dispatched but, because of poor visibility, the Master Bomber ordered the raid to be abandoned before any of the heavies bombed. No aircraft lost.

2 Wellington R.C.M. and 1 Hudson Resistance sorties were flown without loss.

9/10 September 1944

MÖNCHENGLADBACH

113 Lancasters and 24 Mosquitoes of 5 and 8 Groups carried out a devastating raid on the centre of this target without loss.

Minor Operations: 39 Mosquitoes to Brunswick and 6 to Steenwijk, 22 R.C.M. sorties, 30 Mosquito patrols. No aircraft lost.

10 September 1944

LE HAVRE

992 aircraft – 521 Lancasters, 426 Halifaxes, 45 Mosquitoes – attacked 8 different German strong points. Each target was separately marked by the Pathfinders and then accurately bombed. No aircraft lost.

8 R.C.M. and 24 Resistance sorties were flown without loss.

10/11 September 1944

MINOR OPERATIONS

47 Mosquitoes to Berlin, 11 R.C.M. sorties, 24 Mosquito patrols, 2 Lancasters minelaying off Texel. No aircraft lost.

11 September 1944

LE HAVRE

218 aircraft – 105 Halifaxes, 103 Lancasters, 10 Mosquitoes – of 4, 5, 6 and 8 Groups attacked German positions outside Le Havre. The bombing was carried out accurately in conditions of good visibility but the Master Bomber ordered the final wave to cease bombing because of smoke and dust. 171 aircraft bombed; none were lost.

Two British divisions were now making an attack on Le Havre and the German garrison surrendered a few hours later, but the port was not cleared for Allied use until several weeks later because of German mining and demolitions.

SYNTHETIC-OIL PLANTS

379 aircraft – 205 Halifaxes, 154 Lancasters, 20 Mosquitoes – carried out attacks on the Castrop-Rauxel, Kamen and Gelsenkirchen (Nordstern) plants. The first 2 targets were clearly visible and were accurately bombed but the Nordstern plant was partially protected by a smoke-screen which hindered bombing and prevented observation of the results.

The 3 forces were escorted by 26 squadrons of fighters – 20 squadrons of Spitfires and 3 each of Mustangs and Tempests. No German fighters were encountered. 5 Halifaxes of 4 Group and 2 Pathfinder Lancasters were lost from the Nordstern raid and 1 Lancaster was lost from each of the other raids. These losses were caused by Flak or by 'friendly' bombs.

Minor Operations: 5 R.C.M. sorties, 19 aircraft on Resistance operations. No losses.

11/12 September 1944

DARMSTADT

226 Lancasters and 14 Mosquitoes of 5 Group. 12 Lancasters lost, 5·3 per cent of the Lancaster force.

A previous 5 Group attack in August had failed to harm Darmstadt but, in clear weather conditions, the group's marking methods produced an outstandingly accurate and concentrated raid on this almost intact city of 120,000 people. A fierce fire area was created in the centre and in the districts immediately south and east of

41. Messages about dead and bombed-out relatives on the steel door of a German air-raid shelter.

42. Mobile cookers – traditionally called *Gulaschkanonen* in Germany – provide emergency meals for bombed-out air-raid victims.

the centre. Property damage in this area was almost complete. Casualties were very heavy. The deaths of 8,433 people were actually reported to police stations. This figure was made up of: German civilians – 1,766 men, 2,742 women and 2,129 children, 936 service personnel, 492 foreign workers and 368 prisoners of war. The United States Strategic Bombing Survey,* which quotes these figures, adds that the actual death figure may have been 5,000 more, because many deaths were not immediately reported by the 49,200 homeless people who were evacuated from Darmstadt, most of whom did not return until after the war, if at all. A present-day Darmstadt city guide says: '12,300 dead, 70,000 homeless.'

The Darmstadt raid, with its extensive fire destruction and its heavy casualties, was held by the Germans to be an extreme example of R.A.F. 'terror bombing' and is still a sensitive subject because of the absence of any major industries in the city. Bomber Command defended the raid by pointing out the railway communications passing through Darmstadt; the directive for the offensive against German communications had not yet been issued to Bomber Command, although advance notice of the directive may have been received. Darmstadt was simply one of Germany's medium-sized cities of lesser importance which succumbed to Bomber Command's improving area-attack techniques in the last months of the war when many of the larger cities were no longer worth bombing.

Minor Operations: 47 Mosquitoes to Berlin and 7 to Steenwijk, 13 R.C.M. sorties, 44 Mosquito patrols, 76 Halifaxes and Lancasters minelaying in the Kattegat. 3 Lancaster minelayers and 1 Mosquito lost on the Berlin raid.

---

* *Effects of City Raids, Darmstadt*, p. 9a.

12 September 1944

SYNTHETIC-OIL PLANTS

412 aircraft – 315 Halifaxes, 75 Lancasters, 22 Mosquitoes – of 4, 6 and 8 Groups attacked plants at Dortmund, Scholven/Buer and Wanne-Eickel. The Dortmund raid was particularly successful, but smoke-screens prevented observation of results at the other targets. 7 aircraft were lost – 3 Lancasters and 1 Halifax from the Wanne-Eickel raid and 2 Halifaxes and 1 Lancaster from the Scholven raid.

MÜNSTER

119 Halifaxes of 4 Group and 5 Pathfinder Lancasters carried out the first raid by R.A.F. heavies on Münster since June 1943. 2 Halifaxes were lost.

Many fires were seen but smoke prevented an accurate assessment of the bombing results. A brief report from Münster describes a 'sea of fire' in the southern part of the town which could not be entered for several hours and tells of water mains destroyed by high-explosive bombs so that 'the firemen could only stand helpless in front of the flames'. 144 people died.

Minor Operations: 9 R.C.M. sorties, 2 aircraft on Resistance operations. No losses.

12/13 September 1944

FRANKFURT

378 Lancasters and 9 Mosquitoes of 1, 3 and 8 Groups on the last major R.A.F. raid of the war against Frankfurt. 17 Lancasters lost, 4·5 per cent of the Lancaster force.

The local report says that the raid occurred when many of the city's firemen and rescue workers were away working in Darmstadt. The bombing caused severe destruction in the western districts of the city, which contained many industrial premises. Property damage was extensive. A troop train was hit at the West Station. 469 people were killed, including 172 inside a public shelter in the Bockenheim district, the 2-metre-thick concrete side wall of which was blown in by a high-explosive bomb. The last fires were not extinguished until the evening of the 15th.

The next entry in the Frankfurt diary, for mid-September, says that members of the Hitler Youth, the Reichsarbeitsdienst (a labour service) and the Organisation Todt were being sent to work on the strengthening of the *Westwall* (Siegfried Line) fortifications, a sign that Allied troops were approaching the German homeland.

STUTTGART

204 Lancasters and 13 Mosquitoes of 1 and 5 Groups. 4 Lancasters lost.

Our local Stuttgart expert, Heinz Bardua, writes that 'the northern and western parts of the centre were erased' in this concentrated attack and that a firestorm occurred. Several valuable cultural buildings were destroyed, including the Schloss Rosenstein and the Prinzenbau. Other property damage was extensive, though no industrial buildings are mentioned. 1,171 people were killed, Stuttgart's highest fatal casualty figure of the war.

SUPPORT AND MINOR OPERATIONS

138 training aircraft on a diversionary sweep over the North Sea, 29 Mosquitoes to Berlin and 6 to Steenwijk, 31 R.C.M. sorties, 81 Mosquito patrols, 12 Halifaxes minelaying in Oslo harbour. 2 Halifaxes were lost, 1 from the diversionary sweep and 1 from the minelaying operation.

Total effort for the night: 901 sorties, 23 aircraft (2·6 per cent) lost.

---

13 September 1944

GELSENKIRCHEN

140 aircraft – 102 Halifaxes of 4 Group and 28 Lancasters and 10 Mosquitoes of 8 Group – attacked the Nordstern oil plant. Large explosions were seen through the smoke-screen. 2 Halifaxes lost.

OSNABRÜCK

98 Halifaxes and 20 Lancasters of 6 and 8 Groups attacked the town, with the cutting of railway communications being one of the raid's objectives. The marking and bombing were accurate but no details are available. No aircraft lost.

13 aircraft flew R.C.M. sorties without loss.

13/14 September 1944

MINOR OPERATIONS

36 Mosquitoes to Berlin and 3 to Karlsruhe, 29 R.C.M. sorties, 41 Mosquito patrols. 2 Mosquitoes lost from the Berlin raid.

---

14 September 1944

WILHELMSHAVEN

184 aircraft – 133 Halifaxes, 51 Lancasters – of 4, 6 and 8 Groups dispatched but recalled while still over the North Sea; no reason for this is given in Bomber Command records. All aircraft returned safely.

WASSENAR

35 Lancasters and 10 Mosquitoes of 3 and 8 Groups bombed 'an ammunition dump' (possibly a suspected V-2 store) near The Hague. The bombing was considered to be accurate until smoke and dust covered the target.

6 aircraft flew R.C.M. sorties without loss.

---

15 September 1944

TIRPITZ

38 Lancasters of 9 and 617 Squadrons and a 5 Group Mosquito for weather reconnaissance had set out on 11 September to fly to Northern Russia in preparation for this raid on the 45,000-ton battleship *Tirpitz*, which was at anchor in Kaa Fjord in Northern Norway. 1 aircraft returned to Britain and 6 crash-landed in Russia but their

crew members were not seriously hurt. Only 27 Lancasters and a further Lancaster with a cameraman on board were available for the raid on the *Tirpitz*, which eventually took place on 15 September. 20 aircraft were loaded with the 12,000-lb *Tallboy* bomb and 6 (or 7, the records are not clear) carried several '*Johnny Walker*' mines – of 400–500 lb weight developed for attacking capital ships moored in shallow water.

The attack caught the *Tirpitz* by surprise and her smoke-screens were late in starting. One *Tallboy* hit the *Tirpitz* near the bows and caused considerable damage. The shock caused by the explosion of this bomb, or possibly from other bombs which were near misses, also damaged the battleship's engines. The Germans decided that repairs to make *Tirpitz* fully seaworthy were not practicable and she was later moved to an anchorage further south in Norway, but only for use as a semi-static heavy-artillery battery. These results of the raid were not known in England at the time and further raids against *Tirpitz* would take place.

None of the Lancasters were shot down on the raid and all returned safely to the airfield in Russia but the 617 Squadron aircraft of Flying Officer F. Levy crashed in Norway while returning to Lossiemouth 2 days later with 11 men on board.

(This raid, with its outward and return transit flights across enemy-held territory and its Mosquito weather flights, is counted as 97 operational sorties in the statistical résumé of this diary and the aircraft lost are estimated as 11 – 1 crashed in Norway and 10 crash-landed or abandoned in Russia.)

9 R.C.M. sorties and 1 Resistance operation flight were also carried out on 15 September without loss.

15/16 September 1944

KIEL

490 aircraft – 310 Lancasters, 173 Halifaxes, 7 Mosquitoes – of 1, 4, 6 and 8 Groups. 4 Halifaxes and 2 Lancasters lost.

The evidence of returning crews and of photographs caused Bomber Command to record this as 'a highly concentrated raid' with 'the old town and modern shopping centre devastated'. The local report confirms this as a heavy attack, and records damage in the centre and port areas, but describes how much of the bombing fell outside Kiel. Unusually low numbers of 12 deaths and 28 people injured were recorded.

SUPPORT AND MINOR OPERATIONS

164 aircraft on a diversionary sweep over the North Sea, 27 Mosquitoes to Berlin, 9 to Lübeck and 8 to Rheine airfield, 34 R.C.M. sorties, 56 Mosquito patrols, 68 Halifaxes and Lancasters minelaying near Oslo, in the Kattegat and in the River Elbe. 5 aircraft lost – 3 Mosquitoes and 1 Stirling of 100 Group and 1 Mosquito from the Berlin raid.

Total effort for the night: 856 sorties, 11 aircraft (1·3 per cent) lost.

---

16 September 1944

MINOR OPERATIONS

9 aircraft on R.C.M. flights, 2 Mosquitoes on Ranger patrols, 14 Stirlings and 4 Hudsons on Resistance operations. No aircraft lost.

16/17 September 1944

OPERATION *MARKET GARDEN*

Bomber Command's main operations on this night were in support of the landings by British and American airborne troops at Arnhem and Nijmegen which took place the following morning.

200 Lancasters and 23 Mosquitoes of 1 and 8 Groups bombed the airfields at Hopsten, Leeuwarden, Steenwijk and Rheine, and 54 Lancasters and 5 Mosquitoes of 3 and 8 Groups bombed a Flak position at Moerdijk. The runways of all the airfields were well cratered but there were only near misses at the Flak position, although its approach road was cut. 2 Lancasters lost from the Moerdijk raid.

Minor Operations: 29 Mosquitoes to Brunswick and 4 to Dortmund, 14 R.C.M. sorties, 29 Mosquito patrols. 1 Mosquito lost from the Brunswick raid.

17 September 1944

BOULOGNE

762 aircraft – 370 Lancasters, 351 Halifaxes, 41 Mosquitoes – dropped more than 3,000 tons of bombs on German positions around Boulogne in preparation for an attack by Allied troops. The German garrison surrendered soon afterwards. 1 Halifax and 1 Lancaster lost.

OPERATION *MARKET GARDEN*

112 Lancasters and 20 Mosquitoes of 1 and 8 Groups attacked German Flak positions in the Flushing area without loss.

EIKENHORST

27 Lancasters and 5 Mosquitoes of 1 and 8 Groups attacked a V-1 rocket depot without loss.

Minor Operations: 9 R.C.M. sorties, 6 Mosquito patrols, 10 Stirlings and 1 Hudson on Resistance operations. No losses.

Total effort for the day: 952 sorties, 2 aircraft (0·2 per cent) lost.

17/18 September 1944

OPERATION *MARKET GARDEN*

241 aircraft made 2 diversionary sweeps – 1 to the Dutch coast and 1 into Holland – in order to draw up German fighters from Southern Holland. This intention was not achieved. No aircraft lost.

Minor Operations: 42 Mosquitoes to Bremen and 6 to Dortmund, 29 R.C.M. sorties, 29 Mosquito patrols. No aircraft lost.

18 September 1944

WALCHEREN

74 aircraft – 34 Lancasters, 30 Halifaxes, 10 Mosquitoes – of 6 and 8 Groups attempted to bomb a coastal battery at Domburg but the Master Bomber abandoned the raid after 8 Mosquitoes had attempted to mark the target in poor weather conditions. No aircraft lost.

7 R.C.M. sorties were flown without loss.

18/19 September 1944

BREMERHAVEN

206 Lancasters and 7 Mosquitoes of 5 Group. 100 Group's R.C.M. operations successfully kept German night fighters away from the force and only 1 Lancaster and 1 Mosquito were lost.

This was another successful 5 Group method raid and Bremerhaven, which had not been seriously bombed by the R.A.F. before, required only this one knock-out blow by the comparatively small force of aircraft carrying fewer than 900 tons of bombs. The centre of the town, the port area and the suburb of Geestemünde were gutted by fire. 2,670 buildings were destroyed and 369 seriously damaged. 30,000 people lost their homes; the local report says that, fortunately, the weather remained warm and the many people who had to sleep in the open for several nights until they were evacuated did not suffer too much from exposure. 618 people were killed and 1,193 were injured, the latter putting a severe strain on the only hospital left intact.

Minor Operations: 33 Mosquitoes to Berlin and 6 to Rheine, 30 R.C.M. sorties, 67 Mosquito patrols, 4 Lancasters minelaying in the River Weser. No losses.

---

19 September 1944

WALCHEREN

56 aircraft – 28 Lancasters, 27 Halifaxes, 1 Mosquito – of 6 and 8 Groups set out to attack the Domburg coastal battery but were recalled. 1 Halifax crashed in England.

There were 8 R.C.M. sorties and 6 Hudsons and 4 Stirlings flew Resistance operations without loss.

19/20 September 1944

MÖNCHENGLADBACH/RHEYDT

227 Lancasters and 10 Mosquitoes of 1 and 5 Groups to these twin towns. 4 Lancasters and 1 Mosquito lost. Bomber Command claimed severe damage to both towns, particularly to Mönchengladbach. The only report from Germany states that between 267 and 271 people were killed in Mönchengladbach.

The Master Bomber for this raid was Wing Commander Guy Gibson, V.C., D.S.O., D.F.C., flying a 627 Squadron Mosquito from Coningsby, where he was serving as Base Operations Officer. Gibson's instructions over the target were heard throughout the raid and gave no hint of trouble, but his aircraft crashed – in flames according to a Dutch eyewitness – before crossing the coast of Holland for the homeward flight over the North Sea. There were no German fighter claims for the Mosquito; it may have been damaged by Flak over the target or on the return flight, or it may have developed engine trouble. It was possibly flying too low for the crew to escape by parachute. Gibson and his navigator, Squadron Leader J. B. Warwick, D.F.C., were both killed and were buried in the Roman Catholic Cemetery at Steenbergen-en-Kruisland, 13 km north of Bergen-op-Zoom. Theirs are the only graves of Allied servicemen in the cemetery.

Aircraft of 100 Group flew 15 R.C.M. and 17 Mosquito sorties without loss.

---

20 September 1944

CALAIS

646 aircraft – 437 Lancasters, 169 Halifaxes, 40 Mosquitoes – attacked German positions around Calais. Visibility was good and the bombing was accurate and concentrated. 1 Lancaster lost.

Minor Operations: 7 R.C.M. sorties, 5 Hudsons and 2 Lysanders on Resistance operations. No losses.

20/21 September 1944

100 Group Operations

2 Mosquitoes and 1 Fortress took off but were quickly recalled because of the widespread fog in England which prevented major operations being mounted.

---

21 September 1944

Minor Operations

2 Fortresses and 2 Wellingtons on R.C.M. sorties and 12 Stirlings and 1 Hudson on Resistance operations. No aircraft lost. Bad weather – rain and low cloud – prevented any major operation during the next 48 hours.

---

22 September 1944

7 aircraft of 100 Group flew signals investigation patrols without loss.

22/23 September 1944

9 R.C.M. sorties and 5 Mosquito Intruder patrols were flown without loss.

---

23 September 1944

WALCHEREN

50 aircraft – 34 Halifaxes, 10 Mosquitoes, 6 Lancasters – of 1 and 6 Groups carried

out a good attack on the Domburg coastal batteries without loss. One particularly large explosion was seen.

Minor Operations: 6 R.C.M. sorties, 2 Mosquitoes on Ranger patrols, 5 Hudsons on Resistance operations. No losses.

23/24 September 1944

NEUSS

549 aircraft – 378 Lancasters, 154 Halifaxes, 17 Mosquitoes – of 1, 3, 4 and 8 Groups. 5 Lancasters and 2 Halifaxes lost. Bomber Command's report states that most of the bombing fell in the dock and factory areas. A short local report only says that 617 houses and 14 public buildings were destroyed or seriously damaged, and that 289 people were killed and 150 injured.

DORTMUND–EMS CANAL

136 Lancasters and 5 Mosquitoes of 5 Group to bomb the banks of the 2 parallel branches of the canal at a point near Ladbergen, north of Münster, where the level of the canal water was well above the level of the surrounding land. Despite the presence of 7/10ths cloud in the target area, breaches were made in the banks of both branches of the canal and a 6-mile stretch of it was drained. Most of this damage was caused by 2 direct hits by 12,000-lb *Tallboy* bombs dropped by aircraft of 617 Squadron at the opening of the raid.

14 Lancasters – more than 10 per cent of the Lancaster force – were lost.

MÜNSTER/HANDORF AIRFIELD

113 aircraft – 107 Lancasters, 5 Mosquitoes, 1 Lightning – of 5 Group carried out a supporting raid on the local German night-fighter airfield just outside Münster. 1 Lancaster lost. No photographic reconnaissance flight was carried out after this raid. Some of the bombs fell in Münster itself; the town records 100 high-explosive bombs but no fatal casualties.

Minor Operations: 38 Mosquitoes to Bochum and 6 to Rheine night-fighter airfield, 31 R.C.M. sorties, 45 Mosquito patrols. No aircraft lost.

Total effort for the night: 923 sorties, 22 aircraft (2·4 per cent) lost.

---

24 September 1944

CALAIS

188 aircraft – 101 Lancasters, 62 Halifaxes, 25 Mosquitoes. The German positions were completely covered by cloud at 2,000 ft and only 126 aircraft bombed. Most of these bombed *Oboe*-aimed sky-markers, but some aircraft came below cloud to bomb visually and 7 Lancasters and 1 Halifax were shot down by light Flak, which was very accurate at such a height.

2 Hudsons flew Resistance operations without loss.

25 September 1944

CALAIS

872 aircraft – 430 Lancasters, 397 Halifaxes, 45 Mosquitoes – were again sent to bomb German defensive positions but encountered low cloud. Only 287 aircraft were able to bomb, through breaks in the cloud. No aircraft lost.

PETROL-CARRYING

70 Halifaxes of 4 Group started a series of flights to carry petrol in jerricans from England to airfields in Belgium, in order to alleviate the severe fuel shortage being experienced by Allied ground forces. 4 Group would fly 435 such sorties during an 8-day period. Each Halifax carried about 165 jerricans, approximately 750 gallons of petrol, on each flight. The total amount of petrol lifted during the period was approximately 325,000 gallons, about the same amount of fuel that the Halifaxes themselves consumed. No aircraft were lost during these operations.

Minor Operations: 4 R.C.M. sorties, 5 Hudsons on Resistance operations. No losses.

Total effort for the day: 951 sorties, no losses.

25/26 September 1944

MINOR OPERATIONS

48 Mosquitoes to Mannheim and 4 to a chemical factory at Höchst, just west of Frankfurt, 3 R.C.M. sorties, 30 Mosquito patrols. 1 Mosquito lost from the Mannheim raid.

26 September 1944

CALAIS AREA

722 aircraft – 388 Lancasters, 289 Halifaxes, 45 Mosquitoes – carried out 2 separate raids. 531 aircraft were dispatched to 4 targets at Cap Gris Nez and 191 aircraft to 3 targets near Calais. Accurate and concentrated bombing was observed at all targets. 2 Lancasters lost.

Minor Operations: 5 R.C.M. sorties, 2 Ranger patrols, 5 Hudsons on Resistance operations, 74 Halifaxes on petrol-carrying flights. No aircraft lost.

Total effort for the day: 808 sorties, 2 aircraft (0·2 per cent) lost.

26/27 September 1944

KARLSRUHE

226 Lancasters and 11 Mosquitoes of 1 and 5 Groups. 2 Lancasters lost.
 Bomber Command claimed a concentrated attack, with a large area of the city

devastated. A short local report says that there was damage throughout Karlsruhe, mentions damage to the Schloss, the Rathaus, the Orangerie, the Stefanskirche and the Kunsthalle, but gives no statistics other than a vague estimate of 50 people killed.

Minor Operations: 50 Mosquitoes to Frankfurt and 6 to Hamburg, 26 R.C.M. sorties, 50 Mosquito patrols. No aircraft lost.

---

27 September 1944

CALAIS AREA

341 aircraft – 222 Lancasters, 84 Halifaxes, 35 Mosquitoes – of 1, 3, 4 and 8 Groups. The target areas were covered by cloud but the Master Bomber brought the force below this to bomb visually. The attacks on the various German positions were accurate and only 1 Lancaster was lost.

BOTTROP

175 aircraft – 96 Halifaxes, 71 Lancasters, 8 Mosquitoes – of 6 and 8 Groups attacked the Ruhroel A.G. synthetic-oil plant in the Welheim suburb of Bottrop. The target was almost entirely cloud-covered and most of the bombing was aimed at *Oboe* sky-markers, although a few aircraft were able to bomb through small breaks in the cloud. Explosions and black smoke were seen. No aircraft lost.

STERKRADE

171 aircraft – 143 Halifaxes, 21 Lancasters, 7 Mosquitoes – of 6 and 8 Groups attempted to bomb the Sterkrade oil plant. Only 83 aircraft bombed the main target, through thick cloud; 53 aircraft bombed alternative targets, most of them aiming at the approximate position of Duisburg. No aircraft lost.

Minor Operations: 6 R.C.M. sorties, 5 Hudsons on Resistance operations, 73 Halifaxes on petrol-carrying flights. No aircraft lost.

Total effort for the day: 771 sorties, 1 aircraft (0·1 per cent) lost.

27/28 September 1944

KAISERSLAUTERN

217 Lancasters and 10 Mosquitoes of 1 and 5 Groups in the only major raid carried out by Bomber Command during the war on this medium-sized target. 1 Lancaster and 1 Mosquito lost.

909 tons of bombs were dropped in an accurate raid and widespread destruction was caused; the post-war British Bombing Survey Unit estimated that 36 per cent of the town's built-up area was destroyed. The local report complains that the town was not a military objective but then lists the typical catalogue of small factories, public buildings, churches, etc. destroyed or seriously damaged, which larger German communities had long got used to being hit in area-bombing raids. The report concludes with the statement that 144 people, predominantly women and children died, *'der meist lebendig verbrannten Opfer'* – 'victims mostly burnt alive'.

Minor Operations: 46 Mosquitoes to Kassel, 6 to Aschaffenburg and 6 to Heilbronn, 12 R.C.M. sorties, 27 Mosquito patrols. No aircraft lost.

---

28 September 1944

CALAIS AREA

494 aircraft – 230 Lancasters, 214 Halifaxes, 50 Mosquitoes – of 1, 3, 6 and 8 Groups to attack 4 German positions at Calais and 6 battery positions at Cap Gris Nez; approximately 50 aircraft were allocated to each position. Only 68 aircraft bombed at Calais before the Master Bomber cancelled the raid because of worsening cloud conditions and only 198 (from 301) aircraft bombed at Cap Gris Nez. No aircraft were lost. Calais surrendered to the Canadian Army soon after this raid and all the French Channel ports were thus in Allied hands, although most of the facilities required extensive clearance and repair. This, and the continuing presence of German troops along the River Scheldt between Antwerp and the sea, would cause the Allied ground forces serious supply difficulties for several more weeks.

Minor Operations: 2 Liberators and 2 Wellingtons on signals investigation patrols, 10 Hudsons and 2 Lysanders on Resistance operations, 75 Halifaxes on petrol-carrying flights. No aircraft lost.

Total effort for the day: 585 sorties, no aircraft losses.

28/29 September 1944

MINOR OPERATIONS

44 Mosquitoes to Brunswick, 5 to Heilbronn and 4 to Aschaffenburg, 43 R.C.M. sorties, 52 Mosquito patrols. 1 Mosquito Intruder lost.

---

29 September 1944

MINOR OPERATIONS

3 Liberators and 2 Wellingtons on R.C.M. sorties, 3 Lysanders on Resistance operations, 72 Halifaxes on petrol-carrying flights. 1 Lysander lost.

29/30 September 1944

MINOR OPERATIONS

40 Mosquitoes to Karlsruhe, 25 R.C.M. sorties, 42 Mosquito patrols, 15 Lancasters minelaying in the Kattegat and off Heligoland. No aircraft lost.

---

30 September 1944

STERKRADE

139 aircraft – 108 Halifaxes, 21 Lancasters, 10 Mosquitoes – of 4 and 8 Groups

attempted to attack the oil plant but the target was cloud-covered. Only 24 aircraft attacked the main target; other aircraft bombed the general town area of Sterkrade. 1 Halifax lost.

BOTTROP

136 aircraft – 101 Halifaxes, 25 Lancasters, 10 Mosquitoes – of 6 and 8 Groups encountered similar conditions at this target. Only 1 aircraft attempted to bomb the oil plant; the remainder of the force bombed the estimated positions of various Ruhr cities. No aircraft lost.

Minor Operations: 3 R.C.M. sorties, 2 Ranger patrols (flown from a forward airfield in France), 6 Hudsons on Resistance operations, 74 Halifaxes on petrol-carrying flights. The two Ranger aircraft, from 515 Squadron, were lost; they both force-landed in Switzerland.

---

30 September/1 October 1944

MINOR OPERATIONS

46 Mosquitoes to Hamburg, 6 each to Aschaffenburg and Heilbronn and 5 to Sterkrade, 1 R.C.M. sortie, 20 Mosquito patrols, 14 aircraft on Resistance operations. 1 Mosquito of 100 Group lost.

Hans Brunswig's history of raids on Hamburg* describes an incident in the raid by *'die berüchtigten Mosquitos'* – 'the notorious Mosquitoes'. Hamburg had a huge, above-ground multi-storey concrete air-raid shelter close to the centre of the city. When the Flak battery situated on top of the bunker opened fire and the first bomb fell near by, the crowd of people waiting to enter the bunker panicked; 7 people were trampled to death and further deaths were caused by the collapse of some scaffolding in the shelter, and then even more by bomb splinters. Total casualties at this place were 30 dead and 75 injured. 73 other people were killed in the city by the Mosquito raid that night and more than 2,000 were bombed out. Mosquitoes carried out dozens of raids similar to this in the last year of the war; the results of this raid just happened to be available.

---

1 October 1944

MINOR OPERATIONS

2 Liberators and 1 Wellington on signals investigation patrols, 6 Hudsons on Resistance operations, 73 Halifaxes on petrol-carrying flights. No aircraft lost.

1/2 October 1944

MINOR OPERATIONS

48 Mosquitoes to Brunswick, 8 each to Heilbronn and Krefeld and 6 each to Dortmund and Koblenz, 2 R.C.M. sorties. No aircraft lost.

---

* *Feuersturm über Hamburg*, op. cit., p. 340.

2 October 1944

MINOR OPERATIONS

3 Liberators and 2 Wellingtons on signals investigation patrols, 8 Hudsons on Resistance operations, 71 Halifaxes on petrol-carrying flights. No aircraft lost.

2/3 October 1944

MINOR OPERATIONS

34 Mosquitoes to Brunswick, 7 to Pforzheim and 4 each to Dortmund and Frankfurt, 3 R.C.M. sorties, 39 Mosquito patrols, 1 aircraft on a Resistance operation. No aircraft lost.

3 October 1944

WALCHEREN

252 Lancasters and 7 Mosquitoes commenced the attack on the sea walls of Walcheren island. Coastal gun batteries at Walcheren dominated the approaches to the port of Antwerp, whose facilities could handle 40,000 tons per day of much-needed supplies when ships could safely use the approaches. The intention was to flood the island, most of which was reclaimed *polder* below sea level. The flooding would submerge some of the gun batteries and also hamper the German defence against eventual ground attack.

The target for this first raid was the sea wall at Westkapelle, the most western point of Walcheren. The main bombing force was composed of 8 waves, each of 30 Lancasters, with marking provided by *Oboe* Mosquitoes and Pathfinder Lancasters, with the whole operation being controlled by a Master Bomber. The attack went well and a great mass of high-explosive bombs, mainly 1,000- and 500-pounders but with some 4,000-pounders, forced a gap during the fifth wave of the attack. Later waves widened the breach until the sea was pouring in through a gap estimated to be 100 yards wide. 8 Lancasters of 617 Squadron which were standing by were not needed and carried their valuable *Tallboy* bombs back to England. No aircraft were lost from this successful operation.

Minor operations: 6 R.C.M. sorties, 5 Hudsons on Resistance operations. No losses.

3/4 October 1944

MINOR OPERATIONS

43 Mosquitoes to Kassel, 6 each to Aschaffenburg and Pforzheim, 5 to Münster and 4 to Kamen, 1 R.C.M. sortie, 19 Intruder patrols. No aircraft lost.

4 October 1944

BERGEN

German U-boats had been forced out of the Biscay ports following the Allied liberation of France and Bergen was one of several Norwegian ports now being used as the forward operating bases for the U-boats. The pens at Bergen were being enlarged, with an influx of German technicians and a large labour force. 93 Halifaxes and 47 Lancasters of 6 and 8 Groups were dispatched to attack Bergen, most of the aircraft being allocated to the pens but 14 Halifaxes and 6 Lancasters were ordered to bomb individual U-boats known to be moored in the harbour. 12 Mosquitoes of 100 Group acted as a long-range fighter escort.

The raid appeared to be successful and only 1 Lancaster was lost. A detailed report from the city of Bergen supplies the actual results. 7 bombs hit the U-boat pens, causing little structural damage because of the thickness of the concrete roof, but the electrical-wiring system in the pens was completely put out of action. Nearby ship-repair yards were seriously damaged. 3 U-boats were damaged by the bombing but they did not sink. 3 other small ships were hit; two of them sank and the third, the German auxiliary *Schwabenland*, had to be put in dry dock for repair.

But, as so often in raids on targets in the Occupied Countries, the bombing spread to civilian areas. The local report continues: 'As regards civilian casualties and damage, the raid is still remembered with horror. Bergen suffered little damage in comparison with other occupied towns and cities in Europe but the raid of 4th October was the worst of the war for us.' 60 houses were destroyed or so badly damaged that they had to be demolished; 600 people lost their homes. Civilian casualties are recorded at only 2 places but they were tragic. A school, opened only that day after a break, received a direct hit in the basement where 2 classes were sheltering; 60 children, 2 teachers and 17 air-raid workers in the same shelter were killed. Another shelter, at a nearby factory, was also hit and a further 34 people were killed and about 100 were injured there. 7 of the dead Norwegians were members of the local Resistance Movement. The Germans admitted the deaths of 12 of their own men.

2 Wellingtons and 1 Liberator flew R.C.M. sorties without loss.

4/5 October 1944

MINOR OPERATIONS

6 Mosquitoes to Pforzheim and 5 to Heilbronn, 4 R.C.M. sorties, 36 Mosquito patrols, 47 Lancasters and 31 Halifaxes minelaying off Oslo and in the Kattegat, 15 aircraft on Resistance operations. 4 aircraft were lost: 1 Mosquito from the Heilbronn raid and 2 Lancasters and 1 Halifax from the minelaying operations.

---

5 October 1944

WILHELMSHAVEN

227 Lancasters and 1 Mosquito of 5 Group attempted to bomb Wilhelmshaven through 10/10ths cloud. Marking and bombing were all based on *H2S* and the raid appeared to be scattered. 18 Lancasters did not join in the main attack but bombed a group of ships seen through a break in the cloud over the sea. Wilhelmshaven's diary only states that 12 people died. 1 Lancaster lost.

Minor Operations: 5 R.C.M. sorties, 5 aircraft on Resistance operations. No losses.

5/6 October 1944

SAARBRÜCKEN

531 Lancasters and 20 Mosquitoes of 1, 3 and 8 Groups on the first major R.A.F. raid to this target since September 1942. 3 Lancasters lost.

The raid was made at the request of the American Third Army which was advancing in this direction; the intention was to cut the railways and block supply routes generally through the town. The bombing was accurate and severe damage was caused in the main town area north of the River Saar, the area through which the main railway lines ran. Damage was particularly severe in the *Altstadt* and Malstatt districts. 5,882 houses were destroyed and 1,141 were seriously damaged. 344 people were killed, a figure which suggests that much of the population may have been evacuated from this town, which was situated right on the Siegfried Line.

Minor Operations: 20 Mosquitoes to Berlin and 26 to 5 other German targets, 36 R.C.M. sorties, 47 Mosquito patrols, 10 Halifaxes minelaying off Heligoland and 9 Mosquitoes of 8 Group minelaying in the Kiel Canal. No aircraft lost.

---

6 October 1944

SYNTHETIC-OIL PLANTS

320 aircraft – 254 Halifaxes of 4 Group and 46 Lancasters and 20 Mosquitoes of 8 Group – attacked the plants at Sterkrade and Scholven/Buer. Both raids took place in clear conditions and the bombing was considered to be accurate. 9 aircraft were lost – 4 Halifaxes and 2 Lancasters at Scholven and 3 Halifaxes at Sterkrade.

4 Liberators and 3 Wellingtons flew signals investigation patrols without loss.

6/7 October 1944

DORTMUND

523 aircraft – 248 Halifaxes, 247 Lancasters, 28 Mosquitoes – of 3, 6 and 8 Groups. 6 Group provided 293 aircraft – 248 Halifaxes and 45 Lancasters, the greatest effort by the Canadian group in the war. This raid opened a phase which some works refer to as 'The Second Battle of the Ruhr'. 5 aircraft – 2 Halifaxes (of 6 Group), 2 Lancasters and 1 Mosquito – lost, less than 1 per cent of the force raiding this Ruhr target on a clear night.

The Pathfinder marking and the bombing were both accurate and severe damage was caused, particularly to the industrial and transportation areas of the city, although residential areas also suffered badly. Civilian casualties were 191 dead, 38 missing and 418 injured.

BREMEN

246 Lancasters and 7 Mosquitoes of 1 and 5 Groups carried out the last of 32 major Bomber Command raids on this target during the war. 5 Lancasters lost.

The raid, based on the 5 Group marking method, was an outstanding success. 1,021 tons of bombs were dropped, of which 868 tons were incendiaries. A detailed local report is available. The local official who compiled this report after the war writes that the night was so clear, with a three-quarters-full moon, that, 'Bremen lay before the bombers like a presentation dish ... the bomb aimers could not have wished for better conditions to carry out their task'. A huge fire area was started throughout the town centre and the surrounding areas but the effects of this were lessened by the extensive property damage caused in this area by the Bomber Command raid of 18/19 August. Classed as destroyed or seriously damaged were: 4,859 houses, 5 churches, 1 hospital, 18 schools and 16 public and historic buildings. Casualties were: 65 killed – a figure which again suggests many evacuations – 766 injured and 37,724 bombed out. Severe damage was also caused to the A.G. Weser shipyard, the two Focke-Wulf factories, the Siemens Schuckert electrical works and other important war industries. The 'transport network' was described as being seriously disrupted. (It is interesting to note the increased efficiency and hence destructive power of Bomber Command at this time. Bremen – with its shipyards and aircraft factories – had been the target for many carefully planned Bomber Command raids earlier in the war and was the target for one of the much publicized 1942 1,000-bomber raids. Now this raid by no more than a quarter of the total strength of Bomber Command, hardly mentioned in the history books, had finished off Bremen and this city need not be attacked by Bomber Command again.)

Two days later the *Bremer Zeitung* published this passage in typical German propaganda style: 'But we know that we must bear all misfortunes with courage, since this is the best way we can contribute to a speedy victory, a victory which will repay us for the blows we have suffered. A victory which will also see the walls of Bremen duly rebuilt providing us with a future in freedom within a new abode.'

Minor Operations: 22 Mosquitoes to Berlin, 11 to Ludwigshafen and 2 to Saarbrücken, 35 R.C.M. sorties, 76 Mosquito patrols, 19 aircraft minelaying off Texel and Heligoland and in the River Weser, 6 aircraft on Resistance operations. 2 Mosquitoes were lost – 1 from the Berlin raid and 1 *Serrate* aircraft.

Total effort for the night: 947 sorties, 12 aircraft (1·3 per cent) lost.

---

7 October 1944

KLEVE

351 aircraft – 251 Halifaxes, 90 Lancasters, 10 Mosquitoes – of 3, 4 and 8 Groups to bomb this small German town which, together with Emmerich, stood on the approach routes by which German units could threaten the vulnerable Allied right flank near Nijmegen which had been left exposed by the failure of Operation *Market Garden*. Visibility was clear and the centre and north of the town were heavily bombed, although some crews bombed too early and their loads actually fell in Holland near Nijmegen. 2 Halifaxes lost.

EMMERICH

340 Lancasters and 10 Mosquitoes of 1, 3 and 8 Groups carried out an even more accurate attack on Emmerich. 3 Lancasters were lost. A local report says that 2,424 buildings in the town were destroyed and 689 damaged, with 680,000 cubic metres of rubble having to be cleared away after the raid. 641 German civilians and 96 soldiers were killed.

WALCHEREN

121 Lancasters and 2 Mosquitoes of 5 Group continued the attack, without any aircraft losses, on the sea walls which were breached near Flushing.

The Kembs Dam

This was another 617 Squadron special operation. The Kembs Dam on the Rhine, just north of Basle, held back a vast quantity of water and it was feared that the Germans would release this to flood the Rhine valley near Mulhouse, a few miles north, should the American and French troops in that area attempt an advance. 617 Squadron was asked to destroy the lock gates of the dam. 13 Lancasters were dispatched. 7 aircraft were to bomb from 8,000 ft and draw the Flak, while the other 6 would come in below 1,000 ft and attempt to place their *Tallboys*, with delayed fuzes, alongside the gates. American Mustang fighters would attempt to suppress Flak positions during the attack. The operation went according to plan. The gates were destroyed but 2 Lancasters from the low force were shot down by Flak.

Minor Operations: 5 R.C.M. sorties, 2 Ranger patrols, 2 Hudsons on Resistance operations. No aircraft lost.

Total effort for the day: 846 sorties, 7 aircraft (0·8 per cent) lost.

7/8 October 1944

FEINT ATTACK

46 aircraft of 100 Group flew an operation in which various electronic devices and *Window* were used in an attempt to lure the German night-fighter force into the air to waste its fuel. The feint was made in the direction of Bremen, using the same route as had been used in the raid carried out the previous night. Radio listening stations in England heard the German controllers plotting the supposed force 'vigorously', but few night fighters were scrambled. Mosquito Intruders and *Serrate* aircraft, which were part of the 100 Group force, then flew on towards Bremen and claimed an Me 110 destroyed and a Ju 88 damaged. 1 further R.C.M. Halifax flew a signals listening patrol. No aircraft were lost on this night.

---

8 October 1944

Minor Operations

2 Mosquitoes flew Ranger patrols over Schleswig-Holstein and Denmark, shooting down an Me 109 in Schleswig-Holstein; 1 Wellington flew a signals patrol. No aircraft lost.

---

9 October 1944

2 Liberators and 2 Wellingtons flew uneventful signals patrols.

9/10 October 1944

BOCHUM

435 aircraft – 375 Halifaxes, 40 Lancasters, 20 Mosquitoes – of 1, 4, 6 and 8 Groups. 4 Halifaxes and 1 Lancaster lost.

This raid was not successful. The target area was covered by cloud and the bombing was scattered. The local report says that there was some damage in the southern districts of Bochum, with 140 houses destroyed or seriously damaged and approximately 150 people killed.

Minor Operations: 47 Mosquitoes to Wilhelmshaven, 5 to Krefeld, 4 to Saarbrücken and 3 to Düsseldorf, 34 R.C.M. sorties, 57 Mosquito patrols. No aircraft lost.

---

10 October 1944

Minor Operations

2 Wellingtons and 1 Liberator on R.C.M. sorties, 2 Ranger patrols, 4 Hudsons and 3 Stirlings on Resistance operations. No aircraft lost.

10/11 October 1944

MINOR OPERATIONS

49 Mosquitoes to Cologne, 6 each to Aschaffenburg and Pforzheim, 5 to Duisburg and 2 to Düsseldorf, 1 Liberator on an R.C.M. sortie. No aircraft lost.

The raid by 49 Mosquitoes on Cologne, which took place through thick cloud, is not recorded in a comprehensive Cologne report and it is possible that the bombs all missed the city, but, by contrast, the 6 Mosquitoes which attacked Pforzheim caused much damage in the northern and eastern parts of the town and killed 64 people.

---

11 October 1944

RIVER SCHELDT GUN BATTERIES

160 Lancasters and 20 Mosquitoes of 1 and 8 Groups attacked the Fort Frederik Hendrik battery position at Breskens, on the south bank of the Scheldt, and 115 Lancasters of 5 Group attacked guns near Flushing on the north bank. Both attacks started well but more than half of the Breskens force had to abandon the raid because their target was covered by smoke and dust. Two large explosions were seen at Flushing. 1 Lancaster lost from the Breskens raid.

WALCHEREN

61 Lancasters and 2 Mosquitoes of 5 Group attempted to breach the sea walls at Veere on the northern coast of the island but were not successful. No aircraft lost.

Minor Operations: 3 R.C.M. sorties, 1 Ranger patrol, 2 Hudsons on Resistance operations. No losses.

11/12 October 1944

MINOR OPERATIONS

46 Mosquitoes to Berlin, 8 to Wiesbaden and 4 to Heilbronn. 1 aircraft lost from the Berlin raid.

12 October 1944

WANNE-EICKEL

111 Halifaxes and 26 Lancasters of 6 and 8 Groups attacked the oil plant. A direct hit on a storage tank early in the raid produced dense cloud and smoke which hindered later bombing. A German report says that the refinery itself was not seriously damaged but that the GAVEG chemical factory was destroyed; it is possible that the bombers were aiming at the wrong target. The report also states that 24 buildings were hit in nearby housing areas and that 103 German civilians, 2 foreign workers and 1 prisoner of war were killed, most of them being in makeshift 'earth shelters'

43. A Halifax of 6 Group attacking the Wanne-Eickel oil refinery, which is covered by smoke, on 12 October 1944.

RIVER SCHELDT GUN BATTERIES

86 Lancasters and 10 Mosquitoes of 1 and 8 Groups attacked a battery near Breskens and destroyed 2 of the 4 gun positions. No aircraft lost.

Minor Operations: 3 R.C.M. sorties, 1 Hudson on a Resistance operation. No losses.

44. A railway-mounted Flak battery on the coast. The white rings around the barrels of the main guns represent eleven R.A.F. bombers claimed as shot down by this battery – a Wellington, a Stirling, six Halifaxes and three Lancasters.

12/13 October 1944

MOSQUITO OPERATIONS

Mosquitoes went to bomb the following targets: Hamburg, 52 aircraft; Düsseldorf and Wiesbaden, 6 aircraft each; Koblenz, 4 aircraft; Schweinfurt, 2 aircraft. 1 aircraft lost from the Hamburg raid.

13 October 1944

2 Wellingtons and 1 Liberator carried out uneventful signals patrols.

13/14 October 1944

MOSQUITO OPERATIONS

57 Mosquitoes to Cologne and 4 to Stuttgart. No aircraft lost. A report from Cologne shows that bombs were scattered across the city, causing mostly minor damage. 32 people were killed, however, most of them in an old persons' home which sustained a direct hit.

14 October 1944

DUISBURG

This raid was part of a special operation which has received little mention in the history books. On 13 October, Sir Arthur Harris received the directive for Operation *Hurricane*: 'In order to demonstrate to the enemy in Germany generally the over-whelming superiority of the Allied Air Forces in this theatre . . . the intention is to apply within the shortest practical period the maximum effort of the Royal Air Force Bomber Command and the VIIIth United States Bomber Command against objec-tives in the densely populated Ruhr.' Bomber Command had probably been fore-warned of the directive because it was able to mount the first part of the operation soon after first light on 14 October. No heavy bombers had flown on operations for 48 hours and 1,013 aircraft – 519 Lancasters, 474 Halifaxes and 20 Mosquitoes – were dispatched to Duisburg with R.A.F. fighters providing an escort. 957 bombers dropped 3,574 tons of high explosive and 820 tons of incendiaries on Duisburg. 14 aircraft were lost – 13 Lancasters and 1 Halifax; it is probable that the Lancasters provided the early waves of the raid and drew the attention of the German Flak before the Flak positions were overwhelmed by the bombing.

For their part in Operation *Hurricane*, the American Eighth Air Force dispatched 1,251 heavy bombers escorted by 749 fighters. More than 1,000 of the American heavies bombed targets in the Cologne area. American casualties were 5 heavy bombers and 1 fighter. No Luftwaffe aircraft were seen.

2 Bomber Command R.C.M. sorties and 2 Resistance operations were also flown on this day.

14/15 October 1944

DUISBURG

Bomber Command continued Operation *Hurricane* by dispatching 1,005 aircraft – 498 Lancasters, 468 Halifaxes, 39 Mosquitoes – to attack Duisburg again in 2 forces, 2 hours apart. 941 aircraft dropped 4,040 tons of high explosive and 500 tons of incendiaries during the night. 5 Lancasters and 2 Halifaxes were lost.

Nearly 9,000 tons of bombs had thus fallen on Duisburg in less than 48 hours. Local reports are difficult to obtain. The Duisburg Stadtarchiv does not have the important *Endbericht* – the final report. Small comments are available: 'Heavy casualties must be expected.' 'Very serious property damage. A large number of people buried.' 'Thyssen Mines III and IV: About 8 days loss of production.' 'Duisburg-Hamborn: All mines and coke ovens lay silent.'

BRUNSWICK

Not only could Bomber Command dispatch more than 2,000 sorties to Duisburg in less than 24 hours, but there was still effort to spare for 5 Group to attack Brunswick with 233 Lancasters and 7 Mosquitoes. The various diversions and fighter support operations laid on by Bomber Command were so successful that only 1 Lancaster was lost from this raid.

Bomber Command had attempted to destroy Brunswick 4 times so far in 1944 and 5 Group finally achieved that aim on this night, using their own marking methods. It was Brunswick's worst raid of the war and the old centre was completely destroyed. A local report says 'the whole town, even the smaller districts, was particularly hard hit'. It was estimated by the local officials that 1,000 bombers had carried out the raid. Reliable statistics on damage are sparse; instead of quoting the normal number of buildings destroyed, the destruction was measured by hectares (150 hectares of the historic town area is mentioned). 561 people are believed to have died but there were near miraculous escapes when, 4 hours after the raid, firemen reached the first of 8 large public shelters which had been cut off in the 'sea of fire' in the centre of the town. An estimated 23,000 people were in these shelters and all but about 200 of them were rescued. Among the relief which arrived to help the 80,000 people bombed out was the *Hilfzug Bayern*, a train from far-away Bavaria equipped with technical help and kitchens for mass-feeding arrangements.

Brunswick was not raided again in strength by Bomber Command.

SUPPORT AND MINOR OPERATIONS

141 training aircraft on a diversionary sweep to Heligoland, 20 Mosquitoes to Hamburg, 16 to Berlin, 8 to Mannheim and 2 to Düsseldorf, 132 aircraft of 100 Group on R.C.M., *Serrate* and Intruder flights (no sub-totals are available), 8 aircraft on Resistance operations. 1 Halifax was lost on the diversionary sweep – it was seen to dive into the sea in flames – and 1 Mosquito was lost from the Berlin raid.

Total effort for the night: 1,572 sorties, 10 aircraft (0·6 per cent) lost. Total effort for the 24 hours: 2,589 sorties, 24 aircraft (0·9 per cent) lost. Total tonnage of bombs dropped in 24 hours: approximately 10,050 tons. These record totals would never be exceeded in the war.

15 October 1944

Sorpe Dam

18 Lancasters of 9 Squadron, 5 Group, to attack the dam at the Sorpe reservoir, the second most important supply of water for the Ruhr and one of the targets for the original Dams Raid by 617 Squadron in 1943. 16 aircraft dropped *Tallboys* or other bombs from 15,000 ft and hits were seen on the face of the earth dam but no breach was made. No aircraft lost.

Minor Operations: 3 R.C.M. sorties, 4 Hudsons on Resistance operations. No losses.

15/16 October 1944

WILHELMSHAVEN

506 aircraft – 257 Halifaxes, 241 Lancasters, 8 Mosquitoes – from all groups except 5 Group on the last of 14 major Bomber Command raids on Wilhelmshaven that began in early 1941.

Bomber Command claimed 'severe damage' to the business and residential areas. A short local report mentions only that the Rathaus was completely destroyed and that 30 people were killed and 92 injured. A further report from Wilhelmshaven, giving overall air-raid details, shows that this port town – a major naval base – escaped relatively lightly in the war. In 26 R.A.F. and American raids, only 510 civilians, 24 servicemen and 30 foreign workers were killed.

Minor Operations: 44 Mosquitoes to Hamburg, 6 to Saarbrücken and 2 each to Düsseldorf and Kassel, 33 R.C.M. sorties, 42 Mosquito patrols, 22 Halifaxes and 15 Lancasters minelaying off Denmark, 2 aircraft on Resistance operations. 2 Halifaxes and 2 Lancasters lost from the minelaying operation.

16 October 1944

9 Mosquitoes of 100 Group dispatched, 5 on Ranger patrols and 4 on anti-minesweeper operations off Denmark where mines were laid the previous night; they attacked 2 coastal vessels with cannon-fire. No aircraft lost.

16/17 October 1944

COLOGNE

39 Mosquitoes dispatched. 38 aircraft bombed on the estimated position of Cologne. A local report describes minor property damage but 29 people were killed and 56 injured. No Mosquitoes lost.

17 October 1944

WALCHEREN

47 Lancasters and 2 Mosquitoes of 5 Group attacked the sea wall at Westkapelle. Bombing appeared to be accurate but no major result was observed. No aircraft lost.

Minor Operations: 5 R.C.M. sorties, 4 Ranger patrols to Denmark, 4 Hudsons on Resistance operations. No aircraft lost.

17/18 October 1944

12 Mosquitoes of 100 Group flew anti-flying-bomb patrols. (The Germans were releasing flying bombs from aircraft over the North Sea.) No interceptions made.

---

18 October 1944

BONN

This was the first major operation by 3 Group in the new independent role which its commander, Air Vice-Marshal R. Harrison, had been granted. Approximately one third of the group's Lancasters were now fitted with the *G-H* blind-bombing device and 3 Group were to operate on days when the ground was concealed by cloud but when the cloud tops did not exceed 18,000 ft. Aircraft with *G-H* had their tail fins painted with a prominent design; aircraft without *G-H* found a *G-H* 'leader' to follow into the target area and bombed when that aircraft bombed. *G-H* was a relatively accurate, easy-to-operate and very useful device and 3 Group were to make good use of it in the remaining months of the war. The device had been used before, but not by a large force.

Air Vice-Marshal Harrison requested that the almost unbombed and unimportant town of Bonn should be the target for this first operation, possibly so that post-raid reconnaissance photographs could show the results of the first *G-H* raid without the effects of other bombing confusing the interpretation of the photographs. 128 Lancasters were dispatched; the raid appeared to go well and only 1 aircraft was lost.

The attack was a complete success. The heart of old Bonn was destroyed, with its university, many cultural and public buildings and a large residential area being burnt out. The local report says that the home in which Beethoven lived was saved 'by the courageous actions of its caretakers'. 700 buildings were destroyed and 1,000 were seriously damaged. 313 people were killed.

Minor Operations: 4 R.C.M. sorties, 1 Hudson on a Resistance operation. No losses.

18/19 October 1944

MOSQUITO OPERATIONS

19 Mosquitoes to Hannover, 18 to Mannheim, 8 to Düsseldorf, 5 to Pforzheim and 4 to Wiesbaden. 1 aircraft lost from the Pforzheim raid.

---

19 October 1944

4 Wellingtons and 1 Liberator on signals patrols, 2 Hudsons on Resistance operations. No aircraft lost.

19/20 October 1944

STUTTGART

565 Lancasters and 18 Mosquitoes of 1, 3, 6 and 8 Groups in 2 forces, 4½ hours apart. 6 Lancasters lost.

The bombing was not concentrated but serious damage was caused to the central and eastern districts of Stuttgart and in some of the suburban towns. Among individual buildings hit were the important Bosch factory, 4 churches and the Karl-Olga Hospital. 376 people were killed and 872 injured.

NUREMBERG

263 Lancasters and 7 Mosquitoes of 5 Group. 2 Lancasters lost.

This was only a partial success for the 5 Group method and the knock-out blow on Nuremberg, which had eluded Bomber Command for so long, was not achieved. The target area was found to be almost completely cloud-covered. The aiming point is believed to have been the centre of the city but the local report says that the bombing fell almost entirely in the southern districts, but this was the industrial area of Nuremberg. 397 houses and 41 industrial buildings were destroyed. 306 people were killed – 122 civilians, 28 soldiers and air-raid workers, 91 foreign workers and 65 Russian officer prisoners who were killed, with 5 of their guards, when their earth shelter was hit.

Minor Operations: 48 Mosquitoes to Wiesbaden and 6 to Düsseldorf, 49 R.C.M. sorties, 82 Mosquito patrols. 1 Mosquito Intruder was lost but other Mosquitoes claimed 2 Ju 88s, 1 Ju 188 and 1 Me 110 destroyed and 3 other night fighters damaged, a better-than-average night's success.

Total effort for the night: 1,038 sorties, 9 aircraft (0·9 per cent) lost.

---

21 October 1944

WALCHEREN

75 Lancasters of 3 Group carried out accurate visual bombing of a coastal battery at Flushing. 1 Lancaster lost.

2 Wellington flew signals patrols.

21/22 October 1944

HANNOVER

242 Halifaxes of 4 and 6 Groups and 21 Pathfinder Lancasters dispatched but recalled because of deteriorating weather in England. All aircraft landed safely.

Minor Operations: 4 Mosquitoes to Pforzheim and 2 each to Cologne and Düsseldorf but only Pforzheim (where 11 people were killed) was reached, 7 aircraft minelaying in an unrecorded area. No aircraft lost.

---

22 October 1944

NEUSS

100 Lancasters of 3 Group; none lost.

This *G-H* raid was not as concentrated as the recent Bonn raid and bombing was scattered. The local report says that 94 houses and 3 industrial buildings were destroyed and 545 houses, 18 industrial buildings and 1 public building were seriously damaged. 65 people were killed and 175 injured.

Minor Operations: 3 R.C.M. sorties, 1 Hudson on a Resistance operation. No losses.

22/23 October 1944

MINOR OPERATIONS

45 Mosquitoes to Hamburg, 4 to Wiesbaden, 3 to Düsseldorf and 2 to Cologne, 6 *Serrate* patrols, 20 Lancasters and 19 Halifaxes minelaying in the Kattegat, 6 Stirlings on Resistance operations. No aircraft lost.

---

23 October 1944

WALCHEREN

112 Lancasters of 5 Group attacked the Flushing battery positions but visibility was poor and the bombing was scattered. 4 Lancasters lost.

Minor Operations: 4 R.C.M. sorties, 6 Ranger patrols. No losses.

23/24 October 1944

ESSEN

1,055 aircraft – 561 Lancasters, 463 Halifaxes, 31 Mosquitoes. This was the heaviest raid on Essen so far in the war and the number of aircraft dispatched was also the greatest number to any target so far; these new records were achieved without the Lancasters of 5 Group being included. 5 Lancasters and 3 Halifaxes were lost.

4,538 tons of bombs were dropped. More than 90 per cent of this tonnage was high explosive (and included 509 4,000-pounders) because it was now considered that most of the burnable buildings in Essen had been destroyed in earlier raids. The greater proportion of high explosive, against all the trends in earlier area-bombing raids, was now quite common in attacks on targets which had suffered major fire damage in 1943. A report from Essen states that 607 buildings were destroyed and 812 were seriously damaged; 662 people were killed, a figure which included 124 foreign workers, and 569 people were injured. Other details from Essen and Bomber Command's own claims for bombing results are given in the report for a further raid on 25 October.

Minor Operations: 38 Mosquitoes to Berlin, 10 to Wiesbaden and 2 to Aschaffenburg, 41 R.C.M. sorties, 50 Mosquito patrols, 1 Hudson on a Resistance operation. No aircraft lost.

Total effort for the night: 1,197 sorties, 8 aircraft (0·7 per cent) lost.

24 October 1944

2 Wellingtons and 1 Liberator on signals patrols.

24/25 October 1944

MINOR OPERATIONS

57 Mosquitoes to Hannover, 6 to Aschaffenburg and 4 to Oberhausen, 3 R.C.M. sorties, 11 Mosquito patrols, 25 Lancasters and 9 Halifaxes minelaying in the Kattegat and off Oslo, 1 aircraft on a Resistance operation. No aircraft lost.

---

25 October 1944

ESSEN

771 aircraft – 508 Lancasters, 251 Halifaxes, 12 Mosquitoes. 2 Halifaxes and 2 Lancasters lost.

The bombing was aimed at sky-markers, because the target area was covered by cloud. The Bomber Command report states that the attack became scattered, but the local Essen report shows that more buildings were destroyed – 1,163 – and more people were killed – 820 – than in the heavier night attack which had taken place 36 hours previously. The foreign workers, who were now present in large numbers in German industrial cities and who usually had poorer air-raid shelters than the German people, once again suffered heavy casualties; 99 foreigners and 2 prisoners of war were killed. A photographic reconnaissance flight which took place after this raid showed severe damage to the remaining industrial concerns in Essen, particularly to the Krupps steelworks. Some of the war industry had already moved to small, dispersed factories but the coal mines and steelworks of the Ruhr were still important.

The Krupps steelworks were particularly hard-hit by the two raids and there are references in the firm's archives to the 'almost complete breakdown of the electrical-supply network' and to 'a complete paralysis'. The Borbeck pig-iron plant ceased work completely and there is no record of any further production from this important section of Krupps.

Much of Essen's surviving industrial capacity was now dispersed and the city lost its role as one of Germany's most important centres of war production.

HOMBERG

243 aircraft – 199 Halifaxes, 32 Lancasters, 12 Mosquitoes – of 6 and 8 Groups attacked the oil plant at Meerbeck. The target was covered by cloud. Bombing was scattered in the early stages but later became more concentrated on the sky-markers. The results of the raid are not known. No aircraft were lost.

Minor Operations: 6 R.C.M. sorties, 1 Hudson on a Resistance operation. No losses.

Total effort for the day: 1,021 sorties, 4 aircraft (0·4 per cent) lost.

26 October 1944

LEVERKUSEN

105 Lancasters of 3 Group carried out a *G-H* raid on Leverkusen, with the chemical works as the centre of the intended bombing area. The raid appeared to proceed well but cloud prevented any observation of the results. No aircraft lost.

Minor Operations: 4 R.C.M. sorties, 1 Hudson on a Resistance operation. No losses.

26/27 October 1944

MINOR OPERATIONS

26 R.C.M. sorties, 42 Mosquito patrols, 10 Lancasters of 1 Group minelaying off Heligoland. 1 Lancaster minelayer lost.

27/28 October 1944

MOSQUITO OPERATIONS

60 Mosquitoes to Berlin and 21 in small numbers to 6 other targets. No aircraft lost.

---

28 October 1944

COLOGNE

733 aircraft – 428 Lancasters, 286 Halifaxes, 19 Mosquitoes. 4 Halifaxes and 3 Lancasters lost.

The bombing took place in 2 separate waves and the local report confirms that enormous damage was caused. The districts of Mülheim and Zollstock, north-east and south-west of the centre respectively, became the centre of the 2 raids and were both devastated. Classed as completely destroyed were: 2,239 blocks of flats, 15 industrial premises, 11 schools, 3 police stations and a variety of other buildings. Much damage was also caused to power-stations, railways and harbour installations on the Rhine. 630 German people were killed or their bodies never found and 1,200 were injured. The number of foreign casualties is not known.

WALCHEREN

277 aircraft – 155 Halifaxes, 86 Lancasters, 36 Mosquitoes – of 4 and 8 Groups carried out raids on gun positions at 5 places on the rim of the newly flooded island. Most of the bombing appeared to be successful. 1 Halifax and 1 Lancaster lost.

Minor Operations: 4 R.C.M. sorties, 1 Hudson on a Resistance operation. No losses.

Total effort for the day: 1,015 sorties, 9 aircraft (0·9 per cent) lost.

28/29 October 1944

BERGEN

237 Lancasters and 7 Mosquitoes of 5 Group to attack the U-boat pens. It is probable that 5 Group had been waiting to attack this important target for several days; the Group had not flown any operations since 23 October. Clear conditions were forecast for the target area, although there were some doubts about this. Unfortunately the area was found to be cloud-covered. The Master Bomber tried to bring the force down below 5,000 ft but cloud was still encountered and he ordered the raid to be abandoned after only 47 Lancasters had bombed. 3 Lancasters lost.

The town of Bergen again provides a good report. 4 bombs did hit the roofs of the U-boat pens but the operations of the base were not affected. 35 houses were destroyed and 50 were damaged around the harbour area but the population here may have been evacuated; no one was killed in that area. There was a second bombing area, however, in the town centre. Further houses were hit and 52 civilians and 2 Germans were killed. A particularly sad loss for the people of Bergen was the Engen Theatre, 'an old wooden theatre – a magnificent, large building and the oldest theatre in Europe'.

Minor Operations: 30 Mosquitoes to Cologne, 4 to Karlsruhe and 3 to Rheine, 8 R.C.M. sorties, 5 Mosquito patrols, 14 Lancasters minelaying off Oslo. No aircraft lost.

---

29 October 1944

WALCHEREN

358 aircraft – 194 Lancasters, 128 Halifaxes, 36 Mosquitoes – of 1, 3, 4 and 8 Groups attacked 11 different German ground positions. Visibility was good and it was believed that all the targets were hit. 1 Lancaster lost.

TIRPITZ

37 Lancasters – 18 from 9 Squadron, 18 from 617 Squadron and a film unit aircraft from 463 Squadron – were dispatched from Lossiemouth in Scotland to attack the battleship Tirpitz, which was now moored near the Norwegian port of Tromsö. The removal of the Lancasters' mid-upper turrets and other equipment and the installation of extra fuel tanks, giving each aircraft a total fuel capacity of 2,406 gallons, allowed the Lancasters to carry out this 2,250-mile operation.

A weather-reconnaissance Mosquito had reported the target area free of cloud and the Lancasters formed up at a lake near the bay in which the Tirpitz was moored and commenced their attack. Unfortunately the wind had changed and a bank of cloud came in to cover the battleship 30 seconds before the first Lancaster was ready to bomb. 32 aircraft released Tallboy bombs on the estimated position of the battleship but no direct hits were scored. 1 of 617 Squadron's Lancasters, which was damaged by Flak, crash-landed in Sweden and its crew were later returned to Britain.

Minor Operations: 3 R.C.M. sorties, 4 Ranger patrols, 1 Hudson on a Resistance operation. No aircraft lost.

29/30 October 1944

MINOR OPERATIONS

59 Mosquitoes to Cologne and 6 to Mannheim, 55 Mosquitoes on *Serrate* and Intruder patrols. No aircraft lost.

---

30 October 1944

WALCHEREN

102 Lancasters and 8 Mosquitoes of 5 Group successfully attacked gun batteries. 1 Mosquito lost. This was the last Bomber Command raid in support of the Walcheren campaign and the opening of the River Scheldt. The attack by ground troops on Walcheren commenced on 31 October and the island fell after a week of fighting by Canadian and Scottish troops, including Commandos who sailed their landing craft through the breaches in the sea walls made earlier by Bomber Command. It required a further 3 weeks before the 40-mile river entrance to Antwerp was cleared of mines and the first convoy did not arrive in the port until 28 November.

45. Gunlaying equipment at a Flak site in Holland. The white symbols on the radar shield represent successes attributed to this unit. The activities of Bomber Command tied down a vast amount of German armaments and manpower.

WESSELING

102 Lancasters of 3 Group carried out a *G-H* raid on the oil refinery. No results were seen because of the cloud but the bombing was believed to be accurate. No aircraft lost.

Minor Operations: 7 R.C.M. sorties, 1 Hudson on a Resistance operation. No losses.

30/31 October 1944

COLOGNE

905 aircraft – 438 Halifaxes, 435 Lancasters, 32 Mosquitoes. No aircraft lost.

This was an *Oboe*-marked raid through cloud, and Bomber Command estimated that only 'scattered and light' damage was caused in the western parts of the city. But the local report shows that enormous damage was caused in the suburbs of Brauns-feld, Lindenthal, Klettenberg and Sülz, which were *'regelrecht umgepflügt'* –'thor-oughly ploughed up' – by the huge tonnage of high explosive dropped (3,431 tons of high explosive and 610 tons of incendiaries were dropped). A vast amount of property, mostly civilian housing, was destroyed but railways and public utilities were also hit. There was little industry in the area which was bombed. Among the buildings de-stroyed or seriously damaged were Cologne University, the local army-garrison headquarters and the 1,000-year-old St Gereon church, struck by a heavy bomb which blew 'an enormous hole'; the damage took 35 years to repair! 497 Germans were killed and 57 were 'missing'. The number of foreigners killed is not known but a prisoner-of-war camp in the Heliosstrasse was destroyed.

Minor Operations: 62 Mosquitoes to Berlin and 3 each to Heilbronn and Oberhausen, 42 R.C.M. sorties, 57 Mosquito patrols. 2 Mosquitoes were lost – 1 from the Berlin raid and 1 Intruder.

Total effort for the night: 1,072 sorties, 2 aircraft (0·2 per cent) lost.

---

31 October 1944

BOTTROP

101 Lancasters of 3 Group carried out a good *G-H* attack on the oil plant. 1 Lancaster lost.

Minor Operations: 1 Wellington carried out a signals patrol and 1 Hudson flew a Resistance operation.

---

31 October/1 November 1944

COLOGNE

493 aircraft – 331 Lancasters, 144 Halifaxes, 18 Mosquitoes – of 1, 3, 4 and 8 Groups. 15 further Mosquitoes carried out a feint attack just before the main raid. 2 Lancasters lost.

This was another *Oboe*-marked attack through thick cloud. Most of the bombing fell in the southern districts, with Bayental and Zollstock, according to the local report, being the hardest hit, although damage was not as severe as in other recent raids. Firm details are now harder to obtain. The recording system in Cologne was becoming less reliable, mainly because so many people had now left the city. The only item of outstanding interest mentioned is the blowing up of an ammunition train in the Klettenberg district. 98 Germans were killed; the foreign casualties were not recorded though it is known that a number were killed at the Eifeltor Station.

Minor Operations: 49 Mosquitoes to Hamburg, 4 to Saarbrücken and 2 to Schweinfurt, 36 R.C.M. sorties, 59 Mosquito patrols. No aircraft lost.

---

1 November 1944

HOMBERG

226 Lancasters and 2 Mosquitoes of 5 Group, with 14 Mosquitoes of 8 Group, attempted to attack the Meerbeck oil plant. The marking was scattered and only 159 of the Lancaster crews attempted to bomb. 1 Lancaster lost.

Minor Operations: 2 R.C.M. sorties, 1 Hudson on a Resistance operation.

1/2 November 1944

OBERHAUSEN

288 aircraft – 202 Halifaxes, 74 Lancasters, 12 Mosquitoes – of 6 and 8 Groups. 3 Halifaxes and 1 Lancaster lost.

The target area was cloud-covered and the bombing was not concentrated. 36 houses were destroyed in Oberhausen and 4 people were killed but other places in the Ruhr may have been hit as well.

Minor Operations: 49 Mosquitoes to Berlin, 12 to Cologne and 4 each to Karlsruhe and Mülheim, 28 R.C.M. sorties, 46 Mosquito patrols, 25 aircraft on Resistance operations. No aircraft lost.

---

2 November 1944

HOMBERG

184 Lancasters of 3 Group carried out a *G-H* attack on the oil plant. Large fires and a thick column of smoke were seen. 5 Lancasters lost.

2 Wellingtons flew R.C.M. sorties without loss.

2/3 November 1944

DÜSSELDORF

992 aircraft – 561 Lancasters, 400 Halifaxes, 31 Mosquitoes. 11 Halifaxes and 8 Lancasters were lost, 4 of the losses being crashes behind Allied lines in France and Belgium.

This heavy attack fell mainly on the northern half of Düsseldorf. More than 5,000 houses were destroyed or badly damaged. 7 industrial premises were destroyed and 18 were seriously damaged, including some important steel firms. At least 678 people were killed and more than 1,000 were injured.

This was the last major Bomber Command raid of the war on Düsseldorf.

Minor Operations: 42 Mosquitoes to Osnabrück and 9 to Hallendorf (only 1 aircraft reached this target), 37 R.C.M. sorties, 51 Mosquito patrols. No aircraft lost.

Total effort for the night: 1,131 sorties, 19 aircraft (1·7 per cent) lost.

---

3 November 1944

1 Wellington flew an R.C.M. sortie and returned safely.

3/4 November 1944

MOSQUITO OPERATIONS

55 Mosquitoes to Berlin and 9 to Herford but only 3 aircraft reached Herford. No aircraft lost.

---

4 November 1944

SOLINGEN

176 Lancasters of 3 Group were dispatched but the raid was not successful and the bombing was badly scattered. 4 Lancasters lost.

2 Wellingtons and 1 Halifax flew R.C.M. sorties.

4/5 November 1944

BOCHUM

749 aircraft – 384 Halifaxes, 336 Lancasters, 29 Mosquitoes – 1, 4, 6 and 8 Groups. 23 Halifaxes and 5 Lancasters were lost; German night fighters caused most of the casualties. 346 (Free French) Squadron, based at Elvington, lost 5 out of its 16 Halifaxes on the raid.

This was a particularly successful attack based upon standard Pathfinder marking techniques. Severe damage was caused to the centre of Bochum. More than 4,000 buildings were destroyed or seriously damaged; 980 Germans and 14 foreigners were killed. Bochum's industrial areas were also severely damaged, particularly the important steelworks. This was the last major raid by Bomber Command on this target.

DORTMUND–EMS CANAL

174 Lancasters and 2 Mosquitoes of 5 Group. 3 Lancasters lost.

The Germans had partly repaired the section of the canal north of Münster after the 5 Group raid in September, so this further attack was required. The banks of both branches of the canal were again breached and water drained off, leaving barges stranded and the canal unusable. A report from Speer to Hitler, dated 11 November 1944, was captured at the end of the war and described how the bombing of the canal was preventing smelting coke from the Ruhr mines reaching 3 important steelworks – 2 near Brunswick and 1 at Osnabrück. In his post-war interrogation, Speer stated that these raids on the Dortmund–Ems Canal, together with attacks on the German railway system, produced more serious setbacks to the German war industry at this time than any other type of bombing.

Minor Operations: 43 Mosquitoes to Hannover and 6 to Herford, 39 R.C.M. sorties, 68 Mosquito patrols. No aircraft lost. The 100 Group Mosquitoes claimed 4 Ju 88s and 2 Me 110s destroyed and 2 other night fighters damaged, possibly their most successful night of the war.

Total effort for the night: 1,081 sorties, 31 aircraft (2·9 per cent) lost.

---

5 November 1944

SOLINGEN

173 Lancasters of 3 Group carried out a *G-H* raid. 1 Lancaster lost.

Results of the raid were not observed, because of the complete cloud cover, but German reports show that this was an outstanding success. Most of the bombing fell accurately into the medium-sized town of Solingen. 1,300 houses and 18 industrial buildings were destroyed and 1,600 more buildings were severely damaged. Between 1,224 and 1,882 people were killed (accounts vary) and approximately 2,000 people were injured. A proportion of the bombs fell outside Solingen, however, and 150 people were killed in nearby Remscheid and Wuppertal.

1 Wellington flew an R.C.M. sortie and returned safely.

These 3 near-perfect raids in 24 hours – the area-bombing raid on Bochum marked by Pathfinders, the selective attack on the Dortmund–Ems Canal by 5 Group and the 3 Group *G-H* raid on Solingen – are good examples of the versatility and striking power now possessed by Bomber Command. All groups had taken part, dispatching 1,098 sorties and dropping 5,130 tons of bombs accurately on the targets. The loss of 28 bombers from the Bochum raid also shows, however, that the German defences could still be effective.

5/6 November 1944

MOSQUITO OPERATIONS

65 Mosquitoes to Stuttgart – in 2 waves – and 6 to Aschaffenburg. No aircraft lost.

---

6 November 1944

GELSENKIRCHEN

738 aircraft – 383 Halifaxes, 324 Lancasters, 31 Mosquitoes. 3 Lancasters and 2 Halifaxes lost.

This large daylight raid had, as its aiming point, the Nordstern synthetic-oil plant. The attack was not well concentrated but 514 aircraft were able to bomb the approximate position of the oil plant before smoke obscured the ground; 187 aircraft then bombed the general town area of Gelsenkirchen.

The Gelsenkirchen war diarist, who often recorded interesting titbits, tells of how this Protestant town had celebrated the Reformation Feast the previous day, a Sunday. The celebration had been held back from its proper date, 31 October, so as not to interfere with industrial production. The diarist wrote: 'For many pious people, this was their last church service. Catastrophe broke over Gelsenkirchen the following day.' The diary then proceeds to give several pages describing the severe damage throughout the town. The number of people killed was 518. The diarist then comments, perhaps with some pride, that Gelsenkirchen was mentioned by name in the O K W (German High Command) communiqué for the first time in the war.

1 Wellington flew an R.C.M. sortie.

6/7 November 1944

MITTELLAND CANAL

235 Lancasters and 7 Mosquitoes of 5 Group attempted to cut the Mittelland Canal at its junction with the Dortmund–Ems Canal at Gravenhorst. The marking force experienced great difficulty in finding the target. The crew of a low-flying Mosquito – pilot: Flight Lieutenant L. C. E. De Vigne; navigator: Australian Squadron Leader F. W. Boyle, 627 Squadron – found the canal and dropped their marker with such accuracy that it fell into the water and was extinguished. Only 31 aircraft bombed, before the Master Bomber ordered the raid to be abandoned. 10 Lancasters were lost.

KOBLENZ

128 Lancasters of 3 Group to this new target, making a night *G-H* attack. 2 Lancasters lost.

This was a successful raid with most of the damage being caused by a large area of fire in the centre of the town. The British Bombing Survey Unit later estimated that 303 acres, 58 per cent of the town's built-up area, were destroyed. The local report (from Dr Helmut Schnatz) states that destruction in an area 2 miles across was almost complete, with 'nearly all of the historic courts of the ancient nobility, 3 old churches and the Castle of the Electors burnt out'. 104 people were killed – 89 civilians, 8 soldiers and 7 French and Italian prisoners of war – and 585 people were injured. Fire raids sometimes produced low casualty figures in towns with properly constructed shelters, but 25,000 people lost their homes.

Minor Operations: 48 Mosquitoes to Gelsenkirchen, 18 to Hannover, 11 to Rheine and 8 to Herford, 32 R.C.M. sorties, 82 Mosquito patrols, 12 Lancasters minelaying off Heligoland. 4 aircraft lost – 1 Mosquito from the Gelsenkirchen raid, 2 Mosquito Intruders and 1 R.C.M. Fortress.

---

7 November 1944

1 Wellington flew an uneventful R.C.M. sortie.

8 November 1944

HOMBERG

136 Lancasters of 3 Group attacked the Meerbeck oil plant. 1 Lancaster lost. The raid opened well and 2 large fires were seen but smoke then concealed the target and later bombing was scattered.

1 Wellington R.C.M. sortie.

8/9 November 1944

MINOR OPERATIONS

59 Mosquitoes to Herford and 50 to Hannover, 4 R.C.M. sorties, 24 aircraft on Resistance operations. 2 Stirlings on Resistance work were lost.

9 November 1944

WANNE-EICKEL

256 Lancasters and 21 Mosquitoes of 1 and 8 Groups to attack the oil refinery. Cloud over the target was found to reach 21,000 ft and the sky-markers dropped by the *Oboe* Mosquitoes disappeared as soon as they ignited so the Master Bomber ordered the force to bomb any built-up area. The town of Wanne-Eickel reports only 2 buildings destroyed, with 4 civilians and 6 foreigners killed. It must be assumed that other towns in the Ruhr were hit but no details are available. 2 Lancasters lost.

9/10 November 1944

MINOR OPERATIONS

6 Mosquitoes each to Gotha and Pforzheim, 4 to Schwelm (which was not reached) and 3 to Kassel, 22 aircraft of 100 Group on a *Window* feint to draw up German fighters, 8 Mosquito patrols, 3 Stirlings on Resistance operations. No aircraft lost.

10 November 1944

Minor Operations

2 Wellington R.C.M. sorties, 2 Mosquito Rangers. No losses.

10/11 November 1944

MINOR OPERATIONS

59 Mosquitoes to Hannover and 4 each to Gotha and Erfurt (Erfurt was not reached), 30 R.C.M. sorties, 40 Mosquito patrols. 1 Mosquito from the Hannover raid was lost.

11 November 1944

CASTROP-RAUXEL

122 Lancasters of 3 Group carried out a *G-H* attack on the synthetic-oil refinery. The bombing was believed to be accurate and no aircraft were lost.

2 Wellington R.C.M. sorties.

11/12 November 1944

HARBURG

237 Lancasters and 8 Mosquitoes of 5 Group. 7 Lancasters lost.

The aiming point for this raid was the Rhenania-Ossag oil refinery, which had been attacked several times by American day bombers. Brunswig's history of the Hamburg–Harburg air raids gives this raid only a brief mention,* saying that considerable damage was caused in Harburg's residential and industrial areas but the oil refinery is not mentioned. 119 people were killed and 5,205 were bombed out.

DORTMUND

209 Lancasters and 19 Mosquitoes of 1 and 8 Groups. No aircraft lost.

The aiming point was the Hoesch Benzin synthetic-oil plant in the Wambel district. A local report confirms that the plant was severely damaged. Other bombs hit nearby housing and the local airfield. 83 people were killed and 85 injured.

Minor Operations: 41 Mosquitoes to the Kamen oil refinery, 12 to Osnabrück, 9 to Wiesbaden, 6 to Gotha and 3 to Erfurt, 36 R.C.M. sorties, 59 Mosquito patrols, 26 Lancasters and 24 Halifaxes minelaying off Oslo, in the Kattegat and in the River Elbe. No aircraft lost.

---

12 November 1944

TIRPITZ

30 Lancasters of 9 and 617 Squadrons and a 463 Squadron Lancaster with cameramen on board flew from Lossiemouth to attack the *Tirpitz*, which was still moored near Tromsö. The weather was clear. *Tirpitz* was hit by at least 2 *Tallboys* and then suffered a violent internal explosion. She capsized to remain bottom upwards – a total loss. Approximately 1,000 of the 1,900 men on board were killed or injured. German fighters which were stationed near by to protect the *Tirpitz* failed to take off in time and only 1 Lancaster, of 9 Squadron, was severely damaged, by Flak; it landed safely in Sweden with its crew unhurt.

Minor Operations: 2 R.C.M. sorties, 2 Mosquitoes on Ranger patrols. No losses.

---

* *Feuersturm über Hamburg*, op. cit., p. 346.

13 and 14 November 1944

1 Wellington flew an uneventful signals patrol on each of these days.

15 November 1944

DORTMUND

177 Lancasters of 3 Group carried out a *G-H* attack on the oil plant. The raid, through thick cloud, was believed to have been accurate. 2 Lancasters lost.

Minor Operations: 5 R.C.M. sorties, 2 Ranger patrols to the Copenhagen area. No losses.

15/16 November 1944

MINOR OPERATIONS

36 Mosquitoes to Berlin, 6 each to Gotha and Wanne-Eickel, 5 to Karlsruhe and 4 to Scholven/-Buer, 29 R.C.M. sorties, 30 Mosquito patrols. 1 Mosquito lost from the Berlin raid.

16 November 1944

AMERICAN ARMY SUPPORT

Bomber Command was asked to bomb 3 towns near the German lines which were about to be attacked by the American First and Ninth Armies in the area between Aachen and the Rhine. 1,188 Bomber Command aircraft attacked Düren, Jülich and Heinsburg in order to cut communications behind the German lines. Düren was attacked by 485 Lancasters and 13 Mosquitoes of 1, 5 and 8 Groups, Jülich by 413 Halifaxes, 78 Lancasters and 17 Mosquitoes of 4, 6 and 8 Groups and Heinsberg by 182 Lancasters of 3 Group. 3 Lancasters were lost on the Düren raid and 1 Lancaster on the Heinsberg raid. 1,239 American heavy bombers also made raids on targets in the same area, without suffering any losses. More than 9,400 tons of high-explosive bombs were dropped by the combined bomber forces.

The R.A.F. raids were all carried out in easy bombing conditions and the 3 towns were virtually destroyed. Düren, whose civilian population was still present, suffered 3,127 fatal casualties – 2,403 local civilians, 398 civilians from other places temporarily staying in Düren and 326 unidentified, of whom at least 217 were soldiers. Heinsberg, described in the British press with other targets as 'a heavily defended town', contained only 110 civilians and a local military unit of 1 officer and a few soldiers; 52 of the civilians were killed. No report is available from Jülich.

The American advance was not a success. Wet ground prevented the use of tanks and the American artillery units were short of ammunition because of supply difficulties. The infantry advance was slow and costly.

18 November 1944

MÜNSTER

479 aircraft – 367 Halifaxes, 94 Lancasters, 18 Mosquitoes – of 4, 6 and 8 Groups. 1 Halifax crashed in Holland.

The raid was not concentrated and bombs fell in all parts of Münster. The only item of interest mentioned in the local report was a direct hit on a concrete shelter which killed 68 people. The total number of deaths in the town was 138.

3 Halifaxes flew R.C.M. sorties.

18/19 November 1944

WANNE-EICKEL

285 Lancasters and 24 Mosquitoes of 1 and 8 Groups. 1 Lancaster lost.

The intention of the raid was to hit the local oil plant. Large explosions seemed to erupt in the plant and post-raid reconnaissance showed that some further damage was caused to it. The local report does not mention the oil plant but states that the Hannibal coal mine was destroyed and that 57 people were killed, 35 of them in a *'Bunkerpanik'*.

Minor Operations: 31 Mosquitoes to Wiesbaden (a 'spoof' raid), 21 to Hannover and 6 to Erfurt, 29 R.C.M. sorties, 44 Mosquito patrols. No aircraft lost.

19 November 1944

1 Hudson Resistance flight.

20 November 1944

HOMBERG

183 Lancasters of 3 Group made a *G-H* attack on the oil plant but the weather was stormy and many aircraft were not able to maintain formation with the *G-H* aircraft on the bombing run. The bombing, through cloud, was believed to have been scattered. 5 Lancasters lost.

Minor Operations: 3 R.C.M. sorties, 2 Mosquito Ranger patrols, 3 Hudsons on Resistance operations. No aircraft lost.

20/21 November 1944

KOBLENZ

43 Lancasters of 8 Group made an unusual Pathfinder solo raid on Koblenz without loss. The purpose of the raid was not recorded. It is possible that either the large road and rail bridges over the Rhine and Mosel or the local railway yards were the targets. Only high-explosive bombs were carried. Koblenz was completely covered by cloud and all bombing was by *H2S* from 15,000 ft.

The local report states that some bombs fell in the town, blocking several roads and railways and scoring hits on a road and a rail bridge, although these remained usable. Part of the bombing fell well outside the town. 62 civilians, 1 female Ukrainian worker and 5 or 6 German soldiers were killed and 48 people were injured.

Minor Operations: 63 Mosquitoes to Hannover, 14 each to Homberg and Castrop-Rauxel oil plants and 9 to Eisenach, 17 R.C.M. sorties, 17 Mosquito patrols. No aircraft lost.

---

21 November 1944

HOMBERG

160 Lancasters of 3 Group to attack the oil refinery. 3 Lancasters lost.

The bombing was scattered at first but then became very concentrated, culminating, according to the Bomber Command report, in 'a vast sheet of yellow flame followed by black smoke rising to a great height'. This was a very satisfactory raid after several previous attempts by Bomber Command to destroy this oil refinery.

2 Wellingtons on R.C.M. sorties.

21/22 November 1944

This was a night of mainly good visibility in which Bomber Command operations were directed strictly according to priorities given in recent directives.

ASCHAFFENBURG

274 Lancasters and 9 Mosquitoes of 1 and 8 Groups. 2 Lancasters lost.

The object of this raid was to destroy the local railway yards and lines. The local report says that 50 bombs fell in the railway area, causing much damage to the marshalling yards and railway workshops but the main through lines were not cut. Many other bombs fell in the centre and north of the town. About 500 houses were destroyed and 1,500 seriously damaged. Many old buildings were hit, including the local castle, the Johannisburg, which was hit by 5 high-explosive bombs and had a 4,000-lb 'blockbuster' burst near by; the roof and upper storeys of the castle were burnt out. 344 people were killed, of whom 221 were in the northern district of Damm. 3 Catholic priests died when their church was hit.

CASTROP-RAUXEL

273 aircraft – 176 Halifaxes, 79 Lancasters, 18 Mosquitoes – of 1, 6 and 8 Groups. 4 Halifaxes lost.

The target was the oil refinery. The local report says that 216 high-explosive bombs, 78 duds and many incendiaries hit the oil plant and caused such a large fire that the fire-fighters could do little more than allow it to burn itself out. It is believed that the refinery produced no more oil after this raid. Bombs fell in many other places, including some important industrial and coal-mining premises. 15 people were killed and 31 injured.

STERKRADE

270 aircraft – 232 Halifaxes, 20 Mosquitoes, 18 Lancasters – of 4 and 8 Groups. 2 Halifaxes lost.

The target was again the synthetic-oil refinery. Bomber Command's report says that the plant was not damaged, though some labour barracks near by were hit. No local details are available.

MITTELLAND CANAL

138 Lancasters and 6 Mosquitoes of 5 Group. 2 Lancasters lost.

The canal banks were successfully breached near Gravenhorst. Later photographs showed that water drained off over a 30-mile stretch and that 59 barges were stranded on one short section alone.

DORTMUND–EMS CANAL

123 Lancasters and 5 Mosquitoes of 5 Group. No aircraft lost.

The canal near Ladbergen was attacked, some of the Lancasters coming down to 4,000 ft to get beneath the cloud. A breach was made in the only branch of the aqueduct here which had been repaired since the last raid and the water once again drained out of the canal.

Minor Operations: 29 Mosquitoes to Stuttgart, 26 to Hannover, 19 to Worms and 4 to Wesel, 38 R.C.M. sorties, 80 Mosquito patrols, 24 Halifaxes and 18 Lancasters minelaying off Oslo, 9 aircraft on Resistance operations. 4 aircraft were lost – 2 Mosquitoes and 1 Halifax of 100 Group and 1 Lancaster from the minelaying force.

Total effort for the night: 1,345 sorties, 14 aircraft (1·0 per cent) lost.

---

22 November 1944

1 Wellington R.C.M. sortie and 1 Hudson Resistance flight. No losses.

22/23 November 1944

TRONDHEIM

171 Lancasters and 7 Mosquitoes of 5 Group were dispatched to attack the U-boat pens but the target was covered by a smoke-screen and the Master Bomber ordered the raid to be abandoned after the illuminating and marking force had been unable to find the target. 2 Lancasters and 1 Mosquito lost.

17 Lancasters minelaying off Heligoland and in the mouth of the River Elbe without loss.

---

23 November 1944

GELSENKIRCHEN

168 Lancasters of 3 Group carried out a *G-H* raid through cloud on the Nordstern oil plant. The bombing appeared to be accurate. 1 Lancaster lost.

Minor Operations: 4 Mosquitoes on Ranger patrols in the Heligoland area, 1 Hudson on a Resistance operation. No aircraft lost.

23/24 November 1944

MINOR OPERATIONS

61 Mosquitoes to Hannover, 9 to Eisenach and 6 each to Göttingen and Hagen, 43 aircraft of 100 Group on R.C.M. and Mosquito operations (separate figures not available). 1 Mosquito lost from the Hannover raid.

---

24 November 1944

1 Wellington R.C.M. sortie and 1 Hudson Resistance flight.

24/25 November 1944

MINOR OPERATIONS

58 Mosquitoes to Berlin and 6 to Göttingen, 13 Halifaxes minelaying off Denmark. No aircraft lost.

25/26 November 1944

MINOR OPERATIONS

68 Mosquitoes to Nuremberg, 10 to Hagen and 9 each to Erfurt and Stuttgart, 36 R.C.M. sorties, 38 Mosquito patrols. 1 Mosquito lost from the Nuremberg raid.

---

26 November 1944

FULDA

75 Lancasters of 3 Group were sent on a trial raid to attack the railway centre at Fulda to establish whether *G-H* signals could reach to this distance, 160 miles from the German frontier. The distance was too great, however, and the bombs were scattered over a wide area. No aircraft lost.

1 Hudson flew a Resistance operation.

26/27 November 1944

MUNICH

270 Lancasters and 8 Mosquitoes of 5 Group. 1 Lancaster crashed in France.

Bomber Command claimed this as an accurate raid in good visibility with much fresh damage, particularly to railway targets. It has not been possible to obtain a local report. The Munich Stadtarchiv refused to provide any help (the only large city in West Germany to do so) and the waiting time for reports from the Bundesarchiv at Freiburg was more than a year!

Minor Operations: 7 Mosquitoes to Erfurt and 6 to Karlsruhe (a 'spoof' raid), 20 R.C.M. sorties, 20 Mosquito patrols, 31 aircraft on Resistance operations. 1 Intruder Mosquito was lost and 1 Hudson on a Resistance flight crashed behind Allied lines in Belgium.

---

27 November 1944

COLOGNE

169 Lancasters of 3 Group carried out a *G-H* raid on the Kalk Nord railway yards. Good results were observed. 1 Lancaster lost.

27/28 November 1944

FREIBURG

341 Lancasters and 10 Mosquitoes of 1 and 8 Groups. 1 Lancaster lost.

Freiburg was not an industrial town and had not been bombed before by the R.A.F. It was attacked on this night because it was a minor railway centre and because many German troops were believed to be present in the town; American and French units were advancing in the Vosges, only 35 miles to the west. The marking of the medium-sized town was based on *Oboe* directed from caravans situated in France. Flak defences were light and 1,900 tons of bombs were dropped on Freiburg in 25 minutes. Photographs showed that the railway targets were not hit but that the main town area was severely damaged. German reports say that 2,000 houses were destroyed and 453 seriously damaged. Casualties were 2,088 people killed, 858 missing and 4,072 injured. 75 German soldiers were also killed and 61 were injured. The high casualty rate suggests that the population were taken by surprise and had not been properly prepared for air attack. The ratio of more than 8 people dead for each heavy bomber attacking is unusually high.

NEUSS

290 aircraft – 173 Halifaxes, 102 Lancasters, 15 Mosquitoes – of 1, 6 and 8 Groups. 1 Mosquito lost.

The central and eastern districts of Neuss were heavily bombed and many fires were started. A brief local report says that 145 houses and 4 industrial buildings were destroyed and 586 houses, 16 industrial buildings and 5 public buildings were seriously damaged. 41 people were killed and 44 injured, figures which suggest a high degree of air-raid preparedness in this town on the western edge of the Ruhr.

Minor Operations: 67 Mosquitoes to Berlin, 7 each to Hallendorf and Ludwigshafen and 5 to Nuremberg, 35 R.C.M. sorties, 61 Mosquito patrols, 18 Halifaxes and 12 Lancasters minelaying off Danish and Norwegian coasts. No aircraft lost.

Total effort for the night: 853 sorties, 2 aircraft (0·2 per cent) lost.

28/29 November 1944

ESSEN

316 aircraft – 270 Halifaxes, 32 Lancasters, 14 Mosquitoes – of 1, 4 and 8 Groups. No aircraft lost.

Bomber Command documents claim further damage to industrial areas, including the Krupps works. Essen reports 405 houses destroyed and 673 seriously damaged, with 135 people killed and 207 injured. An interesting little item in the local fire-brigade report congratulates the team working in the burning headquarters of the local Gestapo for saving valuable documents.

NEUSS

145 Lancasters of 3 Group and 8 Lancasters of 1 Group carried out a mainly *G-H* attack. No aircraft lost.

The brief local report gives details of modest property damage, mainly in residential areas, and states that 65 people were killed and 43 injured.

Minor Operations: 75 Mosquitoes to Nuremberg and 9 to Hallendorf, 35 R.C.M. sorties, 35 Mosquito patrols. 1 Mosquito lost from the Nuremberg raid.

Total effort for the night: 623 sorties, 1 aircraft (0·2 per cent) lost.

---

29 November 1944

DORTMUND

294 Lancasters and 17 Mosquitoes of 1 and 8 Groups. 6 Lancasters lost.

Bad weather caused the marking and resultant bombing to be scattered but fresh damage was caused in Dortmund.

DUISBURG

30 Mosquitoes of 8 Group attempted to bomb a tar and benzol plant in the Meiderich district, using the *Oboe*-leader method for the first time on a German target, but 2 of the 3 formations of Mosquitoes failed to link up with their *Oboe* leaders and bombed on timed runs from the docks south of Duisburg. Most of the bombs were believed to have fallen beyond the target. No Mosquitoes lost.

1 Hudson flew a Resistance operation.

29/30 November 1944

MINOR OPERATIONS

67 Mosquitoes to Hannover and 4 to Bielefeld, 27 R.C.M. sorties, 38 Mosquito patrols, 19 aircraft on Resistance operations. 6 Mosquitoes of 5 Group to lay mines in the River Weser were unable to carry out the operation because of 10/10ths cloud over the target area. No aircraft lost.

---

30 November 1944

BOTTROP

60 Lancasters of 3 Group attacked a coking plant without loss.

OSTERFELD

60 Lancasters of 3 Group attacked a benzol plant. 2 Lancasters lost.

DUISBURG

39 Mosquitoes of 8 Group attacked the oil plant at Meiderich without loss.

---

30 November/1 December 1944

DUISBURG

576 aircraft – 425 Halifaxes, 126 Lancasters, 25 Mosquitoes – of 1, 4, 6 and 8 Groups. 3 Halifaxes lost.

The target area was completely cloud-covered and the attack was not concentrated but much fresh damage was still caused. Duisburg reports 528 houses destroyed and 805 seriously damaged, but no industrial buildings are mentioned in the report. 246 people were killed, including 55 foreign workers and 12 prisoners of war.

Minor Operations: 53 Mosquitoes to Hamburg and 7 to Hallendorf, 88 aircraft of 100 Group on R.C.M. and Mosquito operations (separate figures not available), 9 aircraft on Resistance operations. 1 Intruder Mosquito lost.

Total effort for the night: 733 sorties, 4 aircraft (0·5 per cent) lost.

1/2 December 1944

MINOR OPERATIONS

71 Mosquitoes to Karlsruhe, 6 to Hallendorf and 4 to Duisburg, 24 R.C.M. sorties, 22 Mosquito patrols. No aircraft lost.

---

3 December 1944

DORTMUND

93 Lancasters of 3 Group attacked the Hansa benzol plant through thick cloud; the bombing was believed to be accurate. No aircraft lost.

1 Hudson flew a Resistance operation.

2/3 December 1944

HAGEN

504 aircraft – 394 Halifaxes, 87 Lancasters, 23 Mosquitoes – of 1, 4, 6 and 8 Groups. 1 Halifax and 1 Lancaster crashed in France.

The town of Hagen, not too heavily bombed before this raid, supplied 22 pages of detail and a large map showing the location of every high-explosive bomb which fell in the town. (There was even a full-page veterinary report.) Most of the bombing was in the central, eastern and southern areas of Hagen. There were 53 large fires.

Classed as destroyed or seriously damaged were: 1,658 houses, 92 industrial buildings, 21 schools, 14 cultural buildings, 5 hospitals, 5 banks, etc. 483 Germans and 100 foreigners were killed; 997 Germans and 88 foreigners were injured.

The effect upon industrial production was serious. Many of the firms shown in the Hagen report are recorded as having lost up to 3 months' production. In addition, it was found by the Allies after the war that a factory making U-boat accumulator batteries – of which large numbers were needed by the new types of U-boats – was completely destroyed in this raid.

Minor Operations: 66 Mosquitoes to Giessen, 44 R.C.M. sorties, 62 Mosquito patrols, 10 Stirlings on Resistance operations. 1 Stirling on Resistance work and 1 Intruder Mosquito lost.

Total effort for the night: 686 sorties, 4 aircraft (0·6 per cent) lost.

---

3 December 1944

HEIMBACH

183 Lancasters and 4 Mosquitoes of 1 and 8 Groups to bomb this small town in the Eifel region, probably in support of an American ground attack in this area. The Master Bomber and the Pathfinders could not identify the target and the Lancasters were ordered to abandon the raid. No aircraft lost.

1 Hudson flew a Resistance operation.

3/4 December 1944

11 *Oboe* Mosquitoes bombed a steelworks at Hallendorf without loss.

---

4 December 1944

OBERHAUSEN

160 Lancasters of 3 Group carried out a *G-H* raid but no results could be seen because of cloud. 1 Lancaster lost.

A short local report says that heavy damage was caused in the centre of the town, around the railway station. 472 houses were destroyed and 483 seriously damaged and several industrial and public premises were hit. The number of casualties is difficult to determine; 266 people are recorded as being killed, 642 as injured and 169 as missing in a composite report for this part of Germany, *Wehrkreis VI*, but the casualties for an American raid on Soest are included in this figure.

URFT DAM

27 Lancasters and 3 Mosquitoes of 8 Group carried out the first of several raids on this large reservoir dam in the Eifel, the destruction of which was required so that the Germans could not release water to flood areas through which American troops wished to advance. The series of raids did blast 13 ft off the top of the dam but no large breach was ever made and the Germans were able to release large quantities of

water whenever they wished to interfere with American advances being attempted further downstream.

No aircraft were lost from this raid.

4/5 December 1944

KARLSRUHE

535 aircraft – 369 Lancasters, 154 Halifaxes, 12 Mosquitoes – of 1, 6 and 8 Groups. 1 Lancaster and 1 Mosquito lost.

The marking and bombing were accurate and severe damage was caused, particularly in the southern and western districts of the city. Among individual buildings destroyed were the important Durlacher machine-tool factory, the main Protestant church and the concert hall. 375 Germans and 39 foreigners were killed.

HEILBRONN

282 Lancasters and 10 Mosquitoes of 5 Group. 12 Lancasters lost.

This was a crushing blow on Heilbronn which stood on a main north–south railway line but was otherwise of little importance. It was the first and only major raid by Bomber Command on this target. 1,254 tons of bombs fell in a few minutes and the post-war British Bombing Survey Unit estimated that 351 acres, 82 per cent of the town's built-up area, were destroyed, mainly by fire. Much investigation by various people resulted in the reliable estimate that just over 7,000 people died. Most of these victims would have died in fires so intense that there was probably a genuine firestorm.

Minor Operations: 54 Mosquitoes to Hagen and 12 to Bielefeld and Hamm (the figure was not subdivided), 47 R.C.M. sorties, 60 Mosquito patrols. No aircraft lost.

Total effort for the night: 1,000 sorties, 14 aircraft (1·4 per cent) lost.

---

5 December 1944

HAMM

94 Lancasters of 3 Group carried out a *G-H* raid through cloud. No aircraft lost.

The British Bombing Survey Unit estimated that 140 acres, 39 per cent of Hamm's built-up area, were destroyed by this attack.

SCHWAMMENAUEL DAM

56 Lancasters of 3 Group attempted to bomb this dam on the River Roer (sometimes called the River Rur) to help the American Army, but the target was covered by cloud and only 2 aircraft bombed. No aircraft lost.

1 Hudson flew a Resistance operation.

5/6 December 1944

SOEST

497 aircraft – 385 Halifaxes, 100 Lancasters, 12 Mosquitoes – of 1, 4, 6 and 8 Groups. 2 Halifaxes lost.

This was a successful raid, with the local report confirming that most of the bombing was in the northern part of the town where the railway installations were situated. Approximately 1,000 houses and 53 other buildings were completely destroyed and 198 Germans and 88 foreign workers were killed.

Minor Operations: 53 Mosquitoes to Ludwigshafen, 32 to Nuremberg and 4 to Duisburg, 36 R.C.M. sorties, 40 Mosquito patrols, 1 Stirling on a Resistance operation. No aircraft lost.

Total effort for the night: 663 sorties, 2 aircraft (0·3 per cent) lost.

6 December 1944

1 Hudson flew a Resistance operation.

6/7 December 1944

LEUNA

475 Lancasters and 12 Mosquitoes of 1, 3 and 8 Groups. 5 Lancasters lost.

This was the first major attack on an oil target in Eastern Germany; Leuna, near the town of Merseburg, just west of Leipzig, was 250 miles from the German frontier and 500 miles from the bombers' bases in England. There was considerable cloud in the target area but post-raid photographs showed that considerable damage had been caused to the synthetic-oil plant.

OSNABRÜCK

453 aircraft – 363 Halifaxes, 72 Lancasters, 18 Mosquitoes – of 1, 4, 6 and 8 Groups. 7 Halifaxes and 1 Lancaster lost.

This was the first major raid on Osnabrück since August 1942. The raid was only a partial success. The railway yards were only slightly damaged but 4 factories were hit, including the Teuto-Metallwerke munitions factory, and 203 houses were destroyed. 39 people were killed.

GIESSEN

255 Lancasters and 10 Mosquitoes of 5 Group. 8 Lancasters lost.

There were two aiming points for this raid. 168 aircraft were allocated to the town centre and 87 to the railway yards. Severe damage was caused at both places but the town of Giessen was unable to provide a local report.

Minor Operations: 42 Mosquitoes to Berlin, 10 to Schwerte and 2 to Hanau, 37 R.C.M. sorties, 47 Mosquito patrols. 2 Mosquitoes lost – 1 from the Berlin raid and an Intruder aircraft which crashed in France.

Total effort for the night: 1,343 sorties, 23 aircraft (1·7 per cent) lost.

7 December 1944

1 Hudson flew a Resistance operation.

7/8 December 1944

MINOR OPERATIONS

53 Mosquitoes to Cologne and 7 to Hanau, 3 R.C.M. sorties. No losses.

---

8 December 1944

URFT DAM

205 Lancasters of 5 Group; 1 aircraft lost. Bombing was affected by 9/10ths cloud and no results were seen.

DUISBURG

163 Lancasters of 3 Group carried out a *G-H* raid through cloud on the railway yards. 30 Mosquitoes of 8 Group attacked the Meiderich oil plant near Duisburg, probably using the *Oboe*-leader technique. No aircraft lost.

1 Hudson flew a Resistance operation.

9/10 December 1944

MINOR OPERATIONS

60 Mosquitoes to Berlin, 8 to Koblenz and 4 to Meiderich (Duisburg) oil plant, 36 R.C.M. sorties, 28 Mosquito patrols. 1 R.C.M. Halifax lost.

---

10 December 1944

1 Hudson flew a Resistance operation.

---

11 December 1944

URFT DAM

233 Lancasters of 5 Group and 5 Mosquitoes of 8 Group. Hits were scored on the dam but no breach was made. 1 Lancaster lost.

OSTERFELD

150 Lancasters of 3 Group on *G-H* raids through cloud on the railway yards (98 aircraft) and on the benzol plant (52 aircraft). The bombing appeared to be accurate. 1 Lancaster lost.

DUISBURG

80 Mosquitoes of 8 Group on *Oboe*-leader raids to a coking plant (48 aircraft) and to the Meiderich benzol plant. Most of the bombing on the benzol plant and approximately half on the coking plant appeared to be accurate. No aircraft lost.

Total effort for the day: 468 sorties, 2 aircraft (0·4 per cent) lost.

11/12 December 1944

MOSQUITO OPERATIONS

38 Mosquitoes to Hannover, 28 to Hamburg, 9 to Schwerte, 8 to Bielefeld and 6 to Duisburg. 1 aircraft lost from the Hamburg raid.

---

12 December 1944

WITTEN

140 Lancasters of 3 Group on a *G-H* raid to the Ruhrstahl steelworks. German fighters intercepted the force in the target area and 8 Lancasters were lost.

Witten provided a report for this raid. It was the town's first major raid of the war. The steelworks were not hit and bombs fell all over the town, destroying 126 houses and 5 industrial premises. 334 people were killed, 64 were missing and 345 were injured.

12/13 December 1944

ESSEN

540 aircraft – 349 Lancasters, 163 Halifaxes, 28 Mosquitoes – of 1, 4 and 8 Groups. 6 Lancasters lost.

This was the last heavy night raid by Bomber Command on Essen (though 2 day raids were still to come in 1945). During the post-war interrogations of Albert Speer, Hitler's Armaments Minister, he was asked which forms of attack were most effective in weakening the German war effort. After referring to the effectiveness of daylight raids and to some of the *Oboe* Mosquito attacks, Speer paid a compliment to the accuracy of this raid on Essen:

The last night attack upon the Krupp works, which was carried out by a large number of 4-engined bombers, caused surprise on account of the accuracy of the bomb pattern. We assumed that this attack was the first large-scale operation based on *Oboe* or some other new navigational system.*

A report from Essen shows that, besides the industrial damage caused on this raid, 696 houses were destroyed and 1,370 seriously damaged. The fatal casualty details are unusual. The total number of people killed was 463, made up of 160 German civilians, 89 prisoners of war, 13 foreign workers and 201 prisoners who were killed when the city prison was hit; a further 39 prisoners were 'missing'.

---

*The Speer interrogations are recorded in the British Official History, Vol. IV, pp. 378–95.

Minor Operations: 49 Mosquitoes to Osnabrück, 43 R.C.M. sorties, 43 Mosquito patrols. No aircraft lost.

Total effort for the night: 675 sorties, 6 aircraft (0·9 per cent) lost.

13/14 December 1944

OSLO FJORD

52 Lancasters and 7 Mosquitoes of 5 Group were sent to attack the German cruiser *Köln* but, when the bombers reached Oslo Fjord, the *Köln* had moved to another location. Other ships were bombed instead but the results were not observed. No aircraft lost.

10 Lancasters and 9 Halifaxes minelaying in the Kattegat without loss.

14/15 December 1944

MINELAYING

30 Lancasters and 9 Halifaxes minelaying in the Kattegat without loss.

---

15 December 1944

SIEGEN

138 Lancasters of 3 Group set out on this raid but were recalled because bad weather prevented their fighter escorts from taking off.

Ijmuiden

17 Lancasters of 617 Squadron attacked the E-boat pens with *Tallboys* but a smoke-screen hindered the bombing and no results were seen. No aircraft lost.

15/16 December 1944

LUDWIGSHAFEN

327 Lancasters and 14 Mosquitoes of 1, 6 and 8 Groups. 1 Lancaster lost.
  The target area for this raid was the northern part of Ludwigshafen and the small town of Oppau in which two important I.G. Farben chemical factories were situated. The local report shows that the raid was very successful, with 450 high-explosive bombs and many incendiaries falling in the premises of I.G. Farben. Severe damage was caused and fierce fires were started. The report states that no other attack since the start of the war had caused such a setback to I.G. Farben production, which included synthetic oil at this factory. The Oppau factory ceased production completely 'until further notice'. 5 other industrial firms were also badly hit. Some damage was also caused to housing areas around the various factories but this was not serious and the fatal casualty figure was only 57 people; 50 of these may have been foreign workers who were killed in one of the factories (the records are not clear

on this point). Damage was also caused to installations and ships at the nearby Rhine quays.

It would be difficult to find a Bomber Command night raid which caused so much industrial damage but so little in civilian housing areas.

Minor Operations: 62 Mosquitoes to Hannover, 11 to Osnabrück and 3 to Duisburg, 31 R.C.M. sorties, 38 Mosquito patrols, 15 Lancasters and 8 Halifaxes minelaying off north-eastern Denmark. 1 Lancaster minelayer lost.

Total effort for the night: 509 sorties, 2 aircraft (0·4 per cent) lost.

---

16 December 1944

The great German offensive in the Ardennes started on this day, with the object of capturing Brussels and the port of Antwerp and splitting the Allied armies into two parts. The attack was launched under cover of poor weather conditions, with low cloud and mist, and it would be several days before the R.A.F. and American bomber forces could intervene in the battle.

SIEGEN

108 Lancasters of 3 Group in a *G-H* raid on the railway yards. 1 Lancaster lost.

The bombing was accurate enough to hit Siegen and the neighbouring town of Weidenau but not to destroy the railway yards which were hit by only a few bombs. Many public buildings and houses were destroyed in Siegen, which had not been bombed seriously before, and 348 people were killed – 290 civilians, 26 servicemen and 32 foreign workers. The further number of dead in Wiedenau is not known.

1 Hudson flew on a Resistance operation.

16/17 December 1944

Minor Operations

1 Mosquito attempted to bomb Wiesbaden but did not reach the target and 2 Wellingtons flew R.C.M. sorties. No aircraft lost.

17/18 December 1944

DUISBURG

523 aircraft – 418 Halifaxes, 81 Lancasters, 24 Mosquitoes – of 4, 6 and 8 Groups. 8 Halifaxes lost.

Duisburg was badly hit again. 346 houses were destroyed and 524 seriously damaged; industrial premises were probably hit also but few details are available. 92 people, including 18 foreigners, were killed.

ULM

317 Lancasters and 13 Mosquitoes of 1 and 8 Groups. 2 Lancasters lost.

This was Bomber Command's first and only raid on Ulm, an old city but also the home of 2 large lorry factories – Magirius-Deutz and Kässbohrer – several other important industries and some military barracks and depots. The report from Ulm states that the local *Gauleiter* had urged an evacuation of women and children from the inner-city area following the recent bombing of Heilbronn, a city similar in character to Ulm. The *Ortsgruppenleiter* delayed the evacuation until 18 December, a Monday, so that families in this Catholic city could observe Advent Sunday together. On that Sunday, however, there was a further change of mind and loudspeaker vans were sent out into the streets of the inner city, urging the people to leave at once and thousands of people departed by train or on foot even though 'a cold, damp wind blew through the streets of the city'.

46. Teenagers from the anti-Nazi 'Cathedral Firefighting Group' at Aachen.

1,449 tons of bombs were dropped during the 25-minute raid, starting in the centre and then creeping back to the west, across the industrial and railway areas and out into the country. 1 square kilometre in the city was completely engulfed by fire. 81·8 per cent (it was a very detailed report) of all Ulm's property was affected in some way, including 29 industrial premises, among which were the two important lorry factories. The Gallwitz Barracks and several military hospitals were among 14 Wehrmacht establishments destroyed. The casualty figures were not as high as might have been expected; the evacuation which took place a few hours before the raid must have saved many lives. The dead were listed as follows: 606 civilians (291 women, 201 men, 114 children under the age of 14), 51 soldiers, police and air-raid workers, 50 foreigners. 613 people were injured and 20,000–25,000 were bombed out.

MUNICH

280 Lancasters and 8 Mosquitoes of 5 Group. 4 Lancasters lost.

Again, no local report could be obtained. Bomber Command claimed 'severe and widespread damage' in the old centre of Munich and at railway targets.

Minor Operations: 44 Mosquitoes to Hanau (a 'spoof' raid), 26 to Münster and 5 to Hallendorf, 44 R.C.M. sorties, 50 Mosquito patrols. No aircraft lost.

Total effort for the night: 1,310 sorties, 14 aircraft (1·1 per cent) lost.

18/19 December 1944

GDYNIA

236 Lancasters of 5 Group attacked this distant port on the Baltic coast and caused damage to shipping, installations and housing in the port area. 4 Lancasters lost.

Minor Operations: 40 Mosquitoes to Nuremberg and 16 to Münster, 34 R.C.M. sorties, 11 Mosquito patrols, 14 Lancasters of 5 Group minelaying in Danzig Bay. 1 Mosquito Intruder lost.

---

19 December 1944

TRIER

32 Lancasters of 3 Group carried out a *G-H* raid on the railway yards in this town behind the front on which the Germans were attacking in the Ardennes. No Lancasters lost.

A short local report states that many of the bombs fell in the town. Casualties were 60 dead, 300 injured and 20 missing. 30 of the dead were nurses who were in the 'vaulted winecellar' of the Town Hospital when it was penetrated by a bomb.

19/20 December 1944

12 Lancasters of 3 Group minelaying in the Kadet Channel off Denmark without loss.

---

21 December 1944

TRIER

113 Lancasters of 3 Group again attempted to bomb the railway yards in 2 waves. No Lancasters lost.

The bomber crews were unable to observe results because of the cloud, although a large column of smoke eventually appeared. The Trier report can only state that the second wave of the bombing caused heavy casualties, but no other details are available.

1 Hudson flew a Resistance operation.

21/22 December 1944

PÖLITZ

207 Lancasters and 1 Mosquito of 5 Group attacked the synthetic-oil refinery at Pölitz, near Stettin. 3 Lancasters were lost and 5 more crashed in England.

Post-raid reconnaissance showed that the power-station chimneys had collapsed and that other parts of the plant were damaged.

COLOGNE/NIPPES

136 aircraft – 67 Lancasters, 54 Halifaxes, 15 Mosquitoes – of 4, 6 and 8 Groups attacked the important Nippes marshalling yards which were being used to serve the German offensive in the Ardennes. No aircraft lost.

The target was cloud-covered and only a few bombs hit the railway yards but these caused the destruction of 40 wagons, a repair workshop and several railway lines. The city slaughterhouse in nearby Ehrenfeld was also destroyed. 14 people were killed and 13 injured.

BONN

97 Lancasters and 17 Mosquitoes of 1 and 8 Groups attempted to attack railway areas but thick cloud cover prevented an accurate raid and later reconnaissance showed that the railway target was not hit. No other details are available. No aircraft lost.

Minor Operations: 4 Lancasters of 5 Group to Schneidmühl as a diversion for the Pölitz raid, 15 R.C.M. sorties, 12 Mosquito patrols, 30 Lancasters and 23 Halifaxes minelaying in the Kattegat. No aircraft lost.

Total effort for the night: 542 sorties, 3 aircraft (0·6 per cent) lost.

22/23 December 1944

KOBLENZ

166 Lancasters and 2 Mosquitoes, mostly from 1 Group but with some Pathfinders. No aircraft lost.

The aiming point was the Mosel railway yards. There was some cloud in the target area and the local report says that the main weight of the attack fell in farming areas between 2 and 4 kilometres to the west, where the villages of Güls and Rübenach were badly hit. But the fringes of the bombing fell on the railway yards, several main lines and 2 important road bridges. Fatal casualties were: 40 people in Koblenz (including 34 policemen and air-raid workers and a French labourer), 90 in Güls and 19 in Rübenach.

BINGEN

106 aircraft – 90 Halifaxes of 4 Group and 14 Lancasters and 2 Mosquitoes of 8 Group. 2 Halifaxes and 1 Lancaster lost.

The railway yards were again the objective of the raid. The attack was extremely accurate and all the bombs fell into the yards or into the nearby Rhine, where 2 barges were sunk. All movement of supplies by rail through Bingen to the Ardennes battle front ceased. About 150 houses in the town suffered blast damage but not one civilian was killed or injured. The town wine store was, however, hit.

Minor Operations: 44 aircraft of 100 Group flew R.C.M. sorties and Mosquito patrols (the figure cannot be broken down). No aircraft lost.

---

23 December 1944

TRIER

153 Lancasters of 3 Group attempted to attack the railway yards through cloud. The bombing appeared to be accurate and concentrated but Trier could only report that it was the town's worst raid of the war. 1 Lancaster lost.

COLOGNE/GREMBERG

27 Lancasters and 3 Mosquitoes of 8 Group to attack the Gremberg railway yards.

The raid went very badly. The force was split into 3 formations, each led by an *Oboe*-equipped Lancaster with an *Oboe* Mosquito as reserve leader. During the outward flight, 2 Lancasters of 35 Squadron collided over the French coast and their crews were all killed. On approaching the target, it was found that the cloud which had been forecast had cleared and it was decided to allow the bombers to break formation and bomb visually; this move was made because the formations would have been very vulnerable to Cologne's Flak defences during the long, straight *Oboe* approach. Unfortunately the order to abandon the *Oboe* run did not reach the leading Lancaster, a 582 Squadron aircraft piloted by Squadron Leader R. A. M. Palmer, D.F.C. (on loan from 109 Squadron), who continued on with his designated role, even though his aircraft was already damaged by Flak. German fighters, who were being directed to intercept an American bomber force, also appeared and attacked. The bombs from Squadron Leader Palmer's aircraft were eventually released and hit the target but his plane went down out of control and only the tail gunner escaped, by parachute. Squadron Leader Palmer, on his 110th operation, was awarded a posthumous Victoria Cross, the only *Oboe* V.C. of the war; his body is buried in the Rheinberg War Cemetery with the other men who died in the Lancaster.

The formation suffered further losses when another Lancaster and a Mosquito were shot down by Flak and fighters and a further Lancaster had to be abandoned by its crew over Belgium. The losses were thus 6 aircraft out of the 30 dispatched.

23/24 December 1944

MINOR OPERATIONS

52 Mosquitoes to Limburg railway yards, 40 to Siegburg and 7 on 'training flights' to Bremen, Hannover, Münster and Osnabrück, 62 aircraft of 100 Group on R.C.M. and Mosquito operations (the figures cannot be broken down), 6 aircraft on Resistance operations. No aircraft were lost. Each of the Mosquitoes shown as being on 'training flights' visited all 4 targets and dropped 1 bomb on each; these operations later became known as 'siren-sounding tours'.

---

24 December 1944

GERMAN AIRFIELDS

338 aircraft – 248 Halifaxes, 79 Lancasters, 11 Mosquitoes – of 4, 6 and 8 Groups attacked the airfields at Lohausen and Mülheim (now Düsseldorf and Essen civil airports). The purpose of the raids was not recorded; it is possible that they were to hinder the movement of supplies by transport aircraft from the Ruhr to the Ardennes battle area. Both attacks took place in conditions of good visibility and the bombing was accurate. 6 aircraft lost – 2 Lancasters and 1 Halifax from the Lohausen raid and 3 Halifaxes from the Mülheim raid.

24/25 December 1944

HANGELAR AIRFIELD

104 Lancasters of 3 Group carried out an accurate attack on Hangelar airfield near Bonn. 1 Lancaster lost. No results are known.

COLOGNE/NIPPES

97 Lancasters and 5 Mosquitoes of 1 and 8 Groups. 5 Lancasters were lost and 2 more crashed in England.

The *Oboe* marking and the resultant bombing were extremely accurate. The local report says that the railway tracks were severely damaged and that an ammunition train blew up. The nearby Butzweilerhof airfield was also damaged. 18 civilians and 1 soldier were killed, probably when houses near the railway yards were hit.

Minor Operations: 2 Mosquitoes to Münster, 42 R.C.M. sorties, 42 Mosquito patrols, 12 Halifaxes of 6 Group minelaying off Oslo, 8 aircraft on Resistance operations. No aircraft lost.

26 December 1944

ST-VITH

The weather at last improved and allowed Bomber Command to intervene in the Ardennes battle. 294 aircraft – 146 Lancasters, 136 Halifaxes, 12 Mosquitoes – of all the bomber groups (not 100 Group) attacked German troop positions near St-Vith. This was the first time since mid-October that aircraft from all the bomber groups had joined together in one raid. The bombing appeared to be concentrated and accurate. 2 Halifaxes lost.

1 Halifax flew a signals patrol.

27 December 1944

RHEYDT

200 Lancasters and 11 Mosquitoes of 1, 3, 5 and 8 Groups attacked the railway yards. 1 Lancaster was lost and 1 Mosquito crashed behind the Allied lines in Holland.

27/28 December 1944

OPLADEN

328 aircraft – 227 Halifaxes, 66 Lancasters, 35 Mosquitoes. 2 Lancasters lost. 9 of the Mosquitoes bombed 3½ hours before the main raid. The aiming point for the attack was the marshalling yards but results are not known.

Minor Operations: 7 Mosquitoes on *Oboe* trials to Bonn, Eisenach, Frankfurt and Kassel (probably calibrating new *Oboe* stations in France and Belgium), 7 Mosquitoes on 'siren tours' of Hamburg, Hannover, Münster and Osnabrück, 32 R.C.M. sorties, 37 Mosquito patrols. No aircraft lost.

28 December 1944

COLOGNE/GREMBERG

167 Lancasters of 3 Group attacked the marshalling yards with accurate bombing. No aircraft lost.

1 Hudson flew on a Resistance operation.

28/29 December 1944

MÖNCHENGLADBACH

186 aircraft – 129 Lancasters, 46 Halifaxes, 11 Mosquitoes – of 1, 4 and 8 Groups. No aircraft lost.

The railway yards were the aiming point but little damage was caused there. Scattered bombing throughout Mönchengladbach and the neighbouring town of Rheydt destroyed 128 houses and 19 public buildings in Mönchengladbach and, in Rheydt, 45 houses, the Catholic church, a school and the office block of the local power-station. 21 (or 24, accounts differ) people were killed in Mönchengladbach and 30 in Rheydt. 200 bombs were also recorded in the village of Wickrath, 7 km south-west of Mönchengladbach; 5 people were killed there.

BONN

162 Lancasters and 16 Mosquitoes of 1 and 8 Groups. 1 Lancaster lost.

The intention again was to bomb the railway installations. Bomber Command's report states that the main weight of the attack fell on the railway yards, causing 'considerable damage'. This is not borne out by a report from Bonn to which is attached a police document (secret at that time) which is in great detail and would be unlikely to omit serious damage to railways. The only railway incident mentioned is the collapse of the Victoria road bridge across the main line from Cologne to Koblenz. A great deal of general damage, on buildings ranging from the university to a slaughterhouse, is listed. 486 people were killed; many of them were in 2 public shelters which received direct hits.

OSLO FJORD

67 Lancasters and 1 Mosquito of 5 Group attacked a 'large naval unit' and some merchant ships but no direct hits were claimed. No aircraft lost.

Minor Operations: 87 Mosquitoes to Frankfurt – 79 to the city generally and 8 to the railway yards – 35 R.C.M. sorties, 45 Mosquito patrols, 16 Halifaxes of 6 Group minelaying in the Skagerrak and 11 Lancasters of 5 Group off Oslo, 12 aircraft on Resistance operations. 1 minelaying Halifax was lost and 1 Mosquito from the Frankfurt raid crashed in France.

Total effort for the night: 638 sorties, 3 aircraft (0·5 per cent) lost.

---

29 December 1944

KOBLENZ

Two separate forces bombed railway yards in Koblenz, one of the main centres serving the Ardennes battlefront. 192 aircraft – 162 Halifaxes, 22 Lancasters, 8 Mosquitoes – of 4 and 8 Groups attacked the Mosel yards, near the main city, and 85 Lancasters of 3 Group attacked the Lützel yards north of the city. No aircraft were lost from either operation.

At least part of the bombing of each raid hit the railway areas. The local report (from Dr Helmut Schnatz) says: 'The raids completed the severe damage inflicted by the American attack of the previous day. The whole railway system was blocked . . . The Koblenz–Lützel railway bridge was out of action for the rest of the war and the cranes of the Mosel Harbour were also put out of action.' Only 39 people were killed: 32 civilians, 6 servicemen and 1 Italian worker; 50 people were injured.

Minor Operations: 16 Lancasters of 617 Squadron attacked the E-boat pens at Rotterdam, scoring several hits; 1 Hudson flew a Resistance operation. No aircraft lost.

29/30 December 1944

SCHOLVEN/BUER

324 Lancasters and 22 Mosquitoes of 1, 6 and 8 Groups. 4 Lancasters lost.

The raid took place in difficult conditions. There was thick cloud over the target but *Oboe* sky-markers were accurately placed and the oil refinery was badly hit. The local report says that 300 high-explosive bombs fell within the oil-plant area. There were two large and 10 small fires and much damage to piping and storage tanks. The local report records a further 3,198 bombs falling in other parts of Scholven and Buer, causing much property and some industrial damage; the surface buildings of the Hugo I and Hugo II coal mines were severely damaged. 93 people were killed, of whom 24 were prisoners of war; 41 people were injured and 1,368 people had to leave their homes, 1,178 through bomb damage and 190 because of unexploded bombs.

TROISDORF

197 aircraft – 159 Halifaxes, 24 Lancasters, 14 Mosquitoes – of 6 and 8 Groups attempted to bomb the railway yards but most of the attack missed the target. No other details are available. No aircraft lost.

Minor Operations: 28 R.C.M. sorties, 28 Mosquito patrols, 16 aircraft of 6 Group minelaying in the River Elbe, 8 Mosquitoes of 5 Group minelaying off Oslo. No aircraft lost.

Total effort for the night: 623 sorties, 4 aircraft (0·6 per cent) lost.

---

30 December 1944

13 Lancasters of 617 Squadron set out to bomb the U-boat pens at Ijmuiden but the raid was abandoned because of bad weather.

30/31 December 1944

COLOGNE/KALK

470 aircraft – 356 Halifaxes, 93 Lancasters, 21 Mosquitoes – of 4, 6 and 8 Groups to attack the area in which the Kalk-Nord railway yards were situated. 1 Halifax and 1 Lancaster lost.

The presence of cloud caused difficulties for the Pathfinders and the outcome of the raid could not be observed. But the local report shows that the Kalk-Nord yards, as well as the 2 passenger stations near by, were severely damaged. At least 2 ammunition trains blew up. Nearby *Autobahnen* were also badly damaged, all adding to the effect upon the German transportation system. Bombing which fell around the railway targets destroyed 116 houses, 3 industrial premises, 5 police or postal buildings, 2 schools and 2 churches. 24 people were killed.

HOUFFALIZE

154 Lancasters and 12 Mosquitoes of 5 Group attacked a German supply bottleneck in a narrow valley at Houffalize. The results of the raid are not known. 1 Lancaster crashed in France.

Minor Operations: 68 Mosquitoes to Hannover, 9 to Bochum and 8 to Duisburg, 32 R.C.M. sorties, 36 Mosquito patrols, 11 Lancasters minelaying off Heligoland, 21 aircraft on Resistance operations. No aircraft lost.

Total effort for the night: 821 sorties, 3 aircraft (0·4 per cent) lost.

---

31 December 1944

VOHWINKEL

155 Lancasters of 3 Group carried out a *G-H* raid on the railway yards at Vohwinkel, near Solingen. A strong wind carried much of the bombing south of the target. 83 people were killed and 97 were injured in Solingen but no other details are available. 2 Lancasters lost.

OSLO

12 Mosquitoes of 627 Squadron, 5 Group, set out to bomb the Gestapo Headquarters in Oslo. 8 aircraft actually bombed, in 2 waves, and hits were believed to have been scored. No aircraft lost.

---

31 December 1944/1 January 1945

OSTERFELD

149 Lancasters and 17 Mosquitoes of 1 and 8 Groups to attack the railway yards. The only details available are Bomber Command's estimates that the railway sidings were 35 per cent damaged and the 'facilities' 20 per cent damaged. 2 Lancasters lost.

OSLO FJORD

28 Lancasters of 5 Group attacked cruisers in the fjord but no hits were scored. 1 Lancaster lost.

Minor Operations: 77 Mosquitoes to Berlin and 12 to Ludwigshafen, 33 R.C.M. sorties, 33 Mosquito patrols, 16 Halifaxes and 10 Lancasters minelaying in the Kattegat. 1 minelaying Lancaster lost.

Operational Statistics, 16/17 August 1944
to the night of 31 December 1944/1 January 1945 (137½ days/nights)

Number of nights with operations: 115
Number of days with operations: 116 (20 of these involved fewer than 10 sorties)
Number of night sorties: 43,819, from which 497 aircraft (1·1 per cent) were lost
Number of day sorties: 28,992, from which 199 aircraft (0·7 per cent) were lost
Total sorties: 72,881, from which 696 aircraft (1·0 per cent) were lost
Approximate bomb tonnage in period: 265,708 tons
Averages per 24-hour period: 530·0 sorties, 5·1 aircraft lost, 1,932·4 tons of bombs dropped

21. VICTORY

1 January to 7/8 May 1945

The final period of these diaries does not open with a clearly defined change in Bomber Command's policy or operations; the last four months of the war in Europe were really a continuation of that phase which had commenced with the Allied break-out from Normandy. But the opportunity is taken to split this final phase of the opening of that bright New Year of 1945, so that the progress of the war, the background of the direction of the bomber operations and other changes affecting the final few months of Bomber Command's efforts during the Second World War can be described.

The offensive in the Ardennes ran its course; the Germans failed to capture either Brussels or Antwerp. Their units were harried from the air, ran out of supplies, and were eventually stopped by a determined defence, mainly by the American troops on whose sector the blow had fallen, though some British troops were involved. Hitler's last gamble in the West had failed but the Germans had imposed a setback to the Allied timetable. The Ardennes front was not finally stabilized until the end of January 1945 and the Allied armies then took several weeks to close up to the Rhine, ready for the assault on Germany's last main line of defence on that broad river. It was not until late in March that the Rhine was crossed in strength and the final breakthrough into Germany commenced, but then events moved fast. The Ruhr was encircled at the beginning of April but held out for eighteen days before the 325,000 troops trapped there finally surrendered those ruined cities to the Allies. American troops linked up with the Russians a few days later on the River Elbe. Berlin fell to the Russians. Montgomery's British and Canadian troops liberated the remainder of Holland and raced northwards to capture Bremen, Hamburg and Lübeck and to meet the Russians on the Baltic coast. Hitler committed suicide and a few days later the war in Europe was over.

But the arguments over the use of Bomber Command continued, almost to the very end. The official priority of attack against oil targets, with the second priority against transportation, remained unchanged. There was a small scare in January when Bomber Command and the Americans were ordered to attack targets associated with the production of German jet aircraft and the new types of '*Schnorkel*'-equipped U-boats. These were difficult targets for Bomber Command but some effort was devoted to them. The real argument, however, was over the employment of Bomber Command's main strength. The Air Ministry was still disappointed that Sir Arthur Harris was devoting so much effort to the general attack on German cities at this late stage of the war, at a time when so many improvements in bombing techniques had become available and when the Combined Chiefs of Staff were ordering the all-out attack on oil and transportation targets. The Official History* describes a long

* Vol. III, pp. 81–94.

47 (a and b). The aircraft repair organization. A Lancaster which crash-landed on returning from Germany is recovered and repaired. According to the notice on the wall of the workshop, the aircraft should be ready for operation within a month of the crash-landing.

exchange of correspondence between Sir Charles Portal and Sir Arthur Harris on this subject. But a study of the diary entries for the last few weeks of the war shows that Harris was devoting more effort to the attack on oil and communications than is popularly believed. The weather was often a problem. Harris may not have sent every sortie possible against the selective targets, but he certainly dispatched a very high proportion of the effort available *when conditions were suitable*. Comment in the Official History, the tenor of the correspondence between Portal and Harris and the view of many post-war publications tend to obscure that fact. But it is still true to say that great raids were sometimes sent, both in good and not-so-good weather conditions, to carry out area attacks on German cities, some of which had little industrial importance. These remarks do not apply to the raid on Dresden, which later caused such a furore; Dresden was attacked in special circumstances which will be described in the appropriate diary entry.

The outcome of this continued area bombing at such a late stage of the war led to Harris being immediately shuffled off into the sidelines as soon as the war was over. It led to the present-day R.A.F. preference for honouring the men of the Battle of Britain – in which fewer airmen died than in one Bomber Command raid to Nuremberg in March 1944 – and the long official reluctance to acknowledge the years of effort and sacrifice by the men of Bomber Command.

So Harris remained to the end but the opportunity was taken to change some of the long-serving group commanders. Air Vice-Marshals Rice of 1 Group, Carr of 4 Group and Cochrane of 5 Group all went in February. There was no criticism of performance in these changes, merely the desire to give experience of command to a new generation of leaders before the war finished. One long-serving group commander –'Pathfinder' Bennett – was not rested; the R.A.F. had no plans for the Pathfinders after the war. (8 Group was disbanded in December 1945. Also to go in 1945 were 4 Group – to become part of Transport Command; 5 Group – surplus to requirement; 6 (Canadian) Group – its squadrons all returned to Canada; and 100 Group – its functions incorporated into other units.)

The final months of operations were flown. January was a quieter month, because of the weather, but then the level of operations rose to a crescendo. March, with a hectic round of raids by day as well as by night, produced a greater weight of bombs dropped by Bomber Command – 67,637 tons – than in any month of the war, the same tonnage as the command had dropped in the first thirty-four months of the war! New cities were visited – places like Hanau, Würzburg, Pforzheim, Wiesbaden, Worms in the West and, further away, Chemnitz, Dresden, Dessau and Potsdam. Oil plants of various kinds were still bombed; many of these targets were now deep in Eastern Germany. Railway yards, canals and bridges were still attacked. German towns near the battle front were reduced to ruins. The German defences continued to decline in effectiveness, although there were occasional flashes of action by the night fighters and some sharp losses were suffered. The weather remained a constant enemy. It was almost all over by the end of March and most of Bomber Command's targets in the remaining five weeks of the war were strictly military ones. The strategic bomber offensive was over.

---

1 January 1945

DORTMUND–EMS CANAL

102 Lancasters and 2 Mosquitoes of 5 Group were dispatched to attack the stretch of

the canal near Ladbergen which the Germans had once more repaired. The raid was successful and the canal was breached again. 2 Lancasters lost.

One of the Lancaster casualties – a 9 Squadron aircraft piloted by Flying Officer R. F. H. Denton – was hit by Flak shortly after bombing and was set on fire. Flight Sergeant George Thompson, the wireless operator, rescued both gunners from their burning turrets but suffered severe burns in doing so. The Lancaster crash-landed at Brussels and Thompson was rushed to hospital but he died 3 weeks later. The mid-upper gunner, Sergeant E. J. Potts, also died of his burns. Flight Sergeant Thompson was awarded a posthumous Victoria Cross for his courage. This was the second Victoria Cross awarded to a 5 Group man while attacking the Dortmund–Ems Canal; Flight Lieutenant R. A. B. Learoyd of 49 Squadron received the decoration for his bravery in an August 1940 raid.

Railway Tunnels

17 Mosquitoes of 8 Group to bomb the mouths of tunnels in the wooded and hilly Eifel region between the Rhine and the Ardennes battle area. Each Mosquito was to dive and attempt to place its 4,000-lb bomb fitted with a short delayed-action fuze in the mouth of a tunnel. 14 tunnels were attacked in this way. 1 Mosquito lost.

1/2 January 1945

MITTELLAND CANAL

152 Lancasters and 5 Mosquitoes of 5 Group carried out an accurate attack on the Gravenhorst section of the canal. Half a mile of banks were pitted with bomb craters and some parts were breached. No aircraft lost.

VOHWINKEL

146 aircraft of 3 Group successfully attacked the railway yards. 1 Lancaster lost.

DORTMUND

105 Halifaxes of 4 Group and 18 Lancasters and 16 Mosquitoes of 8 Group attempted to bomb a benzol plant but the attack was scattered and the plant was not hit. No aircraft lost.

Minor Operations: 28 Mosquitoes to Hanau and 27 to Hannover (both 'spoof' raids), 42 R.C.M. sorties, 59 Mosquito patrols. No aircraft lost. The 100 Group Mosquitoes claimed 6 German night fighters destroyed.

Total effort for the night: 598 sorties, 1 aircraft (0·2 per cent) lost; 5 aircraft crashed in England.

---

2 January 1945

2 Hudsons flew on Resistance operations without loss.

2/3 January 1945

NUREMBERG

514 Lancasters and 7 Mosquitoes of 1, 3, 6 and 8 Groups. 4 Lancasters were lost and 2 crashed in France.

Nuremberg, scene of so many disappointments for Bomber Command, finally succumbed to this attack. The Pathfinders produced good ground-marking in conditions of clear visibility and with the help of a rising full moon. The centre of the city, particularly the eastern half, was destroyed. The castle, the Rathaus, almost all the churches and about 2,000 preserved medieval houses went up in flames. The area of destruction also extended into the more modern north-eastern and southern city areas. 4,640 houses (mostly blocks of flat) were destroyed. The industrial area in the south, containing the important M.A.N. and Siemens factories, and the railway areas were also severely damaged. 415 separate industrial buildings were destroyed. It was a near-perfect example of area bombing. 1,838 people were killed and at least 50 more were missing; the number of injured was not recorded.

LUDWIGSHAFEN

389 aircraft – 351 Halifaxes, 22 Lancasters, 16 Mosquitoes – of 4, 6 and 8 Groups. 1 Halifax which crashed in France was the only loss.

The aiming point for this raid was the area of the two I.G. Farben chemical factories. A good local report shows that the bombing was accurate, with severe damage to the main I.G. Farben factory and to the same firm's factory at nearby Oppau. Estimated totals of 500 high-explosive bombs and 10,000 incendiaries fell inside the limits of the 2 factories, causing much damage. 10 large, 30 medium and 200 small fires were recorded at the main factory. Production failure at both plants was complete because of 'loss of power'. 13 other industrial firms and several railway installations were also hit; the train of a railway repair unit was destroyed. Only a small proportion of the bombing fell in housing areas. 103 houses were destroyed and 251 seriously damaged. 1,800 people were bombed out. The people of Ludwigshafen must have been provided with very good shelters; only 5 people were killed and 50 injured.

Minor Operations: 53 Mosquitoes to Berlin, 9 to Castrop-Rauxel and 7 to Hanau, 49 R.C.M. sorties, 41 Mosquito patrols. 2 Mosquitoes were lost, 1 each from the Berlin and Castrop-Rauxel raids.

Total effort for the night: 1,069 sorties, 9 aircraft (0·8 per cent) lost.

3 January 1945

BENZOL PLANTS

99 Lancasters of 3 Group made *G-H* attacks through cloud on the Hansa plant at Dortmund and the Castrop-Rauxel plant. Bombing appeared to be accurate at both targets. 1 Lancaster lost from the Dortmund raid.

3/4 January 1945

Mosquito Operations

3 *Oboe* Mosquitoes each to the railway yards at Ludwigshafen and Neuss. No aircraft lost.

---

4 January 1945

1 Hudson flew on a Resistance operation.

4/5 January 1945

ROYAN

347 Lancasters and 7 Mosquitoes of 1, 5 and 8 Groups. 4 Lancasters were lost and 2 more collided behind Allied lines in France and crashed.

This was a tragic raid with a strange – and disputed – background. Royan was a town situated at the mouth of the River Gironde in which a stubborn German garrison was still holding out, preventing the Allies from using the port of Bordeaux. The task of besieging the town had been given to 12,000 men of the French Resistance commanded by Free French officers appointed by General de Gaulle. The commander of the German garrison recognized the Resistance units as regular forces and the normal rules of warfare were observed. The French, lacking artillery, made little progress with their siege. The German commander gave the inhabitants of the town the opportunity to leave but many preferred to stay in order to look after their homes. It is believed that there were 2,000 civilians at the time of the raid.

The request that Bomber Command should attack the town has a tortuous background and it must be stressed that the version given here may be disputed by some of the participants.* On 10 December 1944, a meeting took place at the town of Cognac between French officers and an American officer from one of the tactical air force units in France. After a meal, at which much alcohol is supposed to have been consumed, the American officer suggested that the German garrison at Royan should be 'softened up' by bombing. He was assured by the French that the only civilians remaining in the town were collaborators – which was not correct. The suggestion that the town be bombed was passed to S.H.A.E.F. (Supreme Headquarters Allied Expeditionary Force), which decided that the task should be given to Bomber Command: 'To destroy town strongly defended by enemy and occupied by German troops only.' It is said that S.H.A.E.F. ordered a last-minute cancellation because of doubts about the presence of French civilians but the order, if issued, was not received by Bomber Command in time.

The attack was carried out by 2 waves of bombers, in good visibility conditions, in the early hours of 5 January. 1,576 tons of high-explosive bombs – including 285 'blockbuster' (4,000-lb bombs) – were dropped. Local reports show that between 85 and 90 per cent of the small town was destroyed. The number of French civilians killed is given as '500 to 700' and as '800' by different sources. Many of the casualties

---

* Acknowledgement is made to MM. Robert Colle, Curator of the Royan Museum, and Pierre Lis, Mayor of Royan in 1982, for their research.

were suffered in the second part of the raid, which took place an hour after the first and caught many people out in the open trying to rescue the victims of the first wave of the bombing trapped in their houses. The number of Germans killed is given as 35 to 50. A local truce was arranged and, for the next 10 days, there was no fighting while the search for survivors in wrecked houses continued.

There were many recriminations. Bomber Command was immediately exonerated. The American air-force officer who passed on the original suggestion to S.H.A.E.F. was removed from his command. The bitterest disputes took place among the Free French officers and accusations and counter-accusations continued for many years after the war. A French general committed suicide. De Gaulle, in his *Mémoires*, blamed the Americans: 'American bombers, on their own initiative, came during the night and dropped a mass of bombs.'* The German garrison did not surrender until 18 April.

Minor Operations: 66 Mosquitoes to Berlin and 7 to Neuss, 2 Halifax R.C.M. sorties. No aircraft lost.

Some of the Light Night Striking Force (8 Group) Mosquitoes which attacked Berlin on this night flew 2 sorties each. These Mosquitoes took off in the early evening, bombed Berlin, returned and changed crews, and then flew to Berlin again. This method of augmenting the Mosquito campaign against Berlin was used several times during the long nights of midwinter.

---

5 January 1945

LUDWIGSHAFEN

160 Lancasters of 3 Group attacked the railway-yards area. 2 Lancasters lost.

The local report shows that the railways were hit but bombs also fell in the northern suburbs of Ludwigshafen, which were partially industrial in nature, and in nearby villages. 535 houses and 87 industrial buildings were destroyed or seriously damaged and 3,500 people were bombed out. 267 people were killed, of whom no less than 229 were foreign workers or prisoners of war.

1 Hudson flew a Resistance operation.

5/6 January 1945

HANNOVER

664 aircraft – 340 Halifaxes, 310 Lancasters, 14 Mosquitoes – of 1, 4, 6 and 8 Groups. 23 Halifaxes and 8 Lancasters lost, 4·7 per cent of the force.

This was the first large raid on Hannover since October 1943. Bombs fell all over the city and the local report, based on messages from 16 of the 18 police districts, shows that 493 buildings, containing 3,605 flats/apartments, were destroyed and that approximately 250 people were killed. No further details are available.

HOUFFALIZE

131 Lancasters and 9 Mosquitoes of 5 Group attacked this bottleneck in the German supply system in the Ardennes. The target was bombed with great accuracy. 2 Lancasters lost.

*Charles de Gaulle, *Mémoires de Guerre*, Plon Presse, 1959, Vol. III, p. 159.

Minor Operations: 69 Mosquitoes to Berlin, 8 to Neuss and 6 to Castrop-Rauxel, 58 R.C.M. sorties, 55 Mosquito patrols. 4 Mosquitoes lost, 2 from the Berlin raid and 2 from 100 Group.

Total effort for the night: 1,000 sorties, 37 aircraft (3·7 per cent) lost.

---

6 January 1945

1 Hudson flew a Resistance operation.

6/7 January 1945

HANAU

482 aircraft – 314 Halifaxes, 154 Lancasters, 14 Mosquitoes – of 1, 4, 6 and 8 Groups. 4 Halifaxes and 2 Lancasters lost.

The attack was aimed at that part of Hanau in which an important junction in the German railway system was situated. The local report says that many bombs did fall in this area but also states that a large proportion of the bombing was scattered in the south – into the centre of Hanau – and to the north – into an area of countryside and villages. The report states that 'approximately 40 per cent' of Hanau was destroyed, with 90 people being killed. The village of Mittelbuchen was also badly hit.

NEUSS

147 Lancasters of 1 and 3 Groups. 1 Lancaster crashed in Belgium.

As in Hanau, some of the bombing fell into the railway area but most was scattered over surrounding districts. 1,749 houses, 19 industrial premises and 20 public buildings were destroyed or seriously damaged. 39 people were killed and 91 injured.

Minor Operations: 20 Mosquitoes to Kassel (a 'spoof' raid) and 6 to Castrop-Rauxel, 52 R.C.M. sorties, 32 Mosquito patrols, 49 Lancasters minelaying off Baltic ports. 2 R.C.M. Halifaxes and 2 Lancaster minelayers lost.

Total effort for the night: 788 sorties, 11 aircraft (1·4 per cent) lost.

7/8 January 1945

MUNICH

645 Lancasters and 9 Mosquitoes of 1, 3, 5, 6 and 8 Groups. 11 Lancasters lost and 4 more crashed in France.

Bomber Command claimed a successful area raid, with the central and some industrial areas being severely damaged. No local details are available. This was the last major raid on Munich.

Minor Operations: 54 Mosquitoes to Hannover, 18 to Nuremberg and 12 to Hanau, 39 R.C.M. sorties, 45 Mosquito patrols. 2 Mosquitoes lost – 1 from the Hannover raid and a 100 Group aircraft.

The last Bomber Command Wellington operation was flown on this night by Flying Officer B. H. Stevens and his crew of 192 Squadron. The Wellington was on an R.C.M. flight over the North Sea 'to investigate enemy beam signals connected with the launching of flying bombs and believed to emanate from marker buoys'. Bad weather over the North Sea caused the flight to be curtailed but the Wellington landed safely, the last of more than 47,000 sorties carried out by this type of aircraft in Bomber Command.

Total effort for the night: 822 sorties, 17 aircraft (2·1 per cent) lost.

10/11 January 1945

MOSQUITO OPERATIONS

50 Mosquitoes to Hannover and 3 each to Cologne, Koblenz, Mannheim and Wiesbaden. No aircraft lost.

---

11 January 1945

KREFELD

152 Lancasters of 3 Group carried out a *G-H* raid on the railway yard in the Uerdingen suburb of Krefeld. A composite report from Krefeld describes this raid as a *'Grossangriff'*, one of only 3 such classifications in the whole war and the report confirms that the bombing was in the 'eastern districts' where Uerdingen is located. No other information is available. No aircraft lost.

1 Stirling flew on a Resistance operation.

---

12 January 1945

BERGEN

32 Lancasters and 1 Mosquito of 9 and 617 Squadrons attacked U-boat pens and shipping in Bergen harbour. 3 Lancasters of 617 Squadron and 1 from 9 Squadron were lost; the Germans told the local people that 11 bombers had been shot down.

A local report says that 3 *Tallboys* penetrated the 3½-metre-thick roof of the pens and caused severe damage to workshops, offices and stores inside. 2 U-boats – U-775 and U-864 – were slightly damaged. The minesweeper *M-1* was sunk in the harbour and the 3,347-ton German cargo ship *Olga Simers* was damaged and had to be either beached or brought into dry dock (the expression used in the Bergen report is 'had to be shored').

Bergen had suffered many civilian casualties in 2 earlier raids but the more accurate bombing on this day resulted in no deaths or damage to civilian houses being incurred in the town. 20 of the 34 German sailors in the minesweeper's crew were killed and 2 other Germans died.

2 Mosquito fighters of 100 Group flew long-range escort for an air–sea rescue operation and 2 Stirlings flew R.C.M. sorties, all without loss.

12/13 January 1945

MINOR OPERATIONS

11 Mosquitoes to Bochum and 9 to Recklinghausen, both forces to bomb synthetic-benzol plants, and 32 Halifaxes minelaying off Flensburg and Kiel. 4 Halifaxes lost.

13 January 1945

SAARBRÜCKEN

158 Lancasters of 3 Group attacked the railway yards. The bombing appeared to be accurate, though with some overshooting. 1 Lancaster crashed in France.

1 Hudson flew on a Resistance operation.

13/14 January 1945

SAARBRÜCKEN

274 aircraft – 242 Halifaxes, 20 Lancasters, 12 Mosquitoes – of 4, 6 and 8 Groups. 1 Halifax crashed in France.

48. This Halifax of 51 Squadron had its nose smashed off in a collision with another bomber after bombing Saarbrücken on the night of 13/14 January 1945. The bomb aimer and the navigator were killed but the pilot, Flying Officer Wilson, was able to bring the aircraft back to what appears to be an airfield near Brussels where many damaged bombers were able to land in this period of the war.

Bomber Command assessed this raid, on the railway yards, as being extremely accurate and effective. The only local report says that 20 people – 18 men and 2 women – were killed.

PÖLITZ

218 Lancasters and 7 Mosquitoes of 5 Group attacked this oil plant, near Stettin. 2 Lancasters lost.

This raid had been planned as a blind-bombing attack but, because the weather conditions were better than forecast, low-level marking was carried out and very accurate bombing followed. Bomber Command, on the basis of photographic reconnaissance, states that the oil plant was 'reduced to a shambles'.

Minor Operations: 19 R.C.M. sorties, 22 Mosquito patrols, 10 Lancasters minelaying off Swinemünde. 1 Mosquito of 100 Group lost.

Total effort for the night: 550 sorties, 4 aircraft (0·7 per cent) lost.

---

14 January 1945

SAARBRÜCKEN

134 Lancasters of 3 Group attacked the railway yards in clear visibility and without loss.

14/15 January 1945

LEUNA

573 Lancasters and 14 Mosquitoes of 1, 5, 6 and 8 Groups carried out two attacks, 3 hours apart, on the synthetic-oil plant. The attacks caused severe damage throughout the plant. Albert Speer, in his post-war interrogations, stated that this was one of a group of most damaging raids on the synthetic-oil industry carried out during this period. 10 Lancasters lost.

GREVENBROICH

151 aircraft – 136 Halifaxes, 12 Mosquitoes, 3 Lancasters – of 6 and 8 Groups attacked the railway yards. The raid was successful and no aircraft were lost.

DÜLMEN

115 aircraft – 100 Halifaxes, 12 Mosquitoes, 3 Lancasters – of 4 and 8 Groups attempted to bomb a Luftwaffe fuel-storage depot at Dülmen, near Münster, but most of the bombing fell in open country south and south-east of the target. Only slight damage was caused to the fuel dump. 1 Halifax lost.

SUPPORT AND MINOR OPERATIONS

126 training aircraft on a diversionary sweep over the North Sea, 83 Mosquitoes to Berlin and 9 to Mannheim, 58 R.C.M. sorties, 54 Mosquito patrols, 21 Halifaxes and 10 Lancasters minelaying off Oslo and in the Kattegat. 1 Lancaster from the diversionary sweep and 1 Mosquito of 100 Group were lost; 3 Mosquitoes from the Berlin raid crashed in Belgium and 1 R.C.M. Liberator crashed in Holland. A further 7 aircraft from the sweep and 5 Mosquitoes from the Berlin raid crashed in England because of bad weather.

Total effort for the night: 1,214 sorties, 17 aircraft (1·4 per cent) lost and 14 aircraft crashed in England.

---

15 January 1945

RECKLINGHAUSEN

82 Lancasters of 3 Group attacked a benzol plant. The bombing appeared to be excellent. No aircraft lost.

BOCHUM

63 Lancasters of 3 Group carried out a *G-H* raid through thick cloud on the Robert Muser benzol plant. No results known. No aircraft lost.

1 Hudson on a Resistance operation.

16/17 January 1945

MAGDEBURG

371 aircraft – 320 Halifaxes, 44 Lancasters, 7 Mosquitoes – of 4, 6 and 8 Groups. 17 Halifaxes lost, 4·6 per cent of the total force, 5·3 per cent of the Halifax force.

This was an area raid. Bomber Command claimed that it was successful, with 44 per cent of the built-up area being destroyed. No local report is available.

ZEITZ

328 Lancasters of 1, 6 and 8 Groups. 10 Lancasters lost, 3·0 per cent of the force.

The target was the Braunkohle-Benzin synthetic-oil plant near Leipzig. Much damage was caused to the northern half of the plant.

BRÜX

231 Lancasters and 6 Mosquitoes of 1 and 5 Groups attacked this synthetic-oil plant in Western Czechoslovakia. The raid was a complete success. Speer also mentioned this raid as causing a particularly severe setback to oil production. 1 Lancaster lost.

WANNE-EICKEL

138 Lancasters of 3 Group attacked the benzol plant. No results known. 1 Lancaster lost.

Minor Operations: 17 Mosquitoes to Mannheim and 9 to Hamburg, 55 R.C.M. sorties, 52 Mosquito patrols, 23 Halifaxes and 8 Lancasters minelaying off Oslo and in the Kattegat. 1 Mosquito of 100 Group lost.

Total effort for the night: 1,238 sorties, 30 aircraft (2·4 per cent) lost.

---

17 January 1945

1 Hudson on a Resistance operation.

17/18 January 1945

MINOR OPERATIONS

72 Mosquitoes to Magdeburg, 8 to Ruthen oil-storage depot and 3 each to Cologne, Frankfurt, Koblenz and Mannheim, 33 R.C.M. sorties, 13 Mosquito patrols. No aircraft lost.

18/19 January 1945

MOSQUITO OPERATIONS

56 Mosquitoes to Sterkrade oil refinery, 12 each, on *H2S* trials, to Düsseldorf, Kassel and Koblenz and 7 to Ruthen oil depot. 1 Mosquito from the Sterkrade raid crashed in Belgium.

21/22 January 1945

MINOR OPERATIONS

76 Mosquitoes to Kassel and 4 to Mainz, 23 R.C.M. sorties, 9 Mosquito patrols, 2 Hudsons on Resistance operations. 1 Mosquito lost from the Kassel raid.

---

22 January 1945

1 Halifax flew an R.C.M. sortie.

22/23 January 1945

DUISBURG

286 Lancasters and 16 Mosquitoes of 1, 3 and 8 Groups. 2 Lancasters lost.

This raid was intended for the benzol plant in the Bruckhausen district of Duisburg. This target was identified visually by moonlight and much damage was inflicted on it. Further bombing also hit the nearby Thyssen steelworks, either by misidentification or by a simple spread of the bombing. Duisburg's local report assumed that the steelworks were the primary target and stated that 500 high-explosive bombs fell on the Thyssen premises. 163 houses around the target areas were destroyed and 289 seriously damaged. 152 people were killed; 115 of these were foreign workers or prisoners of war.

GELSENKIRCHEN

152 aircraft – 107 Halifaxes, 29 Lancasters, 16 Mosquitoes – of 4, 5 and 8 Groups. No aircraft lost.

This was a small area-bombing raid. The Bomber Command report states that 'moderate' damage was caused to residential and industrial areas. No further details are available.

Minor Operations: 48 Mosquitoes to Hannover and 6 to Dortmund, 50 R.C.M. sorties, 40 Mosquito patrols. No aircraft lost.

Total effort for the night: 598 sorties, 2 aircraft (0·3 per cent) lost.

26/27 January 1945

8 Mosquitoes bombed the Castrop-Rauxel synthetic-oil refinery without loss.

---

27 January 1945

1 Lightning of 100 Group flew on a signals-investigations patrol.

27/28 January 1945

12 Mosquitoes to Berlin; 8 bombed this target and 3 bombed alternative targets. No aircraft lost.

---

28 January 1945

COLOGNE/GREMBERG

153 Lancasters of 3 Group attacked the railway yards in conditions of good visibility. Some of the bombing fell on the target but some overshot. 3 Lancasters were lost and 1 crashed in France.

28/29 January 1945

STUTTGART AREA

602 aircraft – 316 Halifaxes, 258 Lancasters, 28 Mosquitoes – of 1, 4, 6 and 8 Groups. 11 aircraft – 6 Lancasters, 4 Halifaxes, 1 Mosquito – lost.

This raid was split into 2 parts, with a 3-hour interval. The first force – of 226 aircraft – was directed against the important railway yards at Kornwestheim, a town to the north of Stuttgart, and the second was against the north-western Stuttgart suburb of Zuffenhausen, where the target is believed to have been the Hirth aero-engine factory. The target area was mostly cloud-covered for both raids and the bombing, on sky-markers, was scattered.

There are some interesting local reports. Bombs fell in many parts of Stuttgart's northern and western suburbs. The important Bosch works, in the suburb of Feuerbach, was hit. The attack on Kornwestheim was the worst suffered by that town during the war; the Kornwestheim local report shows that the local people felt they had been bombed by mistake and that the main target was in Stuttgart. 14 high-explosive bombs fell in the industrial area of the town and in the railway yards. Fires burned for up to 12 hours. 123 people were killed in Stuttgart and 41 in Kornwestheim. A large number of bombs fell outside Stuttgart, particularly in the east around a decoy fire site which was also firing dummy target-indicator rockets into the air. The village of Weilimdorf, situated not far away, complained bitterly about its damage and casualties!

Our local expert, Heinz Bardua, also tells the story of the newly promoted Flak Leutnant at his battery position at Vaihingen, situated just south of the decoy fire site. With bombs falling all around his position, the Leutnant thought that the raid was directed against the Flak positions. He ignored regulations about conservation of ammunition and shot his entire stock at the radar echoes of the attacking bombers. 2 Lancasters and a Halifax crashed in the immediate vicinity, much to the relief of the officer, who had feared a court martial because of his prodigious use of ammunition.

This was the last large R.A.F. raid on Stuttgart. Herr Bardua says that the city had endured 53 major raids, most of them by the R.A.F., during which 32,549 blocks of flats or houses were destroyed (67·8 per cent of the total). After the war, 4·9 million cubic metres of rubble had to be cleared. 4,562 people died in the air raids, among them 770 prisoners of war or foreign workers. Stuttgart's experience was not as severe as other German cities. Its location, spread out in a series of deep valleys, had consistently frustrated the Pathfinders and the shelters dug into the sides of the surrounding hills had saved many lives.

Minor Operations: 67 Mosquitoes to Berlin and 8 to Mainz (a 'spoof' raid for the Stuttgart attacks), 51 R.C.M. sorties, 36 Mosquito patrols, 6 Lancasters of 1 Group minelaying in the Kattegat. 1 Mosquito of 100 Group crashed in France.

Total effort for the night: 770 sorties, 12 aircraft (1·6 per cent) lost.

---

29 January 1945

KREFELD

148 Lancasters of 3 Group attacked the Uerdingen railway yards without loss. Bombing was claimed to be accurate but a short Krefeld report states that bombs fell over a wide area. No other details are available.

29/30 January 1945

BERLIN

59 Mosquitoes; 50 aircraft reached and bombed the city without loss.

---

31 January/1 February 1945

Mosquito Operations

8 Mosquitoes to the Hansa benzol plant at Dortmund and 6 Mosquitoes to Duisburg. 1 aircraft from the Dortmund raid crashed in Holland.

The weather started to improve at the beginning of February and Bomber Command commenced an almost unbroken period of operations of the most intense and concentrated nature which would continue until a halt was called to the strategic-bombing offensive in April. The first round of raids, however, was not very effective because of poor weather at the targets.

1 February 1945

MÖNCHENGLADBACH

160 Lancasters of 3 Group attacked the general town area through 8–10/10ths cloud, using *G-H*. The results of the raid are not known. 1 Lancaster crashed in France.

1 Halifax flew an R.C.M. sortie.

1/2 February 1945

LUDWIGSHAFEN

382 Lancasters and 14 Mosquitoes of 1, 6 and 8 Groups. 6 Lancasters lost.

Most of the force aimed their loads at sky-markers and the local report shows that bombs fell in many parts of Ludwigshafen, with much property damage of a mixed nature. The 900 houses destroyed or seriously damaged were the main item in the report but it also states that the railway yards were seriously damaged and one of the Rhine road bridges was hit by 2 bombs and temporarily closed to traffic. 25 people were killed and 6 injured, figures which might indicate that the population either had been evacuated or were extremely well provided with shelters.

MAINZ

340 aircraft – 293 Halifaxes, 40 Lancasters, 8 Mosquitoes – of 4, 6 and 8 Groups. No aircraft lost.

A few early crews were able to bomb target indicators seen through a gap in the clouds, but the gap soon closed and most of the raid was on sky-markers. The local report states that a few buildings were destroyed, including the Christuskirche, which burnt out, and the town hospital was damaged, but most of the bombing fell outside Mainz. 33 people were killed.

SIEGEN

271 Lancasters and 11 Mosquitoes of 5 Group. 3 Lancasters and 1 Mosquito lost.

This raid also experienced difficult marking and bombing conditions. Some damage was caused to the railway station but the local report says that the markers were either carried away from Siegen by a strong wind or that dummy markers and a decoy fire site attracted much of the bombing. Most of the raid fell in country areas outside Siegen. 128 people died.

Minor Operations: 122 Mosquitoes to Berlin, 8 to Bruckhausen benzol plant, 6 to Hannover, 4 to Nuremberg and 4 dropping dummy target indicators at both Mannheim and Stuttgart, 64 R.C.M. sorties, 47 Mosquito patrols. No aircraft lost.

Total effort for the night: 1,273 sorties, 10 aircraft (0·8 per cent) lost.

---

2 February 1945

2 Mosquito Ranger patrols over Northern Germany without loss.

2/3 February 1945

WIESBADEN

495 Lancasters and 12 Mosquitoes of 1, 3, 6 and 8 Groups. 3 Lancasters crashed in France.

This was Bomber Command's one and only large raid on Wiesbaden. There was complete cloud cover but most of the bombing hit the town. A brief local report states that 520 houses and about 30 other buildings were destroyed, and 400 houses and 50 other buildings were seriously damaged. 5 important war industries along the banks of the Rhine were untouched but the railway station was damaged. Casualties were recorded as 'approximately 1,000 killed and 350 injured'.

WANNE-EICKEL

323 aircraft – 277 Halifaxes, 27 Lancasters, 19 Mosquitoes – of 4, 6 and 8 Groups. 4 Halifaxes lost.

This target was also cloud-covered and the attack, intended for the oil refinery, was not accurate. The local report assumed that the target was a local coal mine – Shamrock 3/4; most of the bombing fell in the open ground around the mine, although 21 houses were hit and 68 people were killed.

KARLSRUHE

250 Lancasters and 11 Mosquitoes of 5 Group. 14 Lancasters lost. 189 Squadron, from Fulbeck, lost 4 of its 19 aircraft on the raid.

Cloud cover over the target caused this raid to be a complete failure. Karlsruhe reports no casualties and only a few bombs. The report mentions 'dive bombers', presumably the Mosquito marker aircraft trying to establish their position. This was a lucky escape for Karlsruhe in its last major R.A.F. raid of the war.

Minor Operations: 43 Mosquitoes to Magdeburg and 20 to Mannheim, 54 R.C.M. sorties, 44 Mosquito patrols. No aircraft lost.

Total effort for the night: 1,252 sorties, 21 aircraft (1·7 per cent) lost.

3 February 1945

U-BOAT PENS

36 Lancasters of 5 Group attacked pens at Ijmuiden (9 Squadron) and Poortershaven (617 Squadron) with *Tallboy* bombs. It was believed that these pens, in that part of Holland still occupied by the Germans, were sheltering midget submarines. The weather was clear and hits were claimed at both targets without loss.

1 Halfax flew an R.C.M. sortie.

3/4 February 1945

BOTTROP

192 Lancasters and 18 Mosquitoes of 1 and 8 Groups attacked the Prosper benzol plant. A local report confirms that severe damage was caused in an accurate raid. 2 people died. 8 Lancasters lost.

DORTMUND

149 Lancasters of 3 Group attacked the Hansa benzol plant but the bombing fell north and north-west of the target. 4 Lancasters lost.

Minor Operations: 42 Mosquitoes to Wiesbaden and 20 to Osnabrück, 42 R.C.M. sorties, 28 Mosquito patrols, 19 Halifaxes of 4 Group minelaying off German ports. No aircraft lost.

Total effort for the night: 510 sorties, 12 aircraft (2·4 per cent) lost.

4/5 February 1945

BONN

238 aircraft – 202 Halifaxes, 20 Lancasters, 16 Mosquitoes – of 4, 6 and 8 Groups. 3 Lancasters lost.
    This was a poor attack, with most of the bombing falling to the south of the target or over the Rhine in the Beuel area. 19 people were killed.

OSTERFELD

123 aircraft – 100 Halifaxes, 12 Mosquitoes, 11 Lancasters – of 6 and 8 Groups attacked a benzol plant but caused no fresh damage. No aircraft lost.

GELSENKIRCHEN

120 aircraft – 96 Halifaxes, 12 Lancasters, 12 Mosquitoes – of 4 and 8 Groups attacked the Nordstern synthetic-oil plant. Some minor damage was caused but most of the bombs fell south of the target. No aircraft lost.

Minor Operations: 50 Mosquitoes to Hannover, 12 to Dortmund, 4 to Magdeburg and 3 to Würzburg, 59 R.C.M. sorties, 42 Mosquito patrols, 15 Lancasters and 12 Halifaxes minelaying off Heligoland and in the River Elbe. 2 Mosquitoes lost, 1 each from the Hannover and Würzburg raids.

Total effort for the night: 678 sorties, 5 aircraft (0·7 per cent) lost.

---

5 February 1945

1 Halifax flew an R.C.M. sortie.

5/6 February 1945

MINOR OPERATIONS

63 Mosquitoes to Berlin, 7 to Magdeburg and 6 to Würzburg, 1 R.C.M. sortie. 1 Mosquito lost from the Berlin raid.

---

6 February 1945

RAILWAY VIADUCTS

35 aircraft of 5 Group (9 and 617 Squadrons) to attack viaducts at Bielefeld and Altenbeken were recalled because of bad weather.

---

7 February 1945

WANNE-EICKEL

100 Lancasters of 3 Group to attack the oil plant. Only 75 aircraft were able to bomb in wintry conditions which scattered the force. The results of the raid are not known. 1 Lancaster lost.

7/8 February 1945

GOCH

464 aircraft – 292 Halifaxes, 156 Lancasters, 16 Mosquitoes – of 4, 6 and 8 Groups. 2 Halifaxes lost.

This raid was preparing the way for the attack of the British XXX Corps across the German frontier near the Reichswald. The Germans had included the towns of Goch and Kleve in their strong defences here. The Master Bomber ordered the Main Force to come below the cloud, the estimated base of which was only 5,000 ft, and the attack opened very accurately. The raid was stopped after 155 aircraft had bombed, because smoke was causing control of the raid to become impossible.

Considerable damage was caused in Goch but most of the inhabitants had probably left the town. Approximately 30 local people died. There were heavy casualties among Russians, Italians and Dutchmen who had been brought in as forced workers to dig the local defences; they were quartered in 2 schools, which were bombed, and more than 150 of them died. The number of German soldiers killed is not known.

KLEVE

295 Lancasters and 10 Mosquitoes of 1 and 8 Groups. 1 Lancaster lost.

285 aircraft bombed at Kleve, which was battered even more than Goch. Few details are available from local reports and casualties may not have been heavy (most of the civilian population were absent), but, after the war, Kleve claimed to be the most completely destroyed town in Germany of its size.

The British attack, led by the 15th (Scottish) Division, made a successful start a few hours later but quickly ground to a halt because of a thaw, which caused flooding on the few roads available for the advance, and also because of the ruins which blocked the way through Kleve. Lieutenant-General B. G. Horrocks, the corps commander in charge of the attack, later claimed that he had requested that Kleve should only be subjected to an incendiary raid but Bomber Command dropped 1,384 tons of high explosive on the town and no incendiaries.

DORTMUND–EMS CANAL

177 Lancasters and 11 Mosquitoes of 5 Group attacked the canal section near Ladbergen with delayed-action bombs. Later photographs showed that the banks had not been damaged; the bombs had fallen into nearby fields. 3 Lancasters were lost.

Minor Operations: 38 Mosquitoes to Magdeburg, 16 to Mainz and 41 in small numbers to 5 other targets, 63 R.C.M. sorties, 45 Mosquito patrols, 30 Lancasters and 15 Halifaxes minelaying in Kiel Bay. 4 Mosquitoes lost – 3 from 100 Group and 1 from the raid on Mainz.

Total effort for the night: 1,205 sorties, 10 aircraft (0·8 per cent) lost.

---

8 February 1945

IJMUIDEN

15 Lancasters of 617 Squadron dropped *Tallboys* on the U-boat pens without loss.

1 R.C.M. sortie was flown.

8/9 February 1945

PÖLITZ

475 Lancasters and 7 Mosquitoes of 1, 5 and 8 Groups. 12 Lancasters lost, 1 of them coming down in Sweden.

The attack took place in 2 waves, the first being marked and carried out entirely by the 5 Group method and the second being marked by the Pathfinders of 8 Group. The weather conditions were clear and the bombing of both waves was extremely accurate. Severe damage was caused to this important synthetic-oil plant. It produced no further oil during the war. Speer mentioned this raid, in his post-war interrogations, as being another big setback to Germany's war effort.

WANNE-EICKEL

228 aircraft – 200 Halifaxes, 20 Mosquitoes, 8 Lancasters – of 4, 6 and 8 Groups. 2 Halifaxes crashed in France.

This raid was not a success. The local report says that the bombing was scattered, with only light damage to the oil refinery. 45 Germans and 17 foreigners were killed.

KREFELD

151 Lancasters of 3 Group attacked the Hohenbudberg railway yards but photographic reconnaissance was unable to detect any new damage. 2 Lancasters lost.

Minor Operations: 47 Mosquitoes to Berlin, 9 to Neubrandenburg (a 'spoof' for the Pölitz raid) and 4 to Nuremberg, 47 R.C.M. sorties, 42 Mosquito patrols, 10 Lancasters of 5 Group minelaying off Swinemünde. 1 R.C.M. Halifax lost.

Total effort for the night: 1,020 sorties, 17 aircraft (1·7 per cent) lost.

---

9 February 1945

1 Halifax flew an R.C.M. sortie.

9/10 February 1945

Minor Operations

7 Stirlings of 3 Group flew on Resistance operations but none were able to carry out their tasks (the reasons were not recorded) and 1 Stirling was lost. 1 Mosquito flew an R.C.M. sortie.

---

10 February 1945

1 Halifax flew an R.C.M. sortie.

10/11 February 1945

MINOR OPERATIONS

82 Mosquitoes to Hannover and 11 to Essen, 24 R.C.M. sorties, 22 Mosquito patrols. No aircraft lost.

12/13 February 1945

MOSQUITO OPERATIONS

72 Mosquitoes to Stuttgart, 11 to Misburg, 4 to Würzburg and 3 each 'on *H2S* trials' to Cologne, Frankfurt, Koblenz and Wiesbaden, 1 Mosquito on an R.C.M. sortie. No aircraft lost.

13/14 February 1945

DRESDEN

The Air Ministry had, for several months, been considering a series of particularly heavy area raids on German cities with a view to causing such confusion and consternation that the hard-stretched German war machine and civil administration would break down and the war would end. The general name given to this plan was Operation *Thunderclap*, but it had been decided not to implement it until the military situation in Germany was critical. That moment appeared to be at hand. Russian forces had made a rapid advance across Poland in the second half of January and crossed the eastern frontier of Germany. The Germans were thus fighting hard inside their own territory on two fronts, with the situation in the East being particularly critical. It was considered that Berlin, Dresden, Leipzig and Chemnitz – all just behind the German lines on the Eastern Front now – would be suitable targets. They were all vital communications and supply centres for the Eastern Front and were already packed with German refugees and wounded from the areas recently captured by the Russians. As well as the morale aspect of the attacks, there was the intention of preventing the Germans from moving reinforcements from the West to face the successful Russian advance. The Air Ministry issued a directive to Bomber Command at the end of January. The Official History * describes how Winston Churchill took a direct hand in the final planning of Operation *Thunderclap* – although Churchill tried to distance himself from the Dresden raid afterwards. On 4 February, at the Yalta Conference, the Russians asked for attacks of this kind to take place, but their involvement in the process only came after the plans had been issued. So, Bomber Command was specifically requested by the Air Ministry, with Churchill's encouragement, to carry out heavy raids on Dresden, Chemnitz and Leipzig. The Americans were also asked to help and agreed to do so. The campaign should have begun with an American raid on Dresden on 13 February but bad weather over Europe prevented any American operations. It thus fell to Bomber Command to carry out the first raid.

796 Lancasters and 9 Mosquitoes were dispatched in two separate raids and dropped 1,478 tons of high explosive and 1,182 tons of incendiary bombs. The first attack was carried out entirely by 5 Group, using their own low-level marking methods. A band of cloud still remained in the area and this raid, in which 244 Lancasters dropped more than 800 tons of bombs, was only moderately successful. The second raid, 3 hours later, was an all-Lancaster attack by aircraft of 1, 3, 6 and 8 Groups, with 8 Group providing standard Pathfinder marking. The weather was now clear and 529 Lancasters dropped more than 1,800 tons of bombs with great accuracy. Much has been written about the fearful effects of this raid. Suffice it to say here that a firestorm, similar to the one experienced in Hamburg in July 1943, was created and large areas of the city were burnt out. No one has ever been able to discover how many people died but it is accepted that the number was greater than the 40,000 who died in the Hamburg firestorm and the Dresden figure may have exceeded 50,000.

Bomber Command casualties were 6 Lancasters lost, with 2 more crashed in France and 1 in England.

311 American B-17s dropped 771 tons of bombs on Dresden the next day, with

* Vol. IV, pp. 112–13.

the railway yards as their aiming point. Part of the American Mustang-fighter escort was ordered to strafe traffic on the roads around Dresden to increase the chaos. The Americans bombed Dresden again on the 15th and on 2 March but it is generally accepted that it was the R.A.F. night raid which caused the most serious damage.

BÖHLEN

368 aircraft – 326 Halifaxes, 34 Lancasters, 8 Mosquitoes – of 4, 6 and 8 Groups attempted to attack the Braunkohle-Benzin synthetic-oil plant at Böhlen, near Leipzig. Bad weather – 10/10ths cloud to 15,000 ft with icing – was encountered and the marking and bombing were scattered. No post-raid photographic reconnaissance was carried out. 1 Halifax was lost.

Minor Operations: 71 Mosquitoes to Magdeburg, 16 to Bonn, 8 each to Misburg and Nuremberg and 6 to Dortmund, 65 R.C.M. sorties, 59 Mosquito patrols. No aircraft lost.

Total effort for the night: 1,406 sorties, 9 aircraft (0·6 per cent) lost.

---

14 February 1945

RAILWAY VIADUCTS

36 Lancasters and 1 photographic Mosquito of 9 and 617 Squadrons dispatched to attack Bielefeld and Altenbeken viaducts abandoned the raids because of cloud. 1 Lancaster of 9 Squadron lost.

14/15 February 1945

CHEMNITZ

499 Lancasters and 218 Halifaxes of 1, 3, 4, 6 and 8 Groups to continue Operation *Thunderclap*. 8 Lancasters and 5 Halifaxes lost.

This raid took place in two phases, 3 hours apart. A very elaborate diversion plan succeeded in keeping bomber casualties down but Chemnitz – now called Karl-Marx-Stadt – was also spared from the worst effects of its first major R.A.F. raid. Both parts of the bomber force found the target area covered by cloud and only sky-marking could be employed. Post-raid reconnaissance showed that many parts of the city were hit but that most of the bombing was in open country. The Stadtarchiv of Karl-Marx-Stadt was unable to provide a local report.

ROSITZ

224 Lancasters and 8 Mosquitoes of 5 Group attacked the oil refinery in this small town near Leipzig. 4 Lancasters were lost. Damage was caused to the southern part of the oil plant.

DIVERSIONARY AND MINOR OPERATIONS

95 aircraft of 3 Group and of Heavy Conversion Units on a sweep into the Heligoland Bight, 46 Mosquitoes to Berlin, 19 to Mainz, 14 to Dessau, 12 to Duisburg, 11 to Nuremberg and 8 to

Frankfurt, 21 R.C.M. sorties, 87 Mosquito patrols, 30 Lancasters and 24 Halifaxes minelaying in the Kadet Channel. 5 Halifaxes and 1 Lancaster lost from the minelaying force.

Total effort for the night: 1,316 sorties, 23 aircraft (1·7 per cent) lost.

---

15 February 1945

1 Halifax flew an R.C.M. sortie.

15/16 February 1945

MINOR OPERATIONS

37 Lancasters and 18 Halifaxes minelaying in Oslo Fjord and the Kattegat, 2 R.C.M. sorties, 6 Mosquito patrols. 1 Mosquito fighter crashed in France.

---

16 February 1945

WESEL

100 Lancasters of 3 Group and 1 Mosquito of 8 Group attacked this town on the Rhine, near the fighting area. No aircraft lost.

The raid took place in clear conditions and 'the town and the railway were seen to be smothered in bomb bursts'. No local details are available other than the information that the local population was still present and presumably suffered heavy casualties. The number of civilians killed in Wesel during the war numbered 562. Most of the survivors were evacuated after this raid.

---

17 February 1945

WESEL

298 aircraft – 247 Halifaxes, 27 Lancasters, 24 Mosquitoes – of 4, 6 and 8 Groups. The target area was covered in cloud and the Master Bomber ordered the raid to be stopped after only 8 Halifaxes had bombed. No aircraft were lost but 3 Halifaxes crashed in England.

17/18 February 1945

Bremen

6 *Oboe* Mosquitoes attacked the Deschimag shipyard but no results were seen because of ground fog. No aircraft lost.

---

18 February 1945

WESEL

160 Lancasters of 3 Group carried out a *G-H* attack through cloud. No Lancasters lost.

18/19 February 1945

MINOR OPERATIONS

32 Mosquitoes to Mannheim, 6 each to Berlin and Bremen and 3 on 'siren tours' of various towns in Central Germany, 34 R.C.M. sorties, 18 Mosquito patrols, 21 Lancasters and 4 Halifaxes minelaying in the German Bight. 2 Lancasters were lost from the minelaying force.

---

19 February 1945

WESEL

168 Lancasters of 3 Group carried out a good attack with the best concentration of bombs being in the railway area. 1 Lancaster lost.

1 Halifax flew an R.C.M. sortie.

19/20 February 1945

BÖHLEN

254 Lancasters and 6 Mosquitoes of 5 Group. 1 Mosquito lost.

This raid was not successful, probably because the aircraft of the Master Bomber, Wing Commander E. A. Benjamin, was shot down by Flak over the target. Post-raid reconnaissance showed that damage to the target was 'superficial'; there was no evidence to show where the main bombing fell. (The body of Wing Commander E. A. Benjamin, D.F.C. and Bar, is buried in the Berlin War Cemetery.)

Minor Operations: 82 Mosquitoes to Erfurt and 24 in small numbers to 6 other targets, 9 R.C.M. sorties, 29 Mosquito patrols. No aircraft lost.

---

20 February 1945

1 Halifax flew an R.C.M. sortie.

20/21 February 1945

DORTMUND

514 Lancasters and 14 Mosquitoes of 1, 3, 6 and 8 Groups. 14 Lancasters lost.

The intention of this raid was to destroy the southern half of Dortmund and Bomber Command claimed that this was achieved. It appears that the Dortmund air-raid recording service had now broken down completely; the local Stadtarchiv has no details of any kind of this raid.

This was the last large Bomber Command raid of the war on Dortmund.

DÜSSELDORF

173 aircraft – 156 Halifaxes, 11 Mosquitoes, 6 Lancasters – of 4 and 8 Groups attacked the Rhenania Ossag refinery in the Reisholz district of Düsseldorf. The raid was accurate and it was later established that all oil production was halted. 7 people died in the raid. 4 Halifaxes and 1 Lancaster lost.

MONHEIM

128 aircraft – 112 Halifaxes, 10 Mosquitoes, 6 Lancasters – of 6 and 8 Groups attacked the Rhenania Ossag refinery at Monheim with similar results to the Reisholz raid. 2 Halifaxes lost.

MITTELLAND CANAL

154 Lancasters and 11 Mosquitoes of 5 Group were ordered to attack the canal section near Gravenhorst but the raid was ordered to be abandoned by the Master Bomber because the area was covered by cloud. No aircraft lost.

DIVERSIONARY AND MINOR OPERATIONS

91 aircraft from Heavy Conversion Units in a sweep over the North Sea, 66 Mosquitoes to Berlin and 16 to Mannheim, 65 R.C.M. sorties, 45 Mosquito patrols, 6 aircraft on Resistance operations. 1 aircraft of 100 Group (type not recorded) lost.

Total effort for the night: 1,283 sorties, 22 aircraft (1·7 per cent) lost.

---

21 February 1945

1 Halifax flew an R.C.M. sortie.

21/22 February 1945

DUISBURG

362 Lancasters and 11 Mosquitoes of 1, 6 and 8 Groups. 7 Lancasters were lost and 3 crashed behind Allied lines in Europe.

This was a successful area-bombing raid and much damage was caused. No other details are available. This was the last major Bomber Command raid on Duisburg.

WORMS

349 aircraft – 288 Halifaxes, 36 Lancasters, 25 Mosquitoes. 10 Halifaxes and 1 Lancaster lost.

This was the first and only large Bomber Command raid on Worms. The raid was an area attack in which 1,116 tons of bombs were accurately dropped. A post-war survey estimated that 39 per cent of the town's built-up area was destroyed. The local report says that a considerable part of the bombing fell just outside the town, to the south-west, but it confirms that the remainder caused severe damage in Worms. 64 per cent of the town's buildings were destroyed or damaged, including the cathedral, the town museum, and most of the churches and cultural buildings in the old centre. Much of the town's industry was also destroyed, including the only firm devoted completely to the production of war material, one making sprocket wheels for tanks. 239 people were killed and 35,000 bombed out from a population of approximately 58,000.

MITTELLAND CANAL

165 Lancasters and 12 Mosquitoes of 5 Group again attempted to breach the canal near Gravenhorst. Visibility was clear and the attack was successful. Bomber Command claimed that the canal was rendered '100 per cent unserviceable'. 9 Lancasters were lost and 4 crashed in France and Holland, 7·9 per cent of the Lancaster force. One of the Lancasters which crashed in Holland was piloted by Group Captain A. C. Evans-Evans, D.F.C., the station commander at Coningsby, flying an 83 Squadron aircraft. The Lancaster was shot down by a German fighter and crashed near Eindhoven. One of the gunners was the only survivor.

Minor Operations: 77 Mosquitoes to Berlin and 5 to Bremen, 66 R.C.M. sorties, 35 Mosquito patrols, 28 aircraft on Resistance operations. No aircraft lost.

Total effort for the night: 1,110 sorties, 34 aircraft (3·1 per cent) lost.

---

22 February 1945

OIL REFINERIES

167 Lancasters of 3 Group in forces of 85 and 82 aircraft to Gelsenkirchen and Osterfeld. A Film Unit Lancaster of 463 Squadron, 5 Group, accompanied the Gelsenkirchen force. Both targets were accurately bombed in clear weather conditions. 1 Lancaster lost from the Gelsenkirchen raid.

22/23 February 1945

MINOR OPERATIONS

73 Mosquitoes to Berlin, 6 to Bremen, 4 to Erfurt and 3 on 'siren tours' of various German towns, 35 Lancasters to railway viaducts at Altenbeken and Bielefeld, 48 R.C.M. sorties, 23 Mosquito patrols, 19 aircraft on Resistance operations. 1 Mosquito from the Erfurt raid crashed in Belgium.

---

23 February 1945

ESSEN

342 aircraft – 297 Halifaxes, 27 Lancasters, 18 Mosquitoes – of 4, 6 and 8 Groups. 1 Halifax crashed in Holland.

The target area was cloud-covered and all of the bombs were dropped on skymarkers. The marking must have been extremely accurate; a German report states that 300 high-explosive and 11,000 incendiary bombs fell on the Krupps works. 155 people were killed in Essen. No other details are available.

GELSENKIRCHEN

133 Lancasters of 3 Group carried out a *G-H* attack on the Alma Pluto benzol plant but no results were seen. No aircraft lost.

1 Lightning flew an R.C.M. sortie.

23/24 February 1945

PFORZHEIM

367 Lancasters and 13 Mosquitoes of 1, 6 and 8 Groups and a Film Unit Lancaster carried out the first, and only, area-bombing raid of the war on this target. 10 Lancasters were lost and 2 more crashed in France.

The marking and bombing, from only 8,000 ft, were particularly accurate and damage of a most severe nature was inflicted on Pforzheim. 1,825 tons of bombs were dropped in 22 minutes. Local records show that an area measuring 3 km by 1½ km was completely engulfed by fire and that 'more than 17,000 people met their death in a hurricane of fire and explosions'.* Fire Officer Brunswig from Hamburg, usually reliable, says that 17,600 people died. This was probably the third heaviest air-raid death toll in Germany during the war, following Hamburg and Dresden. The postwar British Bombing Survey Unit estimated that 83 per cent of the town's built-up area was destroyed, probably the greatest proportion in one raid during the war.

Bomber Command's last Victoria Cross of the war was won on this night. The Master Bomber was Captain Edwin Swales, D.F.C., a South African serving with 582 Squadron. His Lancaster was twice attacked over the target by a German fighter. Captain Swales could not hear the evasion directions given by his gunners because he was broadcasting his own instructions to the Main Force. 2 engines and the rear turret of the Lancaster were put out of action. Captain Swales continued to control the bombing until the end of the raid and must take some credit for the accuracy of the attack. He set out on the return flight but encountered turbulent cloud and ordered his crew to bale out. This they all did successfully but Captain Swales had no opportunity to leave the aircraft and was killed when it crashed. He is buried at the Leopold War Cemetery at Limburg in Belgium.

HORTEN

73 Lancasters and 10 Mosquitoes carried out an accurate attack on a possible U-boat base on the Oslo Fjord. 1 Lancaster was lost.

The local report makes no mention of a U-boat base but describes very accurate bombing of the port area with a shipyard severely damaged by fire, a large warehouse which burned 'like a massive torch' and an old naval hospital, now used by the Germans as a military hospital, also on fire. A tanker was hit and a floating crane

---

*Quoted from page 9 of a diary provided by the Pforzheim Stadtarchiv.

49. The blazing port area of Horten, in Norway, after being attacked by Lancasters and Mosquitoes of 5 Group on the night of 23/24 February 1945.

capsized. The local people came out after the raid and, from some high ground, 'looked out over the sea of fire in the place which had been Horten's main source of employment for generations'. If the wind had been from the wrong direction, much of the wooden town would have been destroyed, but there is no mention of civilian damage or casualties.

Minor Operations: 70 Mosquitoes to Berlin, 6 to Worms and 4 each to Darmstadt, Essen and Frankfurt, 54 R.C.M. sorties, 25 Mosquito patrols, 22 Lancasters minelaying in Norwegian waters, 13 aircraft on Resistance operations. 4 aircraft lost – 2 R.C.M. Halifaxes, 1 Resistance operation Stirling and 1 Mosquito from the Berlin raid.

Total effort for the night: 666 sorties, 17 aircraft (2·6 per cent) lost.

---

24 February 1945

KAMEN

340 aircraft – 290 Halifaxes, 26 Lancasters, 24 Mosquitoes – of 4, 6 and 8 Groups. 1 Halifax lost.

The target was a synthetic-oil plant which was actually in Bergkamen, just north of Kamen. The target area was covered by cloud and the raid was based on *Oboe* and *H2S* markers. Kamen reports heavy damage in several areas of the town and in the nearby village of Bergkamen. It is a very emotional report which does not mention damage to the oil refinery but stresses the damage in the centre of Kamen, where most of the churches were destroyed and a hospital was hit. The public utilities all failed and the report says, 'we had to go to bed when the chickens went, like our forefathers'. 199 people were killed in Kamen and 33 in Bergkamen during this raid and the one of the following day.

DORTMUND–EMS CANAL

166 Lancasters and 4 Mosquitoes of 5 Group were ordered to abandon this raid without bombing because of cloud which covered the target area. All aircraft landed safely.

24/25 February 1945

MINOR OPERATIONS

74 training aircraft on a diversionary sweep over Northern France to draw German fighters into the air, 63 Mosquitoes to Berlin, 18 to Neuss and 3 on 'siren tours' of Dessau, Erfurt and Halle, 37 R.C.M. sorties, 23 Mosquito patrols, 35 Lancasters minelaying in the Kattegat and off Norwegian ports. 5 R.C.M. aircraft – 4 Halifaxes and 1 Fortress – lost; these aircraft were operating in association with the diversionary sweep of training aircraft and were probably victims of German fighters drawn up by that sweep. The 4 lost Halifaxes were all from 462 (Australian) Squadron, based at Foulsham; they had been sent ahead of the diversionary force to drop *Window*, bombs and incendiaries in a 'spoof' raid on the Ruhr.

25 February 1945

KAMEN

153 Lancasters of 3 Group carried out a *G-H* attack on the synthetic-oil refinery. 1 Lancaster lost.

25/26 February 1945

MINOR OPERATIONS

63 Mosquitoes to Erfurt, 10 each to Berlin and Mainz and 6 to Bremen, 8 R.C.M. sorties, 23 Mosquito patrols, 10 Halifaxes of 6 Group minelaying in Oslo Fjord, 20 aircraft on Resistance operations. 1 Halifax minelayer lost.

26 February 1945

DORTMUND

149 Lancasters of 3 Group carried out a *G-H* attack on the Hoesch benzol-oil plant through cloud. No results were seen but the bombing appeared to be concentrated. No aircraft lost.

26/27 February 1945

MINOR OPERATIONS

38 Mosquitoes each to Berlin and Nuremberg, 3 Mosquitoes on 'siren tours' of Northern Germany, 1 R.C.M. sortie, 6 Mosquito patrols, 18 aircraft on Resistance operations. 1 Stirling lost on a Resistance flight.

27 February 1945

MAINZ

458 aircraft – 311 Halifaxes, 131 Lancasters, 16 Mosquitoes – of 4, 6 and 8 Groups. 1 Halifax and 1 Mosquito lost.

Mainz was covered by cloud and the bombing was aimed at sky-markers dropped on *Oboe*. No results were seen by the bomber crews but the bombing caused severe destruction in the central and eastern districts of Mainz; this was the city's worst raid of the war. 1,545 tons of bombs were dropped. 5,670 buildings were destroyed, including most of the historic buildings in the *Altstadt*, but the industrial district was also badly hit. At least 1,122 people were killed; other accounts say 1,200. The 1,122 figure was made up of: 647 women, 437 men, 5 children, 21 servicemen and 12 foreigners; most of the city's children had probably been evacuated. Among the dead were 41 nuns in a convent which was bombed; there were only 3 survivors. This was the last heavy raid on Mainz. The city's total number of air-raid deaths in 14 major R.A.F. and U.S.A.A.F. raids and several minor raids numbered 2,482.

GELSENKIRCHEN

149 Lancasters of 3 Group carried out a *G-H* attack through thick cloud on the Alma Pluto benzol plant but no results were seen. 1 Lancaster lost.

27/28 February 1945

MINOR OPERATIONS

82 training aircraft on a sweep over the North Sea to draw up German fighters, 96 Mosquitoes to Berlin and 6 to Bremen, 62 R.C.M. sorties, 32 Mosquito patrols. No aircraft lost.

---

28 February 1945

GELSENKIRCHEN

156 Lancasters of 3 Group in a *G-H* raid on the Nordstern synthetic-oil plant. No aircraft lost.

---

28 February/1 March 1945

MINOR OPERATIONS

98 training aircraft on a sweep over the North Sea, 74 Mosquitoes to Berlin, 8 to Nuremberg and 4 to Munich, 44 R.C.M. sorties, 31 Mosquito patrols, 5 Mosquitoes of 5 Group minelaying in the Kiel Canal, 20 aircraft on Resistance operations. 1 Mosquito lost from the Berlin raid.

---

1 March 1945

MANNHEIM

478 aircraft – 372 Lancasters, 90 Halifaxes, 16 Mosquitoes – of 1, 6 and 8 Groups. 3 Lancasters lost.

This was a general attack on the city area. Sky-marking was used because of the complete cloud cover. Nothing is known of what happened in Mannheim. The city's recording procedure, one of the best in Germany until now, appears to have broken down completely and, if any report was prepared, it did not survive the war. This was the last large Bomber Command raid on Mannheim.

The neighbouring town of Ludwigshafen, however, was also hit by many bombs.

A considerable amount of damage was caused right across the town and in nearby villages. Public, domestic and industrial buildings were all hit – 424 buildings destroyed, nearly 1,000 seriously damaged. Only 5 people were killed and 17 injured but 6,000 people lost their homes.

KAMEN

151 Lancasters of 3 Group attacked the oil plant through cloud. No aircraft were lost. The local report says only that 9 people died.

1/2 March 1944

MINOR OPERATIONS

55 Mosquitoes to Berlin, 40 to Erfurt and 3 on 'siren tours' of Northern Germany, 32 R.C.M. sorties, 13 Mosquito patrols. No aircraft lost.

---

2 March 1945

COLOGNE

858 aircraft – 531 Lancasters, 303 Halifaxes, 24 Mosquitoes. 6 Lancasters and 2 Halifaxes were lost and 1 Halifax crashed in Belgium.

There were 2 raids on Cologne, now almost a front-line city. The first raid was carried out by 703 aircraft and the second by 155 Lancasters of 3 Group. In the second raid, however, only 15 aircraft bombed, because the *G-H* station in England was not working correctly. The main raid was highly destructive, with the Pathfinders marking in clear weather conditions. Our local expert, Erich Quadflieg, describes the great 'carpet of bombs', mostly high explosive, which stretched right across the main city on the west bank of the Rhine; '*Das war das Ende von Köln,*' Herr Quadflieg writes. Not surprisingly, details of the exact extent of the damage are non-existent and casualty figures are vague. The number of dead civilians is given as 'hundreds' and the American troops who entered the city a few days later cleared at least 400 bodies from the streets; the warning sirens had sounded only 2 minutes before the first bombs fell. In addition, at least 160 German soldiers were killed, mostly S.S. men. Many of these died in the basement of the Krebsgasse Police Station, which was being used as the local air-raid control room; this building was hit by 5 bombs. Many German military units were affected by the bombing.

This was the last R.A.F. raid on Cologne, which was captured by American troops 4 days later.

2/3 March 1945

MINOR OPERATIONS

69 training aircraft on a sweep, 67 Mosquitoes to Kassel and 3 to Berlin, 48 R.C.M. sorties, 31 Mosquito patrols, 10 Halifaxes and Lancasters minelaying off Norway and 6 Mosquitoes in the Kiel Canal, 21 aircraft on Resistance operations. No aircraft lost.

3/4 March 1945

This was the 2,000th night of the war.

KAMEN

234 aircraft – 201 Halifaxes of 4 Group and 21 Lancasters and 12 Mosquitoes of 8 Group. No aircraft lost over Germany.

The synthetic-oil refinery at Bergkamen was severely damaged in this accurate raid and no further production of oil took place. 17 people died in Kamen.

DORTMUND–EMS CANAL

212 Lancasters and 10 Mosquitoes of 5 Group attacked the Ladbergen aqueduct, breached it in 2 places and put it completely out of action. 7 Lancasters lost.

The gunners in the 619 Squadron Lancaster of Wing Commander S. G. Birch claimed to have shot down a V-1 flying bomb near the target area; the V-1 was probably aimed at the port of Antwerp.

SUPPORT AND MINOR OPERATIONS

95 training aircraft on a diversionary sweep, 64 Mosquitoes to Berlin and 32 to Würzburg, 61 R.C.M. sorties, 29 Mosquito patrols, 31 Lancasters minelaying in the Kattegat and in Oslo Fjord, 17 aircraft on Resistance operations. 1 Lancaster lost from the minelaying operation.

The Luftwaffe mounted their Operation *Gisella* on this night, sending approximately 200 night fighters to follow the various bomber forces to England. This move took the British defences partly by surprise and the Germans shot down 20 bombers – 8 Halifaxes of 4 Group, 2 Lancasters of 5 Group, 3 Halifaxes, 1 Fortress and 1 Mosquito of 100 Group and 3 Lancasters and 2 Halifaxes from the Heavy Conversion Units which had been taking part in the diversionary sweep. 3 of the German fighters crashed, through flying too low; the German fighter which crashed near Elvington airfield was the last Luftwaffe aircraft to crash on English soil during the war.

Total effort for the night: 785 sorties, 8 aircraft lost over Germany and the sea, 20 aircraft shot down by Intruders over England, a total casualty rate of 3·6 per cent.

---

4 March 1945

WANNE-EICKEL

128 Lancasters of 3 Group carried out a *G-H* attack through cloud. No results were seen. No aircraft lost.

4/5 March 1945

MINOR OPERATIONS

31 Mosquitoes to Berlin, 24 to Essen and 28 in small numbers to 5 ports in Northern Germany,

6 Mosquito patrols, 12 Halifaxes minelaying off Heligoland, 16 aircraft on Resistance operations. 2 Stirlings on Resistance operations were lost.

---

5 March 1945

GELSENKIRCHEN

170 Lancasters of 3 Group carried out a *G-H* attack on the Consolidation benzol plant. No results were seen. 1 Lancaster lost.

5/6 March 1945

CHEMNITZ

760 aircraft – 498 Lancasters, 256 Halifaxes, 6 Mosquitoes – to continue Operation *Thunderclap*. The operation started badly when 9 aircraft of 6 Group crashed near their bases soon after taking off in icy conditions. 426 Squadron, at Linton-on-Ouse, lost 3 out of their 14 Halifaxes taking part in the raid in this way, with only 1 man surviving. 1 of the Halifaxes crashed in York, killing some civilians. 22 further aircraft were lost in the main operation – 14 Lancasters and 8 Halifaxes.

The city of Karl-Marx-Stadt was unable to supply any local details but it is known that the centre and the south of the city suffered severe fire damage. Several important factories were situated in the fire area and the Siegmar factory, which made tank engines, was destroyed.

BÖHLEN

248 Lancasters and 10 Mosquitoes of 5 Group attacked the synthetic-oil refinery. The target area was covered by cloud but some damage was caused to the refinery. 4 Lancasters lost.

Minor Operations: 75 Mosquitoes to Berlin, 15 to Gelsenkirchen and 36 in small numbers to 6 other targets, 52 R.C.M. sorties, 27 Mosquito patrols. 5 aircraft lost – 2 Mosquito bombers from the Berlin raid, 1 Mosquito lost from a small raid to Hallendorf, 2 R.C.M. aircraft (1 Halifax and 1 Stirling, of which the latter was believed to have been shot down over France by an American artillery unit).

Total effort for the night: 1,223 sorties, 31 aircraft (2·5 per cent) lost and 10 more crashed in England.

---

6 March 1945

SALZBERGEN

119 Lancasters of 3 Group carried out a *G-H* attack through cloud on the Wintershall oil refinery. 1 Lancaster lost.

WESEL

48 Mosquitoes of 8 Group attacked Wesel, which was believed to contain many German troops and vehicles. The target had been cloud-covered for several days. *Oboe* Mosquitoes provided the marking. 1 aircraft lost.

6/7 March 1945

SASSNITZ

191 Lancasters and 7 Mosquitoes of 5 Group attacked this small port on the island of Rügen, in the Baltic. Considerable damage was caused to the northern part of the town and 3 ships were sunk in the harbour. 1 Lancaster lost.

WESEL

87 Lancasters of 3 Group and 51 Mosquitoes of 8 Group continued the attack on Wesel with two separate raids. No aircraft lost.

Minor Operations: 42 Mosquitoes to Berlin, 2 R.C.M. sorties, 5 Mosquito patrols, 15 Lancasters minelaying off Sassnitz. No aircraft lost.

7/8 March 1945

DESSAU

526 Lancasters and 5 Mosquitoes of 1, 3, 6 and 8 Groups. 18 Lancasters lost, 3·4 per cent of the force.

This was another devastating raid on a new target in Eastern Germany with the usual town centre, residential, industrial and railway areas all being hit. Few further details are available.

HEMMINGSTEDT

256 Halifaxes and 25 Lancasters of 4, 6 and 8 Groups attempted to attack the Deutsche Erdoel refinery at Hemmingstedt, near Heide, but the bombing fell 2 to 3 miles from the target. 4 Halifaxes and 1 Lancaster lost.

HARBURG

234 Lancasters and 7 Mosquitoes of 5 Group carried out an accurate attack on the oil refinery. 14 Lancasters lost. 189 Squadron, from Fulbeck, lost 4 of its 16 Lancasters on the raid.

Brunswig's local report (pp. 362 and 456) states that a rubber factory was seriously damaged as well as the oil targets. 422 people were killed, including 44 who died in the rubber factory's air-raid shelter. There were 99 fires, 37 of them classified as large.

Minor Operations: 80 Mosquitoes to Berlin, 10 to Frankfurt, 9 to Münster and 5 to Hannover, 56 R.C.M. sorties, 43 Mosquito patrols, 15 Halifaxes and 5 Lancasters minelaying off Eckernförde and Flensburg. 4 aircraft were lost – 2 Halifaxes and 1 Fortress of 100 Group and 1 Mosquito from the Berlin raid.

Total effort for the night: 1,276 sorties, 41 aircraft (3·2 per cent) lost.

8/9 March 1945

HAMBURG

312 aircraft – 241 Halifaxes, 62 Lancasters, 9 Mosquitoes – of 4, 6 and 8 Groups. 1 Halifax lost.

The purpose of this raid was to hit the shipyards which were now assembling the new Type XXI U-boats, whose parts were prefabricated in many parts of inland Germany. Thanks to the *Schnorkel* breathing tube and a new type of battery-driven electric engine, the Type XXI could cruise under water for long periods and was capable of bursts of high speed. Its development in numbers would have posed great problems for Allied convoy defence if the war had lasted longer.

The Hamburg area was found to be cloud-covered and the bombing was not expected to be accurate enough to cause much damage to the shipyards. Brunswig (pp. 362–3 and 456) mentions only a serious fire which almost destroyed the liner *Robert Ley*, built in Hamburg before the war as a cruise liner for the Strength Through Joy movement, and gives statistics of 118 people killed, 172 wounded, 54 fires (38 of them large ones).

KASSEL

262 Lancasters and 14 Mosquitoes of 1 and 8 Groups carried out the first large raid on Kassel since October 1943; it was also the last large R.A.F. raid on this target. 1 Mosquito lost.

This target was also covered by cloud. The only local report available is a short one which says that many fires were started in the western parts of Kassel. No casualties or other details are given.

Minor Operations: 39 Mosquitoes to Berlin, 33 to Hannover, 7 to Hagen and 5 each to Bremen and Osnabrück, 50 R.C.M. sorties, 36 Mosquito patrols, 23 Halifaxes and 14 Lancasters minelaying in the Rivers Elbe and Weser, 5 aircraft on Resistance operations. 1 R.C.M. Halifax lost. The 5 Stirlings of 161 Squadron, which were carrying supplies to Resistance units at unrecorded destinations, but probably in Denmark and Norway, were the last Resistance operations flights of the war.

Total effort for the night: 805 sorties, 3 aircraft (0·4 per cent) lost.

---

9 March 1945

DATTELN

159 Lancasters of 3 Group bombed the North and South plants of the Emscher Lippe benzol plant. The target area was cloud-covered and *G-H* was used. The bombing appeared to be accurate but no results were seen. 1 Lancaster lost.

Bielefeld Viaduct

21 Lancasters and 2 Mosquitoes of 5 Group set out to this target but the raid was abandoned because of low cloud.

9/10 March 1945

MINOR OPERATIONS

92 Mosquitoes to Berlin and 16 Mosquitoes on 'siren tours' of Bremen, Hannover, Osnabrück and Wilhelmshaven, 29 R.C.M. sorties, 12 Mosquito patrols, 21 Halifaxes minelaying in the Kattegat and off Oslo. No aircraft lost.

10 March 1945

SCHOLVEN/BUER

155 Lancasters of 3 Group carried out a *G-H* attack on the oil refinery. Photographs taken later showed this to have been a very accurate and effective raid. No aircraft lost.

10/11 March 1945

MINOR OPERATIONS

60 Mosquitoes to Berlin, 4 each to Gotha, Jena and Weimar, 35 R.C.M. sorties, 10 Mosquito patrols. No aircraft lost.

11 March 1945

ESSEN

1,079 aircraft – 750 Lancasters, 293 Halifaxes, 36 Mosquitoes – of all bomber groups. This was the largest number of aircraft sent to a target so far in the war. 3 Lancasters lost.

4,661 tons of bombs were dropped on *Oboe*-directed sky-markers through complete cloud cover. The attack was accurate and this great blow virtually paralysed Essen until the American troops entered the city some time later. Essen's recording system produced no proper reports but 897 people are said to have been killed.

This was the last R.A.F. raid on Essen, which had been attacked so many times, though often in the early years of the war with such disappointing and costly results. Most of the city was now in ruins. 7,000 people had died in air raids. The pre-war population of 648,000 had fallen to 310,000 by the end of April 1945; the rest had left for quieter places in Germany.

11/12 March 1945

MINOR OPERATIONS

90 Mosquitoes to Berlin and 6 each to Brunswick, Hannover and Magdeburg, 4 Mosquito patrols, 22 Lancasters minelaying in the Kattegat and off Oslo. No aircraft lost.

12 March 1945

DORTMUND

1,108 aircraft – 748 Lancasters, 292 Halifaxes, 68 Mosquitoes. This was another new record to a single target, a record which would stand to the end of the war. 2 Lancasters lost.

Another record tonnage of bombs – 4,851 – was dropped through cloud on to this unfortunate city. The only details available from Dortmund state that the attack fell mainly in the centre and south of the city. A British team which investigated the effects of bombing in Dortmund after the war says that, 'The final raid ... stopped production so effectively that it would have been many months before any substantial recovery could have occurred.'*

12/13 March 1945

MINOR OPERATIONS

81 Mosquitoes to Berlin and 3 each to Halle, Magdeburg and Stendal, 2 R.C.M. sorties, 16 Lancasters and 3 Halifaxes minelaying in the Kattegat. 3 Lancaster minelayers lost.

13 March 1945

WUPPERTAL/BARMEN

354 aircraft – 310 Halifaxes, 24 Lancasters, 20 Mosquitoes – of 4, 6 and 8 Groups. No aircraft lost.

This attack also took place over a cloud-covered target and the bombs fell slightly east of the area intended, covering the eastern half of the Barmen district and extending into Schwelm. Much property damage was caused and 562 people were killed. No other details are available.

Bomber Command had now dispatched 2,541 sorties by daylight to Ruhr targets in a 3-day period. Approximately 10,650 tons of bombs had been dropped through cloud with sufficient accuracy to cripple 2 cities and 1 town. The bomber losses were only 5 aircraft, a casualty rate of 0·2 per cent. These results show the great power now wielded by Bomber Command, its technical efficiency and the weakness of the German defences.

RAILWAY VIADUCTS

38 Lancasters of 5 Group to bomb the Arnsberg and Bielefeld viaducts encountered bad weather. 1 aircraft bombed at Arnsberg and 2 further aircraft bombed alternative targets. No aircraft lost.

13/14 March 1945

BENZOL PLANTS

195 Lancasters and 32 Mosquitoes of 1 and 8 Groups attacked plants at Herne and

* Official History, Vol. III, p. 264.

Gelsenkirchen. The Gelsenkirchen attack was successful but not the Herne raid. 1 Lancaster lost from the Gelsenkirchen raid.

Minor Operations: 50 Mosquitoes to Berlin, 26 to Bremen and 6 to Erfurt, 58 R.C.M. sorties, 37 Mosquito patrols. 1 Mosquito from the Berlin raid crashed in Belgium and 1 Halifax R.C.M. aircraft in France.

---

14 March 1945

BENZOL PLANTS

169 Lancasters of 3 Group carried out *G-H* attacks through cloud on plants at Datteln and Hattingen (near Bochum). Both attacks appeared to be accurate but no results were seen. 1 Lancaster lost from the Hattingen raid.

RAILWAY VIADUCTS

32 Lancasters and 1 Mosquito of 5 Group, with 4 *Oboe* Mosquitoes of 8 Group, to attack the Bielefeld and Arnsberg viaducts. 28 Lancasters dropped *Tallboy* bombs and the 617 Squadron Lancaster of Squadron Leader C. C. Calder dropped the first 22,000-lb bomb, named the *Grand Slam*, at Bielefeld. The Arnsberg viaduct, 9 Squadron's target, was later found to be undamaged but more than 100 yards of the Bielefeld viaduct collapsed through the 'earthquake effect' of the *Grand Slam* and *Tallboys* of 617 Squadron. No aircraft lost.

14/15 March 1945

LÜTZKENDORF

244 Lancasters and 11 Mosquitoes of 5 Group attacked the Wintershall synthetic-oil refinery at this distant target. Photographic reconnaissance showed that 'moderate damage' was caused. 18 Lancasters were lost, 7·4 per cent of the Lancaster force.

ZWEIBRÜCKEN

230 aircraft – 121 Lancasters, 98 Halifaxes, 11 Mosquitoes – of 6 and 8 Groups. No aircraft lost.

This attack was directed on to the town area to block the passage through it of German troops and stores to the nearby front line. The raid took place in good visibility and was very effective. The local report shows that *every* public building and inn and 80 per cent of the houses in the town were destroyed or damaged. Most of the civilian population had been evacuated; those remaining took shelter in 2 large caves in the north and south of the town or in the normal basement shelters of their houses. The people in the caves all survived but 192 bodies had been removed from the basement shelters by the time the local report was prepared on 20 May 1945. It must be assumed that some German troops were also killed by the bombing.

HOMBERG

161 aircraft – 127 Halifaxes, 23 Lancasters, 11 Mosquitoes – of 4 and 8 Groups on

the same task as the Zweibrücken raid. No local report is available but it is believed that this attack was equally successful. 2 Halifaxes lost.

Minor Operations: 75 Mosquitoes to Berlin and 6 each to Bremen and Brunswick, 52 R.C.M. sorties, 27 Mosquito patrols. 100 Group lost 2 Mosquitoes and 1 Fortress.
    The last Stirling operation of Bomber Command was flown on this night when Stirling LJ 516, from 199 Squadron at North Creake, flew a *Mandrel* screen operation; Squadron Leader J. J. M. Button, the Australian pilot, and his crew landed safely.

Total effort for the night: 812 sorties, 23 aircraft (2·8 per cent) lost.

---

15 March 1945

BENZOL PLANTS

188 aircraft – 150 Halifaxes, 24 Mosquitoes, 14 Lancasters – of 4, 6 and 8 Groups attacked plants at Bottrop and Castrop-Rauxel. Both raids were believed to have been successful. 1 Halifax of 4 Group lost from the Bottrop raid.

Arnsberg

16 Lancasters of 9 and 617 Squadrons attacked the viaduct. Two aircraft of 617 Squadron each carried a *Grand Slam*; the 14 aircraft of 9 Squadron carried *Tallboys*. The viaduct was not cut. No aircraft lost.

15/16 March 1945

HAGEN

267 aircraft – 134 Lancasters, 122 Halifaxes, 11 Mosquitoes – of 4, 6 and 8 Groups. 6 Lancasters and 4 Halifaxes lost.
    This area attack took place in clear visibility and caused severe damage; the local report estimated that the bomber force was 800 aircraft strong! The main attack fell in the centre and eastern districts. There were 1,439 fires, of which 124 were classified as large. 493 Germans and 12 foreigners were killed. 30,000–35,000 people were bombed out.

MISBURG

257 Lancasters and 8 Mosquitoes of 1 and 8 Groups attacked the Deurag refinery at Misburg, on the outskirts of Hannover. Visibility was good and some fires were started but the main weight of the raid fell south of the target. 4 Lancasters lost.

Minor Operations: 54 Mosquitoes to Berlin, 27 to Erfurt, 16 to Mannheim and 5 each to Jena and Weimar, 53 R.C.M. sorties, 37 Mosquito patrols. 1 R.C.M. Fortress lost.

Total effort for the night: 729 sorties, 14 aircraft (1·9 per cent) lost.

16/17 March 1945

NUREMBURG

231 Lancasters of 1 Group and 46 Lancasters and 16 Mosquitoes of 8 Group. 24 Lancasters, all from 1 Group, lost, 8·7 per cent of the Lancaster force and 10·4 per cent of the 1 Group aircraft involved. Most of these losses were due to German night fighters, which found the bomber stream on its way to the target.

The local report (from Dr Erich Mulzer) states that the southern and south-western districts were hit as well as the ruins of the *Altstadt* which was destroyed in a previous raid. A serious 'fire area' was established in the Steinbuhl district. The main railway station was also on fire and the city's gasworks were so badly damaged that they did not resume production before the end of the war. There are no figures for property damage and the only casualty figure given is 529 dead.

This was the last heavy Bomber Command raid on Nuremberg.

WÜRZBURG

225 Lancasters and 11 Mosquitoes of 5 Group. 6 Lancasters lost.

This was another dramatic and devastating blow by 5 Group. 1,127 tons of bombs were dropped with great accuracy in 17 minutes. According to a post-war survey, the old cathedral city with its famous historic buildings suffered 89 per cent of its built-up area destroyed. Würzburg contained little industry and this was an area attack. Estimates of the number of dead vary from 4,000 to 5,000. No further details are available.

Minor Operations: 56 Mosquitoes to Berlin, 24 to Hanau and 6 each to Brunswick and Osnabrück, 32 R.C.M. sorties, 40 Mosquito patrols, 12 Halifaxes and 12 Lancasters minelaying in the Kattegat and off Heligoland. No aircraft lost.

Total effort for the night: 717 sorties, 30 aircraft (4·2 per cent) lost.

---

17 March 1945

BENZOL PLANTS

167 Lancasters of 3 Group carried out *G-H* attacks through cloud on plants at Dortmund and Hüls. Both raids appeared to be accurate. No aircraft lost.

17/18 March 1945

MINOR OPERATIONS

66 Lancasters and 29 Halifaxes from training units on a sweep over Northern France to draw up German fighters, 39 Mosquitoes to Nuremberg, 38 to Berlin and 2 each to Mannheim and Stuttgart, 6 R.C.M. sorties, 15 Mosquito patrols. 1 Intruder Mosquito of 100 Group lost.

18 March 1945

BENZOL PLANTS

100 Lancasters of 3 Group carried out *G-H* attacks on plants at Hattingen and Langendreer. Both raids appeared to be accurate. No aircraft lost.

18/19 March 1945

WITTEN

324 aircraft – 259 Halifaxes, 45 Lancasters, 20 Mosquitoes – of 4, 6 and 8 Groups. 8 aircraft – 6 Halifaxes, 1 Lancaster, 1 Mosquito – lost.

This was a successful area raid carried out in good visibility. 1,081 tons of bombs were dropped, destroying 129 acres, 62 per cent of the built-up area (according to the post-war British Bombing Survey Unit). The only German report states that the Ruhrstahl steelworks and the Mannesmann tube factory were severely damaged.

HANAU

277 Lancasters and 8 Mosquitoes of 1 and 8 Groups. 1 Lancaster lost.

This was another accurate area raid. The local report states that 50 industrial buildings and 2,240 houses were destroyed. The *Altstadt* was completely devastated and, says the report, all of the town's churches, hospitals, schools and historic buildings were badly hit. Approximately 2,000 people were killed, of whom 1,150 were regular residents of Hanau; the remaining dead were presumably evacuees or refugees from bombed cities.

SUPPORT AND MINOR OPERATIONS

70 aircraft on a sweep over France, 30 Mosquitoes to Berlin, 24 to Kassel and 18 to Nuremberg, 40 R.C.M. sorties, 53 Mosquito patrols. No aircraft lost.

Total effort for the night: 844 sorties, 9 aircraft (1·1 per cent) lost.

---

19 March 1945

GELSENKIRCHEN

79 Lancasters of 3 Group attacked the Consolidation benzol plant. Smoke and dust from the bombing prevented observation of the results. No aircraft lost.

RAILWAYS

37 Lancasters of 5 Group attacked the viaduct at Arnsberg and the bridge at Vlotho, near Minden. The 617 Squadron attack at Arnsberg, using 6 *Grand Slams*, was successful and a 40-foot gap was blown in the viaduct. The 9 Squadron attack at Vlotho was not successful. No aircraft lost.

19/20 March 1945

Berlin

34 Mosquitoes. No losses.

20 March 1945

RECKLINGHAUSEN

153 aircraft – 125 Halifaxes, 16 Lancasters, 12 Mosquitoes – of 4 and 6 Groups attempted to hit the railway yards but cloud and a strong wind spoiled the Pathfinder marking and the bombing was well scattered. No aircraft lost.

RAILWAYS

99 Lancasters of 3 Group attacked the railway yards at Hamm and 14 Lancasters of 9 Squadron attacked the railway bridge at Arnsberg. Bombs were seen to explode in the target area at both targets. No aircraft lost.

20/21 March 1945

BÖHLEN

224 Lancasters and 11 Mosquitoes of 5 Group attacked the synthetic-oil plant. This accurate attack put the plant out of action and it was still inactive when captured by American troops several weeks later. 9 Lancasters lost.

HEMMINGSTEDT

166 Lancasters of 1, 6 and 8 Groups carried out an equally effective attack upon the oil refinery at this target. 1 Lancaster lost.

SUPPORT AND MINOR OPERATIONS

70 training aircraft on a diversionary sweep over France, 12 Lancasters in a feint raid on Halle, 38 Mosquitoes to Berlin, 27 to Bremen and 16 to Kassel, 47 R.C.M. sorties, 55 Mosquito patrols, 9 Lancasters minelaying off Heligoland. 3 aircraft lost – 1 Lancaster from the Halle raid and 1 Fortress and 1 Liberator R.C.M. aircraft.

Total effort for the night: 675 sorties, 13 aircraft (1·9 per cent) lost.

21 March 1945

RHEINE

178 aircraft – 150 Halifaxes, 16 Lancasters, 12 Mosquitoes – of 4, 6 and 8 Groups carried out an accurate attack upon the railway yards and the surrounding town area. 1 Lancaster lost.

MÜNSTER

160 Lancasters of 3 Group attacked the railway yards and a nearby railway viaduct. 3 Lancasters lost. The only information available from Münster is that 17 people were killed.

BREMEN

133 Lancasters and 6 Mosquitoes of 1 and 8 Groups attacked the Deutsche Vacuum oil refinery. This appeared to be an accurate raid in clear weather conditions. No aircraft lost.

20 Lancasters of 617 Squadron attacked the Arbergen railway bridge just outside Bremen. 2 piers of the bridge were destroyed. 1 Lancaster lost.

Total effort of the day: 497 sorties, 5 aircraft (1·0 per cent) lost.

21/22 March 1945

HAMBURG

151 Lancasters and 8 Mosquitoes of 5 Group. 4 Lancasters lost.

The target for this raid was the Deutsche Erdölwerke refinery. The attack was accurate; 20 storage tanks were destroyed and the plant was still out of action at the end of the war. Some bombs fell in the nearby Wilhelmsburg district, where 31 Germans were killed and at least 100 foreign workers died when their camp was hit.

BOCHUM

131 Lancasters and 12 Mosquitoes of 1 and 8 Groups carried out an accurate attack on the benzol plant. 1 Lancaster lost.

Minor Operations: 142 Mosquitoes in 2 attacks on Berlin (with some aircraft making 2 sorties), 3 Mosquitoes to Bremen, 26 R.C.M. sorties, 56 Mosquito patrols, 7 Mosquitoes of 5 Group minelaying in Jade Bay and the River Weser. 1 Mosquito from the Berlin raid and 1 R.C.M. Fortress lost.

Total effort for the night: 536 sorties, 7 aircraft (1·3 per cent) lost.

---

22 March 1945

HILDESHEIM

227 Lancasters and 8 Mosquitoes of 1 and 8 Groups. 4 Lancasters lost.

The target was the railway yards; these were bombed but the surrounding built-up areas also suffered severely in what was virtually an area attack. This was the only major Bomber Command raid of the war on Hildesheim and the post-war British survey found that 263 acres, 70 per cent of the town, had been destroyed. The local report states that the inner town suffered the most damage. The Cathedral, most of the churches and many historic buildings were destroyed. A total of 3,302 blocks of flats (containing more than 10,000 apartments) were destroyed or seriously damaged. 1,645 people were killed.

DÜLMEN

130 aircraft – 106 Halifaxes, 12 Lancasters, 12 Mosquitoes – of 4 and 8 Groups. No aircraft lost.

This was an area attack and the town was soon burning after a concentrated raid in clear weather conditions. No other details are available.

DORSTEN

124 aircraft – 100 Halifaxes, 12 Lancasters, 12 Mosquitoes – of 6 and 8 Groups. No aircraft lost.

Dorsten was a rail and canal centre and also the location of a Luftwaffe fuel dump. All these targets were believed to have been hit but the town probably suffered as well.

BOCHOLT

100 Lancasters of 3 Group carried out a *G-H* attack on the town area, probably with the intention of cutting communications. The town was seen to be on fire. No aircraft lost.

RAILWAY BRIDGES

102 Lancasters of 5 Group attacked bridges at Bremen (82 aircraft) and Nienburg (20 aircraft of 617 Squadron). The bridge at Nienburg was destroyed; the bombing at the Bremen bridge appeared to be accurate but no results were seen. No aircraft lost.

Total effort for the day: 708 sorties, 4 aircraft (0·6 per cent) lost.

22/23 March 1945

MINOR OPERATIONS

56 Mosquitoes to Berlin, 8 to Paderborn and 6 to Bochum, 39 R.C.M. sorties, 30 Mosquito patrols, 21 Lancasters and 8 Mosquitoes minelaying in Oslo Fjord. 2 Intruder Mosquitoes of 100 Group lost.

---

23 March 1945

RAILWAY BRIDGES

128 Lancasters of 1 and 5 Groups attacked bridges at Bremen (117 aircraft) and Bad Oeynhausen (11 aircraft). Both bridges were hit. 2 Lancasters were lost from the Bremen raid. (The Bad Oeynhausen bridge may have been the one described as 'at Vlotho' in a raid 4 days earlier; the two places are close to each other, both near Minden.)

WESEL

80 Lancasters of 3 Group attacked the town, which was an important troop centre

behind the Rhine front in an area about to be attacked by British troops. The raid was accurate and no aircraft were lost.

23/24 March 1944

WESEL

195 Lancasters and 23 Mosquitoes of 5 and 8 Groups carried out the last raid on the unfortunate town of Wesel. No aircraft lost.

Wesel claims to have been the most intensively bombed town, for its size, in Germany. 97 per cent of the buildings in the main town area were destroyed. The population, which had numbered nearly 25,000 on the outbreak of war, was only 1,900 in May 1945. No casualty figures or any other details of the raids are available.

SUPPORT AND MINOR OPERATIONS

78 training aircraft on a sweep across France and as far as Mannheim, 65 Mosquitoes to Berlin and 23 to Aschaffenburg, 41 R.C.M. sorties, 39 Mosquito patrols. 2 Mosquitoes lost from the Berlin raid.

---

24 March 1945

The final phase of the land war opened on this day, with the amphibious crossing of the Rhine on the Wesel sector and the airborne landings among the enemy defences a few hours later. British Commandos captured Wesel in the early hours, just after the Bomber Command raid had left the defenders dead or too dazed to fight properly.

The weather remained good for further Bomber Command operations. It is interesting to observe that the Ruhr was still supplying fuel and munitions for the fighting front which was now only 15 miles away and that tactical bombing and strategic bombing were taking place almost side by side.

STERKRADE

177 aircraft – 155 Halifaxes, 16 Lancasters, 6 Mosquitoes – of 4 and 8 Groups attacked the railway yards so successfully that, according to Bomber Command, there was 'complete destruction of a well packed marshalling yard'. No aircraft lost.

GLADBECK

175 aircraft – 153 Halifaxes, 16 Lancasters, 6 Mosquitoes – of 6 and 8 Groups attacked this town situated on the northern edge of the Ruhr and not far from the new battle area. The target was 'devastated'. 1 Halifax lost.

BENZOL PLANTS

173 Lancasters and 12 Mosquitoes of 1, 6 and 8 Groups attacked the Harpenerweg plant at Dortmund and the Mathias Stinnes plant at Bottrop. 3 Lancasters were lost on the Dortmund raid.

Total effort for the day: 537 sorties, 4 aircraft (0·7 per cent) lost.

24/25 March 1945

MINOR OPERATIONS

67 Mosquitoes to Berlin, 8 to Nordheim and 2 which bombed both Berlin and Magdeburg on a 'siren tour', 38 R.C.M. sorties, 33 Mosquito patrols. No aircraft lost.

---

25 March 1945

The Bomber Command operations on this day were directed to towns on the main reinforcement routes into the Rhine battle area. Heavy attacks were made on the railway routes through these towns and on the surrounding built-up areas.

HANNOVER

267 Lancasters and 8 Mosquitoes of 1, 6 and 8 Groups. The bombing was observed to fall in the target area. 1 Lancaster lost.

MÜNSTER

175 aircraft – 151 Halifaxes, 14 Lancasters, 10 Mosquitoes – of 4, 6 and 8 Groups. 3 Halifaxes lost.

Few results were seen by the bombers because the target area rapidly became smoke-covered. Münster reports a large number of bombs but only 2 people dead.

OSNABRÜCK

156 aircraft – 132 Halifaxes, 14 Lancasters, 10 Mosquitoes – of 4 and 8 Groups. No aircraft lost.

Osnabrück reports extensive property damage throughout the town. 175 people were killed – 143 civilians, 22 soldiers and 10 foreign workers – and 244 people were injured.

Total effort for the day: 606 sorties, 4 aircraft (0·7 per cent) lost.

25/26 March 1945

Minor Operations

8 Mosquitoes to Berlin and 1 Lancaster dropping leaflets over The Hague. No losses.

26/27 March 1945

MOSQUITO OPERATIONS

86 Mosquitoes to Berlin, 2 each to Erfurt and Paderborn, and 2 which bombed both Berlin and Magdeburg on a 'siren tour'. No aircraft lost.

---

27 March 1945

PADERBORN

268 Lancasters and 8 Mosquitoes to attack this town where American troops were attempting to complete the encirclement of the Ruhr. No aircraft lost.

Paderborn was covered by cloud but the raid was still carried out with almost perfect accuracy and this old town was virtually destroyed in less than a quarter of an hour. A local report, compiled a few hours after the raid, estimated that there were 3,000 separate fires and 330 people, including 50 foreigners, were dead or buried in the ruins.

HAMM

150 Lancasters of 3 Group carried out *GH* raids on 2 benzol plants in the Hamm area. No results were seen, because of cloud, but dense black smoke rose through the cloud from both targets. No aircraft lost.

FARGE

115 Lancasters of 5 Group attacked an oil-storage depot (95 aircraft) and a U-boat shelter (20 aircraft of 617 Squadron) at this small port on the River Weser north of Bremen. Both attacks appeared to be successful. The results of the raid on the oil depot were not known because this target was attacked with delayed-action bombs so that clouds of smoke would not obscure the target. The U-boat shelter was a particularly interesting target. It was a huge structure with a concrete roof 23 ft thick. It was almost ready for use when 617 Squadron attacked it on this day and penetrated the roof with 2 *Grand Slams* which brought down thousands of tons of concrete rubble and rendered the shelter unusable.

No aircraft were lost in these attacks.

Total effort for the day: 541 sorties, no aircraft lost.

27/28 March 1945

MINOR OPERATIONS

82 Mosquitoes to Berlin, 7 to Bremen, 4 to Erfurt and 3 each to Hannover and Magdeburg, 46 R.C.M. sorties, 23 Mosquito patrols, 8 Mosquitoes of 5 Group minelaying in the River Elbe. 4 Mosquitoes lost – 3 from the Berlin raid and 1 from the minelaying operation.

29 March 1945

SALZGITTER

130 Lancasters of 3 Group carried out a *G-H* raid on the Hermann Goering benzol plant. No results were seen through the cloud. No aircraft were lost.

29/30 March 1945

MOSQUITO OPERATIONS

48 Mosquitoes to Berlin, 7 to Harburg and 3 each to Bremen and Hannover. No aircraft lost.

30/31 March 1945

MINOR OPERATIONS

43 Mosquitoes to Berlin, 43 to Erfurt, 4 to Nordingen and 3 each to Hamburg and Kiel, 36 R.C.M. sorties, 31 Mosquito patrols, 6 Mosquitoes minelaying in Jade Bay and the River Weser. 1 Mosquito was lost from the Berlin raid.

31 March 1945

HAMBURG

469 aircraft – 361 Lancasters, 100 Halifaxes, 8 Mosquitoes – of 1, 6 and 8 Groups attempted to attack the Blohm & Voss shipyards, where the new types of U-boats were being assembled, but the target area was completely cloud-covered. The local report describes 'considerable damage' to houses, factories, energy supplies and communications over a wide area of southern Hamburg and Harburg. 75 people were killed.

8 Lancasters and 3 Halifaxes were lost, a number being victims of an unexpected intervention by the Luftwaffe day-fighter force. This was Bomber Command's last double-figure aircraft loss of the war from a raid on one city.

1/2 April 1945

Intruders

4 Mosquitoes of 100 Group, operating from a forward airfield in France, patrolled airfields in Southern Germany. 1 Mosquito was lost, hit by Flak and seen to crash at Leipheim, a small airfield near Ulm.

2/3 April 1945

MINOR OPERATIONS

59 training aircraft on a sweep over the North Sea, 54 Mosquitoes to Berlin, 50 to Magdeburg, 8 to Lüneburg and 1 each to Hamburg and Lübeck, 55 R.C.M. sorties, 26 Mosquito patrols. 1 Mosquito lost from the Berlin raid.

3 April 1945

NORDHAUSEN

247 Lancasters and 8 Mosquitoes of 1 and 8 Groups to attack what were believed to be military barracks near Nordhausen. Unfortunately, the barracks housed a large

number of concentration-camp prisoners and forced workers of many nationalities who worked in a complex of underground tunnels where various secret weapons were made. The camp and the tunnel workshops had been established immediately after Bomber Command attacked the rocket-research establishment at Peenemünde in August 1943.

The bombing was accurate and many people in the camp were killed; the exact number is not known. The men working in the tunnels were unhurt. 2 Lancasters lost.

3/4 April 1945

MINOR OPERATIONS

95 Mosquitoes to Berlin, 8 to Plauen and 5 to Magdeburg, 17 Mosquito patrols. 9 Lancasters sent to lay mines in the Kattegat were recalled because of weather conditions. 1 Mosquito lost from the Magdeburg raid.

---

4 April 1945

NORDHAUSEN

243 Lancasters and 1 Mosquito of 5 Group, with 8 Pathfinder Mosquitoes, attacked the barracks and the town, which was severely damaged. 1 Lancaster lost.

4/5 April 1945

LEUNA

327 Lancasters and 14 Mosquitoes of 3, 6 and 8 Groups attacked the synthetic-oil plant. The target was cloud-covered, the bombing was scattered and only minor damage was caused. 2 Lancasters lost.

HARBURG

327 aircraft – 277 Halifaxes, 36 Lancasters, 14 Mosquitoes – of 4, 6 and 8 Groups attacked the Rhenania oil plant. The target was easily identified and severe damage was caused to it. 2 Lancasters and 1 Halifax lost.

LÜTZKENDORF

258 Lancasters and 14 Mosquitoes of 1 and 8 Groups attacked the oil refinery. Bomber Command claimed 'moderate damage'. 6 Lancasters lost.

Minor Operations: 35 Mosquitoes to Berlin and 31 to Magdeburg, 70 R.C.M. sorties, 66 Mosquito patrols, 30 Lancasters minelaying in the Oslo Fjord and the Kattegat. 5 aircraft lost – 2 Mosquitoes from the Magdeburg raid and 3 Lancasters of 1 Group from the Kattegat minelaying operation. The 136 aircraft dispatched by 100 Group on this night were that group's largest effort of the war.

Total effort for the night: 1,172 sorties, 16 aircraft (1·4 per cent) lost.

---

6 April 1945

IJMUIDEN

54 Lancasters and 1 Mosquito of 5 Group to attack a ship or ships which had broken the naval blockade around that large part of Western Holland where German forces were cut off. The raid was abandoned because of bad weather.

7 April 1945

IJMUIDEN

15 Lancasters (617 Squadron) and 2 Mosquitoes of 5 Group carried out an accurate attack on the ships at Ijmuiden. No aircraft lost.

7/8 April 1945

MOLBIS

175 Lancasters and 11 Mosquitoes of 5 Group attacked the benzol plant at Molbis, near Leipzig. The weather was clear and the bombing was so effective that all production at the plant ceased. No aircraft lost.

6 R.C.M. sorties and 14 Mosquito patrols were flown by 100 Group without loss.

8/9 April 1945

HAMBURG

440 aircraft – 263 Halifaxes, 160 Lancasters, 17 Mosquitoes – of 4, 6 and 8 Groups. 3 Halifaxes and 3 Lancasters lost.

This attack was intended for the shipyard areas but partial cloud caused the raid to become dispersed. Some damage was probably caused to the shipyards but, as an American raid on the yards had taken place a few hours earlier, damage seen in photographs could not be allocated between the two forces. Other areas of Hamburg, particularly the Altona district, were badly damaged and 292 people were killed.

This was the last major Bomber Command raid of the war on Hamburg.

LÜTZKENDORF

231 Lancasters and 11 Mosquitoes of 5 Group attacked the oil refinery, which had escaped serious damage the previous night. The refinery was rendered 'inactive'. 6 Lancasters lost.

Minor Operations: 22 Halifaxes of 4 Group in a diversionary raid on Travemünde, 71 Mosquitoes to Dessau, 28 to Berlin (where *Oboe* from forward ground stations was used for the first time) and 8 to Munich, 64 R.C.M. sorties, 43 Mosquito patrols. No aircraft lost.

Total effort for the night: 918 sorties, 12 aircraft (1·3 per cent) lost.

50. The empty ruins of Hamburg typify the vast amount of damage wreaked in German cities by Bomber Command.

9 April 1945

HAMBURG

57 Lancasters of 5 Group attacked oil-storage tanks (40 aircraft) and U-boat shelters (17 aircraft of 617 Squadron with *Grand Slams* and *Tallboys*). Both attacks were successful. 2 Lancasters were lost from the raid on the oil tanks.

9/10 April 1945

KIEL

591 Lancasters and 8 Mosquitoes of 1, 3 and 8 Groups. 3 Lancasters lost.

This was an accurate raid, made in good visibility on two aiming points in the harbour area. Photographic reconnaissance showed that the Deutsche Werke U-boat yard was severely damaged, the pocket battleship *Admiral Scheer* was hit and capsized, the *Admiral Hipper* and the *Emden* were badly damaged. The local diary says that all 3 shipyards in the port were hit and that the nearby residential areas were severely damaged. 81 civilians were killed; there were probably naval casualties as well. The Kiel diarist comments on the effects of shortages – the shoes removed from the body of a dead woman, the flesh all cut from a dead horse.

Minor Operations: 22 Halifaxes in a diversionary raid to Stade, 44 Mosquitoes to Berlin, 37 to Plauen and 24 to Hamburg, 45 R.C.M. sorties, 37 Mosquito patrols, 70 Lancasters and 28

Halifaxes minelaying in Kiel Bay and the Little Belt. 1 Halifax from the diversion raid crashed in France.

Total effort for the night: 906 sorties, 4 aircraft (0·4 per cent) lost.

---

10 April 1945

LEIPZIG

230 aircraft – 134 Lancasters, 90 Halifaxes, 6 Mosquitoes – attacked the Engelsdorf and Mockau railway yards. The weather was clear and the bombing was accurate. 1 Halifax and 1 Lancaster lost.

10/11 April 1945

PLAUEN

307 Lancasters and 8 Mosquitoes of 1 and 8 Groups. No aircraft lost.

The bombing fell around the railway yards in the northern half of the town. The railways were hit and 365 acres, 51 per cent, of the town's built-up area were also destroyed.

LEIPZIG

76 Lancasters and 19 Mosquitoes of 5 and 8 Groups attacked the Wahren railway yards. The eastern half of the yards was destroyed. 7 Lancasters lost.

Minor Operations: 77 Mosquitoes to Berlin, 21 to Chemnitz and 7 to Bayreuth, 53 R.C.M. sorties, 26 Mosquito patrols. 1 Mosquito from the Berlin raid and 1 R.C.M. Halifax were lost.

Total effort for the night: 594 sorties, 9 aircraft (1·5 per cent) lost.

---

11 April 1945

NUREMBERG

129 Halifaxes of 4 Group and 14 Pathfinder Lancasters attacked the railway yards with great accuracy. No aircraft lost.

BAYREUTH

100 Halifaxes of 4 Group and 14 Lancasters and 8 Mosquitoes of 8 Group also carried out a very good attack on railway yards without loss.

11/12 April 1945

MOSQUITO OPERATIONS

107 Mosquitoes attacked Berlin in 3 waves. Large fires were seen. 1 Mosquito lost. 8 Mosquitoes attacked Munich without loss.

12/13 April 1945

MINOR OPERATIONS

97 Mosquitoes to Berlin and 10 to Munich, 13 Mosquitoes on Intruder patrols. No aircraft lost.

---

13 April 1945

SWINEMÜNDE

34 Lancasters of 5 Group (9 and 617 Squadrons) set out to attack the warships *Prinz Eugen* and *Lützow* in Swinemünde harbour but the raid was abandoned because of cloud over the target. All aircraft returned safely.

13/14 April 1945

KIEL

377 Lancasters and 105 Halifaxes of 3, 6 and 8 Groups. 2 Lancasters lost.

This raid was directed against the port area, with the U-boat yards as the main objective. Bomber Command rated this as 'a poor attack' with scattered bombing. The local diary states that the main bombing was in and around the suburb of Elmschenhagen, 2 miles from the port area, but some damage was caused nearer the harbour, including a hit on an ammunition depot at the northern end. 50 people were killed.

Minor Operations: 20 Halifaxes and 8 Mosquitoes in a diversionary raid on Boizenburg, 87 Mosquitoes to Hamburg, 20 to Stralsund and 12 to Reisa, 62 R.C.M. sorties, 55 Mosquito patrols, 82 Lancasters and 27 Halifaxes minelaying in Kiel Bay and the Kattegat. 1 Mosquito of 100 Group lost.

Total effort for the night: 855 sorties, 3 aircraft (0·4 per cent) lost.

---

15 April 1945

Swinemünde

20 Lancasters of 617 Squadron again found their target covered by cloud and returned without bombing. No aircraft lost.

14/15 April 1945

POTSDAM

500 Lancasters and 12 Mosquitoes of 1, 3 and 8 Groups. This was the first time that Bomber Command 4-engined aircraft had entered the Berlin defence zone since March 1944 but the approach, across parts of Germany recently captured by Allied troops, and the Cuxhaven diversion led to only 1 Lancaster being lost; it was shot down by a night fighter.

This was the last raid of the war by a major Bomber Command force on a German city. The aiming point was the centre of Potsdam and the intention was to destroy the local barracks (depot of the old German Guards regiments) and the railway facilities. The attack was reasonably successful and severe damage was caused in Potsdam but bombs also fell in the nearby northern and eastern districts of Berlin. No information is obtainable from Potsdam (now in Eastern Germany) but a figure of 5,000 dead has been mentioned. This high figure, if true, was caused by the fact that the people of this community had seen Berlin and not themselves bombed so often that they failed to take proper cover when the sirens sounded.

Minor Operations: 24 Lancasters and 4 Mosquitoes in a diversion raid to Cuxhaven, 62 Mosquitoes to Berlin and 10 to Wismar, 54 R.C.M. sorties, 50 Mosquito patrols. No aircraft lost.

Total effort for the night: 716 sorties, 1 aircraft (0·1 per cent) lost.

15/16 April 1945

MINOR OPERATIONS

106 Mosquitoes to Berlin, 8 to Oranienburg airfield and 4 to Lechfeld airfield, 27 R.C.M. sorties, 19 Mosquito patrols. 1 Mosquito of 100 Group lost.

---

16 April 1945

Swinemünde

18 Lancasters of 617 Squadron flew to Swinemünde to attack the pocket battleship *Lützow*. The force flew through intense Flak; 1 Lancaster was shot down (617 Squadron's last loss of the war) and all but 2 aircraft were damaged. 15 aircraft managed to bomb the target with *Tallboys* or with 1,000-pounders. The effects of one near miss with a *Tallboy* tore a large hole in the bottom of the *Lützow* and she sank in shallow water at her moorings.

16/17 April 1945

PILSEN

222 Lancasters and 11 Mosquitoes of 5 Group carried out an accurate attack on the railway yards. 1 Lancaster crashed in France.

SCHWANDORF

167 Lancasters and 8 Mosquitoes of 6 and 8 Groups attacked the railway yards, causing severe damage. 1 Lancaster lost.

Minor Operations: 19 Halifaxes of 6 Group and 4 Pathfinder Mosquitoes to Gablingen airfield, 64 Mosquitoes to Berlin and 23 to Munich, 57 R.C.M. sorties, 35 Mosquito patrols. 2 Halifaxes and 1 Fortress of 100 Group were lost.

Total effort for the night: 610 sorties, 5 aircraft (0·8 per cent) lost.

17/18 April 1945

CHAM

90 Lancasters and 11 Mosquitoes of 5 Group attacked the railway yards in this small town deep in south-eastern Germany. The attack was completely successful, with tracks torn up and rolling stock destroyed. No aircraft lost.

Minor Operations: 61 Mosquitoes to Berlin and 43 to Ingoldstadt airfield, 28 R.C.M. sorties, 40 Mosquito patrols. 2 Mosquitoes lost from the Berlin raid.

18 April 1945

HELIGOLAND

969 aircraft – 617 Lancasters, 332 Halifaxes, 20 Mosquitoes – of all groups attacked the naval base, the airfield and the town on this small island. The bombing was accurate and the target areas were turned almost into crater-pitted moonscapes. The present-day Bürgermeister was unable to supply any local details; it is probable that the civilian population had been evacuated long before this raid. 3 Halifaxes were lost.

18/19 April 1945

KOMOTAU

114 Lancasters and 9 Mosquitoes of 5 Group attacked the railway yards in this Czechoslovak town (now known as Chomutov). This was the last major raid in the long communications offensive to which 5 Group had made a particularly effective contribution. The raid was completely successful and all the aircraft involved returned safely.

Minor Operations: 57 Mosquitoes to Berlin and 36 to Schleissheim airfield near Munich, 35 R.C.M. sorties, 33 Mosquito patrols. 1 Mosquito of 141 Squadron was lost while carrying out a napalm attack on an airfield in Northern Germany; this was a new form of weapon being used by the Mosquito squadrons of 100 Group.

19 April 1945

MUNICH

49 Lancasters of 3 Group carried out a *G-H* raid on the Pasing railway yards. The bombing appeared to be concentrated. No aircraft lost.

HELIGOLAND

36 Lancasters of 9 and 617 Squadrons attacked coastal battery positions with *Tallboy* bombs. All targets were hit and no aircraft were lost.

19/20 April 1945

MINOR OPERATIONS

79 Mosquitoes to Berlin, 35 to Wittstock airfield and 8 to Schleswig airfield, 34 R.C.M. sorties, 40 Mosquito patrols. No aircraft lost.

---

20 April 1945

REGENSBURG

100 Lancasters of 3 Group bombed the fuel-storage depot accurately. 1 Lancaster lost.

This was the last raid in the current campaign against German oil targets which had been waged since June 1944. Much of Bomber Command's effort during this period, sometimes at considerable loss, had been devoted to these oil operations, which had helped not only the Allied ground forces on the Western Front but also those fighting in Italy and on the Eastern Front.

20/21 April 1945

BERLIN

76 Mosquitoes made 6 separate attacks on Berlin. This was the last R.A.F. raid of the war on Berlin; the Russians were about to enter the city. Mosquito XVI M L 929, of 109 Squadron, claimed the last bombs – 4 500-pounders – at 2.14 a.m. British Time. The crew were Flying Officer A. C. Austin, pilot, and Flying Officer P. Moorhead, navigator. All aircraft returned safely.

Minor Operations: 36 Mosquitoes to Schleissheim airfield, 3 R.C.M. sorties, 2 Mosquito patrols. No aircraft lost.

21/22 April 1945

KIEL

107 Mosquitoes. 2 aircraft lost.

The local diarist recorded details of this raid. The sirens did not sound until after the first bombs had exploded. The worst damage was in the Elmschenhagen suburb, 'but', he wrote plaintively, 'there are new ruins all over the town. It is no longer possible to spot which damage is new. One sometimes asks oneself whether there are any intact houses left.' 50 people were killed.

Minor Operations: 16 Mosquitoes to Eggebek airfield near Flensburg, 3 R.C.M. sorties, 16 Mosquito patrols, 20 Lancasters of 6 Group minelaying in the Kattegat. No aircraft lost.

22 April 1945

BREMEN

767 aircraft – 651 Lancasters, 100 Halifaxes, 16 Mosquitoes – of 1, 3, 6 and 8 Groups. 2 Lancasters lost.

This raid was part of the preparation for the attack by the British XXX Corps on Bremen. The bombing was on the south-eastern suburbs of the city, where the ground troops would attack 2 days later. The raid was hampered by cloud and by smoke and dust from bombing as the raid progressed. The Master Bomber ordered the raid to stop after 195 Lancasters had bombed. The whole of 1 and 4 Groups returned home without attacking.

The Bremen city officials were, amazingly, still recording the effects of the raid in great detail, even though the city would be in British hands within 5 days and the intervening period would be filled with a continuous artillery bombardment, fighter-bomber attacks and the British assault! 3,664 houses were carefully listed under 5 categories of air-raid damage from 'destroyed' to 'broken windows'. 'At least 172 civilians' were killed, of whom 26 died in a concrete shelter whose side was blown in by a heavy bomb exploding just outside. There are, unfortunately, no notes on casualties to the German troops or on the effect upon their defences but Bremen soon fell after 3 days of ground attack, with 6,000 German troops surrendering. It was the first major German port to be captured.

22/23 April 1945

MINOR OPERATIONS

40 Mosquitoes to Bremen and 11 to Kiel, 56 R.C.M. sorties, 39 Mosquito patrols. No aircraft lost.

---

23 April 1945

FLENSBURG

148 Lancasters of 5 Group set out to attack the railway yards and port area but the operation was abandoned because of cloud which covered the target on the bomb run. All aircraft returned safely.

23/24 April 1945

KIEL

60 Mosquitoes; none lost. The Kiel report says that bombs fell in many parts of the town but no one was killed. Many of the inhabitants of the remaining German targets were spending these last few days of the war permanently in air-raid shelters.

Minor Operations: 38 Mosquitoes to Rendsburg, 32 to Travemünde and 8 to Schleissheim airfield, 45 R.C.M. sorties, 35 Mosquito patrols. No aircraft lost.

---

24 April 1945

BAD OLDESLOE

110 Lancasters attacked the railway yards. No aircraft lost.

A short report from Germany states that this town, midway between Hamburg and Lübeck, was unprepared for air attack and its precautions were 'slack'. Approximately 700 people were killed and 300 were injured when bombs fell in areas near the railway yards.

24/25 April 1945

PRISONER-OF-WAR CAMPS

30 Mosquitoes and 7 Lancasters dropped leaflets on 8 camps in which British prisoners-of-war were waiting to be liberated. Medical supplies were also dropped at the Neubrandenburg camp, north of Berlin. No aircraft were lost.

Minor Operations: 40 Mosquitoes to Schleissheim airfield, 38 to Pasing airfield and 17 to Kiel, 27 R.C.M. sorties, 19 Mosquito patrols. 1 Mosquito from the Schleissheim raid crashed in Belgium.

25 April 1945

WANGEROOGE

482 aircraft – 308 Halifaxes, 158 Lancasters, 16 Mosquitoes – of 4, 6 and 8 Groups. 5 Halifaxes and 2 Lancasters lost.

The raid was intended to knock out the coastal batteries on this Frisian island which controlled the approaches to the ports of Bremen and Wilhelmshaven. No doubt the experience of Antwerp, when guns on the approaches had prevented the port being used for several weeks, prompted this raid.

The weather was clear and bombing was accurate until smoke and dust obscured the target area. A good local report is available (from Hans-Jürgen Jürgens, proprietor of a restaurant at the present-day holiday resort). The areas around the batteries were pitted with craters but the concreted gun positions were 'hardly damaged'; they were all capable of firing within a few hours. Part of the bombing hit a camp for forced workers and the holiday resort and many buildings were destroyed, including several hotels and guest houses, the Catholic church and two children's holiday homes, although these do not appear to have been occupied at the time of the bombing. Detailed casualty figures are provided. 306 people died: 59 civilians, 132 service personnel – including 6 female naval auxiliaries – 95 foreign workers (48 Dutch, 36 Belgian, 11 Polish) and 20 prisoners of war (16 French and 4 Moroccan).

6 of the 7 bombers lost were involved in collisions – 2 Halifaxes of 76 Squadron, 2 Lancasters of 431 Squadron and 2 Halifaxes of 408 and 426 Squadrons (both from Leeming airfield). There was only 1 survivor, from one of the 76 Squadron aircraft. 28 Canadian and 13 British airmen were killed in the collisions. The seventh aircraft lost was a Halifax of 347 (Free French) Squadron, whose crew were all killed.

BERCHTESGADEN

359 Lancasters and 16 Mosquitoes of 1, 5 and 8 Groups. 2 Lancasters lost.

This raid was against Hitler's 'Eagle's Nest' chalet and the local S.S. guard barracks. Among the force were 16 Lancasters of 617 Squadron dropping their last *Tallboys*. 8 *Oboe* Mosquitoes were also among the bombing force, to help with the marking, but mountains intervened between one of the ground stations transmitting the *Oboe* signals and the Mosquitoes could not operate even though they were flying at 39,000 ft! There was some mist and the presence of snow on the ground also made it difficult to identify targets, but the bombing appeared to be accurate and effective. No other deatils are available.

Total effort for the day: 857 sorties, 9 aircraft (1·0 per cent) lost. Most of the squadrons taking part in the raids on this day were flying their last operations of the war.

25/26 April 1945

TONSBERG

107 Lancasters and 12 Mosquitoes of 5 Group attacked the oil refinery in this town in Southern Norway in the last raid flown by heavy bombers. The attack was accurately carried out and the target was severely damaged. A Lancaster of 463 Squadron came down in Sweden, the last of more than 3,300 Lancasters lost in the war; Flying Officer A. Cox and his all-British crew all survived and were interned in Sweden until the end of the war – only a few days away.

Minor Operations: 82 Mosquitoes to Pasing airfield and 18 to Kiel, 9 R.C.M. sorties, 35 Mosquito patrols, 14 Lancasters minelaying in Oslo Fjord (the last minelaying operation of the war), 12 Mosquitoes of 8 Group dropping leaflets over prisoner-of-war camps.

---

26 April to 7 May 1945

OPERATION *EXODUS*

Bomber Command Lancasters now started flying to Brussels, and later to other airfields, to collect British prisoners of war recently liberated from their camps. 469 flights were made by aircraft of 1, 5, 6 and 8 Groups before the war ended and approximately 75,000 men were brought back to England by the fastest possible means (unlike the end of the First World War when some British ex-prisoners were still not home by Christmas, although the Armistice was signed on 11 November 1918). There were no accidents during that part of Operation *Exodus* which was carried out before the war ended. (These flights are not included in the statistical surveys of this diary.)

26/27 April 1945

MOSQUITO OPERATIONS

31 Mosquitoes to Husum, 28 each to Eggebek and Grossenbrode and 12 to Neumünster (all airfields in Schleswig-Holstein), 12 Mosquitoes to Kiel, 4 Mosquito Intruders on patrols. No aircraft lost.

---

29 April to 7 May 1945

OPERATION *MANNA*

A large pocket in Western Holland was still in German hands and the population was approaching starvation; many old or sick people had already died. A truce was arranged with the local German commander and Lancasters of 1, 3 and 8 Groups started to drop food supplies for the civilian population. Pathfinder Mosquitoes 'marked' the dropping zones. 2,835 Lancaster and 124 Mosquito flights were made before the Germans surrendered at the end of the war and allowed ships and road transport to enter the area. Bomber Command delivered 6,672 tons of food during Operation *Manna*. (These flights are not included in statistical surveys.)

30 April 1945

Hitler committed suicide in Berlin on this day, after handing over the leadership to Admiral Doenitz, who was in the Kiel–Flensburg area.

2/3 May 1945

KIEL

There had been no offensive operations by Bomber Command since 26/27 April and most squadrons thought that their war in Europe was over, but it was feared that the Germans were assembling ships at Kiel to transport troops to Norway in order to carry on the war there. A last raid by 8 Group Mosquitoes was thus organized, with a large supporting effort being provided.

16 Mosquito bombers of 8 Group and 37 Mosquitoes of 100 Group were first dispatched to attack airfields in the Kiel area. A Mosquito of 169 Squadron, 100 Group, was lost while carrying out a low-level napalm attack on Jagel airfield; its crew – Flying Officer R. Catterall, D.F.C., and Flight Sergeant D. J. Beadle – were killed.

126 Mosquitoes of 8 Group then attacked Kiel in 2 raids, 1 hour apart. The target area was almost completely cloud-covered but *H2S* and *Oboe* were used. Large fires on the ground were seen through the cloud. No Mosquitoes were lost on these raids. The Kiel diarist, Detlef Boelck, performing his duty to the end, provides an interesting report. Bombs fell in several parts of the town, killing 18 civilians. The tower of the Rathaus collapsed and other buildings were hit. Towards morning, a large column of military vehicles departed in the direction of Flensburg on the Danish frontier. 'The upsurge in the population's morale was indescribable.' There was a final spasm of fear when explosions were heard from the harbour but these turned out to be all the Flak guns and warships in the harbour firing off their ammunition; after this, Kiel was declared an open, undefended town. As soon as this happened, all the military stores and some of the civilian ones containing rationed goods were thrown open to the public before Allied troops arrived, but there was much confusion and Herr Boelck reports that people often reached home to find that they had two left or two right shoes instead of a pair. British and Canadian troops entered the town quietly 36 hours later.

Meanwhile, there had been a final small tragedy for Bomber Command. 89

R.C.M. aircraft of 100 Group had been sent to support the Mosquito bomber force and 2 Halifaxes from 199 Squadron, each with 8 men on board, were lost. The Halifaxes had been part of the *Mandrel* screen and were also carrying 4 500-lb bombs and large quantities of *Window*. The 2 aircraft crashed at Meimersdorf, just south of Kiel, and it is probable that they collided while on their bomb runs. They were the last Bomber Command aircraft to be lost in the war. There were only 3 survivors. 13 airmen, 12 from the United Kingdom and one from the Irish Republic, mostly second-tour men, died. They were: Warrant Officer W. F. Bolton; Flight Sergeant A. A. Bradley; Flight Lieutenant W. E. Brooks; Sergeant F. T. Chambers; Flying Officer K. N. J. Croft; Warrant Officer K. A. C. Gavin; Flight Sergeant D. Greenwood; Flying Officer A. S. J. Holder, D.F.C.; Flight Sergeant J. R. Lewis; Flight Sergeant J. Loth; Pilot Officer W. H. V. Mackay; Warrant Officer R. H. A. Pool; and Flight Sergeant D. Wilson. These men are now buried in the Kiel War Cemetery, together with the crew of the 169 Squadron Mosquito who were killed earlier in the night.

On 4 May, German officers came to the Tactical Headquarters of Montgomery's 21st Army Group on Lüneburg Heath and signed a surrender document for all German forces in North-West Germany, Denmark and Holland, to be effective from the following day. Various local surrenders took place elsewhere. On 7 May General Eisenhower, with representatives from Britain, Russia and France, accepted the unconditional surrender of all German forces on all fronts, to be effective from 00.01 hours on 9 May. But the fighting was effectively already over. Allied troops, fully supported by Bomber Command, had liberated the whole of Western Europe in just eleven months of hard fighting. The British Army lost nearly 40,000 men during this

51. An R.A.F. officer enters the ruined Krupps works in Essen at the end of the war.

campaign. Bomber Command had lost 2,128 aircraft during the same period, with approximately 10,000 airmen being killed.

Many of the bomber squadrons were now earmarked for Tiger Force, to continue the war against Japan, but the dropping of two atom bombs three months later brought the surrender of Japan and the end of the Second World War before Tiger Force left England.

Operational Statistics, 1 January to 7/8 May 1945
(127 days/nights)

Number of nights with operations: 100
Number of days with operations: 81
Number of night sorties: 44,289, from which 611 aircraft (1·4 per cent) were lost
Number of day sorties: 18,545, from which 100 aircraft (0·5 per cent) were lost
Total sorties: 62,824, from which 711 aircraft (1·1 per cent) were lost
Approximate bomb tonnage in period: 181,740 tons
Average per 24-hour period: 494·6 sorties, 5·6 aircraft lost, 1,431·0 tons of bombs dropped

Part Two
Statistics

OPERATIONAL STATISTICS

3 September 1939 to 7/8 May 1945
(2,074 days/nights)

(These statistics have been compiled by first totalling the operational statistics printed at the end of each period of the diaries and then adding 2,654 sorties and 73 aircraft lost on Resistance Operations between 29/30 August 1941 and 7/8 January 1944 and 1,364 sorties and 3 aircraft lost by 1409 (Meteorological) Flight since 2 April 1943; these further figures were not included in the periodic statistics. For reasons of convenience, it has been assumed that all the Resistance Operations were flown at night and those of the Met Flight by day.)

Number of nights with operations: 1,481 (71·4 per cent of all nights in the war)
Number of days with operations: 1,089 (52·5 per cent of all days in the war)
Number of night sorties: 307,253, from which 7,953 aircraft (2·6 per cent) were lost
Number of day sorties: 80,163, from which 1,000 aircraft (1·2 per cent) were lost
Total sorties: 387,416, from which 8,953 aircraft (2·3 per cent) were lost
Approximate bomb tonnage in war: 955,044 tons
Averages per 24-hour period: 186·8 sorties, 4·3 aircraft lost, 460·5 tons of bombs dropped

Comment. The overall loss rate for daylight sorties – 1·2 per cent – is deceptive. The majority of daylight sorties were flown in the last year of the war when the Allies held complete air supremacy by day. Losses in daylight operations in the first three and a half years of the war were much heavier than night losses.

AIRCRAFT SORTIES AND CASUALTIES

Aircraft Type	Sorties[1]	Lost (percentage of sorties)	Operational Crashes[2] (percentage of sorties)
Lancaster	156,192	3,431 (2·20)	246 (0·16)
Halifax	82,773	1,884 (2·28)	199 (0·24)
Wellington	47,409	1,386 (2·92)	341 (0·72)
Mosquito	39,795	260 (0·65)	50 (0·13)
Stirling	18,440	625 (3·39)	59 (0·32)
Hampden	16,541	424 (2·56)	209 (1·26)
Blenheim	12,214	442 (3·62)	99 (0·81)
Whitley	9,858	317 (3·22)	141 (1·43)
Boston	1,609	42 (2·61)	4 (0·25)
Fortress	1,340	14 (1·04)	4 (0·30)
Manchester	1,269	64 (5·04)	12 (0·95)
Ventura	997	39 (3·91)	2 (0·20)
Liberator	662	3 (0·45)	nil
Others	710	22 (3·10)	2 (0·28)
Total	389,809	8,953	1,368 (0·35)

Notes

1. Figures quoted for sorties are taken from the War Room Manual. They are slightly higher than those quoted by us in our Final Operational Statistics on page 707. The reason for this is the different interpretations of what constituted an operational sortie. For example, the petrol-carrying flights by Halifaxes in 1944 and the Lancaster flights in Operations *Manna* and *Exodus* in 1945 were not counted as operational sorties in our figures.
2. 'Operational Crashes' are the numbers of aircraft recorded in Bomber Command documents as having crashed in the United Kingdom while outward or inward bound on operational flights. It is impossible to say how many of these aircraft became total losses. It is interesting to note the dramatic decrease in the proportion of operational crashes as the war progressed, due to better crew training, improved flying control and diversion procedures, and the introduction of more reliable aircraft. Compare, for example, the Whitley's crash rate of 1·43 per cent and the Lancaster's of 0·16 per cent. Overall figures for the first half of the war were 1·05 per cent compared with 0·20 per cent for the second half of the war.

AIRCREW CASUALTIES

Approximately 125,000 aircrew served in the squadrons and the operational training and conversion units of Bomber Command during the war.* Nearly 60 per cent of Bomber Command aircrew became casualties. Approximately 85 per cent of these casualties were suffered on operations and 15 per cent in training and other accidents. The Air Ministry was able to compile the following figures up to 31 May 1947:†

Killed in action or died while prisoners of war	47,268	
Killed in flying or ground accidents	8,195	
Killed in ground-battle action	37	
Total fatal casualties to aircrew		55,500
Prisoners of war, including many wounded		9,838
Wounded in aircraft which returned from operations	4,200	
Wounded in flying or ground accidents in U.K.	4,203	
Total wounded, other than prisoners of war		8,403
Total aircrew casualties		73,741

---

* The figures for aircrew in Bomber Command are quoted by Sir Arthur Harris in *Bomber Offensive*, p. 267.

† Letter to Martin Middlebrook from Air Historical Branch, 25 June 1969, and Appendix 41 of the British Official History, Vol. IV, pp. 440–44.

52 (a and b). The British War Cemetery being constructed at Rheinberg after the war. The crew in the communal grave in the foreground is that of Sergeant Guy Fisher of 51 Squadron, whose Halifax was lost while attacking Duisburg on the night of 26/27 April 1943.

Rheinberg from the air. Of the 3,326 graves 2,895 belong to R.A.F. men, nearly all lost in Bomber Command raids on targets in the Ruhr. It was not far from here that the biggest wartime decoy fire site for the Ruhr was situated.

53 (a and b). The Reichswald War Cemetery, near Kleve, contains 3,971 R.A.F. men, more than any other cemetery in Germany. The airmen on the front row of temporary crosses were not Bomber Command men. The communal grave on the left of the second row contains Pilot Officer George Burgess, an Australian, and five other members of a 460 Squadron crew lost when their Lancaster was shot down by Flak while attacking Dortmund in daylight on 12 March 1945. Flight Sergeant Harold Dyer was a Canadian air gunner in a 50 Squadron Lancaster shot down while raiding Duisburg on 8/9 January 1943; five other members of this crew are also buried here.

54. The Berlin War Cemetery, in which more than 80 per cent of the graves are those of Bomber Command men, many lost in the costly Battle of Berlin.

The graves in the foreground belong to Sergeant George Jeffrey, Sergeant Harry Coffey (Canadian) and Flight Sergeant Alan Drake, killed when their Lancaster of 630 Squadron was shot down on the Nuremberg raid of 30/31 March 1944.

AIRCREW CASUALTIES BY NATIONALITY

The Bomber Command men who died were serving with the following Air Forces at the time of their deaths (these figures include 73 men who died of natural causes; it is not possible to extract that figure from the nationality totals):

Royal Air Force	38,462	(69·2 per cent)
Royal Canadian Air Force	9,919	(17·8 per cent)
Royal Australian Air Force	4,050	(7·3 per cent)
Royal New Zealand Air Force	1,679	(3·0 per cent)
Polish Air Force	929	(1·7 per cent)
Other Allied Air Forces	473	(0·9 per cent)
South African Air Force	34 ⎱	(0·1 per cent)
Other Dominions	27 ⎰	

CASUALTIES BY RANK

From a random study of Bomber Command names in the registers of nine war cemeteries in Germany, the following were the approximate proportions of dead aircrew:

Officers	27·6 per cent
Warrant Officers	3·3 per cent
Non-commissioned officers	69·1 per cent

This table includes promotions which were being processed when airmen were shot down and which were applied after the man had died.

ESCAPERS AND EVADERS

During the war 156 R.A.F. men successfully escaped from German prison camps in Western Europe and 1,975 men evaded capture after having been shot down in Western Europe (source: Public Record Office AIR 40/1897). No breakdown by commands is available but it is probable that more than half of the escapers and evaders were Bomber Command men.

GROUNDCREW

It is not known how many men and women ground staff served with Bomber Command during the war but 1,479 men and 91 W.A.A.F.s died while on duty and 52 male ground staff became prisoners of war.

55. The Durnbach War Cemetery. Probably the most beautiful setting of any of the war cemeteries in Germany, the mountains of Bavaria. Nine out of every ten of these graves are of Bomber Command men killed while raiding targets in Southern Germany or on the way to Italy.

Part Three

Operational Performances
of Units

SQUADRONS

NOTES

Service. Only details of a squadron's service in Bomber Command during the years of the Second World War in Europe are given; an excellent reference book for earlier and later periods is *Bomber Squadrons of the R.A.F. and Their Aircraft* by Philip Moyes (Macdonald, 1964). 'Original squadrons on the outbreak of war' do not include 'group pool' squadrons or those which were in reserve on the outbreak of war; only front-line, operational squadrons are given the 'original' title.

Raids Flown. If a squadron's aircraft were split between several targets in any one night, as happened frequently in the early war years, only one 'raid' has been counted for that night. Sometimes, for convenience, 'armed recces' or 'sweeps' over the sea are classed as 'bombing raids' even though no bombs were dropped.

Sorties and Losses. Sorties and losses have been counted by Chris Everitt in the squadron Operations Record Books (AIR 27 series) at the Public Record Office in a research effort which required nearly 400 hours of work. The petrol-carrying flights made by Halifax squadrons in September and October 1944, and the food-carrying flights to Holland and the prisoner-of-war evacuation flights made by Lancasters in April and May 1945, have not been included. The definition of a 'lost' aircraft is the same as that used throughout these diaries: crashed into enemy territory, into the sea or behind Allied lines in Europe; shot down over Britain by German Intruders or by 'friendly' defences.

The total number of sorties shown in the squadron record books agrees, within a small margin, with the totals recorded in Bomber Command's records (already quoted in Part Two: Statistics). But the total number of aircraft shown as lost in the individual squadron record books are well below Bomber Command's totals for the relevant aircraft types. Losses of some types in the squadron records were under-recorded by as much as 20 per cent! This serious shortfall required that further searches be made. Two reliable reference books quoted the serial numbers of all the Manchesters, Lancasters and Stirlings made during the war and the eventual fate of each aircraft.* Most of the shortages for other types were found by Chris Everitt in the Bomber Command Day and Night Bombing Sheets (Public Record Office AIR 14/2664–76 and 3360–65). As a result of this further work, we have been able to bring up individual squadron losses to within 2·4 per cent of Bomber Command's overall totals.

---

*The reference books were *Lancaster – The Story of a Famous Bomber* by Bruce Robertson (Harleyford, 1964) and *The Stirling File* by Bryce Gomersall (Air Britain and Aviation Archaeologists Publications, 1979); Robertson's work covered Manchesters as well as Lancasters.

Figures for aircraft destroyed in operational and non-operational crashes were recorded in some reference books and this information has been added where available.

Points of Interest. To receive a mention for most raids, sorties or losses and for highest and lowest percentage losses in Bomber Command or in a group, a squadron had to have flown a minimum of 2,500 sorties in the regular bomber groups and 500 in 2 Group and 1,000 in 100 Group. To qualify for similar mentions in comparisons of a particular aircraft type, the squadron had to have flown 1,000 sorties on Wellingtons, Stirlings, Halifaxes or Lancasters and 500 sorties on most other types.

7 SQUADRON

SERVICE

In 3 Group from October 1940; first operation on 10/11 February 1941 to Rotterdam. To 8 Group in August 1942 and served as a Pathfinder squadron until the end of the war. Equipped with Stirlings from October 1940 to August 1943 and with Lancasters from July 1943 (there was an overlapping of types in July and August 1943). Based at Oakington throughout its operational service.

OPERATIONAL PERFORMANCE

Raids Flown
3 Group Stirlings – 167 bombing, 11 minelaying
8 Group Stirlings – 82 bombing, 7 minelaying
8 Group Lancasters – 279 bombing
_____

Total – 528 bombing, 18 minelaying = 546 raids

Sorties and Losses
3 Group Stirlings – 918 sorties, 41 aircraft lost (4·5 per cent)
8 Group Stirlings – 826 sorties, 37 aircraft lost (4·5 per cent)
8 Group Lancasters – 3,316 sorties, 87 aircraft lost (2·6 per cent)
_____

Total – 5,060 sorties, 165 aircraft lost (3·3 per cent)

27 Stirlings were destroyed in crashes.

POINTS OF INTEREST

Introduced the Stirling to operational service.
An original Pathfinder squadron.
Introduced (with 35 Squadron) *H2S* to operations.
Suffered third highest percentage losses in Bomber Command.
Carried out most bombing raids in 8 Group heavy-bomber squadrons.

Suffered highest overall and percentage losses in 8 Group.
Suffered highest percentage losses in Stirling squadrons.

9 SQUADRON

SERVICE

In 3 Group from the outbreak of the war to August 1942, with a short detachment to Lossiemouth in April 1940 for service with Coastal Command. In 5 Group from August 1942 to the end of the war. Equipped with Wellingtons in 3 Group and with Lancasters in 5 Group. Based at Honington in 3 Group and at Waddington and Bardney in 5 Group.

OPERATIONAL PERFORMANCE

Raids Flown
3 Group Wellingtons – 272 bombing, 7 minelaying, 8 leaflet
5 Group Lancasters – 289 bombing, 12 minelaying

Total – 561 bombing, 19 minelaying, 8 leaflet = 588 raids

Sorties and Losses
3 Group Wellingtons – 2,333 sorties, 66 aircraft lost (2·8 per cent)
5 Group Lancasters – 3,495 sorties, 111 aircraft lost (3·2 per cent)

Total – 5,828 sorties, 177 aircraft lost (3·0 per cent)

22 Lancasters were destroyed in crashes.

POINTS OF INTEREST

Continuous service in Bomber Command throughout the war except for the short detachment to Coastal Command in April 1940. Flew operations and sustained casualties on the second day of the war.

Victoria Cross: Flight Sergeant G. Thompson, posthumously, Dortmund–Ems Canal, 1 January 1945.

The squadron's Lancasters were fitted with bomb bays capable of taking *Tallboy* bombs in 1944 and 1945 and were the only Main Force aircraft to carry out precision bombing with 617 Squadron.

10 SQUADRON

SERVICE

In 4 Group from the outbreak of the war until the end, though with short detachments to Coastal Command and the Middle East. Equipped with Whitleys until December 1941 and then with Halifaxes. Based at Dishforth, Leeming and Melbourne.

OPERATIONAL PERFORMANCE

Raids Flown
Whitleys – 208 bombing, 15 leaflet
Halifaxes – 325 bombing, 61 minelaying

Total – 533 bombing, 61 minelaying, 15 leaflet = 609 raids

Sorties and Losses
Whitleys – 1,430 sorties, 47 aircraft lost (3·3 per cent)
Halifaxes – 4,803 sorties, 109 aircraft lost (2·3 per cent)

Total – 6,233 sorties, 156 aircraft last (2·5 per cent)

POINTS OF INTEREST

An operational squadron from the outbreak of war, flying night operations in the
first week.
Made the first flights over Berlin, dropping leaflets on 1/2 October 1939.
Pioneered what were later known as 'pathfinder' techniques in 1941.
Carried out most bombing raids in 4 Group and flew only four sorties less than the
highest number in 4 Group (by 78 Squadron).

12 SQUADRON

SERVICE

Returned from the Advanced Air Striking Force in France (where the squadron had
won two V.C.s, Flying Officer D. E. Garland and Sergeant T. Gray) in June 1940
and posted to 1 Group; remained with 1 Group to the end of the war. Equipped with
Battles, Wellingtons and Lancasters. Based at Binbrook (three times), Thorney Island
and Eastchurch (both for raids by Battles to the Channel ports) and Wickenby.

OPERATIONAL PERFORMANCE

Raids Flown
Battles – 8 bombing
Wellingtons – 137 bombing, 24 minelaying, 6 leaflet
Lancasters – 282 bombing, 27 minelaying

Total – 427 bombing, 51 minelaying, 6 leaflet = 484 raids

Sorties and Losses
Battles – 36 sorties, 1 aircraft lost (2·8 per cent)
Wellingtons – 1,242 sorties, 59 aircraft lost (4·8 per cent)
Lancasters – 3,882 sorties, 111 aircraft lost (2·9 per cent)

Total – 5,160 sorties, 171 aircraft lost (3·3 per cent)

18 Lancasters were destroyed in crashes.

Continuous wartime service as a bomber squadron with the Advanced Air Striking
   Force and Bomber Command.
Suffered second highest percentage losses in Bomber Command.
Suffered highest percentage losses in 1 Group.
Suffered highest losses in 1 Group Wellington squadrons.

15 SQUADRON

SERVICE

After flying Battles in the reconnaissance role with the Advanced Air Striking Force
in France, returned to England in December 1939 and was re-equipped with Blenheims. Flew with 2 Group in the Battle of France and the invasion-threat period and
suffered heavy losses. Transferred to 3 Group in November 1940 and flew Wellingtons, Stirlings and Lancasters until the end of the war. While with Bomber Command,
based at Wyton (twice), Alconbury, Bourn and Mildenhall.

OPERATIONAL PERFORMANCE

Raids Flown
2 Group Blenheims – 97 bombing and reconnaissance
3 Group Wellingtons – 38 bombing
3 Group Stirlings – 263 bombing, 85 minelaying, 5 leaflet
3 Group Lancasters – 208 bombing, 18 minelaying

Total – 606 bombing, 103 minelaying, 5 leaflet = 714 raids

Sorties and Losses
2 Group Blenheims – 543 sorties, 27 aircraft lost (5·0 per cent)
3 Group Wellingtons – 173 sorties, 3 aircraft lost (1·7 per cent)
3 Group Stirlings – 2,231 sorties, 91 aircraft lost (4·1 per cent)
3 Group Lancasters – 2,840 sorties, 45 aircraft lost (1·6 per cent)

Total – 5,787 sorties, 166 aircraft lost (2·9 per cent)

5 Blenheims, 38 Stirlings and 11 Lancasters were destroyed in crashes.

POINTS OF INTEREST

Continuous wartime service with the Advanced Air Striking Force and Bomber
   Command, flying five different types of aircraft on operations.
Carried out more bombing raids than any other Stirling squadron.
Suffered (with 218 Squadron) the heaviest losses in Stirling squadrons.

18 (BURMA) SQUADRON

SERVICE

Returned from the Advanced Air Striking Force in France in May 1940. Served with

2 Group until August 1941 but then posted to the Middle East where the squadron was absorbed into other units and lost its identity. Reformed in 2 Group in August 1942 but only operated in that month before being sent to the Middle East again. Equipped with Blenheims during both spells with 2 Group. Based at Gatwick, West Raynham (twice), Great Massingham, Oulton (twice), Horsham St Faith (twice), Manston and Wattisham.

OPERATIONAL PERFORMANCE

Raids Flown
Blenheims – 170 bombing, 4 reconnaissance, 1 leaflet, 1 fighter escort. (Some of the 'bombing' raids were night Intruder raids to airfields in Holland.)

Sorties and Losses
Blenheims – 1,242 sorties, 40 aircraft lost (3·2 per cent), 7 destroyed in crashes.

21 SQUADRON

SERVICE

With 2 Group from the outbreak of the war until December 1941 but detached to Coastal Command three times during this period. Sent to Malta in December 1941, disbanded there on 14 March 1942 and re-formed the same day in England to fly with 2 Group again until 2 Group left Bomber Command in May 1943. Equipped with Blenheims and Venturas and based at Watton, Bodney, Methwold and Oulton while with Bomber Command.

OPERATIONAL PERFORMANCE

Raids Flown
Blenheims – 155 bombing
Venturas – 10 bombing
_____

Total – 165 bombing raids

Sorties and Losses
Blenheims – 1,050 sorties, 29 aircraft lost (2·8 per cent)
Venturas – 369 sorties, 10 aircraft lost (2·7 per cent)
_____

Total – 1,419 sorties, 39 aircraft lost (2·7 per cent)

10 Blenheims were destroyed in crashes.

POINTS OF INTEREST

An operational squadron on the outbreak of war; flew photographic reconnaissance sorties over the Ruhr on 27 September 1939.
Introduced the Ventura to operational service and flew more Ventura sorties than any other squadron.

23 SQUADRON

SERVICE

Returned from duty as a fighter squadron in Italy and posted to 100 Group as a *Serrate* and Intruder squadron and flew in those roles from July 1944 until the end of the war. Equipped with Mosquitoes and based at Little Snoring.

OPERATIONAL PERFORMANCE

Carried out 70 *Serrate* and 125 Intruder operations (although it is sometimes difficult to differentiate between the two types of operation); also carried out 8 daylight bomber-escort operations. Flew 1,067 sorties and lost 8 aircraft (0·7 per cent). Claimed 3 enemy aircraft destroyed and 1 damaged in the air and 15 aircraft destroyed on the ground; also carried out numerous bomb and cannon-fire attacks on airfields and railways.

35 (MADRAS PRESIDENCY) SQUADRON

SERVICE

A bomber training unit on the outbreak of war, later absorbed into an O.T.U. Reformed as a bomber squadron in 4 Group on 5 November 1940; transferred to 8 Group in August 1942 and served as a Pathfinder squadron for the remainder of the war. Equipped with Halifaxes and Lancasters; based at Leeming and Linton-on-Ouse in 4 Group, and at Graveley in 8 Group.

OPERATIONAL PERFORMANCE

Raids Flown
4 Group Halifaxes – 109 bombing, 6 leaflet
8 Group Halifaxes – 146 bombing, 5 minelaying
8 Group Lancasters – 202 bombing

Total – 457 bombing, 6 leaflet, 5 minelaying = 468 raids

Sorties and Losses
4 Group Halifaxes – 717 sorties, 35 aircraft lost (4·9 per cent)
8 Group Halifaxes – 1,776 sorties, 65 aircraft lost (3·7 per cent)
8 Group Lancasters – 2,216 sorties, 27 aircraft lost (1·2 per cent)

Total – 4,709 sorties, 127 aircraft lost (2·7 per cent)

6 Lancasters were destroyed in crashes.

POINTS OF INTEREST

Introduced the Halifax to operational service.
An original Pathfinder squadron and suffered 8 Group's first operational loss, in the group's first raid to Flensburg on 18/19 August 1942.
Introduced (with 7 Squadron) *H2S* into operational service.

37 SQUADRON

SERVICE

In 3 Group on the outbreak of war, flying Wellingtons from Feltwell, until posted to the Middle East in November 1940.

OPERATIONAL PERFORMANCE

Raids Flown
Wellingtons – 80 bombing and shipping sweeps, 8 leaflet

Sorties and Losses
Wellingtons – 688 sorties, 15 aircraft lost (2·2 per cent)

POINTS OF INTEREST

Operated on the first day of the war when 6 Wellingtons carried out a shipping sweep over the North Sea.

38 SQUADRON

SERVICE

In 3 Group on the outbreak of the war, flying Wellingtons from Marham, until posted to the Middle East in November 1940.

OPERATIONAL PERFORMANCE

Raids Flown
Wellingtons – 88 bombing and shipping sweeps, 3 leaflet

Sorties and Losses
Wellingtons – 659 sorties, 7 aircraft lost (1·1 per cent)

POINTS OF INTEREST

An operational squadron on the outbreak of war.
Suffered unusually low casualties for a squadron operating in the early months of the war.

40 SQUADRON

SERVICE

After a brief period flying Battles with the Advanced Air Striking Force in France, returned to England and converted to Blenheims in 2 Group, flying operations from March 1940. Transferred to 3 Group and converted to Wellingtons in November 1940. Posted to Malta in October 1941. Part of the squadron then appears to have returned to England in January 1942 (the squadron records are vague on this point) and resumed operations with 3 Group. This part of the squadron was then re-numbered 156 Squadron on 11 or 12 March 1942. Based at Wyton while with 2 Group and at Alconbury with 3 Group.

OPERATIONAL PERFORMANCE

Raids Flown
2 Group Blenheims – 93 bombing, 13 reconnaissance, 3 sweeps
3 Group Wellingtons – 90 bombing

Total – 186 bombing and sweeps, 13 reconnaissance = 199 raids

Sorties and Losses
2 Group Blenheims – 526 sorties, 22 aircraft lost (4·2 per cent)
3 Group Wellingtons – 730 sorties, 31 aircraft lost (4·2 per cent)

Total – 1,256 sorties, 53 aircraft lost (4·2 per cent)

3 Blenheims were destroyed in crashes.

44 (RHODESIA) SQUADRON

SERVICE

In 5 Group from the outbreak until the end of the war. Detachments of 6 aircraft were twice sent for short periods to Coastal Command but the main part of the squadron continued to operate with Bomber Command. Equipped with Hampdens and Lancasters; based at Waddington, Dunholme Lodge and Spilsby.

OPERATIONAL PERFORMANCE

Raids Flown
Hampdens – 246 bombing, 81 minelaying, 7 leaflet, 4 'night-fighter' over English cities
Lancasters – 272 bombing, 27 minelaying

Total – 518 bombing, 108 minelaying, 7 leaflet, 4 'night-fighter' = 637 raids

Sorties and Losses
Hampdens – 2,043 sorties, 43 aircraft lost (2·1 per cent)
Lancasters – 4,362 sorties, 149 aircraft lost (3·4 per cent)

Total – 6,405 sorties, 192 aircraft lost (3·0 per cent)

21 Lancasters were destroyed in crashes.

POINTS OF INTEREST

Continuous, unbroken service with Bomber Command throughout the war, one of only two squadrons to claim this honour (see 149 Squadron); the only squadron with continuous service in 5 Group. Operated on the first day of the war when 9 Hampdens flew a shipping search over the North Sea.

Introduced the Lancaster to operational service and sustained heavy casualties on this aircraft.

Victoria Cross: Squadron Leader J. D. Nettleton, daylight raid on Augsburg, 17 April 1942; later, as Wing Commander Nettleton, killed in action returning from a raid to Turin on 13 July 1943.

Had two holders of the Victoria Cross – Wing Commander Learoyd and Wing Commander Nettleton – as squadron commanders.

Suffered third highest overall losses in Bomber Command (sharing this distinction with 78 and 102 squadrons).

Suffered heaviest Lancaster losses and highest percentage Lancaster losses both in 5 Group and in Bomber Command.

Suffered heaviest overall losses in 5 Group.

49 SQUADRON

SERVICE

With 5 Group from the outbreak until the end of the war, except for two periods of squadron detachment to Coastal Command in early 1940. Equipped with Hampdens, Manchesters and Lancasters and based at Scampton, Fiskerton and Fulbeck.

OPERATIONAL PERFORMANCE

Raids Flown
Hampdens – 241 bombing, 82 minelaying, 19 leaflet
Manchesters – 4 bombing, 2 minelaying, 4 leaflet
Lancasters – 298 bombing, 21 minelaying, 3 leaflet

Total – 543 bombing, 105 minelaying, 26 leaflet = 674 raids

Sorties and Losses
Hampdens – 2,636 sorties, 55 aircraft lost (2·1 per cent)
Manchesters – 47 sorties, 6 aircraft lost (12·8 per cent)
Lancasters – 3,818 sorties, 102 aircraft lost (2·7 per cent)

Total – 6,501 sorties, 163 aircraft lost (2·5 per cent)

18 Lancasters were destroyed in crashes.

POINTS OF INTEREST

An operational squadron on the outbreak of war; 3 Hampdens flew a shipping search over the North Sea on the first day of the war.

Except for two short periods, continuous service in Bomber Command until the end of the war.

Flew more Hampden sorties than any other squadron.

Victoria Cross: Flight Lieutenant R. A. B. Learoyd, Dortmund–Ems Canal, 12/13 August 1940.

50 SQUADRON

SERVICE

In 5 Group from the outbreak until the end of the war but detached for short periods to Coastal Command in late 1939 and in 1940. Equipped with Hampdens, Manchesters and Lancasters; based at Waddington, Lindholme, Swinderby (twice) and Skellingthorpe (twice).

OPERATIONAL PERFORMANCE

Raids Flown
Hampdens – 266 bombing, 88 minelaying, 14 leaflet
Manchesters – 15 bombing, 10 minelaying, 9 leaflet
Lancasters – 339 bombing, 26 minelaying

Total – 620 bombing, 124 minelaying, 23 leaflet = 767 raids

Sorties and Losses
Hampdens – 2,299 sorties, 57 aircraft lost (2·5 per cent)
Manchesters – 126 sorties, 7 aircraft lost (5·6 per cent)
Lancasters – 4,710 sorties, 112 aircraft lost (2·4 per cent)

Total – 7,135 sorties, 176 aircraft lost (2·5 per cent)

26 Hampdens and 27 Lancasters were destroyed in crashes.

POINTS OF INTEREST

Except for three short periods, continuous service in Bomber Command throughout the war.
Victoria Cross: Flying Officer L. T. Manser, posthumously, 1,000-bomber raid on Cologne, 30/31 May 1942.
Carried out most bombing raids in 5 Group and in Bomber Command heavy squadrons.
Flew most Lancaster sorties in 5 Group, most overall sorties in 5 Group and third highest number of sorties in Bomber Command.
Dropped greatest tonnage of bombs in 5 Group (approximately 21,000 tons) and believed fourth greatest tonnage in Bomber Command.

51 SQUADRON

SERVICE

In 4 Group from the outbreak to the end of the war but with detachments to Coastal Command in November/December 1939 and May to October 1942. Equipped with Whitleys and Halifaxes; based at Linton-on-Ouse, Dishforth, Snaith and Leconfield.

OPERATIONAL PERFORMANCE

Raids Flown
Whitleys – 221 bombing, 10 leaflet, 2 parachute dropping
Halifaxes – 255 bombing, 9 minelaying

Total – 476 bombing, 10 leaflet, 9 minelaying, 2 parachute dropping = 497 raids

Sorties and Losses
Whitleys – 1,806 sorties, 50 aircraft lost (2·8 per cent)
Halifaxes – 4,153 sorties, 108 aircraft lost (2·6 per cent)

Total – 5,959 sorties, 158 aircraft lost (2·7 per cent)

POINTS OF INTEREST

An operational squadron on the outbreak of war.
Flew the first sorties over Germany when 3 Whitleys dropped leaflets over Hamburg
  and other places on the first night of the war.
Pioneered operational dropping of airborne forces and dropped the troops who
  carried out the Italian aqueduct raid in February 1941 (actually 51 Squadron crews
  in 78 Squadron aircraft) and the Bruneval raid on 27/28 February 1942.
Flew more Whitley sorties than any other squadron.

57 SQUADRON

SERVICE

Returned from the Advanced Air Striking Force in France in May 1940 and served
with 2 Group until June, flying Blenheims from Wyton and Gatwick. In Coastal
Command from late June to late October 1940. Posted to 3 Group and flew Wellingtons from Feltwell from November 1940 to September 1942. Posted to 5 Group and
flew Lancasters from Scampton and East Kirkby until the end of the war.

OPERATIONAL PERFORMANCE

Raids Flown
2 Group Blenheims – 34 offensive sweeps, 3 bombing
3 Group Wellingtons – 166 bombing, 7 minelaying
5 Group Lancasters – 313 bombing, 35 minelaying

Total – 482 bombing, 42 minelaying, 34 sweeps = 558 raids

Sorties and Losses
2 Group Blenheims – 58 sorties, 10 aircraft lost (17·2 per cent)
3 Group Wellingtons – 1,056 sorties, 54 aircraft lost (5·1 per cent)
5 Group Lancasters – 4,037 sorties, 108 aircraft lost (2·7 per cent)

Total – 5,151 sorties, 172 aircraft lost (3·3 per cent)

31 Lancasters were destroyed in crashes.

POINTS OF INTEREST

57 Squadron served in three different groups but always suffered higher-than-average casualties. Its percentage loss rate was the highest in the squadrons of 2 Group (though with only a small number of sorties), the highest in the Wellington squadrons of 3 Group and the highest, for all aircraft types combined, in Bomber Command.

58 SQUADRON

SERVICE

In 4 Group at the outbreak of the war; detached to Coastal Command in the winter of 1939–40 and posted permanently to Coastal Command in April 1942, where the squadron had a very successful anti-submarine career. Equipped with Whitleys and based at Linton-on-Ouse while with Bomber Command.

OPERATIONAL PERFORMANCE

Raids Flown
Whitleys – 219 bombing, 8 leaflet = 227 raids

Sorties and Losses
Whitleys – 1,757 sorties, 49 aircraft lost (2·8 per cent)

POINTS OF INTEREST

An operational squadron on the outbreak of war and flew leaflet sorties on the first night of the war.

61 SQUADRON

SERVICE

In 5 Group from the outbreak until the end of the war but detached to Coastal Command in November/December 1940 and in July/August 1942. Equipped with Hampdens, Manchesters and Lancasters; based at Hemswell, North Luffenham, Woolfox Lodge, Syerston, Skellingthorpe (twice) and Coningsby.

OPERATIONAL PERFORMANCE

Raids Flown
Hampdens – 229 bombing, 49 minelaying, 3 'night-fighter' over English cities, 2 leaflet
Manchesters – 33 bombing, 11 minelaying
Lancasters – 351 bombing, 25 minelaying, 1 leaflet

Total – 613 bombing, 85 minelaying, 3 'night-fighter', 3 leaflet = 704 raids

Sorties and Losses
Hampdens – 1,339 sorties, 28 aircraft lost (2·1 per cent)
Manchesters – 197 sorties, 12 aircraft lost (6·1 per cent)
Lancasters – 4,546 sorties, 116 aircraft lost (2·6 per cent)

Total – 6,082 sorties, 156 aircraft lost (2·6 per cent)

25 Lancasters destroyed in crashes.

POINTS OF INTEREST

An operational squadron on the outbreak of war.
Victoria Cross: Flight Lieutenant W. Reid, Düsseldorf, 3/4 November 1943.
Carried out more raids that any other Lancaster squadron in Bomber Command and
  second highest number of bombing raids, overall, in Bomber Command heavy
  Squadrons.

75 (NEW ZEALAND) SQUADRON

SERVICE

Formed in April 1940 from the New Zealand Wellington Flight and served in 3
Group until the end of the war. Equipped with Wellingtons, Stirlings and Lancasters;
based at Feltwell, Mildenhall, Newmarket and Mepal.

OPERATIONAL PERFORMANCE

Raids Flown
Wellingtons – 291 bombing, 24 minelaying, 4 leaflet, 1 photo recce
Stirlings – 103 bombing, 107 minelaying
Lancasters – 190 bombing, 18 minelaying, 1 leaflet

Total – 584 bombing, 149 minelaying, 5 leaflet, 1 photo recce = 739 raids

Sorties and Losses
Wellingtons – 2,540 sorties, 74 aircraft lost (2·9 per cent)
Stirlings – 1,736 sorties, 72 aircraft lost (4·1 per cent)
Lancasters – 3,741 sorties, 47 aircraft lost (1·3 per cent)

Total – 8,017 sorties, 193 aircraft lost (2·4 per cent)

8 Lancasters were destroyed in crashes.

POINTS OF INTEREST

First New Zealand squadron and the only New Zealand night-bomber squadron in
  Bomber Command.
Victoria Cross: Sergeant J. A. Ward, Münster, 7/8 July 1941; later killed in action on
  a raid to Hamburg on 15/16 September 1941.

Carried out fourth highest number of bombing raids in Bomber Command heavy Squadrons.

Flew most sorties in 3 Group and in the whole of Bomber Command.

Suffered the second highest casualties in Bomber Command.

Believed to have dropped the third greatest tonnage of bombs (approximately 21,600 tons) in Bomber Command; also dropped 2,344 mines, probably the second highest number in Bomber Command.

76 SQUADRON

SERVICE

After several false starts early in the war, the squadron became operational in 4 Group at Middleton St George in June 1941 and commenced operations with Halifaxes. Most of the squadron was sent to the Middle East in July 1942 and became absorbed into other units, but that part of the squadron which had remained in England was built up again and continued to fly Halifaxes in 4 Group until the end of the war, being based at Linton-on-Ouse and Holme-on-Spalding Moor.

OPERATIONAL PERFORMANCE

Raids Flown
Halifaxes – 376 bombing, 17 minelaying, 3 leaflet = 396 raids.

Sorties and Losses
Halifaxes – 5,123 sorties, 139 aircraft lost (2·7 per cent), 16 destroyed in crashes.

POINTS OF INTEREST

Carried out more bombing raids than any other Halifax squadron.

Dropped Bomber Command's first 8,000-lb bomb, on Essen, 10/11 April 1942.

Aircrew casualties: 787 killed in action or died of wounds, 278 prisoners of war, 27 evaders.*

Contained a flight with Norwegian aircrew during the Halifax period.

77 SQUADRON

SERVICE

In 4 Group from the outbreak until the end of the war but with detachments to Coastal Command at various times between October 1939 and May 1940 and with the whole squadron detached to Coastal Command from May to October 1942. Flew Whitleys and Halifaxes; based at Driffield, Linton-on-Ouse, Topcliffe, Leeming, Elvington and Full Sutton.

---

* 76 Squadron's aircrew casualties are from *To See the Dawn Breaking*, a history of 76 Squadron by W. R. Chorley, published privately in 1981.

OPERATIONAL PERFORMANCE

Raids Flown
Whitleys – 223 bombing, 13 leaflet, 3 reconnaissance
Halifaxes – 220 bombing, 27 minelaying

Total – 446 bombing and recce, 27 minelaying, 13 leaflet = 486 raids

Sorties and Losses
Whitleys – 1,687 sorties, 56 aircraft lost (3·3 per cent)
Halifaxes – 3,692 sorties, 75 aircraft lost (2·0 per cent)

Total – 5,379 sorties, 131 aircraft lost (2·4 per cent)

POINTS OF INTEREST

An original squadron on the outbreak of the war; flew leaflet operations over the
  Ruhr on the third night of the war.
Carried out most bombing raids by a Whitley squadron.
Suffered most losses in Whitley squadrons.

78 SQUADRON

SERVICE

Started the war as a group-pool squadron in 4 Group but became operational in July
1940 and flew Whitleys and Halifaxes with 4 Group until the end of the war. Based at
Dishforth, Middleton St George (twice), Croft, Linton-on-Ouse and Breighton.

OPERATIONAL PERFORMANCE

Raids Flown
Whitleys – 163 bombing
Halifaxes – 323 bombing, 32 minelaying, 7 leaflet

Total – 486 bombing, 32 minelaying, 7 leaflet = 525 raids

Sorties and Losses
Whitleys – 1,117 sorties, 34 aircraft lost (3·0 per cent)
Halifaxes – 5,120 sorties, 158 aircraft lost (3·1 per cent)

Total – 6,237 sorties, 192 aircraft lost (3·1 per cent)

POINTS OF INTEREST

Flew most sorties in 4 Group (but only by 4 sorties from 10 Squadron).
Suffered most losses and highest percentage losses in any Halifax squadron, most
  losses in 4 Group (with 102 Squadron), and third heaviest overall losses in Bomber
  Command (sharing this distinction with 44 and 102 Squadrons).
Believed to have dropped the greatest tonnage of bombs in 4 Group, approximately
  16,900 tons.

82 (UNITED PROVINCES) SQUADRON

SERVICE

In 2 Group from the outbreak of the war until March 1942, flying Blenheims from Watton and suffering heavy losses. Sent to India in the spring of 1942 and operated from there until the end of the war.

OPERATIONAL PERFORMANCE

Raids Flown
Blenheims – 200 bombing and sweeps, 10 photo and weather recces

Sorties and Losses
Blenheims – 1,436 sorties, 62 aircraft lost (4·3 per cent), 11 destroyed in crashes

POINTS OF INTEREST

An original squadron on the outbreak of war, flying photo-recce sorties to Germany
  before the end of September 1939.
Flew most bombing raids and sweeps and suffered most losses in Blenheim squadrons.
Sank U-31 off Borkum on 11 March 1940. (The U-boat was later salvaged and
  returned to service but was depth-charged and sunk by the destroyer H.M.S.
  Antelope in the Atlantic on 2 November 1940.)

83 SQUADRON

SERVICE

In 5 Group at the outbreak of the war and flew Hampdens, Manchesters and Lancasters from Scampton, with a short detachment to Coastal Command at Lossiemouth in February/March 1940. Transferred to 8 Group in August 1942 and flew
Pathfinder operations from Wyton until returned to 5 Group for that group's own
marker force in April 1944 and flew from Coningsby until the end of the war.

OPERATIONAL PERFORMANCE

Raids Flown
5 Group Hampdens – 205 bombing, 72 minelaying, 6 'night-fighter' over English
  cities
5 Group Manchesters – 21 bombing, 10 minelaying, 2 leaflet
5 Group Lancasters (May to August 1942) – 26 bombing, 8 minelaying, 1 leaflet
8 Group Lancasters – 167 bombing
5 Group Lancasters (April 1944 to May 1945) – 105 bombing

Total – 524 bombing, 90 minelaying, 6 'night-fighter', 3 leaflet = 623 raids

Sorties and Losses
5 Group Hampdens – 1,987 sorties, 43 aircraft lost (2·2 per cent)
5 Group Manchesters – 152 sorties, 9 aircraft lost (5·9 per cent)

5 Group Lancasters (May to August 1942) – 262 sorties, 4 aircraft lost (1·5 per cent)
8 Group Lancasters – 1,740 sorties, 56 aircraft lost (3·2 per cent)
5 Group Lancasters (April 1944 to May 1945) – 1,380 sorties, 31 aircraft lost (2·2 per cent)

Total – 5,521 sorties, 143 aircraft lost (2·6 per cent)

25 Lancasters were destroyed in crashes.

POINTS OF INTEREST

An original squadron on the outbreak of war; 6 Hampdens flew a sweep over the North Sea on the first day of the war.
Victoria Cross: Sergeant John Hannah, Antwerp, 15/16 September 1940.
An original Pathfinder squadron.

85 SQUADRON

SERVICE

Came from Air Defence of Great Britain (Fighter Command) on 1 May 1944 for 'bomber support' work with 100 Group as a Mosquito Intruder squadron. Based at Swannington until the end of the war, except when detached to West Malling in the summer of 1944 for anti-flying bomb operations.

OPERATIONAL PERFORMANCE

Carried out 170 bomber support, 48 anti-flying bomb and 2 anti-Intruder operations. Flew 1,190 sorties – 864 bomber support, 326 anti-flying bomb, etc. Lost 7 aircraft, all on bomber-support work. Claimed 71 German aircraft destroyed – 30 Me 110s, 27 Ju 88s, 8 Ju 188s, 4 He 219s, 2 FW 190s and 6 others damaged. This total of claims is greater than that of any other Mosquito squadron in 100 Group. Also claimed 30 flying bombs destroyed and many attacks on railways.

88 (HONG KONG) SQUADRON

SERVICE

Came to 2 Group in July 1941 after service with the Advanced Air Striking Force in France and with Coastal Command in Northern Ireland. Flew Blenheims and Bostons from Swanton Morley (twice), Attlebridge and Oulton until 2 Group left Bomber Command in May 1943.

OPERATIONAL PERFORMANCE

Raids Flown
Blenheims – 15 bombing
Bostons – 47 bombing

Total – 62 bombing

Sorties and Losses
Blenheims – 96 sorties, 5 aircraft lost (5·2 per cent)
Bostons – 559 sorties, 6 aircraft lost (1·1 per cent)

Total – 655 sorties, 11 aircraft lost (1·7 per cent)

POINTS OF INTEREST

Introduced the Boston to Bomber Command operations and flew more Boston sorties than any other squadron.

90 SQUADRON

SERVICE

A training squadron on the outbreak of war and later absorbed into an O.T.U. Re-formed in 2 Group on 7 May 1941 and flew Fortresses in the daylight role but this was not successful and the Fortresses were phased out later in the year; the squadron was disbanded in February 1942. Re-formed again on 7 November 1942, this time in 3 Group, and flew Stirlings and Lancasters in 3 Group until the end of the war. Based at Watton, West Raynham and Polebrook while with 2 Group and at Ridgewell, West Wickham (renamed Wratting Common in August 1943) and Tuddenham while with 3 Group.

OPERATIONAL PERFORMANCE

Raids Flown
2 Group Fortresses – 20 bombing
3 Group Stirlings – 111 bombing and Resistance operations, 100 minelaying
3 Group Lancasters – 162 bombing, 19 minelaying

Total – 293 bombing, etc., 119 minelaying = 412 raids

Sorties and Losses
2 Group Fortresses – 52 sorties, 3 aircraft lost (5·6 per cent)
3 Group Stirlings – 1,937 sorties, 58 aircraft lost (3·0 per cent)
3 Group Lancasters – 2,624 sorties, 25 aircraft lost (1·0 per cent)

Total – 4,613 sorties, 86 aircraft lost (1·9 per cent)

26 Stirlings and 12 Lancasters were destroyed in crashes.

POINTS OF INTEREST

Introduced the B-17 Flying Fortress to R.A.F. service and the only squadron to operate the Fortress in the daylight-bombing role.

97 (STRAITS SETTLEMENTS) SQUADRON

SERVICE

A training squadron on the outbreak of war and lost its identity in April 1940. Re-formed in May 1940 as a Whitley squadron in 4 Group but never operated and was disbanded before the end of that month. Again re-formed, in February 1941, this time in 5 Group, where Manchesters and Lancasters were flown. Transferred to 8 Group in April 1943 and flew Pathfinder operations for a year, suffering heavy losses. Returned to 5 Group in April 1944 as part of 5 Group's own marker force until the end of the war. Based at Waddington, Coningsby and Woodhall Spa in the first spell with 5 Group, at Bourn with 8 Group and at Coningsby again on the return to 5 Group.

OPERATIONAL PERFORMANCE

Raids Flown
5 Group Manchesters – 33 bombing, 3 minelaying
5 Group Lancasters (to 14 April 1943) – 135 bombing, 42 minelaying
8 Group Lancasters – 96 bombing
5 Group Lancasters (April 1944 to May 1945) – 111 bombing, 4 minelaying

Total – 375 bombing, 49 minelaying = 424 raids

(In July 1941, the squadron's Manchesters were grounded and, in the next six weeks, 97 Squadron aircrew flew operations in 106 Squadron Hampdens; these raids, sorties and losses have been included in 106 Squadron's totals.)

Sorties and Losses
5 Group Manchesters – 151 sorties, 8 aircraft lost (5·3 per cent)
5 Group Lancasters – (to 14 April 1943) – 998 sorties, 23 aircraft lost (2·3 per cent)
8 Group Lancasters – 1,465 sorties, 58 aircraft lost (4·0 per cent)
5 Group Lancasters (April 1944 to May 1945) – 1,320 sorties, 20 aircraft lost (1·5 per cent)

Total – 3,934 sorties, 109 aircraft lost (2·8 per cent)

26 Lancasters were destroyed in crashes.

POINTS OF INTEREST

The squadron broke no records but performed a valuable bombing and pathfinding service over a long period. It was not a lucky squadron and often suffered heavy losses until the last few months of the war.

98 SQUADRON

SERVICE

98 Squadron was re-formed as a day-bomber squadron in 2 Group on 12 September 1942, after having served as a training squadron, with the Advanced Air Striking

Force in France and with Coastal Command in Iceland. Flew Mitchells from West Raynham and Foulsham until 2 Group left Bomber Command in May 1943.

OPERATIONAL PERFORMANCE

98 Squadron flew 70 Mitchell sorties and lost 2 aircraft (2·9 per cent) in 5 bombing raids and 7 air–sea rescue searches.

POINTS OF INTEREST

With 180 Squadron, introduced the Mitchell to Bomber Command service.

99 (MADRAS PRESIDENCY) SQUADRON

SERVICE

A Wellington squadron in 3 Group from the outbreak of the war until posted to India in January 1942. A detachment to Lossiemouth for service with Coastal Command took place in November and December 1939. Based at Newmarket and Waterbeach while with 3 Group.

OPERATIONAL PERFORMANCE

Raids Flown
Wellingtons – 228 bombing, 5 leaflet = 233 raids

Sorties and Losses
Wellingtons – 1,786 sorties, 43 aircraft lost (2·4 per cent)

POINTS OF INTEREST

An original squadron on the outbreak of war; 2 Wellingtons dropped leaflets over Hannover on the sixth night of the war.
Part of the squadron was detached to Salon in Southern France in January 1940 and carried out some of the first raids to Italy.

100 SQUADRON

SERVICE

In the Far East from 1939 to 1942 and wiped out while operating Vickers Vildebeest aircraft in Malaya and Java. Re-formed in 1 Group on 15 December 1942 and flew Lancasters until the end of the war. Based at Grimsby until the last few weeks of the war when a move was made to Elsham Wolds.

OPERATIONAL PERFORMANCE

Raids Flown
Lancasters – 267 bombing, 13 minelaying = 280 raids

Sorties and Losses
Lancasters – 3,984 sorties, 92 aircraft lost (2·3 per cent), 21 aircraft destroyed in crashes.

101 SQUADRON

In 2 Group with Blenheims from the outbreak of the war until May 1941, in 3 Group with Wellingtons until September 1942, then in 1 Group with Wellingtons and Lancasters until the end of the war. Based at West Raynham, Oakington, Bourn, Stradishall, Holme-on-Spalding Moor and Ludford Magna.

OPERATIONAL PERFORMANCE

Raids Flown
2 Group Blenheims – 81 bombing
3 Group Wellingtons – 129 bombing, 13 minelaying
1 Group Wellingtons – 4 bombing, 4 minelaying
1 Group Lancasters – 298 bombing, 10 minelaying

Total – 512 bombing, 27 minelaying = 539 raids

Sorties and Losses
2 Group Blenheims – 618 sorties, 15 aircraft lost (2·4 per cent)
3 Group Wellingtons – 1,216 sorties, 42 aircraft lost (3·4 per cent)
1 Group Wellingtons – 37 sorties, 1 aircraft lost (1·7 per cent)
1 Group Lancasters – 4,895 sorties, 113 aircraft lost (2·3 per cent)

Total – 6,766 sorties, 171 aircraft lost (2·5 per cent)

6 Blenheims and 33 Lancasters were destroyed in crashes.

POINTS OF INTEREST

An original squadron on the outbreak of war but it did not fly its first operation until July 1940. In service with Bomber Command until the end of the war but with frequent interruptions for changes of group and aircraft type.

From early October 1943, the squadron operated Lancasters equipped with *A.B.C.* (*Airborne Cigar*). With an extra, German-speaking crew member, they mixed with the bomber stream and jammed German night-fighter communications. The *A.B.C.* aircraft also carried normal bomb loads. 101 Squadron was the only squadron to perform the *A.B.C.* role in Bomber Command and retained the duty even after 100 Group was formed. Because of this role, the squadron was often dispatched on raids when its parent group was being rested and this led to its taking part in more bombing raids than any other Lancaster squadron in 1 Group.

102 (CEYLON) SQUADRON

In 4 Group from the outbreak until the end of the war, though with short detachments to Coastal Command in 1939 and 1940. Flew Whitleys and Halifaxes; based at Driffield, Leeming, Linton-on-Ouse, Topcliffe (twice), Dalton and Pocklington.

OPERATIONAL PERFORMANCE

Raids Flown
Whitleys – 181 bombing, 14 recce/leaflet
Halifaxes – 310 bombing, 84 minelaying, 13 leaflet

Total – 491 bombing, 84 minelaying, 27 recce/leaflet = 602 raids

Sorties and Losses
Whitleys – 1,372 sorties, 52 aircraft lost (3·8 per cent)
Halifaxes – 4,734 sorties, 140 aircraft lost (3·0 per cent)

Total – 6,106 sorties, 192 aircraft lost (3·1 per cent)

POINTS OF INTEREST

An original squadron on the outbreak of the war; 3 Whitleys dropped leaflets over
  the Ruhr on the second night of the war. Served until the end with only short
  breaks on detachment to Coastal Command.
Suffered the third heaviest overall losses in Bomber Command (sharing this distinc-
  tion with 44 and 78 Squadrons).
Suffered most losses in 4 Group (sharing with 78 Squadron).
Suffered highest percentage losses in 4 Group.
Suffered highest percentage losses in any Whitley squadron.

103 SQUADRON

SERVICE

Came to 1 Group in July 1940 after returning from operations in France with the
Advanced Air Striking Force and served continuously with 1 Group until the end of
the war, carrying out intensive operations during that long period and often suffering
heavy casualties. Based at Newton and Elsham Wolds.

OPERATIONAL PERFORMANCE

Raids Flown
Battles – 16 bombing
Wellingtons – 138 bombing, 6 minelaying
Halifaxes – 15 bombing
Lancasters – 317 bombing, 27 minelaying

Total – 486 bombing, 33 minelaying = 519 raids

Sorties and Losses
Battles – 51 sorties, 1 aircraft lost (2·0 per cent)
Wellingtons – 1,116 sorties, 31 aircraft lost (2·8 per cent)
Halifaxes – 137 sorties, 12 aircraft lost (8·8 per cent)
Lancasters – 4,536 sorties, 135 aircraft lost (3·0 per cent)

Total – 5,840 sorties, 179 aircraft lost (3·1 per cent)

22 Lancasters were destroyed in crashes.

POINTS OF INTEREST

Counting service with the Advanced Air Striking Force, unbroken service as a bomber squadron throughout the Second World War.

Only squadron in 1 Group to operate Halifaxes and thus the only squadron to operate all four types of aircraft flown by 1 Group in the war.

Carried out the most bombing raids in 1 Group.

Suffered most losses in 1 Group.

Suffered highest percentage losses in 1 Group Lancaster squadrons.

104 SQUADRON

SERVICE

A training squadron on the outbreak of war and absorbed into an O.T.U. in April 1940. Re-formed as a Wellington squadron in 4 Group on 1 April 1941 and flew operations from Driffield until February 1942, by which time most of the squadron had been posted to the Middle East.

OPERATIONAL PERFORMANCE

104 Squadron flew 373 Wellington sorties and lost 13 aircraft (3·5 per cent) in 60 bombing raids.

105 SQUADRON

SERVICE

Returned from the Advanced Air Striking Force in France in June 1940 and posted to 2 Group. While with 2 Group, flew Blenheims at first and then Mosquitoes in the day-bomber role, sometimes suffering heavy losses. Based at Honington, Watton, Swanton Morley, Horsham St Faith and Marham. The squadron was detached to Malta from July to October 1941 while still equipped with Blenheims.

105 Squadron was retained in Bomber Command when 2 Group left in May 1943 and flew *Oboe* Mosquito night-bomber operations with 8 Group until the end of the war. It was based at Marham and Bourn during this period.

OPERATIONAL PERFORMANCE

Raids Flown
2 Group Blenheims – 99 bombing, 10 reconnaissance
2 Group Mosquitoes – 127 bombing
8 Group Mosquitoes – 487 bombing, mostly using *Oboe*

Total – 713 bombing, 10 reconnaissance = 723 raids

Sorties and Losses
2 Group Blenheims – 692 sorties, 22 aircraft lost (3·2 per cent)

2 Group Mosquitoes – 548 sorties, 26 aircraft lost (4·7 per cent)
8 Group Mosquitoes – 4,947 sorties, 10 aircraft lost (0·2 per cent)

Total – 6,187 sorties, 58 aircraft lost (0·9 per cent)

10 Blenheims were destroyed in crashes.

POINTS OF INTEREST

Continuous duty as a bomber squadron throughout the war, counting the Advanced
Air Striking Force and Malta periods.
Carried out more bombing raids than any other squadron in Bomber Command
(though many of the raids with 8 Group were with small numbers of aircraft and
incurred very light casualties).
Introduced the Mosquito to Bomber Command service and pioneered the Mosquito
in the daylight-bombing role; carried out the first daylight raid to Berlin on 30
January 1943.
Carried out more raids and flew more sorties than any other Mosquito squadron.
Victoria Cross: Wing Commander H. I. Edwards, D.F.C., Bremen, 4 July 1941.
One of only two *Oboe* squadrons in Bomber Command.

106 SQUADRON

SERVICE

A training squadron on the outbreak of war. Became operational in September 1940
and flew continuously with 5 Group until the end of the war. Equipped with Hampdens, Manchesters and Lancasters; based at Finningly, Coningsby, Syerston and
Metheringham.

OPERATIONAL PERFORMANCE

Raids Flown
Hampdens – 106 bombing, 44 minelaying
Manchesters – 19 bombing, 14 minelaying, 3 leaflet
Lancasters – 346 bombing, 24 minelaying, 1 leaflet

Total – 471 bombing, 82 minelaying, 4 leaflet = 557 raids

Sorties and Losses
Hampdens – 1,230 sorties, 55 aircraft lost (4·5 per cent)
Manchesters – 151 sorties, 9 aircraft lost (6·0 per cent)
Lancasters – 4,364 sorties, 105 aircraft lost (2·4 per cent)

Total – 5,745 sorties, 169 aircraft lost (2·9 per cent)

18 Lancasters were destroyed in crashes.

Suffered highest percentage losses in Hampden squadrons.
Victoria Cross: Sergeant N. C. Jackson, Schweinfurt, 26/27 April 1944.

107 SQUADRON

SERVICE

In 2 Group on the outbreak of war and flew Blenheims and Bostons until 2 Group left Bomber Command in May 1943. The squadron was detached to Coastal Command several times and to Malta once. Main bases were at Wattisham and Great Massingham but several other airfields were used for short periods.

OPERATIONAL PERFORMANCE

Raids Flown
Blenheims – 162 bombing and sweeps, 5 general weather recces
Bostons – 63 bombing

Total – 225 bombing, 5 recces = 230 raids

Sorties and Losses
Blenheims – 1,442 sorties, 61 aircraft lost (4·2 per cent)
Bostons – 157 sorties, 23 aircraft lost (14·6 per cent)

Total – 1,599 sorties, 84 aircraft lost (5·3 per cent)

7 Blenheims and 1 Boston were destroyed in crashes.

POINTS OF INTEREST

An original squadron on the outbreak of war; 5 Blenheims were dispatched on the second day of the war and 4 were lost attacking German warships.
Flew most Blenheim sorties in Bomber Command.
Flew most sorties in 2 Group and probably dropped the greatest tonnage of bombs in 2 Group squadrons; flew only one bombing raid less than 105 Squadron's highest number in 2 Group. Suffered most losses in 2 Group.

109 SQUADRON

SERVICE

From December 1940 was a radio countermeasures unit until transferred to Bomber Command in August 1942. Served with 8 Group as an *Oboe* Mosquito squadron until the end of the war, being based at Wyton, Marham and Little Staughton.

OPERATIONAL PERFORMANCE

Raids Flown
Mosquitoes – 522 bombing, mostly using *Oboe*

Sorties and Losses
Mosquitoes – 5,421 sorties, 18 aircraft lost (0·3 per cent)

Introduced *Oboe* to Bomber Command service.

Carried out most raids and flew most sorties in 8 Group.

Victoria Cross: Squadron Leader R. A. M. Palmer, D.F.C., posthumously, Cologne, 23 December 1944; Squadron Leader Palmer was flying in a Lancaster of 582 Squadron in this raid.

110 (HYDERABAD) SQUADRON

SERVICE

In 2 Group on the outbreak of war, flying Blenheims from Wattisham. Numerous small detachments to other airfields and once to Malta in the summer of 1941. Posted to India in March 1942 and flew operations in India and Burma until the end of the war.

OPERATIONAL PERFORMANCE

Raids Flown
Blenheims – 175 bombing and sweeps

Sorties and Losses
Blenheims – 1,402 sorties, 38 aircraft lost (2·7 per cent), 10 aircraft destroyed in crashes.

POINTS OF INTEREST

An original squadron on the outbreak of the war; carried out operations against German warships on the second day of the war and suffered casualties.

114 (HONG KONG) SQUADRON

SERVICE

In 2 Group, at Wyton, from September to December 1939 but did not fly operations and was posted to the Advanced Air Striking Force in France. Returned to 2 Group from France in May 1940. Flew Blenheims from Horsham St Faith, Oulton and West Raynham. Suffered heavy casualties in shipping attacks and was frequently detached to Coastal Command between March 1941 and August 1942 for recuperation. The last operations for Bomber Command were flown at the end of July 1942 and the squadron was posted to North Africa in November.

OPERATIONAL PERFORMANCE

Raids Flown
Blenheims – 124 bombing, sweeps and Intruder, 7 weather recce, 1 photo recce = 132 raids

Sorties and Loses
Blenheims – 731 sorties, 39 aircraft lost (5·3 per cent)

POINTS OF INTEREST

Suffered the highest percentage losses in 2 Group and the highest percentage losses in any Blenheim squadron.

115 SQUADRON

SERVICE

In 3 Group from the outbreak until the end of the war. Flew Wellingtons and Lancasters from Marham, Mildenhall, East Wretham, Little Snoring and Witchford. Detached to Coastal Command for one short period in April 1940.

OPERATIONAL PERFORMANCE

Raids Flown
Wellingtons – 332 bombing, 54 minelaying, 4 leaflet
Lancasters – 261 bombing, 27 minelaying

Total – 593 bombing, 81 minelaying, 4 leaflet = 678 raids

Sorties and Losses
Wellingtons – 3,075 sorties, 98 aircraft lost (3·2 per cent)
Lancasters – 4,678 sorties, 110 aircraft lost (2·4 per cent)

Total – 7,753 sorties, 208 aircraft lost (2·7 per cent)

22 Lancasters were destroyed in crashes.

POINTS OF INTEREST

115 Squadron had one of the finest records of operational service in Bomber Command.

An original squadron on the outbreak of war and, except for one very short period of detachment to Coastal Command, served continuously until the end of the war.

Carried out the first *Gee* trials in August 1941.

Carried out the third highest number of bombing raids in Bomber Command heavy squadrons and the most raids in 3 Group.

Flew the second highest number of sorties in Bomber Command.

Probably dropped the second greatest tonnage of bombs, approximately 23,000 tons, in Bomber Command; dropped more bombs than any other squadron in 3 Group.

Suffered the most losses in the whole of Bomber Command; the only squadron to lose more than 200 aircraft in the war.

Carried out most raids, flew most sorties and suffered most losses of any Wellington squadron in Bomber Command.

Carried out most raids, flew most sorties, suffered most losses and the highest percentage loss rate in any Lancaster squadron in 3 Group.

128 SQUADRON

SERVICE

A maritime squadron in West Africa from October 1941 to March 1943 but then disbanded. Re-formed as a Mosquito squadron in 8 Group's Light Night Striking Force on 15 September 1944 and operated in that role, flying from Wyton, until the end of the war.

OPERATIONAL PERFORMANCE

128 Squadron flew 1,531 sorties and lost 2 aircraft (0·1 per cent) in 157 bombing raids.

138 SQUADRON

SERVICE

Formed from 1419 Flight in August 1941 as the first Special Duty squadron in Bomber Command for what are called Resistance operations in these diaries. Whitleys, Halifaxes and Stirlings were used for the dropping of supplies and agents by parachute, and Lysanders for the delivery and collection of agents and urgent packages from secret landing grounds in the occupied countries. A very few sorties were also flown by Liberators and a Wellington. Early operations were flown from Newmarket and Stradishall but the main base used was Tempsford. The squadron was administered by 3 Group, although 38 Group had some control over the operations.

The squadron gave up its special role in March 1945 and became a normal Lancaster bomber squadron, still in 3 Group and flying from Tuddenham.

OPERATIONAL PERFORMANCE

It is impossible to give a full record of 138 Squadron's operations because the Operations Record Book for the early part of the squadron's life is not complete. It is known that 438 operations were carried out on Resistance work, flying at least 2,578 sorties – 1,788 Halifaxes, 503 Stirlings, 219 Whitleys, approximately 64 Lysanders, 3 Liberators and 1 Wellington. 69 aircraft (2·7 per cent) are known to have been lost – 47 Halifaxes, 11 Lysanders (often after becoming bogged down in soft ground in French fields), 10 Stirlings and 1 Whitley.

In its bomber role from March to May 1945, the squadron dispatched 105 Lancaster sorties on 9 raids and lost 1 aircraft (1·0 per cent).

POINTS OF INTEREST

Carried out more operations in support of Resistance groups than any other squadron.
Had Czechoslovak airmen among its aircrew in late 1941.

139 (JAMAICA) SQUADRON

SERVICE

In 2 Group on the outbreak of war, flying Blenheims from Wyton. Posted to the Advanced Air Striking Force in France in December 1939 and, after being almost wiped out in the Battle of France, returned to England in May 1940. Resumed operations in 2 Group, flying from Horsham St Faith (twice) and Oulton (twice). Posted to Malta in December 1941 and lost its identity. Re-formed in 2 Group again with Mosquito day bombers in June 1942 and again suffered heavy losses flying from Horsham St Faith (twice more), Oulton, Marham and Wyton. Transferred to 8 Group in June 1943 and became a most useful all-purpose night-bomber squadron, dropping markers, *Window* or bombs, often in diversionary raids until the end of the war. Based at Wyton and Upwood while with 8 Group.

OPERATIONAL PERFORMANCE

Raids Flown

2 Group Bostons – 190 bombing, 7 photo recce
2 Group Mosquitoes – 56 bombing, 10 weather/photo recce
8 Group Mosquitoes – 438 bombing and marker

Total – 684 bombing, 17 recce = 701 raids

Sorties and Losses

2 Group Blenheims – 1,112 sorties, 33 aircraft lost (3·0 per cent)
2 Group Mosquitoes – 245 sorties, 14 aircraft lost (5·7 per cent)
8 Group Mosquitoes – 4,187 sorties, 23 aircraft lost (0·5 per cent)

Total – 5,544 sorties, 70 aircraft lost (1·3 per cent)

6 Blenheims were destroyed in crashes.

POINTS OF INTEREST

An original squadron on the outbreak of war and flew Bomber Command's first sortie of the war, a reconnaissance mission over the North Sea and Germany, on the first day of the war. Almost continuous service throughout the war if Advanced Air Striking Force and Malta detachments are included.
Carried out most bombing raids in 2 Group.
Suffered most losses and highest percentage losses in 8 Group Mosquito squadrons.

141 SQUADRON

SERVICE

A night-fighter squadron in Fighter Command which developed the *Serrate* device for detecting and engaging German night fighters. After several months of carrying out such operations independently, the squadron was transferred to 100 Group in December 1943 and flew with Bomber Command until the end of the war, being based at West Raynham.

OPERATIONAL PERFORMANCE

The Squadron operated on 223 occasions, mostly at night, while with 100 Group, flying 12 sorties with Beaufighters and 1,202 with Mosquitoes. Most of these were *Serrate* operations but 84 ordinary Intruder sorties were flown. 11 Mosquitoes (0·9 per cent) were lost.

The squadron claimed 70 German aircraft destroyed, 4 probables and 21 damaged in the air, and 7 aircraft destroyed and 3 damaged on the ground, as well as 58 railway engines, 7 ships and 2 motor vehicles attacked on the ground.

POINTS OF INTEREST

141 Squadron performed a most valuable service in developing *Serrate* and introducing this form of operation to 100 Group. Only one other squadron in 100 Group claimed more German aircraft destroyed, and then by only one aircraft.

142 SQUADRON

SERVICE

Returned from the Advanced Air Striking Force in France in May 1940 and served in 1 Group, flying Battles and Wellingtons from Waddington, Binbrook (twice), Eastchurch, Grimsby and Kirmington. Detached to 38 Group for parachute training in June and July 1942 but no operations were flown and the squadron returned to 1 Group. The main body of the squadron was posted to the Middle East in December 1942 and flew operations there until the squadron was disbanded in October 1944. Re-formed the same month in England and served as a Mosquito squadron in 8 Group's Light Night Striking Force until the end of the war, being based at Gransden Lodge during this period.

OPERATIONAL PERFORMANCE

Raids Flown
1 Group Battles – 16 bombing
1 Group Wellingtons – 132 bombing, 32 minelaying, 1 leaflet
8 Group Mosquitoes – 116 bombing

Total – 264 bombing, 32 minelaying, 1 leaflet = 297 raids

Sorties and Losses
1 Group Battles – 63 sorties, 4 aircraft lost (6·3 per cent)
1 Group Wellingtons – 1,073 sorties, 47 aircraft lost (4·4 per cent)
8 Group Mosquitoes – 1,095 sorties, 2 aircraft lost (0·2 per cent)

Total – 2,231 sorties, 53 aircraft lost (2·4 per cent)

POINTS OF INTEREST

Flew most Battle sorties in Bomber Command.

144 SQUADRON

SERVICE

In 5 Group at the outbreak of the war; flew Hampdens intensively from Hemswell and North Luffenham until April 1942 when the squadron transferred to Coastal Command for training as a torpedo-bomber squadron, in which role it operated with much success until the end of the war.

OPERATIONAL PERFORMANCE

Raids Flown
Hampdens – 276 bombing, 42 minelaying, 6 leaflet = 324 raids

Sorties and Losses
Hampdens – 2,045 sorties, 62 aircraft lost (3·0 per cent)

POINTS OF INTEREST

An original squadron on the outbreak of war, carrying out operations over the North Sea from 25 September 1939. Suffered 100 per cent losses on 28 September 1939 when a formation of 5 Hampdens, including the aircraft of the squadron commander – Wing Commander J. C. Cunningham, was shot down.
Carried out most bombing raids in Hampden squadrons and suffered the most losses.

149 (EAST INDIA) SQUADRON

SERVICE

In 3 Group from the outbreak until the end of the war. Flew Wellingtons, Stirlings and Lancasters from Mildenhall, Lakenheath and Methwold.

OPERATIONAL PERFORMANCE

Raids Flown
Wellingtons – 213 bombing, 3 weather recce, 2 leaflet
Stirling – 244 bombing, 160 minelaying, 6 leaflet
Lancasters – 110 bombing

Total – 567 bombing, 160 minelaying, 8 leaflet, 3 recce = 738 raids

Sorties and Losses
Wellingtons – 1,647 sorties, 40 aircraft lost (2·4 per cent)
Stirlings – 2,628 sorties, 87 aircraft lost (3·3 per cent)
Lancasters – 1,630 sorties, 4 aircraft lost (0·2 per cent)

Total – 5,905 sorties, 131 aircraft lost (2·2 per cent)

40 Stirlings and 1 Lancaster were destroyed in crashes.

An original squadron on the outbreak of war; flew operations over the North Sea on the first day.

Continuous service in Bomber Command throughout the war, one of only two squadrons to claim this honour (see 44 Squadron).

Victoria Cross: Flight Sergeant R. H. Middleton, posthumously, Turin, 28/29 November 1942.

Carried out the fifth highest number of bombing raids in Bomber Command heavy squadrons.

Carried out most minelaying operations in Bomber Command.

Flew the most Stirling sorties in Bomber Command.

Suffered the lowest percentage loss rate among those Bomber Command squadrons which operated continuously from 1940 until the end of the war.

150 SQUADRON

SERVICE

Returned from the Advanced Air Striking Force in France in June 1940 and posted to 1 Group. Flew Battles and Wellingtons from Newton, Snaith and Kirmington until posted to the Middle East in December 1942. Disbanded in Algeria in September 1944 and re-formed, again in 1 Group, on 1 November 1944 and flew Lancasters from Fiskerton (briefly) and Hemswell until the end of the war.

OPERATIONAL PERFORMANCE

Raids Flown
Battles – 16 bombing
Wellingtons – 175 bombing, 25 minelaying
Lancasters – 73 bombing

Total – 264 bombing, 25 minelaying = 289 raids

Sorties and Losses
Battles – 50 sorties, no losses
Wellingtons – 1,667 sorties, 50 aircraft lost (3·0 per cent)
Lancasters – 840 sorties, 6 aircraft lost (0·7 per cent)

Total – 2,557 sorties, 56 aircraft lost (2·2 per cent)

2 Lancasters were destroyed in crashes.

153 SQUADRON

SERVICE

After three years' duty as a night-fighter squadron, disbanded in Algeria in September 1944. Re-formed as a Lancaster squadron in 1 Group on 7 October 1944 and flew from Kirmington (briefly) and Scampton until the end of the war.

OPERATIONAL PERFORMANCE

Raids Flown
Lancasters – 70 bombing, 5 minelaying = 75 raids

Sorties and Losses
Lancasters – 1,041 sorties, 22 aircraft lost (2·1 per cent), 4 aircraft destroyed in crashes.

156 SQUADRON

SERVICE

Formed in February 1942 as a Wellington squadron in 3 Group, flying from Alconbury. Transferred to 8 Group in August 1942 and flew as a Pathfinder squadron until the end of the war, converting to Lancasters in January 1943. Based at Warboys and Upwood while with 8 Group.

OPERATIONAL PERFORMANCE

Raids Flown
3 Group Wellingtons – 38 bombing, 4 minelaying, 1 leaflet
8 Group Wellingtons – 40 bombing
8 Group Lancasters – 230 bombing

Total – 308 bombing, 4 minelaying, 1 leaflet = 313 raids

Sorties and Losses
3 Group Wellingtons – 346 sorties, 22 aircraft lost (6·4 per cent)
8 Group Wellingtons – 305 sorties, 17 aircraft lost (5·6 per cent)
8 Group Lancasters – 3,933 sorties, 104 aircraft lost (2·6 per cent)

Total – 4,584 sorties, 143 aircraft lost (3·1 per cent)

16 Lancasters were destroyed in crashes.

POINTS OF INTEREST

Suffered heavy losses while flying Wellingtons.
An original Pathfinder squadron.
Flew most overall sorties and most Lancaster sorties in Pathfinder heavy squadrons.
Lost four commanding officers in four months, January to April 1944.

157 SQUADRON

SERVICE

This Mosquito night-fighter squadron was posted to 100 Group in May 1944 for bomber-support duties. Based at Swannington and flew Intruder operations until the end of the war, except for two periods in the summer of 1944 when anti-flying-bomb patrols were flown from West Malling.

OPERATIONAL PERFORMANCE

Flew 1,122 bomber-support sorties in 174 separate operations, losing 5 aircraft (0·4 per cent), and 214 anti-flying-bomb sorties with the loss of 1 aircraft (0·5 per cent). All operations were with Mosquitoes. Claimed 37 German aircraft destroyed (18 Ju 88s, 14 Me 110s, 2 Ju 188s, 2 He 119s, 2 FW 190s) and 13 others damaged; claimed 39 flying bombs destroyed and 1 damaged.

158 SQUADRON

SERVICE

Formed in 4 Group on 14 February 1942 and, after flying Wellingtons for four months, converted to Halifaxes which were flown until the end of the war. Based at Driffield, East Moor, Rufforth and Lissett. Several short detachments were made to Coastal Command in November and December 1942.

OPERATIONAL PERFORMANCE

Raids Flown
Wellingtons – 78 bombing, 3 minelaying
Halifaxes – 267 bombing, 8 minelaying

Total – 345 bombing, 11 minelaying = 356 raids

Sorties and Losses
Wellingtons – 207 sorties, 14 aircraft lost (6·8 per cent)
Halifaxes – 5,161 sorties, 145 aircraft lost (2·8 per cent)

Total – 5,368 sorties, 159 aircraft lost (3·0 per cent)

3 Wellingtons and 12 Halifaxes were destroyed in crashes.

POINTS OF INTEREST

Flew most Halifax sorties in Bomber Command. One of the squadron aircraft, Halifax III LV907 – nicknamed *Friday the 13th* from the day of its delivery to the squadron – flew 128 operational sorties and survived the war; this was a record number of sorties for a Halifax.
Suffered the following aircrew casualties: 859 killed, died of wounds or died in prison camps, 308 prisoners of war, 61 evaded capture. 78 of the dead have no known grave; 107 of the fatal casualties were suffered in crashes in the United Kingdom.*

161 SQUADRON

SERVICE

Formed in February 1942 from a nucleus provided by the King's Flight. Operated

---

*The 158 Squadron casualty figures are from a squadron history, *In Brave Company* by W. R. Chorley and R. N. Benwell, published privately in 1977.

until the end of the war as a Special Duty squadron delivering supplies and agents to Resistance units. Based at Tempsford and operated many types of aircraft.

OPERATIONAL PERFORMANCE

The records of 161 Squadron are incomplete and confusing. The number of nights and days on which the squadron operated is not known. The sorties and losses shown below are known to have taken place but the true figure is greater:

Halifaxes – 786 sorties, 17 aircraft lost (2·2 per cent)
Stirlings – 379 sorties, 6 aircraft lost (1·6 per cent)
Lysanders – 266 sorties, 10 aircraft lost (3·8 per cent)
Hudsons – 179 sorties, 10 aircraft lost (5·6 per cent)
Whitleys – 139 sorties, 6 aircraft lost (4·3 per cent)

Total – 1,749 sorties, 49 aircraft lost (2·8 per cent)

The Lysanders and the Hudsons were the most commonly used aircraft for landing in fields to collect agents, which accounts for their high casualties; these aircraft often had to be abandoned by their crews when they crashed or became bogged in soft ground. The Lysanders, and some other types of aircraft, sometimes carried small bomb loads which were dropped on a nearby target after their Resistance loads had been delivered.

In addition to the above figures, at least 125 sorties by Havocs were flown; some of these were agent-landing operations but the Havoc was not suitable for this work and was replaced by the Hudson. Many of the 125 Havoc sorties were flown from St Eval as convoy escorts under Fighter or Coastal Command control. It is also known that the squadron had Albemarles, Ansons and Wellingtons for short periods but details of their operations, if any, were not recorded.

162 SQUADRON

SERVICE

After operating as a radio-countermeasures squadron in the Middle East, the squadron was disbanded in September 1944 but was re-formed in 8 Group on 18 December 1944 and flew Mosquitoes with the Light Night Striking Force until the end of the war. Based at Bourn.

OPERATIONAL PERFORMANCE

162 Squadron flew 913 sorties and lost only 1 aircraft (0·1 per cent) in 89 bombing raids.

POINTS OF INTEREST

Suffered the lowest casualties and the lowest percentage casualties in Bomber Command.

Part of the squadron was equipped with *H2S* and carried markers during the Mosquito campaign against Berlin in the final weeks of the war.

163 SQUADRON

SERVICE

Was a communications squadron in Africa from July 1942 until June 1943 but then disbanded. Re-formed in 8 Group on 25 January 1945 and flew Mosquitoes with the Light Night Striking Force until the end of the war.

OPERATIONAL PERFORMANCE

163 Squadron flew 636 sorties and lost 3 aircraft (0·5 per cent) in 64 bombing raids.

166 SQUADRON

SERVICE

A Whitley training squadron in 4 Group on the outbreak of the war but lost its identity in April 1940. Re-formed in 1 Group on 27 January 1943 and flew its first operation that night. Flew Wellingtons and Lancasters from Kirmington until the end of the war.

OPERATIONAL PERFORMANCE

Raids Flown
Wellingtons – 43 bombing, 33 minelaying
Lancasters – 202 bombing, 13 minelaying

Total – 245 bombing, 46 minelaying = 291 raids

Sorties and Losses
Wellingtons – 789 sorties, 39 aircraft lost (4·9 per cent)
Lancasters – 4,279 sorties, 114 aircraft lost (2·7 per cent)

Total – 5,068 sorties, 153 aircraft lost (3·0 per cent)

3 Wellingtons and 19 Lancasters were destroyed in crashes.

169 SQUADRON

SERVICE

A Mosquito night-fighter squadron, transferred to 100 Group in December 1943. Flew mainly *Serrate* operations from Little Snoring and Great Massingham until the end of the war.

OPERATIONAL PERFORMANCE

Operations flown: 219 *Serrate*, 26 daylight Intruder (known as Rangers), 10 bombing and napalm raids and 2 anti-Intruder operations over Britain. Sorties, 1,247; losses, 13 aircraft (1·0 per cent). Claims: 25 German aircraft destroyed (16 Me 110s, 7 Ju 88s, 1 Do 217, 1 Me 109) and 7 aircraft damaged. Also claimed 1 flying bomb destroyed.

170 SQUADRON

SERVICE

A Mustang Army Co-Operation squadron from June 1942 to January 1944 but then disbanded. Re-formed on 15 October 1944 in 1 Group and flew Lancasters from Kelstern, Dunholme Lodge and Hemswell until the end of the war.

OPERATIONAL PERFORMANCE

170 Squadron flew 980 sorties and lost 13 aircraft (1·3 per cent) in 63 bombing raids. 1 Lancaster was destroyed in a crash.

171 SQUADRON

SERVICE

Formed in September 1944 for R.C.M. operations in 100 Group and flew Stirlings and Halifaxes from North Creake until the end of the war.

OPERATIONAL PERFORMANCE

171 Squadron flew 87 Stirling sorties without loss in 33 R.C.M. operations and 1,496 Halifax sorties with the loss of 4 aircraft (0·3 per cent) in 95 R.C.M. operations.

180 SQUADRON

SERVICE

Formed in 2 Group on 13 September 1942 and flew Mitchells from West Raynham and Foulsham until 2 Group left Bomber Command in May 1943.

OPERATIONAL PERFORMANCE

180 Squadron flew 151 Mitchell sorties and lost 4 aircraft (2·6 per cent) in 9 bombing raids and 14 air–sea searches.

POINTS OF INTEREST

With 98 Squadron, introduced the Mitchell to Bomber Command operations; lost its
  commanding officer in its first Mitchell raid.

186 SQUADRON

SERVICE

An Army Co-Operation squadron from April 1943 until April 1944 but then lost its identity. Re-formed in 3 Group on 5 October 1944 and flew Lancasters from Tuddenham and Stradishall until the end of the war.

OPERATIONAL PERFORMANCE

Raids Flown
Lancasters – 96 bombing, 2 minelaying

Sorties and Losses
Lancasters – 1,254 sorties, 8 aircraft lost (0·6 per cent). 4 aircraft destroyed in crashes.

189 SQUADRON

SERVICE

Formed in 5 Group on 15 October 1944 and flew Lancasters from Bardney and Fulbeck until the end of the war.

OPERATIONAL PERFORMANCE

189 Squadron flew 652 Lancaster sorties and lost 16 aircraft (2·5 per cent) in 48 bombing raids. 2 Lancasters were destroyed in crashes.

192 SQUADRON

SERVICE

Formed from 1474 Flight on 4 January 1943 as a specialist radio-countermeasures squadron. Operated in 3 Group until November 1943, then transferred to the newly formed 100 Group. Flew Wellingtons, Halifaxes and Mosquitoes with both 3 and 100 Groups and contained a detachment of American aircrew flying Lightnings while with 100 Group. Based at Gransden Lodge and Feltwell in 3 Group and at Foulsham in 100 Group.

OPERATIONAL PERFORMANCE

192 Squadron flew 141 operations with 3 Group and 342 operations with 100 Group, a total of 483. The primary purpose of all operations was to carry out some form of radio-countermeasures work but bombs were often carried and dropped on the Main Force targets.

Sorties and Losses
3 Group Wellingtons – 291 sorties, 4 aircraft lost (1·4 per cent)
3 Group Halifaxes – 55 sorties, no losses
3 Group Mosquitoes – 48 sorties, 1 aircraft lost (2·1 per cent)
100 Group Wellingtons – 589 sorties, 1 aircraft lost (0·2 per cent)
100 Group Halifaxes – 937 sorties – 10 aircraft lost (1·1 per cent)
100 Group Mosquitoes – 544 sorties, 1 aircraft lost (0·2 per cent)
100 Group Lightnings – 101 sorties, 2 aircraft lost (2·0 per cent)

Total – 2,565 sorties, 19 aircraft lost (0·7 per cent)

POINTS OF INTEREST

Pioneered Bomber Command's R.C.M. operations, flew more sorties and suffered more losses than any other R.C.M. squadron. The first squadron to fly operations in 100 Group on 30 November 1943.

195 SQUADRON

SERVICE

An Army Co-Operation squadron from November 1942 until disbanded in February 1944. Re-formed as a Lancaster squadron in 3 Group on 1 October 1944 and flew from Witchford and Wratting Common until the end of the war.

OPERATIONAL PERFORMANCE

195 Squadron flew 1,384 Lancaster sorties and lost 14 aircraft (1·0 per cent) in 87 bombing raids. A small number of further sorties were flown by squadron crews using 115 Squadron Lancasters in the first three weeks of October 1944 and some casualties were suffered, but it is not possible to separate these from 115 Squadron's statistics.

196 SQUADRON

SERVICE

Formed on 7 November 1942 as a Wellington squadron in 4 Group and commenced operations in February 1943, flying from Leconfield. Transferred to 3 Group in July 1943 and flew Stirlings from Witchford until November 1943 when the squadron left Bomber Command to become a glider-towing and transport unit.

OPERATIONAL PERFORMANCE

Raids Flown
4 Group Wellingtons – 33 bombing, 23 minelaying
3 Group Stirlings – 12 bombing, 18 minelaying

Total – 45 bombing, 41 minelaying = 86 raids

Sorties and Losses
4 Group Wellingtons – 517 sorties, 13 aircraft lost (2·5 per cent)
3 Group Stirlings – 166 sorties, 11 aircraft lost (6·6 per cent)

Total – 683 sorties, 24 aircraft lost (3·5 per cent)

199 SQUADRON

SERVICE

Formed on 7 November 1942 as a Wellington squadron in 1 Group, based at Blyton and Ingham. Transferred to 3 Group on 21 June 1943 and flew Stirlings until again transferred, in May 1944, to 100 Group as an R.C.M. squadron. Flew Stirlings and Halifaxes from North Creake while in 100 Group.

OPERATIONAL PERFORMANCE

Raids Flown
1 Group Wellingtons – 35 bombing, 23 minelaying
3 Group Stirlings – 30 bombing, 52 minelaying, 16 Resistance operations, 1 leaflet
100 Group Stirlings – 138 R.C.M.
100 Group Halifaxes – 37 R.C.M. (which were combined with some bombing in the last four weeks of the war)

Total – 65 bombing, 75 minelaying, 16 Resistance operations, 1 leaflet, 175 R.C.M. = 332 raids

Sorties and Losses
1 Group Wellingtons – 475 sorties, 12 aircraft lost (2·5 per cent)
3 Group Stirlings – 681 sorties, 14 aircraft lost (2·1 per cent)
100 Group Stirlings – 1,378 sorties, 4 aircraft lost (0·3 per cent)
100 Group Halifaxes – 329 sorties, 2 aircraft lost (0·6 per cent)

Total – 2,863 sorties, 32 aircraft lost (1·1 per cent)

POINTS OF INTEREST

Believed to have carried out a greater variety of operations than any other squadron in Bomber Command.
Suffered Bomber Command's last casualties of the war when 2 Halifaxes collided near Kiel on 2/3 May 1945 and 13 aircrew were killed.

207 SQUADRON

SERVICE

A training squadron on the outbreak of war and lost its identity in April 1940. Re-formed in 5 Group in November 1940 for the introduction of the Manchester and commenced operations in February 1941. Served in 5 Group for the remainder of the war, converting to Lancasters in March 1942. Based at Waddington, Bottesford, Langar and Spilsby.

OPERATIONAL PERFORMANCE

Raids Flown
Manchesters – 76 bombing, 15 minelaying, 4 leaflet
Lancasters – 350 bombing, 35 minelaying, 1 leaflet

Total – 426 bombing, 50 minelaying, 5 leaflet = 481 raids

Sorties and Losses
Manchesters – 360 sorties, 17 aircraft lost (4·7 per cent)
Lancasters – 4,203 sorties, 131 aircraft lost (3·1 per cent)

Total – 4,563 sorties, 148 aircraft lost (3·2 per cent)

8 Manchesters and 19 Lancasters were destroyed in crashes. Some operations flown in 44 Squadron's Hampdens, when 207 Squadron's Manchesters were grounded, are included in 44 Squadron's records.

POINTS OF INTEREST

Introduced the Manchester to operations, the first new bomber to enter Bomber Command service after the outbreak of the war.
Carried out more raids, flew more sorties and suffered more losses than any other Manchester squadron.
207 Squadron was often unlucky and it suffered the fourth highest overall percentage losses in Bomber Command and the highest percentage losses in 5 Group.

214 (FEDERATED MALAY STATES) SQUADRON

SERVICE

A Wellington squadron in 3 Group on the outbreak of the war but did not fly operations until June 1940, the first raid being a fire-raising tour of German forests by 2 Wellingtons on 14/15 June. Served in 3 Group until January 1944, flying Wellingtons and Stirlings from Methwold, Stradishall (twice), Honington, Chedburgh and Downham Market. Transferred to 100 Group as an R.C.M. squadron, flying Fortresses from Sculthorpe and Oulton until the end of the war.

OPERATIONAL PERFORMANCE

Raids Flown
3 Group Wellingtons – 184 bombing, 1 minelaying
3 Group Stirlings – 131 bombing, 88 minelaying, 3 leaflet
100 Group Fortresses – 192 R.C.M.

Total – 315 bombing, 89 minelaying, 192 R.C.M., 3 leaflet = 599 raids

Sorties and Losses
3 Group Wellingtons – 1,532 sorties, 45 aircraft lost (2·9 per cent)
3 Group Stirlings – 1,432 sorties, 54 aircraft lost (3·8 per cent)
100 Group Fortresses – 1,225 sorties, 13 aircraft lost (1·1 per cent)

Total – 4,189 sorties, 112 aircraft lost (2·7 per cent)

29 Stirlings were destroyed in crashes.

Completely unbroken service throughout the war in Bomber Command, though not on operations for the first nine months.

Suffered the highest percentage losses in 3 Group.

218 (GOLD COAST) SQUADRON

SERVICE

Returned from the Advanced Air Striking Force in France in June 1940, posted to 2 Group and converted from Battles to Blenheims. Flew operations from Oakington from August to November 1940 but then transferred to 3 Group, where the squadron remained until the end of the war. Flew Wellingtons, Stirlings and Lancasters with 3 Group and based at Marham, Downham Market, Woolfox Lodge, Methwold and Chedburgh.

OPERATIONAL PERFORMANCE

Raids Flown

2 Group Blenheims – 22 bombing, 3 photo recce, 3 weather recce

3 Group Wellingtons – 115 bombing

3 Group Stirlings – 183 bombing, 153 minelaying, 3 leaflet, 1 *Window* (on the eve of D-Day)

3 Group Lancasters – 127 bombing

Total – 447 bombing, 153 minelaying, 10 others = 610 raids

Sorties and Losses

2 Group Blenheims – 122 sorties, 2 aircraft lost (1·6 per cent)

3 Group Wellingtons – 854 sorties, 21 aircraft lost (2·5 per cent)

3 Group Stirlings – 2,600 sorties, 91 aircraft lost (3·5 per cent)

3 Group Lancasters – 1,726 sorties, 16 aircraft lost (0·9 per cent)

Total – 5,302 sorties, 130 aircraft lost (2·5 per cent)

35 Stirlings and 3 Lancasters were destroyed in crashes.

POINTS OF INTEREST

With Advanced Air Striking Force duty, continuous service as a bomber squadron throughout the war.

Victoria Cross: Flight Sergeant A. A. Aaron, D.F.M., posthumously, Turin, 12/13 August 1943.

Suffered most losses (with 15 Squadron) in Stirling squadrons.

223 SQUADRON

SERVICE

After flying as a bomber squadron in East and North Africa and Italy, 223 Squadron lost its identity in August 1944. Re-formed as an R.C.M. squadron in 100 Group later the same month, mainly from ex-Coastal Command aircrew, and flew Liberators and Fortresses from Oulton until the end of the war.

OPERATIONAL PERFORMANCE

223 Squadron flew 615 Liberator sorties and lost 3 aircraft (0·5 per cent) in 135 R.C.M. operations and 10 Fortress sorties without loss in 6 R.C.M. operations.

226 SQUADRON

SERVICE

Posted to 2 Group in May 1941 after flying Battles in France and in Northern Ireland with Coastal Command. Served in 2 Group until the group left Bomber Command in May 1943. Flew Blenheims, often in the anti-shipping role, and Bostons; based at Wattisham, Manston and Swanton Morley.

OPERATIONAL PERFORMANCE

Raids Flown
Blenheims – 38 bombing and shipping attacks
Bostons – 62 bombing, 1 Intruder

Total – 100 bombing and shipping attacks, 1 Intruder

Sorties and Losses
Blenheims – 241 sorties, 16 aircraft lost (6·6 per cent)
Bostons – 499 sorties, 12 aircraft lost (2·4 per cent)

Total – 740 sorties, 28 aircraft lost (3·8 per cent)

POINTS OF INTEREST

Introduced American bomber crews to operations in June 1942.

227 SQUADRON

SERVICE

After flying Beaufighters from Malta, lost its identity in August 1944. A new 227 Squadron was formed in 5 Group on 7 October 1944 and flew Lancasters from Bardney, Balderton and Strubby until the end of the war.

OPERATIONAL PERFORMANCE

227 Squadron flew 815 Lancaster sorties and lost 15 aircraft (1·8 per cent) in 61 bombing raids. 2 Lancasters were destroyed in crashes.

239 SQUADRON

SERVICE

A home-based Mosquito night-fighter squadron which was transferred to 100 Group on 9 December 1943 for *Serrate* operations. Flew from West Raynham until the end of the war.

OPERATIONAL PERFORMANCE

239 Squadron flew 1,394 Mosquito sorties and lost 9 aircraft (0·6 per cent) in 263 *Serrate* and Intruder operations. The squadron claimed 51 German aircraft destroyed (27 Me 110s, 10 Ju 88s, 14 of seven other types) and a further 9 aircraft probably destroyed or damaged.

POINTS OF INTEREST

Carried out most *Serrate*/Intruder operations and flew most Mosquito sorties in 100 Group.

300 (MASOVIAN) SQUADRON

SERVICE

This Polish squadron was formed in July 1940 and operated in 1 Group from September 1940 until the end of the war. Flew Battles, Wellingtons and Lancasters and was based at Swinderby, Hemswell (twice), Ingham (twice) and Faldingworth. The squadron was entirely Polish in the first part of its career but had to be made up with R.A.F. and other aircrews as the war progressed.

OPERATIONAL PERFORMANCE

Raids Flown
Battles – 7 bombing
Wellingtons – 218 bombing, 105 minelaying
Lancasters – 138 bombing

Total – 363 bombing, 105 minelaying = 468 raids

Sorties and Losses
Battles – 47 sorties, no losses
Wellingtons – 2,421 sorties, 47 aircraft lost (1·9 per cent)
Lancasters – 1,216 sorties, 30 aircraft lost (2·5 per cent)

Total – 3,684 sorties, 77 aircraft lost (2·1 per cent)

6 Lancasters were destroyed in crashes.

The first Polish squadron to be formed in Bomber Command; carried out more raids, flew more sorties and suffered more losses than any other Allied squadron. Carried out most raids and flew most sorties in 1 Group Wellington Squadrons.

301 (POMERANIAN) SQUADRON

SERVICE

This Polish squadron was also formed in July 1940 and became operational in 1 Group in September 1940. Flew Battles and Wellingtons from Swinderby and Hemswell but was disbanded in April 1943 owing to a shortage of Polish aircrews.

OPERATIONAL PERFORMANCE

Raids Flown
Battles – 8 bombing
Wellingtons – 190 bombing, 51 minelaying, 1 leaflet

Total – 198 bombing, 51 minelaying, 1 leaflet = 250 raids

Sorties and Losses
Battles – 40 sorties, no losses
Wellingtons – 1,220 sorties, 29 aircraft lost (2·4 per cent)

Total – 1,260 sorties, 29 aircraft lost (2·3 per cent)

304 (SILESIAN) SQUADRON

SERVICE

Formed in August 1940, mainly from Polish airmen who had been serving in the French Air Force. Operated with Wellingtons in 1 Group from 8 April 1941, being based at Syerston and Lindholme. Transferred to Coastal Command in May 1942 and flew maritime operations until the end of the war.

OPERATIONAL PERFORMANCE

304 Squadron flew 464 Wellington sorties and lost 18 aircraft (3·9 per cent) in 99 bombing raids and 1 leaflet raid.

305 (ZIEMIA WIELKOPOLSKA) SQUADRON

SERVICE

Also formed from ex-French Air Force Poles in August 1940. Flew Wellingtons in 1 Group between April 1941 and August 1943, being based at Syerston, Lindholme, Hemswell and Ingham. Transferred to the 2nd Tactical Air Force and flew Mitchells and Mosquito bombers until the end of the war.

OPERATIONAL PERFORMANCE

305 Squadron flew 1,063 Wellington sorties and lost 30 aircraft (2·8 per cent) in 160 bombing and 51 minelaying raids.

311 (CZECHOSLOVAK) SQUADRON

SERVICE

Formed in July 1940 from Czechoslovak airmen who had been serving in France. Operated with 3 Group from September 1940, flying Wellingtons from Honington and East Wretham. Posted to Coastal Command in April 1942 and flew Liberators on long-range maritime operations until the end of the war.

OPERATIONAL PERFORMANCE

311 Squadron flew 1,029 Wellington sorties and lost 19 aircraft (1·8 per cent) in 152 bombing raids.

POINTS OF INTEREST

The first Allied squadron to fly operations in Bomber Command.
The only Czechoslovak squadron in Bomber Command.

320 (DUTCH) SQUADRON

SERVICE

After serving as a maritime squadron in Coastal Command, 320 Squadron was transferred to 2 Group in March 1943 and started converting to Mitchells, but the squadron was not ready for operations when 2 Group left Bomber Command a few weeks later. The squadron later operated with the 2nd Tactical Air Force until the end of the war. It was the only Dutch squadron in Bomber Command but flew no operational sorties while in Bomber Command. Based at Attlebridge.

342 (LORRAINE) SQUADRON

SERVICE

After serving as a Blenheim squadron in Africa and the Middle East from December 1941 until early 1943, this Free French squadron was posted to 2 Group and started to convert to Bostons, but this process was not complete and no operations had been flown when 2 Group left Bomber Command. The squadron subsequently flew Bostons and Mitchells in the 2nd Tactical Air Force until the end of the war.

346 (FRENCH) SQUADRON

SERVICE

Formed as a Halifax squadron in 4 Group on 16 May 1944 and flew from Elvington until the end of the war.

OPERATIONAL PERFORMANCE

346 Squadron flew 1,371 Halifax sorties and lost 15 aircraft (1·1 per cent) in 121 bombing raids.

347 (FRENCH) SQUADRON

SERVICE

Formed as a Halifax squadron in 4 Group on 20 June 1944 and flew from Elvington until the end of the war.

OPERATIONAL PERFORMANCE

347 Squadron flew 1,355 Halifax sorties and lost 15 aircraft (1·1 per cent) in 110 bombing raids.

All squadrons numbered between 405 and 434 were Royal Canadian Air Force squadrons, serving mostly in 6 (Canadian) Group.

405 (VANCOUVER) SQUADRON

SERVICE

Formed in 4 Group on 23 April 1941 and flew Wellingtons and Halifaxes from Driffield, Pocklington and Topcliffe until posted to Coastal Command in October 1942. Returned to Bomber Command in March 1943 and operated from Leeming in 6 Group from 11/12 March (when the squadron lost 4 out of its 15 Halifaxes flying on the first raid, to Stuttgart). Transferred to 8 Group in April 1943 and operated as a Pathfinder squadron until the end of the war, flying Halifaxes and Lancasters from Gransden Lodge.

OPERATIONAL PERFORMANCE

Raids Flown
4 Group Wellingtons – 86 bombing
4 Group Halifaxes – 34 bombing, 2 leaflet
6 Group Halifaxes – 13 bombing
8 Group Halifaxes – 29 bombing
8 Group Lancasters – 288 bombing

Total – 450 bombing and 2 leaflet raids

Sorties and Losses
4 Group Wellingtons – 522 sorties, 20 aircraft lost (3·8 per cent)
4 Group Halifaxes – 396 sorties, 26 aircraft lost (6·6 per cent)
6 Group Halifaxes – 55 sorties, 4 aircraft lost (7·3 per cent)
8 Group Halifaxes – 330 sorties, 12 aircraft lost (3·6 per cent)
8 Group Lancasters – 2,549 sorties, 50 aircraft lost (2·0 per cent)

Total – 3,852 sorties, 112 aircraft lost (2·9 per cent)

First Canadian squadron in Bomber Command and the only Canadian Pathfinder squadron; carried out more bombing raids than any other Canadian squadron.
Carried out most Wellington bombing raids in 4 Group.
Carried out an unusually high proportion of bombing raids throughout its career and suffered heavy casualties; the only long-serving heavy squadron not to have flown any minelaying operations.

408 (GOOSE) SQUADRON

SERVICE

Formed on 24 June 1941 in 5 Group. Flew Hampdens (and one Manchester sortie on the Thousand-Bomber Raid to Cologne) from Syerston and Balderton from August 1941 until posted to 4 Group in September 1942 in preparation for the formation of 6 Group. Became a founder squadron of 6 Group on 1 January 1943. Flew Halifaxes from Leeming while with 4 Group and Halifaxes, then Lancasters and then back to Halifaxes, from Leeming and Linton-on-Ouse while with 6 Group.

OPERATIONAL PERFORMANCE

Raids Flown
5 Group Hampdens – 117 bombing, 56 minelaying, 15 leaflet, 2 weather recce
5 Group Manchester – 1 bombing
4 Group Halifaxes – 57 bombing, 11 minelaying
6 Group Halifaxes – 98 bombing
6 Group Lancasters – 100 bombing

Total – 373 bombing, 67 minelaying, 15 leaflet, 2 recce = 457 raids

Sorties and Losses
5 Group Hampdens – 1,233 sorties, 35 aircraft lost (2·8 per cent)
5 Group Manchester – 1 sortie returned safely
4 Group Halifaxes – 540 sorties, 33 aircraft lost (6·1 per cent)
6 Group Halifaxes – 1,469 sorties, 20 aircraft lost (1·4 per cent)
6 Group Lancasters – 1,210 sorties, 41 aircraft lost (3·4 per cent)

Total – 4,453 sorties, 129 aircraft lost (2·9 per cent)

10 Lancasters were destroyed in crashes.

POINTS OF INTEREST

Flew most sorties and suffered most losses (with 419 Squadron) in Canadian squadrons.
Suffered most losses and the highest percentage losses in 6 Group Lancaster squadrons.

415 (SWORDFISH) SQUADRON

SERVICE

Came to 6 Group in July 1944 after more than two years duty with Coastal Command. Flew Halifaxes from East Moor until the end of the war.

OPERATIONAL PERFORMANCE

415 Squadron flew 1,526 Halifax sorties and lost 13 aircraft (0·9 per cent) in 104 bombing raids.

419 (MOOSE) SQUADRON

SERVICE

Formed in 3 Group on 15 December 1941 and flew Wellingtons from Mildenhall until the squadron was transferred to 4 Group, being based at several airfields in 4 Group while converting to Halifaxes and waiting for 6 Group to be formed. Started operating again from Middleton St George in January 1943 and flew from there until the end of the war, converting to Lancasters in April 1944.

OPERATIONAL PERFORMANCE

Raids Flown
3 Group Wellingtons – 67 bombing, 18 minelaying, 3 leaflet
6 Group Halifaxes – 105 bombing, 33 minelaying, 1 diversion
6 Group Lancasters – 127 bombing

Total – 299 bombing, 51 minelaying, 4 others = 354 raids

Sorties and Losses
3 Group Wellingtons – 648 sorties, 24 aircraft lost (3·7 per cent)
6 Group Halifaxes – 1,616 sorties, 66 aircraft lost (4·1 per cent)
6 Group Lancasters – 2,029 sorties, 39 aircraft lost (1·9 per cent)

Total – 4,293 sorties, 129 aircraft lost (3·0 per cent)

14 Lancasters were destroyed in crashes.

POINTS OF INTEREST

419 was a very active squadron and holds many records for its heavy casualties. Of all the Canadian squadrons, it suffered the most losses (with 408 Squadron) and suffered the highest percentage loss.
In 6 Group, it carried out the most bombing raids (with 427 Squadron), flew the most sorties and suffered the most losses.
Suffered the most losses and the highest percentage loss in 6 Group Halifax squadrons and the highest percentage loss in all Bomber Command Halifax squadrons.
Carried out the most bombing raids and flew the most sorties in 6 Group Lancaster squadrons.

Victoria Cross: Pilot Officer A. C. Mynarski, posthumously, Cambrai, 12/13 June 1944.

420 (SNOWY OWL) SQUADRON

SERVICE

Formed in 5 Group on 19 December 1941 and flew Hampdens from Waddington. Moved to 4 Group in August 1942 and flew Wellingtons from Skipton-on-Swale and Middleton St George until transferred to 6 Group in January 1943. Detached to the Middle East from May to November 1943 but then returned to 6 Group and converted to Halifaxes; flew from Tholthorpe until the end of the war.

OPERATIONAL PERFORMANCE

Raids Flown
5 Group Hampdens – 44 bombing, 37 minelaying, 8 leaflet, 1 weather recce
4 Group Wellingtons – 13 bombing, 10 minelaying, 1 weather recce
6 Group Wellingtons – 30 bombing, 10 minelaying
6 Group Halifaxes – 160 bombing

Total – 247 bombing, 57 minelaying, 8 leaflet, 2 recce = 314 raids

Sorties and Losses
5 Group Hampdens – 535 sorties, 19 aircraft lost (3·6 per cent)
4 Group Wellingtons – 142 sorties, 2 aircraft lost (1·4 per cent)
6 Group Wellingtons – 325 sorties, 14 aircraft lost (4·3 per cent)
6 Group Halifaxes – 2,477 sorties, 25 aircraft lost (1·0 per cent)

Total – 3,479 sorties, 60 aircraft lost (1·7 per cent)

424 (TIGER) SQUADRON

SERVICE

Formed in 4 Group on 15 October 1942 but did not operate until after transferring to 6 Group in January 1943. Flew Wellingtons from Topcliffe and Leeming until detached to the Middle East in May 1943. Returned to 6 Group in October and converted to Halifaxes at Skipton-on-Swale, flying the first Halifax operation on 15/16 February 1944 when the target was Berlin and 1 aircraft was lost. Converted to Lancasters in February 1945.

OPERATIONAL PERFORMANCE

Raids Flown
Wellingtons – 24 bombing, 13 minelaying
Halifaxes – 123 bombing, 33 minelaying
Lancasters – 29 bombing, 13 minelaying

Total – 176 bombing, 59 minelaying = 235 raids

Sorties and Losses
Wellingtons – 332 sorties, 5 aircraft lost (1·5 per cent)
Halifaxes – 1,811 sorties, 23 aircraft lost (1·3 per cent)
Lancasters – 388 sorties, 5 aircraft lost (1·3 per cent)

Total – 2,531 sorties, 33 aircraft lost (1·3 per cent)

2 Lancasters were destroyed in crashes.

425 (ALOUETTE) SQUADRON

SERVICE

This French Canadian squadron was formed in 4 Group on 22 June 1942 and operated Wellingtons from Dishforth from October 1942. Transferred to 6 Group in January 1943 but then detached to the Middle East from May to November 1943. Returned to 6 Group and converted to Halifaxes. Flew operations from Tholthorpe from February 1944 until the end of the war.

OPERATIONAL PERFORMANCE

Raids Flown
4 Group Wellingtons – 13 bombing, 10 minelaying, 1 recce
6 Group Wellingtons – 28 bombing, 11 minelaying
6 Group Halifaxes – 162 bombing

Total – 203 bombing, 21 minelaying, 1 recce = 225 raids

Sorties and Losses
4 Group Wellingtons – 135 sorties, 3 aircraft lost (2·2 per cent)
6 Group Wellingtons – 347 sorties, 8 aircraft lost (2·3 per cent)
6 Group Halifaxes – 2,445 sorties, 28 aircraft lost (1·1 per cent)

Total – 2,927 sorties, 39 aircraft lost (1·3 per cent)

426 (THUNDERBIRD) SQUADRON

SERVICE

Formed in 4 Group on 15 October 1942 but did not operate until after the transfer to 6 Group in January 1943. Flew Wellingtons, Lancasters (suffering heavy losses in the Battle of Berlin period) and then Halifaxes from Dishforth and Linton-on-Ouse between January 1943 and the end of the war.

OPERATIONAL PERFORMANCE

Raids Flown
Wellingtons – 33 bombing, 19 minelaying
Lancasters – 53 bombing
Halifaxes – 136 bombing

Total – 222 bombing, 19 minelaying = 241 raids

Sorties and Losses
Wellingtons – 467 sorties, 18 aircraft lost (3·9 per cent)
Lancasters – 579 sorties, 28 aircraft lost (4·8 per cent)
Halifaxes – 2,161 sorties, 22 aircraft lost (1·0 per cent)

Total – 3,207 sorties, 68 aircraft lost (2·1 per cent)

7 Lancasters were destroyed in crashes.

POINTS OF INTEREST

Carried out the most Wellington bombing raids in 6 Group.

427 (LION) SQUADRON

SERVICE

Formed in 4 Group on 7 November 1942 but only flew one minelaying operation before being transferred to 6 Group in January 1943. Flew Wellingtons, Halifaxes and Lancasters until the end of the war; based at Croft and Leeming.

OPERATIONAL PERFORMANCE

Raids Flown
4 Group Wellingtons – 1 minelaying
6 Group Wellingtons – 26 bombing, 10 minelaying
6 Group Halifaxes – 190 bombing, 21 minelaying
6 Group Lancasters – 16 bombing, 7 minelaying

Total – 232 bombing, 39 minelaying = 271 raids

Sorties and Losses
4 Group Wellingtons – 3 sorties, no losses
6 Group Wellingtons – 267 sorties, 10 aircraft lost (3·7 per cent)
6 Group Halifaxes – 2,800 sorties, 58 aircraft lost (2·1 per cent)
6 Group Lancasters – 239 sorties, 1 aircraft lost (0·4 per cent)

Total – 3,309 sorties, 69 aircraft lost (2·1 per cent)

1 Lancaster was destroyed in a crash.

POINTS OF INTEREST

Carried out (with 419 Squadron) the most raids in 6 Group.
Carried out the most Halifax raids and flew the most Halifax sorties in 6 Group.

428 (GHOST) SQUADRON

SERVICE

Formed in 4 Group on 7 November 1942 but did not operate until after transferring to 6 Group. Flew Wellingtons, Halifaxes and Lancasters until the end of the war, being based at Dalton and Middleton St George.

OPERATIONAL PERFORMANCE

Raids Flown
Wellingtons – 26 bombing, 9 minelaying
Halifaxes – 69 bombing, 53 minelaying
Lancasters – 111 bombing

Total – 206 bombing, 62 minelaying = 268 raids

Sorties and Losses
Wellingtons – 350 sorties, 17 aircraft lost (4·9 per cent)
Halifaxes – 1,406 sorties, 32 aircraft lost (2·3 per cent)
Lancasters – 1,677 sorties, 18 aircraft lost (1·1 per cent)

Total – 3,433 sorties, 67 aircraft lost (2·0 per cent)

10 Lancasters were destroyed in crashes.

429 (BISON) SQUADRON

SERVICE

Formed in 4 Group on 7 November 1942 but, unlike most Canadian squadrons, did not transfer to 6 Group until 1 April 1943. Flew Wellingtons, Halifaxes and Lancasters until the end of the war; based at East Moor and Leeming.

OPERATIONAL PERFORMANCE

Raids Flown
4 Group Wellingtons – 11 bombing, 8 minelaying
6 Group Wellingtons – 31 bombing, 15 minelaying
6 Group Halifaxes – 172 bombing, 17 minelaying
6 Group Lancasters – 8 bombing, 5 minelaying

Total – 222 bombing, 45 minelaying = 267 raids

Sorties and Losses
4 Group Wellingtons – 158 sorties, 7 aircraft lost (4·4 per cent)
6 Group Wellingtons – 384 sorties, 21 aircraft lost (5·5 per cent)
6 Group Halifaxes – 2,519 sorties, 49 aircraft lost (1·9 per cent)
6 Group Lancasters – 114 sorties, 1 aircraft lost (0·9 per cent)

Total – 3,175 sorties, 78 aircraft lost (2·5 per cent)

Suffered the most Wellington losses in 6 Group.

431 (IROQUOIS) SQUADRON

SERVICE

Formed in 4 Group on 11 November 1942 but did not operate until March 1943, after the transfer to 6 Group. Flew Wellingtons, Halifaxes and Lancasters until the end of the war; based at Burn, Tholthorpe and Croft.

OPERATIONAL PERFORMANCE

Raids Flown
Wellingtons – 25 bombing, 24 minelaying
Halifaxes – 111 bombing, 6 minelaying
Lancasters – 51 bombing

Total – 187 bombing, 30 minelaying = 217 raids

Sorties and Losses
Wellingtons – 321 bombing, 18 aircraft lost (5·6 per cent)
Halifaxes – 1,461 bombing, 46 aircraft lost (3·1 per cent)
Lancasters – 796 bombing, 11 aircraft lost (1·4 per cent)

Total – 2,578 bombing, 75 aircraft lost (2·9 per cent)

POINTS OF INTEREST

Suffered the highest percentage losses in 6 Group.

432 (LEASIDE) SQUADRON

SERVICE

In 6 Group from 1 May 1943 until the end of the war. Flew Wellingtons, Lancasters and Halifaxes from Skipton-on-Swale and East Moor.

OPERATIONAL PERFORMANCE

Raids Flown
Wellingtons – 18 bombing, 29 minelaying
Lancasters – 16 bombing
Halifaxes – 167 bombing

Total – 201 bombing, 29 minelaying = 230 raids

Sorties and Losses
Wellingtons – 494 sorties, 16 aircraft lost (3·2 per cent)
Lancasters – 190 sorties, 8 aircraft lost (4·2 per cent)
Halifaxes – 2,416 sorties, 41 aircraft lost (1·7 per cent)

Total – 3,100 sorties, 65 aircraft lost (2·1 per cent)

3 Lancasters were destroyed in crashes.

POINTS OF INTEREST

Flew the most Wellington sorties in 6 Group.

433 (PORCUPINE) SQUADRON

SERVICE

Formed in 6 Group on 25 September 1943 and flew operations from January 1944 until the end of the war. Flew Halifaxes and Lancasters from Skipton-on-Swale.

OPERATIONAL PERFORMANCE

Raids Flown
Halifaxes – 123 bombing, 39 minelaying
Lancasters – 28 bombing, 14 minelaying

Total – 151 bombing, 53 minelaying = 204 raids

Sorties and Losses
Halifaxes – 1,926 sorties, 28 aircraft lost (1·5 per cent)
Lancasters – 390 sorties, 3 aircraft lost (0·8 per cent)

Total – 2,316 sorties, 31 aircraft lost (1·3 per cent)

4 Halifaxes and 1 Lancaster were destroyed in crashes.

434 (BLUENOSE) SQUADRON

SERVICE

In 6 Group from 13 June 1943 until the end of the war. Flew Halifaxes and Lancasters from Tholthorpe and Croft.

OPERATIONAL PERFORMANCE

Raids Flown
Halifaxes – 135 bombing, 17 minelaying
Lancasters – 41 bombing

Total – 176 bombing, 17 minelaying = 193 raids

Sorties and Losses

Halifaxes – 2,038 sorties, 53 aircraft lost (2·6 per cent)

Lancasters – 559 sorties, 5 aircraft lost (0·9 per cent)

Total – 2,597 sorties, 58 aircraft lost (2·2 per cent)

15 Halifaxes and 2 Lancasters were destroyed in crashes.

455 (AUSTRALIAN) SQUADRON

SERVICE

The ground staff started forming in Australia on 23 May 1941 and the squadron became operational in 5 Group in August 1941. Flew Hampdens from Swinderby and Wigsley until April 1942 when transferred to Coastal Command to become a torpedo-bomber unit, in which role the squadron flew until the end of the war.

OPERATIONAL PERFORMANCE

455 Squadron flew 424 Hampden sorties and lost 14 aircraft (3·3 per cent) in 92 raids – 56 bombing, 29 minelaying and 7 leaflet.

POINTS OF INTEREST

The first Australian squadron to fly in Bomber Command.

458 (AUSTRALIAN) SQUADRON

SERVICE

Ground crew formed in Australia in July 1941 and the squadron became operational in 4 Group in October 1941. Flew Wellingtons from Holme-on-Spalding Moor until December but then transferred to the Middle East in February 1942, the aircraft of the C.O., Wing Commander Mulholland, D.F.C., being shot down into the sea while flying to Malta. Served as a torpedo-bomber squadron in the Middle East until the end of the war.

OPERATIONAL PERFORMANCE

458 Squadron flew 65 Wellington sorties and lost 3 aircraft (4·6 per cent) in 10 bombing raids.

460 (AUSTRALIAN) SQUADRON

SERVICE

Formed as a Wellington squadron in 1 Group and commenced operations on 12/13 March 1942. Flew Wellingtons and Lancasters until the end of the war, a conversion to Halifaxes after the Wellington phase being cancelled before any operations were flown on this type. Based at Breighton and Binbrook.

OPERATIONAL PERFORMANCE

Raids Flown
Wellingtons – 50 bombing, 9 minelaying, 2 leaflet
Lancasters – 280 bombing, 27 minelaying

Total – 330 bombing, 36 minelaying, 2 leaflet = 368 raids

Sorties and Losses
Wellingtons – 538 sorties, 29 aircraft lost (5·4 per cent)
Lancasters – 5,700 sorties, 140 aircraft lost (2·5 per cent)

Total – 6,238 sorties, 169 aircraft lost (2·7 per cent)

31 Lancasters were destroyed in crashes.

POINTS OF INTEREST

Being a three-flight squadron for most of its operational career, and serving in a
   group which strove for maximum efforts and bomb loads, led to 460 Squadron
   being credited with many records.
Flew the most sorties in 1 Group.
Carried out the most bombing raids, flew the most sorties and suffered the most
   losses in Australian squadrons.
Suffered the highest percentage loss in all Bomber Command Wellington squadrons.
Flew the most Lancaster sorties in 1 Group and in Bomber Command; suffered the
   most Lancaster losses in 1 Group.
Believed to have dropped the greatest tonnage of bombs – approximately 24,000 tons
   – in Bomber Command.

462 (AUSTRALIAN) SQUADRON

SERVICE

Formed as a Halifax squadron in the Middle East in September 1942 but lost its
identity in March 1944. Re-formed in 4 Group on 12 August 1944 and flew Halifaxes
from Driffield until December 1944, when the squadron was moved to Foulsham for
radio-countermeasures duties in 100 Group for the remainder of the war.

OPERATIONAL PERFORMANCE

Raids Flown
4 Group Halifaxes – 45 bombing
100 Group Halifaxes – 63 R.C.M.

Total – 108 raids (bombs were sometimes dropped during the R.C.M. operations)

Sorties and Losses
4 Group Halifaxes – 544 sorties, 6 aircraft lost (1·1 per cent)
100 Group Halifaxes – 621 sorties, 7 aircraft lost (1·1 per cent)

Total – 1,165 sorties, 13 aircraft lost (1·1 per cent)

463 (AUSTRALIAN) SQUADRON

SERVICE

Formed in 5 Group on 25 November 1943 and flew Lancasters from Waddington until the end of the war.

OPERATIONAL PERFORMANCE

463 Squadron flew 2,525 Lancaster sorties and lost 69 aircraft (2·7 per cent) in 180 bombing raids. 10 further Lancasters were destroyed in crashes.

POINTS OF INTEREST

The squadron's aircraft often carried cameramen of the R.A.F. Film Unit.
Suffered the highest percentage loss rate in Australian squadrons, but only by a small
 fraction from 460 and 467 Squadrons.

464 (AUSTRALIAN) SQUADRON

SERVICE

Formed in 2 Group and flew Venturas from Feltwell and Methwold until 2 Group left Bomber Command in May 1943. Continued to operate in the 2nd Tactical Air Force until the end of the war, converting to Mosquito fighter-bombers in August 1943.

OPERATIONAL PERFORMANCE

464 Squadron flew 226 Ventura sorties and lost 6 aircraft (1·8 per cent) in 28 bombing raids.

466 (AUSTRALIAN) SQUADRON

SERVICE

Formed in 4 Group on 15 October 1942 and flew Wellingtons and Halifaxes from Driffield (twice) and Leconfield until the end of the war.

OPERATIONAL PERFORMANCE

Raids Flown
Wellingtons – 46 bombing, 43 minelaying
Halifaxes – 168 bombing, 7 minelaying

Total – 214 bombing, 50 minelaying = 264 raids

Sorties and Losses
Wellingtons – 844 sorties, 25 aircraft lost (3·0 per cent)
Halifaxes – 2,484 sorties, 40 aircraft lost (1·6 per cent)

Total – 3,328 sorties, 65 aircraft lost (2·0 per cent)

POINTS OF INTEREST

Flew most sorties and suffered most losses in 4 Group Wellington squadrons.

467 (AUSTRALIAN) SQUADRON

SERVICE

Formed in 5 Group on 7 November 1942 and flew Lancasters from Scampton, Bottesford and Waddington until the end of the war.

OPERATIONAL PERFORMANCE

467 Squadron flew 3,833 Lancaster sorties and lost 104 aircraft (2·7 per cent) in 299 bombing and 15 minelaying raids. 14 further Lancasters were destroyed in crashes.

487 (NEW ZEALAND) SQUADRON

SERVICE

Formed in 2 Group and flew Venturas from Feltwell and Methwold until 2 Group left Bomber Command in May 1943. Continued to operate in the 2nd Tactical Air Force until the end of the war, converting to Mosquito fighter-bombers in August 1943.

OPERATIONAL PERFORMANCE

487 Squadron flew 273 Ventura sorties and lost 15 aircraft (5·5 per cent) in 27 bombing raids. 1 further Ventura was destroyed in a crash.

POINTS OF INTEREST

Victoria Cross: Squadron Leader L. H. Trent, Amsterdam Power Station, 3 May 1943. 487 Squadron lost 10 aircraft on this raid.

514 SQUADRON

SERVICE

Formed in 3 Group on 1 September 1943 and flew Lancasters from Foulsham and Waterbeach until the end of the war.

OPERATIONAL PERFORMANCE

514 Squadron flew 3,675 Lancaster sorties and lost 66 aircraft (1·8 per cent) in 218 bombing and 4 minelaying raids. 14 further Lancasters were destroyed in crashes.

515 SQUADRON

SERVICE

A radio-countermeasures unit flying Defiants and Beaufighters until transferred to 100 Group in December 1943. Flew *Serrate* and Intruder operations, using Mosquitoes, from 5 March 1944 until the end of the war; based at Little Snoring.

OPERATIONAL PERFORMANCE

515 Squadron flew 1,366 Mosquito sorties and lost 21 aircraft (1·5 per cent) in 239 *Serrate*/Intruder and 9 escort operations. The squadron claimed 11 German aircraft destroyed in the air, 18 on the ground and 5 more damaged on the ground.

POINTS OF INTEREST

Suffered the most losses and the highest percentage loss in 100 Group Mosquito squadrons.

550 SQUADRON

SERVICE

Formed in 1 Group on 25 November 1943 and flew Lancasters from Grimsby and North Killingholme until the end of the war.

OPERATIONAL PERFORMANCE

550 Squadron flew 3,582 Lancaster sorties and lost 59 aircraft (1·6 per cent) in 192 raids. 14 further Lancasters were destroyed in crashes.

571 SQUADRON

SERVICE

Formed in 8 Group on 7 April 1944 for the Light Night Striking Force and flew Mosquitoes from Downham Market and Graveley (both briefly), and then Oakington until the end of the war.

OPERATIONAL PERFORMANCE

571 Squadron flew 2,681 Mosquito sorties and lost 8 aircraft (0·3 per cent) in 259 bombing raids and 1 minelaying operation.

576 SQUADRON

SERVICE

Formed in 1 Group on 25 November 1943 and flew Lancasters from Elsham Wolds and Fiskerton until the end of the war.

576 Squadron flew 2,788 Lancaster sorties and lost 66 aircraft (2·4 per cent) in 189 bombing and 2 minelaying raids. 9 further Lancasters were destroyed in crashes.

578 SQUADRON

SERVICE

Formed in 4 Group on 14 January 1944 and flew Halifaxes from Snaith and Burn until the end of the war.

OPERATIONAL PERFORMANCE

578 Squadron flew 2,721 Halifax sorties and lost 40 aircraft (1·5 per cent) in 155 bombing raids.

POINTS OF INTEREST

Victoria Cross: Pilot Officer C. J. Barton, posthumously, Nuremberg, 30/31 March 1944.

582 SQUADRON

SERVICE

Formed as a Pathfinder squadron in 8 Group on 1 April 1944 and flew Lancasters from Little Staughton until the end of the war.

OPERATIONAL PERFORMANCE

582 Squadron flew 2,157 Lancaster sorties and lost 28 aircraft (1·3 per cent) in 165 raids. 8 further Lancasters were destroyed in crashes.

POINTS OF INTEREST

Victoria Cross: Captain E. E. Swales, posthumously, Pforzheim, 23/24 February 1945.

608 (NORTH RIDING) SQUADRON

SERVICE

This pre-war Auxiliary Air Force squadron had flown maritime operations from England and in the Middle East from 1939 until disbanded in Italy on 31 July 1944. Re-formed the following day as a Mosquito squadron for the Light Night Striking Force in 8 Group and flew from Downham Market until the end of the war.

608 Squadron flew 1,726 Mosquito sorties and lost 9 aircraft (0·5 per cent) in 246 bombing raids.

POINTS OF INTEREST

The only Auxiliary Air Force squadron to serve in Bomber Command, but there was little trace of the pre-war Auxiliary character at the time of the Bomber Command service.

617 SQUADRON

SERVICE

Formed on 21 March 1943 as a special squadron in 5 Group specifically for the raid on the German dams which took place on 16/17 May 1943. Retained as a precision-bombing squadron after the Dams Raid and flew Lancasters, Mosquitoes and Mustangs from Scampton, Coningsby and Woodhall Spa until the end of the war.

OPERATIONAL PERFORMANCE

Raids Flown
100 bombing raids and the eve of D-Day 'spoof' raid were carried out.

Sorties and Losses
Lancasters – 1,478 sorties, 32 aircraft lost (2·2 per cent)
Mosquitoes – 75 sorties, no losses
Mustangs – 6 sorties, no losses

Total – 1,599 sorties, 32 aircraft lost (2·1 per cent)

12 Lancasters were destroyed in crashes.

POINTS OF INTEREST

Victoria Crosses:
Wing Commander G. P. Gibson, D.S.O., D.F.C., The Dams Raid, 16/17 May 1943. (Wing Commander Gibson was killed in action on 19/20 September 1944.)
Wing Commander G. L. Cheshire, D.S.O., D.F.C.; the Victoria Cross was awarded on 8 September 1944 for many acts of courage during four tours of operations.

619 SQUADRON

SERVICE

Formed in 5 Group on 18 April 1943 and flew Lancasters from Woodhall Spa, Coningsby, Dunholme Lodge and Strubby until the end of the war.

OPERATIONAL PERFORMANCE

619 Squadron flew 3,011 Lancaster sorties and lost 77 aircraft (2·6 per cent) in 223 bombing and 17 minelaying raids. 12 further Lancasters were destroyed in crashes.

620 SQUADRON

SERVICE

Formed on 17 June 1943 in 3 Group and flew Stirlings from Chedburgh until transferred to 38 Group in November 1943 for duty as a transport and glider-towing squadron.

OPERATIONAL PERFORMANCE

620 Squadron flew 339 Stirling sorties and lost 17 aircraft (5·0 per cent) in 32 bombing and 29 minelaying raids. 9 further Stirlings were destroyed in crashes.

622 SQUADRON

SERVICE

Formed in 3 Group on 10 August 1943 and flew Stirlings and Lancasters from Mildenhall until the end of the war.

OPERATIONAL PERFORMANCE

Raids Flown
Stirlings – 21 bombing, 20 minelaying
Lancasters – 210 bombing, 17 minelaying

Total – 231 bombing, 37 minelaying = 268 raids

Sorties and Losses
Stirlings – 195 sorties, 7 aircraft lost (3·6 per cent)
Lancasters – 2,805 sorties, 44 aircraft lost (1·6 per cent)

Total – 3,000 sorties, 51 aircraft lost (1·7 per cent)

2 Stirlings and 3 Lancasters were destroyed in crashes.

623 SQUADRON

SERVICE

Formed in 3 Group on 10 August 1943 and flew Stirlings from Downham Market until disbanded on 6 December 1943.

623 Squadron flew 150 Stirling sorties and lost 10 aircraft (6·7 per cent) in 19 bombing and 22 minelaying raids. 1 further Stirling was destroyed in a crash.

625 SQUADRON

SERVICE

Formed in 1 Group on 1 October 1943 and flew Lancasters from Kelstern until nearly the end of the war and then 5 raids from Scampton in April 1945.

OPERATIONAL PERFORMANCE

625 Squadron flew 3,385 Lancaster sorties and lost 66 aircraft (1·9 per cent) in 191 bombing and 2 minelaying raids. A further 8 Lancasters were destroyed in crashes.

626 SQUADRON

SERVICE

Formed in 1 Group on 7 November 1943 and flew Lancasters from Wickenby until the end of the war.

OPERATIONAL PERFORMANCE

626 Squadron flew 2,728 Lancaster sorties and lost 49 aircraft (1·8 per cent) in 187 bombing and 18 minelaying raids. A further 11 Lancasters were destroyed in crashes.

627 SQUADRON

SERVICE

Formed at Oakington in 8 Group on 12 November 1943 as a Mosquito squadron for the Light Night Striking Force. Transferred to 5 Group for that group's marker force on 15 April 1944 and flew from Woodhall Spa until the end of the war.

OPERATIONAL PERFORMANCE

Raids Flown

8 Group Mosquitoes – 73 bombing
5 Group Mosquitoes – 121 marking, 6 minelaying, 4 *Window*, 35 weather/photo recce

Total – 121 marking, 73 bombing, 45 others = 239 raids

Sorties and Losses
8 Group Mosquitoes – 477 sorties, 4 aircraft lost (0·8 per cent)
5 Group Mosquitoes – 1,058 sorties, 15 aircraft lost (1·4 per cent)

Total – 1,535 sorties, 19 aircraft lost (1·2 per cent)

630 SQUADRON

SERVICE

Formed in 5 Group on 15 November 1943 and flew Lancasters from East Kirkby until the end of the war.

OPERATIONAL PERFORMANCE

630 Squadron flew 2,453 Lancaster sorties and lost 59 aircraft (2·4 per cent) in 180 bombing and 22 minelaying raids. 11 further Lancasters were destroyed in crashes.

635 SQUADRON

SERVICE

Formed as a Pathfinder squadron in 8 Group on 20 March 1944 and flew Lancasters from Downham Market until the end of the war.

OPERATIONAL PERFORMANCE

635 Squadron flew 2,225 Lancaster sorties and lost 34 aircraft (1·5 per cent) in 189 raids. 7 further Lancasters were destroyed in crashes.

POINTS OF INTEREST

Victoria Cross: Squadron Leader I. W. Bazalgette, D.F.C., posthumously, Trossy-St-Maxim flying-bomb site, 4 August 1944.
Carried out the first operational trials of the Lancaster Mark VI from July to November 1944.

640 SQUADRON

SERVICE

Formed in 4 Group and flew Halifaxes from Lissett (only 2 raids) and Leconfield until the end of the war.

OPERATIONAL PERFORMANCE

640 Squadron flew 2,423 Halifax sorties and lost 40 aircraft (1·7 per cent) in 170 bombing raids.

692 (FELLOWSHIP OF THE BELLOWS) SQUADRON

SERVICE

Formed in 8 Group on 1 January 1944 as a Mosquito squadron for the Light Night Striking Force and flew from Graveley until the end of the war.

OPERATIONAL PERFORMANCE

692 Squadron flew 3,237 Mosquito sorties and lost 17 aircraft (0·5 per cent) in 308 bombing and 2 minelaying raids.

POINTS OF INTEREST

The 'Fellowship of the Bellows' was a patriotic organization of Anglo-Argentine businessmen and families in Buenos Aires who raised money for the purchase of aircraft for the R.A.F. The 'Bellows' were to help 'raise the wind'.

Dropped the first 4,000-lb bombs by Mosquitoes, on Düsseldorf, 23/24 February 1944.

1409 (METEOROLOGICAL) FLIGHT

SERVICE

Formed at Oakington on 1 April 1943 and flew weather-reconnaissance flights for Bomber Command and the American Eighth Air Force until the end of the war. Unarmed Mosquitoes were used for all of these flights.

OPERATIONAL PERFORMANCE

1409 Flight flew 1,364 sorties and lost 3 aircraft (0·2 per cent) on 632 occasions (mostly days).

GROUPS

1 GROUP

Battles – 287 sorties, 6 aircraft lost (2·1 per cent)
Wellingtons – 12,170 sorties, 395 aircraft lost (3·2 per cent)
Halifaxes – 137 sorties, 12 aircraft lost (8·8 per cent)
Lancasters – 43,836 sorties, 1,016 aircraft lost (2·3 per cent)

Total – 56,430 sorties, 1,429 aircraft lost (2·5 per cent)

At least 199 Lancasters were destroyed in crashes; other types not known.

2 GROUP

SORTIES AND LOSSES

Blenheims – 11,311 sorties, 421 aircraft lost (3·7 per cent)
Bostons – 1,215 sorties, 41 aircraft lost (3·4 per cent)
Fortresses – 52 sorties, 3 aircraft lost (4·0 per cent)
Mosquitoes – 793 sorties, 40 aircraft lost (5·0 per cent)
Venturas – 868 sorties, 31 aircraft lost (3·6 per cent)
Mitchells – 221 sorties, 6 aircraft lost (2·7 per cent)

Total – 14,460 sorties, 542 aircraft lost (3·7 per cent)

At least 78 Blenheims, 3 Bostons and 1 Ventura were destroyed in crashes; other types not known.

3 GROUP

SORTIES AND LOSSES

Wellingtons – 20,584 sorties, 608 aircraft lost (3·0 per cent)
Stirlings – 15,895 sorties, 577 aircraft lost (3·6 per cent)
Lancasters – 26,462 sorties, 380 aircraft lost (1·4 per cent)
Other types (mostly on Resistance and R.C.M. operations) – 3,672 sorties, 103 aircraft lost (2·8 per cent)

Total – 66,613 sorties, 1,668 aircraft lost (2·5 per cent)

At least 227 Stirlings and 78 Lancasters were destroyed in crashes; other types not known.

4 GROUP

SORTIES AND LOSSES

Whitleys – 9,169 sorties, 288 aircraft lost (3·1 per cent)
Wellingtons – 2,901 sorties, 97 aircraft lost (3·3 per cent)
Halifaxes – 45,337 sorties, 1,124 aircraft lost (2·5 per cent)

Total – 57,407 sorties, 1,509 aircraft lost (2·6 per cent)

No reliable figures for aircraft destroyed in crashes are available.

5 GROUP

SORTIES AND LOSSES

Hampdens – 15,771 sorties, 417 aircraft lost (2·6 per cent)
Manchesters – 1,185 sorties, 69 aircraft lost (5·8 per cent)
Lancasters – 52,262 sorties, 1,389 aircraft lost (2·7 per cent)
Mosquitoes – 1,133 sorties, 13 aircraft lost (1·1 per cent)
Mustangs – 6 sorties, no aircraft losses

Total – 70,357 sorties, 1,888 aircraft lost (2·7 per cent)

At least 28 Manchesters and 253 Lancasters were destroyed in crashes; other types not known.

6 (CANADIAN) GROUP

SORTIES AND LOSSES

Wellingtons – 3,287 sorties, 127 aircraft lost (3·9 per cent)
Halifaxes – 28,126 sorties, 508 aircraft lost (1·8 per cent)
Lancasters – 8,171 sorties, 149 aircraft lost (1·8 per cent)

Total – 39,584 sorties, 784 aircraft lost (2·0 per cent)

At least 56 Lancasters were destroyed in crashes; other types not known.

8 (PATHFINDER FORCE) GROUP

SORTIES AND LOSSES

Wellingtons – 305 sorties, 17 aircraft lost (5·6 per cent)
Halifaxes – 2,106 sorties, 77 aircraft lost (3·7 per cent)
Stirlings – 826 sorties, 37 aircraft lost (4·5 per cent)
Lancasters – 19,601 sorties, 444 aircraft lost (2·3 per cent)

Total heavies – 22,838 sorties, 575 aircraft lost (2·5 per cent)
Mosquitoes – 28,215 sorties, 100 aircraft lost (0·4 per cent)

Total of all types – 51,053 sorties, 675 aircraft lost (1·3 per cent)

The operations of 1409 (Meteorological) Flight are included in the Mosquito total.

At least 12 Stirlings and 72 Lancasters were destroyed in crashes; other types not known.

100 (BOMBER SUPPORT) GROUP

SORTIES AND LOSSES

R.C.M. Operations
Halifaxes – 3,383 sorties, 23 aircraft lost (0·7 per cent)
Fortresses – 1,465 sorties, 4 aircraft lost (0·3 per cent)
Stirlings – 1,235 sorties, 13 aircraft lost (1·1 per cent)
Liberators – 615 sorties, 3 aircraft lost (0·5 per cent)
Wellingtons – 589 sorties, 1 aircraft lost (0·2 per cent)
Mosquitoes – 544 sorties, 1 aircraft lost (0·2 per cent)
Lightnings – 101 sorties, 2 aircraft lost (2·0 per cent)

Total – 7,932 sorties, 47 aircraft lost (0·6 per cent)

Serrate *and Intruder Operations*
Beaufighters – 12 sorties, no aircraft losses
Mosquitoes – 8,802 sorties, 75 aircraft lost (0·9 per cent)

Total – 8,814 sorties, 75 aircraft lost (0·9 per cent)

Total of all types – 16,746 sorties, 122 aircraft lost (0·7 per cent)

The number of aircraft destroyed in crashes is not known.

TRAINING UNITS

Bomber Command contained a considerable number of its own training units, in which airmen who had received a basic training in their respective speciality – pilots, navigators (earlier known as observers), wireless operators, air gunners, bomb aimers (officially 'air bombers') and flight engineers – were gathered together for crew training at O.T.U.s (Operational Training Units) and, for those crews intended for four-engined aircraft, at H.C.U.s (Heavy Conversion Units). Many of these training units dispatched aircraft on active-service operations. Most of the O.T.U. flights were by pupil crews which carried out a short sortie to a target in Northern France just before finishing their training courses at the O.T.U.; most of these flights only carried leaflets. The H.C.U. operations were mainly flown by mixed crews of pupils and instructors in 1942, when training aircraft were added to Bomber Command's Main Force for the Thousand-Bomber Raids and for other major raids. The O.T.U.s also contributed to the 1942 Main Force raids, but more instructors than pupils provided the crews on these occasions. Most of the operational flights by training units ceased after the invasion of Normandy in June 1944, but O.T.U.s and H.C.U.s sometimes provided aircraft for diversionary sweeps over the North Sea and over France in 1944 and 1945; details of these sweeps, however, are not included in the statistics below because the German lines were never crossed, although there were occasional losses on the sweeps.

Twenty-four O.T.U.s and eight H.C.U.s sent crews on operations:

O.T.U.s

Wellingtons – 3,270 sorties, 95 aircraft lost (2·9 per cent)
Whitleys – 558 sorties, 18 aircraft lost (3·2 per cent)
Hampdens – 240 sorties, 7 aircraft lost (2·9 per cent)

Total – 4,068 sorties, 120 aircraft lost (2·9 per cent)

H.C.U.s

Stirlings – 73 sorties, 5 aircraft lost (6·8 per cent)
Halifaxes – 58 sorties, 4 aircraft lost (6·9 per cent)
Lancasters – 36 sorties, 4 aircraft lost (11·1 per cent)

Total – 167 sorties, 13 aircraft lost (7·8 per cent)

27 O.T.U., which trained Australian aircrew at Lichfield, flew the most sorties – 384

Wellington sorties, losing 7 aircraft. 15 O.T.U. at Harwell and 10 O.T.U. at Abingdon flew 331 sorties with 8 losses and 318 sorties with 8 losses respectively. Twenty-one other O.T.U.s and eight H.C.U.s also flew operations.

NOTES ON SOURCES, BIBLIOGRAPHY, ACKNOWLEDGEMENTS

BRITISH AND ALLIED SOURCES

PUBLIC RECORD OFFICE, KEW

The following records have been consulted:

AIR 14/2664–2680 Night Bombing Sheets
    14/3360–3368 Day Bombing Sheets
    14/3408–3412 Final Raid Reports
AIR 22/31–49 Aircraft Serviceability Returns
    22/203 War Room Manual of Bomber Command Operations
AIR 24/200–209 Bomber Command Headquarters Operations Record Books
    24/214–319 Bomber Command Intelligence Reports
The AIR 25 class of records for group Operations Record Books
The AIR 27 class for squadron Operations Record Books
The AIR 28 class for station Operations Record Books
The AIR 29 class for Operations Record Books of 1409 (Meteorological) Flight and of training
    units

Many other minor files have been consulted; where relevant the references are quoted
in the diaries.

THE UNITED STATES STRATEGIC BOMBING SURVEY

Copies of the Survey are held in the Imperial War Museum, London. The following
individual reports have been studied: ('Effects of Bombing Raids on') Augsburg,
Cologne, Darmstadt, Düsseldorf, Hamburg, Krefeld, Lübeck, Remscheid, Solingen
and Wuppertal.

    Reports of the British Bombing Survey Unit are in Volume IV of the British
Official History (see below), Appendix 49.

BRITISH BIBLIOGRAPHY

The following works, being either official histories or reference books based on
original research from prime sources, have been consulted:

Official Histories
Webster, Sir Charles, and Frankland, Noble, *The Strategic Air Offensive against Germany,
1939–1945*, H.M.S.O., 1961.

Other Works

Bowyer, Michael J. F., *2 Group R.A.F.*, Faber & Faber, 1974.

Brickhill, Paul, *The Dam Busters*, Pan, 1945; Evans, 1951.

Chorley, W. R., *To See the Dawn Breaking – A History of 76 Squadron*, Chorley, 1981.

Chorley, W. R., and Benwell, R. N., *In Brave Company – A History of 158 Squadron*, Chorley & Benwell, 1977.

Cooper, Alan W., *The Men Who Breached the Dams*, Kimber, 1982.

Frankland, Noble, *The Bomber Offensive against Germany*, Faber & Faber, 1965.

Freeman, Roger A., *Mighty Eighth War Diary*, Jane's, 1981.

Garrett, Richard, *Scharnhorst and Gneisenau*, David & Charles, 1978.

Gomersall, Bryce, *The Stirling File*, Air Britain and Aviation Archaeologists, 1979.

Harris, Marshall of the R.A.F. Sir Arthur, *Bomber Offensive*, Collins, 1947.

Lawrence, W. J., *No. 5 Bomber Group R.A.F.*, Faber & Faber, 1951.

Middlebrook, Martin, *The Nuremberg Raid*, Allen Lane, 1973, 1980.

Middlebrook, M., *The Battle of Hamburg*, Allen Lane, 1980.

Middlebrook, M., *The Peenemünde Raid*, Allen Lane, 1982.

Moyes, Philip J. R., *Bomber Squadrons of the R.A.F. and Their Aircraft*, Macdonald, 1964.

Musgrove, Gordon, *Pathfinder Force*, Macdonald & Jane's, 1976.

Robertson, Bruce, *Lancaster – The Story of a Famous Bomber*, Harleyford, 1964.

Sweetman, John, *Operation Chastise*, Jane's, 1982.

Verity, Hugh, *We Landed by Moonlight*, Ian Allen, 1978.

White, A. N., *44 (Rhodesia) Squadron R.A.F. on Operations*, White, 1977.

GERMAN SOURCES

PERSONAL RESEARCH HELPERS

The following local, amateur historians have provided valuable help which is most warmly acknowledged: Arno Abendroth, Berlin; Heinz Bardua, Stuttgart; Hubert Beckers, Aachen; Dieter Busch, Bingen; Werner Dettmar, Kassel; Jürgen E. Dominicus, Düren; Hans-Martin Flender, Siegen; Erwin Folz, Ludwigshafen am Rhein; Ludwig Hügen, Mönchengladbach; Hans-Jürgen Jürgens, Wangerooge; Norbert Krüger, Essen; Heinz Leiwig, Mainz; Gus Lerch, Frankfurt am Main; Dr Erich Mulzer, Nuremberg; Erich Quadflieg, Cologne; Hanfried Schliephake, Augsburg; Dr Helmut Schnatz, Koblenz. Emil Nonnenmacher of Eppstein (Taunus) provided German night-fighter material.

Officials of the following Staat- or Stadtarchivs sent copies of their wartime records or extracts from local histories and, again, we are most thankful for this assistance: Bingen am Rhein, Bonn, Braunschweig (Brunswick), Bremen, Bremerhaven, Castrop-Rauxel, Dortmund, Düsseldorf, Emmerich, Flensburg, Frankfurt am Main, Freiburg im Briesgau, Gelsenkirchen, Goch, Hagen, Hanau, Hannover, Heide, Heilbronn, Heinsberg, Herne, Hildesheim, Kaiserslautern, Kamen, Karlsruhe, Kiel, Kleve, Krefeld, Ludwigshafen am Rhein, Mannheim, Mönchengladbach (and Rheydt), Mülheim an der Ruhr, Münster, Neuss, Osnabrück, Paderborn, Pforzheim, Rheine, Saarbrücken, Saarlouis, Soest, Trier, Ulm, Wesel, Wesseling, Wiesbaden, Wilhelmshaven, Witten, Worms, Zweibrücken. (Only one major community in West Germany, Munich, was unwilling to provide any help at all without a personal visit being made.)

GERMAN BIBLIOGRAPHY

Bardua, Heinz, *Stuttgart im Luftkrieg 1939–45*, Stuttgart, 1967, and *Kriegsschäden in Baden-Württemberg 1939–45*, Stuttgart, 1975.

Braun-Rühling, Max, *Eine Stadt in Feurregen*, Kaiserslautern, no date.

Brunswig, Hans, *Feuersturm über Hamburg*, Motorbuch, 1978.

Ennen, Edith, and Höroldt, Dietrich, *Vom Römerkastell zur Bundeshauptstadt*, Bonn, 1976.

Köhler, Wolfgang, *Wesermünde (Bremerhaven) im Luftkrieg 1939–45*, no date.

Prescher, Rudolf, *Der rote Hahn über Braunschweig 1927–1945*, Braunschweig, 1955.

Rumpf, Hans, *The Bombing of Germany*, German original, Stalling, 1961, English edition, Muller, 1963.

Zenz, Dr Emil, *Geschichte der Stadt Trier in der ersten Hälfte des 20. Jahrhunderts*, NCO Verlag, 1973.

Kiel im Luftkrieg 1939–45, the diary of Detlef Boelck, edited by Jürgen Plöger, Gesellschaft für Kieler Stadtgeschichte, 1980.

Verwaltungsbericht und Statistik der Stadt Pforzheim – Das Stadtgeschehen 1939–45, Stadt Pforzheim, no date.

Zerstörung, Wiederaufbau und Verwaltung der Stadt Kleve 1944–57, Stadt Kleve, 1960.

FRENCH AND BELGIAN SOURCES

All material from municipal archives and other bodies in France and Belgium was obtained on our behalf by M. Philippe Lerat of Ronchin to whom we are most grateful. The French towns which provided M. Lerat with material are: Achères, Amiens, Angers, Argenten, Boulogne-Billancourt, Boulogne-sur-Mer, Cannes, Coutances, Gennevilliers, Laon, Le Havre, Le Mans, Lille, Lisieux, Mantes-la-Jolie, Noisy-le-Sec, Royan (particularly M. Robert Colle), Sochaux (for Montbéliard raids), St-Nazaire, Toulouse (particularly M. Daniel Latapie), Villeneuve-St-Georges. In Belgium: Gand (Ghent), Hasselt, Kortrijk (Courtrai), Leuven (Louvain), Mechelen (Malines). The S.N.C.F. (French Railways) offices at Chambly and Lille, and the S.N.C.B. (Belgian Railways) at Brussels, also provided useful information through M. Lerat.

ITALY

Signore Gino Künzle, of Como, very kindly obtained material from the municipal archives of Genova (Genoa), Milano (Milan) and Torino (Turin). We thank Sig. Künzle and the three city archives.

OTHER COUNTRIES

We acknowledge the following for providing material: Philips International B.V. of Eindhoven, Holland; the Burgemeester of Geleen, a Dutch community which now contains Lutterade, where the first *Oboe* raid was carried out; the towns of Bergen and Horten in Norway; and Anders Bjørnvad of Rude, Denmark.

PERSONAL ACKNOWLEDGEMENTS

We wish to thank the following people for help generously given: James Bamford of Barford, Norwich; Bill Chorley of Dedham, Colchester; Harry Drew of 12 and 626 Squadrons' Association; Dave Gibson of the Coldstream Guards, who carried out research in Germany during a tour of duty in B.A.O.R.; Mike Hodgson of Mareham-le-Fen, Lincoln; Jane Middlebrook; Mary Middlebrook, for many hours of careful typescript and proof checking; Janet Mountain of Swineshead, near Boston, for her diligent typing of a complicated script; Paul Spitzer of Zug, Switzerland, for help with particularly difficult German translations; Peter Strugnell of the 75 (New Zealand) Squadron Museum at Ohakea. We should also like to thank the staffs at the Air Historical Branch, the Adastral Library, Cranwell College Library, the Commonwealth War Graves Commission and the Public Record Office for much patient assistance over a long research period. Finally, Martin Middlebrook would like to thank Chris Everitt who, helped by his wife Margaret, undertook the onerous task of compiling the Index, which needed to be carried out through the Christmas and New Year holiday period.

INDEX

The index is divided into the following sections:

Royal Air Force
  Groups; Squadrons; Flights and Other
  Units; Airfields; Personnel
Place Names
  Belgium; Denmark; France; Germany;
  Holland; Italy; Norway; Other Countries

Luftwaffe
  Units; Personnel
Ships
  British; German and German-controlled
General

Personnel

Place Names

ADDENDA
to the previous edition of *The Bomber Command War Diaries*

14/15 January 1943 – Lorient / Minor Operations. Page 343, last line:

91 O.T.U. should read 29 O.T.U.

26/27 March 1943 – Duisberg raid. Page 370, line 6:

Warrant Officer F. S. Sprouts should read Warrant Officer F. S. Strouts.

27/28 April 1944 – Montzen raid. Page 501, line 5:

Squadron Leader E. M. Blenkinsopp should read Squadron Leader E. W. Blenkinsop.

14/15 June 1944 – 'Troop Positions' entry. Page 528, add the following:

The raid on Aunay-sur-Odon was particularly tragic. The small town had been bombed in daylight two days earlier whan at least 31 people were killed. The mainly 5 Group raid was concentrated and violent and caused massive destruction; 165 inhabitants died. Not a single German was present when the raid took place.

The town has since tried to find the reason for the bombing. It was one week after D-Day and followed immediately on a thrust by the British 7th Armoured Division which penetrated the German lines and reached Villers Bocage, well in the German rear and only four miles from Aunay. But the British withdrew from the area 36 hours before the air raid. The local people believe the raid may have been the result of mistaken identity and should have been directed on Epinay-sur-Oden, only five miles away and described as containing 'a large concentration of German tanks'. This may be so, but Aunay-sur-Odon was a vital road centre with six medium-class and four minor roads radiating from the town. It is likely that the blocking of these roads to German reinforcements expected to arrive on this important sector of the battle front, had been requested by Allied commanders in Normandy.

15 December 1944 – Siegen raid. Page 631, add the following extra paragraph:

It has been suggested that the bomb loads jettisoned over the sea by the Siegen force after being recalled may have been responsible for the death of the famous band-leader, Glenn Miller, who disappeared on this day while a passenger in a light aircraft flying from England to Paris. The 3 Group force jettisoned its bombs in mid-Channel due south of Beachy Head. This location was on a likely route taken by Miller's aircraft, which took off from Twinwood Farm airfield near Bedford at 1.55 pm. 3 Group's squadron records do not all show the recall and jettison times. Those that do mostly show that jettisons took place before Glenn Miller's aircraft could have reached that area. But 115 Squadron's aircraft appear not to have received the recall signal until well into their flight, at 1.45 pm, 70 minutes after other squadrons. The time then taken to fly back to the jettison point over the Channel *might* have coincided with the passage of Glenn Miller's UC-64 Norseman aircraft, well below and probably hidden in the 'very poor visibility' noted in 115 Squadron's records.

29/30 December 1944 – Troisdorf raid. Page 639, add extra paragraphs:

As stated above, Bomber Command's records show that the raid was believed to have been a failure. A letter from Jill Rutter who visited Troisdorf six years after the initial publication of our book shows a different result. The letter is reproduced here:

The village of Troisdorf lies about 19 km South of Cologne. In 1900 Alfred Noble built a dynamite factory (DAG) on land that he had won from local farmers in a card game. The dynamite was initially used by the coal mines in the Ruhr but during World War I the factory expanded.

On the night of December 29th 1944 two waves of bombers came over from the direction of Cologne. The first wave succeeded with the bombs, as at 19.21hrs precisely, all the public clocks stopped. The railway line from Cologne divided in the village, part of it running alongside the Rhine and the other part travelling up into the hills. That night there was a munitions train in the station with many trucks. One end of it caught fire, and about every 20 minutes another truck caught fire and exploded, until the whole train was destroyed. During the raid, between 500 and 700 people lost their lives. This was about one third of the whole population. The dynamite factory was virtually destroyed but rebuilt after the war with the aid of international money and was one of the first factories to make plastic extrusions for windows.

14/15 April 1945 – Potsdam raid. Page 696, delete lines 4 to 8 inclusive and replace with the following:

Information recently in from Potsdam, formerly in East Germany, shows that the number of dead was 1,593, not 5,000 as given by the former Communist authorities, who attempted to attribute victims of Red Army street fighting and artillery bombardment to the R.A.F. The bombing toll was still a high one, partly due to the fact that the people of this community had seen Berlin and not themselves bombed so often that they failed to take proper cover when the sirens sounded.

SURVIVAL OF AIRCREW FROM SHOT DOWN BOMBERS by Martin Middlebrook

In 1979, an article was published in the *New Yorker* magazine and in Britain's *Daily Telegraph Magazine* which aroused much interest among former Bomber Command aircrew. The author of the article was Freeman Dyson, who had served as a civilian scientist in the Operational Research Section at Bomber Command Headquarters in 1944. In his article Dyson described how a colleague had collected statistics on the number of men known to have baled out of bombers shot down over Europe to survive and become prisoners of war. From these statistics, his colleague had submitted reports to his superiors giving his conclusion that, because of the comparative inaccessibility and poor location of its escape hatches, the Lancaster produced the poorest survival rate of the heavy bombers in service at that time. Dyson and his colleague were both disappointed that no modifications were made to improve the Lancaster's escape hatches before the war ended.

The articles provoked some correspondence in various publications, much of it from loyal ex-Lancaster men protesting at the criticism of this beloved aircraft. These men, however, missed the main point. No one disputed that the Lancaster was the safest aircraft to fly and suffered the lowest casualties. What Dyson and his colleagues were contending was that, *once shot down*, the Lancaster was more difficult to escape from than the other four-engined types, the Stirling and the Halifax.

By coincidence, a visitor to my home at the time of the publication of this article had been the Education Officer at Bomber Command Headquarters in 1944 and he remembers the report being submitted. He said that he remembers the case being put, but heard it said that the large number of Lancasters then in squadron service could not be modified, partly for technical reasons, partly because the resulting dislocation would produce an unacceptable loss of operational effort. Similarly, the future production of Lancasters was not to be modified because the necessary re-tooling of factories would cause too much reduction in the flow of new Lancasters.

This subject is only raised here because I happen to have detailed figures on survival rates from the loss of 213 four-engined bombers from six Bomber Command night operations – the four raids of the Battle of Hamburg in July/August 1943, the Peenemünde raid, and the Nuremberg raid of 30/31 March 1944. I do not feel qualified to comment on Mr Dyson's main contentions and there were probably other factors involved, such as the Lancaster's heavier bomb loads, but his statements that, *once shot down*, the Lancaster crew member had a poorer chance of survival than his colleagues in the Stirlings and Halifaxes flying on operations at that time, seems to be confirmed by my figures. Dyson's estimate was that, over a long period of operations, 25 per cent of shot down Stirling and Halifax crew members could expect to survive but only 15 per cent of men in Lancasters would do so. The figures for the Hamburg, Peenemünde and Nuremberg operations are as follows. The loss of nine Wellingtons in the Battle of Hamburg has not been included.

	LANCASTERS			HALIFAXES			STIRLINGS		
Raids	Shot down	Men killed	Men survived	Shot down	Men killed	Men survived	Shot down	Men killed	Men survived
Hamburg (4 raids)	39	267	8	29	171	31	11	67	14
Peenemunde	23	152	14	15	85	22	2	6	9
Nuremberg	64	356	96	30	155	62	– Not operating –		
Total	126	775	118	74	411	115	13	73	23
Percentage Survived		13.2			21.9				24.0

These figures are not based upon a sufficiently large number of aircraft lost to be presented as absolute mathematical proof of Dyson's case, particularly in the smaller number of Stirlings involved, but they do tend to support Dyson's argument. Dyson's figures claimed a 10 per cent advantage for the Stirling and Halifax; the above figures show a remarkably similar 9 per cent advantage over the Lancaster for the combined totals of the Stirlings and Halifaxes.

It does seem, under normal circumstances, that although the Lancaster could expect to return more often from operations it was a more difficult aircraft from which to escape when it was attacked and shot down.

Some interesting figures are also available for the survival rate from the American B-17 Fortresses shot down in a similar series of raids. From four operations carried out by B-17s during July 1943 - two to Hamburg, one to Kiel and one to Hanover - and from the Schweinfurt and Regensburg raids of 17 August 1943, 88 B-17s were shot down over enemy territory. From these aircraft, 262 men (29.7 per cent) were killed while 620 men (70.3 per cent) survived. These figures do not include a further 16 B-17s which made leisurely crash landings many miles from the scene of combat or ditchings in the sea; from these 16 B-17s not one crew member died. If these aircraft had been included, the American survival rate would have risen to nearly 75 per cent!

There was, of course, a world of difference between the average circumstances of the shooting down of the bombers of the two air forces. A single German night-fighter could often approach very close to a R.A.F. night bomber and hit it with a concentrated burst of cannon fire. By contrast, American bombers were usually under attack for a prolonged period by fighters which, because of the massed defensive fire of an American daylight bomber formation, could not approach too closely, and a crippled American bomber was often in trouble for a long time before its crew had to abandon it. Both types of bomber were likely to blow up when sustaining direct hits by Flak, but the R.A.F. aircraft's much heavier bomb load would prove more lethal in these cases also.